RESEARCH HANDBOOK ON MONEY LAUNDERING

Research Handbook on Money Laundering

Edited by

Brigitte Unger

Daan van der Linde

Utrecht University School of Economics, the Netherlands

Edward Elgar

Cheltenham, UK • Northampton, MA, USA

Published by
Edward Elgar Publishing Limited
The Lypiatts
15 Lansdown Road
Cheltenham
Glos GL50 2JA
UK

Edward Elgar Publishing, Inc.
William Pratt House
9 Dewey Court
Northampton
Massachusetts 01060
USA

A catalogue record for this book
is available from the British Library

Library of Congress Control Number: 2013930505

This book is available electronically in the ElgarOnline.com
Law Subject Collection, E-ISBN 978 0 85793 400 0

MIX
Paper from responsible sources
FSC® C013056
www.fsc.org

ISBN 978 0 85793 399 7 (cased)

Typeset by Servis Filmsetting Ltd, Stockport, Cheshire
Printed and bound in Great Britain by T.J. International Ltd, Padstow

Contents

Contributors

Henk Addink is Professor of Good Governance and Administrative Law at Utrecht University, Faculty of Law, Economics and Governance, the Netherlands. His scholarly work focuses on Principles of (European) Administrative Law and the Enforcement of (European) Administrative Law (Good Governance: Concept and Context, Utrecht University 2012). The main topics in his research field are Principles of Good Governance – and in particular the Principle of Properness, the Principles of Transparency, the Principle of Participation, the Principle of Effectiveness, the Principle of Accountability and the Principle of Human Rights – and the compliance and enforcement of these principles. He supervises several PhD studies on these principles and their relation to (European) administrative law public contracts, to supervision and to money laundering (reporting in the legal and accountancy sectors, supervision). He regularly teaches as visiting professor in foreign universities in Europe, Asia and Latin America.

Amedeo Argentiero is Assistant Professor of Economics at the University of Perugia. He was awarded a PhD in Money and Finance from the University of Rome 'Tor Vergata' in 2009. In 2007 (spring semester) he was a visiting PhD student in the Department of Economics of MIT. He was a research fellow at the Italian Institute for Studies and Economic Analyses (ISAE) from 2008 to 2010. From 2010 to 2012 he was an officer at the statistical and econometric analysis of compliance office of the Italian Revenue Agency. He was adjunct professor in risk management and econometrics at the University of Macerata from 2009 to 2012. His research interests deal with dynamic stochastic general equilibrium models, fiscal policy, unobserved economy and banking.

Michele Bagella is an economist and Professor of Monetary Economics at the Faculty of Economics of the University of Rome 'Tor Vergata', where he was Dean from July 2007 to October 2011. From 1991 to 2007 he was the Director of the Department of Economics and Institutions. He has coordinated the Master in European Economy, Finance and Institutions. He has been an Advisor for the Ministry of Industry, the Ministry of Economy and Finance, and a consultant for banks as well as other private and public institutions. He contributes articles to several Italian newspapers. He has published many contributions in scientific journals and books in the field of Industrial Studies, in Finance and in Monetary Economics.

Raymond W. Baker is President of Global Financial Integrity and author of *Capitalism's Achilles Heel: Dirty Money and How to Renew the Free-Market System* (John Wiley & Sons, 2005). He was a guest scholar at the Brookings Institution in Washington for six years and prior to that was in business throughout much of the developing world for 35 years.

John Biggins (BA (Hons), LLM) is a graduate of Dublin City University and Trinity College Dublin. In September 2010 he joined Professors Colin Scott and Blanaid Clarke at the University College Dublin Centre for Regulation and Governance on a transnational research initiative which investigated public and private regulation in the over-the-counter (OTC) derivatives markets in the wake of the global financial crisis. This initiative subsequently resulted in a report with recommendations on OTC derivatives regulation aimed at public policy makers and other stakeholders. In October 2011 John took up a position with the Irish financial services regulatory authority, the Central Bank of Ireland.

Jakub Brettl is a recent graduate of the Utrecht University School of Economics (USE) Master programme specializing in International Financial Economics. As a bachelor student, he worked with Brigitte Unger under whose guidance he wrote his bachelor thesis on money laundering threat assessment, which was accepted at the Student Research Conference 2011 in Eindhoven. Jakub was involved in an EU project on money laundering throughout his Master studies where he continued to work in the field of money laundering risk. His Master thesis was written at the International Monetary Fund in Washington DC, where he tested new methods for the estimation of illicit flows through the financial system. Currently, he is a member of the Risk Analysis team of the Credit Rating Agencies unit at the European Securities and Markets Authority in Paris.

Melissa van den Broek is a PhD candidate at the Institute of Jurisprudence, Constitutional and Administrative Law of Utrecht University, the Netherlands. She has a general research interest in European and administrative law. Next to her involvement in the EU-funded project 'ECOLEF: The Economic and Legal Effectiveness of Anti-Money Laundering and Combating Terrorist Financing Policy' as a legal researcher, she performs a comparative legal study to the effectiveness of supervision and enforcement in the preventive AML/CTF policy in the European Union. Melissa's work in the field of AML/CTF policy and related topics has been published in various European and Dutch legal journals.

Andreas Buehn is Assistant Professor of Public Economics at the Utrecht University School of Economics (USE). He holds a PhD in Economics from the Technische Universität Dresden and was Visiting Research Scholar in the International Center for Public Policy at Georgia State University and in the Office of Tax Policy Research at the University of Michigan. His research interests include Public Economics, especially Tax Evasion, Shadow Economics and Do-it-yourself Activities, and International Economics. Illegal Trade and Smuggling and Applied Econometrics.

Francesco Busato is Associate tenured Professor at the University of Naples Parthenope; he obtained his PhD from Columbia University and covered positions at the University of Aarhus School of Economics and Management, and the University of Rome 3. He is interested in dynamics models, finance, applied theory, and teaches classes in microeconomics and financial derivatives.

Paolo Costanzo is Head of the International Cooperation Unit of the Italian Financial Intelligence Unit, within the Bank of Italy, and Chair of the Legal Working Group of the Egmont Group. He has served in the European Commission (Directorate General Internal Market and Services) as a National Expert on Anti-Money Laundering and Counter-Financing of Terrorism (AML/CFT). He participates in the activities of several international organizations dealing with AML/CFT issues and has contributed to the preparation of international standards and conventions as well as to the negotiation of EU AML/CFT directives.

Stephen Dawe joined the IMF in September 2005. He works on Anti-Money Laundering/Countering the Financing of Terrorism (AML/CFT) issues focusing on ML and FT risk. Previously he worked for the Reserve Bank of New Zealand including as a bank supervisor, financial sector and FDI regulator, and general counsel. He has worked on AML/CFT since 1993, including representing New Zealand at Financial Action Task Force (FATF) meetings. Within FATF Steve has chaired a working group that revised the FATF recommendations, served on its steering group, and co-chaired a project to produce guidance on national ML/FT risk assessments. Steve has an LLB/BCA (Business Administration) from Victoria University of Wellington.

Ioana Deleanu is a PhD candidate at the Utrecht University School of Economics (USE). She holds a diploma in Multidisciplinary Economics with a minor in Law from Utrecht University and is writing a multidisciplinary PhD in Law and Economics. Her PhD focuses on the efficiency of information transmission chains present in various Anti-Money Laundering repressive frameworks and combines principles of economics, criminal law and network theory.

Petrus C. van Duyne is Professor Emeritus of Empirical Criminal Law at Tilburg University and visiting professor at the University of Manchester. Van Duyne has carried out extensive international research on organized crime, fraud, money laundering and corruption. He is the founder and coordinator of the Cross-border Crime Colloquium.

Joras Ferwerda is Assistant Professor at the Utrecht University School of Economics (USE), and wrote his PhD on 'The Multidisciplinary Economics of Money Laundering'. He has been involved in previous studies on money laundering for the Dutch Ministries of Finance, Justice and Inner Affairs, the EU and the World Bank. He has previously published a book with Edward Elgar together with Brigitte Unger called *Money Laundering in the Real Estate Sector: Suspicious Properties*.

Loek Groot is an economist (University of Amsterdam) and philosopher (University of Leuven) and currently Associate Professor of Economics of the Public Sector at the Utrecht University School of Economics (USE). His research focuses on the economics of the welfare state and the interaction with the labour market, with special attention to the proposal of a basic income. His other research interests are environmental economics and sport economics.

Victor van Kommer is Member of the Executive Board and Director Tax Services of the International Bureau of Fiscal Documentation in Amsterdam. He is also Professor of Tax Policy at the Utrecht University School of Economics (USE) and Chairman of the Supervisory Board of the Knowledge Institute for Independent Professionals. He is visiting professor at the universities in Lodz, Poland, Riga, Latvia and the Tax Academy in Kuala Lumpur. Victor van Kommer started his career in the Ministry of Finance and the Dutch Tax and Customs Administration where he performed several management functions in the field of Planning, Finance and Control and Investigation and Intelligence.

Jan van Koningsveld is finishing his PhD on the Misuse of Offshore Companies at the University of Tilburg. He has more than 25 years' experience in financial investigations and has contributed to research at the FATF and the World Bank. Since 2011 he has been the Director of the Offshore Kennis Centrum (www.offshorekenniscentrum.nl).

Tim Krieger is Wilfried Guth Professor for Constitutional Political Economy and Competition Policy at the University of Freiburg, Germany. His publications include *Public Pensions and Immigration: A Public Choice Approach* (Edward Elgar, 2005) as well as several articles in leading economics and political science journals such as *Journal of Public Economics*, *Journal of Conflict Resolution*, *Public Choice*, and *Defense and Peace Economics*.

Michael Levi is Professor of Criminology, School of Social Sciences, Cardiff University, UK. He has been conducting international research on the control of white-collar and organised crime, corruption and money laundering / financing of terrorism since 1972, and has published widely on these subjects as well as editing for major journals. His books include 2013 *Regulating Fraud: White-Collar Crime and the Criminal Process* Routledge Revivals, London: Routledge (first published 1987); 2008 *The Phantom Capitalists: the Organisation and Control of Long-Firm Fraud*, 2nd edition, Andover: Ashgate; 2005 *Drugs and Money: Managing the Drug Trade and Crime-Money in Europe* (with Petrus van Duyne), London: Routledge; 1994 *Money-Laundering in the UK: an Appraisal of Suspicion-Based Reporting* (with M.Gold), London: Police Foundation; and 1991 *Customer Confidentiality, Money-Laundering, and Police-Bank Relationships: English law and practice in a global environment*, London: Police Foundation.

Prince Michael von und zu Liechtenstein is a resident of the Principality of Liechtenstein and holds an MA in Business Administration from the Vienna University of Economics and Business. He is Chairman of Industrie- und Finanzkontor, a company specializing in long-term wealth preservation, and founder and chairman of Geopolitical Information Service AG, a geopolitical information platform. He is also president of the Liechtenstein Think Tank, European Center of Austrian Economics Foundation (www.ecaef.li), Vaduz.

Daan van der Linde has a BSc in Political Science from Radboud Universiteit, Nijmegen and an MSc in Economics of Public Policy and Management from the Utrecht University School of Economics (USE). Currently, he is a PhD candidate at the Chair of Public Sector Economics at the Utrecht University School of Economics (USE).

Donato Masciandaro is full Professor of Economics, Chair in Economics of Financial Regulation and Director of the Paolo Baffi Centre on Central Banking and Financial Regulation, Bocconi University. He is a Member of the Management Board of the SUERF (Société Universitarie Européenne de Recherches Financières) and Associated Editor of the *Journal of Financial Stability*.

Killian J. McCarthy is an Assistant Professor at the University of Groningen, and a scientific adviser with ISPIM (The International Society for Professional Innovation Management). An economist and strategist, he gained a PhD in the Economics of Corporate Strategy, on the topic of merger performance. His research interests include business and industrial organization, and strategy. He has also published, however, on the topics of corporate tax competition, money laundering and criminal finance, as well as the influence of media power on both consumer and business sentiment. Killian earned a BSc in Economics from University College Cork, Ireland, an MSc in Law and Economics from the Utrecht University School of Economics (USE), the Netherlands and a research master in Economics, which he earned jointly at the Utrecht University School of Economics (USE) and the University of Vienna, Austria.

Daniel Meierrieks is a research associate at the University of Freiburg, Germany. His research has been published in leading economics and political science journals such as the *Journal of Conflict Resolution*, the *Journal of Peace Research*, *Public Choice*, and *Defense and Peace Economics*.

Burkhard Mühl is a Senior Specialist at Europol and has longstanding experience in investigating financial crime and in supporting the development of EU policies in this area. He is the project manager of the Europol Criminal Assets Bureau (ECAB) which provides support to European Law Enforcement Agencies in tracing and confiscating criminal proceeds worldwide. He holds a Master of Arts degree in Financial Investigation and Financial Crime from Teesside University.

Ewald Nowotny is the Governor of the Oesterreichische Nationalbank (OeNB) and a Member of the Governing Council of the European Central Bank (ECB). Before taking on his current position in September 2008, Ewald Nowotny held a number of high-level positions in financial institutions. He studied law and government sciences at the University of Vienna and economics at the Institute of Advanced Studies in Vienna. Ewald Nowotny received his postdoctoral qualification (Habilitation) in General Economics and Public Economics in 1973 and subsequently held research tenures and professorships at Harvard University, Technische Universität Darmstadt, Germany, and the University of Linz, Austria. From 1981 to 2008 Ewald Nowotny served as Full Professor at the Vienna University of Economics and Business.

Thomas Pietschmann has a PhD in economics and business administration. He worked as an international money broker and analyst of financial markets before joining the UN system in 1990, and in 1993 the United Nations International Drug Control Program (UNDCP) which later became the United Nations Office on Drugs and Crime (UNODC). He has been, *inter alia*, a key author of UNODC's annual 'World Drug Report' publications (1997–2012) and of UNODC's report on 'Estimating Illicit Financial Flows resulting from Drug Trafficking and other Transnational Organized Crimes' (October 2011) and a contributing author of UNODC's report on 'The Globalization of Crime – A Transnational Organized Crime Threat Assessment' (June 2010).

Peter Reuter is Professor of Public Policy and of Criminology at the University of Maryland. His research is primarily on illegal markets and related policy issues. His books include *Drug War Heresies: Learning from Other Vices, Times and Places* (with Robert MacCoun) and *Chasing Dirty Money* (with Edwin Truman). He served as the founding president of the International Society for the Study of Drug Policy from 2007 to 2011.

Iris van Rossum is an economist and Junior Researcher at the Amsterdam Institute for International Development (AIID). She holds a BA in Economics from the University of Utrecht (UU) and an MA in (Development) Economics from the Free University Amsterdam (VU). Her research interests include Public Policy and Development Economics.

Friedrich Schneider is Professor of Economics of the Johannes Kepler University of Linz, Austria. He obtained his PhD in Economics from the University of Konstanz and has held numerous visiting and honorary positions. He was the European editor of *Public Choice* and he has published extensively in leading economics journals including *The Quarterly Journal of Economics*, *The American Economic Review*, *The Economic Journal*, and *Kyklos*. He has published 67 books, 195 articles in scientific journals and 169 articles in edited volumes.

Maaike Stouten works as a legal counsel at the Netherlands Authority for the Financial Markets. Stouten has written a PhD thesis at Utrecht University, School of Law. The title of her thesis is 'De witwasmeldplicht. Omvang en handhaving van de Wwft-meldplicht voor juridische en fiscale dienstverleners' [The anti-money laundering reporting duty. Scope and enforcement of the Dutch reporting duty for legal and fiscal service providers], (Den Haag: Boom Juridische Uitgevers 2012).

André Tilleman is a trained lawyer and works with a supervisory institution in the Netherlands. In addition, he is active as an academic lecturer and researcher. He has published various articles on money laundering and disciplinary law relating to especially civil law notaries.

Lotte Tromp is currently pursuing an MSc in International Economics at the Erasmus University School of Economics Rotterdam (ESE). She holds a Bachelor's degree in Economics from Utrecht University. Her interests lie in Policy Economics, especially Trade Policy and Development.

Brigitte Unger is Professor of Public Sector Economics at the Utrecht University School of Economics (USE), the Netherlands, and Director of the Institute for Economics and Social Science Research (Wirtschafts- und Sozialwissenschaftliches Institut (WSI)), Germany. She has published diverse articles, three books with Edward Elgar on money laundering and edited a special issue about money laundering in the *Review of Law and Economics*.

John Vervaele is full-time Professor of Economic and European Criminal Law at Utrecht Law School (the Netherlands) and Professor of European Criminal Law at the College of Europe in Bruges (Belgium). He is vice-president of the International Association of Penal Law (AIDP), in charge of the scientific coordination of the world organization for criminal law. His scholarly work focuses on white collar crime and economic offences and European criminal law and procedure. The main topics in his research field are: enforcement of Union law; standards of due process of law, procedural safeguards and human rights; criminal law and procedure and regional integration; comparative economic and financial criminal law; and terrorism and criminal procedure. He has undertaken a great deal of research in these areas, both for Dutch Departments and European

Institutions as well as a working consultant. He regularly teaches as visiting professor in foreign universities, in Europe, the US, Latin America and China.

Barbara Vettori is Assistant Professor in Sociology of Deviance at the Faculty of Political and Social Sciences, Università Cattolica del Sacro Cuore, Milan, Italy. She holds an MSc in Criminology and Criminal Justice from Cardiff University and a PhD in Criminology from the University of Trento. Her main research interests are organised and economic crime. In relation to these criminal phenomena she has undertaken evaluation assessments of counter policies and practices – in particular, anti-money laundering regulation, confiscation legislation and, more recently, legislation on the disposal of confiscated assets and on criminal liability of legal entities.

Frans van Waarden is Professor of Policy and Organization Studies at Utrecht University and Fellow at its honours college, University College Utrecht, the Netherlands. Being a sociologist, he is particularly interested in issues at the interface of economics, politics and law.

John Walker is an independent research consultant, specializing in the development of forecasting models for strategic planning of criminal justice systems, and economic models of the proceeds of crime, the costs of crime, and money laundering. His work has received multiple awards for innovation and commendations for business excellence.

John S. Zdanowicz is the Florida International Bankers Association Professor of Finance at Florida International University and President of International Trade Alert, Inc. He gained his PhD in finance from Michigan State University. Professor Zdanowicz has consulted for US Customs, the CIA, the Internal Revenue Service, the US Department of Justice, and the US Congress Office of Technology Assessment. Professor Zdanowicz is an internationally recognized expert on money laundering, capital flight, income tax evasion, and terrorist financing through international trade flows. Zdanowicz and a colleague were awarded a $2 million research grant from the US Treasury to study transfer pricing and money laundering issues.

Preface

Brigitte Unger and Daan van der Linde

In this *Research Handbook on Money Laundering* we set out to give you a survey of the state of the art in the debate surrounding money laundering. We have invited authors from academia, international organizations, from practice and country representatives to write an 8–15-page contribution on the topic of money laundering. Since it was not possible to find a historian writing (for free) on the history of money laundering, the editors themselves took care of it. However, this still seems a promising field for economic historians to delve into.

We thank all the participants in this volume for their valuable contributions. We would also especially like to thank the student assistants from the Chair of Public Sector Economics, Utrecht University School of Economics, Tom Geijsen and Jorrit Hendriksma. Finally we would like to thank Edward Elgar for the opportunity to publish, and especially Tara Gorvine for her help in the process.

The Utrecht University School of Economics, where we are both employed as Professor and PhD candidate, stands for multidisciplinary research. We hope that through this Handbook, the study of money laundering will become a flourishing field in multidisciplinary academia.

PART I

INTRODUCTION

1. Introduction

Brigitte Unger

Money laundering (ML) is a multidisciplinary topic which has become important since the late 1980s. Covering the political regulatory, social, criminological, anthropological and economic aspects, this volume tries to show the state of the art in the money laundering debate. Why did money laundering become so important (Part II)? To what extent does money laundering pose a problem and what effects does it have (Part III)? For whom is laundering a problem (Part IV)? What is the size of the problem (Part V)? What ways of laundering exist (Part VI)? How can it be combated and what legislation is involved (Part VII)? How effective is anti-money laundering policy? To what extent is it a danger to individual privacy protection? And what improvements can be recommended (Part VIII)?

1.1 INTRODUCTION

Money laundering, being the disguising of the illicit origin of money was criminalized only recently, though it dates back to ancient times. In these ancient times false trading was the way to transport illegal merchandise and proceeds (see Zdanowicz in this volume, Chapter 20). Chicago gangster Al Capone is often cited as the father of the modern form of transferring illegal proceeds, or money laundering. He used the cash intense business of launderettes to disguise his illegal alcohol proceeds in times of prohibition in the 1920s. Al Capone's laundering of money in launderettes might however be a myth – he was convicted in 1931 for tax evasion and not for his bootlegging.

Another potential origin of the term comes from the fact that money laundering may refer to the 'washing' of coins. Coins were washed in casinos in the early 1900s, so ladies wearing white gloves would not get them dirty playing in the casino. It is, however, also not proven whether the term laundering stems from this 'washing' of money. The term 'money laundering' first appeared in newspapers reporting the Watergate scandal in the United States in 1973. The expression first appeared in a judicial or legal context in 1982 in the case *US v $4,255,625.39* (1982) 551 F Supp.314.[1] Since, anti-money laundering measures have taken an amazing route, from fighting Al Capone's alcohol business and drugs to fighting Al Qaeda and other terrorist groups (see Chapter 2).

1.2 THE HISTORY OF MONEY LAUNDERING

Brigitte Unger of Utrecht University gives an overview of the history of anti-money laundering regulation in this volume. It is especially the United States who have a high interest in making money laundering a global issue. The Financial Action Task Force (FATF), an intergovernmental body established by the G-7 in 1989, sets international standards (the '40 + 9 Recommendations', 40 on money laundering plus nine on terrorist financing) and forces compliance of countries by means of blacklisting countries as 'non cooperative'. Compliance with the standards is checked every three years in mutual evaluations reports, while the speed with which countries have implemented these standards is amazing. The European Union complies with the international standards, in addition establishing three anti-money laundering and combating terrorist financing Directives, which force member states to comply through hard law. The Fourth Directive will come into force soon. The EU Directives concern administrative law issues, meaning duties to identify launderers and laundering transactions, e.g. reporting duties of obliged entities, know your customer rules, risk assessment issues, while they leave the repressive part – punishing criminals – to criminal law and law enforcement of the member states.

1.3 THE PROBLEM

To what extent is money laundering a problem: How and for whom does it pose a problem? Is money laundering a serious problem? Are there any victims of money laundering? Does it harm anyone when the Italian or Columbian mafia puts a billion US$ into the European banking system? Or isn't it rather beneficial if more liquidity is put into the dried out banking sector during the financial crisis? In a newspaper interview in 2008, the United Nations Office on Drugs and Crime (UNODC) head of the money laundering section, Antonio Costa, warned about criminal organizations using the financial crisis, in particular the interbank distrust crisis, for laundering purposes. Evidently, there were also benefits for consumers and businesses who could get additional loans from an otherwise dried out banking sector.

Joras Ferwerda, economist at the Utrecht University School of Economics, gives an overview of the potential negative effects that money laundering can have. In this sense it *does* pose a problem. Money laundering can have negative effects, economically, socially and politically. The economic effects, for example, concern unfair competition between honest and dishonest business, distortion of prices, a negative effect on investment, and eventually the crowding out of honest business. Social effects include increases in corruption and bribing. Laundering needs helpers and facilitators, so more and more people are drawn into criminality. Political effects are, for example, that criminals can undermine democratic systems, with drug dealers becoming ministers. Ferwerda does a detailed analysis of the growth effects of money laundering. Here, two opposite mechanisms operate: On the one hand laundering money is simply money, which helps the private sector to grow. On the other hand, more laundering means more crime, which negatively impacts growth.

The impact of money laundering on crime is specified by Donato Masciandaro, Professor of Finance at Bocconi University, Milan, Italy. In his contribution, Masciandaro shows that one has to reconcile two strands of literature related to money laundering: Becker's economics of crime and finance, since money laundering is not only a criminal, but also a financial phenomenon. Masciandaro shows that if criminals reinvest parts of their ill-gotten gains into the real economy, this will result in a multiplicative increase of crime. Since money laundering can lead to an explosion of crime rates, it is a ticking time bomb and therefore creates a serious problem that has to be fought.

The direct effects of money laundering are questioned. Who suffers directly when the Brazilian mafia sends ten million US$ to a country? Whether there are any victims of money laundering is an important question for lawyers and philosophers. Even for practical purposes, this poses a problem. In many countries, a money laundering prosecution can only even be started by either the public prosecutor or by the victims themselves. The Financial Intelligence Unit (FIU), an organization which detects laundering from reports of the obliged entities, often faces the problem that it cannot start a prosecution because it is not the victim. But who is the victim? Money laundering usually does not have direct victims; it can even be interpreted as a 'victimless crime'. This legal philosophical concept from the nineteenth century has not lost its attraction today. The contribution by Loek Groot, Associate Professor of Economics of the Public Sector at Utrecht University School of Economics, on decimating money laundering by legalizing drugs and prostitution, analyzes from a philosophical economic background whether money laundering constitutes a victimless crime. Referring to the debate initiated by John Stuart Mill, who in his 1859 'On Liberty' argued that drugs transactions constitute a victimless crime, since both the buyer and seller of the drug agree on a contract in which the latter is asking a price for a specific amount of drugs, while the former is willing to pay this in order to get drugged. Mill's argument in a nutshell is that since both market participants act voluntarily, and since they do not cheat each other, nobody is harmed, and therefore drugs should be liberalized. A debate on the harmful effects of drugs on society followed, in which Posner (1992) introduced the concept of cost and benefits, which should be weighed against each other. In this tradition, Groot argues that if drugs were to be liberalized, money laundering from drugs would also not constitute a crime anymore. Groot speaks in favor of a cost–benefit analysis which looks at the costs of forbidding victimless crimes and the benefits of doing so. Only if the benefits from prohibiting drugs and money laundering outweighs the costs of so doing, should drugs and money laundering be criminalized. From a liberal point of view, making drugs legal and thereby decriminalizing money laundering should be reconsidered. This liberal, Dutch view on legalizing drugs and thereby reducing the criminal proceeds from drugs definitely diametrically opposes recurrent US politics, which favor a broadening of predicate crimes for laundering rather than a reduction of them. It might, however, be wise to take into account the findings of Groot and to keep an eye on the costs and benefits of anti-money laundering policy, defining who the victims of laundering are.

Michael Levi, criminologist and sociologist from the University of Cardiff in the UK, gives an overview of the most important predicate crime for money laundering: fraud. He distinguishes fraud against individuals, business and authorities and shows ways of estimating the costs of fraud. Technological progress has led to more fraud detection and improvement in data, but there are also more possibilities for larger-scale fraud in a complex society.

Recently, another predicate crime, terrorism financing, has been subsumed under money laundering. Causes for terrorism are found in inequality, lack of education and ideology. Tim Krieger and Daniel Meierrieks from the University of Freiburg, Germany, argue that while terrorist attacks are usually inexpensive, running and maintaining a terrorist organization requires substantial financial means. Countering terrorist financing may thus indeed be a viable counter-terrorism policy. Though 9/11 has traumatized the Western world, and not only Americans, from the viewpoint of sheer costs compared to the whole US economy, the economic effects have been small. It is mainly small and less diversified countries (i.e., less developed economies) characterized by low macroeconomic robustness and facing significant terrorist activity that experience the most severe macroeconomic consequences. Terrorist financing can take place in three ways: (i) *state-financing* (i.e., state sponsorship of terrorism); (ii) *financing by legitimate means* (e.g., from business, charities, diaspora support, etc.); and (iii) *private financing by unlawful means* that usually includes outright *criminal activities* (e.g., bank robberies, drug trafficking, kidnapping, extortion). Anti-money laundering instruments are more likely to help when terrorism is financed by *private, legitimate means*. Terrorists are different from organized crime groups. They often operate in the name of 'higher ideals', they want change, while criminal groups are conservative and want to abuse existing institutions without change. Krieger and Meierrieks argue that anti-money laundering policy can help to prevent the planning and execution of terrorist attacks in the short run.

1.4 WHO IS THREATENED BY LAUNDERING ACTIVITIES?

Which countries are threatened by laundering activities? Which countries bear the costs of laundering and which ones perhaps benefit from the additional financial resources derived from launderers?

A method which distinguishes threats and policy responses and classifies (European) countries into low and high threat areas is carried out in the EU Project 'The Economic and Legal Effectiveness of Anti Money Laundering and Combating Terrorist Financing Policy' (ECOLEF) (see Unger et al., 2011, Second and Third delivery to the EU). One can see that rankings depend very much on the weight different variables get. If, for example, the cash intensity of the economy is weighted highly, the Southern European countries are especially highly threatened by money laundering risk. If, however, big financial centers are considered to have a high money laundering risk, then Northern European countries seem more threatened. Whatever the final model and scheme that wins the threat assessment race, it seems the trend is going in the direction of ranking and benchmarking in this area.

Jakub Brettl, a former student from Utrecht University shows different ways of estimating the country risk of laundering. Compared to the findings of John Walker (see Chapter 13 in this volume), Brettl's findings emphasize the role of cash. The more cash-intense a country, the higher the risk of laundering, he argues, whereas Walker focuses on the role of financial centers for laundering. Stephen Dawe, Senior Financial Sector Expert at the Legal Department of the IMF, in his contribution on conducting national money laundering or the financing of terrorism risk shows the latest approaches of the IMF to assess the likelihood that money laundering occurs. Countries, sectors and transaction types can be scored and ranked on a scale from 1 to 7, showing whether they are highly exposed to money laundering risks or not. The IMF has created a large dataset with several modules for this. It distinguishes between the likelihood that a risky event occurs and the consequences this type of laundering has.

Is money laundering a problem for small or for big countries? Which countries tolerate laundering? In the international debate it is very often small countries and little islands who are blamed for tolerating money laundering. When in 1995 the Seychelles openly advertised 'If you invest more than 10 million US$, we will not inquire where the money originates from', there was uproar in the international community. Under the US threat of blacklisting and of forbidding American banks to do business with the Seychelles, the Seychelles finally gave in to international pressure (see Unger and Rawlings, 2008). Unger and Rawlings (2008) showed that countries might have an incentive to compete for criminal money. Gnutzmann, McCarthy and Unger (2010) distinguished between small and big countries. They showed that while big countries are responsible for larger amounts of laundering due to the volume of their financial markets, small countries have a larger incentive to launder, hence are more likely to launder. This is because they usually bear the benefits from laundering, but not the costs of the underlying crime, which often stays in the country of origin of the money. Killian McCarthy shows in this volume that the argument is reversed when it comes to developing countries, who usually do not suffer from criminal money – neither domestically nor abroad – but from their own crime. One has to look at anti-money laundering policy from the perspective *cui bono?*: 'whom does it serve', McCarthy suggests anti-money laundering policy benefits mostly the rich, large and developed countries.

Two distinguished representatives of small, developed (and rich) countries have been generous enough to provide their view on small countries' role concerning money laundering and financial integrity. His Highness, Prince Michael von und zu Liechtenstein, a big supporter of academics in general and president of the European Center of Austrian Economics Foundation, was kind enough to comment on the role of Liechtenstein: a small country of around 36000 inhabitants, located between Austria and Switzerland, with a large financial sector and high financial expertise. Liechtenstein came into the news when lists of German account holders in Liechtenstein popped up under the suspicion of tax evasion. The scandal grew when it turned out that the Liechtenstein bank employee who had collected this information by violating the bank's confidentiality requirements had received several million euro from the German government to pass on this list. Evidently, the Germans were eager to get at their tax evaders in order to increase tax revenues. However, lawyers were concerned whether a government purchasing stolen lists from criminals was engaged in a criminal activity called *Hehlerei* (dealing in stolen goods) in the German Criminal Code.

His Highness very clearly expresses the view that hard crimes like drugs, fraud and human trafficking should not be intermingled with soft misdemeanors like tax evasion. Since tax evasion is no predicate crime for money laundering in Liechtenstein, the country has not and is not doing money laundering here. The US policy of making tax evasion a crime is not necessarily the road that Europe should be following. It is not by criminalizing tax evasion that one should reduce tax avoidance, the Prince argues, but by making tax laws more transparent and simpler among European (and other) countries. At the moment it is impossible to oversee the different tax loopholes, so how could a Liechtenstein bank possibly find out who evades taxes? Simplifying tax laws and providing legal certainty in this area is, according to the Prince, the right way to go.

The second small European country, Austria, with 8 million inhabitants, located between Germany, Switzerland, Liechtenstein, Czech Republic, Slovakia, Italy, Slovenia and Hungary, also came into the news for not complying with FATF Recommendations and for providing the opportunity for especially the Russian mafia to launder its money.

Austria was mainly criticized for not criminalizing self-laundering and for its banking secrecy, which does not allow official authorities to have access to bank information except when there is already an ongoing lawsuit. The Governor of the Oesterreichische Nationalbank (Austrian Central Bank), and former university Professor of Public Finance, Ewald Nowotny, reflects on the role of small countries for financial integrity. Contrary to the US, which lists as the ultimate goal of anti-money laundering policy to reduce money laundering and crime, the EU has included a third goal: to maintain the integrity of financial markets. The contribution on financial market integrity and the role of small countries shows that under international pressure Austria was able to adapt its laws and regulations very quickly to international standards. The chapter demonstrates the changes that have been made, which are even more amazing when one takes into account Austria's traditionally very legalistic culture, which means that what is written in a law must be practicable and practiced and must be consistent with what is written in other parts of the law. Certain parts of the FATF Standards and of the EU Directives are much more difficult to implement for legalistic countries than for less legalistic cultures who only copy and paste the Directive and leave it up to the national Courts to decide in cases of conflicting norms. To give an example: self-laundering – where the one who commits the crime also does the laundering of its proceeds – was considered double punishment by Austrian Criminal Law, since doing the robbery and doing something with the money from the robbery was seen as one criminal act. Austria, under FATF threat of blacklisting, changed this very fundamental principal of law and abandoned self-laundering. This also means a very far reach of the FATF into countries' national rights; in particular, because the hard-law EU Directives do not oblige countries to abandon self-laundering and the FATF Recommendations are not founded on any legal or democratic base. They are soft law based on the threat of blacklisting in the event of non compliance.

The anti-money laundering law, with its very American origins in adding up punishments is much more difficult to implement in a legalistic culture than in a more pragmatic culture. With regard to implementation, many Eastern European countries only copied and pasted the EU Directive and waited to see how the administration and Courts would deal with it. Austria has a very well functioning bureaucracy, dating back to Empress Maria Theresa, which very meticulously sticks to the law and the room for maneuver it provides. Changing the law in a country with a legalistic culture means a much more binding commitment to international standards than in a more pragmatic culture. Adapting the Austrian anti-money law to adjust to international standards must therefore be seen as a high commitment to the international community. Bank secrecy is a constitutional right in Austria which could only be removed with a two-thirds majority of Parliament. Many of the criticized bearer instruments have been forbidden by law as well.

The chapter illustrates the changes in law and the supervisory body for anti-money laundering policy issues. Furthermore, it claims that for financial integrity small countries have a definite advantage over large countries: it is not only easier to know your customer, but the more essential part of anti-money laundering policy is to know your banks. In a small country with regular meetings of all actors it is much easier to reach agreements and an overview over anti-money laundering threats and to combat them in a consensual style.

1.5 THE SCALE OF THE PROBLEM

The first estimate of global amounts of money laundering was performed in 1995 by the Australian criminologist John Walker from the University of Wollongong. He first estimated the proceeds of crime per type of crime and country and then used a gravity model (see Walker and Unger 2009) in order to find out how much of these proceeds were attracted by which country.

Walker's first estimate amounted to 2.8 trillion US$ laundered worldwide. Ever since, a large debate built up: In 1998, Michael Camdessus of the IMF came up with a guess of 1.5 trillion US$, by then five percent of global GDP. Some countries estimated their amount of laundering and came up with similar amounts (for a survey of this debate and for estimates for the Netherlands, see Unger 2007). Lately, the Walker model was tested (see Ferwerda et al. 2013), refined and a new specification of it was suggested.

In this volume, Andreas Buehn and Friedrich Schneider give a short overview of a large amount of estimates and present their own model of estimating laundering, the MIMIC model. By means of observable variables which are assumed to develop parallel with money laundering, they can calculate how money laundering changes over time. They have to assume a base year in order to calculate the volume of money laundering. The advantage of the MIMIC model is that it is one of the few methods to measure money laundering over time. Another one favored by me and also discussed by Buehn and Schneider is that of Busato, Bagella and Argentiero which is also in this volume (Chapter 17). Buehn and Schneider measure that money laundering increased US$ 273 billion (or 1.33% of official GDP) in 1995 to US$ 603 billion (or 1.74% of official GDP) in 2006 for 20 OECD countries

The contribution of Raymond Baker, Director of Global Financial Integrity (GFI) focuses on estimating money laundering and capital flight from wealth data. Baker wants a broader approach, including all forms of finance that escapes regulation, since especially for developing countries this can be disastrous. Baker shows that for every dollar of development aid sent to developing countries, ten dollars flow back as capital flight. This disequilibrium in world finance deprives developing countries of their chance to catch up.

The latest efforts in this field deal with trying to analyze money laundering routes from assets confiscated. The contribution of Thomas Pietschmann from the UNODC takes this kind of approach. Here, drug seizures are used to identify drug routes. Pietschmann first gives an overview of the efforts of the UNODC to regulate and fight drugs and money laundering. In 2009, the United Nations (UN) developed a new model to estimate drug money flows. In his chapter, Pietschmann presents the efforts of the UN to find out about major routes of drugs and drug money. His model indicates that the most cocaine consumption still takes place in the US, followed by Europe. Using a transport route model fed with data on drug seizures, one can show where the drugs and the drug money flow. According to Pietschmann, in 2009 about 53 billion US$ were available for laundering from the cocaine trade alone. Special attention in this model is also given to transit countries.

A new approach of using a two sector dynamic macroeconomic equilibrium model, where one sector, the legal sector, is known and can be calculated, and the second sector, the criminal sector, can be simulated from the model parameters, has been used for estimating money laundering by the Italian economists Michele Bagella, Francesco Busato and Amedeo Argentiero from the Universities of Rome 'Tor Vergata', Naples Parthenope and Perugia. This model predicts money laundering in percent of GDP for the US and the EU countries.

Despite all the analysis, there is still some doubt as to whether money laundering increases or decreases over time. Unger and den Hertog (2012) showed that it was impossible from all empirical studies done so far to even conclude the direction of money laundering trends. Many opt, as Buehn and Schneider do, for the opinion that laundering is increasing. Yet, when one looks at the development of the proceeds of crime, they seem to be stable over time.

The second unresolved question is whether money laundering is big or small in volume. Here the major divide between economists and criminologists still seems to exist. Money laundering research is performed among many disciplines. Evidently, the methodologies of these disciplines differ a lot, with several scientific 'languages' being used. Unfortunately, there are very few 'translators' between them. The most pronounced and prominent critique of John Walker's estimates (and other large global estimations) is Peter Reuter from the School of Public Policy and Department of Criminology, University of Maryland. In his contribution on whether estimates of the volume of money laundering are either feasible or useful, Reuter criticizes assumptions of the Walker model and generally rejects global estimates of money laundering. Also, when one reads the contribution of Petrus van Duyne, emeritus Professor of Criminology from Tilburg University, the Netherlands on 'Crime-money and Financial Conduct', one sees that he favors a criminological micro, or as he calls it, 'bottom up approach', for discovering crime-money. The Dutch criminologists have been pioneers in studying money launderers and their behavior, and the article of Van Duyne gives an impressive overview of this. From what kind of predicate crime do launderers earn their money, what do launderers do with their money, how do they spend it, and are they rich or poor are questions that have been addressed in several case and file studies. At a micro level one cannot detect the large sums of criminal money proclaimed by international institutions such as the FATF or the IMF, or found in the economic models of Walker (1995) and Walker and Unger (2009), Van Duyne claims. He gives several explanations for this but favors one: methodological mistakes of economists, by simply just inconsistently counting together wrong variables. According to him, the threat of laundering is heavily exaggerated. There are simply far fewer launderers and less crime-money than internationally proclaimed. However, Van Duyne also mentions one argument which might reconcile the debate led by criminological and international economists. It is an argument which Stephen Levitt (2006) elaborated in his famous article 'Why do drug dealers still live with their mom': only very few drug dealers make it to the top. There is a very low chance of becoming the head of a criminal organization and of earning very much. The rest of the dealers remain severely underpaid, often below the minimum wage, clinging to the small chance of getting rich, similar to lotto players. This might explain why internationally respected bottom-up analysts like Petrus van Duyne, Michael Levi and Peter Reuter do not find large amounts of crime-money. They might simply mainly find the many small dealers on the shopfloor.

1.6 WAYS TO LAUNDER

Which techniques do launderers use to launder money? And how much money is laundered and in what ways? John Zdanowicz, Professor of Finance at Florida International University, in Chapter 20 estimates the oldest way of laundering, trade based money laundering, being illicit money hidden in fake invoices for export and import products. He shows that one can detect particular products with very unusual prices or weights, and countries which definitely have more of these dubiously priced products. He establishes risk indicators by product and by country. In the US on average, more than 10 million records per year are analyzed, with each record identifying the item, quantity and US$ value along with the mode of transportation, the US customs district through which the goods passed and the foreign country involved in the trade. Zdanowicz deals with very large datasets, where over 232 columns represent every country in the world, while every import harmonized code and every export harmonized code are represented by over 26 000 rows. If a transaction exceeds a certain threshold it is classified as suspicious. In total, Zdanowicz calculates, about 168 billion US$ moved out from the US due to trade-based money laundering and 233 billion US$ moved into the US: This amounts to about ten percent of US trade.

Unger and Ferwerda (2011) used Zdanowicz's idea of unusual prices for identifying money laundering in the real estate sector. Together with criminologists they developed an instrument to detect suspicious objects and applied this method to two Dutch cities. The same methodology can also be used to estimate the costs of corruption in public procurement. Joras Ferwerda and Brigitte Unger from the Utrecht University School of Economics demonstrate this method in this volume. At the moment, in a small project lasting until June 2013, together with Ioana Deleanu, they are busy applying the same method to estimate corruption in public procurement for the European Union in a joint project with PriceWaterhouseCoopers and Ecorys. A new field to enter the money laundering debate is tax evasion. Some countries see fighting tax evasion as the main purpose of anti-money laundering policy (e.g. the Nordic countries) whereas others focus on combating drug dealers (e.g. Austria). Lately, the US and the FATF have made great efforts to include tax evasion as a predicate offence into the money laundering definition. The concept of money laundering, starting with fighting drug crimes, then extended to all other sorts of other crime among which are human trafficking and corruption and finally terrorism would then be further enlarged. The contribution of Victor van Kommer from the International Bureau of Fiscal Documentation (IBFD) shows how authorities can measure the tax gap and tax compliance. The article also warns against too precise measurements of the tax gap in practice. Especially in less developed countries, hunting for tax money might turn into a war against people. Van Kommer makes the case for applying the principles of good governance in order to raise enough tax income, monitor the compliance of tax payers and still keep enough flexibility for effective administration.

Lotte Tromp, Iris van Rossum, Andreas Buehn and Victor van Kommer analyze to what extent corporations can make use of tax havens to launder money. They investigate the definition of tax havens. Under which conditions, they ask, is a country a tax haven? They survey the literature on tax havens and distinguish three categories of tax havens: the ones with low corporate tax rates; the ones with large secrecy; and the ones with low corporate tax rates *and* large secrecy. With this concept, they test whether the

Netherlands is a tax haven. The Netherlands have repeatedly been accused (especially by the US) of being a tax haven for corporations. Unger (2007) also highlighted special financial constructions, such as special purpose vehicles, to facilitate laundering. The chapter here (chapter 23) concludes that the Netherlands, with its low corporate tax rates and exemptions attract mainly tax avoiders, like famous pop music groups, but less so criminal money. This is quite the opposite from the findings of Unger (2007).

Do launderers profit from developments in financial markets like financial innovations? The contribution of John Biggins working at the financial services regulatory authority at the Central Bank of Ireland, shows that especially the over-the-counter (OTC) derivative market can be abused by criminals. He first explains derivatives and translates the language of financial markets into more accessible language. Buying equals going short, selling equals going long and making a bet for interest rates to fall is a 'plain Vanilla swap'. Since the payoff is derived from a contingent future event (namely the interest rate falling), it is called a derivative. Biggins shows that with the help of a broker this partly unregulated market can easily be abused by paying largely in cash for the bets and booking the winnings as legal income. With this, Biggins points to the most sensitive point of regulating money laundering. Criminals very quickly discover loopholes or as Unger and Den Hertog (2012) put it: water always finds its ways.

In his second contribution, Michael Levi presents e-gaming in the EU and associated money laundering risks. He shows differences relating to risk to exist between land-based and e-gaming, and argues for desirability of different AML regulations for the latter, as opportunities for monitoring are different.

1.7 LEGAL ASPECTS

Paolo Costanzo, a lawyer who has worked at the European Union on money laundering issues and is now employed at the Italian Central Bank, Banca d'Italia, which is also the location of the Italian Financial Intelligence Unit, analyzes the change from a rule-based to a risk-based approach in anti-money laundering policy. Originally, reporting entities, like banks and other financial institutions, had to identify laundering activities by means of a rule-based approach. They had clear rules which dictated under what circumstances they had to report a transaction to the Financial Intelligence Unit. For example a clear rule would be, 'if there is a cash transaction exceeding 8000 euro, this has to be reported'. The problem with this approach was that far too many reports were sent (every grandmother buying a car for her grandson had to be reported).

However, criminals also knew the rules and could use smurfing to circumvent them: just sending 7999 euro in order to stay below the reporting threshold, for example. This is why the US and the EU changed to a risk-based approach. In a risk-based approach the obliged entities, banks financial institutions, but also lawyers, notaries, real estate agents, dealers in goods with large values have to develop their own criteria for when they consider something to be risky. Costanzo shows that a risk-based approach will lead to less uniform compliance patterns, and that it will change the mode of supervision. Controls, like compliance, have an essential judgemental component and require that the competent authority focuses on the whole compliance process to understand when the failure of the measures adopted depends on poor compliance and when it depends on lack of information about risks. Costanzo shows that costs for the banking sector have certainly increased, especially in the 'transition' period. The investments that have to be done, in terms of organization, procedures, staff, training, IT tools, etc. have been, and still are, considerable. Costanzo is positive about the future and thinks that benefits from a better identification of money laundering risks will (over)compensate for these costs in the long term.

Anti-money laundering policy is based on a twin approach. One part concerns criminal law which identifies criminal acts and punishment, and the other part relates to administrative law. The latter aims at preventing laundering happening by making sure that the private sector, such as banks, dealers in large values, real estate agents, notaries and lawyers identify and report laundering activities. In their chapter, 'Prevention of money laundering and terrorist financing from a good governance perspective' Melissa van den Broek and Henk Addink (Institute of Constitutional and Administrative Law of Utrecht University, Faculty of Law, Economics and Governance) give an overview of the administrative law part of AML policy. They identify four administrative law related elements: customer due diligence (know your customer measures); the reporting obligation of entities (entities have to report suspicious transaction to the FIU); the record-keeping obligation of obliged entities; and the enforcement (supervision and sanctioning) of those obligations. Are these elements in line with principles of good governance, a concept which has been promoted by the World Bank in recent years? These principles are put into groups that allow us to test whether legal norms (in our case anti-money laundering regulations) are in line with them.

Principles of proper administration, of transparency, of citizens' participation, of effectiveness, of accountability and of respecting fundamental human rights are first described and then tested. The authors find tensions between some of these principles – in particular the tension between the reporting obligation and the principle of legal privilege (which forms part of the right to a fair trial). Since notaries and lawyers have been included as entities that are obliged to report suspicious transactions, there is a tension between the lawyer's duty of secrecy and the right of the client to confidentiality, that is, the client's right to speak openly with his lawyer and thus to a fair trial, and the lawyer's duty to report a suspicious transaction or client. Another tension they identify is between the effectiveness of anti-money laundering policy and the accountability of politics. Involving the private sector by using a risk-based reporting approach which leaves it up to the private sector to develop criteria for identifying money laundering risks means a strong involvement of private actors in the process, which could jeopardize the classic understanding of accountability. Who can be held accountable for anti-money laundering policy if the public sector shifts responsibilities for combating laundering in a very poorly defined way to the private sector?

From a criminal law perspective, John Vervaele (Utrecht Law School, Utrecht University) shows that money laundering and terrorist financing regulations imply a paradigm change in law. Already the classic AML approach of the FATF has resulted in several substantial changes such as establishing an autonomous offence; the elaboration of asset-freezing, asset-seizure and asset-confiscation into an autonomous control and sanctioning mechanism. The real paradigmatic chance has however been established by enlarging the anti-money laundering approach to combating terrorist financing. With this, criminal law evolves into a proactive law, of a preventive kind. We see an evolution from a judicial criminal law to a criminal law with the strong power of the executive branch of government. We also see an evolution from a criminal law based on the violation of a legally protected interest into a criminal law of the dangerousness of a person. This can imply serious privacy concerns.

1.8 IMPLEMENTATION AND EFFECTIVENESS OF AML

With regard to the implementation and effectiveness of anti-money laundering policy in practice, Brigitte Unger and Frans van Waarden, Professor of sociology at Utrecht University are less optimistic than Paolo Costanzo about the future of the risk-based approach. They agree with Costanzo that the risk-based approach will end up as a book of rules, however, they do not think that this book is the result of the private sector's learning experience, but rather a set of rules emerging from court decisions. More and more private entities and (falsely) accused launderers will go before the courts and finally the court decisions will establish new rules. The risk-based approach will end up as a new rule-based approach with rules set by the courts and not by politicians. The authors show that reporting duties under the risk-based approach have quite different effects in an adversarial system, like the US and a consensual system, like the Netherlands. Reporting increased in the US, since banks are afraid of being punished for not reporting. However, they tend to overdo it, and report too much, and in this way deliver quite useless information to the law enforcement agencies. In the Netherlands, where rules have been developed jointly with the private sectors and where fines are low, the amount of reporting has decreased, but the quality of information has increased.

Maaike Stouten and André Tilleman analyze the first tension mentioned by Broek and Addink in Chapter 27 in more depth. In their contribution on 'Reporting duty for lawyers versus legal privilege – unresolved tension' they first define 'legal privilege' as the right of the client to confidentiality combined with a duty of secrecy on the part of the lawyer. They then give an overview and interpretation of various court decisions on this issue. Particularly interesting is the case they present where the Belgian bar, the 'Ordre des Barreaux', supported by some other bar associations, initiated a court case seeking a preliminary ruling from the European Court of Justice on the legality of the reporting duty to lawyers pursuant to the Second EU Directive in relation to *inter alia* Article 6 ('Right to a fair trial') of the Convention for the Protection of Human Rights and Fundamental Freedoms (ECHR). From this case one can conclude that the question of legal privilege and reporting duty has not been solved in non-contentious circumstances, where there is no link with judicial procedures. Furthermore, the European Court of Justice judgment left the interpretation of 'ascertaining the legal position' open to interpretation by national courts. The Belgian (and similarly the French) court applied a broad interpretation of the ECJ's judgment, whereas the Polish, Finnish and Dutch legislations applied a narrow interpretation. This means that defining what legal privilege is and what exceptions there are is far from being harmonized in Europe.

Jan van Koningsveld, former employee of the Dutch financial police FIOD, now Director of the Research Center Offshore Kennis Centrum, doubts the three-phase money laundering model of the UNODC. He claims that when the executive follows this approach it risks missing important money laundering cases. He tries to rethink the stages of the money laundering process to make enforcement more effective and suggests four instead of three phases for laundering. In particular, the stage before the criminals park their criminal proceeds would give the executive a second chance to trace the illicit proceeds.

From a practical perspective, former Austrian FIU policeman and now employee at EUROPOL, Burkhard Mühl, has analyzed the access by law enforcement agencies to financial data. Is it effective, or in fact the weak link in the investigation of financial crime and the tracing of criminal proceeds? Mühl used the CARIN Network which comprised at the time of the survey 46 countries and jurisdictions, including all 27 countries of the European Union. The research provided general information on how the systems in the respective countries function, supplemented by five cases studies which focused in particular on the identification of bank accounts via central bank account registers, central credit referencing agencies and other means. The research examined procedures, practical questions and obstacles in the daily work of law enforcement in their attempts to obtain financial information. The research findings indicate that two-thirds of the participating countries believe that the procedures they have in place to obtain financial information work well, whereas one-third are of the opinion that their systems do not work well. An increase in the submission of electronically processed and standardized data by the financial institutions as well as shorter response times by financial institutions are commonly seen as areas where improvement is needed. Finally, the study made clear that the establishment of central bank account registers as a tool to identify bank accounts and to trace crime proceeds seems to be an important requirement for law enforcement. At the moment almost all EU countries have established or decided to establish central bank registers. The only two exceptions at the time of writing this introduction are Cyprus and Austria.

Ioana Deleanu from the Utrecht University School of Economics shows differences of access to information by different Financial Intelligence Units. She uses information flow theory to find ways of improving information between the obliged entities, the Financial Intelligence Unit, the police, and the Public Prosecutor.

Barbara Vettori, Assistant Professor in Criminology at the Faculty of Sociology of the Università Cattolica del Sacro Cuore di Milano, Italy, in her chapter gives an overview of the cost–benefit analyses on anti-money laundering policy done so far. How effective is anti-money laundering policy? What are its costs what are its benefits? Little empirical research has been done on this. Legal concepts of how to empirically approach 'effectiveness' are not yet fully developed. Vettori highlights the work of Ferwerda (2009) who for the first time tried to operationalize legal effectiveness for empirical work. Vettori has participated in the first cost–benefit analysis done, the so-called 'Savona project', an EU project under the leadership of Ernesto Savona, which conducted a concise cost–benefit analysis on the ultimate beneficial ownership regulation. The EU project ECOLEF, led by Brigitte Unger, tries to fill in numbers for the variables defined by the 32 FATF Recommendations, by the EU and by Eurostat for European countries.

Money laundering will certainly stay on the international agenda for a while. We hope to disappoint money launderers, as we did with our first book (Unger, 2007). Very quickly after it appeared it was being sold secondhand from the Cayman islands, as it did not contain the practical hints for launderers on where to place their money. With this book we hope to attract the attention of researchers, law enforcers and people interested in this issue.

NOTE

1. See http://www.laundryman.u-net.com/page1_hist.html

REFERENCES

Ferwerda, J. (2009), 'The economics of crime and money laundering: Does anti-money laundering policy reduce crime?', *Review of Law and Economics*, Special issue: Tackling Money Laundering, **5**, (2), Article 5, 903–29.

Ferwerda, J., M. Kattenberg, H. Chang, B. Unger, L. Groot and J. Bikker (2013), 'Gravity models of trade-based money laundering', *Applied Economics*, **45**, (22), 3170–82.

Gnutzmann, H., K.J. McCarthy and B. Unger (2010), 'Dancing with the devil: Country size and the incentive to tolerate money laundering', *International Review of Law and Economics*, **30**, 244–52.

Levitt, S. (2006), *Freakonomics: A Rogue Economist Explores the Hidden Side of Everything*, New York, NY: William Morrow.

Posner, R.A. (1992), *Blackmail, Privacy, and Freedom of Contract*, Chicago Working Paper in Law & Economics, no. 4 (2d series).

Unger, B. (2007), *The Scale and Impacts of Money Laundering*, Cheltenham UK and Northampton, MA, USA: Edward Elgar.

Unger, B. and J. Ferwerda (2011), *Money Laundering in the Real Estate Sector: Suspicious Properties*, Cheltenham, UK and Northampton, MA, USA: Edward Elgar.

Unger, B. and J. Den Hertog (2012), 'Water always finds its way: Identifying new forms of money laundering', *Crime, Law, and Social Change*, **57** (3), 287–304.

Unger, B. and G. Rawlings (2008), 'Competing for criminal money', *Global Business and Economics Review*, **10**, (3), 331–52.

Unger, B., H. Addink, M. Van den Broek, I. Deleanu, and J. Ferwerda (2011), 'The economic and legal effectiveness of anti money laundering and combating terrorist financing policy', EU Project, 2009–2012. Second and Third Delivery.

Walker, J. (1995), 'Estimates of the extent of money laundering in and through Australia', paper prepared for AUSTRAC, Queanbeyan: John Walker Consulting Services.

Walker, J. and B. Unger (2009), 'Measuring global money laundering: The Walker Gravity Model', *Review of Law & Economics*, 5 (2), Article 2.

PART II

THE HISTORY OF MONEY LAUNDERING

2. Money laundering regulation: from Al Capone to Al Qaeda*

Brigitte Unger

2.1 INTRODUCTION

Global regulation of money laundering became an issue only in the late 1990s as a consequence of the liberalization of financial markets, which attracted both legal and illegal capital. The fact that laundering is a global phenomenon which is not directly harmful, and has no direct negative effects on society or business nor is the scale of it known, is a big challenge to the regulators. As a consequence, the support from business and society for a regulatory policy is weak. Laundering regulation was mainly the result of a failed US war on drugs which turned into a fight to reclaim the proceeds of crime. The Financial Action Task Force implemented this regulation by setting international standards and by blacklisting. In the EU hard law was used. Regulation switched from a rule-based to a risk-based approach, but even this is not well supported. Laundering regulation is still a public policy centered within nation states, however it is slowly becoming an issue of global governance where private organizations and the need for legitimacy are assuming more importance.

Money laundering – bringing illicit proceeds from drugs, fraud and other crime, back into the legal economy – owes its name to Al Capone. He used launderettes for disguising illegal alcohol revenues during prohibition in the US. Launderettes, a flourishing cash intensive business in the 1930s, when almost no household had a washing machine, were an ideal location to slip the money from illegal alcohol sales into the cash register. Disguising the origin of such money is, however, even older than Al Capone's 'washing of money'. One of the oldest techniques to circumvent government scrutiny was to use international trade to move money, undetected, from one country to another, by means of fake invoicing or falsely declared merchandise (Zdanowicz 2009).

Though money laundering is an old way of trying to hide the illicit proceeds from crime, it became an issue of international concern only in the last 20 years; and it is only since 09/11 that it figures as a prominent issue of national and international safety on the agenda of international organizations. How was it possible that a problem which existed for centuries was suddenly considered a topic of major international concern which had to be regulated? And how was it possible that its scope expanded from Al Capone's whiskey business to protecting national security and fighting Al Qaeda?

I will discuss the characteristics of the problems to be regulated in the following section and what they mean for the private support and public interest in regulating laundering in section 2.2. Section 2.3 shows the regulatory responses and section 2.4 the problems of the effectiveness, enforcement and legitimacy of anti-money regulation. The conclusions in section 2.5 on regulating global issues focus mainly on the role of the EU.

2.1.1 The Characteristics of the Problem to be Regulated

After criminalization of drug abuse in 1922 in the US, there followed almost a century of hopeless efforts to reduce drug trafficking, which led to the need for combating money laundering to be put on the international agenda. If one could not get at drug dealers and eventually other criminals directly, then at least they should be discouraged by the realization that they could not reap the monetary benefits of their acts. The following four characteristics make money laundering a particular regulatory challenge.

2.1.2 Victimless Crime

While money laundering makes crime pay because the launderer can safely disguise his illicit proceeds, it does not have direct victims. No one suffers from the fact that the Colombian drugs mafia sends $10 billion from one country to another. There are, hence, no victims who would complain, no liability claims that would be raised, and no tort law that could be applied. No direct harm comes from this.

The question heavily debated in legal literature is whether crime without victims should be punished at all and whether punishment is a deterrent (for a survey see Polinsky et al. 1997). Should the government leave people their free will and not forcibly prevent them from engaging in crime that does not harm others (Mill (2008 [1859]), Chapter 1, p. 21) or would society be damaged by this maleficent behavior and fall into decadence? *Public order crime* is now the preferred term for 'victimless' crime, based on the idea that there are always secondary victims such as family, friends, acquaintances, and society at large (for further reading see Siegel 2006; Siegel and Senna 2008)

2.1.3 No Direct Effects of Laundering

The harm of money laundering is only very indirect. Unger (2007) lists 25 negative and positive effects that money laundering can have. It can deter honest business activities, if criminals invest their money in particular sectors like the transport industry, restaurants, housing; it can lead to changes in relative prices, savings, output, employment and growth or it can affect the liquidity, reputation, integrity and stability of the financial sector. The public sector can suffer from unpaid taxes and criminals might buy up public enterprises during privatization efforts.

There are also social and political effects like increased corruption and bribery. Professionals, like lawyers, notary publics, real estate agents, accountants, can become contaminated since laundering needs facilitators. Criminals might undermine political institutions. That none of these effects can be directly observed poses problems for regulation.

2.1.4 Ambiguous Relation between Money Laundering and Terrorism Financing

Money laundering can also increase terrorist activity if the proceeds of crime are used to finance it. Here laundering serves two purposes: concealing the illegal origin of the money as well as the illegal destination of the funds (Masciandaro et al., 2007). Most experts agree that the sale and trade of drugs seem to be a sizable financial contributor to terrorist organizations. The Taliban, for example, profited from the trafficking of opium and taxing the drug trade in areas under its control, and these funds were subsequently used to support terrorist organizations like Al Qaeda (Schneider 2004).

However, very often terrorism is financed with clean money by abusing donations and foreign aid. This involves a process completely different from money laundering: 'money dirtying' which is the reverse of money laundering. Regulating terrorism together with money laundering therefore poses an additional challenge.

2.1.5 Unknown Size of the Problem

The regulator has a difficult business to do: there are no victims, the link between money laundering and crime is only a very vague one, and between money laundering and terrorist financing this link is even more doubtful. The regulator also does not know how big the problem is that he regulates. Estimates on global money laundering are still in their infancy. First, because the underlying crime is unknown, second because the proceeds of this unknown crime can only be estimated. As Reuter and Greenfield (2001, p. 171) observe, 'knowing the value of drug exports from Mexico to the US is \$1–3 billion rather than \$10–20 billion may be very important for purposes of allocating resources for money laundering investigations or even passing money laundering regulations in Mexico'. Global estimates for money laundering range from between \$45 and \$280 billion (Reuter and Greenfield 2001), and \$1.5 trillion in the IMF and Human Development Report 1999 (see TNI 2003) to \$2.85 trillion (Walker 1995, Walker 2002, Walker and Unger 2009).

2.1.6 A Global Phenomenon

Money laundering is a global phenomenon and regulation of it increased with the deregulation of financial markets, which has made countries more vulnerable. Today, money can be pumped around the world in a second through the push of a computer button. The fact that financial capital can move freely between countries has created new ways for organized crime to disguise the origin of illegal proceeds. Instruments like bearer shares, over-the-counter derivatives outside the control of national banks, and techniques like bank to bank loans and international mortgages, also created room for maneuver for criminals. Innovations which benefit legal transfers open doors for illegal moves. The international dimension also implies that regulating money laundering in one country will depend heavily on simultaneous action in other countries. The winners and losers of regulation might differ: some countries might profit from the additional money while others might suffer from increased crime. Loopholes in the anti-money laundering regime will be used by launderers, therefore some sorts of international instruments and cooperation are needed.

2.2 THE POLITICAL ECONOMY OF MONEY LAUNDERING

Yandle (2011) distinguishes five theories of regulation. Public interest theory, which assumes that regulators serve a broad public interest; capture theory which recognizes that politicians are captured by rent seeking groups; special interest theory which specifies which party will be most influential in this process; the money-for-nothing theory which focuses on the financial support politicians can gain by threatening industry with regulation; and the bootleggers and Baptists theory which shows regulation as the outcome of odd alliances which share common interests for quite different reasons. This article focuses on the first three theories.

2.2.1 Lack of Private Interest for Regulating Money Laundering

According to the economic theory of regulation (see Stigler 1971; Becker 1968), special interest groups and other political participants will use the regulatory and coercive powers of government to shape laws and regulations in a way that is beneficial to them. But such a 'capture' by the most influential group evidently does not take place with money laundering, because it is a victimless crime. The lack of victims means that there are also no private groups involved that would specially lobby for regulating money laundering.

Given the lack of private interest in lobbying for money laundering regulation, not much support of the private sector in law implementation and enforcement can be expected. The private sector can quietly ignore the rules, or can actively counteract them but is very unlikely to be supportive, nor contribute voluntarily to the costs of enforcing a government rule which does not have any advantage for them. Economists stress the information problem inherent in such a situation, where the regulator will act as the principal and the private sector as an agent in a 'principal agent setting' (see Rosen 1986; Sappington 1991; Stiglitz 1987; Rees 1985). Political scientists would add the problems of the political and bureaucratic power of the agent (Moe 2006), which can frustrate and even counteract the enforcement of rules.

2.2.2 Public Interest Theory of Regulation and US Interests

Seen from a public interest theoretical point of view, the reason for regulating money laundering was a very pragmatic one. After years of losing the war on drugs, exemplified by the constant or ever increasing amounts of drugs produced and consumed (see UNODC 2009, 2010, 2011), a new strategy has evolved. Now it is a case of 'following the money instead of having to chase the criminal', of hitting international crime the hardest by getting at its money, and 'making crime less profitable'. The grounds for this process are shaky and lobbied for only by the United States, which eventually got international organizations, and some governments to truly, voluntarily comply.

With money laundering, it is the government, and more specifically the US government, and not the private sector, which has an interest in regulation. The government claims it has to protect the public good where the nation's health is threatened by drugs and national security is threatened by terrorism. Those in favor of public choice see this as a problem. Their aim is to protect individual free will and so they are very critical of governmental regulatory intervention which purports to protect public goods (Laffont and Tirole 1991; Levine and Forrence 1990; Bernstein 1955; Huntington 1952).

Money laundering was not considered much of a problem until the 1980s, when the US started criminalizing money laundering in the context of its 'war on drugs'. In 1986, it became the first country to make money laundering a crime (Title 18, US Code Sec. 1956), with penalties of up to 20 years in prison and $500 000 in fines. In addition, the law permits civil penalty lawsuits by the government for the value of the funds or property involved in the transaction (Takats 2007).

From a legal point of view, the Achilles heel in defining money laundering relates to the so-called 'predicate offences' which generate the proceeds that make laundering necessary. Hiding or disguising the source of certain proceeds will of course, not amount to money laundering *unless* these proceeds were obtained from a criminal activity (Busuioc 2007). The United States have developed a 130+ list of predicate crimes for money laundering. Originally mainly crimes with regard to drugs were on the list; eventually fraud, counterfeiting, fencing, illegal work, etc. were added and after 09/11 terrorist financing. The developments in the US explain why money laundering came so late onto the international agenda and why it became an issue in fighting Al Qaeda.

With regard to law enforcement, the Banking Secrecy Act (1970) can be seen as an early starting point. It in fact curbed banking secrecy to fight money laundering, and was followed by a series of laws to further strengthen enforcement: the Money Laundering Control Act (1986), the Annunzio-Wylie Money Laundering Act (1992), the Money Laundering Suppression Act (1994), the Money Laundering and Financial Crimes Strategy Act (1998) and finally the USA Patriot Act (2001) (Takats 2007, fn.1).

It is not surprising that the US, with the largest number of money launderers in the world, has been the first country and the strictest when it comes to money laundering regulations. Half of the globally laundered funds are probably transferred through American banks (Walker 1999; Unger 2007).

2.3 THE REGULATORY RESPONSES

2.3.1 The Reporting System and Problems With It

Originally, the regulations were rule-based. Money laundering enforcement relied on the private sector reporting to public law enforcement agencies. In the US, banks had to file a rule-based Currency Transaction Report (CTR) for cash transactions exceeding $10 000. Rule-based regulation was less risky both for the private sector and the government. As there were explicit criteria for reporting, it was a standard disclosure process. Bank reports were ex-post verifiable.

The precision of rule-based regulation however also had disadvantages. Not only banks but also money launderers were aware of the criteria for suspected money laundering and could circumvent them. Thus they could 'smurf', that is, divide up large cash deposits to keep them under the reporting threshold of $10 000 (Takats 2007, p. 8).

The weaknesses of rule-based reports led the US in 1996 to introduce a discretionary report, the Suspicious Activity Report (SAR). The definition of suspicious was left vague to keep both money launderers and banks in uncertainty (Takats 2007, p. 8).

A rule-based approach provides precise rules and hence legal certainty, but it also encourages, apart from smurfing, formalistic over-reporting. This is why not only the US, but also Europe switched from a rule-based to a risk-based approach. The change to a risk-based approach also happened at a time when governments everywhere introduced supposedly less bureaucratic, more subject-friendly, more responsive regulations (Ayres and Braithwaite 1992; Hutter 2005, 2006).

Yet, the risk-based approach had the opposite effect and encouraged even more relatively useless, over-reporting, also called the 'crying wolf problem' (Takats 2007, Dalla Pellegrina and Masciandaro 2009). The regulation gave private actors more discretion about what to report and instructed them to report transactions that *they* considered suspicious. It gave them vaguer criteria as to which transactions to report. This not only meant that private actors had to estimate the risks of a transaction being suspect; it also meant that they themselves ran the risks of getting accused of false reporting or more generally of being held responsible for whether they did a good job or not. The liability may induce businesses with a reporting duty to play it safe, by reporting as many cases as possible. Reporting units, according to Takats, might behave strategically and on purpose dilute information; by behaving like the little boy in the fairy tale and 'crying wolf' so often, when there is real money laundering no one will take the cry seriously.

Unger and Van Waarden (2009) showed that countries' reactions depend heavily on the legal system within which the private sector has to report. In the US, the fierceness of the legal conflict, the often severe sanctions, and the uncertainty of outcomes induce people to be formalistic and choose to 'go by the book' (Bardach and Kagan 1982). Here the risk-based approach indeed led to an increase of reports and a decline of convictions, indicating a 'crying wolf' problem. In the Netherlands, however, with a consensual legal system, where the regulator worked out the new rules in cooperation with the private sector, and where fines were extremely low, reporting went down drastically and the number of convictions increased (Unger and Van Waarden 2009).

2.3.2 Seeking Alliances and Expanding Regulation: From the War on Drugs to the War on Terror

Aware of the problem's international dimension, the US needed alliances with its anti-money laundering policy. It put pressure on international organizations to fight drugs. Similarly international legislation with respect to money laundering began with the criminalization of the proceeds of drug-related offences, as provided by the 1988 UN Convention against the Illicit Traffic in Narcotic Drugs and Psychotropic Substances (the Vienna Drug Convention). Since money laundering was mainly a problem for rich countries, which provide financial expertise, low corruption and high stability for placing illicit funds, the US pressured its G-7 partners to create an organization that would coordinate their efforts; thus the Financial Action Task Force (FATF) emerged in 1989 (Huelsse 2009). Officially only a task force, the FATF is an intergovernmental organization with a small secretariat based within the OECD building in Paris. Membership of the FATF was initially very exclusive – restricted to the G-7 countries plus other OECD members.

The organization's club-like character (Drezner 2007, pp. 122 and 142) enabled FATF members to agree quickly on a set of common standards, the 'Forty Recommendations', which were intended as a benchmark for national anti-money laundering legislation. As recommendations, they are non-binding rules, standards of behaviour that states can adopt voluntarily (Huelsse 2009).

Over the years, these recommendations have been revised with one important addition: Following the 9/11 attacks, FATF published 'Eight Special Recommendations on Terrorist Finance' (later extended to nine). Though money laundering and the finance of terrorism are two rather distinct activities, linking them has given an enormous boost to combating money laundering. The FATF was now engaged in the 'war on terror' (Winer and Roule 2002).

By 2009 the FATF included 34 members plus five associate members, who represented regions (see www.fatf.org). There are also a number of international organizations particularly involved in combating money laundering, like the Egmont Group which started in 1995 with 14 members and is comprised now of 116 members. It is a network designed to improve interaction among Financial Intelligence Units in the areas of communications, information sharing and training coordination.

2.3.3 Setting an International Standard for Money Laundering: The Forty Plus Nine Recommendations

By now the FATF's 40 recommendations for money laundering and nine on terrorist financing have become the international standard. FATF member states have to adopt these recommendations and compliance is checked through mutual assessments of FATF member countries.

The recommendations include issues regarding the legal system and law enforcement. This is to say, the criminalization of money laundering on the basis of the UN Vienna Convention, the application of the law to corporations, penalties, the possibility of confiscation, the absence of bank secrecy, customer due diligence, the know your customer rule applied by financial institutions, the prosecution of politically exposed persons (PEPs), reporting requirements to financial intelligence units and other reporting units, training, auditing, sanctions for not reporting and non compliance, establishment of a financial intelligence unit, existence of supervision, and the establishment of one central database.

Similarly, regarding the financing of terrorism the requirements are: the criminalization of terrorism, the implementation of the UN instruments on terrorism contained in the 1999 United Nations International Convention for the Suppression of the Financing of Terrorism, the United Nations Security Council Resolution 1373 and others. Countries must have measures in place to detect the physical cross-border transportation of currency and bearer negotiable instruments. There are also recommendations concerning the confiscation of assets (see www.fatf.org).

2.4 ENFORCEMENT, EFFECTIVENESS AND LEGITIMACY PROBLEMS

2.4.1 Instruments to Reach Countries' Compliance

In the absence of any legal instruments to make non-members follow its rules, FATF relied on soft instruments like 'seminar diplomacy' and peer review (Sharman 2008). The cooperation of countries was not always 'voluntary' in the proper sense since the relationship between FATF members and non-members is hardly symmetrical (Tranøy 2002). On the one side we have the world's richest countries led by the global hegemony of the US (Simmons 2000, 2001; Williams 2001; Naylor 2002) and on the other side, there is a heterogeneous group of states, ranging from developing countries to offshore centers, with none of them being anywhere near equal in power to the FATF members. Though legally free to ignore the FATF rules, it may not be very wise for non-members to do so. Hence, there surely exists a shadow of hierarchy, which explains why non-member countries comply even in the absence of explicit threats and coercive measures. 'To call this voluntary compliance hardly seems the correct label for such rule following behavior' (Huelsse 2009, p. 461).

In addition, the FATF also uses direct hierarchical means to enforce non-members' compliance with its rules. In 1995 the government of the Seychelles, an island state of some 80 000 people in the Indian Ocean, passed the Economic Development Act (EDA) through which the islands invited internationals to invest a minimum of US$10 million and in return the Seychelles government would grant immunity from prosecution. The US Department of the Treasury issued an advisory to banks and financial institutions urging them to exercise strict caution in their financial dealings with the Seychelles. The Republic Bank of New York stopped all payments to and from the Seychelles. The FATF issued its first ever public condemnation of an individual country. One year later, the Seychelles also introduced an Anti Money Laundering Act (Unger and Rawlings 2008, p. 333; Simmons 2000, pp. 258–9; Rawlings and Sharman 2006).

By intervening FATF was paving the way for its later strategy of blacklisting countries considered to be tolerant of money laundering (Unger and Rawlings 2008). The blacklist contains 25 'negative' criteria, such as banking secrecy, some loopholes of law and financial regulation (for the complete list see FATF 2000). Countries that succumb to some of these are listed by the FATF as a Non-Cooperative Country and (or) Territory (NCCT). Between its first appearance in 2000 and 2006 this blacklist became shorter and shorter. In October 2006, Myanmar, the only country left on the list, was finally also removed (Unger and Ferwerda 2008).

The blacklist of the FATF suffered from severe problems. First, the list contained only 23 subjectively selected countries and no large country. Second, countries could show compliance with the FATF recommendations by filling in written statements. Thirdly, only when a certain not precisely defined threshold of declared compliance was not reached were they put on the list. Overall, the blacklist, therefore, did not sufficiently fulfill the transparency criteria for being a successful instrument of naming and shaming (Braithwaite 1989; Van Erp 2007). The list was judged discriminatory towards small islands and countries (Unger and Ferwerda 2008). Rawlings (2007) showed that blacklisting might have had reverse effects. Some states have experienced loss of business, but other offshore centers have prospered. Examples of these are the Cayman Islands, Bermuda, Jersey, Guernsey and the Isle of Man. Since all the countries have been removed, the list can be viewed as having failed to identify countries with a lax anti-money laundering policy.

For fairness it has to be mentioned that there are some positive effects. The fact that no country is left on the blacklist suggests that all countries have adjusted and improved their regulatory framework to combat money laundering, perhaps due to FATF (FATF 2006). The fragile legitimacy of FATF was definitely not improved with blacklisting.

It had been looking repeatedly for cooperation with the IMF and the World Bank, which originally did not consider money laundering as within their mandate (Interview Richard Gordon, May 2008). But since 9/11 cooperation started, in particular with writing a common methodology. The IMF and World Bank – their own legitimacy problems notwithstanding (Barnett and Finnemore 2004) – are universal organizations which gives them an advantage over the exclusive FATF (see Reuter and Truman 2004; Huelsse 2009). One condition for this cooperation set by them was that the FATF gave up blacklisting (Interview Richard Gordon, May 2008).

The disappointing experience of blacklisting non-cooperative countries by the FATF confirms earlier findings on ratings under globalization: blacklisting and ratings by international organizations are less powerful than when done by private companies, because the former stand under the influence and pressure of large states which shape and finance them (see Graz and Noelke 2008; Van Waarden 2008, pp. 84–98). Van Waarden (2011) mentions as examples the judgments of rating agencies such as Standard and Poor's, Moody's and Fitch which receive much broader acceptance than rankings of international organizations.

2.4.2 Some Regulatory Weaknesses

The Achilles heel of the AML/CFT regime is the veritable patchwork of national lists of predicate offences. Some countries like China and Italy exclude home country laundering from their money laundering definition. In these countries, a drug dealer who is caught when laundering his own proceeds of crime cannot be prosecuted for money laundering but only for the drug crime itself. Austria only included home country laundering in 2010, under the pressure of criticism from FATF. To find a common denominator of predicate crimes for money laundering that includes the most serious crimes like drugs, weapons, human trafficking and all crimes committed by organized gangs seems a necessary and important step towards legislation that does not create opportunities for avoidance by launderers. Also, whether corporations can be prosecuted as opposed to individuals differs in the laws. Whether politically exposed persons (PEPs) can be prosecuted for money laundering or are under immunity is also differently regulated. This can make it difficult to prosecute corrupt officials for money laundering. Especially in many Asian and African countries the PEPs cannot be prosecuted. Counterfeiting and product piracy is a predicate crime in the US, but it often does not fit into European penal law, since it is considered private law there. This gives rise to irritations with negative FATF evaluations. Often tax evasion is related to money laundering. But in most countries tax evasion is not a predicate crime for laundering (see Unger 2007).

2.4.3 Effectiveness

What started as soft law, became hard law in Europe. In Europe, the EU has transposed the FATF recommendations by establishing three Directives which have to be integrated into national law by its member states. The first EU Directive 91/308/EEG for the prevention of the use of the financial system for the purpose of money laundering, foresaw a need for financial institutions to identify and report any suspicious financial transactions. The second Directive 2001/97/EG for the prevention of the use of the financial system for the purpose of money laundering extended the remit of the first recommendation to other groups. Since 2001 car dealers, sellers of ships, art and antiques, of gold, silver and jewellery, and since June 2003 also lawyers, notaries public, tax consultants, accountants and real estate agents are under a reporting duty.

The third and most recent Directive 2005/60/EG on the prevention of the use of the financial system for the purpose of money laundering and terrorism financing broadened the definition of money laundering, by including financing terrorism. It replaced the first EU Directive.

With regard to cash, the EU regulation 1889/2005 on cash entering or leaving the EU says that any individual entering or leaving the Community and carrying cash of a value of €10 000 or more shall declare that sum to the competent authorities of the member state.

As with the US, enforcement problems also occurred in Europe. Reporting systems are under heavy criticism. With regard to suspicious transactions reporting outputs rather than outcomes are evaluated: what countries do with suspicious transaction report data remains in its infancy (Levi and Reuter 2006). Reuter and Truman (2004) showed that only 7.5 percent of the suspicious reports are used for further investigation in the US. A similar criticism of low performance holds true for the Dutch system of reporting unusual transactions. In a recent report, the Dutch Court of Audit criticized, among other things, the inefficient way of handling reporting data (Algemene Rekenkamer 2008).

The fact that by now also the IMF and World Bank are busy with combating money laundering, has increased in particular the collection and development of data that allows assessment of anti-money laundering policy. An IMF Working Group is at the moment busy developing a methodology to assess the attractiveness of countries and their vulnerability to money laundering. Also a Task Force at Eurostat has started to collect statistical indicators for assessing the effectiveness of the anti-money laundering policy.

2.4.4 Legitimacy Problems

Anti-money laundering policy runs the risk of contravening human rights. Vervaele criticized the paradigm change in law that followed from the incorporation of financing terrorism (see Vervaele, Chapter 28 in this volume). Making laundering an issue of national security means that the enforcement authorities can enter people's houses without notification and can secretly tape phone calls or set up cameras. Today, a person suspected of laundering is treated as a potential terrorist. This can mean a severe violation of people's privacy.

Lawyers in several countries object to their reporting duty. They claim that they are bound to professional privacy protection on behalf of their clients.

The anti-money laundering policy will have to show some success very soon; otherwise it will face serious problems of legitimacy. Policemen in the Netherlands claim that the money laundering law helps them to catch drug dealers, because when suspected of money laundering, the criminal has to provide proof of the origin of his funds, while when suspected of drug dealing, the police must prove the crime, so there seem to be some benefits. But overall the law has to be able to prevent additional laundering or to reduce existing amounts of laundering, or to prevent or reduce predicate crimes. And these benefits of the policy will have to outweigh its costs and are yet to be shown.

2.5 CONCLUSIONS

With money laundering, the EU basically implements US policy rather than export its own policy to other countries. However, the regulatory powers of the EU provide it with the means to increasingly shape international standards (Schimmelfenning, 2011). While money laundering legislation is only, and can only be, soft law at the global regulatory level in the Financial Action Task Force, the EU can and does use hard law and imposes it through Directives on its member states. This development of international soft law becoming hard law at lower levels of governance can also be found in other areas like environmental regulation (see Karlsson-Vinkhuyzen 2011).

So far, money laundering, though a global problem, continues to be handled by cooperation between nation-states and by entities like the EU, which are still public in character, unlike multi-level governance entities like the WTO (see Zürn 2011). The norms imposed on individual nation-states tend to be mostly subjects of discussion at international levels, like that of EU working groups and G20 meetings, where a broad democratic discourse is missing. In money laundering policy, the FATF becomes increasingly important through its evaluation system. Though nation-states influence, through their national legal institutions, implementation and enforcement, international organizations exert a dominant influence on standard setting as well as on monitoring and evaluation. The instruments used so far by the FATF, like blacklisting, have, due to their lack of transparency and fair treatment of all member states, lacked legitimacy. Since monitoring and verification of international rules are increasingly carried out by actors who are not directly under the control of nation-states (Zürn 2011), money laundering issues face more and more problems typical of global regimes. As Coleman (2011) stresses, in a global policy-making context, the term public policy does not refer to state actors anymore. The distinction between private and public organizations also becomes blurred (Scott 2011). Typical examples of this development are private organizations like Transparency International, which rates predicate crimes such as corruption, or private firms that establish risk-based reporting mechanisms for banks. What Marx (2011) finds for business regulation might also eventually hold for money laundering regulation through an increase in private standards. With the switch from rule-based to risk-based money laundering standards, more room is left for private organizations to define these standards and implement them, for example, bank warning systems. However, the standards which form the bases for their evaluation are set by the FATF and display a strong touch of Americanism and lack of knowledge of European legal traditions and institutions.

As such, money laundering regulation displays both the characteristics and the deficiencies of global regulation. Scott (2011) argues that the enforcement of global regulations can imply that actors do not feel bound by these norms and can create problems of compliance and fragmentation. First impressions of the effectiveness of anti-money laundering policy support this view: 'crying wolf' by the over-reporting and copy and pasting of FATF regulations by new member states, in the hope that nobody will monitor the execution of the policy, are examples of this. The FATF seems to define itself as the central coordinator by giving other international institutions some directions. The EU seems to accept these directions willingly. However, it might face problems of legitimacy and lack of compliance with a policy that seems to attract neither business nor citizens but only a public interest perceived by international organizations and governments.

NOTE

* This chapter is a reprint of Unger, B. (2011) 'From Al Capone to Al Qaeda', in Levi-Faur, D. (ed.), *Handbook on the Politics of Regulation*, Cheltenham UK and Northampton, MA, USA: Edward Elgar.

REFERENCES

Algemene Rekenkamer (2008), *Bestrijden witwassen en terrorismefinanciering*. KST118064A, The Hague: Sdu Uitgeuers.

Ayres, I. and J. Braithwaite (1992), *Responsive Regulation: Transcending the Deregulation Debate*, New York: Oxford University Press.

Bardach, E. and R.A. Kagan (1982), *Going by the Book: The Problem of Regulatory Unreasonableness*, Philadelphia, PA: Temple University Press.

Barnett, M. and M. Finnemore M (2004), *Rules for the World: International Organizations in Global Politics*, Ithaca, NY: Cornell University Press.

Becker, Gary (1968), 'Crime and punishment: an economic approach', *The Journal of Political Economy*, **76**, 169–217.

Bernstein, M. (1955), *Regulating Business by Independent Commission*, Princeton, NJ: Princeton University Press.

Braithwaite, J. (1989), *Crime, Shame and Reintegration*, New York: Cambridge University Press.

Busuioc, E.M. (2007), 'Defining money laundering', in Unger, B., *The Scale and Impacts of Money Laundering*, Cheltenham and Northampton, MA: Edward Elgar, 15–280.

Coleman, William D. (2011), 'Governance and global public policy', in Levi-Faur, D. (ed.), *Oxford Handbook of Governance*, Oxford: Oxford University Press.

Dalla Pellegrina, L. and D. Masciandaro (2009), 'The risk based approach in the new European anti money laundering legislation: a law and economics view', *Review of Law and Economics*, December.

Drezner, D.W. (2007), *All Politics is Global: Explaining International Regulatory Regimes*, Princeton, NJ: Princeton University Press.

EC, Regulation (EC) No 1889/2005 of the European Parliament and of the Council of 26 October 2005 on controls of cash entering or leaving the Community.

Erp, J.G. van (2007), *Informatie en Communicatie in het handhavingsbeleid, inzichten uit wetenschappelijk onderzoek*, Boom Juridische Uitgevers.

FATF (Financial Action Task Force on Money Laundering) (2000), 'Report on non-cooperative countries and territories', available at: http://www.fatf-gafi.org/media/fatf/documents/reports/intial%20Report%20on%20NCCTs%2002_2000.pdf

FATF (Financial Action Task Force on Money Laundering) (2006), *Annual Report 2005–2006*, 23 June, Paris.

FFIEC BSA/AML (Federal Financial Institutions Examination Council) (2007), *Bank Secrecy Act Anti-Money Laundering Examination Manual*, available at: http://www.ffiec.gov/bsa_aml_infobase/pages_manual/OLM_079.htm (accessed 24 August, 2007).

Graz, J.C. and A. Noelke (eds) (2008), 'Transnational private governance and its limits', ECPR Studies in European Political Science, London and New York: Routledge.

Helleiner, E. (2002), 'The politics of global financial regulation: lessons from the fight against money laundering', in Eatwell, J., and L. Taylor (eds), *International Capital Markets: Systems in Transition*, Oxford: Oxford University Press, 177–204.

Huelsse, Rainer (2009), 'Even clubs can't do without legitimacy: why the anti-money laundering blacklist was suspended', *Regulation and Governance*, **2** (4), 459–79.

Huntington, S. (1952), 'The marasmus of the ICC: the Commission, the railroads, and the public interest', *Yale Law Journal*, **614**, 467–509.

Hutter, Bridget M. (2005), 'Afterword', in *Governance and NGOs of the Future*, London: European Policy Forum, 73–5.

Hutter, Bridget M. (2006), 'Risk, regulation, and management', in Taylor-Gooby, P. and J.O. Zinn (eds), *Risk in Social Science*, Oxford: Oxford University Press, 202–27.

Karlsson-Vinkhuyzen, Sylvia I. (2011), 'Bridging governance and law: global regulation through a diversity of norms', in Levi-Faur, D. (ed.), *Handbook on the Politics of Regulation*, Cheltenham and Northampton, MA: Edward Elgar.

Laffont, J.J. and J. Tirole (1991), 'The politics of government decision making: a theory of regulatory capture', *Quarterly Journal of Economics*, 106(**4**), 1089–127.

Levi, M. and P. Reuter (2006), 'Money laundering: a review of current controls and their consequences', in Tonry, M. (ed.), *Crime and Justice: An Annual Review of Research*, vol. 34, Chicago: Chicago University Press.

Levine, M.E. and J.L. Forrence (1990), 'Regulatory capture, public interest, and the public agenda: toward a synthesis', *Journal of Law Economics & Organization*, **6**, 167–98.

Marx, Axel (2011), 'Global governance and private regulation of supply chains: types, trends and challenges', in Levi-Faur, D. (ed.), *Handbook on the Politics of Regulation*, Cheltenham and Northampton, MA: Edward Elgar.

Masciandaro, D. (1999), 'Money laundering: the economics of regulation', *European Journal of Law and Economics*, **7**, 225–40.

Masciandaro, D., E. Takats and B. Unger (2007), *Black Finance: The Economics of Money Laundering*, Cheltenham and Northampton, MA: Edward Elgar.

Meier, Robert F. and Gilbert Geis (1997), *Victimless Crime? Prostitution, Drugs, Homosexuality, Abortion*, Los Angeles: Roxbury.

Mill, S. (2008 [1859]), *On Liberty*, Oxford: Oxford University Press.

Moe, Terry (2006), 'Political control and the power of the agent', *Journal of Law, Economics, and Organization*, **22** (1) (Spring), 1–29.

Naylor, RT. (2002), *Wages of Crime: Black Markets, Illegal Finance, and the Underworld Economy*, Ithaca, NY: Cornell University Press.

Polinsky, A. Mitchell (1980), 'Private versus public enforcement of fines', *The Journal of Legal Studies*, (1), 105–27.

Polinsky, A. Mitchell and Steven Shavell (1997), 'On the disutility and discounting of imprisonment and the theory of deterrence', NBER Working Paper 6259, National Bureau of Economic Research, Inc.

Rawlings, G. (2007), 'Taxes and transnational treaties: responsive regulation and the reassertion of offshore sovereignty', *Law and Policy*, (1), 51–66.

Rawlings, G. and J.C. Sharman (2006), 'National tax blacklists: a comparative analysis', *Journal of International Taxation*, **17** (9), 38–47, 64.

Rees, R. (1985), 'The theory of principal and agent – Part I and Part II', *Bulletin of Economic Research*, **37** (1), 3–26 and **37** (2), 75–97.

Reuter, P. and V. Greenfield (2001), 'Measuring global drug markets: how good are the numbers and why should we care about them?', *World Economics*, **2** (4) (October–December), 159–73.

Reuter, P. and E.M. Truman (2004), *Chasing Dirty Money: Progress on Anti-Money Laundering*, Washington, DC: Institute for International Economics.

Rosen, S. (1986), 'Prizes and incentives in elimination tournaments', *American Economic Review*, **76** (4), 701–15.

Sappington, David E.M. (1991), 'Incentives in principal–agent relationships', *Journal of Economic Perspectives*, **5** (2) (Spring), 45–66.

Schimmelfenning, Frank (2011), 'EU external governance and europeanization beyond the EU', in Levi-Faur, D. (ed), *Oxford Handbook of Governance*, Oxford: Oxford University Press.

Schneider, Friedrich (2004), 'Macroeconomics: the financial flows of Islamic terrorism', in Masciandaro, D. (ed.), *Global Financial Crime: Terrorism, Money Laundering and Offshore Centres*, Aldershot, UK: Ashgate.

Schur, E.M. (1965), *Crimes Without Victims: Deviant Behavior and Public Policy: Abortion, Homosexuality, Drug Addiction*. Upper Saddle River, NJ: Prentice Hall.

Scott, Colin (2011), 'Regulating in global regimes', in Levi-Faur, (ed.), *Handbook on the Politics of Regulation*, Cheltenham and Northampton, MA: Edward Elgar.

Sharman, J.C. (2008), 'Power and discourse in policy diffusion: Anti-money laundering in developing states', *International Studies Quarterly*, **52**, 635–56.

Siegel, Larry J. (2006), *criminology: Theories, Patterns, & Typologies*, 9th edition, Belmont, CA: Wadsworth Publishing.

Siegel, L.J. and J.J. Senna (2008), *Introduction to Criminal Justice*, Belmont, CA: Thomson Wadsworth.

Simmons, B.A. (2000), 'International efforts against money laundering', in Shelton, D. (ed.), *Commitment and Compliance: The Role of Non-Binding Norms in the International Legal System*, Oxford: Oxford University Press, 244–63

Simmons, B.A. (2001), 'The international politics of harmonization: the case of capital market regulation', *International Organization*, **55**, 589–620.
Stigler, G. (1971), 'The theory of economic regulation', *Bell Journal of Economics*, **2**: 3–21.
Stiglitz, Joseph E. (1987), 'Principal and agent', *The New Palgrave Dictionary of Economics*, vol. **3**, Basingstoke, UK: Palgrave Macmillan, 966–71.
Takats, Elod (2007), 'A theory of "crying wolf": the economics of money laundering enforcement', IMF Working Paper No 07/81, April, http://ssrn.com/abstract=979035
TNI (Transnational Institute) (2003), 'Crime and globalisation: the economic impact of the illicit drug industry', seminar December 2003, the Netherlands, http://www.tni.org/archives/acts/impact.pdf
Tranøy, B.S. (2002), *Offshore Finance and Money Laundering: The Politics of Combating Parasitic State Strategies*, Oslo: Norwegian Ministry of Foreign Affairs.
Unger, B. (2007), *The Scale and Impacts of Money Laundering*, Cheltenham and Northampton, MA: Edward Elgar.
Unger, B. (2008), 'Illicit financial flows in the context of Afghanistan's Opium Economy', Study prepared for the Paris Pact Expert Round Table on the financial flows to and from Afghanistan linked to the illicit production of and trafficking in opiates in October/November 2008, Vienna: UNODC.
Unger, B. and J. Ferwerda (2008), 'Regulating money laundering and tax havens: The role of blacklisting', paper prepared for the (ECPR) conference June 2008, also published as a Tjallings Koopmans Institute Working Paper at Utrecht University, 2008.
Unger, B. and G. Rawlings (2008), 'Competing for criminal money', *Global Business and Economics Review*, **10** (3), 331–52.
Unger, B. and Van Waarden, F. (2009), 'Attempts to dodge drowning in data: rule- and risk-based anti money laundering policies compared', *Review of Law and Economics*, December.
United Nations (1988), 'UN Convention against the Illicit Traffic in Narcotic Drugs and Psychotropic Substances', Vienna.
United Nations (1998a), 'Social and economics costs of illicit drugs', *United Nations Chronicle, Online Edition*, **35** (2).
United Nations (1998b), 'Report on Financial Havens, Banking Secrecy and Money Laundering', http://www.imolin.org/imolin/finhaeng.html
United Nations Development Programme (1996), *Human Development Report 1996*, New York and Oxford: Oxford University Press.
United Nations Office on Drugs and Crime (UNODC) (2006), *World Drug Report 2006*, 2 volumes, http://www.unodc.org/pdf/WDR_2006/wdr2006_volume1.pdf
United Nations Office on Drugs and Crime (UNODC) (2009), *World Drug Report 2009*, Vienna.
United Nations Office on Drugs and Crime (UNODC) (2010), *World Drug Report 2010*, Vienna.
United Nations Office on Drugs and Crime (UNODC) (2011), *World Drug Report 2011*, Vienna.
Van Waarden, Frans (2008), 'Where to find a "demos" for controlling global risk regulators? From private to public regulations and back', in, Graz J-C. and A. Noelke (eds), *Transnational Private Governance and its Limits*, London and New York: Routledge, 84–97.
Van Waarden, Frans (2011), 'Varieties of private market regulation: Problems and prospects', in Levi-Faur, D. (ed.), *Handbook on the Politics of Regulation*, Cheltenham and Northampton, MA: Edward Elgar.
Walker, J. (1995), 'Estimates of the extent of money laundering in and through Australia', paper prepared for the Australian Transaction Reports and Analysis Centre, September 1995, Queanbeyan: John Walker Consulting Services.
Walker, J. (1999), 'How big is global money laundering?', *Journal of Money Laundering Control*, **3** (1).
Walker, J. (2002), *Just How Big is Global Money Laundering?*, Sydney: Australian Institute of Criminology Seminar.
Walker, J. and B. Unger (2009), 'Estimating money laundering: The Walker Gravity Model', *Review of Law and Economics*, December.
Williams, P. (2001), 'Crime, illicit markets, and money laundering', in Simmons, P.J. and C. de Jonge Oudrat (eds), *Managing Global Issues: Lessons Learned*, Washington DC: Brookings Institution Press, 106–50.
Winer, J.M. and T.J. Roule (2002), 'Fighting terrorist finance', *Survival*, **44**: 87–104.
Yandle, Bruce (2011), 'Bootleggers and Baptists in the Theory of Regulation', in Levi-Faur, D. (ed.), *Handbook on the Politics of Regulation*, Cheltenham and Northampton, MA: and Edward Elgar.
Zdanowicz, John (2009), 'Trade-based money laundering and terrorist financing', *Review of Law and Economics*, December.
Zürn, Michael (2011), 'Global multi level governance', in Levi-Faur, D. (ed.), *Oxford Handbook of Governance*, Oxford: Oxford University Press.

PART III

THE PROBLEM

3. The effects of money laundering

Joras Ferwerda

3.1 INTRODUCTION

Money laundering is defined as the processing of criminal proceeds to disguise their illegal origin (FATF 1996, p. 1). As disguising is the main goal of this criminal act, a successful money laundering scheme goes completely unnoticed. Not only should the process itself go unnoticed, also afterwards nothing should be visible. Most crimes eventually have a clear effect: A dead body (murder), a missing item (theft) or a counterfeit product, yet money laundering should leave no trace at all. On top of that most crimes have a clear victim, whereas in the case of money laundering it is unclear who the actual victim is. These two aspects combine to make money laundering an invisible crime. One could wonder why we are fighting something which is basically invisible and without a clear victim. John Stuart Mill concluded as for back as 1859 that governments should not forcibly prevent people from engaging in victimless crimes, because it does no harm to others (Mill 1859). In order to justify anti-money laundering policies, we have to identify who is harmed by money laundering and to what extent.

This chapter discusses how one can justify the fight against money laundering and lists the effects of money laundering mentioned in the literature.

3.2 LITERATURE OVERVIEW OF THE EFFECTS OF MONEY LAUNDERING

The literature mentions one direct effect of the criminalization of money laundering: law enforcement agencies now have an additional opportunity to catch criminals. Apart from this direct effect of the criminalization of money laundering, the literature mentions many indirect effects. A comprehensive literature review yields one direct and 24 indirect effects that money laundering can have on the real and the financial sector, shown in Table 3.1. Money laundering can affect the real economy by distorting consumption, savings, investment, inflation, competition, trade and employment. Furthermore, money laundering can affect the financial sector with an increased risk on the solvability, liquidity, reputation and integrity of the sector. Money laundering, on the other hand, could also be good for our economy, for example because it increases the profits for the financial sector and leads to a greater availability of credit. The literature is therefore still uncertain whether money laundering would have a net positive or negative effect on the economy in the long run.

Hardly any of the effects listed in Table 3.1 are backed up by empirical evidence. Most of them are theorized and some even seem to have no traceable source at all. Bartlett (2002) might be a good example of this with explanations like 'it is clear from available

Table 3.1 The effects of money laundering as mentioned in the literature

Effect	Type of effect			Effect in which sector?			Short term	Long term
	Economic	Social	Political	Real	Financial	Public and monetary		
1. Law enforcement gets a second chance		X		X			X	
2. Distortion of consumption	X			X			X	
3. Distortion of investment and savings	X			X				X
4. Artificial increase in prices	X			X			X	
5. Unfair competition	X			X			X	
6. Changes in imports and exports	X			X			X	
7. More (or less) economic growth	X			X				X
8. Change in output income and employment	X			X			X	
9. Higher/lower revenues for the public sector	X					X	X	
10. Threatens privatization	X		X			X		X
11. Changes in the demand for money, interest and exchange rates	X					X	X	
12. Increase in the volatility of interest and exchange rates	X					X	X	
13. Greater availability of credit	X			X			X	
14. Higher capital inflows/ outflows	X				X	X	X	

Effect	Type of effect			Effect in which sector?			Short term	Long term
	Economic	Social	Political	Real	Financial	Public and monetary		
15. Changes in foreign direct investment	X			X		X		X
16. Risk for the financial sector, solvability and liquidity	X	X			X			X
17. Profits for the financial sector	X				X			X
18. Reputation of the financial sector		X		X	X			X
19. Illegal business contaminates legal business	X		X	X	X			X
20. Distortion of economic statistics			X			X	X	
21. Corruption and bribery		X		X	X			X
22. Increase in crime		X	X	X		X		X
23. Undermines political institutions			X			X		X
24. Undermines foreign policy goals			X			X		X
25. Increase in terrorism		X	X			X		X

Notes: The sources for each effect mentioned are listed in the Appendix. Although this literature overview is based on an extensive literature research, its completeness can, of course, not be guaranteed. This literature review is based on a systematic reviewing of the publications by international organizations such as the International Monetary Fund (IMF), Organisation for Economic Co-operation and Development (OECD) and the Financial Action Task Force (FATF). In addition we browsed through Econlit, an economic search database that includes about 750 journals and over 44000 working papers. We also used the search engine of the Dutch Central Catalogue (NCC), which includes around 14 million books and 500000 magazines and Google Scholar. We analyzed the *Journal of Money Laundering Control* and the *Journal of Financial Crime*. Moreover, we followed the references that were made in the retrieved articles in order to find more literature on the effects of money laundering. It is not in all sources clear whether the effects of money laundering are described, or also (or only) the effect of anti-money laundering policy. This overview is an updated version of the literature overview that has been published in Unger et al. (2006, p. 110–11). Also the description and explanation that follows is consequently based on Unger et al. (2006) and Unger (2007).

evidence', without ever mentioning this evidence. To my knowledge, this suggested evidence simply does not exist. Empirical research on the effects of money laundering is mainly hampered by the lack of a reliable estimate of the amount of money laundering in every country in every year (Levi and Reuter 2006, p. 294). Unger et al. (2006, p.102) conclude that 'most literature on money laundering effects is pure speculation . . . one source refers to the other source, without much of an empirical solid back up'. All these effects of money laundering are in need of empirical testing. It is mostly economists, like Tanzi (1997), Baker (2005), Quirk (1996) and Ferwerda (2009) who attempt to estimate these effects. The section below describes most of those effects and will highlight relevant empirical studies.

3.2.1 Law Enforcement Agencies Get a Second Chance

The direct effect of fighting money laundering is that the law enforcement agencies have a second chance to catch the criminal. The criminal that got away might still reveal himself when he starts to invest the money he made from his crime. Even if the police are unable to prove the original crime, the criminal can still be convicted for money laundering, and the proceeds of the crime can be confiscated. All's well that ends well. This idea seems to be the reason money laundering was criminalized in the first place. When the US found out that it could not win the 'war on drugs', it decided to go after the money made from the drugs trade. In 1986, the Money Laundering Control Act was enacted, which basically started a 'war on drugs money' (Ferwerda 2012).

It might seem easy to get an idea how big this effect is as we have statistics on how many convictions for money laundering occurred, but the situation is actually more complicated. The criminals convicted for money laundering consist of two subgroups; some of them are detected while laundering their money and convicted consequently for money laundering and possibly also the predicate crime, while others are caught for the predicate crime and subsequently also or only convicted for money laundering. While the size of the former subgroup gives us an idea of how many criminals are actually caught because of the criminalization of money laundering, the latter is simply a different labeling of the crime the criminal is eventually convicted for. To make it even more complicated, it could also happen that a criminal attracts the attention of the law enforcement agencies while laundering the money, but that the criminal is eventually convicted for only the predicate crime. For instance, in Ireland, money laundering is often harder to prove than the predicate crime. Consequently, the authorities normally prosecute only the predicate crime, which results in low conviction rates for money laundering. Basically the opposite is true in the Netherlands, where authorities quite often only charge the criminal for money laundering to increase the chances of getting the criminal behind bars.[1] Therefore, a simple analysis of money laundering conviction rates is uninformative.

3.2.2 Distortion of (Statistics on) Consumption, Investment, Savings, Imports and Exports, Output, Income and Employment

The criminalization of money laundering might make criminals spend their money differently (Walker 1995). Criminals might buy or invest solely for money laundering purposes (like real estate), might not buy something because it might attract the attention of the authorities (e.g. jewelers nowadays have to report possible money laundering transactions), or buy things in a different way or at another supplier to avoid the suspicion of money laundering. When this different spending and investing pattern is related to foreign produced goods, it also has an effect on imports and exports. This appears to particularly be the case in developing countries (Bartlett 2002, p. 20), where rich criminals spend their money on imported luxury goods.

But do criminals really consume significantly different than normal people? Unger (2007, p. 122) did a simple comparison on spending behavior of criminals and normal people to verify this effect. Meloen et al. (2003) analyzes the spending behavior of criminals in the Netherlands, based on confiscated proceeds in 52 court cases. After comparing this spending behavior with the asset ownership of Dutch households (based on Alessie et al. (2002, p. 358), Unger (2007, p. 128) concludes that 'at a first glance, the patterns seem to not be extremely diverse'. Therefore we have to expect that, at least in the Netherlands, the size of these effects is not large.

Walker (1995, p. 33) uses an input output model to estimate that if AU$1 million of laundered money is invested in dwelling properties rather than in more productive sectors of the economy, the Australian economy on average loses AU$1.126 million of output, AU$609,000 income and 25 jobs.

3.2.3 Artificial Increase in Prices and Unfair Competition

Holding on to illegally acquired funds is incriminating, so criminals attempt to convert them into assets (like real estate or a business) that are less conspicuous. Because of their large funds, criminals will outbid honest buyers to acquire such assets (Walker 1995, p. 33). Not only is this unfair competition, it also artificially increases prices. Keh (1996, p. 5) gives anecdotal evidence of this effect by describing land purchases by the Medellin group in the 1980s which pushed up prices from US$500 to US$2000 per hectare.

3.2.4 Higher Capital Inflows/Outflows and their Effects

Walker (1999, p. 25) concludes that worldwide money laundering is 'heavily concentrated in Europe and North America'. The reasons for this probably lie in the more advanced financial systems of the Western world, and the fact that these countries are a good place to enjoy a luxurious life (Baker 2005). This geographic concentration of money laundering has its effect on capital flows worldwide. Proceeds of crime arise from all around the world and when a large proportion of this money finds its way into the Western economies, it means that money is subtracted money from other parts of the world. Baker (2005) estimates that about US$500–800 billion flows from the developing and transitional economies into the financial systems in the West. The money laundering process thus removes a significant amount of capital (and therefore, potential development) from developing countries. He concludes that the rich are getting richer and the poor are getting poorer – as average income globally is increasing, while at the same time the number of people living below the poverty line is increasing – and suggests that this flow of capital might be one of the important reasons behind it. Baker (2005) estimates that, for every US$1 of foreign aid sent to developing nations by the

West, US$10 finds its way back to the West 'under the table' by means of illicit financial flows.

Tanzi (1997) estimates the outflows of cash money from the US by calculating the difference between money printed and the money circulating in the US. This analysis led to the estimate that US$5 billion cash money was flowing out of the US in 1984. Tanzi (1997) allocates this outflow to the illegal drugs trade, but one should not neglect the possibility that cash money was taken out of the US for legal reasons, such as safe investment or for the use of an alternative currency.

These unanticipated inflows and outflows of money lead to volatility in exchange rates and interest rates and directly affect the demand for money in the respective countries (Tanzi 1997, p. 8; McDonell 1998, p. 10; Camdessus 1998, p. 2; FATF 2002, p. 3; Boorman and Ingves 2001, p. 9). It seems that the implicit assumption for these effects is that money laundering flows are irregular in size and destination. Since direct measurement of money laundering is impossible and since our estimation models so far give no indications on the size and destination over time, one can only speculate about the extent to which this is the case.

3.2.5 Effects for the Financial Sector

If launderers' economic behavior is less predictable than those of conventional investors, this could be a risk for the solvability and liquidity of the financial sector (Alldridge, 2002, p. 310). The literature seems to suggest that an even bigger concern for the financial sector is the effect of money laundering on its reputation. When money laundering operations are detected, the financial – sector specifically those financial institution it concerns – will lose credibility and customer confidence (Bartlett, 2002). Economic agents will consequently try to avoid these institutions due to the perceived risk of fraud and corruption associated with money laundering (Unger 2007, pp. 145–6).

3.2.6 Greater Availability of Credit and Changes in Foreign Direct Investment

If money is brought to a specific country for laundering, its financial institutions might have higher profits and deposits, which leads to higher credit availability, even for legitimate businesses (Unger 2007, p. 140). The reputation of being a country with high money laundering inflows however can have a detrimental effect on foreign direct investment (Boorman and Ingves 2001, p. 9).

Although it is not the result of published scientific research, it might be worthwhile to discuss here also another observation, namely that money launderers might have even saved banks. In an interview with the *Observer* (December 13, 2009) Antonio Maria Costa (head of the United Nations Office on Drugs and Crime) stated that drug money saved our banks during the financial crisis. When banks stopped lending money, drug money was the only liquid investment capital available. Costa has seen evidence that €238 billion worth of drug money was laundered during the financial crisis. Adding these amounts of money during financial downtimes actually stabilizes financial markets. Unfortunately, the evidence Costa speaks of has never been made publicly available and therefore is not assessable.

3.2.7 Increases in Crime

Money laundering could increase crime. Money laundering makes criminal activities worthwhile and provides criminal organizations with capital they can use to further expand their criminal activities (Mackrell 1997).

Ferwerda (2009) estimates the effect of anti-money laundering policy on other crimes. If governments succeed in making money laundering difficult, then becoming a criminal will be less attractive[2] since it will be harder to enjoy the ill-gotten gains – even when the crimes that are committed result in large gains and are not detected. Therefore anti-money laundering policy might not only decrease money laundering, but also crime in general.

Ferwerda (2009) theorizes on this reasoning and assesses whether this reasoning can be found empirically. To do so, one needs to quantify the level of crime and the effectiveness of the anti-money laundering policy in each country. Although one can argue crime levels are not precisely measureable, data such as on police records of total crimes committed can be used to approximate levels of crime.

Data on the effectiveness of anti-money laundering policy is more cumbersome to acquire. The information is quite hard to quantify and differs across countries. The only structured and more-or-less consistent information is from the FATF mutual evaluation reports, based on the 40 recommendations of the FATF. If they are all fully implemented these recommendations should provide a country with a complete framework for successfully combating money laundering. The 40 recommendations include, among others, the definition of money laundering, descriptions of the crimes which generate laundering, the sectors that should be monitored more closely, and the regulatory institutions and international co-operation needed (Ferwerda 2009). Although the FATF mutual evaluation reports are based on the same 40 recommendations, 'as a result of the way the assessments were made and even their layout, the assessments differed widely in quality, content, layout, and even across institutions and countries, making it very difficult to make sensible cross-country comparisons and analysis' (Arnone and Padoan 2006, p. 11). The fact that the FATF applies scores to each recommendation for each country creates the opportunity to quantify the degree of anti-money laundering policy for each country, but since these scores are not internationally comparable (mostly because the economic realities of the country are taken into account), Ferwerda and Bosma (2005) completely reapplied these scores. They consistently applied 680 cross-country comparable scores to measure the degree of anti-money laundering policy in 17 countries.

Econometrics was used to analyse the data, taking into account country characteristics such as the legal framework, economic strength, levels of corruption and public enforcement. The conclusion of this econometric research suggests that anti-money laundering policy can be used to reduce crime levels, and that especially more intense international cooperation in the fight against money laundering is associated with lower crime rates. This result is in line with the idea that we can make crime less worthwhile by fighting money laundering.

3.2.8 The Effect of Money Laundering on Economic Growth

Money laundering can dampen economic growth, because of all the above mentioned effects, like its damaging effect on financial institutions (Tanzi 1997, p. 96), distorted investments and facilitation of crime and corruption (Bartlett 2002, p. 1).

Quirk (1997) used the widely cited economic growth model of Barro (1991) to estimate the effect of money laundering on economic growth. Quirk changed Barro's growth model by replacing the human capital variable with a money laundering variable. As he had no estimates of money laundering, he used countries' crime levels as a proxy variable instead. This led him to basically not estimate the effect of money laundering specifically, but the effect of crime in general. Quirk found that money laundering (actually crime) dampens economic growth.

Ferwerda and Bosma (2005) did a follow-up study on the work of Quirk. They also estimated the effect of money laundering on economic growth based on Barro, but used six different actual estimates of money laundering for 17 countries, all based on the Walker Model and the adjusted Walker Model.[3] To test the robustness of Quirk's results, the crime level was also used as a proxy for money laundering. It turned out that the result found in Quirk (1996) – that money laundering dampens economic growth – was consistent with Ferwerda and Bosma's study. Higher values in the six different estimates of money laundering and the crime rate were all associated with lower economic growth rates.

Since Ferwerda and Bosma had estimates of crime *and* money laundering, they were able to estimate their effects separately.[4] Their research showed that while money laundering itself does not dampen economic growth, the crime that is intermingled with it does. Hence, it might not be the actual capital flow from money laundering that is hurting the economy, but the criminals that might follow this money.

3.3 CONCLUSION

The literature mentions many effects of money laundering, but the empirical back-up of these effects is still largely missing. 'The cost of compliance is increasing rapidly but it would be a brave person who steps up to say that it is too high a price to pay for countering terrorism and serious crime' (Whitehouse 2003, p. 144). Now that we have been brave enough to doubt the cost-effectiveness of anti-money laundering policy, it is time for some serious research to find out how real these effects of money laundering really are. The literature tells us that money laundering can dampen our economic growth, destabilize our financial system and increase the general crime level. If anti-money laundering policy would counter all of this, it could easily pay for itself. As long as we are unsure to what extent this is the case, the cost-effectiveness of this world-wide policy can never be determined. So, effectively, at the moment, we leave the public in the dark on whether their tax-money is well spent on anti-money laundering policy.

NOTES

1. Based on interviews conducted in the EU-funded project ECOLEF, 2012.
2. How AML policy influences the incentives of (potential) criminals is modeled in Ferwerda (2009), one can use this model to show algebraically that anti-money laundering policy reduces crime.
3. Walker pioneered estimating the amount of money laundering worldwide, see Walker (1995). His model was modified by Unger et al. (2006).
4. The money laundering estimations that Ferwerda and Bosma (2005) used are from the estimation models of Walker (1995) and Unger et al. (2006). The methodological problem that we should highlight is that one of the main inputs of these estimation models is crime, which could hurt the pureness of the estimations of Ferwerda and Bosma (2005) that include crime and money laundering simultaneously.

REFERENCES

Alessie, R., S. Hochguertel and A. van Soest (2002), 'Household portfolios in the Netherlands', in L. Guiso, M. Haliassos and T. Jappelli (eds) *Household Portfolios*, Cambridge, MA: MIT Press, 340–88.

Alldridge, P. (2002), 'The moral limits of the crime of money laundering', *Buffalo Criminal Law Review*, **5**: 279–319.

Aninat, E., D. Hardy and R. B. Johnston (2002), 'Combating money laundering and the financing of terrorism', *Finance & Development, A Quarterly Magazine of the IMF*, **39**(3).

Arnone, M. and P.C. Padoan (2006), 'Anti-money laundering by international institutions: a very preliminary assessment', paper presented at the Conference Corralling the Economy of Crime and Money Laundering: A Challenge for Banks and International Institutions Into the 21st Century, ECSPC and Research Center for International Economics (CIDEI), Rome, September.

Baker, R.W. (1999), 'The biggest loophole in the free-market system', *Washington Quarterly*, **22**(4), 29–46.

Baker, R.W. (2005), *Capitalism's Achilles Heel, Dirty Money and How to Renew the Free-market System*, Hoboken, NJ: John Wiley.

Barro, R.J. (1991), 'Economic growth in a cross section of countries', *The Quarterly Journal of Economics*, **106**, 407–43.

Bartlett, B.L. (2002), 'The negative effects of money laundering on economic development', *Platypus Magazine*, **77**, 18–23.

Boorman, J. and S. Ingves (2001), 'Financial system abuse, financial crime and money laundering', IMF Background Paper.

Camdessus, M. (1998), 'Money laundering: the importance of international countermeasures', Plenary Meeting of the FATF, Paris, 10 February.

FATF (1996), *The Forty Recommendations*, published online at: www.fatf-gafi.com.

FATF (2002), *Basic Facts about Money Laundering*, published online at: www.fatf-gafi.org.

FATF (2007), *Money Laundering and Terrorist Financing through the Real Estate Market*, published online at: www.fatf-gafi.org.

Ferwerda, J. (2009), 'The economics of crime and money laundering: does anti-money laundering policy reduce crime?', *Review of Law and Economics*, **5**.

Ferwerda, J. (2012), 'The multidisciplinary economics of money laundering', PhD thesis, Utrecht University School of Economics.

Ferwerda, J. and Z. S. Bosma (2005), 'The effect of money laundering on economic growth', paper for applied economics research course, Utrecht University School of Economics.

Gnutzmann, H., K. McCarthy and B. Unger (2010), 'Dancing with the devil: country size and the incentive to tolerate money laundering', *International Review of Law and Economic*, **30**, 244–52.

Keh, D.I. (1996), 'Drug money in a changing world: economic reform and criminal finance', UNODC, http://www.unodc.org/pdf/technical_series_1996-01-01_2.pdf.

Levi, M. (2002), 'Money laundering and its regulation', *Annals of the American Academy of Political and Social Science*, **582**, 181–94.

Levi, M. and P. Reuter (2006), 'Money laundering', University of Chicago Crime and Justice, pp. 292 and 349.

Mackrell, N. (1997), 'Economic consequences of money laundering', in A. Graycar and P. Brabosky (eds), *Money Laundering in the 21st Century: Risks and Countermeasures*, Australian Institute of Criminology, Research and Public Policy Series, Canberra, Australia.

Masciandaro, D. (2004), *Global Financial Crime: Terrorism, Money Laundering, and Offshore Centres*, Global Finance Series, Ashgate: ISPA.

McDonell, R. (1998), 'Money laundering methodologies and international and regional counter-measures', paper presented at the conference on gambling, technology and society, Rex Hotel, Sydney, 7–8 May.
McDowell, J. (2001), 'The consequences of money laundering and financial crime, economic perspectives', *Electronic Journal of the US Department of State*, **6**(2).
Meloen, J., R. Landman, H. de Miranda, J. van Eekelen and S. van Soest (2003), *Buit en Besteding, Een empirisch onderzoek naar de omvang, de kenmerken en de besteding van misdaadgeld*, Den Haag: Reed Business Information.
Mill, J.S. (1859), *On Liberty*, republished as J.S. Mill (1982) *On Liberty*, Penguin classics.
Quirk, P.J. (1996), 'Macroeconomic implications of money laundering', IMF Working Paper, International Monetary Fund, No. 96/66.
Quirk, P.J. (1997), 'Money laundering: muddying the macroeconomy', *Finance & Development*, **34**(1), 7–9.
Takáts, E. (2007), 'A theory of "crying wolf" the economics of money laundering enforcement', IMF Working paper 07/81.
Tanzi, V. (1997), 'Macroeconomic implications of money laundering', in E. U. Savona (ed.), *Responding to Money Laundering: International Perspectives*, Amsterdam: Harwood Academic Publishers.
Unger, B. (2007), *The Scale and Impacts of Money Laundering*, Cheltenham and Northampton, MA: Edward Elgar.
Unger, B. and G. Rawlings (2008), 'Competing for criminal money', *Global Business and Economics Review*, **10**(3), 331–52.
Unger, B., G. Rawlings M. Siegel, J. Ferwerda, W. de Kruijff, M. Busuioc and K. Wokke (2006), *The Amounts and Effects of Money Laundering*, report for the Dutch Ministry of Finance.
Walker, J. (1995), 'Estimates of the Extent of Money Laundering in and through Australia', paper prepared for AUSTRAC, Queanbeyan: John Walker Consulting Services.
Walker, J. (1999), 'How big is global money laundering?', *Journal of Money Laundering Control*, **3**(1), 25–37.
Whitehouse, A. (2003), 'A brave new world: the impact of domestic and international regulation on money laundering prevention in the UK', *Journal of Financial Regulation and Compliance*, **11**(2), 138–45.
Zdanowicz, J.S. (2004), 'Who's watching our back door?', *Business Accents*, *College of Business Administration Magazine*, Florida International University, Fall, **1**, 26–29.

APPENDIX

Effect	Source(s)
1. Law enforcement gets a second chance	Levi (2002) p. 182, Levi and Reuter (2006) pp. 292 and 349
2. Distortion of consumption	Bartlett (2002), Mackrell (1997), Walker (1995)
3. Distortion of investment and savings	Aninat et al. (2002), Bartlett (2002) p. 19, Camdessus (1998), Mackrell (1997), McDonell (1998) pp. 10–11, McDowell (2001), Quirk (1997), Tanzi (1997) pp. 95–6, Walker (1995)
4. Artificial increase in prices	Alldridge (2002) p. 314, FATF (2007), Keh (1996) p. 5
5. Unfair competition	Mackrell (1997), McDowell (2001), Walker (1995)
6. Changes in imports and exports	Baker (1999) p. 33, Baker (2005), Bartlett (2002) pp. 18–20, Walker (1995), Zdanowicz (2004)
7. More (or less) economic growth	Aninat et al. (2002), Bartlett (2002) pp. 18–20, Camdessus (1998), Ferwerda and Bosma (2005), McDonell (1998) p. 10, McDowell (2001), Quirk (1997), Tanzi (1997) pp. 92–96
8. Change in output income and employment	Bartlett (2002) p. 18, Boorman and Ingves (2001) p. 8, McDowell (2001), Quirk (1997), Tanzi (1997)
9. Higher/lower revenues for the public sector	Alldridge (2002) p. 135, Boorman and Ingves (2001) p. 9, Mackrell (1997), McDonell (1998) p. 10, McDowell (2001), Quirk (1997)
10. Threatens privatization	McDowell (2001), Keh (1996) p. 11
11. Changes in the demand for money, interest and exchange rates	Bartlett (2002), p. 18, Boorman and Ingves (2001), Camdessus (1998), FATF (2002), McDonell (1998) p. 10, McDowell (2001), Quirk (1997), Tanzi (1997) p. 97
12. Increase in the volatility of interest and exchange rates	Boorman and Ingves (2001) p. 9, Camdessus (1998) p. 2, FATF (2002) p. 3, McDonell (1998) p. 10, Tanzi (1997) p. 8
13. Greater availability of credit	Levi (2002) pp. 183–4, Tanzi (1997) p. 6
14. Higher capital inflows/ outflows	Baker (2005), Gnutzmann et al. (2010), Keh (1996) p. 4, Tanzi (1997) p. 6, Unger and Rawlings (2008), Levi (2002) pp. 183–4
15. Changes in foreign direct investment	Baker (2005), Boorman and Ingves (2001) p. 9, FATF (2002), Walker (1995)
16. Risk for the financial sector, solvability and liquidity	Alldridge (2002) p. 310, Aninat et al. (2002), Boorman and Ingves (2001) pp. 9–11, Camdessus (1998), FATF (2002), Levi (2002) pp. 183–4, McDonell (1998) p. 10, McDowell (2001), Tanzi (1997) p. 98
17. Profits for the financial sector	Alldridge (2002) p. 310, Levi (2002) pp. 183–4, Takáts (2007)

Effect	Source(s)
18. Reputation of the financial sector	Aninat et al. (2002) p. 19, Bartlett (2002), Boorman and Ingves (2001) pp. 9–11, Camdessus (1998), FATF (2002), Levi (2002) p. 184, McDonell (1998) p. 9, McDowell (2001), Quirk (1997), Tanzi (1997) pp. 92–8, Walker (1995)
19. Illegal business contaminates legal business	Alldridge (2002) p. 315, Camdessus (1998), FATF (2002), Levi (2002) p. 184, McDonell (1998) p. 11, Quirk (1997)
20. Distortion of economic statistics	Alldridge (2002) p. 306, McDonell (1998) p. 10, Quirk (1997), Tanzi (1997) p. 96, Zdanowicz (2004)
21. Corruption and bribery	Alldridge (2002) p. 308, Bartlett (2002) pp. 18–19, Camdessus (1998), FATF (2002), Keh (1996) p. 11, Levi (2002) pp. 183–4, McDowell (2001), Quirk (1997) p. 19, Tanzi (1997) pp. 92–9, Walker (1995)
22. Increase in crime	Bartlett (2002) pp. 18–22, FATF (2002), Ferwerda (2009), Levi (2002) p. 183, Mackrell (1997), Masciandaro (2004) p. 137, McDonell (1998) p. 9, McDowell (2001), Quirk (1997) p. 19
23. Undermines political institutions	Camdessus (1998), FATF (2002), Mackrell (1997), McDonell (1998) p. 9, McDowell (2001), Tanzi (1997) pp. 92–99
24. Undermines foreign policy goals	Baker (1999) pp. 38–9, Baker (2005)
25. Increase in terrorism	Masciandaro (2004) p. 131

4. Money laundering and its effects on crime: a macroeconomic approach

Donato Masciandaro

4.1 INTRODUCTION

In recent times economic analysis has developed a peculiar focus on the financial issues related to the study of crime, thus far completely absent in the international literature. The basic theoretical reason lies in the absence of special treatment of monetary and financial aspects within the traditional Becker model. Furthermore, the complexity of the topic also concerns the need to adopt a multidisciplinary approach, using cognitive instruments associated with different disciplines: economic, legal and social sciences.

In this chapter, I propose a simple macroeconomic approach to analyse the relationship between crime, money laundering and value. The paper builds extensively on different works of the author (see References), which provide considerable details that space precludes presenting here.

The emphasis on the study of money laundering has progressively increased, recognizing its role in the development of any crime that generates revenues. In fact, the conduct of any illegal activity may be subject to a special category of transaction costs, linked to the fact that the use of the relative revenues increases the probability of discovery of the crime and therefore incrimination. Those transaction costs can be minimized through an effective laundering action, a means of concealment that separates financial flows from their origin, an activity whose peculiar economic function is to transform potential wealth into effective purchasing power.

Having defined a microeconomic definition of the money-laundering choices enables the formulation of a macroeconomic model of the relationship between the development of the illegal markets and the laundering activity. The macro analysis can be performed using the classic multiplier approach in a novel analytical framework, which can be developed both in a static and a dynamic way. I will represent the multiplying effects of money laundering with respect to the criminal subject's economic endowment.

The general intuition is quite simple. Starting from the initial crime that produces some dirty revenues, the laundering process allows – given some laundering costs – such capitals to be re-invested in the legal and illegal sectors of the economy. The portion which is destined for the illegal sector will further produce some other dirty revenues to undergo the laundering process; the money-laundering cycle has therefore taken off and each step – provided that no obstacle hinders the process – contributes to strengthening the economic and financial power of criminal subjects.

The chapter is organized as follows. In Section 2 I give the economic definition of money laundering useful to presenting the basic model in Section 3 (Masciandaro 1999) that identifies the macro relations between criminal profits, money laundering and legal investment. In Section 4 the model is developed in a dynamic version (Barone and Masciandaro 2011).

4.2 MONEY LAUNDERING: DEFINITION

First of all, we need a definition of money laundering that points at its distinctiveness compared to other illegal or criminal economic activity involving accumulation and/ or reinvestment. In this chapter it is the following: given that the conduct of any illegal activity may be subject to a special category of transaction costs, linked to the fact that the use of the relative revenues increases the probability of discovery of the crime and therefore incrimination, those transaction costs can be minimized through an effective laundering action, a means of concealment that separates financial flows from their origin.

In other words, whenever a given flow of purchasing power that is potential – since it cannot be used directly for consumption or investment as it is the result of illegal accumulation activity – is transformed into actual purchasing power, money laundering has occurred.

Focusing our attention on the concept of incrimination costs enables us to grasp not only the distinctive nature of this illegal economic activity but also its general features. The definition we have adopted maintains basic unity among three aspects that, according to other points of view, represent three different objects of the anti-laundering action: the financial flows; the wealth and goods intended as terminal moments of those flows; the principal actors, or those who have that wealth and goods at their disposal.

In our scheme of analysis there will always be an agent who, having committed a crime that has generated accumulation of illicit proceeds, moves the flows to be laundered, so as to subsequently increase his financial assets, by investment in the legal sector or re-accumulation in the illegal sector. The agent can be an individual or a criminal organization. By criminal organization we mean a group of individuals and instrumental assets associated for the purpose of exclusively exchanging or producing services and goods of an illicit nature or services and goods of a licit nature with illicit means or of illicit origin.

In general, following the classic intuition à la Becker, we can claim that the choices of an economic agent to invest his resources in illegal activities – as money laundering is – will depend, *ceteris paribus*, on two peculiar magnitudes, given the possible returns: the probability of being incriminated and the punishment he will undergo if found guilty.

Now, to undertake a money-laundering activity, the agent possessing liquidity coming from illegal activity will decide whether to perform a further illicit act, in a given economic system – i.e. money laundering – assessing precisely the probability of detection and relative punishment and comparing that with the expected gains, net of the economic costs of this money-laundering activity.

The choice of the agent requires that the crime in question, and the relative production function be basically autonomous with respect to other forms of crime, those that generated the revenues in the accumulation phase.

Assigning a monetary utility to the crime of money laundering, by giving it a unitary expression, actually summarizes the value of a series of more general services that stimulate the growth of demand for money-laundering services on the part of the agents that accumulate illegal resources. Money laundering, in fact, produces for its users:

1. The economic value, in the strict sense, of minimizing the expected incrimination costs, transforming into purchasing power the liquidity deriving from a wide range of criminal activities (transformation); transformation, in turn, produces two more utilities for the criminal agent;
2. The possibility of increasing his rate of penetration in the legal sectors of the economy through the successive phase of investment (pollution);
3. The possibility of increasing the degree to which the criminal actors and organizations are camouflaged in the system as a whole (camouflaging).

Having defined the micro problem in the most general terms possible, we can now investigate in detail and in depth macro effects of money laundering choices.

4.3 THE BASIC MODEL

To define a macro model of the accumulation-laundering-investment process, we focus on the behaviour of a general Criminal Sector that derives its income from a set of illegal activities, and that, under certain conditions, must launder the income to invest it. We will highlight the role of money laundering as an overall multiplier of the Criminal Sector endowment.

Let us assume that in a given economic system there is a Criminal Sector that controls an initial volume of liquid funds ACI, fruit of illegal activities of accumulation. Let us further suppose that, at least for part of those funds, determined on the basis of the optimal microeconomic choices already discussed above, there is a need for money laundering. Without separating these funds from their illicit origin, given the expected burden of punishment, they have less value. Money-laundering activity is therefore required.

To underscore the general nature of the analysis, we can claim that the demand for money-laundering services could be expressed – distinguishing the different potential components of a criminal sector according to their primary illegal activity – by organized crime in the strict sense, by white collar crime, or by political corruption crime, also considering the relative cross-over and commingling.

Each laundering phase has a cost for the Criminal Sector, represented by the price of the money-laundering supply. The price of the money-laundering service, all other conditions being equal, will depend on the costs of the various money-laundering techniques. Let us suppose that in the money laundering markets the Criminal Sector is a price taker and that the cost of money laundering cR is constantly proportional to the amount of the illicit funds; designating the costs with c, both regulatory and technical, we can write:

$$cR = cACI \tag{1}$$

If the first laundering phase is successful, the Criminal Sector may spend and invest the remaining liquid funds $(1 - c)yACI$ in both legal economic activities (investment) or illicit activities (re-accumulation). The trend to use specialist money launderers – with their explicit or implicit fees – is increasing. These operators use their expertise to launder criminal proceeds. In general the professionals may be witting or unwitting accomplices; but in any case the build-up of the overall procedure represents a cost.

We assume that in general the money laundering procedures represent a cost for organized crime, notwithstanding it is well known that the criminal groups can implement legal businesses also for the concealment of their illegal proceeds and these businesses can produce profits. As will be evident below, the smaller the money laundering costs the greater the multiplier effect.

The Criminal Sector will spend part of the laundered liquidity in consumer goods, equal to d, while a second portion will be invested in the legal sectors of the economy, for an amount of f, and then a third portion, equal to q, will be reinvested in illegal markets (giving, of course, $d + f + q = 1$).

On the one hand, a share of illegal funds has to be spent: minimizing incrimination risks comes at a price; the Criminal Sector has to pay a price. On the other hand, we suppose that a share of dirty money will be reinvested in the illegal market without concealment. For example, in all illicit services, cash is by definition the currency of choice, running in a closed circuit separate from the legitimate market.

Reinvestment in criminal markets is a distinctive feature of actual organized crime groups, given their tendency towards specialization. Organized crime tends to acquire specialist functions to augment their illegal businesses.

If the Criminal Sector makes investment choices according to the classical principles of portfolio theory, indicating with $q(r, s)$ the amount of laundered funds reinvested in illegal activities, with r the actual expected return on the illegal re-accumulation, and with s the relative. Finally, we can assume that the re-accumulation of funds in the illegal sector requires their laundering only in part, thus indicating with the positive parameter y the portion of illegal re-accumulation that requires laundered liquidity.

The Criminal Sector reinvests both clean and dirty money and then a new flow of illegal liquidity will be created. The illegal revenues will be characterized again by incrimination costs, that will generate a new demand for money-laundering services. It will be therefore equal to:

$$(1 + r)(1 - c)^2 q y^2 ACI \tag{2}$$

The crucial assumption is that both the lawful investment and part of the unlawful re-accumulation require financing with 'clean' cash. This assumption can be supported by the presence of rational, informed operators in the supply of services to the Criminal Sector for the illegal re-accumulation, or by rationality of the criminal himself, who wishes to minimize the probability of being discovered.

Repeating infinite times the demand for money-laundering services, which each time encounter a parallel supply, with the values of the parameters introduced remaining constant, the total amount of financial flows generated by money-laundering activity AFI will be equal to:

$$AFI = \frac{yACI(1 - c)}{1 - yq(1 - c)(1 + r)} = mACI \tag{3}$$

with $0 < c, q, y < 1$.

The flow *AFI* represents the overall financial endowment generated by the money-laundering activity, and *m* can be defined as the multiplier of the model. Doing comparative static exercises, it is easy to show that the amount of liquidity laundered will increase as the price of the money-laundering service declines:

$$\frac{\partial AFI}{\partial c} = -\frac{ACIy}{[1 - qy(1 - c)(1 + r)]^2} < 0 \tag{4}$$

If the amount of re-accumulation of laundered cash in illegal activities increases, this in turn depends on expected profits, in terms of return and risk:

$$\frac{\partial AFI}{\partial q} = \frac{(1 - c)^2(1 + r)ACIy^2}{[1 - qy(1 + r)(1 - c)]^2} > 0 \tag{5}$$

If the expected actual return on the re-accumulation in illegal activities rises:

$$\frac{\partial AFI}{\partial r} = \frac{(1 - c)^2 ACIqy^2}{[1 - qy(1 - c)(1 + r)]^2} > 0 \tag{6}$$

If the initial volume of illegal proceeds increases:

$$\frac{\partial AFI}{\partial ACI} = \frac{\mathrm{y}(1 - c)}{[1 - qy(1 - c)(1 + r)]} > 0 \tag{7}$$

If the optimal share of the initial volume of illegal revenues requiring cleaning increases:

$$\frac{\partial AFI}{\partial y} = \frac{(1 - c)ACI}{[1 - qy(1 + r)(1 - c)]^2} > 0 \tag{8}$$

Therefore, the more effective the money-laundering action, the greater the cash flows available to the Criminal Sector for reinvestment, illegal and legal, will be.

Now we look at the volume of investment in the legal sector. Also the legal investment may grow the more effective the money-laundering is. It helps camouflage the illegal organizations within the economic system. Using *ARL* to indicate the total flow of legal investments and r_1 the average rate of return:

$$ARL = \frac{f(1 - c)(1 + r_l)yACI}{1 - yq(1 - c)(1 + r)} \tag{9}$$

So the total investment flow ART – illegal and legal – made possible by the money-laundering activity will be equal to:

$$ART = ARI + ARL = \frac{(1 - c)[q + f(1 + r_l)]yACI}{1 - yq(1 - c)(1 + r)} \tag{10}$$

where:

$$ARI = \frac{q(1 - c)yACI}{1 - yq(1 - c)(1 + r)} \tag{11}$$

Expression (10) grasps the central role of money laundering in favouring the overall growth of revenues for the Criminal Sector. Thanks to laundering, the criminals are able not only to consume and spend but, more importantly, to input capital into the legal and illegal circuits of the economy. Furthermore, the more the investments are successful and profitable, the more the criminals increase their strength, raising the level of pollution in the overall economy.

Returning to the initial expression (3), if the money-laundering multiplier is stable, changes in the initial revenues from the criminal activities of accumulation will have a more-than-proportional effect on the volume of funds laundered. The maximum multiplying effect is obtained when the costs are negligible ($c = 0$), while at the same time all the proceeds from the criminal activities must be laundered ($y = 1$). In this case, the degree of expansion of the volume of activity AFI – which coincides with the maximum flow of liquidity available for reinvestment – produced by laundering is equal to:

$$AFI_{max} = \frac{ACI}{1 - q(1 + r)} \tag{12}$$

4.4 THE DYNAMIC MODEL

In the previous pages the chain that goes from the illegal profits to financial accumulation thanks to money laundering services has been described using a static framework. How should we deal with the time dimension of the problem, which means that the different stages – money laundering, illegal re-investment and legal investment – cannot be perfectly overlapped? A different model can be used, shedding light on the same intuition. Here for the sake of simplicity we will assume that all the re-investment in the illegal markets is done using dirty money.

Let us consider again that in a given country or region the Criminal Sector is involved in illegal activities, and it gains an aggregate monetary profit of K_0.

We assume that the Criminal Sector should launder at least a fraction $0 \leq y < 1$ of its illegal profits, while the rest will be reinvested in illegal markets. We also assume that each laundering operation has a cost for the criminal sector, represented by the price of money-laundering services.

The variable C represents the overall cost of money laundering procedures. The process of money laundering holds one period. The net value of cleaned money available to the criminal sector will be:

$$W_0 = (1 - C)yK_0 \tag{13}$$

A portion f of these assets will be invested in the legal markets while the remaining $(1 - f)W_0$ will be spent on consumption goods. Money laundering is the channel thorough which the criminal profits are funnelled into the legitimate economic sector for business investments or for sustaining the lifestyle of organized crime groups' members.

Organized crime groups are increasingly employing legitimate business structures, using different methods for controlling and influencing them. The exploitation of the real and financial sectors is used for reinvestment of criminal proceeds.

In the second period the legal financial assets, which result from the legal investment, will be:

$$L_1 = fW_0(1 + r_l) \tag{14}$$

where r_l is the legal rate of return. In the meantime the share of illegal revenues $(1 - y)K_0$, which was reinvested in the illegal market in the first period, yielded the overall illegal return:

$$K_1 = (1 - y)K_0(1 + r_i) \tag{15}$$

Afterwards, the legal assets will arise from two sources: the share of starting illegal capital which was laundered in the first period and then invested in the legal sector in the second period; the share of illegal capital which was directly reinvested in the illegal market in the first period and then laundered for use in the legal economy in the second period. Therefore in general we have:

$$L_n = f(1 + r_l)(L_{n-1} + W_{n-1}) \tag{16}$$

where:

$$W_n = (1 - C)yK_n \tag{17}$$

and:

$$K_n = (1 - y)K_{n-1}(1 + r_i) = (1 - y)^n K_0(1 + r_i)^n \tag{18}$$

Let us suppose that every period holds a time interval h; therefore the difference (ΔL) between two successive steps is given by:

$$\Delta L = f(1 + r_l)[L(t) - L(t - h)] + f(1 + r_l)y(1 - C)K_0(1 - y)^t(1 + r_i)^t \left[\frac{(1 - y)^h(1 + r_i)^h - 1}{(1 - y)^h(1 + r_i)^h}\right]$$

$$\frac{\Delta L}{h} = f(1 + r_l)\frac{[L(t) - L(t-h)]}{h} + f(1 + r_l)y(1 - C)K_0(1 - y)^t(1 + r_i)^t$$

$$\left[\frac{(1 - y)^h(1 + r_i)^h - 1}{h(1 - y)^h(1 + r_i)^h}\right]$$

$$\lim_{h\to 0}\frac{\Delta L}{h} \Rightarrow \frac{dL}{dt} = f(1+r_l)\frac{dL}{dt} + f(1+r_l)yK_0(1-C)(1-y)^t(1+r_i)^t\log[(1-y)(1+r_i)]$$

$$\frac{dL}{dt} = \frac{f(1 + r_l)}{1 - f(1 + r_l)}yK_0(1 - C)(1 - y)^t(1 + r_i)^t\log[(1 - y)(1 + r_i)]$$

Given:

$$F = \frac{f(1 + r_l)}{1 - f(1 + r_l)}yK_0(1 - C)$$

we have:

$$\int_0^t \frac{dL}{d\tau}d\tau = F\int_0^t [\log(1 - y) + \log(1 + r_i)](1 - y)^\tau(1 + r_i)^\tau d\tau$$

The overall amount of the legal assets of the Criminal Sector is equal to:

$$L(t) = F[(1 - y)^t(1 + r_i)^t - 1] \tag{19}$$

Expression (19) is relevant when it is a monotonic increasing function of t for:

$$r_i > \frac{y}{1 - y}$$

And for:

$$f < \frac{1}{1 + r_l}.$$

Now we can go further in describing the costs of money laundering procedure, in order to disentangle the role of the regulation. We simply assume that the cost (C) of money laundering, which does not depend on time, is made up of two parts: the first one is the technical cost (C_0) of money-laundering procedures, while the second corresponds to the cost (R) produced by the anti-money-laundering regulation.

We suppose that the latter part depends on the off-shore attitude index δ and the functional relation could be even more complicated, nevertheless we suppose that δ has only small variations, therefore we could consider as a first approximation that this contribution depends linearly on it:

$$C = C_0 + R \text{ with } 0 \leq C < 1$$

$$R = C_1\,(1 - \beta\delta),\ 0 < C_1 < 1 \text{ e } 0 < \beta < 1;\ \delta. \geq 0$$

Where C_0 is the cost of money laundering technology and R depends on the effectiveness of the anti-money-laundering regulation. Technology is becoming a facilitator of organized crime, particularly for money laundering, while anti-money-laundering regulations have forced criminals to invest a great deal of energy and resources in diversifying money-laundering methods.

We can suppose that the former is a fixed cost $0 \leq C_0 < 1$, while the latter is a variable cost that depends on an index which measures the country's attitude to be lax in its money laundering regulation (δ index); the parameter β is a normalizing factor.

We can rewrite the equation (19) as:

$$L(t) = \frac{f(1 + r_l)}{1 - f(1 + r_l)} yK_0\{1 - [C_0 + R(\delta)]\}[(1 - y)^t(1 + r_i)^t - 1]$$

or:

$$L(t) = \frac{f(1 + r_l)}{1 - f(1 + r_l)} yK_0\{1 - [C_0 + C_1(1 - \beta\delta)]\}[(1 - y)^t(1 + r_i)^t - 1]$$

At a time t = n, we will have:

$$L(n) = \frac{f(1 + r_l)}{1 - f(1 + r_l)} yK_0\{1 - [C_0 + C_1(1 - \beta\delta)]\}[(1 - y)^n(1 + r_i)^n - 1]$$

The ratio between the overall legal wealth and the initial illegal profits represents the money laundering multiplier.

Given an initial volume of illegal profits, the more effective the money-laundering process is, the greater the legal assets available to the criminal sector, due the laundering – illegal reinvestment mechanism. The dynamic model shows how the money-laundering mechanism empowers organized crime, when we take into account the time dimension.

The model can be used to explore the possible effects of regulation on the total amount of legal assets held by organized crime. It shows that the costs of money-laundering procedures depend on the effectiveness of the anti-money-laundering regulation, given that the legal regulations and their enforcement increase the transaction costs.

Every improvement in the effectiveness of the anti-money-laundering regulation – given its cost – will produce a decrease in the money-laundering multiplier, consequently in the effects of money-laundering activity, and therefore an increase in the overall public benefits.

Following this line of reasoning it is evident that in the long run the goal of regulation must be to eliminate the multiplier effect – i.e. the optimal value of the multiplier is zero.

In its steady state, the multiplier cannot be less than zero. In fact if the overall legal wealth is negative, this means that money laundering activity destroys economic value. But if money laundering procedures are ineffective the likely consequence is that the criminal sector will progressively change its behaviour – for example in terms of the proportion of illegal revenues to be laundered, share of reinvestment in the illegal economy and its diversification – in order to avoid the destruction of value. It is well recognized that organized crime implements counter-measures to avoid detection and prosecution by the law.

REFERENCES

Barone, R. and D. Masciandaro (2011), 'Organized crime, money laundering and legal economy: theory and simulations', *European Journal of Law and Economics*, **32** (1), 115–42.

Dalla Pellegrina, L. and D. Masciandaro (2009), 'The risk based approach in the new European anti-money laundering legislation: a law and economics view', *Review of Law and Economics*, **5** (2), 932–52.

Masciandaro, D. (1999), 'Money laundering: the economics of regulation', *European Journal of Law and Economics*, **7** (3), 225–40.

Masciandaro, D. (ed.) (2004), *Global Financial Crime: Terrorism, Money Laundering and Offshore Centres*, Aldershot: Ashgate.

Masciandaro, D., E. Takats and B. Unger (2007), *Black Finance: The Economics of Money Laundering*, Cheltenham, UK and Northampton, MA, USA: Edward Elgar.

5. Money laundering, drugs and prostitution as victimless crimes

Loek Groot

5.1 INTRODUCTION

The market for laundered money can be analyzed just as any ordinary good for which there is demand and supply. The supply of money to be laundered ultimately originates from legal money put to use in illegal activities or transactions. This can roughly be subdivided into two categories, the first being tax evasion, in which legal money or legal transactions are hidden to avoid paying taxes. Most of the money involved in tax evasion finds its way back to the official economy easily. Money, for instance earned in the black economy, is simply spent on consumer goods and channeled back in the legal sector. The second stems from the proceeds in the trade of illegal goods and services (drugs, prostitution, weapons) and other illegal activities (such as bank robberies, blackmailing, gambling, counterfeit and fraud). For instance, a citizen who spends part of his legal salary to smoke marijuana in the evening turns legal money into money that will be hidden from the official economy by dealers and drug lords, with them, in turn, transferring part of the revenues back into the official economy through consumption.

Only that part of legal money transformed into illegal money which cannot easily be transferred back in the official economy, stemming either from tax evasion or from the trade of illegal goods, constitutes the supply of money to be laundered. Tax avoiders and criminals both contribute to the supply of money to be laundered and exert a demand for money-laundering services. Financial institutions that facilitate tax evasion and money laundering (henceforth abbreviated as ML) exert a demand for money to be laundered and supply ML services. In some tax havens, but probably also in the financial centers of the world, there is an entire infrastructure that can only be sustained with more or less steady and sufficient streams of money to be laundered.

There is a close parallel between demand and supply of ML and demand and supply of drugs, partly because both are considered illegal: with respect to, for example, cocaine, in the end the (net) supply (e.g. the production in Colombia minus what is captured) must be equal to the demand (e.g. consumption in the US and Europe), and this equality is mediated by the price of cocaine (see e.g. the model of Chumacero 2008). Also with respect to ML, supply must balance demand. If the supply of ML services decreases, for example because an agency delivering ML services is captured, then given the demand, the price of ML will go up and vice versa given the supply of ML services, if there is more money to be laundered and thus an increasing demand for ML services, the market price to launder money will go up. The analogy of supply and demand of ML with supply and demand of drugs, or any other marketable good, suggests that in ML there must also be an 'equilibrium price' which ensures equality between demand and supply. Since in the legal economy the value of money per unit, is unity by definition, and legal money is preferred above illegal money – why would otherwise so many people be busy with risky and intricate ML activities? – it must be the case that the value of illegal money is less than unity, or to state it otherwise, the value of an illegal dollar or euro is less than the value of a legal one. One can think of this price of ML as a conversion factor, like an exchange rate, or as an equivalent ML discount rate. The closer to unity the conversion factor, the cheaper or easier it is to launder money. At the limit, with the conversion factor equal to unity, there is no practical distinction between legal and illegal money and laundering money is costless and without any risk. In general, the lower the conversion factor, the higher is the cost of ML, which in turn is determined by the intensity and efficacy of fighting ML through policing financial institutions and other effective anti-ML policies, including the required compensatory risk premium for the chance of being captured and sentenced.

Taking ML as a market with demand and supply, this chapter argues that if one is prepared to decriminalize activities that qualify as victimless crimes, a significant share of the supply of money to be laundered will vanish, which in turn will lead to a lower demand for ML services. Section 2 explains the notion of a victimless crime, as introduced by Mill and taken up by legal scholars such as Feinberg and Posner, in relation to criminal law. Section 3 focuses on victimless crimes in the economic analysis of law and section 4 deals with the war on drugs. Section 5 provides an additional argument for why the market for ML, or what is left of it after legalizing drugs, prostitution and gambling, should be legalized. Nowhere do I have the ambition to provide a conclusive argument. This contribution is rather meant to lay out the scheme of reasoning to be followed in order to arrive at the proposition that laws prohibiting many activities underlying the market for ML, and prohibiting ML itself, should be repealed. The final section summarizes and concludes.

5.2 VICTIMLESS CRIMES AND CRIMINAL LAW

As point of departure I take John Stuart Mill's Harm Principle, which, because it plays such a prominent role in this chapter, is cited in full length:

> The object of this Essay is to assert one very simple principle, as entitled to govern absolutely the dealings of society with the individual in the way of compulsion and control, whether the means used be physical force in the form of legal penalties, or the moral coercion of public opinion. That principle is, that the sole end for which mankind are warranted, individually or collectively, in interfering with the liberty of action of any of their number, is self-protection. That the only purpose for which power can be rightfully exercised over any member of a civilised community, against his will, is to prevent harm to others. His own good, either physical or moral, is not a sufficient warrant. He cannot rightfully be compelled to do or forbear because it will be better for him to do so, because it will make him happier, because, in the opinions of others, to do so would be wise, or even right. These are good reasons for remonstrating with him, or reasoning with him, or persuading him, or entreating him, but not for compelling him, or visiting him with any evil in case he do otherwise. To justify that, the conduct from which it is desired to deter him must be calculated to produce evil to some one else. The only part of the conduct of any one, for which he is amenable to society, is that which concerns others. In the part which merely concerns himself, his independence is, of right, absolute. Over himself, over his own body and mind, the individual is sovereign. (Mill 2008, pp. 13–14)

After this statement, Mill goes on to say that the doctrine that each should be accorded the maximum liberty and autonomy consistent with the rights of others and subject to the harm to others principle only has to be applied to those 'in the maturity of their faculties', which implies that paternalism is allowed to protect children or the mentally handicapped. Although Mill does not use the term 'victimless crime', if state coercion and state interference with private conduct can only be justified to prevent harm to others, then it follows that there can be no such thing as a victimless crime, an act earmarked as criminal yet imposing no harm to others not involved in the act. This leaves open the possibility that there may be a victim (e.g. an addict in a drugs transaction), but this can only be someone involved in the act itself. Victimless therefore means that there are no so-called third parties, or actors not involved, that suffer harm as a consequence of the act.

For illustrative purposes, suppose someone dumps toxic waste in a river. The harm to others principle justifies state intervention such as environmental laws regulating toxic waste disposal because the interests of others not involved in this act may be harmed. A typical drugs transaction can be described as follows: a drug addict voluntarily makes a contract with the drug dealer to sell and buy a drug, nobody gets cheated and both parties voluntarily consent to the transaction. Is this really a victimless crime? First of all, the drug user might be the victim, which becomes more likely if the drug is addictive. After some time the buyer becomes addicted and one may say that as soon as this is the case, the buyer is turned into a junkie who feels compelled to continue using drugs, as opposed to the rather optional voluntary purchases in normal consumption acts. Strictly, even if there would be consensus that all drug users are victims, this does not imply that the no harm to others principle of Mill is violated. Somewhat crudely said, in a free society, everyone is free to choose their own way to go to hell. Indeed, in the citation above, Mill is rather explicit that even with acts harmful to those involved but without harm to others, there is no case for intervention since '[h]is own good, either physical or moral, is not a sufficient warrant'.

However, since there are very few acts that have no effects on others whatsoever, one has to take into account the harm imposed on friends, family and society. That friends and family may suffer needs no comment, but this stands on an equal footing with when friends and family do not approve of a bad career move or a marriage decision. More relevant is that society at large may incur a loss, for instance the costs of rehab or the cost of providing shelter once an addict is homeless. It is important to note that the cost to fight the use and trade of drugs (all costs falling under the war on drugs), the cost of criminal offenses related to drugs due to the higher propensity of drug addicts involved in criminal acts and the indirect cost of the corruption of police and diminished respect for the law only arise if society decides to criminalize drugs. In measuring the social costs of drugs, these costs would be absent if drugs were legalized and are thus an artifact of their illegality. As Crombag (1983, p. 125) remarks, all these costs are the consequence of the decision to criminalize drugs, and society should pay the price to prohibit drugs. For the harm to society, these are social costs connected to the choice to criminalize drugs, whereas under the alternative these costs do not arise. The proper social cost accounting will be addressed in the next section.

Legal scholars have identified a number of activities that count as criminal offenses under existent laws but nevertheless also may qualify as victimless crimes. Usually, they make a distinction between solitary and consensual victimless crimes. To the first category belong suicide and the possession and use of drugs, to the second euthanasia, abortion, gambling, drugs trade, prostitution, homosexuality and pornography. Apart from all being alleged victimless crimes, the common denominator of this list is that they are considered, if not by all then at least by many, as morally offensive. One may say that in case of victimless crimes, the law basically enforces a particular morality. According to what H.L.A. Hart calls the 'conservative thesis', the majority in society has the right not only to follow its own moral convictions but also to preserve this 'moral environment' as a thing of value and to insist that all members of society abide by their moral convictions.[1] According to what he calls the 'disintegration thesis', where public morality is considered the 'cement of society', public morality must be maintained to prevent social disintegration. For a variety of reasons, Hart does not endorse either the conservative nor the disintegration thesis.[2] What should be clear, however, is that even when the legislator, mandated by a majority of the population, considers drugs, prostitution or homosexuality immoral, as long as it does not bring harm to others, following Mill, it should not be made illegal simply because it is considered as immoral. I reject the morality-based criminalization of victimless crimes. In what follows, I will follow the economic approach to law, which not only descriptively but also prescriptively claims that the substance of law is to maximize efficiency or wealth. This is the position taken by Richard Posner in his economic analysis of law. I will argue that the harm to others principle of Mill can best be interpreted as a cost–benefit argument.

5.3 VICTIMLESS CRIMES AND THE ECONOMIC ANALYSIS OF LAW

A central tenet of economic analysis is that voluntary exchange is conducive to efficiency. With voluntary exchange, resources are allocated to where their value is highest no matter whether it concerns consumer goods or factors of production. An allocation is said to be efficient if there is no other allocation that would increase the value, as measured by the willingness to pay. Posner (2001, p. 111), a major contributor to the economics of law, states that

> [t]he major function of criminal law in a capitalist society is to prevent people from bypassing the system of voluntary, compensated exchange – the 'market,' explicit or implicit – in situations where, because transactions costs are low, the market is a more efficient method of allocating resources than forced exchange. Market bypassing in such situations is inefficient – in the sense in which economists equate efficiency with wealth maximization – no matter how much utility it may confer on the offender . . . I contend, in short, that most of the distinctive doctrines of the criminal law can be explained as if the objective of that law were to promote economic efficiency.

In that sense a market economy as a system of voluntary exchange is said to be efficient.[3]

Among the five principal types of conduct made criminal in the legal system, Posner (2003, p. 217) also includes as a separate category 'Voluntary, and therefore presumptively value maximizing, exchanges incidental to activities that the state has outlawed', on which he comments:

> . . . why punish acts that don't hurt anybody? . . . the answer lies outside economics; it is difficult for an economist to understand why, if a crime is truly 'victimless', the criminal should be punished. (Of course, ostensibly victimless crimes may, like other contractual exchanges, have third-party effects; the sale of liquor to a drunk driver is an example.)

In an earlier version, published in the *Columbia Law Review* in 1985, a similar statement can be found:

> It is hard for an economist to understand why the voluntary exchange of valuable goods should be criminal. Such exchange, prima facie at least, promotes rather than reduces efficiency – whether it concerned hard-core or soft-core pornography, cocaine or cigarettes, common carriage or contract carriage. The qualification is important, however. Voluntary transactions may have such serious effects on third parties that when those effects are taken into account the transaction is not value-maximizing after all.' (Posner 1985, p. 1200)

The important qualification obviously refers to the fact that what *prima facie* seem like efficiency-increasing voluntary exchanges might turn out not to be so, all things considered.

Although Posner hardly refers to Mill,[4] both are in favour of decriminalizing victimless crimes. Mill's criterion that legitimate state interference is subject to the harm to others principle can be aligned with Posner's stance that the purpose of law is to maximize efficiency or wealth if Mill's principle is operationalized as a cost–benefit approach. Most voluntary exchanges increase efficiency, or society's wealth as Posner would say, and would therefore also pass a cost–benefit calculation. The case would be settled for victimless crimes as just voluntary exchanges if all voluntary exchanges were (by definition) efficient and would increase society's wealth. However, not all voluntary exchanges increase wealth. Even Posner, a staunch libertarian, identifies voluntary exchanges that do not increase wealth. One example is that of blackmail: 'Blackmailer possesses information about Victim that Victim would prefer not be made public, Victim values Blackmailer's silence more than Blackmailer values the right to publicize the information, so Blackmailer sells Victim the right to information' (Posner 1972, p. 2). If blackmail were legal, both parties could enter legally enforceable contracts about disclosure of the information, but because it is illegal, they cannot do so and the deviant nature of blackmail compared to normal commerce is an artifact of their illegality. So although blackmail qualifies as a voluntary exchange and also as victimless as far as third parties are concerned, it has to be prohibited because it is wealth reducing. The blackmail act simply transfers resources from the victim to the blackmailer and indirectly reduces wealth because of the wasteful use of resources by the blackmailer to collect the information and to make his threat credible and the resources used by (potential) victims to avoid threats. Unless there is a social benefit, Posner (1972, p. 4) concludes that on economic grounds blackmail should be forbidden because it is 'a sterile redistributive activity, like (simple) theft'.

The main economic function of the legal framework, according to Posner, is not only to limit exchanges to voluntary ones, but to promote efficiency. Property law precludes that resources are wasted in disputes about ownership by giving enforceable rights over property, thus contributing to economic efficiency by channeling resources into production. Without contract law, only Pareto improvements involving the simultaneous exchange of barter trade would take place. Antitrust law prohibits agreements between competing firms that would harm consumers by raising prices and thus reducing efficiency and wealth. By making involuntary exchanges illegal, criminal law contributes to economic efficiency by channeling our efforts into voluntary exchanges that benefit the parties involved (so-called (quasi) Pareto improvements). The system of law outlaws all involuntary exchanges like theft and robbery and confines the subset of possible voluntary exchanges to only those that raise society's wealth. As will be clear, in Posner's approach, the question whether particular provisions of law[5] are desirable or not depends on whether they further efficiency or wealth. In other words, in the end a social cost–benefit analysis is decisive.

To take stock of the terms and concepts introduced so far, we have the harm to others principle, victimless crimes, criminal law, (in)voluntary exchanges and efficiency or wealth. Imagine that the universe of all possible exchanges is divided into involuntary and voluntary exchanges. Criminal and other law prohibits all involuntary exchanges, like theft, rape and a host of other offenses. Voluntary exchanges that are Pareto improvements – at least one agent gains, while no one is worse off – are efficient. There are also voluntary exchanges that are quasi-Pareto efficient: the gains for the winners of the exchange are higher than the losses imposed on third parties, so whether or not they actually do so, the winners can compensate the losers. Quasi-Pareto efficiency, or Kaldor-Hicks efficiency, is the wealth maximizing approach used by Posner in his writings on the economics of law. Both voluntary exchanges that are Pareto improvements or quasi-Pareto efficient should not be prohibited. One may say that the demands of the no harm to others principle are met as long as the harm on others can be compensated. This does not apply to the set of voluntary exchanges in which, although the parties involved gain, a greater loss is imposed on third parties. The example of toxic waste disposal given above belongs to this subset. Among the set of voluntary exchanges there are finally the so-called victimless crimes, as far as third parties are concerned, passing the no harm to others principle, but not increasing efficiency or wealth and therefore possibly prohibited. The example of blackmail belongs to this category. This suggests that the no harm to others principle does not suffice, whereas a social cost–benefit approach provides the guidelines for which acts to legitimize and which to forbid.

For the evaluation of an arrangement, it is the calculus of the total benefits and harms, including those on (potential) victims, that is decisive. The victim of blackmail, although voluntarily consenting to a blackmail deal, would prefer a regime in which blackmail is forbidden. In the evaluation of the costs and benefits of allowing blackmail, we therefore have to compare this situation with the alternative in which blackmail is prohibited. For voluntary exchanges like prostitution, drugs trade or gambling, Posner argues that legalization is more efficient and therefore these exchanges should not be prohibited. The wealth-maximizing approach, or equivalent social cost–benefit approach,[6] shares with Mill's no harm to others principle that the moral intention of an act or the immorality of the act itself is of no concern. Many may detest prostitution, gambling or drugs, but if there are markets for these activities, the sheer existence of these markets suggests that they are potentially wealth increasing. The case for regulation of these markets, with in its most extreme form prohibition, rests on showing that regulation performs better in terms of social cost and benefits than its alternatives.

I do not want to claim that Posner's approach is the only sensible one. Crombag (1983) for instance uses the utilitarian framework and is in favour of legalization of drugs if a convincing case can be made that legalization is better in terms of total welfare than prohibition. Both approaches identify costs and benefits of alternatives, but the latter additionally assumes declining marginal utility of income and the possibility of interpersonal comparison. In theory, an arrangement considered efficient by the criteria of Posner might be welfare decreasing under the utilitarian calculus, for example because the increase in wealth is concentrated among the rich and the losses borne by the poor. However, if for simplicity it is assumed that the government has the instrument of lump sum redistribution, wealth maximizing can be made equivalent with utilitarian welfare maximization. In the next section, the cost–benefit approach will be applied to the market for drugs – probably the most important market with respect to ML.

5.4 THE WAR ON DRUGS

In 2005 and again in 2010 the Becker-Posner blog dealt with the war on drugs and drugs legalization. On 3 May 2005, Becker kicks off to explain why the war on drugs has failed. It failed not due to lack of effort in law enforcement, but due to the fact that the basic property for the demand for drugs is that it is inelastic. The war on drugs has the effect of raising the price of drugs, which, due to the inelastic demand, does not lead to a large drop in the use of drugs and therefore to higher drugs sales (the price rises more than quantity declines). On the supply side the higher sales revenues translate into the use of resources to avoid detection, bribery payments, liquidation of competitors, and so on. On the demand side, the higher prices have a criminalizing effect on the drug addicts. And for the government, Becker refers to own research in which government expenditures for the USA in 2005 on the war on drugs is estimated at about $100 billion per year, including the cost of police, courts and the cost of imprisonment, but excluding intangible costs 'such as the destructive effects on many inner city neighborhoods, the use of the American military to fight drug lords and farmers in Colombia and other nations, or the corrupting influence of drugs on many governments'. Apart from a cost–benefit analysis comparing legalization and prohibition, which leaves open the possibility of legalization with increased drug use, Becker claims that legalization is even superior in reaching the goal of reduced drugs use:

> Our study suggests that legalization of drugs combined with an excise tax on consumption would be a far cheaper and more effective way to reduce drug use. Instead of a war, one could have, for example, a 200% tax on the legal use of drugs by all adults – consumption by say persons under age 18 would still be illegal. That would reduce consumption in the same way as the present war, and would also increase total spending on drugs, as in the current system. But the similarities end at that point. The tax revenue from drugs would accrue to state and federal authorities, rather than being dissipated into the real cost involving police, imprisonment, dangerous qualities, and the like. Instead of drug cartels, there would be legal companies involved in production and distribution of drugs of reliable quality, as happened after the prohibition of alcohol ended. There would be no destruction of poor neighborhoods – so no material for the Wire HBO series, or the movie Traffic – no corruption of Afghani or Columbian governments, and no large scale imprisonment of African-American and other drug suppliers. The tax revenue to various governments hopefully would substitute for other

> taxes, or would be used for educating young people about any dangerous effects of drugs. (Becker-Posner blog)

In the follow-up blog, Posner raises three points. First, since higher prices are the result of the war on drugs, the war on drugs is partially won as far as higher prices lead to reduced consumption. Second, this partial victory has not been worth the considerable social cost. Again classifying a drugs transaction between a willing buyer and seller as a victimless crime, Posner remarks that since these types of crimes have a low probability of apprehension, the sentences must be severe to provide deterrence. The special problem victimless crimes pose is the difficulty in detection if there is no victim to report and lay a claim against the offender (a point that is also made by Unger (2011)). This explains why victimless crimes reside within criminal law, prosecuted by the state, instead of tort or contract law, where the victim sues the offender, and, if convicted, the offender has to pay monetary damages to the victim. At the same time, the deterrence effect of harsher sentences is more limited, the higher the discount rate of criminals. Third, the connections between drugs and violence are 'merely artifacts of the fact that the sale of the drugs in question has been criminalized, so that the suppliers cannot use the usual, peaceable means of enforcing property rights and contracts and are not regulated in the interest of consumer safety, as legal drugs are' (Posner, 03/20/2005). Like Becker, for Posner the outcome of a proper cost–benefit analysis is decisive whether or not to legalize drugs. This becomes manifest in Posner's position with respect to performance-enhancing steroid drugs by athletes. The social cost–benefit approach favors a ban on performance-enhancing steroid drugs by athletes, since each user not only impairs his own health, but also imposes costs on competitors, with no offsetting gain. Note that here Mill's harm to others principle points in the same direction of prohibition.

In December 2010, on the occasion of the release of a study on the budgetary impact of ending drug prohibition (see Miron and Waldock, 2010), the issue of legalization is taken up again in the blog. Posner compares the direct social cost of prohibition as estimated by Miron and Waldock with the social cost of increased drugs consumption under legalization. The budgetary impact of legalization consists of savings in legal enforcement and the increase in tax revenues. Since tax revenues are basically transfer payments, only the savings in legal enforcement should enter the cost–benefit analysis. These savings have to be compared with the social cost of increased drugs consumption under legalization: 'The question would then be whether the external costs of increased consumption of mind-altering drugs would exceed the savings in law enforcement costs from legalization' (Posner, 12/31/2010). The point is that legalization would reduce the stigma of using drugs and being a drug addict, which leads to the full price of drugs (that is, the monetary plus non-monetary cost) approaching the nominal price. In 'The American War on Drugs is Not Only an American Disaster' (Becker, 12/31/2010), Becker responds that the direct social cost is only a small fraction of the total social cost of the war on drugs. First, there are the indirect social costs of the deterioration of neighborhoods due to drugs. Second,

> Legalization of drugs will very likely increase the high school graduation rate because it would reduce these illegal opportunities for dropouts. As a result, drug legalization would radically reduce the numbers of young uneducated persons going into the drug trade, and

increase their numbers in better paying legal jobs since they would be better qualified for these jobs.

Third, the foreign cost of the American war on drugs is immense, just looking at the estimated 30 thousand dead in Mexico's war on drugs.

In conclusion, a cost–benefit analysis for a number of activities that qualify as victimless crimes and still fall under the criminal law might show that legalization (subject to some form of regulation, for example with respect to youngsters) is to be preferred over the present regime of criminalization. The ethical arguments against legalized drugs and prostitution (one could also add gambling and pornography), particularly popular among religious sections of the population, are that the activities involved are vices, if not sins. The libertarian response is that all should have freedom to act, even if others consider these acts as sins. The alleged sinfulness and the problem of addiction does not justify a ban, since people can sin and become addicted to anything. Only a cost–benefit study can show which regulatory regime is best. If legalization turns out to be superior, the prohibitionists impose a net cost on society, which can be seen as the price to be paid if particular moral preferences are imposed on society at large.

For the issue of ML, there are two implications. First, a cost–benefit analysis of ML is flawed in so far as criminalization of activities fueling the market for ML do not pass the cost-benefit test themselves. It would be inconsistent to apply a cost-benefit analysis to ML without applying the same test to the underlying activities. Drugs, prostitution and gambling are probably the most important issues, since these activities are responsible for a major share of the money to be laundered. My rough guess is that from a cost–benefits point of view, legalization of these activities is warranted. If that were indeed to happen, then the market for ML would shrink significantly,[7] if not be decimated. Second, what remains to be answered is whether the act of ML itself can be considered as a victimless crime and whether legalization of ML will pass a cost–benefit analysis. This will be addressed in the next section.

5.5 MONEY LAUNDERING AS A VICTIMLESS CRIME

Victimless crimes are illegal acts in which all involved have consented to perform the act: they all wanted the transaction to happen, so to speak. Now does the act of ML also qualify as a victimless crime? Imagine a criminal with money to be laundered and a money launderer supplying the services, agreeing on a price and striking a deal. The core of the argumentation in the previous section was that many activities contributing to ML should not be prohibited in the first place, so if they are nevertheless considered criminal, we might have a sequence of acts all treated as criminal although victimless. One also has to take into account that it is inevitable that the conversion of legal into illegal capital by drugs users or prostitution consumers sooner or later must be reversed by means of ML, otherwise the stock of illegal capital would continue to grow, unless capturing provides a sufficient offsetting force.[8] As long as law enforcement is not perfect, as it never will be, the phenomenon of ML is a fact of life.

To make the case more clear cut, suppose the money to be laundered is definitely criminal money derived, for example, from fraud or from a bank robbery. Obviously, fraud or bank robbery are not victimless and are rightly considered as criminal activities. Suppose the bank robber uses part of the loot to buy a fancy present for his wife. Either this last act is illegal because the pedigree of the money is illegal, or the act is legal, despite the bank robbery being illegal. The same reasoning can be applied to ML: if the activities (drug trade, prostitution) giving rise to ML are legalized, they no longer contribute to the supply of money to be laundered. The main reason to consider ML still as a crime is to fight tax evasion. If the activities are illegal, following the argument of the pedigree of the money, one may decide that therefore ML is also illegal, or that ML is legal (despite its illegal source, like the purchase of the gift by the bank robber was legal). My hunch with respect to this issue is that by and large ML is a victimless crime, but for the question whether or not it should be legalized or prohibited, as matter of consistency, a cost–benefit analysis has to be performed. Again, the prohibitionists would have to accept not only the direct cost of criminalizing ML, such as the legal enforcement cost, but also the social cost from all secondary effects, such as the emergence of tax havens, turning people into law-breakers, bribery, etc. On the other side of the ledger, one has to take into account that legalization might make criminal activities more attractive, imposing a social cost on society. The legalization of ML would amount to waiving the duty to give a satisfactory explanation to fiscal authorities and banks as to where the money comes from.

If the analysis in this chapter is sound, to answer the question whether ML should be decriminalized or not, the total market for ML first has to be cleared for these (victimless) activities that have to be legalized in the first place based on proper cost–benefit analyses. For what is left, the cost–benefit approach can go either way: prohibition of ML may provide such an important tool to fight tax evasion and criminality, for example terrorism, that it justifies all (in)direct social costs, but if not, ML is to be considered as an ordinary financial transaction.

5.6 CONCLUSION

The problem of ML cannot be tackled without addressing the underlying markets of drugs, prostitution and gambling. John Stuart Mill's harm to others principle and the derived notion of a victimless crime initiated a debate on whether drugs, prostitution and gambling should be forbidden or not. For Mill, every crime needs a victim. If so, victimless crimes pose a problem. One approach is to put forward principled arguments pro and con criminalization of victimless crimes, invoking public morality and society's dominant moral convictions. A more practical approach is to conduct a cost–benefit analysis to decide between criminalization and legalization, or which regulatory regime somewhere in between these two extremes is to be preferred. This is the approach adopted by Posner in his economics of law. It might well turn out that repealing the criminal law for drugs, prostitution and gambling, and maybe also ML itself, passes such a cost–benefit test. The criminal sector of the economy would shrink and so would the amount of ML.

NOTES

1. For a more thorough discussion, see 'Criminalization and decriminalization – a review and typology of criminalization arguments' http://law.jrank.org/pages/838/Criminalization-Decriminalization-review-typology-criminalization-arguments.html
2. One problem is of course whose morality is to be enforced. Even if this problem is solved in democratic deliberation and the majority view were to prevail, one may doubt whether this gives a better outcome than following the harm to others principle.
3. Subject of course to correction for market failures arising from externalities, public goods, asymmetric information, etc.
4. In the 2001 volume of a collection of economic essays by Posner on the economics of public law, there is no reference to Mill at all and in his 2003 textbook *Economic Analysis of Law* there are only two references, but not to Mill's harm to others principle.
5. The thesis of Posner is not limited to the examples given in the main text. As he writes elsewhere (2003, 24–25)

   > Legal writers have . . . argued that many of the doctrines and institutions of the legal system are best understood and explained as efforts to promote the efficient allocation of resources . . . What we may call the efficiency theory of the common law is not that every common law doctrine and decision is efficient. That would be unlikely, given the difficulty of the questions that the law wrestles with and the nature of judges' incentives. The theory is that the common law is best (not perfectly) explained as a system for maximizing the wealth of society.

6. In the economic literature, the Kaldor-Hicks criterion is taken as the rationale for cost–benefit analysis. Selecting only the projects with higher benefits than costs is not different from applying the Kaldor-Hicks criterion, because total benefits must at least be sufficient to pay for all the cost.
7. Suppose that prostitution and the consumption of soft drugs are no longer illegal, as is the case in the Netherlands. Most of this business will then become part of the official economy and, except for reasons of tax evasion, the now legal monetary transactions in these sectors of industry will no longer contribute to ML, as would be the case so long as prostitution or soft drugs were illegal.
8. As an accounting identity, in a closed economy the total amount of legal money turned into illegal money must be equal to the sum of the amount captured by the policy, the amount of ML and the amount hoarded in cash by criminals. Assuming the last one is constant, one can say that given the volume of the criminal business, the amount of ML is the complement of the amount captured; or stated otherwise, the amount of ML is equal to the amount not captured.

REFERENCES

Becker-Posner blog, http://www.becker-posner-blog.com/2005/03/the-failure-of-the-war-on-drugs-becker.html. See also Posner (03/20/2005), http://www.becker-posner-blog.com/2005/03/the-war-on-drugs-posners-comment.html; Posner (12/31/2010), http://www.becker-posner-blog.com/2010/12/drug-legalizationPosner.html; Becker (12/31/2010), http://www.becker-posner-blog.com/2010/12/the-american-war-on-drugs-is-not-only-an-american-disaster-becker.html.

Chumacero, R. (2008), *General Equilibrium Analysis of the Market for Illegal Drugs*, World Bank Policy Research, working paper WPS4565.

Crombag, H.F.M. (1983), *Een manier van overleven: Psychologische grondslagen van moraal en recht*, Tjeenk Willink.

Mill, J.S. (2008) [1859], *On Liberty*, Oxford: Oxford University Press.

Miron, J.A. and K. Waldock (2010), *The Budgetary Impact of Ending Drug Prohibition*, Washington, DC: Cato Institute, available at: http://www.cato.org/pubs/wtpapers/DrugProhibitionWP.pdf.

Posner, R.A.(1972), *Blackmail, Privacy and Freedom of Contract*, Chicago Law & Economics Working Paper No. 4, 1–26.

Posner, R.A. (1985), 'An economic theory of criminal law', *Columbia Law Review*, 85(6), 1193–231.

Posner, R.A. (2001), *The Economics of Public Law: The Collected Economic Essays of Richard A. Posner, Volume Three*, Cheltenham, UK and Northampton, MA, USA: Edward Elgar.

Posner, R.A. (2003), *Economic Analysis of Law*, New York: Aspen Publishers.

Unger, B. (2011), *From Al Capone to Al Qaeda: Regulating Anti Money Laundering*, in D. Levi (ed.), *Handbook of Regulation*, Cheltenham, UK and Northampton, MA, USA: Edward Elgar.

6. The costs of fraud*

Michael Levi

6.1 INTRODUCTION

Fraud is a deceptively simple word covering a very broad territory. It is a way of making money illegally via deception, whether that deception is directly person-to-person in real space or in virtual space; operates by false stories alone or via the use of deceptive real or e-documents or via Personal Identification Numbers; or uses genuine or phoney businesses as tools of fraud. Thus there is a huge range of contexts in which frauds, large and small, lasting milliseconds (like unauthorised electronic funds transfers) or many years (like the Madoff 'Ponzi' scheme),[1] are perpetrated. Some are planned as scams from the start, sometimes as part of an 'organised crime group' activity; others – with or without the involvement of outsiders – are the result of insiders spotting system weaknesses which, if undetected, may spread from there into much larger schemes. After the event, it can be a matter of interpretation into which planning category any given fraud falls. But the level of harm may be independent of that level of planning, and many losses may have been generated by inefficient business activities and poor judgement rather than pure criminal profit: hence, in addition to clever laundering, the fact that such modest amounts are sometimes recovered from corporate losses. It should be borne in mind that long before any criminal trial may take place or even be contemplated, civil investigations by professionals acting for creditors may have failed to find many assets, and it is speculation that these assets really still exist. These observations also apply to the proceeds of corruption, even Grand Corruption, though the funds found abroad in some major cases are huge enough to show the scale of the depredations.

6.2 WHAT IS FRAUD?

There is no space here to review national variations in legislation, but their breadth or narrowness makes a huge difference to the total. Note that many cases of Grand Corruption also involve false accounting and breach of fiduciary duty so could also be labelled as 'fraud'. In England and Wales, 'fraud' was redefined in the Fraud Act 2006, which created a new general offence of fraud and introduced three possible ways of committing it – by false representation (s. 2), failure to disclose information when there is a legal duty to do so (s. 3 e.g. by a solicitor to a client), and abuse of position (s. 4) (see http://www.cps.gov.uk/legal/d_to_g/fraud_act/). The term covers a huge range of both acts and criminal actors, from (a) group-organised frauds, for example 'carousel' VAT, 'boiler room' share manipulation, insider dealing rings, mortgage fraud rings and payment card counterfeiting; through (b) investment 'Ponzi' Schemes, usually committed by several people; to (c) embezzlement and other frauds by individuals that may be sufficiently well organised to obtain funds, but are not usually considered to meet the criteria for 'organised crime'. How does this overlap with other categories of 'serious and organised crime'? Fraud is one area where – depending on logistics related to the form of the crime – well-organised offenders can profit extensively from crime without needing to form larger groups and networks.

6.3 MEASURING THE COSTS OF FRAUD

The UK government and police have become interested in recent years in the cost of fraud, as part of a movement to measure more accurately the cost of different social harms and allocate police and prevention resources more rationally. This has not been matched elsewhere in the world, though there are very modest efforts to look at consumer fraud and corruption rates in international victimisation surveys (van Dijk et al. 2008) and a growing number of corporate fraud surveys by consulting groups (BDO, Ernst & Young, KPMG, Kroll and PwC), some of which produce global measures, as well as a low response rate study in the US biennially by the Association of Certified Fraud Examiners. There are various problems with the validity of such surveys (Levi and Burrows 2008; Levi 2011). Research on the costs of fraud typically disaggregates costs into their various main components (see e.g., NERA 2000). The costs of fraud under consideration in the research of Levi et al. (2007) and Levi and Burrows (2008) were as follows:

- *Fraud losses (transfer costs):* Victims face direct losses as a result of fraud (i.e. the amount defrauded). These losses are sometimes considered transfers (from the victim to the fraudster), and in the economic literature, transfers are typically *excluded* in analyses of the costs of crime. The present research follows Brand and Price (2000) and includes fraud losses in the costs of fraud, as these are unwanted losses (i.e. the victim has not agreed to the transfer), and as such the transfer represents one from the legal to the illegal economy.
- *Costs of preventing fraud before the event (and other anticipatory costs):* Private and public sector entities take certain defensive measures to prevent/deter fraud, all with costs. These costs range from personal expenditures on shredders to corporate membership of (a) service organisations such as the ABI and APACS, one of whose many functions is fraud prevention, and (b) dedicated fraud prevention bodies such as UK fraud prevention body CIFAS (indeed, the running costs of CIFAS itself). Costs also result from precautionary behaviour: consumers may avoid using certain services or avoid visiting certain crime-heavy locations (physically or virtually) to avoid being victims of crime in general and fraud in particular. NERA (2000) notes, for example, that customers might avoid online banking services for fear of being defrauded (which would represent a loss to them and perhaps the banks if the marginal cost of online banking is lower than that of its alternatives).
- *Costs of responding to fraud after the event:* The costs in response to fraud include costs to the criminal justice system (including police, prosecutors, courts, prison service)[2] and of civil remedies in response to fraud. Larger and more complex frauds against firms will typically incur expenditures (e.g. through internal and/or

> out-sourced private sector investigations) even if they are not ultimately reported to the police. In the event, very few sources provided information relating to the costs of fraud prevention and/or in response to fraud, nor do many appear to keep data in this form.

The costs of fraud (and crime in general) are sometimes disaggregated as losses, resource costs, and externalities. Resource costs may relate to expenditures both in anticipation of and in response to fraud (e.g. on fraud prevention systems, on reactive investigative teams), though these distinctions were difficult. Externalities refer to side effects from an activity which have consequences for another activity but are not reflected in market prices. Externalities can be either positive, when an external benefit is generated, or negative, when an external cost is generated. A negative externality of fraud may be a reduction in the use of online banking services (assuming that online banking commands lower marginal costs). Another might be where a corporate and/or national reputation for making or demanding corrupt payments for contracts leads to other firms or countries avoiding doing business with the suspected bribe-payer or bribe-demander. This falls into the category of fraud (as well as corruption) because where a bribe to an agent leads to the deception of the ultimate 'beneficial owner' (citizens, taxpayers, shareholders/private business owners), this is fraud. Furthermore, there is usually some false accounting that accompanies the bribes.

It should also be noted that costs may be estimated by 'bottom-up' and/or 'top-down' methods. *A 'bottom up' approach* seeks to evaluate the costs of fraud from the perspective of the producer or defrauded organisation. An example of the *bottom-up method* might be the use of administrative data on payment card fraud reported to the UK Cards Association (in which the annual volume/value terms simply represent the sum of all reported frauds). *A 'top down' approach* seeks to estimate the economic implications of fraud from a national perspective. An example of a top-down method might be as follows: X per cent of cheques appear to be fraudulent (perhaps determined through some sort of audit), the mean loss per fraudulent cheque is Y GBP, and Z cheques are used in the UK annually, so X*Y*Z would yield the cost of fraudulent cheques.[3]

6.4 TRENDS IN FRAUD

The dimensions of fraud are difficult to determine. Normally, we would look to statistical data on crime and/or cost of crime trends to enable us to judge whether a problem is getting better or worse. However despite attempts to improve fraud statistics, these cannot readily be applied retrospectively to past data, which are really too patchy and unreliable to be confident that the problem is growing in the way that most people think it is. This is compounded by media tendencies to look unhelpfully at 'fraud' as if it were one homogeneous problem, and to swallow ever-larger figures presented under the banner of 'awareness raising'. Despite very large error margins in estimation, what we do know is that fraud is a very large sum, and it is larger than other forms of property crime. However although some fraudulent trading, mortgage frauds, etc., stimulated and were revealed by the global financial crisis, losses from fraud were almost certainly less than those from bad lending decisions.

The National Fraud Authority (2010a) estimated UK fraud losses at about £30 billion in 2009: around £621 a year for every man, woman and child in the UK (though given the uneven distribution of losses, such average figures are forensically valueless). By 2010, this figure had risen to £38.4 billion (National Fraud Authority 2011), and by 2011 to £73 billion (National Fraud Authority 2012). But these figures cover a variety of types of victim. Card fraud losses in 2011 totalled £341 million, 56 per cent of the losses in 2008 (and a record low cost in the past decade as a ratio to turnover); online banking fraud losses totalled £35.4 m, a significant fall from the previous three years, especially taking into account the rise in people banking online; and cheque fraud losses fell by a third from 2008 to £28.9 m in 2010, before rising again to £34.3 m in 2011, due to an increase in fraudsters stealing genuine cheques and altering the payee name, or using details from genuine cheques to create counterfeits (Financial Fraud Action UK 2012). In 2008, 4 per cent of all insurance claims by value (excluding life insurance) were deemed fraudulent, against 3 per cent in 2007; in 2010, insurers uncovered 133,000 fraudulent insurance claims worth £919m – a rise of 9 per cent on 2009. The Association of British Insurers (ABI) found that motor frauds were the most costly, totalling £466m. and claimed that the value of savings from detected frauds represented 5 per cent of all claims, compared to 4 per cent 2009. The number and value of detected insurance frauds rose by more than 100 per cent over the past five years (ABI 2011) and although no figures are given for changes in the number of policies, we can presume that this is a disproportionate rise.

Currently, time series cost data are available in the UK only for payment card frauds (Financial Fraud Action UK), some aspects of identity frauds (CIFAS) and – until 2009 when they were stopped – for external frauds against government departments (UK Treasury). Intermittent or recent data only are available for other data such as social security fraud and error (DWP) and fraud against local authorities and some national non-departmental bodies (Audit Commission). Fraud cost and incidence surveys carried out by accounting firms in many parts of the world are intermittent and have been applied only to large corporate victims, inadvertently altering the shape of fraud costs away from those solely against individuals and small businesses (Levi et al. 2007; Levi and Burrows 2008). And the regular surveys of 'fraud trends' in the UK by BDO and by KPMG are analyses of trends in cases coming to court rather than trends in fraud itself. Given the variable probabilities and elapsed times that cases take to come to court, it would be misleading to read them as trends in financial crime. This may seem to be a rather roundabout way of stating that no reliable or valid data exist that would enable us to tell whether fraud or almost any sub-component of it (other than plastic fraud) was changing. However such warnings may be needed because otherwise opinions – however plausible – may be confused with 'evidence'.

Many estimates of fraud are based on very limited evidence, derive from institutional profile-raising, and take on a life of their own as 'facts by repetition', seldom critiqued either by media always hungry for sensational headlines (Levi 2006) or by pressure groups. On the other hand, if we rely on cases brought to conviction, the data may be absurdly low in both harm caused and case complexity. The most subtle cases of fraud and money laundering are hardest to prove beyond a reasonable doubt in the minds of juries or judges, and therefore may not even be proceeded with under the 'reasonable prospect of conviction' criterion in the Code for Crown Prosecutors. We must be careful to avoid 'throwing the baby out with the bathwater' by using only very low figures from convictions and treating them as 'the figures' rather than just treating them as the validated baseline figures (see Levi and Burrows 2008; Levi and Reuter 2009).

The elapsed time from fraud to discovery and then from discovery to criminal justice action (if any) means that many of the larger frauds coming to light in 2008–2010 will have been committed some years before. This differs from 'volume crimes' such as credit and debit card fraud, which usually come to light promptly (though often not as promptly as burglaries and vehicle thefts). Thus, in the UK, data collected by the fraud prevention service CIFAS (2012) indicate a rise in identity takeover frauds, as 'new credit' becomes harder to get, generating displacement to impersonating existing account-holders.[4] Such frauds emerge quite quickly. Since 2006, payment card fraud data in the UK have displayed a broad downwards trend in fraud on lost or stolen cards, due to the introduction of Chip and PIN. The only type of card fraud having shown an increase in the number of fraudulent transactions between 2009 and 2010 was account take-over (up from 66,000 to 84,000) (Financial Fraud Action UK 2011). In concert with the fall in cheque usage, cheque fraud losses have fallen significantly, while online banking fraud losses rose substantially in 2009 and 2010 – perhaps due to improved awareness and reporting, but also reflecting increased phishing for passwords and sophisticated bank site-cloning – before falling in 2011, as banks worked harder on prevention. Thus, where cost and incidence data are good, we can work out trends in fraud quite quickly and validly.

A contrasting example of much longer elapsed time from fraudulent to business-detected awareness is 'rogue trading' in the form of illicit (and – perhaps more importantly – unsuccessful!) betting on market trends, for example by Nick Leeson at Barings in 1995 (http://www.nickleeson.com) and by Jérôme Kerviel at Société Générale in 2007–8 and by UBS trader Adoboli in 2011.[5] In the earlier cases the primary accused alleged that more senior managers turned a blind eye to the risk taking, because they were incompetent (Barings) or because they stood to gain if the risks paid off (both Barings and Société Générale). In essence, they were cases in which ill-supervised traders found ways of breaching their dealing limits without detection and, having lost significant sums in early trading, carried on trading in the hope that they would be able to recoup those losses. Whether others behaved similarly but were more fortunate in their later dealing (or gambling) and remained forever undetected is unknown.

Technological advances in data linking fuzzy-matching software have shown that what would previously have been seen as isolated frauds, if fraud at all, are actually part of an 'organised' network, for example between accident management companies, car hire firms, valuers, and a pool of people willing *if asked* to make false claims for whiplash and other injuries, implicitly because they do not regard this is as seriously immoral. The fact that there is an overlap between such fraudsters and other banking/social security fraudsters is often asserted and is highly plausible, but no data have been submitted for public review that demonstrate its *extent and detail*. The National Fraud Authority (NFA 2010a) gives data on only two areas in which it has 'organised fraud costs': a £348 million figure from the Insurance Fraud Bureau (IFB) regarding staged motor accidents (based on strong software-linked network data); and the harder-to-validate 'criminal attack' figure – £5 billion – based on an assumed 15.6 per cent of the estimated £32 billion 'tax gap' (HMRC 2012), within an overall estimated £15 billion tax fraud figure consisting of the above, plus 'evasion' and 'hidden economy' (NFA 2010a, p. 15). About £1 in every £10 of Britain's exports in 2006 was linked to VAT carousel fraud, but costs and scale have declined since. The NFA do use data from industry and from the Organised Crime Group Mapping exercise in the UK to estimate how much is lost from 'organised crime', but they ignore the problem of judging what is and is not 'organised crime' (e.g. NFA 2011, pp. 32–3).

Cheque frauds are harder to attribute to *group* 'organised crime' activity, but it seems likely that most of the £46.7 million reported losses from online banking fraud in 2010 were the result of 'organised crime'. Such groups may also be involved in cyber-extortion and commercial espionage, which are not costed here. On a similar logic, a significant proportion of the *estimated* (and disputed by parts of the industry) £1 billion of mortgage fraud (NFA 2010a, pp. 25) will have been committed by at least networks, if not tighter groups, comprising mortgage brokers, valuers, lawyers and property investors, as well as some dishonest staff working for financial institutions and mortgage applicants.

The review for the Association of Chief Police Officers (ACPO) by Levi et al. (2007) calculated the minimum extent of the losses borne (excluding responses to fraud) as £12.9 billion, but the proportion committed by 'organised fraudsters' was not considered. The Office of Fair Trading (OFT 2006) estimated that £3.5 billion (a mid-point) is lost each year as a result of mass-marketing fraud and here victims are reliant for protection on the police, Trading Standards officers, and their own common sense. Holiday club scams, high-risk investment scams and pyramid schemes were the most costly mass-marketing frauds, accounting for almost 60 per cent of all mass-marketing fraud losses. Almost half of the UK adult population is likely to have been targeted by a scam and perhaps 3.2 million people fall victim to a mass-marketing fraud each year, with multiple victimisation being most visible *ex post facto* (and most media-publicised) among the elderly. Due to email and telephone attempts, the percentage at risk over their lifetimes is likely to rise unless interventions occur, and these – like other risks – are unlikely to be constant.

For public bodies at the national level there is much the same variation in the availability and quality of fraud data noted in the private sector. The NFA Annual Fraud Indicator includes all estimated tax fraud, but it is not self-evident how much of this is committed by co-offending networks that one might reasonably label 'organised crime'. Fraud cost and prevalence data are examined more broadly in Levi and Burrows (2008) and are developed in Dorn et al. (2009) in the context of assessing the role of the Financial Services Authority in combating financial crime threats. However, the details of the sub-types of fraud are set out by the NFA, as illustrated in Figure 6.1

Recorded crime statistics are distorted guides to fraud harm or to victimisation rates, since *especially for non-volume frauds*, so many decision-stages lie between the act and its recording by the authorities, and reporting is itself a time-costly business unless benefits are expected. There is an obligation on regulated firms to report 'significant frauds' to the Financial Services Authority as a regulator, but these are risk adjusted for individual firms, the risk levels defined in consultation with the regulators, and are relatively rare; nor is reporting such frauds to the police compulsory except via Suspicious Activity Reports (SARs), which are not currently used to assess financial crime risks (Dorn et al. 2009; NFA 2010a, 2011, 2012).

Opportunity, culture and expectations about others' behaviour are so central to the propensity to defraud that one must be wary of automatic assumptions about international transferability. Fraud, like the value of investments, can go down as well as up. But 'fraud' – like many other crimes – is not a unitary 'thing' but consists of many different

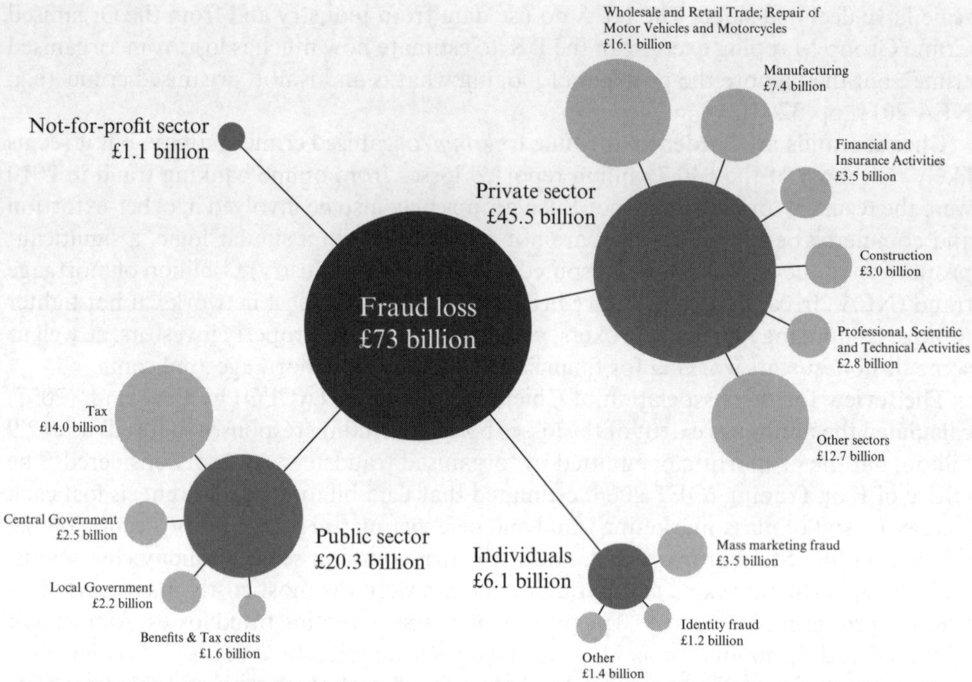

Source: NFA (2012, p. 7, Figure 2).

Figure 6.1 Breakdown of fraud losses by victim group

sorts of harm which were likely to be driven by different factors, including what we do to prevent them and prosecute them. Whereas Levi et al. (2007) were asked merely to review the scientific adequacy of existing data, the National Fraud Authority has been able to stimulate a broader range of bodies to collect and divulge data about fraud during the period covered. But it is a mistake to think that there is a 'true figure of fraud': there will always be frauds that are unrecognised as such by victims and third parties, and even where something is recognised as a suspicious loss, the amount of it that can properly be attributed to intentional or reckless dishonesty may be a legitimate area of dispute.

A rise in crime rates can be an indication that the quality of life has got worse, but in this case, the substantially greater cost of fraud figure is far more likely to reflect improved knowledge of fraud than a real rise. Indeed, on a strict like-for-like comparison of items included in both Levi et al. (2007) and NFA (2010a), there was a slight fall of 3.47 per cent in the period 2005–9 in the costs of fraud. Thanks to improved controls rather than improved social morality, Missing Trader Intra-Community and social security frauds have gone down substantially, while in the private sector, insurance and telecoms frauds have gone up; and in the public sector, NHS patient frauds and frauds against the BBC have gone up. Other than for payment card, cheque and some identity frauds – where the data are more reliable, at least in the UK where not-for-profit organisation CIFAS is permitted to store data for crime prevention purposes under the Data Protection legislation – we cannot know without further work whether these changes reflect better analytical skills in fraud detection by victims or real changes in fraud. But we should appreciate that any given sector of fraud risk consists of the interaction between motivation, criminal ingenuity and the opportunities that we give criminals by the way potential victims and 'third party guardians' watch over our assets and intervene (or otherwise). All three of these can change over time.

6.5 CONCLUSIONS

Though there remain areas of fraud against individuals, business and government that need greater understanding of risks, the UK government has made a more sustained effort than have other countries to measure the direct costs of fraud in private, public and not-for-profit sectors, and we are beginning to understand a little more about the impacts that these costs have upon our businesses, citizens, external investors, public services and visitors, which are not included in these financial totals. However sceptical we are about media and vendor alarmism about the rise in computer-enabled crimes, there is no doubt that this has created a step-change in the possibilities of scaled-up exploitation of vulnerabilities in consumer frauds, and severe damage to company image in business sectors that suffer cyber-attacks, whether from outsiders or insiders mass-copying insecurely held data. However, unless they are done for blackmail or competitive advantage, cyber-damage may be costly but it does not generate profits for offenders and therefore laundering capacities. More conventional forms of fraud also may be on the rise, unless they rely on hard-to-get credit. In a climate of private and public sector spending cuts, there is a risk that controls – public and private – may be cut.

From the perspective of money laundering, fraud offers many benefits, inasmuch as a large proportion of it is obtained electronically from persons and organisations that appear legitimate, making it less problematic to move, – at least via wire transfers that in principle are subject to money laundering regulation. (Other frauds receive cash, but except for cash traders evading the revenue authorities or in 'cash societies' such as China, total sums obtained this way would be relatively modest.) However, to the extent that those movements enhance traceability, laundering in the sense of genuine transformation of legitimacy may paradoxically be more difficult. If we are examining laundering in the sense of savings and investment from crime, we still however need to know the savings ratios of offenders, and, as many of 'my' fraudsters indicated (Levi, 2008), it may be too tempting to save money from the next fraud and instead go out and spend this fraud's proceeds in conspicuous consumption. No one can easily recover money from the legitimate outlets – airlines, bookmakers, casinos, escort agencies, restaurants and wine bars – where the fraudulently obtained money has been spent.

NOTES

* The chapter is based on research carried out under the ESRC Professorial Fellowship RES-051-27-0208.

1. 'Madoff losses totaled so far at $21.2 billion; $530 million paid back', http://voices.washingtonpost.com/economy-watch/2009/10/madoff_losses_totaled_so_far_a.html. The figure paid out to Madoff victims exceeds the Security Industry Protection Corporation's total payouts since it was formed in 1970. However, out of 15,974 claims from people who invested directly with Madoff or through his

feeder funds, only 2335 investors who put more into Madoff's funds than they pulled out were compensated (up to October 2009). The year 2010 saw some very large recoveries, some of them voluntary, and in December 2010, insiders stated that they expected half of the actual losses (as contrasted with the loss of expected gains) to be compensated. The criteria used are subject to heated legal dispute. The investment fraud with almost totally fictitious trades lasted for almost a decade, even on a highly conservative view.

2. Unless the offenders have surplus assets from which costs can be paid, private sector investigative and legal costs will be deducted from compensation for victims; public sector costs are borne by contributors to council and central government taxes.
3. If the costs of the fraudulent cheques are initially met by banks, they would want to recoup such costs by charging more for cheque services or levying a wider interest rate spread (competitive conditions permitting). In both cases, customers end up paying more. This is an externality.
4. There was a 5 per cent increase in overall fraud levels during the first half of 2012. However, identity fraud (the use of a false identity or the identity details of another person) now accounts for 50 per cent of all recorded frauds. In addition, 15 per cent of all recorded frauds in the first half of 2012 related to the takeover or hijacking of a customer's account. This means that frauds relating to the misuse of identity details now account for 65 per cent of all fraud.
5. If the bets had been successful, these might never have been identified as frauds or reported to the regulators and police. Defamation risks apart, would this have made them less fraudulent?

REFERENCES

ABI (2011), *Fraud*, London: Association of British Insurers.

Brand, S. and R. Price (2000), *The Economic and Social Costs of Crime*, Home Office Research Study no.217, London: Home Office.

Cabinet Office (2002), *Identity Fraud*, London: Cabinet Office.

CIFAS (2012), *Fraudscape Bulletin*, London: CIFAS.

Cohen, M. (2005), *The Costs of Crime and Justice*, London: Routledge.

Committee of Public Accounts (2004), *32nd Report: HM Customs and Excise Standard Report*, HC 284, London: TSO.

Dorn, N. and M. Levi (2006), 'From Delphi to Brussels, the policy context: prophecy, crime proofing, impact assessment', *European Journal on Criminal Policy and Research*, **12**, 213–20.

Dorn, N., M. Levi, D. Artingstall and J. Howell (2009), *Impacts of Financial Crimes and Amenability to Control by the FSA: Proposed Framework for Generating Data in a Comparative Manner*, London: Financial Services Authority, available at: http://www.fsa.gov.uk/pubs/other/scale_and_impact_paper.pdf

Ernst and Young (2008), *Corruption or Compliance: Weighing the Costs*, 10th Global Fraud Survey, London: Ernst and Young.

Ernst and Young (2012), *European Fraud Survey 2011: Recovery, Regulation and Integrity*, London: Ernst & Young.

Financial Fraud Action UK (2011), *Fraud – the Facts 2011*, London: Financial Fraud Action UK.

Financial Fraud Action UK (2012), *Fraud – the Facts 2012*, London: Financial Fraud Action UK.

Fraud Review (2006), *Final Report*, London: Attorney General's Office.

Home Office (2006), *Updated Estimate of the Cost of Identity Fraud to the UK Economy*, 2 February 2006, London: Home Office.

HM Treasury (2005), *2004–05 Fraud Report: An Analysis of Reported Fraud in Government Departments*, Norwich: HM Treasury.

HMRC (2012), *Measuring Tax Gaps 2012: Tax Gaps Estimates for 2010 – 2011*, London: HMRC.

Levi, M. (2006), 'The media construction of financial white-collar crimes', *British Journal of Criminology*, **46**, 1037–57.

Levi, M. (2008), *The Phantom Capitalists*, 2nd edn, Andover: Ashgate.

Levi, M. (2011), 'Assessing the costs of frauds', in D. Gadd, S. Karstedt and S. Messner (eds), *The SAGE Handbook of Criminological Research Methods*, London: Sage, 461–74.

Levi, M. and J. Burrows (2008), 'Measuring the impact of fraud: a conceptual and empirical journey', *British Journal of Criminology*, **48**(3), 293–318.

Levi, M. and P. Reuter (2009), 'Money laundering', in M. Tonry (ed.), *Handbook on crime and public policy*, New York: Oxford university press, 356–80.

Levi, M, J., Burrows M. Fleming and M. Hopkins, with the assistance of K. Matthews (2007), *The Extent, Nature and Economic Impact of Fraud in the UK.* Report for the Association of Chief Police Officers'

Economic Crime Portfolio, available at: http://www.cardiff.ac.uk/socsi/resources/ACPO%20final%20nature%20extent%20and%20economic%20impact%20of%20fraud.pdf
National Audit Office (2003), *Tackling Fraud against the Inland Revenue*, London: National Audit Office.
National Fraud Authority (2009), 'Fraud victims voice concerns over lack of support', London: National Fraud Authority.
National Fraud Authority (2010a), *Annual Fraud Indicator*, London: National Fraud Authority.
National Fraud Authority (2010b), 'Identity fraud costs UK £2.7billion every year', London: National Fraud Authority.
National Fraud Authority (2011), *Annual Fraud Indicator*, London: National Fraud Authority.
National Fraud Authority (2012), *Annual Fraud Indicator*, London: Home Office.
NERA (2000), *The Economic Cost of Fraud*, London: Home Office.
OFT (2006), *Research on impact of Mass Marketed Scams*, London: Office of Fair Trading, available at: http://www.oft.gov.uk/shared_oft/reports/consumer_protection/oft883.pdf
PKF (2012), *The Resilience to Fraud of the UK Insurance Sector*, London: PKF.
PricewaterhouseCoopers (2007, 2009, 2011), *Global Economic Crime Survey*, London: PwC.
van Dijk, J., J. van Kesteren and P. Smit (2008), *Criminal Victimisation in International Perspective, Key Findings from the 2004–2005 ICVS and EU ICS*, The Hague: Boom Legal Publishers.

7. Terrorism: causes, effects and the role of money laundering

Tim Krieger and Daniel Meierrieks

7.1 INTRODUCTION

Since the 9/11 attacks on New York and Washington DC, transnational terrorism has been considered particularly dangerous.[1] The direct and indirect costs of terrorism, ranging from the loss of human lives and assets to reduced growth and life satisfaction, are substantial, making it necessary to fight terrorism with a variety of means at the same time.

While eliminating the root causes of terrorism, for example by improving unfavorable socio-economic and politico-institutional conditions which would otherwise make individuals turn to terrorism, appears to be the most promising counter-terrorism strategy, it also takes the longest time to prove successful. In the short run, therefore, other more direct means are needed to tackle the problem. Since running a terrorist organization involves some non-negligible costs (e.g., funds must be raised to maintain the organization), the financing of terrorism has become a new policy focus. Drying out the financial flows from sponsors to terrorist organizations or from an organization's headquarters to terrorist cells around the world may impede the capacities of terrorist groups to attack.

Not surprisingly, in the aftermath of 9/11 national and international pieces of legislation were introduced to intercept financial flows to or from terrorist organizations, the most prominent examples being the UN Security Council Resolution 1373 and the Financial Action Task Force's 'FATF Special Recommendations on Terrorist Financing' (FATF 2001/2010),[2] which extend the international framework for fighting money laundering by organized crime, for example, the *FATF 40 Recommendations* (FATF 2003/2010). At first glance this appears reasonable because there is a direct link between organized crime and terrorism: most terrorist acts are themselves crimes (Dandurand and Chin 2004). However, although the extended FATF framework includes recommendations concerning some issues which are specific to terrorist financing (e.g., charitable organizations or cash couriers), the analogy drawn between money laundering and terrorist financing is still open to debate. On the one hand, it is argued that organized crime and terrorist groups are sufficiently similar (or even close to identical) to justify treating them alike and using a similar set of instruments to disrupt their financial activities. On the other hand, there is a fundamental difference with respect to the 'direction' of financial flows: money laundering by organized crime aims at disguising the criminal identity of funds so that they appear legitimate, while terrorist financing has been called 'almost money laundering in reverse' (J. Sloan, FinCEN Director, cited in Gouvin 2003, p. 973) because it is the use of funds that is criminal, whereas its sources and their transfer are often legitimate. This difference has important practical consequences because money-laundering prosecutors have to correctly predict a dangerous future use of funds, which may be a difficult challenge and requires close cooperation with counter-terrorism intelligence agencies. This difference is aggravated by the differing goals of both types of organizations and by the fact that most terrorist attacks are rather inexpensive, so that the financial flows that prosecutors need to detect are usually small. Also, since nowadays terrorists are increasingly organized in networks of the Al Qaeda type, anti-money laundering instruments may fail to yield the desired results.

This chapter focuses on two areas. First (section 7.2), we conduct a thorough discussion of the causes and costs of terrorism. Our literature review suggests that the economic and non-economic costs of terrorism are indeed substantial. Our review also shows the root causes of terrorism are unlikely to be 'healed' in the short run, which justifies the prosecution of terrorist financing (as one of several instruments against terrorism). Then (section 7.3), we consider the issue of terrorist financing and the associated role of money laundering. We argue that while terrorist attacks are usually inexpensive, running and maintaining a terrorist organization requires substantial financial means, so countering terrorist financing may indeed be a viable counter-terrorism option. We show that there are three forms of terrorist financing: state sponsorship, legitimate financial support through legal channels by private persons, and private financing by unlawful means, with the latter case involving money laundering activities that come closest to those employed by organized crime. Our discussion has some implications for policymakers and prosecutors, also with respect to the role of money laundering in terrorist financing. In section 7.4, we summarize our findings.

7.2 TERRORISM: CAUSES AND CONSEQUENCES

7.2.1 The Causes of Terrorism

Existing empirical studies on the causes of terrorism usually rely on (economic) rational-choice theory to explain terrorist activity and derive hypotheses which may later be tested in statistical analyses. They argue that terrorists are rational actors who resort to terrorism while considering its benefits and (opportunity) costs, subject to certain economic constraints (e.g., Sandler and Enders 2004). From such a perspective, it is plausible to argue that a variety of country-specific factors (i.e., macro variables) may matter to the terrorists' calculus. For instance, poor socio-economic conditions (e.g., poverty) may mean that the opportunity costs of terrorism (e.g., foregone earnings) are comparatively low, while its benefits (e.g., a redistribution of wealth) are comparatively high, meaning that in such an environment terrorism ought to be more likely.

Ameliorating the root causes of terrorism, that is, the socio-economic and politico-institutional conditions that incite terrorism, seems to be the most promising and sustainable strategy for fighting terrorism, as it ought to reduce the incentives and support for terrorism most effectively. However, as Krieger and Meierrieks (2011) show, while a plethora of empirical studies surfaced especially after the 9/11 attacks, the academic debate regarding the roots of terrorism is still inconclusive. In this section, we provide selected evidence from large-*N* studies that try to unveil these root causes. Most of these studies have focused on transnational terrorism due to data constraints (cf. Krieger and Meierrieks 2011), thereby distinguishing between two perspectives. The studies may either analyze why countries are targeted by international terrorism (*target perspective*) or why they produce it (*origin perspective*). In the following, we focus only on those (macro) factors that are argued to be related to the emergence of terrorism, that is, on the origin perspective.

One strand of the empirical literature argues that poor socio-economic development causes terrorism (while controlling for political and demographic conditions). That is to say, poverty and inequality are believed to be among the root causes of terrorism, meaning that they decrease the opportunity costs of terrorism (e.g., in terms of economic participation). Indeed, some empirical analyses support this hypothesis. For instance, Blomberg and Hess (2008) find that economic progress is negatively related to the generation of terrorism. Further studies construct indirect linkages between a country's level of socio-economic development and terrorism. For example, Li and Schaub (2004) show that higher levels of economic integration (e.g., trade openness) are negatively related to terrorism through their beneficial effect on economic development. Similarly, Burgoon (2006) argues that social welfare policies reduce terrorism by ameliorating socio-economic grievances (e.g., through redistribution).

However, the empirical mainstream does not support the idea that terrorism has economic roots (cf. Krieger and Meierrieks 2011). In fact, a significant number of empirical studies find that political and institutional variables trump economic ones in statistical analyses (e.g., Abadie 2006; Basuchoudhary and Shughart 2010; Krueger and Laitin 2008; Krueger and Maleckova 2003; Kurrild-Klitgaard et al. 2006; Li 2005; Piazza 2008; Tavares 2004). That is, even though these studies control for the effect of the economy on terrorism, they do not find that it matters once politico-institutional factors come into play. On the one hand, some of these studies argue that certain unfavorable politico-institutional conditions (e.g., political instability and transformation, low state capacity) offer opportunities for terrorist groups to conduct attacks, since they lower operating costs. For instance, Piazza (2008) finds that political instability is conducive to the emergence of terrorism, given that such instability makes it less likely for a government to react effectively in the face of terrorism. On the other hand, it is also argued that a lack of political participation and poor institutional quality constitute the root causes of terrorism. For instance, Li (2005) finds that democratic participation is detrimental to terrorism. Basuchoudhary and Shughart (2010) find that high levels of economic freedom (e.g., property rights protection) also reduce terrorist activity.

A handful of studies also point to the role of international political factors in terrorism (e.g., foreign policy), again suggesting that such factors matter more than socio-economic variables. For instance, Dreher and Gassebner (2008) find that political proximity to the US makes countries likelier targets of transnational terrorism. The latter finding indicates that international terrorism (e.g., Al Qaeda activity), in particular, is motivated by foreign policy behavior (and not so much by poverty, inequality, etc.), so that such behavior may be yet another root cause of terrorism. The recent trend toward self-radicalization and 'home-grown' terrorism that is often motivated by international political developments seems to support this finding.

Besides socio-economic and politico-institutional factors, demographic conditions are also argued to matter to terrorism. In fact, a very robust finding in the analysis of terrorism is that larger countries are more prone to terrorism (Krieger and Meierrieks 2011). This finding may provide initial evidence that demographic stress (signaled by large populations) creates conflicts over rents and scarce resources. Also, Basuchoudhary and Shughart (2010) find that ethnic tensions are conducive to the emergence of transnational terrorist activity. However, while such findings may imply that demographic stress results in terrorism, the context of ethnically or religiously motivated conflict should not be disregarded. Usually, such conflict is associated with poor socio-economic and politico-institutional conditions (e.g., poverty, inequality, discrimination, lack of representation). As noted by Sen (2008), such poor conditions may exacerbate ethno-religious conflict, which in turn may lead to a further deterioration of these very conditions. Such a view implies that terrorism is rooted in not one but many causes, where these causes may be interrelated and form vicious circles of violence.

In light of these insights, governments are advised to consider addressing the aforementioned root causes of terrorism (e.g., by increasing economic and political participation), as this seems the most promising strategy against terrorism. Given that terrorism may be associated with a variety of economic, political and social costs, as we shall discuss below, it becomes even more important to identify its determinants to develop sound counter-terrorism strategies.

7.2.2 Costs of Terrorism

Schelling (1991) argues that terrorist actions (e.g., assassinations or bombings) are means to achieve economic and political destabilization and attract media attention. That is, they produce costs for affected countries. In this subsection, we want to focus on their negative economic consequences. Terrorist actions aim at enforcing the terrorists' long-run political objectives (e.g., redistributing wealth and power, gaining independence). Economic destabilization is among the terrorists' short-run goals because such damage weakens their enemy (i.e., the government). An attacked government ought to weigh the cost of giving in to (at least some of) the terrorists' demands (i.e., socio-political goals not enforceable in the ordinary political process) against the cost of a prolonged terrorist campaign that results from continued resistance by the government (Sandler and Enders 2008). When terrorists are successful at destabilizing an economy, the (opportunity) costs of continued resistance increase, so that accommodating terrorists' demands becomes comparatively less costly (i.e., more likely) from the government's perspective.

Terrorism may harm the economy directly and indirectly, where the latter refers to the reaction of economic agents (e.g., consumers, foreign investors, governments) to terrorism. There are several transmission channels through which terrorism affects the economy, namely destruction, disruption, diversion, dissaving and portfolio substitution. *Destruction* refers to the direct costs of terrorism. Human and physical capital is destroyed through attacks, resulting in reduced economic output. The other effects refer to the indirect consequences of terrorism that emerge from the response of economic agents. The *disruption* effect may become manifest in higher transaction costs, as the effectiveness of public institutions is challenged and manipulated by terrorism, or as insecurity increases. For instance, given that terrorism creates uncertainty, it may consequently lead to the postponement of long-term investments, reducing economic activity (e.g., Bird et al. 2008). *Diversion* occurs when public resources are shifted from output-enhancing to non-productive expenditures. For instance, a government may increase spending on security at the expense of education and infrastructure expenditures, which may impede future growth. *Dissaving* refers to a decline in savings that affects an economy's capital stock. *Portfolio substitution* means the flight of human, physical and financial capital in the face of conflict (e.g., Dreher et al. 2011). For instance, Abadie and Gardeazabal (2008) argue that terrorism negatively affects an economy's foreign direct investment position since it poses a costly risk and reduces the returns to investment. This withdrawal of capital may hurt economic development, particularly when foreign finance is an important engine of growth (e.g., in developing economies). Economic performance may suffer through all these five channels, particularly because they are expected to reinforce each other.

Several empirical studies indeed suggest that terrorism is detrimental to economic development on sub-national, national and global levels. On a sub-national level, for example, Abadie and Gardeazabal (2003) analyze the negative effects of the terrorist conflict in the Basque Country. They find that due to ETA (Euskadi Ta Askatasuna) terrorism, the Basque Country suffered a per capita GDP decline of about 10 percent relative to a 'counterfactual' Basque region without terrorism. On a national level, for example, Eckstein and Tsiddon (2004) focus on the effect of terrorism on the Israeli economy and find that terrorism reduced per capita output by 10–15 percent, due to the detrimental effects of terrorism on consumption, investments and exports. Finally, several studies find that terrorism is a negative determinant of economic activity on a global (i.e., cross-country) level, too. As one example, Crain and Crain (2006) assess the macroeconomic consequences of terrorism for 147 countries between 1968 and 2002 and find that in the absence of terrorism global GDP could have increased by US$ 3.6 trillion in 2002. Evidently, this indicates that the economic costs of terrorism can be substantial.

Given these (potentially enormous) costs, some empirical studies have analyzed the channels of transaction through which negative repercussions may occur. Given that the direct effects of terrorism through destruction are unquestioned, these studies have centered on terrorism's indirect effects. Here, the disruption effect emerges through, for example, higher transaction costs in international trade. Nitsch and Schumacher (2004) find that a doubling in the number of terrorist incidents in a single year is associated with a decrease in bilateral trade flows of about 4 percent. Further evidence hints at the effect of terrorism on macroeconomic variables such as consumption, investment and public spending (e.g., Blomberg et al. 2004; Crain and Crain 2006; Eckstein and Tsiddon 2004; Gupta et al. 2004), indicating that disruption, diversion and dissaving induced by terrorism also play a role. Finally, there is also evidence of portfolio substitution. For instance, Abadie and Gardeazabal (2008) show that terrorism may harm economic activity by weakening a country's investment position. They estimate that a one standard deviation increase in the intensity of terrorism causes the economy's net FDI position to decline by 5 percent.

However, some qualifications regarding the effect of terrorism on the economy have to be made, particularly given that some studies do not attribute a strong role to terrorism in economic development (e.g., Enders et al. 2006; Tavares 2004). First, terrorism is anticipated to have only localized effects. While it may damage certain sectors of an economy (e.g., the tourism industry) or regions (e.g., the Basque Country), substitution of economic activity away from vulnerable to robust sectors/regions within an attacked economy is likely to take place (accompanied by quick adjustments in prices and capital allocation). A higher intensity of terrorism ought to make such adjustments more difficult. Second, this adjustment is likely to depend on a country's degree of diversification and macroeconomic resiliency. When countries are well diversified and robust, terrorism is less likely to produce notable economic damage. Third, a country's economic size also matters. Even the high costs of the 9/11 attacks (in absolute terms) can be considered small when seen in relation to the economic size of the US (cf., e.g., Sandler and Enders 2008). Smaller countries are more likely to suffer from the economic consequences of terrorism. Overall, as Sandler and Enders (2008) note, small and less diversified countries (i.e., less developed economies) characterized by low macroeconomic robustness and facing significant terrorist activity ought to experience the most severe macroeconomic consequences.[3]

7.3 THE FINANCING OF TERRORISM AND MONEY LAUNDERING

7.3.1 Financial Needs of Terrorist Organizations

Terrorism is a costly venture. As argued above, terrorists are considered rational actors that maximize the utility from violence, subject to certain costs, benefits and budget constraints (all of which are usually governed by socio-economic, politico-institutional and other social conditions). That is, financial means (as they manifest themselves in a group's budget constraint) influence the patterns of terrorist activity. Basically, financial means can be channeled into two activities: (i) aggressive actions (terrorist attacks), and (ii) other operative (also defensive) actions (e.g., secret communication).

Terrorist attacks serve as a prime instrument of 'communication' between terrorists and the general public, intended to win support, demoralize enemies and raise public awareness (e.g., Sirseloudi 2004). Interestingly, it turns out that the costs directly associated with conducting terrorist attacks are comparatively small (Brisard 2002; Whitlock 2008). For instance, even the costs of the highly sophisticated 9/11 attacks amounted to only US$ 400,000–600,000, while smaller attacks such as the *USS Cole* bombing (2000) stood at around US$ 5000–10,000. This shows that terrorism can be a highly cost-efficient way of making one's cause known and of winning support, while simultaneously hurting one's enemy very severely, as indicated in the previous section.

Besides the (supposedly) small cost of conducting attacks, however, running and maintaining a terrorist organization in the long run also requires a significant amount of financial resources. Associated (operative) costs may include, for example, the operation of secret communication systems and training facilities, recruitment, 'wages' for active members of the group and the families of 'martyrs' or the support of sleeper cells. Clearly, it is difficult to estimate these operative (fixed) costs for terrorist groups. Schneider (2010) estimates the financial flows to Islamic terrorist groups amount to US$5–50 million per year. For instance, he estimates that the annual budget of Al Qaeda between 2001 and 2004 was approximately US$20–50 million (cf. also Comras 2005). From these estimates and the comparatively low (assumed) costs of offensive actions (i.e., actual attacks) we may hypothesize that it is especially the 'fixed costs' of terrorism that matter, net of the possibility that terrorist groups use some of their financial resources to build up a 'war chest' to increase financial independence.

In sum and from a policy perspective, these findings show that limiting the availability of financial resources to terrorist groups through appropriate policies may be an effective measure to restrain terrorism at least in the short run. Here, financial flows from terrorism sponsors to group leaders/headquarters are more relevant than flows from the headquarters towards operative units, that is, terrorist cells all around the world.[4]

7.3.2 Sources of Terrorist Financing and the Importance of Money Laundering

In order to intercept terrorists' financial flows effectively, it is necessary to know their sources. In general, terrorist groups may gain financial resources through three channels (Bantekas 2003; Napoleoni 2004; Ward 2004): (i) *state financing* (i.e., state sponsorship of terrorism), (ii) *financing by legitimate means* (e.g., from business, charities, diaspora support, etc.), and (iii) *private financing by unlawful means*, which usually includes outright *criminal activities* (e.g., bank robberies, drug trafficking, kidnapping, extortion). Below, we shall discuss these forms of financing and how money laundering relates to them.

State sponsorship of terrorism means that a state enlists terrorist groups, usually to attack other states that are the sponsor's enemy (e.g., O'Brien 1996). States that sponsor terrorism use it as a foreign policy tool to weaken their enemies through economic and/or political destabilization. For instance, during the Cold War the Soviet Union was alleged to support Palestinian terrorist organizations (e.g., PLO, PFLP) to weaken the position of Israel and the US in the Middle East (cf. O'Brien 1996). Terrorism is most likely to be state-financed when the (tactical and strategic) goals, common interests and ideological beliefs of sponsoring states and sponsored groups coincide (e.g., anti-Americanism, socialism, anti-colonialism). Because this attracts international political repercussions, states are usually expected to mask their financial support, also relying on reverse money laundering, where money from legal sources (i.e., government funds) is used to serve a terrorist purpose (e.g., Casella 2003). The difficulty with proving a link between an alleged state sponsor and a terrorist organization has surely contributed to the attractiveness of terrorism sponsorship as a foreign policy tool in the past (cf. O'Brien 1996). Nowadays, only few groups still receive financial assistance from foreign states. For instance, the Lebanon-based Hezbollah has been estimated to receive US$100–200 million per year from Iran (e.g., Wilson 2004).

Financing through state sponsorship is available only to a small number of terror groups (and state support has been decreasing since the end of the Cold War), so alternative *legitimate private financing sources* are also exploited. Here, on the one hand, income may result from legitimate business activities. For instance, Napoleoni (2004) notes that some terrorist groups in the Middle East own companies to self-finance (e.g., the Egyptian Islamic Jihad owned several honey shops). On the other hand, financing through legitimate activities often refers to the voluntary sponsorship of terrorism by private persons (e.g., through donations to charities). Financial support may come from the country in which the terrorist group operates (domestic support) or from individuals living abroad (the diaspora). Siqueira and Sandler (2006) argue that terrorist groups are likely to gain (voluntary) financial (grassroots) support when they are able to attract a sufficiently high level of popular support by building on a compelling ideology (e.g., national liberation, religious fundamentalism) and/or by referring to poor social conditions (e.g., ethnic/religious discrimination, foreign occupation). Groups that have resorted to financing terrorism through legitimate activities include, for example, several Sikh terrorist groups (e.g., with financial support from the American diaspora), Sri Lanka's LTTE (Liberation Tigers of Tamil Eelam), the PKK (Kurdistan Workers' Party), Al Qaeda and other radical Islamic groups (e.g., Hamas), and terrorist groups fighting for the unification of Northern Ireland with the Irish Republic (e.g., the Provisional IRA). Usually, such support for terrorism by private persons is masked in order to avoid legal repercussions. For instance, according to the National Commission (2004) the Al Qaeda network – at least until 9/11 – was mainly funded through donations by private individuals and religious communities. Comras (2005) reports that after the 9/11 attacks some 100 charities in the Gulf countries were either shut down or came under official surveillance due to unclear connections to Al Qaeda. As another example, terrorist groups in Northern Ireland received financial support from the US-Irish diaspora, where this support was collected legally by front institutions (e.g., Noraid) and then supposedly channeled to terrorist organizations to support their activity in the UK (Napoleoni 2004).

When neither state nor legitimate private financing sources are available, terrorist groups may resort to *private financing by unlawful means*. Terrorist groups are on the one hand likely to resort to criminal activity to obtain financial resources when they are not successful in attracting (or when they lose) domestic and/or international support for their cause. Such isolated groups are expected to rely on limited criminal activity to obtain financial resources (e.g., robberies). For instance, a lack of popular support (and the loss of support from the Soviet bloc at the end of the Cold War) may explain why Western European groups (e.g., the Red Army Faction in Germany) often resorted to ordinary crime to obtain financial resources (e.g., 'revolutionary' bank robberies). On the other hand, terrorist groups may resort to private financing by unlawful means when they are able to exert some territorial control (e.g., Bantekas 2003). That is, not only small and isolated but also large, organized groups with some degree of public support may rely on criminal activity. However, the latter groups are expected to rely on means of large-scale (organized) crime as a source of self-finance. For instance, territorial control allows for the production of drugs, drug trafficking and other forms of smuggling. Social-revolutionary and national liberation movements such as the Colombian FARC (Fuerzas Armadas Revolucionarias de Colombia), the PKK or the Afghan Taliban are argued to use money from drug production and trafficking to finance their armed struggle. The volume of funds appears to be substantial. Dishman (2001) finds that the FARC was able to earn US$100–500 million from drug-related criminal activity (e.g., drug production, trafficking) in the 1990s and early 2000s.

When terrorists resort to criminal activity to gain financial resources, the line between terrorism and (organized) crime may become blurred. According to Makarenko (2004), the *crime–terrorism nexus* is to be placed on a continuum ranging from 'traditional' organized crime to 'traditional' terrorism. In the middle of this spectrum, organized crime and terrorism become difficult to distinguish. Some criminal groups have political motivations ('political crime') and some terrorist groups are rather interested in criminal profits and end up using political rhetoric only as a façade ('commercial terrorism'). In this scenario, private financing by unlawful means (e.g., bank robberies, kidnapping, the production and trafficking of drugs, diamonds, etc., extortion and smuggling) by terrorist groups is most likely to occur. This also includes the possibility that terrorists 'learn' how to obscure illegitimate money flows from their criminal counterparts.

7.3.3 Implications for Prosecutors

The potential sources of terrorist finance pose challenges for prosecutors and policymakers alike, which we discuss below. We also emphasize the role of anti-money laundering measures in counter-terrorism by impairing its financing.

In the case of *state sponsorship*, prosecutors have to recognize the unlawful intensions behind legitimate ominous financial flows, that is, the 'reversed' money laundering pattern of transactions. This requires knowledge of the ultimate intentions of the funds' recipient. From a practical point of view this calls for close cooperation between money laundering prosecutors and counter-terrorism intelligence agencies. For instance, national intelligence agencies of terrorism-sponsoring states usually have sophisticated methods of transferring funds to terrorist cells and/or groups around the world without leaving significant traces. Even more fundamental, however, is the problem that state sponsors play a significant role in providing non-financial support to terrorist groups, for example, by offering training facilities or safe havens (e.g., Byman et al. 2001).

Anti-money laundering instruments are more likely to help when terrorism is financed by *private, legitimate means*. While prosecutors again need to identify the unlawful intension behind legitimate financial flows, these very funds need to be transferred through legal channels, such as the banking system, making interception possible. However, alternative transfer systems such as the *Hawala* banking system may be used by terrorist groups, which largely escape the control of prosecutors. In addition, specific organizational forms of raising funds may be applied, which are again hardly controllable by the state. Funds collected, for example, through contributions to charities or by levying 'revolutionary taxes', are difficult to detect. Finally, given the rather low cost of a single terrorist attack, 'decentralizing' their fund-raising may be a reasonable strategy for terrorists. For instance, the (low) cost of explosives may easily be covered through a single criminal act, such as a bank robbery.[5] Given these caveats, anti-money laundering means may yield only limited success when terrorist funding is obtained through private, legitimate means.

This does not, however, imply that instruments of anti-money laundering policies should be disregarded when fighting terrorism. Arguably, when terrorists finance themselves by *criminal activity* an analogy to money laundering by the organized crime can be drawn. When terrorist organizations (sufficiently) mirror criminal organizations, there is little doubt that approaching terrorist financing with a standard anti-money laundering strategy is promising. It appears reasonable to assume that similar organizational structures, tactics and actors' characteristics in organized crime and terrorist organizations support similar financing structures. In the aftermath of 9/11, in particular, both politicians and scholars argued in favor of a *crime–terrorism nexus* that was predicted to ultimately result in the emergence of an alliance, cooperation, convergence or even symbiosis of criminal and terrorist groups (Schmid 2004). In these cases, anti-money laundering efforts that proved successful against organized crime may also help against terrorist financing. For instance, Thony (2005) argues that the main concern of prosecutors should be the funds themselves (and the organizations behind them), not the illegal *processing* of the funds. Therefore, he claims that the rationale of the anti-money laundering strategy can be applied *mutatis mutandis* to terrorist groups.

However, there are instances where organized crime and terrorism differ substantially, for example with respect to the direction and volume of financial flows and their underlying intensions. The idea of terrorist groups behaving similarly to organized crime has been criticized for being limited to a small number of cases (e.g., Bovenkerk and Chakra 2004; Schmid 2004), mostly in the field of so-called 'narco-terrorism' activities (Bantekas 2003). When moving away from the center of Makarenko's (2004) crime–terror spectrum toward more 'traditional' terrorist groups, ideology matters the most when it comes to the difference between terrorism and crime. Specifically, terrorists operate in the name of 'higher ideals' (Bovenkerk and Chakra 2004; Ignatieff 2002), which may not be beneficial to straightforward criminal activity or can lead to conflicts with criminal groups (Dishman 2001). Also, since terrorist activity is born out of political motives or socio-economic grievances, terrorists seek public attention to communicate their interests or, at least, to convince the world of the justness of their causes (Bovenkerk and Chakra 2004). Political credibility is in fact highly valued by terrorists. Groups may lose credibility when they act as normal criminals or when cooperating with organized crime. Arguably, terrorist groups that care about their 'image' ought to prefer legitimate ways of financing their operations, such as state sponsorship or donations and diaspora support.

Finally, organized crime is usually considered 'conservative' (Bovenkerk and Chakra 2004) with a strong interest in exploiting the imperfections of private and public institutions. Preserving existing structures and institutions is therefore beneficial to organized crime, which runs counter to the terrorists' interest in 'solving' a country's socio-economic and political problems. This difference may indicate that in many cases terrorism and organized crime are sufficiently different from each other, so that anti-money laundering measures (tailored to the fight against organized crime) may not prove successful.

7.4 CONCLUSIONS

This chapter has focused on three areas. First, it discussed the literature on the consequences of terrorism. It argued that terrorists aim at economic destabilization to push their agenda and force governments to give in to their demands. Terrorism may produce direct costs (destruction) and (more importantly) indirect costs, where the latter stem from the reaction of economic agents to the threat of terrorism (through capital flight, diversion of investment, adjustments in government budgets, etc.). While the exact macroeconomic consequences of terrorism depend on country-specific conditions (e.g., macroeconomic size and robustness, intensity of terrorism), developing economies seem particularly vulnerable to terrorism, given that they are often less diversified and weaker in economic and institutional terms. At the same time, the political and social costs of terrorism (e.g., reduced political openness and life satisfaction) should not be disregarded, which may very well also matter to developed countries. In general, the cost of terrorism appears sufficiently high to call for a broad range of counter-measures.

Second, we reviewed the literature on the causes of terrorism. We showed that terrorism is likely to be rooted in a set of unfavorable social conditions (e.g., poor socio-economic development, foreign policy behavior that creates grievances, demographic stress), although a true academic consensus on this issue has yet to emerge. Terrorism is a complex phenomenon rooted in a variety of conditions that are usually linked and potentially mutually reinforcing. Among the factors that may incite terrorism are: (i) poor socio-economic conditions, in particular when they are not addressed (e.g., by means of redistributive policies); (ii) poor politico-institutional frameworks (e.g., lack of economic and political participation); (iii) foreign policy activities that create grievances and possibly lead to the internationalization of domestic conflict and self-radicalization; and (iv) demographic stress. Eliminating terrorism's root causes appears to be the most viable policy option in the long run.

Third, we discussed the sources of terrorist financing and the role of money laundering. Here, we acknowledge that while ameliorating grievances leading to terrorism may prove successful in the long term, in the short run it also seems necessary to pursue policies that aim at interrupting the planning and execution of terrorist attacks. Such strategies resemble the 'stick' in the 'stick-versus-carrot' approach to fighting terrorism (cf. Frey 2004). Their main goal is to raise the material costs of terrorism instead of raising its opportunity costs (the 'carrot' being the removal of the root causes of terrorism). Here, tackling the issue of terrorist financing (and considering the associated role of money laundering) and consequently disrupting financial flows to terrorist organizations is one measure that is expected to make terrorism, at least in the short run, more difficult and expensive and thus less likely.

We have shown that terrorists obtain financial resources through state sponsorship, private legitimate contributions and criminal activity. We argued that anti-money laundering efforts may prove most successful when directed against terrorist groups that behave similarly to criminal groups. In the aftermath of the 9/11 attacks, several measures were introduced that extended the existing anti-money laundering legislation (directed against organized crime) so as to account for the new challenges of terrorist financing. Our analysis has shown, however, that drawing a simple analogy between money laundering by organized crime and terrorist financing may be too simple. Money laundering aims at disguising the criminal identity of funds so that they appear legitimate. There are financial sources of terrorist organizations (e.g., 'narco-terrorism') which are clearly illegitimate and where more traditional forms of money laundering do take place. However, terrorist groups are often financed from legitimate sources (e.g., private sponsorship), while it is their use of funds that is criminal. Because of this, terrorist financing has been referred to as 'money laundering in reverse', which poses a particular challenge for prosecutors who have to anticipate the future misuse of today's legitimate funds. In order to tackle terrorist financing, close cooperation between money-laundering prosecutors and counter-terrorism intelligence agencies appears to be a particularly promising strategy for dealing with terrorists' financial flows.

In sum, the effectiveness of anti-money laundering tools in counter-terrorism appears to be limited. What is more, recent developments in terrorism (e.g., self-radicalization, sleeper cells and 'lone wolf' terrorism) may further reduce its effectiveness. For instance, self-radicalized terrorism is only loosely connected to an overarching network and requires fewer and smaller financial transfers (if any) which cannot be easily detected by money laundering prosecutors. If these trends continue, it becomes questionable whether the rather strict rules introduced in the aftermath of 9/11 should be sustained. There are good reasons why some of the anti-money laundering regulations adopted in the face of the terrorist threat in 2001 had been previously rejected (when legislation against organized crime and money laundering was proposed without connecting it to terrorism).[6] These far-reaching regulations (which also go beyond the issue at stake) were argued to severely constrain civil rights, while substantially raising transaction costs and therefore ultimately hurting economic growth (cf. UN 2007). One decade later, new developments in terrorism and the war on terror may lead to a political reevaluation of these rules, thereby possibly re-strengthening civil rights while improving counter-terrorism intelligence and the fight against the root causes of terrorism.

One shortcoming of existing research on terrorist financing is the lack of reliable data and thus of sound empirical investigations. The few existing studies show an enormous mismatch between the costs of a single attack and the supposed costs of running and maintaining a terror organization. At the same time, estimates of actual financial flows between parties involved in terrorist activities appear rather preliminary. However, this information is urgently needed to provide a sound cost–benefit analysis of measures against terrorist financing. More dedication to empirical work (e.g., field studies) may help to produce a clearer (and unbiased) picture of the financial needs of terrorist organizations. On the basis of convincing empirical findings, open questions regarding terrorist financing (and the associated role of money laundering) can be resolved and sound policy recommendations provided.

NOTES

1. *Transnational terrorism* involves at least two countries (e.g., because foreign targets are attacked or because a group crosses borders to attack). *Domestic terrorism*, by contrast, refers to terrorism that only involves one country. Generally, domestic terrorism is estimated to account for 80–90% of all terrorist activity (e.g., Abadie 2006).
2. Both frameworks refer directly to the 1999 UN Convention for the Suppression of the Financing of Terrorism, which for the first time established a distinct and internationally recognized notion of an 'offense of terrorist financing'.
3. Even though the economic repercussions of terrorism may be low (e.g., because a country is economically robust as is the case for instance in the developed world), its political and social consequences may still matter. For instance, terrorism may jeopardize open and democratic societies, for example as governments overreact to the threat of terrorism (e.g., constraining civil liberties) or as government stability is affected (e.g., Gassebner et al. 2008). Other studies (e.g., Frey et al. 2009) find that terrorism is also accompanied by a decline in life satisfaction, particularly when regions are strongly affected by terrorism (e.g., Northern Ireland).
4. The trend toward loose network structures in terrorism with a stronger reliance on self-organized terrorism tends to reduce *both* the need for funds *and* financial flows (without necessarily reducing the effectiveness of these groups).
5. Recent developments in terrorism point in this direction. There is an increase in 'home-grown' terrorism, that is, terrorists self-organize in diaspora communities with only very loose contact to an overarching terror network (e.g., Sageman 2008). In a process of self-radicalization young people turn into terrorists ('lone wolf terrorists') and conduct major terrorist attacks although no financial flows have taken place (e.g., Homeland Security Institute 2009).
6. Arguably, counter-terrorism instruments improve anti-money laundering prosecution, thus providing a more convincing (political) rationale for treating both issues within the same legal framework. For instance, Vervaele (2009) observes a *paradigm change* in legislation, because including terrorist financing in the definition of money laundering allows the police to use (proactive) instruments of national security for prosecution (including, e.g., data mining) (see also Vervaele in this volume, Chapter 28).

REFERENCES

Abadie, Alberto (2006), 'Poverty, political freedom, and the roots of terrorism', *American Economic Review*, **96** (2), 50–56.

Abadie, Alberto and Javier Gardeazabal (2003), 'The economic costs of conflict: a case study of the Basque Country', *American Economic Review*, **93** (1), 113–32.

Abadie, Alberto and Javier Gardeazabal (2008), 'Terrorism and the world economy', *European Economic Review*, **52**, 1–27.

Bantekas, Ilias (2003), 'The international law of terrorist financing', *The American Journal of International Law*, **97** (2), 315–33.

Basuchoudhary, Atin and William Shughart (2010), 'On ethnic conflict and the origins of transnational terrorism', *Defence and Peace Economics*, **21** (1), 65–87.

Bird, Graham, S. Brock Blomberg and Gregory D. Hess (2008), 'International terrorism: Causes, Consequences and Cures', *The World Economy* **31** (2), 255–274.

Blomberg, S. Brock and Gregory D. Hess (2008), 'From (no) butter to guns: understanding the economic role in transnational terrorism', in P. Keefer and N. Loayza (eds), *Terrorism, Economic Development, and Political Openness*, New York: Cambridge University Press, 83–115.

Blomberg, S. Brock, Gregory D. Hess, are Athanasios Orphanides (2004), 'The macroeconomic consequences of terrorism', *Journal of Monetary Economics*, **51**, 1007–32.

Bovenkerk, Frank and Bashir Abou Chakra (2004), 'Terrorism and organized crime', *Forum on Crime and Society*, **4** (1–2), 3–15.

Brisard, Jean-Charles (2002), 'Terrorism financing – roots and trends of Saudi terrorism financing. Report prepared for the President of the Security Council, United Nations', December 19, 2002.

Burgoon, Brian (2006), 'On welfare and terror: social welfare policies and political-economic roots of terrorism', *Journal of Conflict Resolution*, **50** (2), 176–203.

Byman, Daniel L., Peter Chalk, Bruce Hoffman, William Rosenau and David Brannan (2001), 'Trends in outside support for insurgent movements', Rand Cooperation, Santa Monica.

Casella, Stefan D. (2003), 'Reverse money laundering', *Journal of Money Laundering Control*, **7** (1), 92–4.

Comras, Victor (2005), 'Al Qaeda Finances and Funding of Affiliated Groups', *Strategic Insights*, **IV** (1), 1–16.

Crain, Nicole V. and W. Mark Crain (2006), 'Terrorized economies', *Public Choice*, **128**, 317–49.

Dandurand, Yvon and Vivienne Chin (2004), 'Links between terrorism and other forms of crime'. Report submitted to Foreign Affairs Canada and The United Nations Office on Drugs and Crime. International Centre for Criminal Law Reform and Criminal Justice Policy, Vancouver.

Dishman, Chris (2001), 'Terrorism, crime, and transformation', *Studies in Conflict & Terrorism*, **24** (1), 43–58.

Dreher, Axel and Martin Gassebner (2008), 'Does political proximity to the U.S. cause terror?', *Economics Letters*, **99**, 27–9.

Dreher, Axel, Tim Krieger and Daniel Meierrieks (2011), 'Hit and (they will) run: the impact of terrorism on migration', *Economics Letters*, **113**, 42–6.

Eckstein, Zvi and Daniel Tsiddon (2004), 'Macroeconomic consequences of terror: theory and the case of Israel', *Journal of Monetary Economics*, **51**, 971–1002.

Enders, Walter, Adolfo Sachsida and Todd Sandler (2006), 'The impact of transnational terrorism on U.S. foreign direct investment', *Political Research Quarterly*, **59** (4), 517–31.

FATF: Financial Action Task Force (2001/2010), *FATF IX Special Recommendations*, October 2001 (incorporating all subsequent amendments until February 2008), FATF/OECD, Paris 2010.

FATF: Financial Action Task Force (2003/2010), *FATF 40 Recommendations*, October 2003 (incorporating all subsequent amendments until October 2004), FATF/OECD, Paris 2010.

Frey, Bruno S. (2004), *Dealing with Terrorism: Stick or Carrot?*, Cheltenham, UK and Northampton, MA, USA: Edward Elgar Publishing.

Frey, Bruno S., Simon Luechinger and Alois Stutzer (2009), 'The life satisfaction approach to valuing public goods: the case of terrorism', *Public Choice*, **138**, 317–45.

Gassebner, Martin, Richard Jong-A-Pin and Jochen O. Mierau (2008), 'Terrorism and electoral accountability: one strike, you're out!', *Economics Letters*, **100**, 126–9.

Gouvin, Eric J. (2003), 'Bringing out the big guns: The USA PATRIOT Act, money laundering, and the war on terrorism', *Baylor Law Review*, **55** (3), 955–90.

Gupta, Sanjeev, Clements Benedict, Rina Bhattacharya and Shamit Chakravarti (2004), 'Fiscal consequences of armed conflict and terrorism in low- and middle-income countries', *European Journal of Political Economy*, **20** (2), 403–21.

Homeland Security Institute (2009), 'The internet as a terrorist tool for recruitment and radicalization of youth', White Paper prepared for the U.S. Department of Homeland Security, Science and Technology Directorate, Arlington/VA, April 24, 2009.

Ignatieff, Michael (2002), 'Human rights, the laws of war, and terrorism', *Social Research*, **69**, 1137–58.
Krieger, Tim and Daniel Meierrieks (2011), 'What causes terrorism?', *Public Choice*, **147** (1–2), 3–27.
Krueger, Alan B. and David D. Laitin (2008), 'Kto kogo? A cross-country study of the origins and targets of terrorism'. in P. Keefer and N. Loayza (eds), *Terrorism, Economic Development, and Political Openness*, New York: Cambridge University Press, 148–73.
Krueger, Alan B. and Jitka Maleckova (2003), 'Education, poverty and terrorism: is there a causal connection?', *Journal of Economic Perspectives*, **17** (4), 119–44.
Kurrild-Klitgaard, Peter, Mogens K. Justesen and Robert Klemmensen (2006), 'The political economy of freedom, democracy and transnational terrorism', *Public Choice*, **128**, 289–315.
Li, Quan (2005), 'Does democracy promote or reduce transnational terrorist incidents?', *Journal of Conflict Resolution*, **49** (2), 278–97.
Li, Quan and Drew Schaub (2004), 'Economic globalization and transnational terrorism: a pooled time-series analysis', *Journal of Conflict Resolution*, **48** (2), 230–58.
Makarenko, Tamara (2004), 'The crime–terror continuum: tracing the interplay between transnational organized crime and terrorism', *Global Crime*, **6**, 129–45.
Napoleoni, Loretta (2004), 'The new economy of terror: how terrorism is financed', *Forum on Crime and Society*, **4** (1), 31–48.
National Commission on Terrorist Attacks upon the United States: '9/11 Commission' (2004), *The 9/11 Commission Report*, Washington, DC.
Nitsch, Volker and Dieter Schumacher (2004), 'Terrorism and international trade: an empirical investigation', *European Journal of Political Economy*, **20**, 423–33.
O'Brien, Sean P. (1996), 'Foreign policy crises and the resort to terrorism: a time-series analysis of conflict linkages', *Journal of Conflict Resolution*, **40** (2), 320–35.
Piazza, James A. (2008), 'Incubators of terror: do failed and failing states promote transnational terrorism?', *International Studies Quarterly*, **52**, 469–88.
Sageman, Marc (2008), *Leaderless Jihad: Terror Networks in the Twenty-First Century*, Philadelphia: University of Pennsylvania Press.
Sandler, Todd and Walter Enders (2004), 'An economic perspective on transnational terrorism', *European Journal of Political Economy*, **20**, 301–16.
Sandler, Todd and Walter Enders (2008), 'Economic consequences of terrorism in developed and developing countries: an overview', in P. Keefer and N. Loayza (eds), *Terrorism, Economic Development, and Political Openness*, New York: Cambridge University Press, 17–47.
Schelling, Thomas C. (1991), 'What purposes can "international terrorism" serve?', in R.G. Frey and W.C. Morris (eds), *Violence, Terrorism, and Justice*, Cambridge: Cambridge University Press, 18–32.
Schmid, Alex P. (2004), *Links Between Terrorist and Organized Crime Networks: Emerging Patterns and Trends*, Milan: International Scientific and Professional Advisory Council.
Schneider, Friedrich (2010), 'The (hidden) flows of terrorist and organized crime organizations: a literature review and some preliminary empirical results', IZA Discussion Paper No. 4860.
Sen, Amartya (2008), 'Violence, Identity, and Poverty', *Journal of Peace Research*, **45** (1), 5–15.
Siqueira, Kevin and Todd Sandler (2006), 'Terrorists versus the government: strategic interaction, support, and sponsorship', *Journal of Conflict Resolution*, **50** (6), 878–98.
Sirseloudi, Matenia P. (2004), 'Early detection of terrorist campaigns', *Forum on Crime and Society*, **4** (1), 71–89.
Tavares, José (2004), 'The open society assesses its enemies: shocks, disasters and terrorist attacks', *Journal of Monetary Economics*, **51**, 1039–70.
Thony, Jean-François (2005), 'Money laundering and terrorism financing: an overview', in International Monetary Fund (ed.), *Current Developments in Monetary and Financial Law*, Vol. 3, Washington, DC, 241–64.
United Nations (UN) (2007), 'Report of the Special Rapporteur on the promotion and protection of human rights and fundamental freedoms while countering terrorism', Document A/HRC/6/17, New York, November 21, 2007.
Vervaele, John A.E. (2009), 'Special Procedural Measures and Respect of Human Rights, General Report for the International Association of Criminal Law (AIDP)', *Utrecht Law Review*, **5** (2), 66–109.
Ward, Richard W. (2004), 'The economics of terrorism', *Forum on Crime and Society*, **4** (1), 17–29.
Wilson, Scott (2004), 'Lebanese wary of a rising Hezbollah', *Washington Post Foreign Service*, December 20, 2004.
Whitlock, Craig (2008), 'Al-Qaeda masters terrorism on the cheap', *Washington Post Foreign Service*, August 24, 2008.

PART IV

WHO IS THREATENED BY LAUNDERING ACTIVITIES?

8. Measuring money laundering threat

Jakub Brettl

8.1 INTRODUCTION

The goal of the chapter is two-fold. First we introduce a money laundering (ML) threat assessment method, originally developed by Brettl and Usov (2010) and present its results. Secondly, we will compare the methodology and its results with the one produced by Walker (2011). Both methods were applied to a sample of European Union member states.

The Brettl-Usov method is based on the computation of a so-called Threat Index that measures the degree to which a particular country is attractive to money launderers relative to other countries. The approach is unique in that it explicitly distinguishes between five different types of money laundering offences (e.g. drug crime ML) and hence it can identify not only the overall ML threat a country faces, but also the degree to which each ML offence contributes to the overall threat. As a result, the method produces six different indices – one overall threat index and five threat indices for each ML offence (as classified by Reuter and Truman 2004).

Walker takes a completely different angle when looking at ML threat. His method is based on the application of a gravity model/formula in order to compute the amount of criminal proceeds that can potentially be laundered in a jurisdiction of interest. The gravity model is augmented for a number of factors, besides geographical distance, that ought to influence international money laundering flows.

As shown below, both methodologies, although fundamentally different, produce similar results. Both methods rank rich western EU countries as the most vulnerable/attractive to dirty money, while poorer countries and the new accession countries are ranked as the least threatened countries. The most significant disagreement between the two methodologies is on the relative threat of Nordic countries. The Brettl-Usov method ranks these countries among the least threatened, while Walker's method ranks them as one of the more threatened. Walker's model ranks Nordic countries high as they generate high proceeds of crime – hence a lot threat. Brettl-Usov generates opposite results as these countries have relatively small financial systems and a strong rule of law.

The rest of the chapter is organized as follows. Section 8.2 introduces the methodology and section 8.3 analyses the results. In section 8.4 we compare the results obtained here with those of Walker's method and section 8.5 is a conclusion.

8.2 THE BRETTL-USOV THREAT ASSESSMENT METHOD

The method developed by Brettl and Usov (2010) relies on a computation of a Threat Index that represents the degree of threat of a country becoming a target for money launderers. The approach is markedly different from the approach presented by Walker

(2011) – who argues that threat is represented by the amount of proceeds that can potentially be laundered in a given jurisdiction. Thus, the methodology presented here represents an alternative approach to the measurement of ML threat. According to Brettl and Usov (2010), ML threat is represented by the relative size of the computed threat index and ranked relative to the rest of the sample.

The index is computed as follows:

$$Threat\ Index_i = \sum_{k=1}^{n} (TS_k * w_k)$$

where the threat index equals the sum of weighted Threat Score (TS). The index assigns scores to identified variables (called threat variables) that contribute to threat and that are weighted according to their relative importance.

8.2.1 Identification and Classification of Threat Variables

The scores are assigned to variables that have been identified by literature and professionals as factors that indeed significantly contribute to (or hinder) the attractiveness of a particular country to ML. The authors list altogether 35 threat variables. The variables range from economic factors such as GDP per capita, trade in services and degree of economic globalization, to variables that come under the heading of 'special skills and access', such as common language and history and distance, among others (see the Appendix for complete list).

Threat variables are then sorted into five different categories according to ML offences as identified by Reuter and Truman (2004). The categories are homogenous with respect to the effects of interventions and the seriousness and the distribution of the harm caused by the particular offences to society, but they also differ from each other in these dimensions. Table 8.1 provides a hypothesis about the differences among the five categories of offences in the two dimensions most relevant for the study: reliance on cash and quantities of money involved. The idea behind the use of such classification is that ML offences represent different categories and that money launderers themselves are no homogenous group of actors and as a result different money launderers are attracted to a slightly different set of factors (threat variables).

Major drug traffickers, for instance, are unique in that they must deal with large sums of cash that, according to Reuter and Truman (2004), is often in small bills. Clearly, such money launderers will then be attracted to countries that allow for easy integration of large sums of cash into their economies.

Table 8.1 Classification of threat variables according to ML offences

ML offences	Drug distrib.	Bribery and corruption	Other blue collar	White collar	Terrorism
Use of cash	Exclusively	Mostly	Mix	Sometimes	Mix
Scale	Very large	Small to medium	Mix	Large	Small

Source: Reuter and Truman (2004).

Even though bribery and corruption could in theory be classified as a white-collar crime, the category is different in terms of actors involved, place of occurrence and the nature of the harm (Reuter and Truman 2004). The majority of bribery and corruption occurs in poorer and undeveloped countries. The reason why corruption is distinctly different from white-collar crime is the fact that it mainly involves public officials. Hence, countries with, for instance, a weak rule of law, banking secrecy and low GDP will be among those most threatened by such a category of launderers.

The most significant contributors to demand for money laundering from blue-collar crime include gambling and people smuggling (Reuter and Truman 2004). Such crimes, however, generate substantially smaller revenues than other markets (e.g. drugs). Nevertheless, a country that, for example, had a large gambling sector will indeed be more vulnerable than others.

White-collar crime is a category that includes a rather heterogeneous list of crimes such as embezzlement, fraud and tax evasion (Reuter and Truman 2004). These offences are often closely tied in with the financial sector and electronic transfers of money. Thus, countries with, for instance, developed financial systems and internet banking services are going to be relatively more threatened than countries that do not have these features.

Terrorism is distinctive in that it takes mostly legally generated proceeds and converts them into money that is then used for illicit purposes (Reuter and Truman, 2004). Since terrorism financing usually involves rather smaller amounts of cash compared to countries that have cash intensive economies, the presence of hawalas or maintaining banking secrecy will again contribute to a higher threat to the given country coming from terrorism financing.

8.2.2 Assigning Scores and Weights to Threat Variables

Once the threat variables are identified, each country is assigned a score for each variable according to how much threat the particular variable poses. The scores are assigned the algorithm illustrated in Figure 8.1.

Taking a sample of observations for a particular threat variable and finding its mean effectively splits the sample into two groups: one group with its observations below the mean and the other above the mean. Hence, the group with observations above the mean

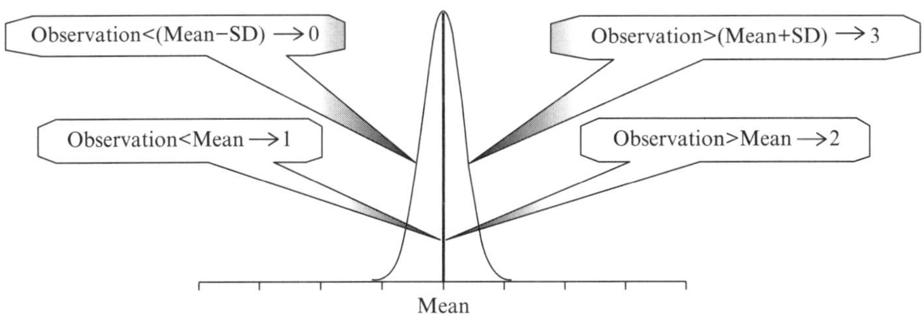

Source: Brettl and Usov (2010).

Figure 8.1 Algorithm of assigning Threat Scores

is relatively more threatened than the other group. Using this logic, scores are assigned as in Figure 8.1. A further set of scores is assigned for country observations that are above the mean plus the standard deviation of the distribution and mean minus the standard deviation of the distribution. The idea behind this step is that countries that are so far out of the main cluster observations virtually signal to the money launderers that they are particularly attractive relative to the rest of the sample. Similar logic applies for countries whose observations are at the opposite side of the distribution. Those countries are the least attractive. The fact that these countries are assigned score 0 does not mean there is no threat. It rather means that the threat is negligible *relative to the sample*.

Weights to threat variables are assigned in a very simple fashion. Clearly, as a result of the classification, it is possible that one particular variable is assigned to more than one category. Hence, threat variables are assigned weights according to how many categories they appear in. For example, the variable GDP per capita is represented in four out of five categories. Therefore, GDP per capita will have assigned weight 4/5 (0.8). Similarly, a variable that is represented in only one category will have weight 1/5 (0.2). The logic here is straightforward: the higher the weight, the more sources of ML threat the country has. As a side effect, the overall threat index is then a weighted average of the five ML offence sub-indices. Hence, the method not only allows for computation of one overall threat index, but for five separate sub-indices according to the ML offences.

8.3 RESULTS

Here we will present the results obtained using the above introduced methodology. We present the results of six different ML threat indices – the overall threat index and five separate indices for each ML offence as classified above. The indices were obtained using a cross-sectional dataset collected for the EU27 countries for the year 2010.[1] Figure 8.2 and Table 8.2 show the results of the overall ML Threat Index.

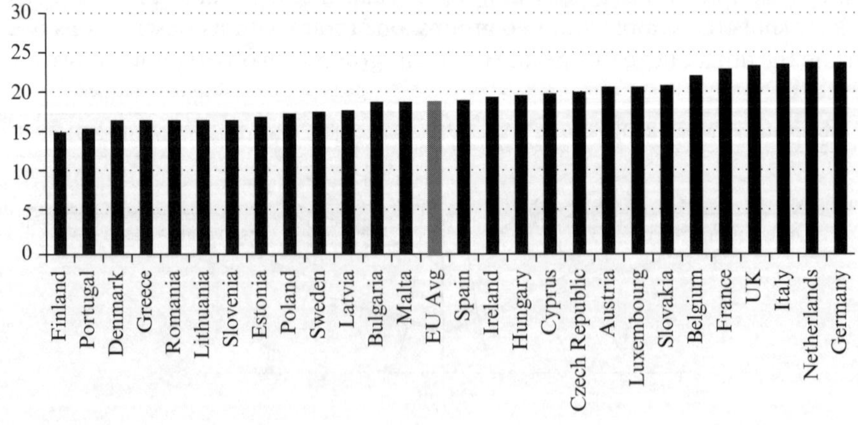

Source: Brettl and Usov (2010).

Figure 8.2 Overall ML threat indices for EU 27, 2010

Table 8.2 Overall ML threat indexes of EU 27 for 2010

Country	Threat Index	Country	Threat Index
Finland	15.2	Spain	19.2
Portugal	15.6	Ireland	19.6
Denmark	16.6	Hungary	19.8
Greece	16.6	Cyprus	20
Romania	16.8	Czech Republic	20.2
Lithuania	16.8	Austria	20.8
Slovenia	16.8	Luxembourg	20.8
Estonia	17.2	Slovakia	21
Poland	17.6	Belgium	22.2
Sweden	17.8	France	23
Latvia	18	UK	23.4
Bulgaria	19	Italy	23.6
Malta	19	Netherlands	23.8
EU Avg	19	Germany	24

Source: Brettl and Usov (2010).

A look at Table 8.2 reveals some similarities with the results obtained by Walker (2011). Clearly, the richest economies again occupy the above average places while the Nordic countries and newcomers are at the bottom.

In order to understand the results, one must examine the composition of the index. The drivers here are threat variables that are the least weighted (the highest weights). According to Brettl and Usov (2010), the least weighted variables are, among others, GDP per capita, trade in services, size of financial sector and the degree of use of cash in the economy (see Appendix). Hence, the richest countries will obviously be the most threatened.

8.3.1 Threat Index for Drug Crime Money Laundering

Drug crime is one of the major forces behind demand for money laundering (Reuter and Truman, 2004). The results, presented in Figure 8.3 and Table 8.3 below, show that the most threatened country for drug crime ML is Germany followed by Italy, the UK, France and the Netherlands. Clearly, the most threatened countries for dirty money coming from drug proceeds are identical to the most overall threatened countries. This is not surprising since drug crime together with white-collar crime consists of variables that are the least weighted (e.g. GDP per capita). The bottom of the graph tells a similar story, where the least threatened country is Denmark followed by Finland, Portugal and Greece.

In order to analyse the outcome further, one must identify the forces behind the demand for drug crime ML. As mentioned above, drug crime offenders deal with vast amounts of cash. Therefore, they will be particularly attracted to countries that allow for an easy integration of cash into their economic systems. There are many ways to do so. For example, should a country use cash as a main payment tool as opposed to electronic

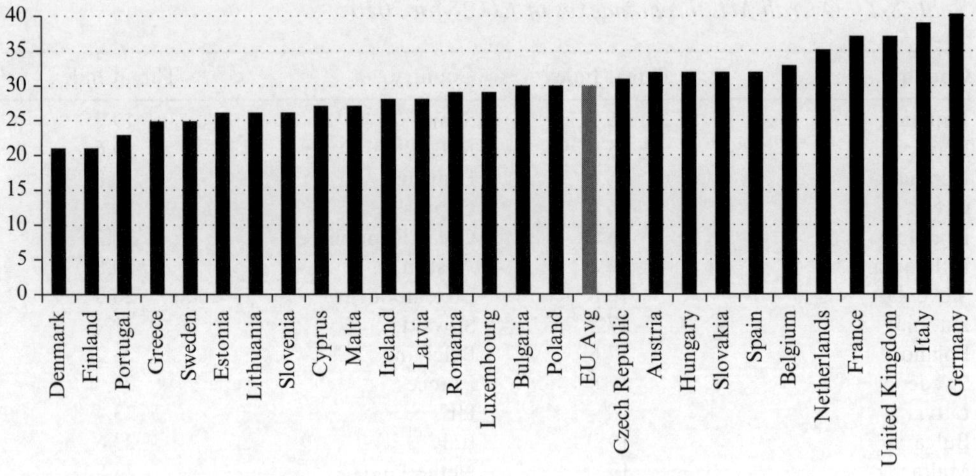

Source: Brettl and Usov (2010).

Figure 8.3 Drug crime ML threat indexes of EU 27 for 2010

Table 8.3 Drug crime ML threat indexes of EU 27 for 2010

Country	Threat Index	Country	Threat Index
Denmark	21	Bulgaria	30
Finland	21	Poland	30
Portugal	23	EU Avg	30
Greece	25	Czech Republic	31
Sweden	25	Austria	32
Estonia	26	Hungary	32
Lithuania	26	Slovakia	32
Slovenia	26	Spain	32
Cyprus	27	Belgium	33
Malta	27	Netherlands	35
Ireland	28	France	37
Latvia	28	UK	37
Romania	29	Italy	39
Luxembourg	29	Germany	40

Source: Brettl and Usov (2010).

transfers, such a country is then more vulnerable than others. Other factors that come into play are a large number of banks, a developed services sector and postal/cash transfer services. Also, the existence of specific sectors such as real-estate and jewellery sectors – sectors ideal for laundering large amounts of cash – further increase countries vulnerability to money laundering coming from drug proceeds.

The above mentioned factors are, among others, the major reason why countries like

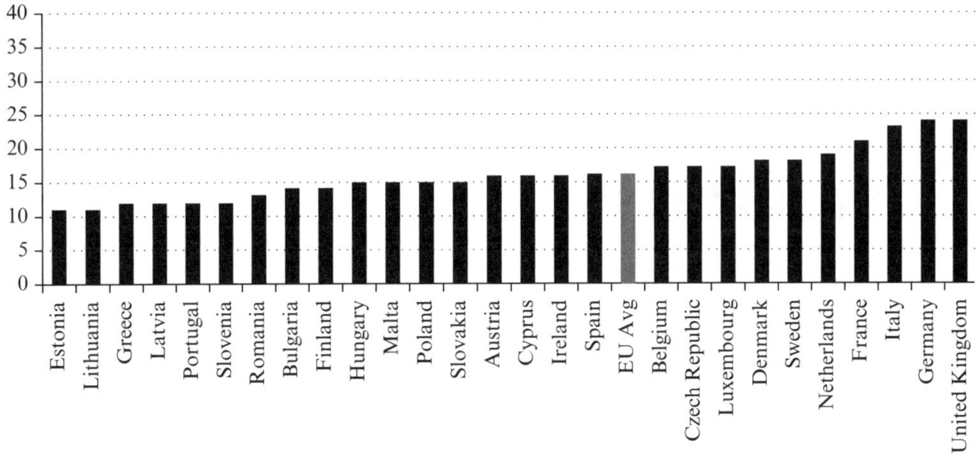

Source: Brettl and Usov (2010).

Figure 8.4 Other blue-collar crime ML threat indexes of EU 27 for 2010

Table 8.4 Other blue-collar crime ML threat indexes of EU 27 for 2010

Country	Threat Index	Country	Threat Index
Estonia	11	Cyprus	16
Lithuania	11	Ireland	16
Greece	12	Spain	16
Latvia	12	EU Avg	16
Portugal	12	Belgium	17
Slovenia	12	Czech Republic	17
Romania	13	Luxembourg	17
Bulgaria	14	Denmark	18
Finland	14	Sweden	18
Hungary	15	Netherlands	19
Malta	15	France	21
Poland	15	Italy	23
Slovakia	15	Germany	24
Austria	16	UK	24

Source: Brettl and Usov (2010).

Germany are most threatened, while Portugal is at the bottom. The case of Portugal is particularly interesting since the country is considered to be one of the EU's organized crime hubs, a place where potentially large amounts of cash could be laundered (OCTA 2009). However, using the methodology, this particular factor is simply outweighed by others.

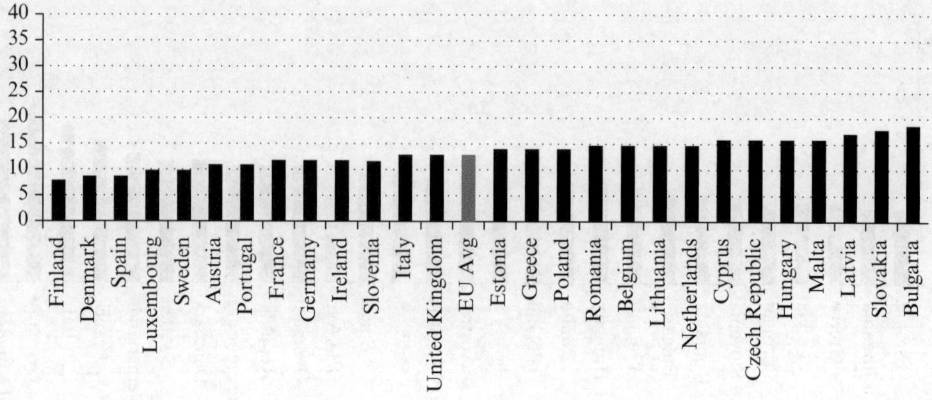

Source: Brettl and Usov (2010).

Figure 8.5 Bribery and corruption ML threat indexes of EU 27 for 2010

8.3.2 Threat Index for Other Blue-Collar Crime Money Laundering

These images are mirrored in Figure 8.4 and Table 8.4, where the most vulnerable countries for ML coming out of blue-collar offences are the richest economies of the EU. The top places, however, this time belong to the UK and Germany, followed by Italy and France. The least threatened countries are Estonia and Lithuania followed by Greece and Latvia.

The factors that come in to play here are similar to the drug crime ML factors, because blue-collar ML offenders also deal predominantly with cash. Nevertheless, there are also specific factors such as the number of casinos and the spread of gambling in each country.

Hence the fact that Italy, Germany and the UK occupy the highest spots in gambling revenues is one of the reasons behind their respective rank. The opposite holds for counties such as Lithuania and Estonia, whose volume of revenues is negligible relative to the rest of the EU.

8.3.3 Threat Index for Corruption and Bribery Money Laundering

The computed threat index for corruption and bribery ML tells a somewhat different story from previous indices. The top positions are occupied by the newcomers to the EU. More specifically Bulgaria, Slovakia, Latvia, Malta and Hungary take the first five spots. The bottom belongs to Finland followed by Denmark, Spain, Luxemburg and Sweden, being the least vulnerable to ML coming from bribery and corruption (see Figure 8.5 and Table 8.5).

As in the case of drug and blue-collar crime ML, bribery and corruption is conducted predominantly by the use of cash (Reuter and Truman 2004). For that reason, countries that use cash as a main medium of transactions will clearly be threatened more. Also, it is essential to keep in mind that due to the nature of bribery and corruption, economic size, development of financial sector and other economic indicators are not the key determinants here. Variables that in fact contribute to a higher threat are, among others, the rule of law and the persistence of corruption itself.

Table 8.5 Bribery and Corruption ML threat indexes of EU 27 for 2010

Country	Threat Index	Country	Threat Index
Finland	8	Estonia	14
Denmark	9	Greece	14
Spain	9	Poland	14
Luxembourg	10	Romania	15
Sweden	10	Belgium	15
Austria	11	Lithuania	15
Portugal	11	Netherlands	15
France	12	Cyprus	16
Germany	12	Czech Republic	16
Ireland	12	Hungary	16
Slovenia	12	Malta	16
Italy	13	Latvia	17
UK	13	Slovakia	18
EU Avg	13	Bulgaria	19

Source: Brettl and Usov (2010).

8.3.4 Threat Index for White-Collar Crime Money Laundering

As mentioned above, white-collar crime ML is, together with the drug crime ML, the most significant contributor to the overall ML demand. This category, due to its characteristics, is very different from the preceding ones. When one speaks of white-collar crime, one is usually referring to illicit activities such as tax evasion, fraud, etc. Generally speaking, the more economically developed a country is, the more threatened a country will be by white-collar money laundering. Furthermore, cash is not being used in such activities, as the vast majority of these activities are likely to be conducted electronically. Thus, a country that has very advanced systems of electronic payments, that allows for Bearer securities, and that maintains banking and financial secrecy will automatically be classified as more vulnerable than others.

The results for the white collar ML Threat Index are consistent with the ones obtained for the overall ML Threat Index. The top spots are occupied by the Netherlands, Germany, Italy, Luxemburg and France. The bottom spots belong to Sweden, Romania, Denmark, Estonia and Finland (see Figure 8.6 and Table 8.6). The position of the Nordic countries is somewhat surprising, but again should be seen in the light of the fact that the absolute size of their financial sector and economic size is subpar relative to the largest countries. Furthermore, these countries do not have weaknesses such as Bearer security, as many western European countries do, and feature a strong rule of law.

8.3.5 Threat Index for Terrorism Money Laundering

Finally, the terrorism ML threat index indicates that the most threatened countries in this category of ML are the Netherlands, Belgium, the UK, Luxemburg and Austria. It is, however, important to keep in mind that, as in the case of all the other predicate crime

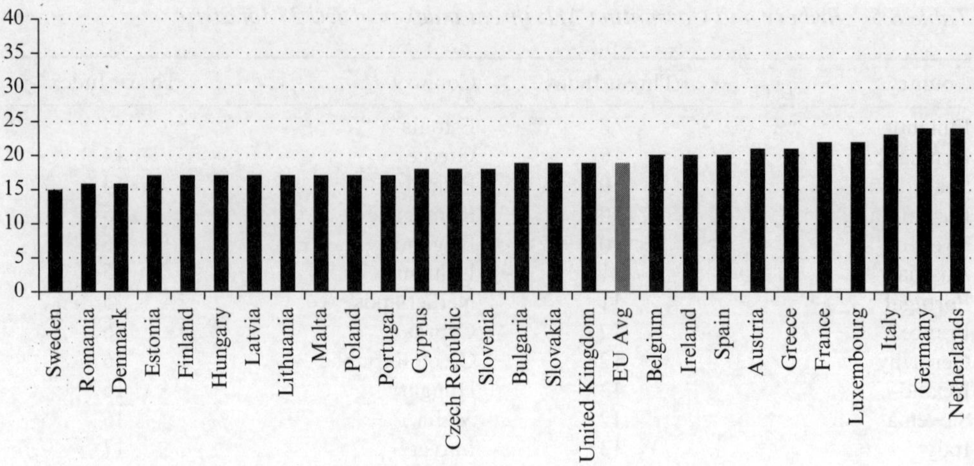

Source: Brettl and Usov (2010).

Figure 8.6 White-collar ML threat indexes of EU 27 for 2010

Table 8.6 White-collar ML threat indexes of EU 27 for 2010

Country	Threat Index	Country	Threat Index
Estonia	11	Cyprus	16
Lithuania	11	Ireland	16
Greece	12	Spain	16
Latvia	12	EU Avg	16
Portugal	12	Belgium	17
Slovenia	12	Czech Republic	17
Romania	13	Luxembourg	17
Bulgaria	14	Denmark	18
Finland	14	Sweden	18
Hungary	15	Netherlands	19
Malta	15	France	21
Poland	15	Italy	23
Slovakia	15	Germany	24
Austria	16	UK	24

Source: Brettl and Usov (2010).

indices, the index does not indicate how a particular country is vulnerable to terrorist attacks. It merely indicates to what degree the EU countries are prone to becoming a source of terrorist financing.

According to the computed index, the least threatened countries are Lithuania, Estonia, Slovenia, Bulgaria and Romania (see Figure 8.7 and Table 8.7). These countries are among the least developed ones in the EU. As the trends show, global terrorism is predominantly being financed from the richest countries and from countries that

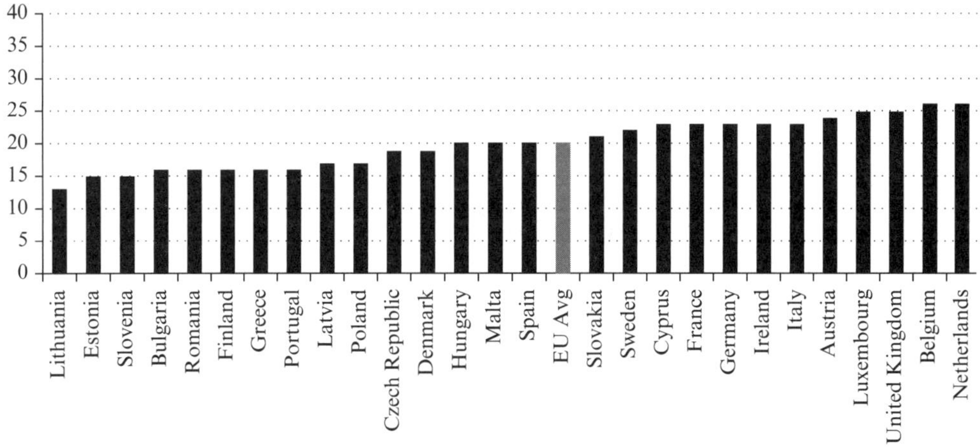

Source: Brettl and Usov (2010).

Figure 8.7 Terrorism ML threat indexes of EU 27 for 2010

Table 8.7 Terrorism ML threat indexes of EU 27 for 2010

Country	Threat Index	Country	Threat Index
Lithuania	13	Spain	20
Estonia	15	EU Avg	20
Slovenia	15	Slovakia	21
Bulgaria	16	Sweden	22
Romania	16	Cyprus	23
Finland	16	France	23
Greece	16	Germany	23
Portugal	16	Ireland	23
Latvia	17	Italy	23
Poland	17	Austria	24
Czech Republic	19	Luxembourg	25
Denmark	19	UK	25
Hungary	20	Belgium	26
Malta	20	Netherlands	26

Source: Brettl and Usov (2010).

feature large minorities (Gurulé 2008). This is in line with the computed index presented here.

8.4 COMPARISON OF WALKER AND BRETTL-USOV RESULTS

The two methods offer the different views on how to perceive threat. The elegance of Walker's method lies in the direct estimation of the volume of dirty money that can be

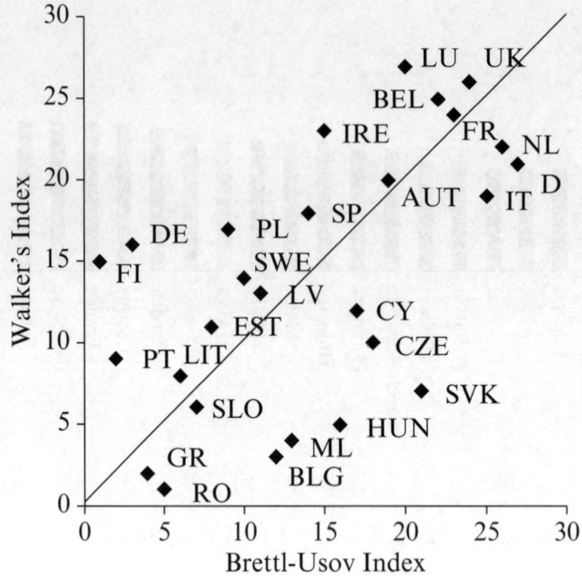

Figure 8.8 Comparison of Walker's and Brettl-Usov results

laundered in a particular jurisdiction as opposed to an estimation of a rather ambiguous number that represents relative threat. However, the strength of Brettl-Usov lies in the fact that it takes into account different types of money launderers – threat indices can be as easily estimated for white-collar as for drug crime. Furthermore, there is no way of checking the accuracy of the results obtained by Walker. Hence, for now, it seems 'safer' to rely on an index that would merely indicate the level of relative threat. Also, the Brettl-Usov method is computationally much simpler and it does not require a world-wide dataset in order to obtain the results, as is the case in Walker's approach.

The chart shown in Figure 8.8 depicts a relationship between the results of both methods. Outcomes of both methods were indexed, so that they are comparable. Clearly there is a positive relationship between the two: countries ranked high according to one method tend to be ranked high by the other method as well, and vice versa. In other words, mostly rich western economies are ranked by both methods as the relatively most threatened, while the newcomers with lower levels of GDP per capita, relatively small financial sectors and lower levels of trade are ranked lower.

There are, however, exceptions: Nordic countries, for instance, are ranked higher by Walker. The reason is that Walker argues that those countries have relatively high levels of crime leading to high levels of generated proceeds of crime and thus a higher 'home-grown' threat. The reason behind low rankings in the Brettl-Usov is that these countries feature both rather small financial sectors and strong rule of law–characteristics that, in theory, should limit ML demand.

8.5 CONCLUSION

This chapter introduces a new approach to measuring money laundering threat. The method views threat as the relative level of attractiveness of a country measured by the Threat Index. The method is innovative in that it takes into account different kinds of money launderers. In other words, the method assumes that dirty money coming from different sources (crimes) needs to be integrated into licit economies in different ways, hence different sources of dirty money will seek different attributes of respective national economies. As an outcome, the method does not produce one, but six different indices – one for an overall ML threat and five for each ML offence (as classified by Reuter and Truman 2004).

The results indicate that rich western countries tend to be among those most threatened by money laundering, while the poorer Baltic and Eastern European countries are among those that are threatened least. Nordic countries also tend to be among those least threatened countries which, according to the methodology, is a result of their small financial sectors and strong rules of law. The results are rather similar across all ML offence-specific threat indices, with the exception of the corruption and bribery threat index. The reason behind this is that bribery and corruption is a phenomenon that is fundamentally different from the other ML offences. Hence, the index is composed of a much different set of threat variables then the rest of the indices.

A comparison of the results of the Brettl-Usov and Walker's method shows that even though both methods are computationally different, they yield similar results. Both methods tend to rank rich western countries at the top while eastern countries are at the bottom. Once again, the Nordic countries are exceptions here, as Walker's results put them in the category of the most threatened countries, while, as mentioned above, Brettl-Usov ranks these countries rather low. Walker argues that Nordic countries have a lot of crime, hence generate a lot of proceeds of crime and as a result produce a lot of threat. On the other hand, Brett and Usov (2010) reason that factors such as strong rule of law and relatively small financial sector are strong enough to hinder the demand for ML.

Altogether, the two key methods introduced certainly bring a new dimension to the world of threat assessments. As such they should not be viewed as competing methodologies, but as complementary to each other – especially in the light of a rather low level of understanding of the money laundering phenomenon.

NOTE

1. For detailed description of the dataset, see Brettl and Usov (2010).

REFERENCES

Brettl, J. and A. Usov (2010), 'Money laundering threat assessment for EU 27', Mimeo.
Gurulé, J. (2008), Unfunding Terror: The Legal Response to the Financing of Global Terrorism, Cheltenham, UK and Northampton, MA, USA: Edward Elgar Publishing.

OCTA (2009), 'EU organized crime threat assessment'. Available at: http://www.drugsandalcohol.ie/12532/1/OCTA2009.pdf
Reuter, P. and E.M. Truman (2004), *Chasing Dirty Money: The Fight Against Money Laundering*, Washington DC: Institute for International Economics.
Walker, J. (2011), 'Measuring money laundering threat', Mimeo.

APPENDIX: THREAT VARIABLES

	Threat var.\ ML offence	Drug distribution	White collar	Other blue collar	Bribery	Terrorism
Opportunity factors						
Economic factors	GDP per capita	X	X	X		X
	Stable economy		X			
	Developed trade in services	X	X		X	
	Developed financial sector		X			
	Population	X				
	Economic globalization	X	X			X
Government conditions	Corruption	X			X	
	Government attitude	X	X	X	X	X
Law enforcement and legal environment	EMU member	X	X			X
	Rule of law	X	X	X	X	X
	Bearer security		X			
	Banking secrecy	X	X			X
	Exchange rate controls	X	X			X
Social or techno-logical change	Social globalization	X		X	X	X
Criminal environment	Drugs	X				
	Organized crime hub	X				X
	Global peace index	X	X		X	
	Theft			X		
	Terrorism					X
Special skills or access	Postal services	X		X		X
	Large borders					
	Number of large companies	X	X			
	History and culture			X	X	X
	Offshore centre	X	X			X
	Use of cash	X		X	X	X
	Electronic banking			X		X
	Gambling/casinos			X		
	Prevalence of specific sectors	X				
	Prepaid or gift cards					
	Number of banks	X	X			
	Geographical distance	X				
	Language					
	Political globalization				X	
	Hawala	X	X			X

9. Conducting national money laundering or financing of terrorism risk assessment*

Stephen Dawe

9.1 INTRODUCTION

How much risk is posed by the money laundering that occurs in certain countries, sectors and transaction types? This chapter summarizes the main components of a framework that International Money Fund (Fund) staff is developing for conducting national ML or FT risk assessment (NRA). Although the FATF standard recognizes that it is appropriate in many contexts to apply a risk-based approach to AML/CFT, it has proved difficult to apply risk-management concepts to the AML/CFT field in a rigorous way. The undertaking is complicated by the fact that ML and FT processes are many faceted and – since they are often intentionally hidden from view – inherently difficult to document or quantify. Moreover, different stakeholders in the AML/CFT community see ML and FT risks from different perspectives: financial firms are concerned about legal, operational and reputational risk posed by their clients, products and services; financial regulators are concerned about the risk that regulated entities will be compromised by dealing (wittingly or unwittingly) with the proceeds of crime; law enforcement and security services are concerned about the risk that criminals and security threats will escape detection and enjoy the fruits of their illicit activity; national policymakers may be concerned about the consequences of any or all of the above. From the Fund's perspective, the application of traditional risk-management concepts to AML/CFT serves several purposes. First, it can help staff focus limited resources on countries that pose and/or face the most substantial ML or FT risks. Second, in connection with an assessment of a given country, it can help focus attention on those aspects of the financial sector, and legal and institutional framework that constitute particularly significant vulnerabilities. Third, through technical assistance, it can help member countries understand, assess and mitigate the ML and FT risks that they face. Finally, it can help the international community to more effectively articulate and focus on the underlying purposes of AML/CFT regimes, and to assess the effectiveness of AML/CFT controls against these purposes. The enterprise is inherently limited by the issues outlined above as well as difficulties associated with the application of imperfect proxies and the use of estimates that may involve very wide ranges. With these caveats, however, and with the attendant recognition that critiques are welcome and further refinements will need to be made, Fund staff are nevertheless convinced of the benefits of undertaking the work. These benefits relate largely to the focused attention that the attempt of conducting a risk assessment using a disciplined process to make informed judgments can bring to officials responsible for outlining strategies and making decisions concerning the allocation of resources.

The chapter discussion begins by briefly discussing the key features of the money laundering (ML) and financing of terrorism (FT) processes (section 9.2). It then describes the key elements of risk management and the Fund staff's preferred approach to applying risk management to ML and FT (section 9.3), and outlines the main components of the framework for assessing ML and FT risk.

9.2 THE MONEY LAUNDERING AND FINANCING OF TERRORISM PROCESSES

Money laundering (ML) is a process that transforms illegal inputs into supposed legitimate outputs and often involves the abuse of financial institutions as instrumentalities. ML broadly encompasses a wide range of activities that may be involved in disguising the origin of proceeds of crime (IMF 2001). The proceeds of crime, thus, represent an 'input' to the process, and the 'output' is a pool of assets with an aura of legitimacy.[1] The laundering process may involve a series of transactions conducted in both the informal and formal sectors. Any provider of a product or service that can be used to store or transfer value can itself be abused as an instrumentality in the laundering process. ML is, thus, commonly associated with the businesses of the core financial sector (i.e., banks and deposit takers, and securities and insurance firms), other financial businesses (e.g., money transfer agents), businesses and professions operating with links to the financial sector (e.g., so-called gatekeepers such as lawyers and accountants), and other businesses (e.g., casinos, dealers in high value assets).

Financing of terrorism (FT) involves raising and processing funds to supply terrorists with the resources to carry out their attacks. It involves the abuse of many of the same instrumentalities as ML but differs in one key respect. In the case of ML, funds are always of illicit origin (and the purpose of ML is to make them appear to be legally acquired), whereas in the case of FT, funds can stem from both legal and illicit sources.

9.3 THE THREE KEYS TO RISK ASSESSMENT: THREAT, VULNERABILITY AND CONSEQUENCES – AND THEIR APPLICATION TO MONEY LAUNDERING AND FINANCING OF TERRORISM

International risk management standards define risk as a function of the likelihood of occurrence and the consequence of risk events,[2] where likelihood of occurrence is a function of the coexistence of threat and vulnerability. In other words, risk events occur when a threat exploits vulnerability. Formally, R, a jurisdiction's level of ML or FT risk, can be represented as:

$$R = f\,[(T), (V)] \times C$$

where T represents threat, V represents vulnerability, and C represents consequence. Accordingly, the level of risk can be mitigated by reducing the size of the threats, vulnerabilities, or their potential consequences. To give an example, the likelihood of a single drug dealer spending illicit money (the threat, T) through exploiting vulnerabilities to purchase a car is probably high in many jurisdictions but the consequences of that single transaction are relatively small. This would therefore rank as a lower money laundering risk, *R*, than say the lower likelihood occurrences of a drug trafficking organization successfully purchasing a large commercial property or a substantial amount of government bonds, both of which have relatively higher consequences in terms of enabling the organization to grow its power and influence.

In the following, the components of the formula *R*, *T*, *V* and *C* will be explained in more detail.

R: The level of ML or FT risk measured is net risk – the risk taking into account the effect of controls on the level of inherent risk. Controls are anything implemented to modify (usually intended to reduce) the level of inherent risk. Controls, thus, reduce inherent risk but the lack of them cannot increase inherent risk levels. In ML and FT controls fall into two categories: first, general controls and mitigants (such as general regulatory requirements); and second, specific AML/CFT controls implementing the FATF 40+9 Recommendations. Since one of the main purposes of risk management is to allocate resources effectively to mitigate the most important risks, the staff's ML/FT risk management framework focuses on the risk from substantial, successful occurrences of ML or FT. Substantial ML refers to the amount of ML measured in its own right, in the context of some relevant circumstance (such as the size of gross domestic product, or the financial sector), or in relation to its consequences on the achievement of an objective. Substantial ML can refer to a single ML transaction or to a series of transactions that allow a substantial amount to be laundered over a 12-month period, either as part of a single ML scheme or a series of unrelated ML schemes, wherever the events take place.[3] Unlike ML, potentially all successful FT likely matters for risk management.[4] Hence, the generic objective that underpins staff's ML and FT risk management framework is to minimize the amount of ML or FT that occurs.

T: In ML, a 'threat' is largely related to the nature and scale of potential demand for ML, that is, the pool of illegally acquired assets that need to be laundered. For the purposes of FT risk assessment, threat is mainly related to the nature and scale of the funds raised for use by terrorists that are in a jurisdiction in need of processing. With respect to ML there are two components that determine the proceeds of crime (POC) that need to be laundered in any given jurisdiction: (i) the nature and types of domestic predicate crime that exist and the scale of proceeds that they generate;[5] and (ii) the nature and scale of proceeds generated outside of the jurisdiction that are likely to enter the jurisdiction for laundering. The two similar components for FT are the nature and types of domestic fundraising efforts and the funds that they generate, and the amount of funds raised outside of the jurisdiction that are likely to enter the jurisdiction for further processing or use. Thus, for both ML and FT risk management it is necessary to obtain estimates or proxies for these two components in order to generate indicators of likely ML of FT activity as inputs to an assessment of the level of ML or FT risk for a jurisdiction. Producing such indicators involves reaching an understanding about the key characteristics of the predicate crime and terrorist financing environments and their drivers and enablers. It also helps identify whether the likely level of ML or FT that will be attempted will be substantial.

V: 'Vulnerability' in ML or FT risk assessment encompasses the intrinsic properties in products, services, distribution channels, customer bases, institutions, systems, structures and jurisdictions (including weaknesses in systems, controls or measures) that enable ML or FT abuse. The staff's framework for assessing ML or FT vulnerability therefore involves assessing the factors across these areas associated with successful ML or FT and generating vulnerability indicators for them. The vulnerability indicators are numerous but they can be grouped into categories such as geographic location, financial services and products, levels of informality in various sectors, weaknesses in the AML/CFT systems and the adequacy of existing AML/CFT controls, general levels of corruption, the effectiveness of law enforcement agencies (LEAs) and the criminal justice system (CJS), and other characteristics of the jurisdiction that could facilitate successful ML or FT (e.g., the level of organized crime). In the staff's framework, vulnerability indicators are aggregated and combined with the threat indicators to produce an overall analysis of the likelihood of substantial ML or of FT occurring successfully.

C: 'Consequences' relate to the outcomes that result from the occurrence of risk events. Consequences can relate to cost, damage caused, or the significance of outcomes – either through enabling the associated criminal and terrorist acts, or through their effect on financial systems and institutions, as well as jurisdictions more generally. From one perspective, ML and FT processes generate two types of consequence: first, those associated with carrying out the ML or FT process; and, second, those associated with the use of the assets after they have been successfully processed. The consequences of laundering proceeds of crime may involve short-term distortion of demand for various products, services, or assets, including those in the financial sector. Using the successfully laundered assets tends to have broader, longer-term, social, economic and political consequences that may apply to citizens, businesses, communities or national or international interests, including encouraging further criminal activity and, thus, further laundering (Masciandaro, 1999). The relevance of any particular consequence depends on the objective(s) of a given risk management exercise. The consequences of ML have been further elaborated in the literature into 25 categories as set out in Box 9.1 (Unger 2007). The consequences of FT likely vary from this list.

9.4 APPLYING RISK MANAGEMENT TO ML OR FT

Applying risk management to ML or FT is complex, due in large part to the lack of sufficient data or information about past ML or FT events. This lack means that, unlike many other risk management fields, it is not feasible to build systems to make meaningful estimates of the likelihood of substantial ML or of FT occurring, or the consequences of its occurrence (FATF 2007). Moreover, ML and FT processes are often too complex to enable analysis of every risk event associated with each type of ML or FT scheme.

Accordingly, the staff's framework relies on a semi-qualitative risk-scoring system that focuses on the key risk events associated with the ML or FT process that are thought to make a difference to ML or FT risk profiles. This approach involves gaining a better understanding and modeling of the ML and FT processes, disaggregating the overall process by identifying the key contributing events that increase the likelihood of substantial ML or of FT being successful, and analyzing these events carefully. By generating scores for a range of objective and subjective indicators that are used to suggest

BOX 9.1 25 SOCIAL, ECONOMIC AND POLITICAL CONSEQUENCES OF MONEY LAUNDERING

1. Losses to the victims and gains to the perpetrator
2. Distortion of consumption
3. Distortion of investment and savings
4. Artificial increase in prices
5. Unfair competition
6. Changes in imports and exports
7. Effects on growth rates
8. Effects on output, income and employment
9. Lower public sector revenues
10. Threats to privatization
11. Changes to demand for money, exchange rates and interest rates
12. Increases in exchange and interest rate volatility
13. Greater availability of credit
14. Higher capital in- and out-flows
15. Changes in FDI
16. Risks for financial sector solvency and liquidity
17. Profits for the financial sector
18. Financial sector reputation
19. Illegal business contaminates legal business
20. Distortion of economic statistics
21. Corruption and bribery
22. Increases in crime
23. Undermining of political institutions
24. Undermining of foreign policy goals
25. Increases in terrorism

the level of threats, vulnerabilities, and consequences related to the drivers and enablers associated with the events, it is possible to assess the overall likelihood of substantial ML or of FT being successful and its potential nature, magnitude and consequences. The analysis is used to create two proxy variables for each of ML and FT: one for likelihood of substantial ML or of FT occurring and one for consequences. These two proxies are combined to measure the national level of ML or FT risk. The staff's framework contains a common approach for how to assess ML and FT risk, but produces a separate assessment for each. This is due to the varying nature of the threats, vulnerabilities and consequences of ML and FT. The rest of this chapter describes in more detail the staff's framework for ML and FT risk analysis and illustrates aspects of the framework using primarily the ML risk assessment process. It describes:

a. The approach to deriving a proxy indicator of likelihood of substantial ML or of FT being successful, based around key ML and FT risk events, and the use of analysis modules of factors and their indicators to analyze and score the likelihood of the key risk events occurring.

b. The approach to deriving a proxy indicator of the relevant consequences in the case of substantial ML or FT being successful.
c. The approach for measuring the overall level of ML or FT risk.

9.5 DETAILS OF THE STAFF'S FRAMEWORK FOR ASSESSING MONEY LAUNDERING AND FINANCING OF TERRORISM RISK

9.5.1 Deriving a Proxy Indicator for the Likelihood of Substantial ML or of FT Being Successful

For operationalizing risk, *R*, risk events have to be identified along with their associated threats and vulnerabilities. The key risk events in the staff's proposed framework for ML and FT risk management derive from three circumstances that co-exist to encourage attempts of ML or FT abuse. These three circumstances, which are a mix of threat, *T*, and associated vulnerabilities, *V*, provide the framework in ML and FT risk assessment for analyzing the likelihood of substantial ML or of FT being successful. The events are based around the dynamics of the ML or FT process. First, the launderer holds illegally obtained assets or the terrorist financier holds illegally obtained or legitimate assets that need processing (a threat). Second, the launderer or financier perceives that there are products, services, assets or other circumstances that can be abused to meet his or her processing needs (a vulnerability). Third, the launder or financier perceives that there is little likelihood of being caught by the authorities during the process and, thus, of being sanctioned and losing the assets (due to other vulnerabilities). Thus, substantial ML or FT is successful if the following interrelated events occur:

a. ML or FT is attempted:
   i. Due to a co-existence of substantial amounts of proceeds of crime or of terrorist funds that need processing, and
   ii. Due to the existence of products, services, assets or other circumstances that the launderer or terrorist financier perceives can be abused to meet their needs; and
b. The perpetrator(s)[6] of the ML or FT is not caught:
   i. if it is attempted, ML or FT will not be detected by the authorities (either directly or indirectly via the efforts of businesses that are required to make suspicious reports),[7] or
   ii. if it is detected, ML or FT will not be investigated adequately by the authorities, or
   iii. if investigated, the perpetrator(s) will not be prosecuted, or
   iv. if prosecuted, the perpetrator(s) will not be convicted or
c. The perpetrator(s) of the ML or FT is not sanctioned adequately:[8]
   i. if convicted, the perpetrator(s) will not be punished adequately, or
   ii. if punished, the perpetrator(s) will not be deprived of their assets.

9.5.2 Analysis Modules for Analyzing Key ML or FT Risk Events

The proxy for the likelihood of substantial ML abuse being successful is derived from analysis modules linked to the key ML or FT risk events containing factors, sub-factors and their indicators, organized in nested hierarchies. The organization and grouping of the ML risk events and analysis modules used to derive the proxy indicator of ML likelihood is set forth in Table 9.1. The modules are listed under the third column entitled 'Areas to analyze'. Each module identifies unique risk factors that are linked to the threats and vulnerabilities and that affect the likelihood of the contributing risk event(s) occurring during any typical 12-month period, taking into account the effectiveness of existing controls, including AML controls. Each risk factor has a range of indicators. Risk factors and their indicators are organized within the analysis modules into nested hierarchies. The highest level comprises those factors that impact directly on the likelihood of the relevant ML or FT risk event occurring. The next level down in any nest within the hierarchy comprises those sub-factors that impact on the first-level factors, and so on. The last column of Table 9.1 summarizes key factors from the highest level for each analysis module.[9]

9.5.3 Approach for Scoring Factors and Indicators of the Likelihood of Substantial ML or of FT Being Successful

Within each risk analysis module, each risk factor is analyzed by reference to its relevant indicators and then scored based on pre-determined decision-making criteria linked to the likelihood of substantial ML or FT occurring. Each indicator for risk factors, including for controls, has its own pre-determined decision-making criteria for scoring. Those criteria are as generic as possible for similar types of indicator. The pre-determined decision-making criteria are descriptive. They fit measurement scales that score factors and their indicators based on a seven-point semi-qualitative ordinal scale. The scoring of each indicator is designed such that there is a meaningful difference between points in the scale. This approach, in part, is premised on an understanding that detecting ML or FT activity is analogous to looking for a proverbial needle in a haystack, meaning that it is easier for launderers and financiers to hide their needles in larger haystacks, given their incentives to act surreptitiously, and therefore, the scoring system should recognize the different scale of potential activity within jurisdictions. Some scales, particularly for AML/CFT controls, are anchored based on 'effectiveness' benchmarks, derived from analysis of the effectiveness statistics presented in a selection of mutual evaluation reports and detailed assessment reports. Scoring is based on the concept of using the best available data. The approach involves scoring those indicators for which data are readily available, and using the available results to score the relevant factor or sub-factor. Scoring does not require that each indicator for a factor or sub-factor has to be scored.[10]

The framework's analysis modules use both quantitative and qualitative indicators drawn from public and private sources. Where possible the indicators are drawn from public sources (e.g., IMF, World Bank, United Nations, assessed country databases and published documents). Otherwise, non-public data are used (e.g., provided by the authorities) or generated for use (e.g., surveys of informed officials and calculations based on other data).

Table 9.1 ML risk analysis framework: risk events and analysis modules of factors

Risk event (that might happen) (1) ML or FT events will be attempted:			
(because of) **contributing risk events**	(due to) **threats (t)** or **vulnerabilities (v)** that increase the likelihood of occurrence	**Area(s) to analyze** (modules of risk factors)	Further broken down by: (factors, and sub-factors)
(1a) Domestic proceeds being generated or available	(t) Presence of domestic proceeds	(A) Amount of domestic proceeds generated or available[a]	Crime type; Cash, financial and physical assets; Organized and other crime
	(v) Inadequate suppression of domestic predicate crime	(B1) LEA (Crime suppression)[b]	Powers, Resources, Effectiveness[c]
(1b) Foreign proceeds entering the jurisdiction	(t) Presence of foreign proceeds	(C) Amount of foreign proceeds entering the jurisdiction[a]	Jurisdiction of origin, and same factors as for domestic POC
	(v) Existence of cross-border products, services, assets, and circumstances that can be abused to meet ML's importing and exporting needs	(D) Cross-border products, services, assets, circumstances[d]	Unique cross-border aspects of all areas to analyze[e]
	(v) Cross-border scrutiny does not suppress cross-border ML	(E) Border security measures and scrutiny	Currency, Financial transactions, Physical assets, People
(1c) Abuse of jurisdiction's products, services, assets or other circumstances for ML events	(v) Jurisdiction and its institutions providing goods, services, assets and other circumstances that can be abused to meet the ML's needs	(F) General jurisdiction environment	Economy, Legal system & rule of law, Business environment & Regulatory quality, Political environment, Culture & integrity, AML/CFT commitment
		(G) Products, services, assets and circumstances offered[f]	Sectors, Institution types, Scale, Customer base, Delivery channels, General mitigants
(1d) Corruption to facilitate ML occurring	(v) Corruption in LEA, cross-border scrutiny, institutions	(H1) Corruption[g]	

Table 9.1 (continued)

Risk event (that might happen) (2) that, if attempted, the perpetrator(s) of the ML or FT events will not be caught				
(because of) **contributing risk events**	(due to) **threats (t)** or **vulnerabilities (v)** that increase the likelihood of occurrence		**Area(s) to analyze** (modules of risk factors)	Further broken down by: (factors, and sub-factors)
(2a) if attempted, ML event(s) not being detected by the authorities	(v) LEAs do not detect ML events directly	(v) LEAs only investigate predicate crime (v) LEAs not told of foreign enquires or don't treat as ML leads	(B2) LEA (Detecting ML directly)	Effectiveness focuses on ML, Domestic cooperation
	(v) LEAs or other investigating authorities do not receive quality information on suspected ML events from the FIU	(v) FIU does not receive sufficient quality reports on suspected ML events from institutions due to: (v) Insufficient reporting. (v) Poor quality, including over-reporting	(I) STR system	Requirements, Volumes, Quality Sectors, Institution type[h]
		(v) Inadequate monitoring of transactions	(J) Transaction & Account Monitoring	Requirements, Effectiveness[i]
		(v) Inadequate information about customers	(K) Customer Identification, profiling, ongoing and enhanced due diligence	Requirements, Effectiveness
		(v) Institution incapacity	(L) Capacity and competence of institutions	Systems & controls, Resources, Guidance received,

		(v) Inadequate supervision of reporting firms	(M) Supervision	Effectiveness, especially when deficiencies identified
		(v) Ineffective processing of reports by the FIU	(N) FIU	Effectiveness of analysis, dissemination
(2b) if detected, ML event(s) not being investigated adequately by the authorities	(v) LEA ineffective at conducting POC & ML investigations		(B3) LEA (ML suppression) [j]	Effectiveness of investigations
	(v) LEA POC & ML investigators cannot obtain leads or evidence	(v) Poor access to or records in reporting firms	(O) Record-keeping & secrecy	Requirements, effectiveness, secrecy
		(v) Inability to obtain beneficial ownership information	(P) Ownership transparency[k]	Entity and asset types, Register requirements, powers to obtain information
		(v) Inability to obtain information and evidence from foreign jurisdictions	(E2) Cross-border cooperation	Effectiveness of administrative cooperation, MLA,[l] and extradition to obtain evidence and people
(2c) if investigated, perpetrators of ML event(s) not being prosecuted	(v) Perpetrators are outside jurisdiction	(v) Inability to extradite or prosecute in absentia		
	(v) Prosecutor not pursuing ML charge		(R1) CJS (Prosecution &Judiciary)	Prosecution and convictions, ML & predicate crimes. CJS priorities, constitution, law, & jurisprudence
	(v) Prosecutor not pursuing any charge			
	(v) Inefficient or ineffective CJS or court system			
(2d) if prosecuted, perpetrators of ML event(s) not being convicted	(v) Ineffective prosecution			
	(v) Incompetent judiciary (v)			
	(v) Inadequate wording of criminal laws		(R2) CJS (Laws)[m]	Adequacy of laws
(2e) Corruption to facilitate ML occurring	(v) Corruption in LEAs, FIU, CJS, institutions and the authorities supervising or monitoring institutions		(H2) Corruption [g]	

Table 9.1 (continued)

Risk event (that might happen) (3) that, once caught, the perpetrator(s) of ML event(s) are not sanctioned adequately.				
(because of) **contributing risk events**	(due to) **threats (t)** or **vulnerabilities (v)** that increase the likelihood of occurrence		**Area(s) to analyze** (modules of risk factors)	Further broken down by: (factors, and sub-factors)
(3a) Convicted perpetrator(s) of ML event(s) not being punished adequately	(v) Inadequate sanctions	(v) Inadequate prison terms being imposed (v) Inadequate fines or other sanctions imposed	(R3) CJS (Sentencing)	Powers, Sanctions imposed[n]
	(v) Ineffective system for implementing sanctions	(v) Ineffective prison system (v) Ineffective systems for collecting fines	(R4) CJS (Enforcing Sanctions)	Length and average of prison terms served Amount and average of fines collected
(3b) Convicted perpetrator(s) of ML event(s) not being deprived of their assets	(v) Inadequate confiscation orders being made		(R5) CJS (Asset confiscation)	Powers, Policy, Sanctions imposed, Effectiveness focus on assets confiscated[n]
	(v) Inadequate recovery of assets	(v) Inadequate resources for asset recovery		
		(v) Inability to recover assets from foreign jurisdictions	(E3) Cross-border asset recovery	Effectiveness of administrative cooperation, MLA to recover assets
		(v) Ineffective use of provisional measures	(B4) LEA (Provisional measures)	Assets seized or frozen
(3c) Corruption to facilitate ML occurring	(v) Corruption within the authorities		(H3) Corruption[g]	

Notes:

(a) This involves identifying all proceeds generating offenses even if laundering those proceeds is not a domestic criminal offense. It is unlikely that a figure for proceeds entering the jurisdiction can be estimated accurately. However, the size of this threat for any jurisdiction is a function of the world proceeds (which for most countries is a constant omnipresent threat), the jurisdiction's cross-border vulnerabilities, and the other general issues impacting on domestic ML events. The actual amount that eventuates, and hence the overall risk, is also a function of the capacity of the jurisdiction to absorb ML events (i.e., process transactions and store assets that are in the process of being, or that have been, laundered).

(b) The level of crime suppression is taken into account implicitly in identifying the level of domestic POC. Additionally, it is a separate vulnerability for understanding the freedom criminals have to go about their business, including carrying out ML or FT.

(c) All modules that look at AML/CFT agencies look at each agency's powers, resources and effectiveness (output and performance). Thus, the rest of the agency entries in this column list only what the effectiveness aspect focuses on.

(d) Cross-border products and services facilitate the transfer or proceeds from one jurisdiction to another or allow a launderer based in one jurisdiction to control proceeds in another. Domestic criminals who export proceeds may also use them.

(e) This module analyzes and scores factors that differentiate cross-border ML events from domestic ML events. General issues relating to the jurisdiction apply to domestic and cross-border ML events. However, there are some factors that only impact on cross-border ML events. A higher 'score' in this module would reflect a higher chance that the jurisdiction will attract ML from other jurisdictions, facilitate the exporting of ML from domestic sources, or both, thus increasing the amount of ML events that occur in the jurisdiction. The level of actual ML events that occur will be constrained by the capacity of the jurisdiction to process and store ML assets. That capacity will also be affected by any actions or limitations on cross-border financial flows. Examples of factors that uniquely facilitate cross-border ML events include: geographical location, language, trade and cultural ties, ease of currency convertibility, ability of non-residents to operate domestic accounts and residents to operate foreign accounts, treatment of foreign PEPs, whether foreign predicate crimes are recognized as predicates for domestic ML, ability of jurisdiction to carry out international cooperation (e.g., extradition), etc.

(f) The first prototype of this module mainly identifies the existence of higher-risk products and services. Subsequent development will broaden the analysis to take account of the potential volume of activity that can be conducted.

(g) Corruption influences all of the ML process, giving launderers the potential to override all controls. It can also be a source of proceeds. For this reason, the existence of corruption is treated as a separate contributing risk event.

(h) Modules that analyze preventive measures imposed on institutions break the analysis down by sector and institution type.

(i) Effectiveness analysis includes in relation to feedback and guidelines from the authorities. Effectiveness would also look at technical issues such as whether the institution can monitor transactions across accounts, across its full network, monitor for unique identifiers, monitor using fuzzy logic for identifiers, monitor for cumulative transactions and other patterns, etc.

(j) Emphasis on and success for proceeds generating crimes (i.e., powers, resources and reported crime clearance rates).

(k) Also relevant for risk events 1c and 2a.

(l) Mutual Legal Assistance.

(m) Also relevant for and taken into account in the investigation and prosecution stages.

(n) For ML and predicate crimes. Sanctions may be less critical than the chance of being caught, and that incarcerating members of criminal groups without confiscating assets may lead to higher levels of organized crime and corruption (see *Eide*, 2000 and Buscaglia, 2008).

A higher score indicates a higher likelihood that substantial ML abuse will occur. The indicators used are suggestive of that likelihood, not perfectly representative of the actual likelihood. The proposed scoring system results in a 'relative' likelihood score (i.e., scores are only meaningful in relation to other similar scores, across the modules, sectors, factors, regions, products, etc.).

9.5.4 Aggregating Factor and Module Scores to Derive Proxy for Overall Likelihood of Substantial ML or of FT Being Successful

Scores across indicators are aggregated by deriving the geometric mean for all indicators within a nested hierarchy. The scoring is aggregated upwards to sub-factor, factor, module and, finally, overall likelihood level, starting at the lowest level of each hierarchy of indicators. This is done using the nth root equation, $\sqrt[n]{A}$ – where, n is the number of indicators, factors or risk events, and A is their product.[11] This method of aggregation is preferred for three reasons. First, it maintains the appropriate relationships between the ML or FT modules and factors, such as those for ML set out in Table 9.1. By combining factor scores using this method any one factor's influence is limited to its primary area of impact. Second, the geometric mean produces a more appropriate result than a simple average because it smoothes outlying indicator scores, which is desirable at this stage of the development of the framework because many of the indicators still need to be tested for their suitability as proxies for estimating actual ML or FT activity. Finally, this approach always results in a score on the seven-point scale, making results easier to understand.

The scores for each analysis module are aggregated to produce a score for the overall likelihood of substantial ML or FT abuse occurring in each jurisdiction. For ML, the aggregated likelihood score calculates the geometric mean from each module listed in the third column of Table 9.1. The equation used, which follows, mirrors the outline structure of the key risk events in that table and calculates the geometric means within brackets first:

$$ML\ likelihood = geometric\ means\ of: [[(A,B1),(C,D,E),(F,G)],\ [H],\ [(B2,((I,J,K,L,M),N)),(B3,(O,P,E2)),\ R1,\ R2],\ [(R3,R4),(R5,E3,B3)]].$$

9.5.5 Deriving Proxies for the Consequences of Substantial ML or of FT Being Successful

In order to identify the relevant consequences, choices must be made among the various consequences of ML and FT when conducting risk management. (See Box 9.1, above, which lists 25 categories of consequence.) The framework has, thus, been developed with flexibility to deal with varying objectives.

The framework focuses first on the generic objective of minimizing the amount of ML or FT that occurs successfully during any typical 12-month period. This objective is likely common across most AML/CFT regimes and it also provides a simple short-term consequence for analysis. This analysis focuses on the immediate consequences of the volume or value of the transactions produced during the process and the value of funds that are laundered or provided to terrorists. The framework provides for more complex indicators of consequence to be derived by collecting subjective views from experts about the potential effect of the likely level of successful ML or FT on various social, economic and political objectives. Thus, an important step when conducting a national risk assessment is to identify which objectives that can be affected by successful ML and FT are of most interest to the authorities.

For analyzing the relevant consequences, the proxy indicators for consequence are derived largely from the perceptions of officials, using a structured approach to make informed judgments and involving the use of pre-determined decision-making criteria and measurement scales. The process consists of informing the officials of the results of the likelihood analysis, presenting them with some, often general, information about the potential impact of successful ML or FT, and asking them to choose, using pre-determined decision-making criteria and measurement scales, how each objective of interest to the authorities is affected by the amount of successful ML or FT that is likely occurring.

The generic short-term consequences of the volume or value of the transactions produced and value of funds that are laundered is analyzed using a mix of objective data and surveys of perceptions.[12] The objective data relates mainly to information about the nature and size of the business conducted by the institutions that might be abused as intermediaries in the ML process. The surveys ask informed officials to make their best informed judgment of the volume and value of ML transactions likely taking place within those institutions, taking into account previous analysis of the POC environment, and of the identified vulnerabilities.

The broader consequences of ML or FT abuse on relevant social, economic and political objectives are analyzed almost exclusively by gathering the authorities' perceptions.

For scoring the relevant consequences, the approach for organizing and scoring indicators for consequences is similar to the approach taken for indicators of likelihood. That is, each relevant consequence is analyzed and scored using a structure of factors and sub-factors, and their indicators, relevant to that consequence. The decision-making criteria, measurement scales and scoring for factors and their indicators are also based on a seven-point semi-qualitative ordinal scale. A higher score indicates that the consequences from successful ML or FT will be more severe on the identified objective.

Finally, we aggregate scores to derive an overall proxy for consequences of substantial ML or of FT being successful. The framework enables ML consequences to be analyzed for any one social, economic or political objective, or for an overall proxy for ML or FT consequences to be derived using the same aggregation method used for likelihood analysis. That is, for any relevant consequence, if there is more than one indicator, these are aggregated using their geometric mean to produce a score for that consequence. An overall proxy for all ML or FT consequences can be derived by aggregating all of the scores for the identified consequences based on their geometric mean.[13]

9.6 DERIVING AND ASSESSING THE LEVEL OF NATIONAL ML OR FT RISK

The overall level of national ML or FT risk is derived by combining the jurisdiction's ML or FT likelihood and consequences proxy scores, and assessing whether the

Table 9.2 Risk level scores

Risk level score	Risk level descriptor	Risk mitigation priority
> 6–7	Extremely higher risk	Urgent priority
> 5–6	Much higher risk	Much higher priority
> 4–5	Higher risk	Higher priority
> 3–4	Medium risk	Medium priority
> 2–3	Lower risk	Lower priority
> 1–2	Much lower risk	Much lower priority
> 0–1	Very much lower risk	Very much lower priority

result falls within acceptable bounds. The combination can be done in two ways to aid understanding:

a. First, the two proxy scores can be combined using their geometric mean. This results in a one-dimensional score which can be compared against the pre-determined scale in Table 9.2 to assess whether the overall ML risk fits within acceptable bounds, or whether it indicates that further steps need to be taken to mitigate the risk.
b. Second, the two proxy scores can be combined and presented via a risk matrix. This still allows for an assessment of whether the level of risk is acceptable–but with the added dimension of identifying the relative contribution of likelihood and consequences.

The framework also provides for national ML or FT risk to be assessed using different combinations of component parts of likelihood and consequences to facilitate understanding of the nature of ML or FT risk. Thus, it is possible to present a risk matrix or graph that shows the likelihood score plotted against the score for each of the identified consequences. The opposite approach can also be taken – to show the overall consequence score plotted against each of the likelihood analysis module scores. In addition, consequences may vary depending on whether the context is domestic or international. Hence, the framework also enables some consequences to be measured against both absolute scales and gross domestic product. In addition, the framework can also produce more granular information for use in other exercises, such as sector or product ML or FT risk assessments.

9.7 CONCLUSION

The Fund staff's framework for conducting national assessments of ML and FT risk is based upon international standards for risk management. The framework defines ML and FT through specific, contextual definitions of threats, vulnerabilities and consequences. Application of the framework is based upon deconstructing the ML or FT process to focus on key ML or FT risk events, then analyzing the drivers and enablers of those events via indicators of risk analysis modules that collectively produce a proxy of the likelihood of substantial ML or of FT occurring successfully. That proxy for likelihood is combined with a proxy for the consequences of successful ML or FT abuse to produce the national level of ML or FT risk. Implementing the framework involves the collection of objective and subjective data for analysis against pre-determined decision-making criteria to enable scoring within the analysis modules on a seven-point ordinal scale.

The framework will continue to evolve through its application in the context of technical assistance, assessments and surveillance. Thus far, the framework has been tested mainly in the context of assisting members to conduct national risk assessments, but it has also been informed by ongoing discussions within the FATF concerning risk-based approaches to AML/CFT controls, and it should prove helpful to staff providing AML/CFT support to the Fund's surveillance mission. Going forward, staff remain particularly interested in validating and refining various aspects of the framework, including, in particular, the range of indicators, and the decision-making criteria involved in defining their interrelationships. Over time it is expected that the application of the framework will help member countries to focus their scarce AML/CFT resources on risk mitigation initiatives where there is the most to gain.

NOTES

* The views expressed herein are those of the author and should not be attributed to the IMF, its Executive Board, or its management.

1. The proceeds derive from a 'predicate crime', which is described in the FATF Recommendations as encompassing 20 categories of offenses.
2. The framework developed by Fund staff is based on ISO 31000, 'Risk management – principles and guidelines, which was adopted by the International Standards Organization (ISO) and published on November 13, 2009.
3. The staff's pilot tests of the proposed framework suggest that a substantial ML amount in absolute terms might be at least $100 million annually for a given product, service or sector within a jurisdiction and perhaps $1 billion for any given jurisdiction.
4. The amount of $10 million annually is suggested as substantial FT activity – based on the cost of substantial one-off terrorist incidents and estimates of the annual operating costs of major terrorist organizations.
5. Under the proposed framework any transfer of domestic POC out of the jurisdiction is considered to be a ML transaction, so the full amount of domestic POC is considered to be potentially launderable.
6. Including associates and advisers.
7. The FATF recognizes that preventive and suppressive (i.e., the criminal justice operational chain) measures must interact to ensure that perpetrators are caught. First, the effectiveness of the CJS operational chain is impacted directly by the quantity and quality of information fed to the law enforcement intelligence function by reporting entities. Second, FATF preventive measures to deter launderers and financiers from abusing the financial system are only effective if the launderers and terrorists perceive that the information being collected about them and reported is used to secure convictions and impose sanctions (see FATF 2010).
8. The focus in the staff's framework is analyzing whether the ML or FT criminal behavior is being effectively pursued and suppressed through applying criminal sanctions rather than focusing on which criminal offense the sanction used derived from.
9. A similar table will be developed subsequently for FT.
10. Where it is not possible to obtain data to score any indicators for a factor or sub-factor, scores default to a preliminary value of five on the seven-point scale (this equates to 'higher likelihood' – unless there is compelling information justifying a different view (e.g., regional or peer results may be more appropriate). Where there is indecision about which score to assign on the pre-determined scale, the preferred approach is to adopt the higher score of those being considered.
11. Note that for the modules that analyze indicators broken down by institution types there is an intermediate step to aggregate the score in proportion to the scale of activity being undertaken within each type.

12. Conducted either as formal one-on-one surveys or within group sessions in workshops.
13. This approach assumes that all relevant consequences carry equal weight. It may need modification to assign weights reflecting the relative importance of each consequence that are of interest to the national authorities.

REFERENCES

Buscaglia, E. (2008), 'The paradox of expected punishment: legal and economic factors determining success and failure in the fight against organized crime', *Review of Law and Economics*, **4** (1) 290–317.

Eide, E. (2000), 'Economics of criminal behaviour', in B. Bouckaert and G. De Geest (eds), *Encyclopedia of Law and Economics*, Cheltenham, UK and Northampton, MA, USA: Edward Elgar Publishing.

FATF (2007), *Guidance on the Risk-Based Approach to Combating Money Laundering and Terrorist Financing: High-Level Principles and Procedures*, Paris: FATF.

FATF (2010), *Working Group of Typologies, Operational Issues: Recommendations*, 27 & 28 October 2010 Q Paris: FATF.

International Monetary Fund (IMF) (2001), 'Financial system abuse, financial crime and money laundering', Background Paper (SM/01/46), February 12, 2001.

Masciandaro, D. (1999), 'Money laundering: the economics of regulation', *European Journal of Law and Economics*, **7**, 225–40.

Unger, B. (2007), *The Scale and Impacts of Money Laundering*, Cheltenham, UK and Northampton, MA, USA: Edward Elgar Publishing.

10. Why do some states tolerate money laundering? On the competition for illegal money

Killian J. McCarthy

10.1 INTRODUCTION

Money laundering is the lifeline of the criminal industry. It is the mechanism through which criminals and criminal organisations 'conceal or disguise the nature, location, source, ownership or control' of their ill-gotten gains, so as to make it possible to invest or to consume the proceeds of crime (Gnutzmann et al. 2010).[1]

As such, it would seem to be self-evident that every country would want to tackle money laundering. Even more so when the existence of a money laundering market is said to destabilise the legitimate economy, and to act as a multiplier for crime, corruption, bribery and terrorism. The costs of money laundering, in fact, are so significant that European legislators have suggested the money laundering market threatens to 'shake the very foundations of society' (Directive 2005/60/ EC).

It is perhaps surprising, therefore, to learn that the enthusiasm with which national governments apply international anti-money laundering policies (hereafter AML) varies significantly from country to country. The variance in AML regimes is so significant, in fact, that the Financial Action Task Force (FATF) – the anti-money laundering organisation founded by the then G7, and now located in the OECD – felt it necessary to identify a number of 'Non-Cooperative Countries and Territories' (NCCT); that is, countries which had 'severe deficiencies' in their AML regimes.[2] The most extreme of these, the Seychelles, was actively encouraging money laundering and, once upon a time, was seen to have publicly invited criminals to invest their ill-gotten gains, under the promise of immunity from prosecution.

The Seychelles long ago caved to international pressures. But others remain problematic. In 2009, the FATF noted its 'concerns' over Iran, Turkmenistan, Pakistan, Uzbekistan, São Tomé and Príncipe, and has requested greater compliance on their behalf.[3] In addition, the FATF Grey List (2011) – which was constructed to monitor the application of standards on financial transparency – adds Nauru, Niue, Guatemala and Uruguay to the list of suspect states. These four states have committed to international standards, but have not yet substantially implemented them. But dozens more have only partially implemented FATF agreements and standards.[4]

But why should money laundering be tolerated in some jurisdictions and not in others? In this chapter we attempt to answer this question by reviewing some of the recent developments from the literature on the economics of money laundering. In section 10.2 we profile the industry, and introduce the key players. In section 3 we then employ the investigative technique of asking 'cui bono' – that is 'who benefits' – from a policy of toleration. And, finally, in section 4, on the basis of previous discussions, we present our conclusions and policy recommendations.

10.2 MONEY LAUNDERING

To answer the question of why some states tolerate money laundering while others do not, we first review the literature on crime and criminal behaviour and on the attraction of money laundering as well as the paradox of the state tolerating its existence. In doing so, the purpose of this section is to introduce the industry and its players.

10.2.1 The Market for Money Laundering

10.2.1.1 Crime and criminalisation

Variously defined as 'deviant behaviour [which] violates the prevailing norms and cultural standards on how humans ought to behave', as a 'public wrong', and as an exploit 'injurious to the community' (Ormerod 2005), crime exists and crime endures, because crime offers the individual an opportunity for private gain. Crime provides the individual with power, influence and authority. And so crime is the unavoidable consequence of human ambition and creativity, and the dark side of the human entrepreneurial spirit. It is held to be 'wrong' and 'injurious' because the private gain it creates for the individual typically benefits the criminal far less then they cost society. Estimates place the cost of crime to the US, for example, at about $1 trillion per annum (Takats 2007; Reuter and Truman 2004; Anderson 1999).

Thus, inevitable as it may be, society can tolerate only the lowest level of crime. And as a result, it is forced to 'tip the scales' in favour of legitimate activity by criminalising all 'injurious' behaviour. In observing that crime is profit motivated, however, 'balance' can be achieved through the manipulation of the criminal profit formula. By increasing the risks of capture, for example, or the duration and severity of punishment, it is suggested that the costs of crime can be made to outweigh the benefits and crime can be discouraged (Ehrlich 1973; Blumstein and Nagin 1977; Wolpin 1978).

10.2.1.2 The money laundering market

Not all criminals can, however, be as easily manipulated. In a world where the proceeds of crime are measured in the tens of billions (Unger, and Rawlings 2008), and where the sheer complexity of the criminal operation often makes the risk of detection and the threat of punishment too remote a possibility to act as a serious deterrent, other measures are necessarily instituted. The creation of a distinction between money earned in the legitimate and illegitimate sectors is then often touted as the solution.

The distinction between legal and illegal monies means that a 'dirty dollar' earned in the criminal economy is worth less than a 'clean' one earned in the legitimate economy. 'Dirty money' has fewer functions. And so the distinction reduces the profitability of crime. Criminal incomes then are 'taxed' at a rate equal to the state's enthusiasm for a crime-free society. Because crime already pays less (Wilson and Abrahamse 1992), any loss in profitability implies an adverse shock to the supply of crime. And because of this, profit motivated criminal activity will be reduced.

As an unintended consequence, however, a demand for 'money laundering' services will be created. These services, defined as financial services conducted 'to conceal or disguise the nature, location, source, ownership or control' of money, aim to make it possible for criminals to invest or to consume the proceeds of crime.[5]

Table 10.1 The scale of the money laundering industry

Study	Period	Value (billions)
Schuster	1994	500–800
United Nations	1994	700–1000
IMF/Interpol	1996	500
Kerry	1997	420–1000
the Economist	1997	400
Walker	1998	2850
United Nations	1998	700–1000
United Nations	1998	700–1000
NCIS	1998	1300
NCIS	2001	1900
the Economist	2001	600
CITE	2002	1000–1600
Schneider	2002	640
Agarwal & Agarwal	2002	500–1000
Agarwal & Agarwal	2002	2000–2500
NCIS	2003	2100
Schneider	2003	680
Schneider	2004	720
Schneider	2005	760
Schneider	2006	790
Baker	2007	1000–1600

Source: Reproduced from Schneider (2008).

As discussed elsewhere in this volume, the Bank of International Settlements (BIS), the Organisation for Economic Co-operation Development (OECD), the G8 and G20, the European Union (EU), several departments of the United Nations (UN), the World Bank (WB), the International Monetary Fund (IMF) and the Financial Stability Forum (FSF) are all involved in efforts to assess (and reduce) the scale of the money laundering industry. And while it has been suggested that measuring money laundering is no more possible than measuring a 'fata morgana' (van Duyne 2006), a number of heroic attempts (see Table 10.1) have been made 'to measure the immeasurable' (Unger 2007).

The IMF and the World Bank, for example, have estimated that some 2–4 per cent of the world's GDP stems from illicit sources. Agarwal and Agarwal (2004; 2006), using regression analysis and forecasts, suggest an even higher level of 5–6, per cent. At this rate somewhere between $2.0–2.5 trillion should flow through the money laundering market on an annual basis. Walker (1999, 2004, 2007) however, claims that this is too low a figure and, using input-output and gravity models, proposes that the true amount is more like $3 trillion per annum. Each estimate is subject to some criticism (cf. Reuter 2007), and are variously said to be overblown – either by media hype, or measurement errors – by as much +/−20 per cent (Schneider 2008). Despite all this the consensus remains that the market for money laundering is a significant one.

10.2.1.3 On the effects of money laundering

Irrespective of its actual scale, and unintended as its very existence may be, money laundering is of tremendous economic significance to the domestic economy. In the short term money laundering distorts prices, rates of consumption, saving and investment; it increases import/export volatility, the demand for money and interest and exchange rates; and it alters the availability of credit. In the short run, money laundering therefore negatively impacts the operation of the legitimate economy.

However, in the long term money laundering endangers the survival of the host countries' financial sector – not only because of the risk it poses in terms of solvability and liquidity, but also in terms of reputation and profitability – which, in turn, threatens the continuance of foreign direct investment (FDI) flows into the country and denies it an instrument for growth. Additionally, money laundering acts as a multiplier for crime, corruption, bribery and terrorism, which at its worst can undermine both the democratic institutions of the state and the foreign policy objectives of its people. Therefore, in the long term money laundering can be seen to pose an existential threat to the state. And for this reason, it must be tackled by the civilised state.

10.2.2 The Money Launderer

10.2.2.1 On the irrepressibility of the money launderers

The supplier of such services – the criminal agent – is referred to as the money launderer. Supplying the market for money laundering is quite clearly a profitable venture, of which the income is derived in cash. The disposal of this cash can sometimes be problematic. *Forbes Magazine* estimated (in 1989) that the Colombian drugs lord, Pablo Escobar, amassed a personal wealth of $25bn. The problem is that only so much of this can be used to purchase tangible assets, like jewellery, cars, boats and houses. In fact, research suggests that as little as 20 per cent of criminal incomes are consumed (Unger 2007). Because of the distinction between clean and dirty money, criminals looking to 'conceal or disguise the nature, location, source, ownership or control' of their ill-gotten gains are forced to 'invest' the remainder of their resources with money launderers (Gnutzmann et al. 2010). Estimates show that criminals are willing to pay at least 5 to 10 per cent – and possibly as much as 50 per cent – above the international rates of return on capital to procure such services (Unger 2007).

In a world where no 'big bills [are] left on the side walk' (Olson 1996) and where estimates suggest that as much as 80 per cent of criminal proceeds are laundered (Walker 2004), the presence of a positive interest rate differential means that there will always be an enterprising arbitrageur willing to supply the money laundering market. Entrepreneurs are ubiquitous (Baumol 1996), and as long as this positive differential exists, the attraction to money laundering will remain constant.

10.2.2.2 On the role of government regulation

The costs incurred by the enterprising arbitrageur – that is, the money launderer – will vary, and will depend directly upon the costs of circumventing anti-money laundering (AML) regulation. As such, the money launderers' costs will be directly proportional both to the levels of financial transparency, and to the levels of AML regulation. Because both of these can be set by government policy, it is suggested that government can indirectly control the supply of national money laundering services.

10.2.3 The Paradox of Toleration

From the preceding discussion it is clear that the money laundering industry comes with some huge costs and benefits. On the one hand the industry is of an immense scale: in 1999, Walker valued the industry at almost $3 trillion. More than a decade of inflation and economic, financial, political and legal integration later, it is likely to be even higher today. This creates some huge opportunities for the unscrupulous to profit. On the other hand, tolerating money laundering multiplies crime and corruption, and threatens the national economy. The externalities that a policy of toleration creates are therefore not to be sneezed at. The paradox then is: if crime is destructive, if government can control the levels of money laundering and if money laundering is a threat to the state, why is the market for money laundering tolerated?

10.3 MONEY LAUNDERING: CUI BONO?

In this section we attempt to answer this question. We follow the money laundering trail from beginning to end, and employ an age-old investigative technique for understanding criminal behaviour – the concept of 'cui bono'[6] – to see who profits from money laundering. We consider the effects of money laundering on three distinct regions: (a) the crime-producing countries, that is, the countries in which criminal goods are produced; (b) the developed countries; and (c) the small economies. In each of these we consider the incentives for three actors: (a) the criminal producer; (b) the money laundering agent; and (c) the domestic government.

10.3.1 The Crime-Producing Countries

In some parts of the world, legal, political and economic forces collide and conspire to create a situation hostile to the development of legitimate business. Demand in the developed world for counterfeit goods, prostitutes and drugs, however, creates a number of alternative opportunities for criminal entrepreneurs driven by human ambition and unhindered by human morality. The result is the creation of what we refer to as the *crime-producing countries*. These countries are almost entirely sustained by black-market businesses. In a study of the period 1990–1993, Fleming et al. (2000) identify Guatemala, Mexico, Peru, Panama and Nigeria as major crime-producing countries. While as little as 8 per cent of GDP in the developed world was derived from black-market businesses, it was around 60 per cent of GDP in Guatemala, Mexico, Peru and Panama, and as much 76 per cent in Nigeria.

Crime is clearly a profitable venture in these countries. The 'problem' is that black-market businesses pay in cash and therefore crime generates an income that requires the services of a money laundering agent. Any one of the black markets identified in Table 10.2 could be used to understand the origins of money laundering and the effect of

Table 10.2 Estimating the black market

Black-market goods	Estimated annual market value ($ billions)
Illegal drugs	322
Piracy & counterfeiting	288
Prostitution	108
Prescription drugs	73
Smuggling–other	50

the market on the crime-producing countries of the world.[7] But of the various markets, the illegal drugs trade accounts for the most sizeable portion.

Globally, and on an annual basis, the illegal drugs industry generates something in the region of $300–400 billion (UNODC, 2010). And according to US government figures,[8] 21 countries – namely, Afghanistan, The Bahamas, Belize, Bolivia, Burma, Colombia, Costa Rica, Dominican Republic, Ecuador, Guatemala, Haiti, Honduras, India, Jamaica, Laos, Mexico, Nicaragua, Pakistan, Panama, Peru, and Venezuela – compete to supply this trade. These countries are described as being the 'major drugs producers' – or, in our case, the crime-producing countries – and are responsible, it is suggested, for supplying the lion's share of the illegal drugs market (see Figure 10.1).

Eighty per cent of the revenues created through the trade in illegal drugs are laundered (Unger 2007). And so – minus the launderer's fees and the other operational costs of supplying the market – a large part of the $300–400 billion created in the industry is returned to the criminal producers in cash. But for the governments of these countries, this is one investment that is not to be welcomed.

Firstly, crime breeds crime, and leads to corruption; a $300–400 billion industry needs employees, supporting services, and political allies. Political corruption, however, further reduces the probability of legitimate investment, and increases the state's dependency on the black market. Secondly, normal 'trickle down economics' can hardly be seen to apply in the criminal sector. The beneficiaries of the drugs trade do not pay taxes, and so the wealth is not shared. In fact, the industry is famous for a centralisation of vast amounts of wealth and power; as noted above, the Colombian drugs dealer, Pablo Escobar, amassed a personal wealth of $25 billion during his reign as head of the Medellín Cartel, in a country that was known to be one of the poorest and most unequal in South America. And finally, supplying the industry comes with some huge external costs: there were 61,333 drug-related arrests in Colombia in 1992, and 27,100 violent deaths, including some 600 policemen.[9] Taken together, the total social costs of crime clearly outweigh its benefits.

Money laundering is the lifeline that allows the drugs industry to survive. So, in the crime producing countries, cui bono from the existence of money laundering?

Clearly, the government, the legitimate economy, and the general populous do not benefit from money laundering; for the vast majority, black-market industries lead to death and destruction, and lost opportunity. And so, in following the money-laundering trail back to its origins, we can see that the producers of crime – that is, the drugs lords that supply the trade – and the money launderers – the criminal agents that make it profitable and allow it to survive – have an incentive to encourage money laundering. But not

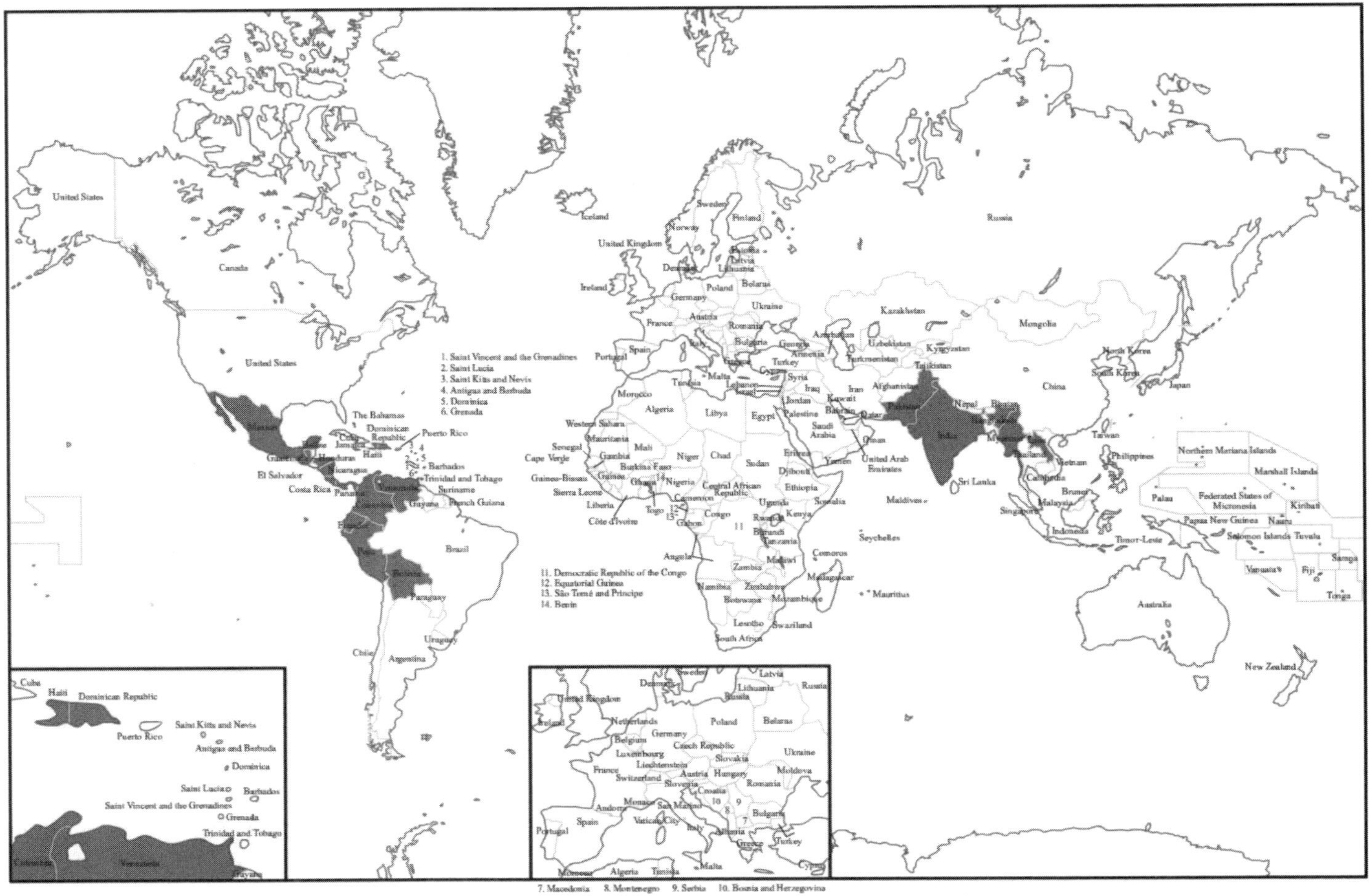

Figure 10.1 The major drugs producing countries

the states that harbour them. In the crime-producing countries, and from an economic perspective, the state has an incentive to tackle crime.

10.3.2 The Developed Countries

In the developed world, the story is somewhat more complex. Because in the developed world, the number of interests, and the number of opportunities, multiply.

In the first place it is demand from the developed world that fuels the illegal drugs trade. Drugs may originate in the crime-producing centres of the world, but only because consumers in the developed world are willing and able to pay for them. According to UN estimates, somewhere between 155 and 250 million people (or 3.5–5.7 per cent of people aged 15–64) used illicit substances at least once in 2008 (UNODC 2011). And the vast majority of these were based in the developed countries (Table 10.3).

The drug barons of the crime-producing countries, and their suppliers in the developed world, clearly have an interest in supplying the illegal drugs trade. And obviously, so too do the money launderers. Some 80 per cent of the revenues raised in the black market cross the money launderer's desk. And with rates of at least 5–10 per cent, and as much as 50 per cent above the international rates of return, each country's domestic entrepreneurs have a clear incentive to profit from the crimes in other jurisdictions. Money launderers – often legitimate bankers sitting in Amsterdam, Frankfurt, London or Zürich – face little more than the decision to invest legal or illegally generated money. Because *pecunia non olet*,[10] and because the money laundering industry offers money launderers high profits at low risk, the temptations for those in-the-know in the developed world to engage in money laundering are high.

But what about the state? The producers of crime (Figure 10.1) and the suppliers of money-laundering services (Figure 10.2) are not one in the same: clearly, it is the developed countries that wash most of the world's criminal monies. But is there state involvement? Or a competition between states to attract criminal investment?

On the face of it, there are huge incentives for the government of an open economy to tolerate money laundering. In a closed economy, the state will be forced to 'internalise' the total costs of crime. And, as a result, the state will suffer the (negative) net consequence of criminal activity. Accordingly, crime prevention will quickly become a political priority. And financial transparency – as a tool for tackling crime – will be set at a higher level.

Few economies today, however, can be described as being closed; even North Korea has trade relations with the Russian Federation, the People's Republic of China, Syria, Iran and Vietnam. Globalisation and economic integration means that the incident and effect of crime can be separated from the positive cash flows that they create. In other words, the dirty business of creating criminal profits can be done in one part of the world, while the 'odour-less' profits that it creates can be transferred and invested somewhere else. Since money does not stink, every government has an incentive to tackle domestic crime, while simultaneously encouraging their domestic arbitrageur to profit from the criminal revenues created in other jurisdictions. By lowering regulatory standards on financial transparency, governments can therefore increase the likelihood of attracting criminal investment. Moving from the closed to the open economy, openness and globalisation are thus seen to erode the incentive for higher levels of financial transparency,

Table 10.3 The major drug consuming countries

Region/subregion	Cannabis users in the past year		Opiate users in the past year		Cocaine users in the past year		Amphetamines-group users in the past year		Ecstasy users in the past year	
	Number (lower)	Number (upper)	Number (lower)	Number (upper)	Number (lower)	Number (upper)	Number (lower)	Number (upper)	Number (lower)	Number (upper)
Africa	**27,680,000**	**52,790,000**	**680,000**	**2,930,000**	**1,020,000**	**2,670,000**	**1,550,000**	**5,200,000**	**350,000**	**1,930,000**
North Africa	4,680,000	10,390,000	130,000	540,000	30,000	50,000	260,000	540,000	estimate cannot be calculated	
West and Central Africa	14,050,000	22,040,000	160,000	340,000	640,000	830,000	estimate cannot be calculated		estimate cannot be calculated	
Eastern Africa	4,490,000	9,190,000	150,000	1,730,000	estimate cannot be calculated		estimate cannot be calculated		estimate cannot be calculated	
Southern Africa	4,450,000	11,170,000	240,000	320,000	290,000	900,000	310,000	1,090,000	220,000	420,000
Americas	**38,210,000**	**40,030,000**	**2,290,000**	**2,440,000**	**8,720,000**	**9,080,000**	**4,760,000**	**5,890,000**	**3,040,000**	**3,280,000**
North America	29,950,000	29,950,000	1,290,000	1,380,000	6,170,000	6,170,000	3,090,000	3,200,000	2,490,000	2,490,000
Central America	580,000	600,000	100,000	110,000	120,000	140,000	320,000	320,000	20,000	30,000
The Caribbean	430,000	-1,730,000	60,000	90,000	110,000	320,000	30,000	510,000	10,000	240,000
South America	7,300,000	7,530,000	840,000	870,000	2,330,000	2,450,000	1,320,000	1,860,000	510,000	530,000
Asia	**31,510,000**	**64,580,000**	**6,460,000**	**12,540,000**	**430,000**	**2,270,000**	**4,430,000**	**37,990,000**	**2,370,000**	**15,620,000**
East/South-East Asia	5,370,000	23,940,000	2,830,000	5,060,000	390,000	1,070,000	3,430,000	20,680,000	1,460,000	6,850,000
South Asia	16,490,000	27,550,000	1,390,000	3,310,000	estimate cannot be calculated		estimate cannot be calculated		estimate cannot be calculated	
Central Asia	1,890,000	2,140,000	340,000	340,000	estimate cannot be calculated		estimate cannot be calculated		estimate cannot be calculated	
Near and Middle East	7,790,000	10,950,000	1,890,000	3,820,000	estimate cannot be calculated		estimate cannot be calculated		estimate cannot be calculated	
Europe	**29,370,000**	**29,990,000**	**3,290,000**	**3,820,000**	**4,570,000**	**4,970,000**	**2,500,000**	**3,190,000**	**3,850,000**	**4,080,000**
West/Central Europe	20,850,000	20,990,000	1,090,000	1,370,000	4,110,000	4,130,000	1,600,000	1,710,000	2,180,000	2,190,000
East/South-East Europe	8,520,000	9,010,000	2,210,000	2,460,000	470,000	840,000	900,000	1,480,000	1,680,000	1,890,000
Oceania	**2,140,000**	**3,410,000**	**120,000**	**150,000**	**330,000**	**390,000**	**470,000**	**630,000**	**840,000**	**910,000**
GLOBAL ESTIMATE	**128,910,000**	**190,750,000**	**12,840,000**	**21,880,000**	**15,070,000**	**19,380,000**	**13,710,000**	**52,900,000**	**10,450,000**	**25,820,000**

Source: UNODC (2011).

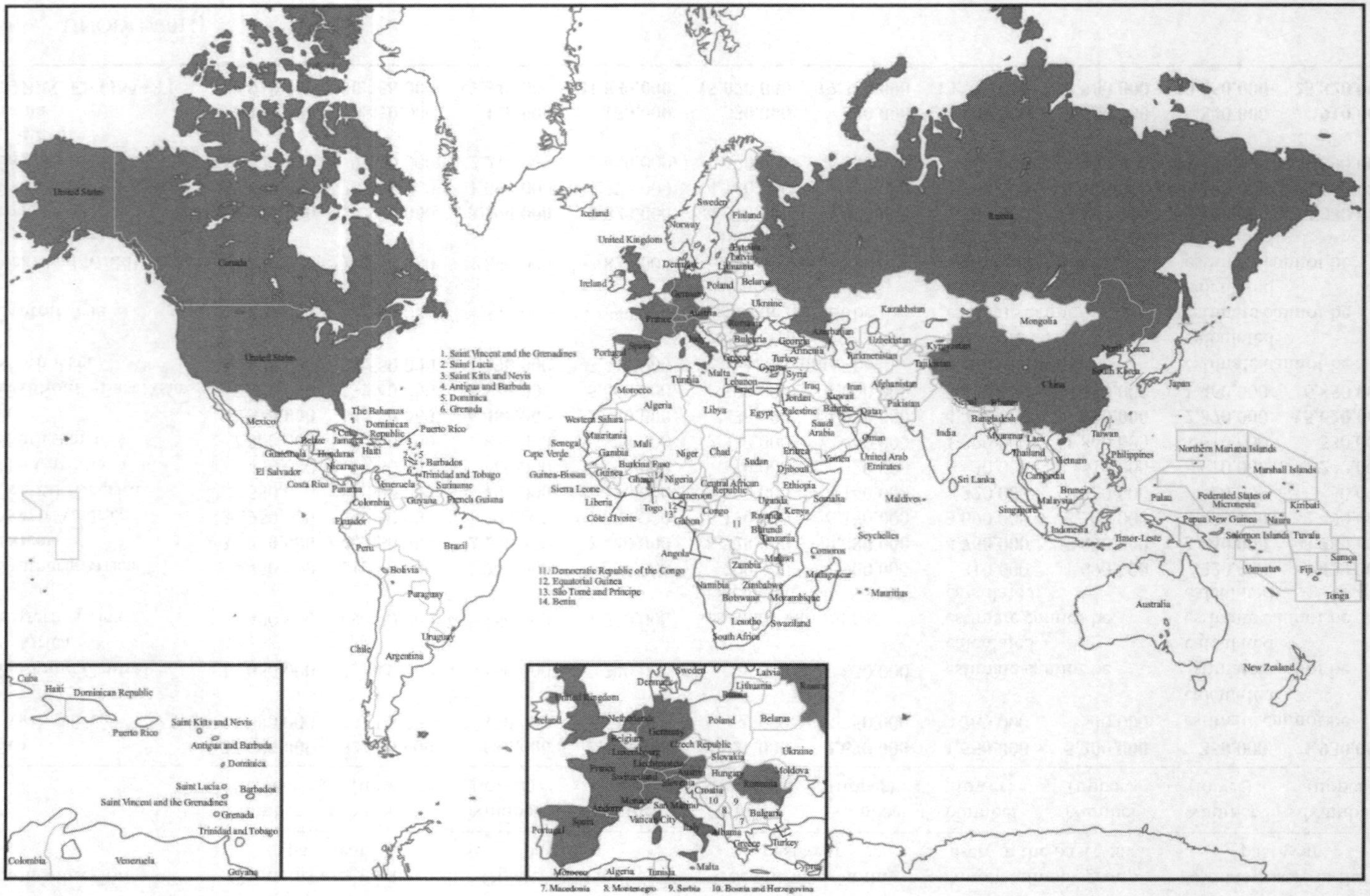

Figure 10.2 The centres of money laundering

simply because those countries with a lower level of regulatory standards will attract a higher level of criminal investment.

For the developed countries, following this logic, we thus come to a number of conclusions on the incentives for governments to engage with crime. Firstly, we see that governments in the developed world will permit domestic money laundering in order to attract criminal investment flows. Secondly, we see that these governments will take advantage of the confused multitude of rules and definitions that govern the market to increase their comparative advantage in the market. As a consequence, we would expect to observe a 'beggar-thy-neighbour' policy in relation to the competition for criminal monies, and an international 'regulatory race to the bottom' (Sinn 2003). Thirdly, we see that while developed countries will tackle crime in their own jurisdictions, they have few incentives to tackle the crime – and in the process reduce the profitability of crime – in other jurisdictions. And finally, and because those countries that 'defect' from the internationally agreed standards will attract more investment, every developed country will be incentivised to make international declarations and agreements on tackling money laundering in their neighbours' economies, while tolerating criminal investment in their own. However, as explained by Gnutzmann et al. (2010), such an analysis is incomplete.

10.3.3 The Small Economies

Traditionally, the money-laundering trail ends at the identification of the major drugs producing countries (Figure 10.1), and the conclusion that the developed world is the source of the problem. Such a conclusion is, however, incomplete because there is an important distinction yet to be made between two types of money laundering: 'intended' and 'unintended'.

To actively attract money laundering, the state must lower its financial standards. In an open and developed economy, low standards of financial transparency do not merely affect the market for money laundering, but will affect all sectors of the economy. Poor financial standards are likely, for example, to encourage the diversion of assets in businesses, to lead to poor supervision of companies (and hence reduce the quality of governance), and to encourage directly unproductive, profit-seeking activities. Because the state has only a few policy instruments with which to fight complex, white-collar crime – one of which is the level of financial transparency – these effects are the inescapable consequence of its decision to tolerate money laundering. As a result, we observe that there is a significant trade-off in the decision to tolerate money laundering, in so far as countries with large and developed economies have more to lose from money laundering then developing countries. In other words, countries with a large legal economy sector in absolute terms will be more affected by low financial standards, and will have more to lose by dropping them, and so the costs of tolerating money laundering for small economies vis-à-vis their larger counterparts will be reduced. Countries with a large legitimate economy can therefore be expected to avoid the money laundering market, while smaller economies, with less to lose, will be incentivised to embrace it. And it is this finding which provides an explanation for the varying zeal with which AML policy is pursued: not all countries will attempt to court criminal capital, because for some countries – the larger developed economies – the costs of doing so will outweigh the benefits.

It should be noted, however, that this does not mean that the 'giants [don't] wash more' (Unger 2007, p. 79). As Unger (2007, p. 191) points out, and as is confirmed by Figure 10.2, 'it is not [the] small states like Liechtenstein, Anguilla and Bermuda' . . . [but] large, industrialised OECD economies that are the main conduits for laundering money'. Walker (1999) estimates that 46.3 per cent of the world's money laundering originates in the Unites States. And as Unger (2007) shows, Luxembourg – home to the European Court of Justice and the secretariat of the European Parliament – is the most attractive destination for money launderers in the world. Of the top 20 largest economies, as ranked in terms of nominal GDP by the World Bank, only Sweden, in fact, is not listed as a 'Major Money Laundering Country' by the US Department of Justice, and of the top 50 largest economies, only five more join it.[11]

As Gnutzmann et al. (2010) show, however, there is an important distinction to be made between 'intended' and 'unintended' money laundering in terms of incentives. And the list of offenders, which are produced for the 'intended' and 'unintended' money launderers, are quite markedly different. The level of money laundering is, they recognise, probably far larger in the US, Switzerland and the UK than it is in most of the Pacific/Caribbean put together. But the key here is that this is 'unintended' money laundering, which arises out of the complexity and scale of the financial systems that these countries operate. The incentives for the state to sponsor money laundering are substantially weaker for the developed countries – simply because in doing so the developed countries will hurt their more significant legitimate sector – and because of this the incidence of 'intended' money laundering will be substantially lower.

Small, open, or developing economies, on the other hand, have a very strong incentive to actively promote 'intended' money laundering, to flaunt international anti-money laundering agreements, to participate in the international deregulatory race to the bottom, to free-ride on the crime-stopping efforts of the developed nations, and to attract investment, almost at any cost. Therefore, while the small island, transitional or developing economies may – potentially at least – represent only a small proportion of the total money laundering market, they are, we suggest, more likely to have a far higher share in relation to their economic importance. For these reasons, the 'Seychelles strategy' of states deliberately inviting capital under the guarantee of immunity from prosecution (Unger and Rawlings 2008) is, it is suggested, far more dangerous to both the rule of law and the legitimate economy of other territories.

10.3.4 Cui Bono?

Thus, in following the money-laundering trail back to its origin, we see that: (1) the crime-producing countries have no incentive to tolerate crime, or money laundering, and that the governments of these countries are incentivised to fight crime, and to tackle money laundering; (2) that the developed countries have an incentive to tackle both crime and money laundering, because money laundering threatens to undermine the operation of their far more significant legitimate economies; and finally (3) we see that small, open, or developing countries, with less to lose, or few other sources of growth, have an incentive to fight domestic crime, while profiting from the criminal revenues created in other countries. Criminals and money launderers everywhere have an incentive to permit money laundering, but only the governments of the small economies, we conclude, have an incentive to tolerate money laundering.

10.4 CONCLUSIONS

10.4.1 Summary

In this chapter we have argued that crime is the flip-side of human ambition, drive and enterprise, and that it is an almost unavoidable consequence of human interaction. Criminals are entrepreneurs, we suggest, who pursue unproductive or destructive behaviour (Baumol 1990). And in making a distinction between 'clean' and 'dirty' money, government attempts to fight crime simply create a market for money laundering, which aims to conceal the sources of criminal profits, so that the proceeds of crime to be enjoyed by the criminal in the legitimate economy.

Money laundering is the lifeline of the criminal industry. As such, it would seem to be self-evident that every country would want to tackle money laundering. Even more so when money laundering is said to destabilise the legitimate economy, and to act as a multiplier for crime, corruption, bribery and terrorism, to the point of threatening to 'shake the very foundations of society' (Directive 2005/60/ EC).

So why should money laundering be tolerated in some jurisdictions and not in others? This chapter has attempted to answer this question, by following the money-laundering trail from beginning to end, and employing an age-old investigative technique for understanding criminal behaviour – the concept of 'cui bono' – to see who profits from money laundering. The effects of money laundering were considered on: (a) the crime-producing countries, that is, the countries in which criminal goods are produced; (b) the developed countries; and (c) the small, open economies. And in each of these we considered the incentives for three key actors: (a) the criminal producer; (b) their money laundering agents; and (c) the domestic government.

In doing so, and as summarised by Table 10.4, we see that: (1) the crime-producing countries have no incentive to tolerate crime or money laundering, and that the government of these countries are incentivised to fight crime and to tackle money laundering; (2) that the developed countries have an incentive to tackle both crime and money laundering, because money laundering threatens to undermine the operation of their legitimate economies; and finally (3) we see that developing countries, with few other sources of foreign direct investment have an incentive to fight domestic crime, while profiting

Table 10.4 Government incentives

Regions	Government Incentives		
	To tackle domestic crime	To tackle foreign crime	To tackle money laundering
Developed countries	X	X	X
Crime-producing countries	X	X	
Small, open economies	X		

from the criminal revenues created in other countries. In other words, as Gnutzmann et al. (2010) put it, the governments of the developing world are the only ones with an incentive to 'dance with the devil'.

10.4.2 Policy Recommendations

At first glance, the implications of our findings do not leave much room for celebration. We have argued that crime will endure, and that the money laundering market is the unavoidable consequence of criminal acts. We have shown that the incentives to tolerate money laundering vary quite significantly between countries, and that criminals need only find the weakest link in the international financial system to have their funds cleared. Only one country is needed to break the international 'chain of accountability', whereas effective anti-money laundering policy requires perfect collusion amongst nearly two hundred sovereign nation states.

Gnutzmann et al. (2010) offer three mechanisms for tackling money laundering. The first way, they suggest, is the legalistic approach to tackling money laundering, which would see international organisations draft conventions to challenge those states within which money laundering occurs. To date, this approach has, however, failed to bear much fruit, simply because many of the large and economically more powerful transgressors – such as the US and the UK – are too difficult to prosecute for any 'legal' violations of the convention.

The second approach documented by Gnutzmann et al. (2010), the so-called political approach has been slightly more successful. This chapter has argued that although the developed world is in absolute terms accountable for the largest part of the money laundering market, it is the smaller economies which should be targeted – for actively encouraging the practice, and for disregarding the international rule of law. Because smaller nations are more easily influenced by bilateral or multilateral pressure, the implication here is that money laundering could be reduced one country at a time. This has already happened with the Seychelles, which bowed to international political pressure over its money laundering policy. Because the political approach could be accused of allowing large and wealthy transgressors to persecute small and less significant ones, however, this approach has its ethical drawbacks.

Far more equitable is the third option, described by Gnutzmann et al. (2010) as the 'economic approach' to tackling money laundering. Large, developed countries, it suggests, bear the majority of the costs of money laundering – in so far as the money laundering market feeds those criminal industries that threaten the developing world – while the smaller countries bare the majority of the benefits – in terms of an inflow of criminal investment. Rich and developed countries thus suffer a money laundering 'externality', and as with optimal environmental protection policy, the solution is that the rich should pay the poor to internalise this externality. The economic approach proposed by Gnutzmann et al. (2010) would thus see small, open countries compensated for voluntarily turning their back on criminal investment, and for losing the lucrative investment that this brings, and would simultaneously reward them for embracing international law. The added benefit from such a measure, of course, would be that the anti-money laundering transfer could be used to provide the developing countries with financial aid, free from the stigma of being mere charity.

10.4.3 Final Words

The purpose of this chapter was understanding cui bono from the market in money laundering. In the process of following the money laundering trail, we see that both the crime-producing countries and the developed countries suffer from black-market trade, and have little incentive to tolerate money laundering. It is only the small, open, or developing countries that benefit from the market for money laundering. But convincing these to tackle the trade is a delicate business. Following Gnutzmann et al. (2010), however, we suggest that the most equitable way to tackle money laundering would be the economic solution – with its emphasis on funding 'carrots' rather than 'sticks' – and that only when this occurs can money laundering be effectively challenged. Convincing the richest countries to pay the weaker countries the trillions necessary to internalise the problem is, however, quite another question.

NOTES

1. See Stages of the Money Laundering Process, A Report to Congress in Accordance with 356(c) of the USA PATRIOT Act, December 2002.
2. There are currently no countries on the list of NCCTs. It has been suggested, however, that this may be due to political considerations, and that many of the countries listed in 2000/2001 may have been removed for 'apparently' rather than actually complying with AML best practice.
3. See: http://www.fatf-gafi.org/topics/high-riskandnon-Cooperativejurisdictions/documents/fatfstatement-concerningiranuzbekistanturkmenistanpakistanandsaotomeandprincipe-october-october2009.html
4. Including Andorra, Anguilla, Antigua and Barbuda, Argentina, Aruba, Australia, Austria, The Bahamas, Bahrain, Barbados, Belgium, Belize, Bermuda, Brazil, British Virgin Islands, Brunei, Canada, Cayman Islands, Chile, China, Cook Islands, Costa Rica, Cyprus, Czech Republic, Denmark, Dominica, Estonia, Finland, France, Germany, Gibraltar, Greece, Grenada, Guernsey, Hong Kong, Hungary, Iceland, India, Indonesia, Ireland, Isle of Man, Israel, Italy, Japan, Jersey, South Korea, Liberia, Liechtenstein, Luxembourg, Macao, Malaysia, Malta, Marshall Islands, Mauritius, Mexico, Monaco, Montserrat, Netherlands, Netherlands Antilles, New Zealand, Norway, Panama, Philippines, Poland, Portugal, Qatar, Russian Federation, St Kitts and Nevis, St Lucia, St Vincent and the Grenadines, Samoa, San Marino, Seychelles, Singapore, Slovakia, Slovenia, South Africa, Spain, Sweden, Switzerland, Turkey, Turks and Caicos Islands, United Arab Emirates, the United Kingdom, United States, US Virgin Islands, Vanuatu.
5. See Stages of the Money Laundering Process, A Report to Congress in Accordance with 356(c) of the USA PATRIOT Act, December 2002. Within the European legal framework: (1) the conversion or transfer of property; (2) the concealment or disguise of the true nature, source, location, disposition, movement, rights with respect to property; or (3) the acquisition, possession or use of property, knowing that such property is derived from criminal activity, are all activities which, when committed intentionally, are considered to be acts of money laundering. See also Council Directive 91/308/EEC of 10 June 1991 on the prevention of the use of the financial system for the purpose of money laundering.
6. Cui bono – or literally, to whose benefit – is a Latin adage, the usage of which dates back at least to Cicero, and is typically used to suggest that the person guilty of committing a crime may be found among those who have something to gain, chiefly with an eye towards financial gain.
7. See: http://www.havocscope.com/ranking/
8. Presidential Memorandum – Major Illicit Drug Transit or Major Illicit Drug Producing Countries, September 15, 2011, available at: http://www.whitehouse.gov/the-press-office/2011/09/15/presidential-memorandum-major-illicit-drug-transit
9. See the Inter-American Commission on Human Rights, http://www.cidh.org/countryrep/colombia93eng/chap.2.htm
10. *Pecunia non olet* ('money does not stink') is a Latin saying. The phrase originally related to the tax levied by the Roman emperor Vespasian upon the collection of urine in the 1st century.
11. See the website of the US Department of Justice: http://www.state.gov/j/inl/rls/nrcrpt/2005/vol2/html/42388.htm

REFERENCES

Agarwal, J.D. and A. Agarwal (2004), 'Globalization and international capital flows', *Finance India*, **19**, 611–41.

Agarwal, J.D. and A. Agarwal (2006), 'Money laudering: new forms of crime, victimization', presentation at the National Workshop on New Forms of Crime, Victimization, with reference to Money Laundering. Indian Society of Victimology, Department of Criminology, University of Madras, India.

Anderson, D. (1999), 'The aggregate burden of crime', *The Journal of Law and Economics*, **42**(2), 611–42.

Baumol, W.J. (1990), 'Entrepreneurship, productive, unproductive and destructive', *Journal of Political Economy*, **98**(5), 893–921.

Baumol, W. (1996), 'Entrepreneurship: productive, unproductive, and destructive', *Journal of Business Venturing*, **11**(1), 3–22.

Blumstein, A. and D. Nagin (1977), 'The deterrent effect of legal sanctions on draft evasion', *Stanford Law Review*, 241–76.

Ehrlich, I. (1973), Participation in illegitimate activities: a theoretical and empirical investigation, *Journal of Political Economy*, **81**(3), 521.

Fleming, M.H., J. Roman, and G. Farrell (2000), 'The shadow economy', *Journal of International Affairs*, **53**(2), 387–409.

Gnutzmann, H., K.J. McCarthy and B. Unger (2010), 'Dancing with the devil: country size and the incentive to tolerate money laundering', *International Review of Law and Economics*, **30**(3), 244–52.

Jenner, M.S. (2011), 'International drug trafficking: a global problem with a domestic solution', *Indianna Journal of Global Legal Studies*, **18**(2), 901–27.

Olson, M. (1996), 'Big bills left on the sidewalk: why some countries are rich and others poor', *Journal of Economic Perspectives*, **10**(2), 3–24.

Ormerod, D. (2005), *Smith and Hogan's Criminal Law*, Oxford: Oxford University Press.

Reuter, P. (2007), 'Are estimates of the volume of money laundering either useful or feasible?', Tackling Money Laundering Conference, University of Utrecht.

Reuter, Peter and E.M. Truman (2004), *Chasing Dirty Money: The Fight against Money Laundering*, Washington, DC: The Institute for International Economics.

Schneider, F. (2008), 'Money laundering and financial means of organized crime: some preliminary empirical findings', Paolo Baffi Centre Research Paper Series No. 2008–16.

Sinn, H-W. (2003), *The New Systems Competition*, Oxford: Blackwell Publishers.

Stages of the Money Laundering Process, A Report to Congress in Accordance with 356(c) of the USA PATRIOT Act, December 2002.

Takats, E. (2007), 'A theory of "crying wolf": the economics of money laundering enforcement', IMF working paper WP/07/81.

Unger, B. (2007), *The Scale and Impacts of Money Laundering*, Cheltenham, UK and Northampton, MA, USA: Edward Elgar Publishing.

Unger, B. and G. Rawlings (2008), 'Competing for criminal money'. *Global Business and Economics Review*, **10**(3), 331–52.

UNODC (2010), *World Drug Report.*

UNODC (2011), *World Drug Report.*

Van Duyne, P. (2003), 'Organizing cigarette smuggling and policy making, ending up in smoke', *Crime, Law and Social Change*, **39**(3), 285–317.

Van Duyne, P. (2006), 'The organization of business crime', in P.C. van Duyne, A. Maljevic, M. van Dijck, K. Von Lampe and J. Newel (eds), *The Organization of Crime for Profit: Conduct, Law and Measurement*, Nijmegen: Wolf Legal Publishers, 69–98.

Van Duyne, P. (2007), 'Criminal finances in the state-of-the-art: case for concern?', in P.C. van Duyne, A. Maljevic, M. van Dijck, K. von Lampe and J. Harvey (eds), *Crime Business and Crime Money in Europe: The Dirty Linen of Illegal Enterprise*, Wolf Legal Publishers, 69–98.

Walker, J. (1999), 'How big is global money 'laundering?', *Journal of Monetary Laundering Control*, **3**, 84–101.

Walker, J. (2004), *A Very Tentative Exploration of the Relationship between Shadow Economy and the Production and Transit of Illicit drug*, New York: UNODC.

Walker, J. (2007), 'Measuring global money laundering', Tackling Money Laundering Conference, University of Utrecht.

Wilson, J. and A. Abrahamse (1992), 'Does crime pay?', *Justice Quarterly*, **9**(3), 359–77.

Wolpin, K. (1978), 'An economic analysis of crime and punishment in England and Wales, 1894–1967', *The Journal of Political Economy*, **86**(5) 815–40.

11. Money laundering and small states: the practical experience of Liechtenstein

Prince Michael von und zu Liechtenstein

11.1 INTRODUCTION

In this chapter the author explains the experiences of Liechtenstein with regard to anti-money laundering (AML) policy from a practical point of view, since the author is not a lawyer, but an entrepreneur and business economist.

11.2 LIECHTENSTEIN AT A GLANCE[1]

Liechtenstein is a small and independent Principality, lying in the heart of Europe, nestled between the neighboring states of Switzerland and Austria. The Principality has a total area of 160 km^2 and a population of around 36,000 inhabitants.

Liechtenstein's origin dates back to the seventeenth century when Prince Johann Adam I acquired the Lordship of Schellenberg. In 1806, Liechtenstein became a member of the Confederation of the Rhine and obtained its sovereignty. Until the early twentieth century Liechtenstein was bound up with Austria, due to the Austrian origins of the Liechtenstein princes. After World War I, when the Austrian-Hungarian monarchy collapsed, Liechtenstein lost its economic support. In consequence, in 1924 Liechtenstein concluded a customs treaty with Switzerland and introduced the Swiss franc as the official currency, thereby opening the door to the Swiss Economic Area. As a further consequence, Liechtenstein became member of the UN, the WTO, the EEA, the Council of Europe, EFTA and the OSCE.

Liechtenstein is a constitutional hereditary monarchy on a democratic and parliamentary basis. The power of the state is exercised in accordance with the constitution by both the Reigning Prince and the people. Furthermore, Liechtenstein has a Parliament which is elected by the people for a period of four years. The Parliament's duty is to represent and assert the rights and interests of the people in relation to the Government. The main responsibility of the Parliament is legislation. The Government is appointed by the Reigning Prince on the recommendation of Parliament. The Government is the Principality's executive power and is responsible for the national administration. Finally, the Administration of Justice completes the legislative and executive powers as the country's judicial power.

Liechtenstein's economy is highly developed and diversified in the fields of industry and goods production, financial services, general services and agriculture, whereby industry and goods production is the largest economic field. Internationally renowned industries and global market leaders have their headquarters or subsidies in Liechtenstein, such as: Hilti, Ivoclar Vivadent, Thyssen Krupp Presta, Swarovski, etc.

Financial services represent an important, albeit not the largest, economic sector in the Liechtenstein national economy. The financial service sector contributes about 30% to Liechtenstein's gross domestic product. The financial center has evolved into a financial services center with globally operating banks, trust companies, investment companies and insurance companies, fulfilling the highest standards with respect to quality of services, competence, security and diligence.

11.3 DEFINITION OF THE TERM 'MONEY LAUNDERING'

The Liechtenstein penal law outlines 'Money Laundering' as money resulting from criminal activities, infringement of the market abuse law or any offence such as forgery of documents, corruption, terrorist financing, etc.

The Swiss Bankers Association (2001) defines the term Money Laundering in a practical way:

> Money laundering is the term applied to the act of concealing the origins of money earned through criminal activities and of releasing it unnoticed into legitimate business activities. Money laundering is most commonly associated with drug trafficking. However, any number of criminal activities may give rise to money laundering, e.g. embezzlement, corruption, blackmail, trafficking in people, to name just a few. (p. 2)

11.4 THE HISTORY OF THE ANTI-MONEY LAUNDERING PROCEDURE IN LIECHTENSTEIN

Money laundering is not a new phenomenon. AML rules have existed in Liechtenstein for some time and were included in the term *fencing* (cf. § 164, penal law, 1987), which is considered an element of crime.

However, what is new in this context is the complexity of money laundering techniques resulting from growing organized crime. Due to modern technology capital, transfers have a far more global character. The importance of AML guidelines has increased because of the improvement of money laundering techniques (e.g. the disguise of criminal activities in the trade in the petroleum markets). Some regulators believe that crime can be reduced only by fighting against money laundering. Although the necessity of the fight against money laundering is inescapable, it is an illusion to believe that those procedures alone will significantly reduce crime.

Due to Liechtenstein's EEA membership, Liechtenstein is bound to implement EU Directives. With regard to money laundering, Liechtenstein has implemented the first EU Anti Money Laundering Directive in 1995 with specific anti-money laundering legislation. The Due Diligence Law was adopted in 1997 with further modifications in the years 2004 and 2008. The second and third EU Anti Money Laundering Directives were implemented in the years 2005 and 2008, respectively. Furthermore, Liechtenstein is a longstanding member state of MONEYVAL, which is an intergovernmental organization in Strasbourg. The aim of MONEYVAL is to ensure that its member states have in place effective systems to counter money laundering and terrorist financing and comply with the relevant international standards in these fields.

11.5 SMALL STATES AS FINANCIAL CENTERS

In order to analyze the possible implications of money laundering on smaller states it is necessary to review the financial system of such states. For a long time, smaller states have been attractive financial centers because of their greater internal stability. Smaller countries are less likely to be affected by the damage of subjecting economic and financial decisions to short-term party politics. That fact enhances the stability of smaller countries. The wish to have a 'safe haven' is justified and a hedge against political risks is therefore provided.

Smaller financial centers like Liechtenstein will always pursue a niche strategy. Because of the size of their population they do not have a sufficient human capacity for extensive asset management. The home market for investment banking is too small. In addition, best performance can only be achieved where there is a high concentration of asset managers or a funding requirement. One typical niche strategy is a strategy for wealth preservation. Wealth has always been in jeopardy for a variety of reasons, for example extravagance, family problems such as divorce, unfavourable business decisions or claims from third parties. Particular risks to wealth preservation, however, come from the outside: political risks, economic instability, confiscation of property by governments or attacks from so-called 'creditors', criminals or kidnappers. Discretion is manifestly the best protection for wealth because if people are unaware of its existence it cannot be attacked. Why else did our ancestors bury their treasure and valuables?

Asset protection can only be provided in a politically and economically stable environment, with a legal and customer-friendly background. Furthermore, the correct infrastructure is needed to implement and provide the necessary background asset protection systems.

A financial system (money) has two functions: to provide facilities in the form of money to support trade and to provide a 'storage-facility', like a battery, between such trades. A financial center accumulates capital (private and institutional) to optimize the allocation of capital and to provide these funds to the economy. Financial centers specialize and compete with each other. Private assets were, and still are, under threat and need special protection. Confidentiality and privacy are essential, alongside a stable and economically liberal environment with good international relations. A financial center also needs appropriate institutions and qualified staff. This explains why small states are attractive as financial centers.

11.6 SMALL STATES AND MONEY LAUNDERING

The most common way of laundering money is to hide it through apparently legitimate commercial transactions. Due to their size and the actual role of private banks, Liechtenstein banks are certainly not suitable as a platform for money laundering. The fiduciary trust business specializes in foundations and trusts, which are not commercial vehicles. In addition, Liechtenstein institutions are extremely strict in the application of AML procedures. The main role of the two financial centers Switzerland and Liechtenstein is to be a jurisdiction for long-term wealth preservation. Especially in

Liechtenstein, assets which are placed in financial institutions or are vested in trusts, foundations or other legal instruments are supposed to be kept for the long term.

Therefore, the major challenge for Liechtenstein is to avoid already laundered money being brought in. From quite an early stage, as set out before, AML legislation was introduced in Liechtenstein. Key to that legislation are proper '*Know-Your-Customer*' procedures, because no formalities can replace having a good knowledge of the client, his environment and his economic activities.

Liechtenstein's financial intermediaries, therefore, apply not only formal controls but also plausibility controls based on the knowledge of their clients. The majority of assets in Liechtenstein are held in foundations and trusts. In order to properly administer a trust or foundation, a trustee additionally needs to understand the whole personal context of the client. This then provides an additional screen.

11.7 EVOLUTION OF THE PROCEDURES

Criminals are very creative. This creativity is problematic, and as a consequence a constant update of AML procedures is necessary. The great danger is that the procedures are too complicated and too distant from the reality of financial life, with the effect that they lose their efficiency.

One thing, however, never changes: the best way to control money laundering is to apply economic plausibility and common-sense. The pure Know-Your-Customer Rule is and remains the essence. The danger of too sophisticated procedures is that through excessive formalities common-sense and overview may get lost. Control in Private Banking (besides the problem of money laundering) is additionally strengthened as this overview and economic common-sense is the key to commercial success for these institutions. This has the important added benefit that private banking places are not so attractive for money launderers.

11.8 LIECHTENSTEIN'S ANTI-MONEY LAUNDERING POLICY

The close compliance of Liechtenstein to the AML rules is shown by the number of Suspicious Transaction Reports sent to the Liechtenstein Financial Intelligence Unit (FIU). In 2009 there were 235 Suspicious Transaction Reports with respect to the Due Diligence Law, 328 in 2010 and 289 in 2011. In relation to the Market Abuse Act there were 21 suspicious transactions reported in 2009, 19 in 2010 and six in 2011. Looking at the size of the Liechtenstein financial center, this shows that the financial intermediaries are applying the regulations very effectively.

11.9 CONCLUSION

As set out before, Liechtenstein as a private banking place and because of its diminutive size is less prone to money laundering. This does not mean that Liechtenstein should not continue to be one of the forerunners in the fight against money laundering.

A problem – which is less a Liechtenstein problem but more a problem for the whole financial sector – is the tax issue. As tax systems in the industrialized world become more and more complicated – even contradictory – and controlling and collection procedures become more unpredictable, the risk of tax avoidance or evasion increases. This can be seen in the large increase in the share of the shadow economy in industrialized economies. Because of the complexity of the law, a considerable share of the population is pushed into illegality. Another indicator is the increasing desire to escape bureaucracy, exaggerated control and the limitation of freedom, which is underlined by a strong 'brain drain' and migration to countries providing more freedom – countries such as Switzerland.

The US now is a forerunner in enforcing tax-compliance and requests that financial institutions ensure the tax compliance of their clients. This will place an overhead burden on financial institutions. On top of that, it is impossible to have sufficient tax know-how of all the world's countries. As an example, the German tax code has more than 73,000 paragraphs. If the German tax code alone has that many paragraphs, how can international financial institutions, guarantee tax-compliance for all their world-wide clients? As one can see, as a result of the discussion on the Foreign Account Tax Compliance Act (FATCA) in the US, many financial institutions in Europe and Asia do not accept American clients anymore.

If issues of direct taxes are considered an underlying crime for money laundering, the danger exists that it will distract attention from the essential part of the fight against money laundering (corruption, drugs, terrorism, etc.). This is an issue for financial institutions and citizens worldwide. The problem will not and should not be solved by making every tax payer a suspect, but rather by simplifying the tax laws and by providing legal certainty in this area.

NOTE

1. Information from this section is taken from www.liechtenstein.li.

REFERENCE

Swiss Bankers Assocation (2001), *Switzerland and the Fight Against Money Laundering*, Basel, September.

12. The role of small states for financial market integrity: Austria

Ewald Nowotny

12.1 AUSTRIA'S SIZE AND ECONOMY

Austria lies at the heart of central Europe, has a size of roughly 84,000 km² and a population of some 8.42 million inhabitants. In this regard, Austria is among the medium-range member countries of the European Union. Austria is a parliamentary republic that consists of nine provinces. Its economy is dominated by the service sector, with the Austrian GDP totaling €300,241 million on December 31, 2011, which translates into roughly €35,700 in terms of GDP per capita. At the end of 2011, a total of 824 credit institutions with more than 5,200 banking offices were operating in Austria. Between them, they held assets worth approximately €1,014.28 billion.

Austria has, for historical reasons, typically had close ties with Central, Eastern and Southern Europe countries (CESEE). Before the fall of the Iron Curtain, the country served as a neutral hub between the east and the west of Europe. This role became obsolete as the Iron Curtain was dismantled and many CESEE economies joined the EU as well. Still, the degree of economic integration continues to be high, and Austrian companies, above all financial sector companies, have been highly active in the CESEE area.

12.2 FINANCIAL MARKET INTEGRITY AS A GOAL OF ANTI-MONEY LAUNDERING POLICY

Every economy is fundamentally dependent on the integrity of its financial sector. Or, in the words of the third EU money laundering directive: 'The soundness, integrity and stability of credited and financial institutions and confidence in the financial system as a whole could be seriously jeopardised by the efforts of criminals and their associates either to disguise the origin of criminal proceeds or to channel lawful or unlawful money for terrorist purposes.'[1] Money laundering activities may endanger the integrity of a financial center and thus the economy as a whole.

The integrity of a financial market will be determined, among other things, by the underlying legal framework that creates a level playing field. Austria has duly transposed Community law on the prevention of money laundering and terrorist financing into national law to create adequate framework conditions. At the same time, it takes more than statutory regulations to secure and maintain the integrity of financial markets; financial market participants must also develop the right mindset – that is, they must be committed to conducting only 'sound' financial transactions. In Austria, there is a consensus among financial market participants that maintaining the integrity of the financial market – that is, leaving no room whatsoever for money laundering and terrorism financing – is a precondition for the stability of the financial market.

12.3 AUSTRIA'S ANTI-MONEY LAUNDERING POLICY

Like other small countries, Austria is frequently the subject of media reports on money laundering. The implementation of measures to prevent money laundering is, of course, particularly important in Austria, given the country's geopolitical location and its banks' and financial institutions' business activity in Central and Eastern Europe, even though no studies with figures on the incidence of money laundering in Austria are available. Likewise, the particular legal conditions prevailing in Austria are cited as a reason why the prevention of money laundering deserves special attention. For instance, tax fraud is considered a predicate offense of money laundering only under certain conditions. These conditions include deliberate financial crimes which are punishable by more than three years imprisonment. Moreover, Austria's name is linked with the use of products that are considered to have a higher inherent risk of being misused for money laundering purposes, which may be another reason that media reports about Austria are often critical. People still remember that it was possible to have an anonymous savings passbook in Austria, even though opening such an account has been prohibited for over a decade and even though no transactions can be made with assets held on old passbooks. The available evidence shows that the identity of account holders has been established for about 98 percent of all savings deposits.[2] Any deposits on or withdrawals from remaining anonymous savings passbooks are subject to extremely rigid legal requirements; for instance, withdrawals of €15,000 or more require prior authorization by the authorities.[3] Another popular example of a product prone to money laundering is a numbered account whose owner is purportedly unknown to the bank maintaining the account. In fact, though, banks are prohibited from maintaining anonymous numbered accounts.[4]

The mere suspicion that Austria takes too few measures to combat money laundering may represent a substantial risk – in particular the risk of a loss of reputation – to the integrity of the country's financial market. In addition to the classical risks resulting from banking operations (such as market risk and credit risk), the risk of a loss of reputation represents a massive danger and could cause other risks to materialize. Austria could be affected not just by sanctions at the international political level, but also by economic consequences at the individual institution level, for example causing a bank to lose customers and consequently to suffer capital withdrawals or to be excluded from accessing international business. This, in turn, would have negative business consequences and would entail high subsequent costs.

Therefore, Austria has always met the challenges of fighting money laundering. However, all stakeholders in Austria – from legislators through the financial industry itself – have taken comprehensive measures, signaling that Austria considers the prevention of money laundering highly important. These measures have established a modern framework that meets international requirements to counteract money laundering in the Austrian financial market. It is true, however, that it is not possible to fully prevent money laundering: against the background of increasingly globalized capital markets, the incidence of many types of crime has skyrocketed in recent years, such as firearm and drug trafficking, but also securities fraud. Those who would claim that money laundering can be fully eliminated are driven by wishful thinking, as there are so many ways to launder money, and these ways do not necessarily involve financial intermediaries.[5] The main objective in combating money laundering is to have every institution involved – from lawmakers to the financial industry – contribute commensurately to upholding the integrity of the financial market by helping to establish the measures and framework to prevent the Austrian financial market from being used to launder money.

The steps Austria has taken to prevent money laundering through banks will be described below to dispel once and for all the prejudice that Austria has not accorded the topic of preventing money laundering enough importance, to prove that even though it is a small country, Austria is aware of its responsibility, and to show that Austria is consistently striving to preserve the integrity of its financial market.

12.4 LEGAL FRAMEWORK

Unlike other countries, Austria opted to transpose the money laundering provisions by inserting corresponding clauses into the respective laws and regulations (such as the Trade Code, the Gambling Act or the Securities Supervision Act) rather than passing a single Money Laundering Act. Austria has implemented the EU directive on money laundering[6] and relevant EU regulations in the Austrian Banking Act, and it regularly amends the relevant provisions. Integrating the provisions to prevent money laundering into the respective laws and regulations ensures that market participants are addressed directly in the relevant context.

Austria is a founding member of the Financial Action Task Force (FATF), whose recommendations are implemented in national law. The FATF's last mutual evaluation report on Austria, which was published in 2009, principally gives Austria good scores for combating money laundering.[7] In its consistent efforts to achieve further improvements, Austria rectified the deficits identified in the Austrian anti-money laundering legal framework during the FATF review as quickly as possible by amending the respective laws. The potential for improvement identified in the report led to the passing of what was referred to as the transparency package, a set of provisions that provided for amendments of numerous laws,[8] among other things the expansion of suspicious transactions reports, the identification of self-laundering as a crime, the granting of more competences to the Austrian Financial Intelligence Unit (FIU) and to the Financial Market Authority, and more clearly detailed powers for anti-money laundering compliance officers.

The measures ensured that Austrian laws were updated to represent a modern set of rules in line with international standards.[9] However, a legal framework and provisions are useless in themselves without proper surveillance by supervisory authorities.

12.5 ORGANIZATIONS INVOLVED IN COMBATING MONEY LAUNDERING

In Austria, numerous institutions are involved in taking countermeasures against money laundering, in monitoring compliance with the regulatory framework, and in taking action against lawbreakers. Because money laundering methods evolve so quickly, all organizations involved – from the supervisory authorities to the law enforcement agencies – make every effort necessary to safeguard Austria's integrity as a financial center.

The Financial Market Authority (FMA) and the Oesterreichische Nationalbank (OeNB) are the institutions charged with the ongoing supervision of the implementation of banking laws in Austria. To ensure that Austrian banks in fact implement the relevant anti-money laundering provisions, the FMA and the OeNB regularly conduct on-site inspections and off-site analyses and evaluate banks' compliance. Both institutions look back on many years of experience with supervisory activity in the fight against money laundering. The objective is not simply to punish wrongdoers, but rather to prevent money laundering in the first place. As a supervisory authority, the FMA is in charge of monitoring compliance with the specific legal provisions and general due diligence obligations in combating money laundering and of taking the appropriate steps if these obligations are violated.[10] The Oesterreichische Nationalbank has been solely entrusted with bank inspections and off-site analyses since January 2008. Compliance with money laundering provisions is a standard component of this supervisory activity.[11] The FMA takes any official steps required on the basis of the prudential or the analysis reports. In addition, the supervisory authorities are obligated to immediately notify the FIU if they suspect that a transaction of which they have received information in performing their duties of banking supervision serves the purpose of money laundering.[12]

The Austrian Federal Ministry of Finance is responsible for supervisory legislation. The FIU, which is located in Austria's Bundeskriminalamt at the Federal Ministry of the Interior, conducts comprehensive analyses on the basis of reports of transactions suspected of being used to launder money or to finance terrorism. If the suspicion that a transaction could serve to finance terrorism is substantiated, the Federal Agency for State Protection and Counter-Terrorism is also involved. The courts and the federal prosecutors handle criminal proceedings.

As the demands on supervisory staff are rising steadily, the FMA and the OeNB have drawn up a university-level joint training program for their institutions' staff to provide for professional, state-of-the-art training of financial market supervisors. This university-level program also covers money laundering issues.

Further important aspects in combating money laundering are deterrence, and the heightened awareness of bank staff of money laundering issues. The supervisory authorities address these concerns by organizing events covering money laundering issues, and by giving presentations at seminars offered by external providers or by the respective professional associations. Moreover, the FMA publishes circulars on money laundering topics. These circulars present the FMA's view of the statutory due diligence obligations to counter money laundering. The FMA has published four such circulars directed at credit institutions since 2008:[13] the Circular on Verification and Ascertainment of Identity, the Circular on the Risk-Sensitive Approach to the Prevention of Money Laundering and Terrorist Financing, the Circular on the Transmission of Payer Information pursuant to Regulation (EC) No 1781/2006 on information on the payer accompanying transfers of funds, and the Circular on Suspicious Transaction Reports in Connection with Money Laundering, the Financing of Terrorist Activities and Violation of the Disclosure Requirements for Trusteeships. Moreover, credit institutions have the option of addressing legal inquiries to the FMA.

In recent years, within the framework of their evaluation of financial institutions, the FMA and the OeNB have noted a continuous improvement in institutions' systems and in their implementation of provisions to deter money laundering, not simply because of pressure applied by the authorities, but also because institutions themselves have recognized the need for action. The institutions, moreover, benefit from the fact that the comparatively small size of Austria also facilitates a regular informal exchange of information among market participants. For instance, many AML officers tend to know each other in person, and they tend to meet at events and in inter-institutional working groups. Moreover, the public authorities are well informed about the activities of the individual institutions, and there is a consensus among all institutions involved about the need to prevent money laundering and terrorism financing.

The following section describes how banks have implemented the main anti-money laundering provisions provided for in the supervisory framework.

12.6 IMPLEMENTATION OF ANTI-MONEY LAUNDERING PROVISIONS AT BANKS

12.6.1 Risk Analysis

Risk analysis – both of banks' activities and of individual customers' activities – represents the cornerstone of every system to prevent money laundering at banks.[14] Comprehensive risk analysis encompasses not just portfolio analysis, but is the result of all deterrent measures taken by an institution. Therefore, risk analysis must present the measures and systems an institution uses. One objective of risk analysis is to identify customer relationships that represent an elevated risk for an institution and that must consequently be treated as high-risk.[15] The provisions of the risk-based AML/CFT (anti-money laundering and counter-terrorist financing) approach obligate credit institutions to classify all customers according to the specific risk they represent.[16] The Banking Act stipulates that credit and financial institutions must subject their business to risk analysis using suitable criteria (in particular products, customers, the complexity of transactions, customer business and geography) with regard to the risk of misuse for the purposes of money laundering.[17]

12.6.2 Organizational Design

The structural and process organization of credit institutions is another key component of the system to prevent money laundering. Here, not just the quality and amount of infrastructure of the units charged with the prevention of money laundering are important; the design of the processes used is also significant. The organization of the credit institution must be such that all information about customers can be ascertained and measures can be taken to prevent transactions linked to money laundering. The money laundering officer or unit plays a key role in this procedure. In addition to having the proper qualification, the money laundering officer must have comprehensive competences and must be obliged to report directly to management. By law, the money laundering officer must be given unrestricted access to all information, data, records and systems that could possibly be linked to money laundering.[18] The fact that the failure to report suspicious transactions and all infractions of money laundering provisions carry legal penalties under the Banking Act underlines the importance of these provisions.[19]

The money laundering officer also counts the conduct of examinations among his duties. Under no circumstances should account managers assume the duties of the money laundering officer. However, in classic banking business, the account manager has a very important role to play – no other bank staff member is closer to customers or knows customers as well. Indeed, most of the suspicious transaction reports originate at banks' 'point of sale'. Hence, in addition to an adequate IT infrastructure, having well-trained staff is an important prerequisite for improving structural efficiency in preventing money laundering at a bank. Money laundering legislation stipulates that staff must complete training programs.[20] The training programs cover not just units in charge of money laundering prevention issues, they apply to all staff members. As a matter of course, participation in the training programs must also be founded on a risk-based approach, and must be geared toward the job specifications of the respective staff members. Staff employed in especially susceptible areas, such as private banking, must regularly complete training courses. These measures are all the more important because money laundering methods change rapidly, and staff must of course be up to date on the latest developments. The money laundering officer and the other members of the organizational unit to which he belongs must be subject to more stringent qualification demands.

12.6.3 Customer Due Diligence

The internationalization of capital markets and financial linkages between countries designed to exploit tax advantages has led to customer relations extending beyond the European Union. Such relationships are not particular to Austria, as some people have claimed; they are simply the consequence of the globalization of financial markets. Such customer relations are not a negative thing in themselves, but they do call for particular safeguards in systems and processes in order to prevent money laundering. The overarching principle in accepting a customer's business is the know-your-customer (KYC) principle. Comprehensive customer due diligence procedures that need to be followed already during the process of taking on a new customer serve to implement KYC policy.[21]

Already at the start of a possible customer relationship, a financial institution must take measures to identify and verify the customer's identity and to understand the customer's circumstances and business.[22] Identification and verification of identity are an essential part of these due diligence measures. The relevant FMA circular describes how the identity of customers is to be ascertained and verified properly.[23] Among other things, financial institutions must ascertain the identities of customers, beneficiaries and trustees. During the identification and verification procedure, the bank must also determine whether the customer is a politically exposed person (PEP)[24] or whether any restrictions preclude a business relationship.

One of the key issues of KYC policies is the above-mentioned analysis of the type and purpose of the business relationship, including the source of the funds. This is an essential feature of the procedure without which the bank cannot ascertain whether the purpose of a customer's relationship with the bank is a clearly commercial one (e.g. asset protection, an increase or diversification of assets, exploitation of tax advantages, conduct of a business activity) or whether it is being misused to launder money. Apart from money laundering, there may also be another unlawful motivation for entering a business relationship with a bank that must not be tolerated under any circumstances, for instance circumventing exchange controls or capital flight. If the bank has obtained knowledge about the customer's business model and purpose of the relationship, it has established the prerequisite for verifying whether the funds stem from criminal activity. In practice, it has frequently been shown that submitting proof of origin documentation for funds is no problem; such documents are quickly drawn up in a professional form. Therefore, it is all the more important to validate such documents. Only if the proof of origin documents agree with the verified data provided by the customer and the account of his business, asset situation, and the like, can a bank be certain that the customer will not misuse the institution for money laundering purposes.

To comply with customer due diligence standards, the institution must perform adequate checks, not just of the customer, but also of the persons standing behind the customer, meaning that they have to verify the identity of any beneficial owner. Under no circumstances must the bank accept customers who will not divulge the identity of their beneficial owners, as this contravenes statutory requirements. The beneficial owner of all types of company must be clearly ascertained. The legal requirements are restrictive on this point, as credit institutions must not execute any transactions or establish a business relationship, or they must terminate a business relationship, if they are not in a position to comply with the provisions on customer identification and on obtaining any required additional information about the business relationship. If banks have to end a business relationship, they will have to determine whether they need to report the matter to the federal crime office.[25]

12.6.4 Monitoring Measures

Once a bank has engaged in a business relationship with a customer, it will be faced with additional commitments. According to the legal provisions, credit institutions must take appropriate risk-based measures to ensure that the business relationship is continuously monitored, including the monitoring of transactions executed during the course of the business transaction.[26]

Banks must use their IT systems not just for regular reviews of customers' primary data, but also to perform ongoing monitoring of transactions. Transaction monitoring represents a key component of the procedure to prevent money laundering at a credit institution. Monitoring consists in tracking customers' transactions on the basis of a risk-sensitive system. The parameters of these systems may be a combination derived on the one hand from customer primary data and on the other hand from the transactions themselves, including information about the type of transaction, transaction size and the frequency of transactions. Within these monitoring rules, various levels may have been implemented to ensure that the approach is risk-based. The results of the transaction analysis serve as the basis for the money laundering officer to initiate examination procedures or to take measures, the most severe of which is a report to the FIU.

To ensure that the procedures are the same throughout the group, all anti-money laundering measures applied at the credit institution's branches and subsidiaries located in third countries are equivalent to those taken at the credit institution itself.

12.7 SUMMARY

By implementing the third EU directive on money laundering and the related regulation, Austria has complied with the EU and international standards in every respect. In recent years, numerous accompanying measures have established an efficient and effective system to prevent money laundering. In reacting rapidly to weaknesses in this system – for example by implementing a package of measures in 2010 – Austria has shown that it is a reliable, recognized partner on an equal footing with other countries for which financial market integrity is a fundamentally important concern. Moreover, the organizations involved in the fight against money laundering, from lawmakers to the institutions charged with supervising Austria's financial market, keep a watchful eye on the quality of legislation and consistently monitor compliance with the laws against money laundering.

Austria's approach to preventing money laundering and terrorism financing shows that a small country in particular can do more than transpose international provisions into national law to secure the integrity of the financial market; a small country also benefits in particular from the commitment shared by all market participants.

NOTES

1. Directive 2005/60/EC of the European Parliament and of the Council of 26 October 2005 on the prevention of the use of the financial system for the purpose of money laundering and terrorist financing.
2. FATF, Mutual Evaluation Report, Anti-Money Laundering and Combating the Financing of Terrorism, AUSTRIA, 26 June 2009, p. 113.
3. Article 40 para. 6 Austrian Banking Act ('Banking Act') prohibits deposits on such accounts, and Article 41 para. 1a Banking Act details the procedure governing withdrawals from such accounts.
4. Cf. Article 40d para. 2 Banking Act, which explicitly prohibits the maintenance of such accounts.
5. Cf. UNODC, *The Globalization of Crime: A Transnational Organized Crime Threat Assessment*, United Nations Office on Drugs and Crime, Vienna 2010.
6. Directive 2005/60/EC, see note 1.
7. Cf. FATF, *Mutual Evaluation Report: Austria*, published 1 December 2009.
8. Cf. Federal Law Gazette I no. 37/2010 of 15 June 2010.
9. Cf. European Commission, *DG Internal Market and Services – Budget: Final Study on the Application of the Anti-Money Laundering Directive*, published 24 January 2011.
10. Cf. the *Annual Report of the Financial Market Authority 2010*, p. 122f, Vienna.
11. Cf. Oesterreichische Nationalbank/Financial Market Authority, *Banking Supervision in Austria*, p. 22f. Vienna, 2009.
12. Cf. Article 41 para. 5 Banking Act.
13. In addition, the FMA published the Circular on Verification and Ascertainment of Identity for Insurance Undertakings in 2008.
14. Cf. FATF publication *Guidance on the Risk-Based Approach to Combating Money Laundering and Terrorist Financing*, June 2007.
15. Cf. FMA Circular on the Risk-Sensitive Approach to the Prevention of Money Laundering and Terrorist Financing of 23 December 2009.
16. Cf. FMA Circular on the Risk-Sensitive Approach to the Prevention of Money Laundering and Terrorist Financing of 23 December 2009.
17. Cf. Article 40 para. 2b Banking Act.

18. Cf. Article 41 para. 4 no. 6 Banking Act.
19. Cf. Article 98 para. 5 Banking Act.
20. Cf. Article 41 para. 4 no. 3 Banking Act.
21. FATF publication *Guidance on the Risk-Based Approach to Combating Money Laundering and Terrorist Financing*, June 2007.
22. Cf. Article 40 para. 2a no. 2 Banking Act.
23. FMA Circular on Verification and Ascertainment of Identity of 3 July 2008.
24. For a definition of PEP, see Article 2 no. 72 Banking Act.
25. Cf. Article 40 para. 2d Banking Act.
26. Cf. Article 40 para. 2a no. 3 Banking Act.

PART V

THE SCALE OF THE PROBLEM

13. Measuring global money laundering: the 'Walker Gravity Model'*

John Walker and Brigitte Unger

13.1 INTRODUCTION

Data on crime and crime prevention which are a prerequisite for measuring money laundering have improved substantially within the last two decades. In particular, the international community now has a detailed knowledge base on the illicit drug economy. The UN calculates the cultivation and production of opium and cocaine worldwide quite accurately (see UN *World Drugs Report 2008*; UNDOC 2011). The annual UNODC International Crop Monitoring Programme Surveys provide annual statistics on the cultivation and production of drugs, as well as prices, yield and the farm gate, wholesale and retail market valuations that are calculated from them (see also the contribution of Pietschmann in this volume for the Cocaine market, Chapter 16).

The economics of money laundering which aims at exploring the scale and impact of illicit funds is a relatively new field (see e.g. Masciandaro et al. 2007; Unger 2007). Producing reliable estimates of laundering is essential for this strand of literature.

In 1998, the Managing Director of the IMF, Michel Camdessus, stated that '2 to 5 per cent of global GDP would probably be a consensus range', thus about US$1.5 trillion of money laundering at that time (www.imf.org/external/np/speeches/1998/021098.htm). The basis for this estimate could, however, not be established (see Thoumi 2003; Truman and Reuter 2004).

The Walker Model (Walker, 1995, 1999, 2002, 2003) was the first serious attempt at quantifying money laundering worldwide. The 1995 'prototype' model suggested that US$ 2.85 trillion were laundered globally – exceeding the upper-range figure suggested by Camdessus' statement, and raising questions on the underestimation of the global extent of fraud.

This model has gained popularity recently. In 2005, Walker used a similar methodology to predict global drug money flows (see UNODC 2005); in 2006 Unger et al used the 'Walker Model' to estimate money laundering for the Netherlands, the UNODC used the model and at the moment the IMF is engaged in improving variables and data collection for this model, which until today is still the leading model for international global money laundering measuring. In the following we will describe ways to measure laundering, explain this model and its theoretical foundation, and demonstrate and explore its strengths and weaknesses for measuring money laundering.

13.2 METHODS FOR ESTIMATING MONEY LAUNDERING

In 1989, the Financial Action Task Force's 'Working Group on Statistics and Methods' report *Narcotics Money Laundering – Assessment of the Scale of the Problem* noted the lack of reliable data to measure money laundering. In 1990, the European Union introduced its Convention on laundering, search, seizure and confiscation of the Proceeds from Crime, and the FATF's 'Forty Recommendations' were published on the prevention of money laundering.

It was in this context that, in 1995, AUSTRAC, the Australian Financial Intelligence Unit, commissioned *Estimates of the Extent of Money Laundering in Australia* and, in 1996, presented it to the FATF as a potential model for other countries to follow. Criticism focused on the poor quality of the data and the methodology's reliance on 'expert knowledge', but it was generally agreed that expert knowledge was a reasonable approach if used only to fill in gaps in statistical evidence.

While other researchers (e.g. Levi and Gold 1994) were trying to analyse financial data, including data on 'suspicious transactions', to identify the extent of money laundering, the Walker Model approach was quite different. Since money laundering involves many stages – 'placement' (e.g. putting the illicit cash money in a bank), 'layering' (pumping the money around the globe to hide its illicit origin) and 'integration' (investing the cleaned money) – and the same money could go through many different transactions in the laundering process, counting financial transaction data was therefore certain to involve double – or even multiple – counting. Worse, counting suspicious transactions was certain to include large errors both ways ('suspicious' transactions that are actually legitimate, and 'legitimate' transactions that are actually criminal).

By focusing only on 'suspicious transactions', such researchers heavily underestimated the scale of money laundering. In the Netherlands, criminologists Meloen et al. (2003) analysed 52 criminal cases wherein property had been confiscated (*ontnemingszaken* in Dutch) from criminals related to money laundering. These 52 cases totalled €100 million in laundered funds. The problem with this kind of approach is that it is unclear how representative the data are. Do the 52 launderers who were caught stand for 0.5 per cent, 5 per cent, 10 per cent or 50 per cent of the launderers in the Netherlands? Are the money launderers caught representative of all money launderers, or are only specific offenders (the stupid ones) caught? Guided by this study which gives very interesting insights into the behaviour of money launderers, Dutch criminologists up until 2007 thought that money laundering in the Netherlands was negligible and heavily underestimated the problem (see the contribution of van Duyne, in this volume and his criticism on our method, Chapter 19).

Analysis of police files also results in underestimation of the size of the problem. They are useless for estimating national or global money laundering, because they have an intrinsic logical problem when aggregated. The stricter the fight against launderers, the more eagerly the police record money laundering cases. This would mean that money laundering, illogically, increases with stricter anti-money laundering policy.

Money laundering can also be measured by means of surveys of experts and law enforcement agents. However, surveys also suffer from diverse biases, including sampling error and interviewee biases. For example, those authorities responsible for combating money laundering might overestimate the scale of the problem because fighting laundering is their daily business and centre of focus. Alternatively, the same people might underestimate the problem if they feel that they fulfil their task of fighting crime efficiently and do their job well. Perception biases, interpretation biases, biases from non-response and sample biases might be included in these data. However, sometimes they can provide important insights especially when dealing with otherwise unobservable facts.

Money laundering has also been estimated using proxy variables. Tanzi (1997) from the IMF used the difference between money supply and money circulating in the US economy to estimate that US$5 billion per year was being taken out of the US in cash through the illegal drugs trade in 1984 and was thus missing from the money supplied. He warned that this creates a potential instability for the world financial system because these dollars could be unloaded in exchange for foreign currency. However, his analysis ignores offence types other than drugs, restricts itself to the money which leaves a country in cash, and does not take into account using the regular financial system or trade to transfer illicit funds.

Another way to measure money laundering is to use approaches from measuring the shadow economy to measure money laundering, like the DYMIMIC (dynamic multiple-indicators multiple causes) model. It uses two sets of observable variables and links them as a proxy to the unobservable variable. One set of observable variables is the causes (for the shadow economy or for money laundering) such as regulations, taxation and prosecutions. The other set is called indicators. These observable variables parallel money laundering and include the growing demand for money, less official growth and/or increases in crime rates (see Buehn and Schneider in this volume who use this approach, Chapter 14). One problem with this approach is that the choice of cause and indicator variables is arbitrary and not reinforced theoretically. Statistics decide which indicators form the relevant bundle of causes of the shadow economy (or money laundering) and which are relevant for the parallel indicators of a shadow economy (or money laundering). Nevertheless, the method identifies the variables that are highly correlated and measure the same part of the proxy variable, and reduces redundancies in the choice of proxy variables.

So far, out of all the models the 'Walker Model' still seems the most promising, because it can be used for all countries and jurisdictions in the world and because it can be given a theoretical underpinning that is much stronger and more promising than other global money laundering measuring approaches identified so far. Measuring money laundering needs a combination of criminology, economics and finance, which are all included in the 'Walker Model'. The minus side of the model is that it is complicated to calculate and in order to generate time series one has to calculate the model every year anew.

13.3 THE 'WALKER MODEL' FOR ESTIMATING MONEY LAUNDERING

The gravity model says that the amount of trade from place A to place B depends on the population in place A, the 'attractiveness' of place B to people based in A, and the distance between the two places.

Walker's 'prototype' gravity formula assumes the following:

$$\frac{F_{ij}}{M_i} = \frac{Attractiveness_j}{Distance_{ij}^2}$$

$$\frac{F_{ij}}{M_i} = \left(\frac{GNP}{capita}\right)_j * \frac{(3BS_j + GA_j + SWIFT_j - 3CF_j - CRj + 15)}{Distance_{ij}^2}$$

where F_{ij}/M_i is the share of proceeds of crime that country I sends to country j. *GNP/capita* is GNP per capita, *BS* is Banking Secrecy, *GA* is Government Attitude, *SWIFT* is SWIFT member, *CF* is Conflict, *CR* is Corruption. The 'distance' factor in the model is the number of kilometres between the countries.

Walker and Unger (2009) showed that the Walker formula comes close to Newton's Law of Universal Gravity. In 1687, Newton proposed that the attractive force between two objects *i* and *j* depends on their masses M_i and M_j, the square distance between these objects D_{ij} and a gravitational constant *G*, which depends on the units of measurement for mass and attractive force (see Head 2003).

$$Atttractive\ Force\ F_{ij} = G * M_i * M_j/(D_{ij})^2$$

where

F_{ij} Attractive Force between object *i* and *j*
M_i Mass of object *i*
M_j Mass of object *j*
D_{ij} Distance between object *i* and object *j*
G Gravitational constant

In 1962, the Dutch Nobel prize winner Tinbergen transformed understanding of the newly established economics of international trade by applying Newton's formula to bilateral trade flows. The trade from country *i* to country *j* depends on the economic mass of the two countries (measured by GDP) and the distance between the two locations (see Head, 2003).

$$F_{ij} = G * M_i^{\alpha} * M_j^{\beta}/(D_{ij})^{\theta}$$

The export flows from country*i*to country*j*depend on the GDP of both the exporting and importing country and the distance between them. Note that if $\alpha, \beta = 1$, and $\theta = 2$, then this is the same as the original Newton formula.

Distance is important for trade flows because it is a proxy for transport costs, communication costs, and for the possibilities of personal contact between managers and customers, that is for informal contacts which cannot be sent over a wire. Distance can also be seen in a wider perspective as transaction costs, as the searching for trading opportunities, the establishment of trust between partners.

The distance indicator used by Walker (1995) assumes a similar importance for money laundering flows. Though physical distance is less important for money flows, since money cannot perish, and transportation costs are negligible given that money can be sent around the globe at the click of a mouse, the communication costs, transaction costs and cultural barriers might still be important. Therefore, the roles of cultural distance (clashes in negotiation style, language etc. (Head 2003, p. 8)), of historical common backgrounds, and of trade relations have to be emphasized more in money laundering gravity models.

Speaking a common language and sharing a common history and cultural background can lower transaction costs. 'Two countries that speak the same language will trade twice to three times as much as pairs that do not share a common language' (Head 2003; see especially the works of Helliwell, e.g. Helliwell 2000). This aspect seems captured well in the 'Walker Model'. The only assumption is that what holds for legal trade also holds for illegal transactions.

The gravity model has been augmented by welfare concerns, expressed in the variable 'income per capita' reflecting that richer countries tend to trade more. The 'Walker Model' assumes the same for money laundering. Richer countries attract more money laundering funds from poorer countries. However, gravity models usually also include a variable for mass, that is, income and not only for welfare (income per capita). The original 'Walker Model' did not include a mass variable, since the money laundering of small islands would be overwhelmed by a giant like the US if one included volume variables. But it will certainly need some serious thought about how to justify this dropping of one of the apples' masses in the formula.[1]

13.4 MODELLING MONEY LAUNDERING: LESSONS LEARNED FROM INTERNATIONAL TRADE THEORY

The formula that was suggested in Walker (1995) is very similar to the gravity model.

Walker's 'prototype' gravity formula assumes:

$$\frac{F_{ij}}{M_i} = \left(\frac{GNP}{capita}\right)_j * \frac{(3BS_j + GA_j + SWIFT_j - 3CF_j - CR_j + 15)}{Distance_{ij}^2}$$

where *GNP/capita* is GNP per capita, *BS* is Banking Secrecy, *GA* is Government Attitude, *SWIFT* is SWIFT member, *CF* is Conflict, *CR* is Corruption.

If one compares this to the original gravity model, the 'Walker Model' assumes $R_j = (3BS_j + GA_j + SWIFT_j - 3CF_j - CR_j + 15)$ and $M_j = (GNP/capita)_j$.The flow formula is divided by M_i. M_i represents the proceeds of crime in the sending country. In the receiving country the 'mass' is welfare (GNP per capita). All the variables relevant for money laundering have been captured in the remoteness variable. The gravitational 'masses' of the two objects country *i* and country *j* have been assumed to be GNP per capita and money generated for laundering, respectively.

For the distance indicator D_{ij}, the original 'Walker Model' assumed $\theta = 2$ and used the squared kilometre distance between capitals. As mentioned above, this can overestimate the effective distance due to intense cross border trade. Unger et al. (2006) opted for θ = 1, using linear and not squared distance, backed up by the fact that many trade gravity equations also come up with this coefficient (Helliwell 2000).[2]

What is still not captured in this and the 'Walker Model' of money laundering is the full layering phase of money laundering (money laundering is measured at the first phase, at placement, when it is generated and invested domestically or sent abroad). However, the second phase of money laundering, when money is transferred all over the globe in order to hide its origin, is much higher in volume and much more prone to all kinds of financial tricks and sophisticated constructions, but is only sporadically treated. The advantage of avoiding double counting faces the disadvantage of underestimating actual gross criminal flows.

13.4.1 Assumptions of the 'Walker Model'

- Crime generates income in all countries.
- Income from crime depends on the prevalence of different types of crime and the average proceeds per crime.
- Sophisticated and organized crimes generate more income per crime than simpler and individual crimes.
- In general, richer countries generate more income per crime than poor ones.
- Income inequality or corruption may support a rich criminal class even in a poor country.
- Not all criminal income is laundered – even criminals have to eat, sleep, drive fast cars, and pay accountants and lawyers.

These are all supportable assumptions, in the absence of any existing research in this area. Walker populated the model using the crime data from the UN's most recent survey results for each country, using regional average rates per population, multiplied by UNDP population data, for countries where no crime data were available. He took the relative 'proceeds per recorded crime', for each type of crime, from his own Australian analysis, adjusted by UNDP data on GDP per capita.

The assumptions built into the model about laundering processes were:

- Not all laundered money leaves the country – some countries' finance sectors provide perfect cover for local launderers.
- Countries where official corruption is common provide benign environments for launderers.
- Laundered money seeks countries with attractive banking regimes:
  - Tax havens
  - 'No questions asked' banking
  - Countries with stable economies and low risk.
- Trading, ethnic and linguistic links will determine launderers' preferred destinations – other things being equal, 'hot' money will be attracted to havens with trading, ethnic, linguistic or geographic links to the generating country.

13.4.2 Estimates of Money Laundering from the 'Walker Model'

Walker updated his model in 2005, again involving surveys of Australian law enforcement officials and researchers both in Australia and overseas along with analysis of some official statistics, including data held by AUSTRAC, the Australian Financial Intelligence Unit, but this time also including requests for information from foreign Financial Intelligence Units. A literature review was conducted to identify any methodological breakthroughs that might have occurred in the intervening decade – with little to indicate any major progress. The process again provided a range of estimates, suggesting that crime in Australia in 2004 generated between AU$2.8 billion and AU$6.3 billion, with the most likely figure being in the vicinity of AU$4.5 billion.

13.5 REVISIONS OF THE 'WALKER MODEL'

13.5.1 A Revised 'Walker Model' for the Netherlands

The 'Walker Model' has two parts. It calculates firstly the proceeds from domestic crime that are laundered and secondly the proceeds from foreign crime that flow into a country for laundering. This second part is the more controversial one in the debate on money laundering.

Money can be laundered in the country in which it was generated or sent to another country for laundering. An important point within this model is that as soon as money has travelled (flowed) at least once, it is 'white washed', or laundered. This model only counts this first transaction involving the placement of funds. Although 'hot money' can be moved on multiple occasions in an effort to disguise its criminal origins, this model does not count each of these transactions, or movement of funds, in order to avoid double counting. The model was slightly revised and calculated for the Netherlands by Unger et al. (2006) following Walker's 1995 advice to improve some of the variables.

Percentage of World Criminal Money Flowing into a country X (the Netherlands):

$$P(X, y_i) = \frac{1}{\sum_{i=1}^{n}\left[\dfrac{attractiveness\ y_i}{dist(X, y_i)}\right]} * \frac{attractiveness\ y_i}{dist(X, y_i)}$$

$$Country\ X,\ countries\ y_i, i = 1, \ldots, n$$

attractiveness = *f* (GDP per capita, Bank Secrecy, Anti-Money Laundering Policy, Swift Membership, **Financial deposits**, Conflict, Corruption, **Egmont Group**)[3].

Distance deterrence = *f* (**Language, Colonial Background**, Physical Distance)

The formula shows the percentage *P* of country y_i's (e.g. the US) criminal money flowing to a country *X* (the Netherlands). This percentage of the US total money for laundering sent to the Netherlands depends on how attractive the Netherlands are for the US (attractiveness y_i) and on the distance between the Netherlands and the US (dist (X, y_i)). The first part of the right hand side of the equation just guarantees that all shares sent by each country add up to 100 per cent. The Netherlands will be more attractive for launderers based in foreign countries like the US if it has a higher GDP per capita, because money hides more easily in rich economies than in poor ones, if it has high bank secrecy, if it has technological means to transfer money quickly, like being a SWIFT member, and if it has low conflicts and corruption so that criminals do not have to fear losing their laundered money. We added to this another two variables for strict anti-money laundering policy, namely membership of the Egmont Group, a group established in order to combat money laundering, and financial deposits. This last variable is meant to express the fact that large financial centres will be more attractive for launderers because they have the expertise and financial skills to handle large amounts of money discreetly.

For the distance deterrence index, Walker's 1995 suggestions were followed by including social and cultural distance variables as well as geographical distance. If two countries speak the same language, share a common colonial background and are top trading partners for each other, they have more common links and hence less 'distance' between each other, than if they do not have these joint experiences. The closer countries are to each other, the smaller the distance between them, the more laundering will take place. A precise description of how we measured the variables is found in Unger et al. (2006), according to which about €14.5 billion of dirty money was sent to the Netherlands in 2005, mainly from the US, Russia, Italy, Germany, the UK and France. In the Netherlands another €4 billion were laundered from the proceeds of Dutch crime (drugs and fraud mainly). This means that the Netherlands has to face about €18.5 billion of money laundering yearly, which amounts to about 5 per cent of the Dutch GDP. The Netherlands seem to be mainly a through flow country for laundering. From suspicious transaction reports of the Dutch FIU (MOT 2005) one can assume that money goes mainly to the Dutch Antilles, Colombia, Turkey and Spain and to Suriname. The 'Walker Model' would also allow the calculation of money flows by destination, but for this, it must be calculated for all countries and for all (cultural, social and geographic) distances between all countries of the world; something, that was not done in the study.

13.6 THE ROBUSTNESS OF THE 'WALKER MODEL'

To test the quality of estimates of unobservable variables like money laundering, one can compare the estimates to other estimates to see how far apart they lie. In particular, where the unobservable variable is logically a sub-set of another variable that has been quantified (or vice versa), then the observable variable provides an upper (or lower) limit for the unobservable one. Thus, obviously, total money laundering must be at least as large as 'known' money laundering, based on the amounts for which criminal convictions have been obtained. But there are many other – more interesting – triangulations that can be made.

In 2006, Austrian economist Friedrich Schneider published some interesting estimates of shadow economy – the economic activity in a country that is hidden from authorities (particularly from tax agencies) for 145 different countries (Schneider 2006). In many

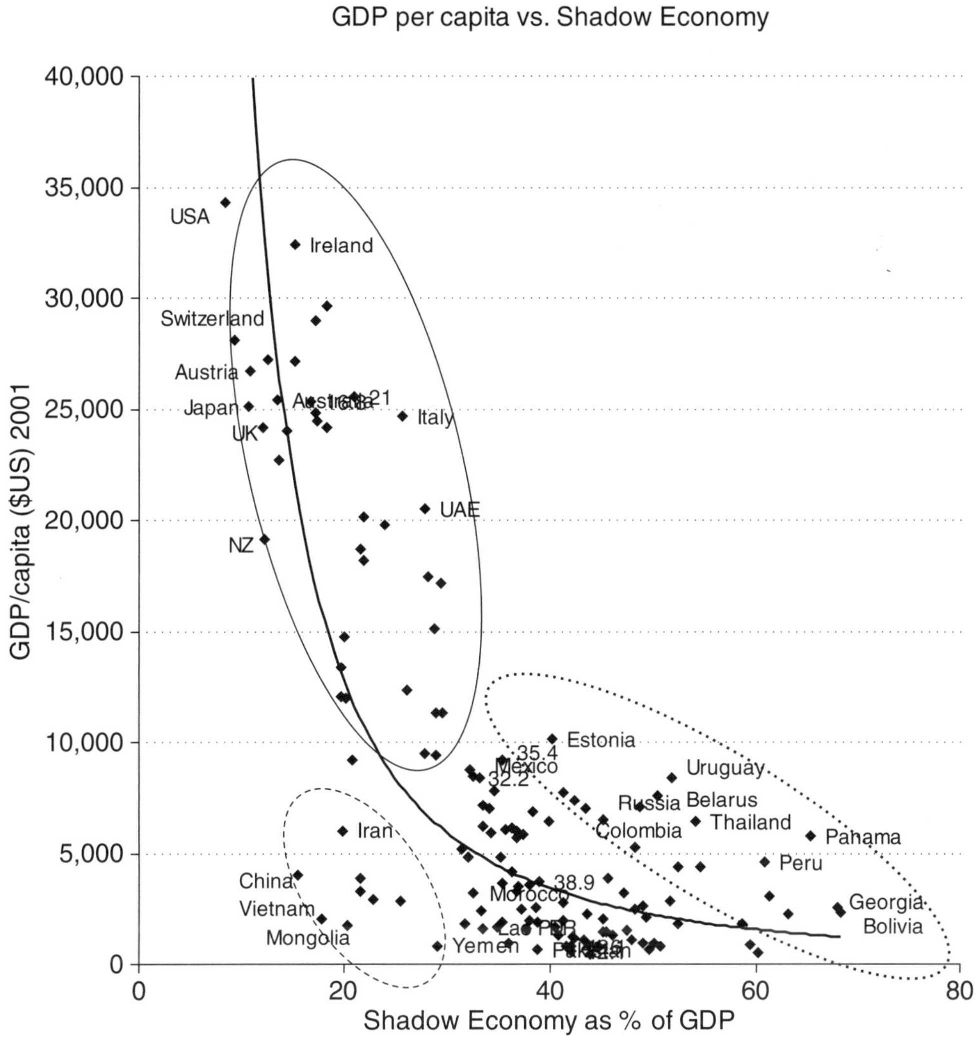

Figure 13.1 The concept of 'excess shadow economy' as a potential measure of the proceeds of crime

countries, the shadow economy consists mostly of legal activities kept hidden for tax avoidance purposes, but logically, since criminals do not report their illegal incomes to tax authorities, the proceeds of crime should be a sub-set of the shadow economy. Some interesting results can be derived by comparing Schneider's estimates of the shadow economy as a proportion of GDP against GDP per capita.

This analysis suggests that poorer countries have higher percentages of shadow economy than rich countries, and there appears to be a nice 'J'-curve on the graph (see Figure 13.1). Countries to the lower left of the curve – lower than expected shadow economy – (including China) tend to have 'command' economies in which the shadow economy is suppressed. In theory, economic crime should be a sub-set of the shadow economy, and those countries to the right of the line appear to have significant transnational crime, illicit drug production and corrupt business practices.

This analysis seems to identify 'excess' shadow economy in some countries, often those with a reputation for 'mafia-type' organized crime, including Italy, Russia and Colombia, and the excess can be measured as a proportion of the countries' GDPs. It is too soon to know whether this form of analysis can successfully identify the proceeds of organized crime in specific countries – but on this basis, the shadow economy in Australia would amount to around AU$20 billion per year, which is not inconsistent with the earlier AU$6–8 billion from crime alone. For the Netherlands the shadow economy estimated by Schneider is 10 per cent of GDP, compared to 5 per cent of GDP estimated for money laundering, which also seems consistent (see Unger 2007).

As Walker and Unger (2009) also showed, triangulation with other studies like the UN Statistics on Service Exports confirms the Walker model (see Figure 13.2). As percentages of GDP, these figures clearly identify countries with unusually strong financial services exports or other services, such as tourism, that could be used for money laundering, including most of the Caribbean tax havens and some of the larger financial centres including Luxembourg, Switzerland and Singapore. These data can be interpreted as measuring the *capacity* of the financial sector to support money laundering, which should be an integral part of their 'attractiveness' to money launderers.

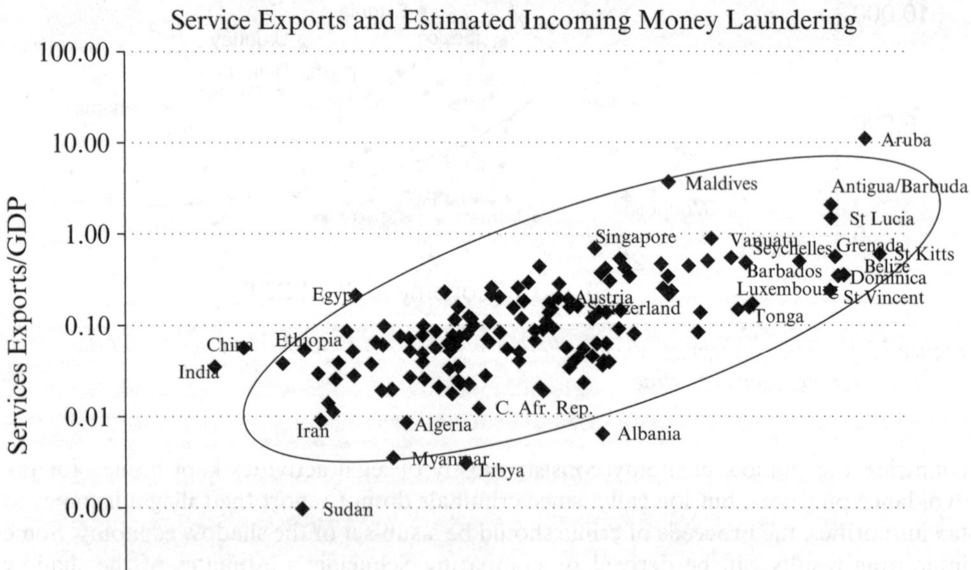

Figure 13.2 The concept of 'capacity to provide money laundering services'

13.7 TRIANGULATION WITH BAKER'S FINDINGS

Raymond Baker's 2005 work on cross-border flow analysis is based on a review of studies of transnational crime, and the data may not be internally consistent, but this is another essential research technique. Each of these figures can potentially serve as a credibility check on any estimates we are able to generate (see Table 13.1).

Baker estimates that criminals in rich countries are transferring from poorer countries around ten times the amount of aid given by the rich countries to the poor. Baker's estimate for illicit flows from developing countries, US$800 billion, closely matches the corresponding results obtained from the 'Walker Model', US$850 billion. The most important reason why we need to focus on the economics of crime and money laundering is that international crime prevention strategies should not only benefit the rich countries (see the contribution of Baker in this volume, Chapter 15).

13.8 FUTURE CHALLENGES

The 'Walker Model' still seems to be the most reliable and robust method to estimate global money laundering and the effects of transnational crime on economic, social and political institutions. Ferwerda, Kattenberg, Chang, Unger, Groot and Bikker (forthcoming) have tested the Walker model and found that it would be better to formulate it in a multiplicative way as is usual for gravity models. They also overcame the problem of ad hoc chosen weights of the variables. They also tested which of Walker's variables explain most, finding that, for example, corruption is an important indicator, while SWIFT membership is not.

A better micro-foundation of the 'Walker Model' will be needed in the future. For this

Table 13.1 Summary of estimates of global flows of illicit finance

Global flows	Low (US$ bn)	High (US$ bn)
Drugs	120	200
Counterfeit goods	80	120
Counterfeit currency	3	4
Human trafficking	12	15
Illegal arms trade	6	10
Smuggling	60	100
Racketeering	50	100
Crime subtotal	331	549
Mispricing	200	250
Abusive transfer pricing	300	500
Fake transactions	200	250
Commercial subtotal	700	1000
Corruption	30	50
Grand Total	1061	1599

Source: Baker (2005).

the behaviour of money launderers, including what makes them send their money to a specific country, is important. To give an example: if Italian launderers always send their drug money only to Turkey and if Dutch launderers sent their ecstasy pill proceeds only to the UK, then the 'Walker Model', which assumes a large spread of flows of money would have to be corrected for this.

It seems, therefore, crucial to continue to collaborate with criminologists in studying criminal behaviour. The variables in the attractiveness indicator are, though plausible, still arbitrary. In particular, the weights of the variables in the attractiveness and distance indicator are still arbitrary. Maybe large financial centres attract far more laundered money, or small islands without financial centres are far more attractive for launderers than is indicated by the global criminal flow model used by the 'Walker Model'.

NOTES

* This chapter is a shortened version of 'Measuring Global Money Laundering: "The Walker Gravity Model"' in *Review of Law and Economics*, Vol. 5, December 2009.

1. We owe this point to Jaap Bikker.
2. We owe this point to Thijs Knaap. Economists usually claim to be very precise. They have applied Newton's principles to economics when creating a theory of exchange. It is therefore not without irony that physicists rightly complain that economists turn the universe around when modifying Newton's formula. The universe would collapse if Newton's distance square term were to be changed by only a marginal amount, let us say from 2 to 1.999. When this is done in trade equations the economic system apparently appears to be quite robust.
3. Modifications to the original 'Walker Model' are in bold.

REFERENCES

Baker, R. (2005), *Capitalism's Achilles Heel: Dirty Money and How to Renew the Free-Market System*, Hoboken, NJ: Wiley.

Ferwerda, J., M. Kattenberg, H. Chang, B. Unger, L. Groot and J. Bikker (forthcoming), 'Gravity models of trade-based money laundering', *Applied Economics* (accepted 29 May 2012).

Head, K. (2003), 'Gravity for beginners', version prepared for UBC Econ 590a students, February 5, 2003, Faculty of Commerce, University of British Columbia, Vancouver, Canada.

Helliwell, J.F. (2000), 'Language and trade, gravity modelling of trade flows and the role of language', The Department of Canadian Heritage.

Levi, M. and M. Gold (1994), *Money-Laundering in the UK: An Appraisal of Suspicion-Based Reporting*, London: Police Foundation.

Masciandaro, Donato, Elod Takats and Brigitte Unger (2007), *Black Finance: The Economics of Money Laundering*, Cheltenham, UK and Northampton, MA, USA: Edward Elgar Publishing.

Meloen, J., R., Landman, H. de, Miranda, J. van Eekelen and S. van Soest (2003), *Buit en Besteding, Een empirisch onderzoek naar de omvang, de kenmerken en de besteding van misdaadgeld*. Den Haag: Reed Business Information.

MOT (Meldpunt Ongebruikelijke Transacties) (2005), Jaarverslag 2004, vooruitblik 2005, Ministerie van Justitie. Breda: Koninklijke Drukkerij Broese & Peereboom.

Schneider, F. (2006), 'Shadow economies of 145 countries all over the world: what do we really know?', revised version May 2006, http://www.econ.jku.at/Schneider/ShadEconomyWorld145_2006.pdf.

Tanzi, V. (1997), 'Macroeconomic implications of money laundering', in E.U. Sarona (ed.), *Responding to Money Laundering: International Perpectives*, Amsterdam: Harwood Academic Publishers.

Thoumi, F. (2003), 'The numbers' game: let's all guess the size of the illegal drugs industry!', paper prepared for TNI seminar on The Economic Impact of the Illicit Drug Industry, December 2003.

Tinbergen, J. (1962), *Shaping the World Economy: Suggestions for an International Economic Policy*, New York: Twentieth Century Fund.

Truman, E.M. and P. Reuter (2004), *Chasing Dirty Money: Progress on Anti-Money Laundering*, Washington DC: Institute for International Economics.

Unger, B. (2007), *The Scale and Impact of Money Laundering*, Cheltenham, UK and Northampton, MA, USA: Edward Elgar Publishing.

Unger, B., J. Ferwerda, W. de Kruijf, G. Rawlings, M. Siegel and K. Wokke (2006), *The Amounts and the Effects of Money Laundering, Report for the Dutch Ministry of Finance*, February 2006, http://www.minfin.nl/binaries/minfin/assets/pdf/old/06_011a.pdf

United Nations Office on Drugs and Crime (UNODC) (2005), *World Drug Report 2005*, Vienna: UNODC.

UNODC, (2011), *World Drug Report 2008*, Vienna: UNODC.

Walker, J. (1995), 'Estimates of the Extent of Money Laundering in and through Australia', paper prepared for the Australian Transaction Reports and Analysis Centre, September 1995, Queanbeyan: John Walker Consulting Services.

Walker, J. (1999), 'How Big is Global Money Laundering?', *Journal of Money Laundering Control*, **3**, (1), 25–37.

Walker, J. (2002), *Just How Big is Global Money Laundering?*, Sydney: Australian Institute of Criminology Seminar.

Walker, J. (ed.) (2003), *The Profits & Losses of Global Crime*, Ontario: de Sitter Publications.

Walker, J. and B. Unger (2009), 'Estimating money laundering: the Walker Gravity Model', *Review of law and Economics*, December.

14. A preliminary attempt to estimate the financial flows of transnational crime using the MIMIC method

Andreas Buehn and Friedrich Schneider

14.1 INTRODUCTION

Until 2008, growth of the world economy was quite high and improved economic well-being all over the globe. This development was, however, accompanied by some risks too. One of them is transnational organized crime (TOC), which has risen remarkably in the last 20 years.[1] This raises the following two questions:

(1) From where does transnational crime get its proceeds; and
(2) What do we know about their size and development?

In this chapter, question (1) will be briefly answered, but the main focus lies on providing a more detailed answer to question (2) on the size and development of the finances of transnational crime. A detailed analysis of the financial proceeds of TOC and its sources is crucial in order to reduce its possibilities, so that the basis of its operations is at least limited.

Our chapter is structured as follows: section 14.2 provides a literature review on the types of transnational crime proceeds. Section 14.3 provides first estimates of the size and development of money laundering for 20 OECD countries from 1995 to 2006 using the MIMIC method, which is also explained in that section. In section 14.4 some conclusions are drawn and policy recommendations made.

14.2 TRANSNATIONAL CRIME PROCEEDS[2]

Dirty money from crime is earned through various underground activities, for instance drugs and weapons trade and human trafficking. How much illicit crime money in all its forms can be observed?[3] Baker (2005) estimates that this illicit crime money ranged between US$ 1.0 and 1.6 trillion in 2000/2001, an estimate that has been adopted by the World Bank. Moreover, Baker estimates that half – US$500 to 800 billion a year – comes out of developing and transitional economies. These are countries that often have the weakest legal and administrative structures, the largest criminal gangs of drug dealers, and, far too often, economic and political elites who want to take their money out of the country by any means possible. In table 14.1, Baker's global flows from illicit activities are shown. According to Baker, the proceeds of bribery and theft are the smallest quantities, at only perhaps 3 per cent of the global total. Generated funds from classical crime activities (Nos 1–7) account for some 30 to 35 per cent of

Table 14.1 Global flows from illicit activities worldwide, years 2000/2001

Number	Global Flows	Low (US$ bn)	%	High (US$ bn)	%
1.	Drugs	120	11%	200	12.5%
2.	Counterfeit goods	80	7.5%	120	7.5%
3.	Counterfeit currency	3	0.2%	3	0.2%
4.	Human trafficking	12	1.1%	15	0.9%
5.	Illegal arms trade	6	2.0%	10	0.6%
6.	Smuggling	60	5.6%	100	6.3%
7.	Racketeering	50	4.7%	100	6.3%
	Crime subtotal	*331*	*31.2%*	*548*	*34.3%*
8.	Mispricing	200	18.9%	250	15.6%
9.	Abusive transfer pricing	300	28.3%	500	31.2%
10.	Fake transactions	200	18.9%	250	15.6%
	Commercial subtotal	*700*	*66.0%*	*1,000*	*62.5%*
11.	*Corruption*	*30*	*2.8%*	*50*	*5.1%*
	Grand Total	*1,061*	*100.0%*	*1,598*	*100.0%*

Source: Baker (2005).

Table 14.2 Estimates of out-of-country illicit financial flows, in billion US$

		2002	2005	2006	2006 in % of total illicit outflows	2006 in % of GDP
Developing countries	Min	372.5	674.9	858.6	100%	6%
	Max	435.4	805.8	1,056.2	100%	7%
Sub-Saharan Africa	Min	12.7	10.2	11.0	1.3%	1%
	Max	21.9	19.0	22.7	2.1%	3%
Asia and the Pacific	Min	192.9	364.0	400.0	46.6%	7%
	Max	219.1	448.9	546.3	51.7%	9%
Europe	Min	60.0	78.2	186.2	21.7%	7%
	Max	67.6	87.5	190.9	18.1%	7%
Middle East and North Africa	Min	22.1	125.3	164.8	19.2%	10%
	Max	25.1	143.1	187.4	17.7%	12%
Americas ('Western Hemisphere')	Min	84.8	97.2	97.3	11.3%	3%
	Max	101.7	107.2	108.9	10.3%	3%

Sources: Kar and Cartwright-Smith (2009) and World Bank Indicators (GDP current US$).

the global total crime activities. Commercial criminal activities, like tax evasion, in particular driven by abusive transfer pricing and fake transactions, as well as mispricing, are by far the largest components, accounting for 60 to 65 per cent of the global total crime activities.

In table 14.2 the estimates of illicit flows out of developing counties and out of countries in transition over the period 2000 to 2006 are presented. As it is quite difficult to calculate exact figures, the table provides minimum and maximum values. Table 14.2

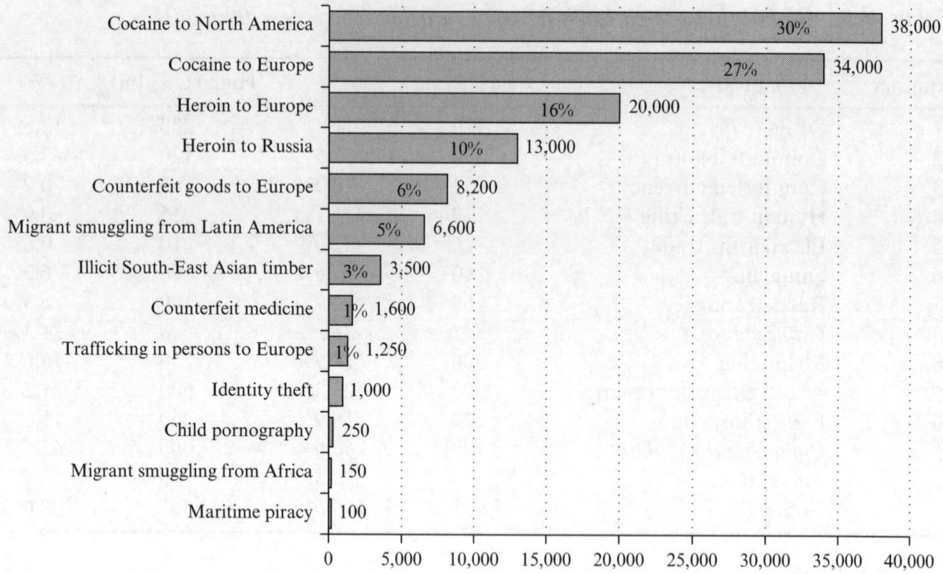

Note: Total sum 127,773 million US$. Other crime types: Ivory to Asia 62 million (0.05%), Firearms from Eastern Europe 33 million (0.03%), Firearms to Mexico 20 million (0.02%), Rhino horn to Asia 8 million (0.01%).

Source: UNODC (2010, p. 200).

Figure 14.1 TOC value estimates in US$ millions

clearly shows that between 46.6 and 51.7 per cent of all illicit financial outflows come from the 'Asia and the Pacific' region, followed by Europe, where the share is between 18.1 and 21.7 per cent. In the year 2006 between US$858.6 and 1056.2 billion left the developing countries. This is a range between 6 and 7 per cent of the GDP of the developing countries – quite a remarkable sum. It is also amazing that over time there is a strong increase in these illicit outflows. Whereas in the year 2002 the minimum value only amounted for US$372.5 billion, it increased to US$858.6 billion in the year 2006, which means the value had more than doubled.

In Figure 14.1 an overview of the most important import crime types and their proceeds on a worldwide basis for the year 2008 is given. The most profitable business is drug trafficking to North America, to Europe and to Russia. Cocaine trafficking to America has an estimated value of US$38 billion and to Europe of US$34 billion heroin trafficking to Europe, makes US$20 billion and to Russia US$13 billion, followed by counterfeit goods to Europe with US$8.2 billion and then migrant smuggling from Latin America with US$6.6 billion and illicitly traded South Asian timber which has a value of US$3.5 billion.[4] Figure 14.1 clearly demonstrates that the worldwide crime scene is a lively one, but also that drug trafficking is the most profitable business.

14.3 MONEY LAUNDERING

14.3.1 Methods of Money Laundering

The main goal of money laundering is to make dirty money appear legal (Walker 1999). There are many methods of money laundering. In Table 14.3 the 12 most common methods are shown, according to Walker and Unger (2009) Which of these methods is chosen depends on the type of crime activity and on the specific institutional arrangements of the country where the criminal money is 'earned'. For example, in the drug business, method 8, that is business ownership, is quite often used.[5] In the drug business and in big cities smaller amounts of cash are earned by drug dealers in a lot of different places, which they infiltrate into cash intensive operations such as restaurants which are especially well suited for money laundering purposes. However, cash deposits, the so-called smurfing method, or illegal gambling are also quite often used.

14.3.2 Estimating Financial Flows of Transnational Crime Organizations

As the size of the financial flows of transnational crime organizations is an unknown (hidden) figure, a latent estimator approach using the MIMIC (i.e. **m**ultiple **i**ndicators, **m**ult**i**ple **c**auses estimation) procedure is applied. This method has quite successfully been used to estimate the size of the shadow economy and is based on the statistical theory of unobserved variables. The statistical idea behind such a model is to compare a sample covariance matrix, that is, a covariance matrix of observable variables, with the parametric structure imposed on this matrix by a hypothesized model.[6] Using covariance information among the observable variables, the unobservable variable is in the first step linked to observable variables in a factor analytical model also called measurement model. Second, the relationships between the unobservable variable and observable variables are specified through a structural model. Therefore, a MIMIC model is the simultaneous specification of a factor and a structural model. In this sense, the MIMIC model tests the consistency of a 'structural' theory through data and is thus a confirmatory, rather than an exploratory technique. An economic theory is thus tested examining the consistency of actual data with the hypothesized relationships between the unobservable (latent) variable or factor and the observable (measurable) variables.[7] In general, a confirmatory factor analysis has two goals: (i) to estimate parameters such as coefficients and variances; and (ii) to assess the fit of the model. For the analysis of TOC activities these two goals mean (i) to estimate the relationships between a set of observable variables, divided into causes and indicators, and the TOC activity (unobservable variable); and (ii) to test if the researcher's theory or the derived hypotheses as a whole fit the data. MIMIC models are, compared to regression models, a rarely used method by economists, which might be due to an under-evaluation of their capabilities with respect to their potential contribution to economic research.

The idea of the MIMIC model application is to examine the relationships between the latent variable size of financial flows of transnational organized crime (TOC) and observable variables in terms of the relationships among a set of observable variables by using their covariance information. The observable variables are divided into causes and indicators of the latent variable (see Figure 14.2). The key benefits of the MIMIC model

Table 14.3 The methods of money laundering

1. Wire transfers or electronic banking	The primary tool of money launderers to move funds through the banking system. These moves can conceal funds' illicit origins or just place the money where the launderers need it. Often the funds go through several banks and even different jurisdictions.
2. Cash deposits	Money launderers need to deposit cash advances in bank accounts prior to wire transfers. Due to anti-money-laundering regulations they often 'structure' the payments, i.e. break down large amounts into smaller sums. This is also called 'smurfing'.
3. Informal value transfer systems (IVTSs)	Money launderers need not rely on the banking sector, other transfer providers, such as the Hawala or Hindi are readily available to undertake fund transfers. These systems consist of shops (mainly selling groceries, phone cards or other similar items), which are also involved in transfer services. IVTSs enable international fund transfers, as these shops are present in several jurisdictions.
4. Cash smuggling	Money launderers might mail, Fedex or simply carry cash with them from one region to another, or even to different jurisdictions.
5. Gambling	Casinos, horse races and lotteries are ways of legalizing funds. The money launderer can buy (for 'dirty' cash) winning tickets – or in the case of casinos, chips – and redeem the tickets or the chips in a 'clean' bank cheque. Afterwards, the cheque can be easily deposited in the banking sector.
6. Insurance policies	Money launderers purchase single premium insurance (with dirty cash) and redeem early (paying some penalty) in order to receive clean cheques to deposit. Longer-term premium payments might make laundering even harder to detect.
7. Securities	Usually used to facilitate fund transfers, where underlying security deals provide cover (and legitimate-looking reason) for transfers.
8. Business ownership	Money might be laundered through legitimate businesses where laundering funds can be added to legitimate revenues. Cash-intensive operations, such as restaurants, are especially well suited for laundering.
9. Shell corporations	Money launderers might create companies exclusively to provide cover for fund moves without legitimate business activities.
10. Purchases	Real estate or any durable good purchases can be used to launder monies. Typically, the item is bought for cash and resold for clean monies, like bank cheques.
11. Credit card advance payment	Money launderers pay money in advance with dirty money, and receive clean cheques on the balance from the bank
12. ATM operations	Banks might allow other firms to operate their ATMs, i.e. to maintain and fill them with cash. Money launderers fill ATMs with dirty cash, and receive clean cheques (for the cash withdrawn) from the bank.

Source: Unger (2007, pp. 195–6).

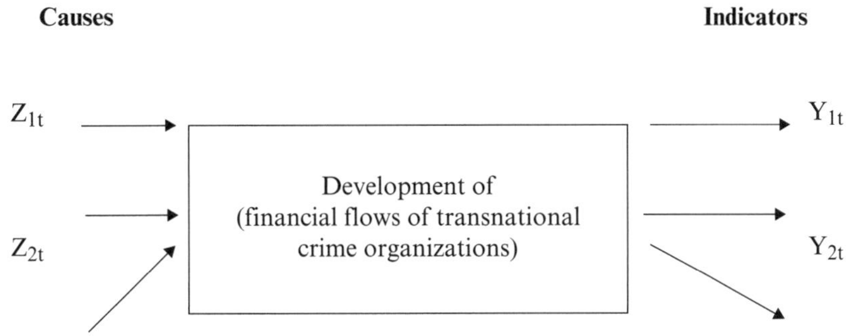

Figure 14.2 The MIMIC model

are that it allows modelling financial flows of TOC as an unobservable (latent) variable and that it takes into account its multiple determinants (causes) and multiple effects (indicators). A factor-analytic approach is used to measure the size of financial flows of transnational organized crime as an unobserved variable over time. The unknown coefficients are estimated in a set of structural equations, as the 'unobserved' variable, that is, the size of the financial flows of TOC cannot be measured directly. Formally, the MIMIC model consists of two parts: the structural equation model and the measurement model. In the measurement model, the unobservable variable η_t determines a p vector $y_t' = (y_{1t}, y_{2t}, \ldots, y_{pt})'$ of indicators, that is, observable variables that reflect the TOC flows, subject to a p vector of random error terms $\varepsilon_t' = (\varepsilon_{1t}, \varepsilon_{2t}, \ldots, \varepsilon_{pt})'$. The unobservable variable η_t is a scalar and λ is a p column vector of parameters that relates y_t to η_t. The measurement equation is given by:

$$y_t = \lambda \eta_t + \varepsilon_t. \tag{1}$$

The structural model determines the unobservable variable η_t by a set of exogenous causes $x_t' = (x_{1t}, x_{2t}, \ldots, x_{qt})'$ that may be useful in predicting its movement and size, subject to a structural disturbance error term ς_t. The structural equation is given by:

$$\eta_t = \gamma' x_t + \varsigma_t, \tag{2}$$

where γ' is a q row vector of structural parameters.[8] In equations (1) and (2) it is assumed that ς_t and the elements of ε_t are normally, independently and identically distributed, the variance of the structural disturbance term ς_t is denoted by ψ, and $\Theta_\varepsilon = E(\varepsilon_t \varepsilon_t')$ is the $(p \times p)$ covariance matrix of the measurement errors.[9] Figure 14.2 shows the path diagram of the MIMIC model.

The MIMIC model of TOC flows estimated in this paper uses three indicators and nine causes. Hence, within this model, equations (1) and (2) are specified as follows:

$$\begin{bmatrix} y_{1t} \\ y_{2t} \\ y_{3t} \end{bmatrix} = \begin{bmatrix} \lambda_1 \\ \lambda_2 \\ \lambda_3 \end{bmatrix} . \eta_t + \begin{bmatrix} \varepsilon_{1t} \\ \varepsilon_{2t} \\ \varepsilon_{3t} \end{bmatrix}, \tag{3}$$

$$\eta_t = [\gamma_1\ \gamma_2\ \gamma_3\ \gamma_4\ \gamma_5\ \gamma_6\ \gamma_7\ \gamma_8\ \gamma_9] \cdot \begin{bmatrix} x_{1t} \\ x_{2t} \\ x_{3t} \\ x_{4t} \\ x_{5t} \\ x_{6t} \\ x_{7t} \\ x_{8t} \\ x_{9t} \end{bmatrix} + \varsigma_t. \tag{4}$$

Substituting (1) into (2) yields a reduced form equation which expresses the relationships between the observed causes and indicators, that is, between x_t and y_t. This is shown in equation (5):

$$y_t = \Pi x_t + z_t, \tag{5}$$

where: $\Pi = \lambda\gamma'$ is a (3×9) reduced form coefficient matrix and $z_t = \lambda\varsigma_t + \varepsilon_t$ is a reduced form vector of a linear transformation of disturbances that has a (3×3) reduced form covariance matrix Ω given as:

$$\Omega = \mathrm{Cov}(z_t) = \mathrm{E}[(\lambda\varsigma_t + \varepsilon_t)(\lambda\varsigma_t + \varepsilon_t)'] = \lambda\psi\lambda' + \Theta_\varepsilon. \tag{6}$$

In equation (6), $\psi = \mathrm{Var}(\varsigma_t)$ and $\Theta_\varepsilon = \mathrm{E}(\varepsilon_t\varepsilon_t')$ is the measurement error's covariance matrix.

In general, estimation of a MIMIC model uses covariance information of sample data to derive estimates of population parameters. Instead of minimizing the distance between observed and predicted individual values, as in standard econometrics, the MIMIC model minimizes the distance between an observed (sample) covariance matrix and the covariance matrix predicted by the model the researcher imposes on the data. The idea behind that approach is that the covariance matrix of the observed variables is a function of a set of model parameters:

$$\Sigma = \Sigma(\theta), \tag{7}$$

where Σ is the population covariance matrix of the observed variables, θ is a vector that contains the parameters of the model and $\Sigma(\theta)$ is the covariance matrix as a function of θ, implying that each element of the covariance matrix is a function of one or more model parameters. If the hypothesized model is correct and the parameters are known, the population covariance matrix would be exactly reproduced, that is, Σ will equal $\Sigma(\theta)$. In practice, however, one does not know either the population variances and covariances or the parameters, but instead uses the sample covariance matrix and sample estimates of the unknown parameters for estimation (Bollen 1989, p. 256).

Estimation is thus performed by finding values for $\hat{\theta} = f(\hat{\lambda},\hat{\gamma},\hat{\psi},\hat{\Phi},\hat{\Theta}_\varepsilon)$ producing an estimate of the models covariance matrix $\hat{\Sigma}$ that most closely corresponds to the sample covariance matrix S. During this estimation procedure, all possible matrices that meet the imposed restrictions are considered. If an estimate Σ^* of $\hat{\Sigma}$ is close to S, one might conclude that θ^* is a reasonable estimate of the model's parameters. Hence, estimation of a MIMIC model is reduced to the problem of measuring how close Σ^* is to S and if this estimate is the most accurate, that is, if it is the best estimate given the set of all possible estimates that meet the imposed restrictions (Long 1983b, pp. 42–5). The covariance equation of the MIMIC model can be derived and has the following functional form:

$$\hat{\Sigma} = \left[\begin{array}{c|c} \hat{\lambda}(\hat{\gamma}'\hat{\Phi}\hat{\gamma} + \hat{\psi})\hat{\lambda}' + \hat{\Theta}_\varepsilon & \hat{\lambda}\hat{\gamma}'\hat{\Phi} \\ \hline \hat{\Phi}\hat{\gamma}\hat{\lambda}' & \hat{\Phi} \end{array}\right]. \tag{8}$$

The function measuring how close a given Σ^* is to the sample covariance matrix S is called the fitting function $F(S;\Sigma^*)$. The $\theta^*$of all possible θ^* that meets the imposed constraints on λ, γ,Φ, ψ and Θ_ε and minimizes the fitting function, given the sample covariance matrix S, is the sample estimate $\hat{\theta}$ of the population parameters. This means that if one set of estimates θ^*_1 produces the matrix Σ^*_1 and a second set θ^*_2 produces the matrix Σ^*_2 and if $F(S;\Sigma^*_1) < F(S;\Sigma^*_2)$, Σ^*_1 is then considered to be closer to S than Σ^*_2 (Long 1983a, p. 56).

The most widely used fitting function is the Maximum Likelihood (ML) function.[10] Under the assumption that $\Sigma(\theta)$ and S are positive definite, that is, nonsingular, and S has a Wishart distribution, the following fitting function is minimized:

$$F_{ML} = \log|\Sigma(\theta)| + tr[S\Sigma^{-1}(\theta)] - \log|S| - (p + q), \tag{9}$$

where log|| is the log of the determinant of the respective matrix and $(p + q)$ is the number of observed variables. In general, no closed form or explicit solution for the structural parameters that minimize F_{ML} exists. Hence, the values of λ, γ,Φ, ψ and $\hat{\Theta}_\varepsilon$ that minimize the fitting function are estimated applying iterative numerical procedures.[11] The ML estimator is widely used because of its desirable properties.[12] First, the ML estimator is asymptotically unbiased. Second, the ML estimator is consistent, that is, plim $\hat{\theta} = \theta$ ($\hat{\theta}_\varepsilon$ is the ML estimator and θ is the population parameter). Third, the ML estimator is asymptotically efficient, that is, among all consistent estimators no other has a smaller asymptotic variance. Fourth, the ML estimator is asymptotically normally distributed, meaning that the ratio of the estimated parameter and its standard error approximate a z-distribution in large samples. Fifth, a final important characteristic of the ML estimator is scale invariance (Swaminathan and Algina 1978). The scale invariance property implies that changes in the measurement unit of one or more of the observed variables do not change the value of the fitting function. This means that $\hat{\lambda}$, $\hat{\gamma}$, $\hat{\Phi}$, $\hat{\psi}$ and $\hat{\Theta}_\varepsilon$ are the same for any change of scale.

It is widely accepted by most scholars who estimate the size and development of informal economic activities such as the shadow economy using the MIMIC model or more general Structural Equation Models (SEMs) with more than one unobservable variable, that such an empirical exercise is a 'minefield', regardless of which method is used. For example, in evaluating the currently available shadow economy estimates of different scholars, one should keep in mind that there is no best or commonly accepted method. Each approach has its strengths and weaknesses and can provide specific insights and results. Although SEM/MIMIC model applications in economics are 'accompanied' by criticisms, they are increasingly used for estimating the shadow economy and other informal economic activities.

In comparison to other statistical methods, SEMs/MIMIC models offer several advantages for the estimation of informal economic activities. According to Giles and Tedds (2002), the MIMIC approach is a wider approach than most other competing methods, since it allows one to take multiple indicator and causal variables into consideration at the same time. Moreover, it is quite flexible, allowing one to vary the choice of causal and indicator variables according to the particular features of the informal economic activity studied, the period in question, and the availability of data. SEMs/MIMIC models lead to a formal estimation and to testing procedures, such as those based on the method of maximum likelihood. These procedures are well known and are generally 'optimal', if the sample is sufficiently large (Giles and Tedds 2002). Schneider and Enste (2000) emphasize that these models lead to some progress in estimation techniques for the size and development of the shadow economy, because this methodology allows a wide flexibility in its application. Therefore, they consider it potentially superior to other estimation methods. Cassar (2001) argues that, when compared to other methods, SEMs/MIMIC models do not need restrictive assumptions to operate. Analogously, Thomas (1992, p. 168) argues that the only real constraint of this approach is not in its conceptual structure, but the choice of variables. These positive aspects of the SEM approach in general and the MIMIC model in particular do not only apply in its application to the shadow economy, but to all informal economic activities.

Of course this method has its disadvantages or limitations, which are identified in the literature. The three most important points of criticism focus on the model's implementations, the sample used, and the reliability of the estimates:

(1) The most common objection estimating informal economic activities using SEMs concerns the meaning of the latent variable (e.g. Helberger and Knepel 1988; Dell'Anno 2003). The confirmatory rather than exploratory nature of this approach means that one is more likely to determine whether a certain model is valid than to 'find' a suitable model. Therefore, it is possible that the specified model includes potential definitions or informal economic activities other than the one studied. For example, it is difficult for a researcher to ensure that traditional crime activities such as drug dealing are completely excluded from the analysis of the shadow economy. This criticism, which is probably the most common in the literature remains difficult to overcome as it goes back to the theoretical assumptions behind the choice of variables and empirical limitations on data availability.

(2) Helberger and Knepel (1988) argue that SEM/MIMIC model estimations lead to unstable coefficients with respect to changes of the sample size and alternative model specifications. Dell'Anno (2003) shows, however, that instability disappears asymptotically as the sample size increases. Another issue is the application of SEMs to time series data because only simple analytical tools such as q- and stemleaf plots are available to analyse the properties of the residuals (Dell'Anno 2003).[13]

(3) Criticism is also related to the benchmarking procedure used to derive 'real world' figures of informal economic activities (Breusch 2005a, 2005b). As the latent vari-

> able and its unit of measurement are not observed, SEMs just provide a set of estimated coefficients from which one can calculate an index that shows the dynamics of the unobservable variable. Application of the so-called calibration or benchmarking procedure, regardless which one is used, requires experimentation, and a comparison of the calibrated values in a wide academic debate. Unfortunately, at this stage of research on the application of the SEM/MIMIC approach in economics it is not clear which benchmarking method is the best or the most reliable.[14]

The economic literature using SEMs is well aware of these limitations. Consequently, it acknowledges that it is not an easy task to apply this methodology to an economic dataset, but also argues that this does not mean one should abandon the SEM approach. On the contrary, following an interdisciplinary approach to economics, SEMs are valuable tools for economic analysis, particularly when studying informal (unobservable) economic activities. However, the mentioned objections should be considered as an incentive for further (economic) research in this field rather than as a suggestion to abandon this method.

In Figure 14.3, the MIMIC estimation results of the turnover of transnational crime for 20 highly developed OECD countries over the period 1994/95 to 2005/06 are shown. Figure 14.3 clearly shows that the amount of criminal activities of illegal weapon selling, illegal drug selling, and illegal trade with human beings have the expected positive and highly statistically significant influence on the turnover of transnational crime activities. The amount of criminal activities of fake products, the functioning of the legal system, and real police expenditures per capita per country are statistically significant as well. If we switch to the indicator variables, the amount of confiscated money has the expected positive sign and is highly statistically significant. The amount of prosecuted persons has the expected negative sign, but is not statistically significant using a strict measure. In general, this MIMIC estimation shows that the single crime types like illegal weapon selling, drug selling and trade with human beings have a highly statistically significant influence on the financial turnover of transnational criminal activities.

If we discuss the econometric result of the MIMIC estimation in detail, we clearly see that seven out of the nine cause variables have a statistically significant influence on the turnover of transnational criminal activities. The amount of criminal activities of illegal drug selling has the largest and most significant influence, followed by the amount of criminal activities of illegal trade with human beings and the amount of criminal activities of illegal weapon selling. Also the real police expenditures have the expected negative and highly statistically significant influence together with the per capita income and the functioning of the legal system. The amount of criminal activities of fraud and computer crime turns out not to be significant, as well as the amount of domestic crime activities. If we consider the indicators, confiscated money has a strongly positive significant influence and the variable 'prosecuted persons' is not statistically significant, but has the predicted negative sign.

With the help of the MIMIC estimation procedure (cf. Figure 14.3), Schneider (2008) estimates that money laundering and/or financial turnover from transnational crime has increased from US$273 billion (1.33% of the total official GDP) in 1995 to US$603 billion (or 1.74% of the official GDP) in 2006 for 20 OECD countries (Australia, Austria,

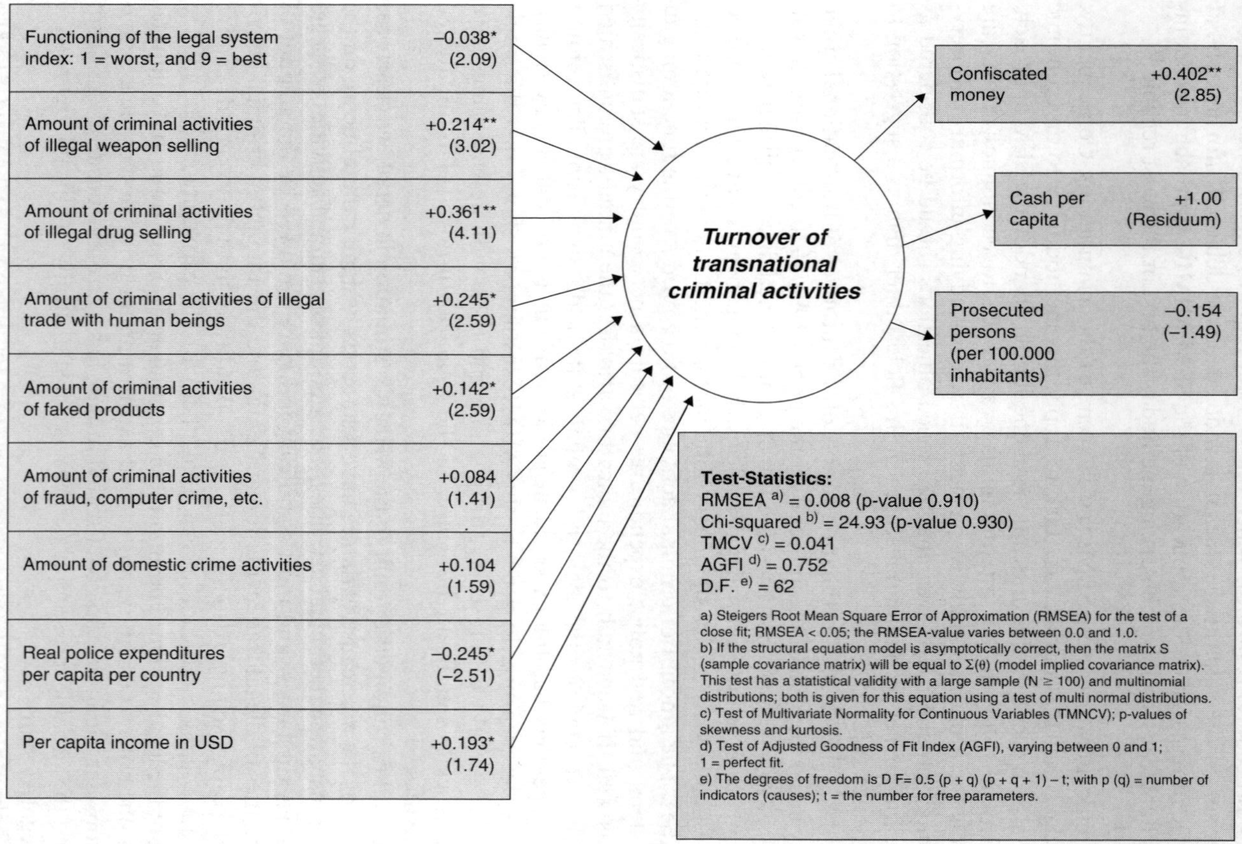

Notes: * Significant at the 5% level; ** Significant at the 1% level.

Figure 14.3 MIMIC estimation of the turnover of transnational crime for 20 highly developed OECD countries over the periods 1994/95, 1997/98, 2000/01, 2002/03, 2003/04 and 2004/05

Table 14.4 Estimated turnover of transnational crime using the MIMIC model

Year	Volume of money laundering (billion US$ for 20 OECD countries)	Volume of money laundering in % of GDP)
1995	273	1.33%
1996	294	1.37%
1997	315	1.40%
1998	332	1.42%
1999	359	1.46%
2000	384	1.47%
2001	412	1.52%
2002	436	1.56%
2003	475	1.63%
2004	512	1.66%
2005	561	1.72%
2006	603	1.74%

Note: 20 OECD Countries: Australia, Austria, Belgium, Canada, Denmark, Germany, Finland, France, Greece, Great Britain, Ireland, Italy, Japan, Netherlands, New Zealand, Norway, Portugal, Switzerland, Spain and USA.

Source: Own calculations, calibrated figures from the MIMIC estimations.

Belgium, Canada, Denmark, Germany, Finland, France, Greece, Great Britain, Ireland, Italy, Japan, Netherlands, New Zealand, Norway, Portugal, Switzerland, Spain and the United States). These figures are presented in Table 14.4, which nicely shows the steady increase of the volume of laundered money from 1995 to 2006. On a worldwide basis, in 2006 the IMF estimated US$600 billion as being laundered coming only from the drug (crime) business.

Unger (2007) estimates the amount of laundered money and its top 20 destination countries; these figures are shown in Table 14.5, covering the time span 1997–2005. In this table two estimates are presented, one by Walker (1999, 2007) and one by the IMF. The Walker figure of US$ 2,850 billion is much larger than the IMF figure of US$1,500 billion (both figures are for the year 2005). Walker's figures have been criticized as much too high, which is one reason why the IMF estimates are shown too. Table 14.5 clearly demonstrates that two-thirds of worldwide money laundering was sent to the top 20 countries listed. One should realize that most of these countries are highly developed and have quite sizeable legal/official economies. What is also amazing is that there are only a few microstate offshore countries and tax heavens among them (Cayman Islands, Vatican City, Bermuda and Liechtenstein).[15] The majority of countries that attract money laundering flows are economically big players. The United States has the largest worldwide share of money laundering at almost 19 per cent, followed by the Cayman Islands (4.9%) Russia (4.2%), and Italy (3.7%), but smaller countries like Switzerland (2.1% of worldwide money laundering), Liechtenstein (1.7%) and Austria (1.7%) are also quite attractive. If one takes the lower IMF value for Austria, Switzerland and the United Kingdom, roughly 5.5 per cent of the total amount is laundered, which comes close to roughly 10 per cent of official GDP of the three countries.

Table 14.5 The amount of laundered money and top 20 destinations of laundered money, year 2005

Rank	Destination	% of world wide money laundering	Walker estimate of 2.85 trillion US$ Amount in billion US$	IMF estimate of 1.5 trillion worldwide Amount in billion US$
1	United States	18.9%	538,145	283,500
2	Cayman Islands	4.9%	138,329	73,500
3	Russia	4.2%	120,493	63,000
4	Italy	3.7%	105,688	55,500
5	China	3.3%	94,726	49,500
6	Romania	3.1%	89,595	46,500
7	Canada	3.0%	85,444	45,000
8	Vatican City	2.8%	80,596	42,000
9	Luxembourg	2.8%	78,468	42,000
10	France	2.4%	68,471	36,000
11	Bahamas	2.3%	66,398	34,500
12	Germany	2.2%	61,315	33,000
13	Switzerland	2.1%	58,993	31,500
14	Bermuda	1.9%	52,887	28,500
15	Netherlands	1.7%	49,591	25,500
16	Liechtenstein	1.7%	48,949	25,500
17	Austria	1.7%	48,376	25,500
18	Hong Kong	1.6%	44,519	24,000
19	United Kingdom	1.6%	44,478	24,000
20	Spain	1.2%	35,461	18,000
	Total	67.1%	1,910,922	1,006,500

Source: Unger (2007, p. 80).

However, it needs to be emphasized that it is not clear whether this money is 'only' laundered in these countries or remains in these countries; it may well leave these countries after the laundering process. In general, Table 14.5 demonstrates how substantial the amount of laundered money is and that two-thirds of these funds are concentrated in only 20 countries.

Bagella, Busato and Argentiero (2009, pp. 881) use a two-sector dynamic general equilibrium model to measure money laundering for the United States and the EU-15 macro areas over the sample 2000:01-2007:01 at a quarterly data basis. Their series are generated through a fully micro-founded dynamic model, which is appropriately calibrated to replicate selected stochastic properties of the two economies. Their model (and the analysis) has a short-run perspective. Bagella et al. (2009, pp. 881) find the following results: first the simulations show that money laundering accounts for approximately 19 per cent of the GDP measured for the EU-15, while it accounts for 13 per cent in the US economy, over the sample 2000:01-2007:04. Second, the simulated money laundering appears less volatile than the corresponding GDP. As regards the EU-15 macro area, the simulated statistics suggest that money laundering volatility is one-third of the GDP volatility; for the US economy, the same statistics produce a figure of two-fifths. Considering these estimates we admit that they are pretty high.

From a global perspective for 2000, the IMF (2001, 2003), as well as the World Bank, estimate that 2–4 per cent of the world gross domestic product (GDP) stems from illicit (criminal) sources. Agarwal and Agarwal (2006) estimate from economic intelligence units that global money laundering amounts to more than US$2.0 to 2.5 trillion annually or about 5–6 per cent of World GDP in 2006 (US$4,444 trillion in 2006) to be contrasted against an observed figure of US$500 billion to one trillion in 2004 from the same authors (Agarwal and Agarwal, 2004). Recent IMF estimates on money laundering by drug traffickers who 'introduce' the proceeds gained through the selling of drugs into the legitimate financial market, amount to US$600 billion annually. The IDB (2004) reaches the conclusion that for Latin America a rough estimate of illicit flows appears to be somewhere between 2.5 and 6.3 per cent of the annual GDP of Latin American countries. Besides the figures from Agarwal and Agarwal, which are much higher, the others seem to be plausible considering their size.

In their latest study, Walker and Unger (2009, p. 821) again undertake an attempt to measure global money laundering and/or the proceeds from transnational crime that are pumped through the financial system worldwide. They criticize methods such as case studies, proxy variables, or models for measuring the crime economy, arguing that they all tend to under- or overestimate money laundering. They present a model, which is a gravity model and which makes it possible to estimate the flows of illicit funds from and to each jurisdiction in the world and worldwide. This 'Walker Model' was first developed in 1994, and was recently updated. The authors show that it belongs to the group of gravity models, which have recently become popular in international trade theory. The authors demonstrate that the original Walker Model estimates are compatible with recent findings on money laundering. Once the scale of money laundering is known, its macroeconomic effects and the impact of crime prevention, regulation and law enforcement effects on money laundering and transnational crime can also be measured. Walker and Unger (2009, pp. 849–50) conclude that their model still seems to be the most reliable and robust method to estimate global money laundering, and thereby the important effects of transnational crime on economic, social and political institutions. Rightly they argue that the attractiveness of the distance indicator in the Walker model is a first approximation, but is still quite ad hoc. A better micro-foundation for the Walker Model will be needed in the future. A micro foundation means that, the behaviour of money launderers is analysed, and in particular what makes them send their money to a specific country. Hence, Walker and Unger (2009, p. 850) argue that an economics of crime micro-foundation for the Walker Model would mean that, similarly to international trade theory, behavioural assumptions about money launderers have to be made. Their gravity model must be the (reduced form) outcome of the money launderer's rational calculus of sending their money to a certain country and potentially making large profits.

14.4 SUMMARY AND CONCLUSIONS

In our chapter an attempt is made to estimate the finances of transnational organized crime (TOC). Our paper reaches the following results:

First, the necessity of money laundering is obvious as a great number of illegal (criminal) transactions are done by cash. Hence, this amount of cash from criminal activities must be laundered in order to have some 'legal' profit, or for the purposes of investment or consumption in the legal world.
Second, to get an estimate of the extent and development of the amount of the financial means of transnational crime over time is particularly difficult.[16] This paper collects some findings and demonstrates that money laundering from transnational crime has increased from US$273 billion (or 1.33% of official GDP) in 1995 to US$603 billion (or 1.74% of official GDP) in 2006 for 20 OECD countries (Australia, Austria, Belgium, Canada, Denmark, Germany, Finland, France, Greece, Great Britain, Ireland, Italy, Japan, Netherlands, New Zealand, Norway, Portugal, Switzerland, Spain and the United States). On a worldwide basis, in 2006, US$600 billion alone is estimated to be laundered from the total drug (crime) business. These figures are very preliminary with a relatively large margin of error, but give a clear indication of how important money laundering and the turnover of transnational crime is.

From these preliminary results we draw three conclusions:

(1) The revenues of transnational crime are extremely difficult to estimate scientifically. They are defined differently in almost every country, the measures taken against it are different and vary from country to country and, therefore, it is not clear how large the revenues of transnational crime are.[17] Moreover, we have little empirical evidence, where these dirty or 'white-washed' financial means stay or are transferred to.
(2) Fighting transnational crime is extremely difficult, as there are no efficient and powerful international organizations which can effectively fight against transnational crime.[18]
(3) Hence, this chapter should be seen as a preliminary attempt in order to shed some light on the grey area of the revenues of transnational crime and to provide some better empirical knowledge.

NOTES

1. See for an example Walker and Unger (2009) and Masciandaro (2004).
2. For a detailed analysis see Schneider (2008), Schneider and Windischbauer (2008), and Takats (2007).
3. Smith (2011) estimates that this amount is US$1.5 trillion per year. However, no clear sources are given and, even more important, the procedure of calculation is not shown or critically discussed.
4. Buehn and Eichler (2009) present an interesting application of a MIMIC model to study illegal immigration and drug smuggling across the US–Mexico border.
5. Cf. Schneider (2004) and Masciandaro (2004).
6. Estimation of a MIMIC model with a latent variable can be done by means of a computer program for the analysis of covariance structures, such as LISREL (Linear Structural Relations). A useful overview of the LISREL software package in an economics journal is Cziraky (2004).
7. On the contrary, in an exploratory factor analysis a model is not specified in advance, i.e., beyond the specification of the number of latent variables (factors) and observed variables the researcher does not specify any structure of the model. This means that one assumes that all factors are correlated, all observable variables are directly influenced by all factors, and all measurement errors are uncorrelated with each

other. In practice, however, the distinction between a confirmatory and an exploratory factor analysis is less strong. Facing poorly fitting models, researchers using the MIMIC model often modify their models in an exploratory way in order to improve the fit. Thus, most applications fall between the two extreme cases of exploratory (non-specified model structure) and confirmatory (ex-ante specified model structure) factor analysis (Long 1983a, 11–17).

8. Without loss of generality, all variables are taken as standardized deviations from their means.
9. In the standard MIMIC model the measurement errors are assumed to be independent of each other, but this restriction could be relaxed (Stapleton 1978, 53).
10. Other estimation procedures such as Unweighted Least Squares (ULS) and Generalized Least Squares (GLS) are also available. ULS has the advantage that it is easier to compute and leads to a consistent estimator without the assumption that the observed variables have a particular distribution. Important disadvantages of ULS are, however, that ULS does not lead to the asymptotically most efficient estimator of θ and that F_{ULS} is not scale invariant. The GLS estimator has similar statistical properties like the ML estimator but the significance tests are no longer accurate if the distribution of the observed variables has very 'fat' or 'thin' tails. Moreover, F_{GLS} accepts the wrong model more often than ML and parameter estimates tend to suffer when using F_{GLS}. Thus, ML seems to be superior (see, e.g. Bollen 1989, 111–15; Olssen et al. 1999, 2000; Jöreskog and Sörbom 2001, 20–4).
11. See Appendix 4C in Bollen (1989) for details.
12. The properties are only briefly reviewed. For a detailed discussion see Bollen (1989, 107–23).
13. Particularly critical are the assumptions $E(\varsigma_{ik}^2) = \mathrm{Var}(\varsigma_i)$ for all k (homoscedasticity assumption) and for all $\mathrm{Cov}(\varsigma_{ik}, \varsigma_i) = 0$ for all $k \neq l$ no autocorrelation in the error terms). Unfortunately, corrections for autocorrelated and heteroscedastic error terms have not yet received sufficient attention in models with unobservable variables (Bollen 1989, 58). An interesting exception is Folmer and Karmann (1992).
14. See Dell'Anno and Schneider (2009) for a detailed discussion on different benchmarking procedures.
15. See also Masciandaro (2005), Zdanowicz (2009), Truman and Reuter (2004) and Walker and Unger (2009).
16. All estimated figures have a large error; the estimation procedures are very difficult to use. Hence the published figures should be interpreted with great care. Compare also the first conclusion.
17. Money laundering definitions vary considerably from country to country; also there are no internationally organized and harmonized processes to fight money laundering, with the result that little has been done so far.
18. Some first attempts have been made, like the FATF, or some sub-organizations of the UN, cf. e.g. UNODC (2005), FATF (2005) and FATF–GAFI (2006).

REFERENCES

Agarwal, J.D. and Aman Agarwal (2004), 'Globalization and international capital flows', *Finance India*, **19**(1), 65–99.

Agarwal, J.D. and Aman Agarwal (2006), 'Money laundering: new forms of crime and victimization', paper presented at the National Workshop on New Forms of crime, Victimization, Department of Criminology, University of Madras, India.

Bagella, Michele, Francesco Busato and Amedeo Argentiero (2009), 'Money laundering in a microfounded dynamic model: simulations for the US and the EU-15 economies', *Review of Law and Economics*, **5**(2), 879–902.

Baker, Raymond W. (2005), *Capitalism's Achilles Heel: Dirty Money and How to Renew the Free-Market System*, Hoboken, NJ: John Wiley and Sons.

Bollen, K.A. (1989), *Structural Equations with Latent Variables*, New York: Wiley.

Breusch, T. (2005a), 'The Canadian underground economy: an examination of Giles and Tedds', *Canadian Tax Journal*, **53**, 367–91.

Breusch, T. (2005b), 'Estimating the underground economy using MIMIC models', Working Paper, available at: http://econwpa.wustl.edu/eps/em/papers/0507/0507003.pdf

Buehn, A. and S. Eichler (2009), 'Smuggling legal versus illegal goods across the U.S.–Mexico border: a structural equations model approach', *Southern Economic Journal*, **76**(2), 328–50.

Cassar, A. (2001), 'An index of the underground economy in Malta', *Bank of Valletta Review*, **23**, 44–62.

Cziraky, D. (2004), 'LISREL 8.54: a program for structural equation modelling with latent variables', *Journal of Applied Econometrics*, **19**, 135–41.

Dell'Anno, R. (2003), 'Estimating the shadow economy in Italy: a structural equation approach', Working Paper 2003-7, Department of Economics, University of Aarhus, Aarhus.

Dell'Anno, R. and F. Schneider (2009), 'A complex approach to estimate the shadow economy: the structural equation modelling', in M. Faggini and T. Lux (eds), *Coping with the Complexity of Economics*, Springer: Heidelberg, 110–30.

FATF (2005), *Money Laundering and Terrorist Financing Typologies*, 2004–2005, Paris: FATF.

FATF – GAFI (2006), *Third Mutual Evaluation Report on Anti-Money Laundering and Competing the Financing of Terrorism*, Portugal, Paris: FATF, 1–165.

Folmer, H. and A. Karmann (1992), 'The permanent income hypothesis revisited – a dynamic LISREL approach', *Methods of Operations Research*, **64**, 355–9.

Giles, D.E.A. and L.M. Tedds (2002), 'Taxes and the Canadian underground economy', *Canadian Tax Foundation*, Toronto.

Helberger, C. and H. Knepel (1988), 'How big is the shadow economy? A re-analysis of the unobserved-variable approach of B.S. Frey and H.Weck-Hannemann', *European Economic Review*, **32**, 965–76.

IDB (2004), *A First Estimation of Illicit Flows in Latin America*, Study, Washington DC.

IMF (2001), *Financial System Abuse, Financial Crime and Money Laundering*, Report, Washington, D.C.: Monetary and Exchange Affairs and Policy Development.

IMF (2003), *Money Laundering: New Facts*, Study, Washington DC.

Jöreskog, K.G. and D. Sörbom (2001), *LISREL 8: User's Reference Guide*, Lincolnwood: Scientific Software International.

Kar, D. and D. Cartwright-Smith (2009), *Global Financial Integrity, Illicit Financial Flows from Developing Countries, 2002–2006*, Study, Washington DC.

Long, J.S. (1983a), *Confirmatory Factor Analysis*, Beverly Hills, CA: Sage.

Long, J.S. (1983b), *Covariance Structure Models: An Introduction to LISREL*, Beverly Hills, CA: Sage.

Masciandaro, D. (2004), *Global Financial Crime: Terrorism, Money Laundering and Off Shore Centres*, Aldershot, UK and Burlington, UT, USA: Ashgate.

Masciandaro, D. (2005), 'Financial supervisory unification and financial intelligence units', *Journal of Money Laundering Control*, **8**(4), 354–71.

Olssen, U.H., S.V. Troye and R.D. Howell (1999), 'Theoretic fit and empirical fit: the performance of Maximum Likelihood versus Generalized Least Squares estimation in Structural Equations Models', *Multivariate Behavioral Research*, **34**, 31–58.

Olssen, U.H., T. Foss, S.V. Troye and R.D. Howell (2000), 'The performance of ML, GLS, and WLS estimation in structural equation modeling under conditions of misspecification and nonnormality', *Structural Equation Modeling*, **7**, 557–95.

Schneider, Friedrich (2004), 'The financial flows of Islamic Terrorism', in Donato Masciandaro (ed.), *Global Financial Crime: Terrorism, Money Laundering and Offshore Centres*, Aldershot, UK: Ashgate, 97–126.

Schneider, Friedrich (2008), 'Money laundering from revenues from organized crime: some preliminary empirical findings', revised version of a paper presented at the Conference 'Illicit Trade and Globalization', CES-ifo Venice Summer Workshop, Venice National University, San Servolo, July 14–15.

Schneider, F. and D. Enste (2000), 'Shadow economies: size, causes, and consequences', *The Journal of Economic Literature*, **38**, 77–114.

Schneider, Friedrich and Ursula Windischbauer (2008), 'Money laundering: some facts', *European Journal of Law and Economics*, **26**(4), 387–404.

Smith, David (2011), 'Black money: the business of money laundering', Economy Watch.com, available at http:// www.economywatch.com.

Stapleton, D.C. (1978), 'Analyzing political participation data with a MIMIC Model', *Sociological Methodology*, **15**, 52–74.

Swaminathan, H. and J. Algina (1978), 'Scale freeness in factor analysis', *Psychometrika*, **43**, 581–3.

Takats, Ilöd (2007), 'A theory of 'crying wolf': the economics of money laundering enforcement', paper presented at the conference 'Tackling Money Laundering', University of Utrecht, The Netherlands, November 2–3.

Thomas, J.J. (1992), *Informal Economic Activity*, Handbooks in Economics, London School of Economics, London: Harvester Wheatsheaf.

Truman, E.M. and Peter Reuter (2004), *Chasing Dirty Money: Progress on Anti-Money Laundering*, Washington DC: Institute for International Economics.

Unger, Brigitte (2007), *The Scale and Impacts of Money Laundering*, Cheltenham, UK and Northampton, MA, USA: Edward Elgar Publishing.

UNODC (2005), *World Drug Report*, United Nations Office for Drug and Crime Prevention (UDCCP), Report, Oxford and New York.

UNODC (2010), *The Globalization of Crime: A Transnational Organized Crime Threat Assessment*, Documentation, New York.

Walker, John (1999), 'How big is global money laundering?', *Journal of Money Laundering Control*, **3**(1), 64–85.
Walker, John (2007), 'Measuring global money laundering', paper presented at the conference 'Tackling Money Laundering', University of Utrecht, The Netherlands.
Walker, John and Brigitte Unger (2009), 'Measuring global money laundering: the Walker Gravity Model', *Review of Law and Economics*, **5**(2), 821–53.
Zdanowicz, John (2009), 'Trade-based money laundering and terrorist financing', *Review of Law and Economics*, **5**(2), 854–78.

15. The scale of the global financial structure facilitating money laundering

Raymond W. Baker

What do we mean by money laundering? Are we referring to money that breaks anti-money laundering laws? Or are we referring to money that breaks any laws in its origin, movement, or use and therefore is handled in a secretive manner to avoid detection of its illegal trail?

The former concept leaves out many forms of illegally generated money. For example, in the United States AML legislation bars principally the knowing receipt of the foreign proceeds of drugs, corruption, terrorist funds, trafficking, bank fraud, and certain treaty violations. Not barred are funds arising from some other forms of racketeering such as handling stolen property, credit fraud, counterfeiting, contraband, environmental crimes, tax evasion, and more.

I prefer the latter concept and thus refer to illicit financial flows. Illicit money is money that is illegally earned, transferred, or utilized in any country where it is generated, through which it moves, or into which it arrives. In my use of the term 'money laundering', I am referring to the whole gamut of illicit financial flows.

There are three forms of cross-border illicit money – the proceeds of bribery and theft by government officials, the proceeds of criminal activity by drug dealers, racketeers, and terrorists financiers, and the proceeds of tax evading and laundered commercial transactions.

Since the 1960s, we in the West have built and expanded a global structure to facilitate the movement of illicit money. A few elements of this system were available before then, but the evolution of the structure accelerated in the 1960s for two reasons. First, it was the period of decolonization. From the late 1950s to the end of the 1960s, 48 countries gained their independence from European powers. Many political leaders and wealthy businesspeople wanted to take their money out of these newly independent countries, a desire which was well serviced by our western financial institutions. Second, corporations began to spread their flags across the planet. Certainly there were international companies before the 1960s, but typically an international oil or trading company had overseas branches in only 12 or 15 countries. The great thrust to expand all over the globe took off in the 1960s and has continued up to the present. Most multinational corporations utilize abusive transfer pricing and tax evading techniques to relocate profits across borders at will. For these two reasons – decolonization and the spread of multinational corporations – the 1960s marked the point at which the expansion of the illicit financial structure took off in earnest.

This illicit financial structure, more commonly referred to as the global shadow financial system, consists of a number of interrelated parts:

- **Tax havens**, more than 60 in number across the globe, allowing non-functioning entities to buy and sell and accumulate profits without tax consequences.

- **Disguised corporations**, now numbering in the millions across the world.
- **Offshore secrecy jurisdictions**, where such entities can be set up behind nominees and trustees so that no one knows who are the real owners and managers.
- **Flee clauses**, allowing disguised entities to instantly relocate from one secrecy jurisdiction to another when anyone tries to discover the identity of natural persons owning accounts.
- **Anonymous trust funds**, shielding both the donor and the beneficiary.
- **Fake foundations**, enabling creators and beneficiaries of charitable entities to be one and the same.
- **False documentation**, used in all sorts of trade and capital transactions.
- **Falsified pricing**, by far the most commonly used element in the illicit financial structure, enabling mispriced imports and exports to be used to shift capital across borders.
- **Money laundering techniques**, specialized devices created to facilitate disguised transfers of funds.
- **Loop holes left in western laws**, allowing movement of money through the illicit financial structure and ultimately into western economies.

All three forms of illicit money – corrupt, criminal, and commercial – use this structure, developed in the West originally for the purpose of moving flight capital and tax evading money across borders. In the late 1960s and 1970s drug dealers stepped into these same channels to move their illicit money across borders. In the 1980s and 1990s, seeing how easy it was for the drug dealers to do it, other kinds of racketeers stepped into these same structures to move their illicit money across borders. In the 1990s and in the early years of this new century, again seeing how easy it was for drug dealers and racketeers, terrorist financiers also stepped into these same channels to move their illicit money across borders. Drug dealers, criminal syndicate heads, and terrorist masterminds have not invented any new ways of shifting illicit money across borders. They merely utilize the mechanisms we originally created to move corrupt and commercially tax evading money across borders.

How much illicit money in all its forms does this structure move? The very conservative estimate of Global Financial Integrity is $1 to $2 trillion a year. Roughly half, approaching $1 trillion a year, comes out of developing and emerging market economies. These are countries that often have the weakest legal and administrative structures, the largest gangs of drug dealers and racketeers, and, far too often, economic and political elites who want to take their money out by any means possible.

In cross-border illicit financial flows, the proceeds of bribery and theft are the smallest, at only perhaps three to five percent of the global total. Criminally generated funds account for some 30 to 35 percent of the global total. Commercially tax evading money, driven in particular by abusive transfer pricing, is by far the largest component, at some 60 to 65 percent of the global total.

The consequences of global illicit financial flows are staggering:

- This reality eviscerates foreign aid, with an estimated $10 in illicit money draining out of poor countries for every $1 of development assistance going in (Figure 15.1).

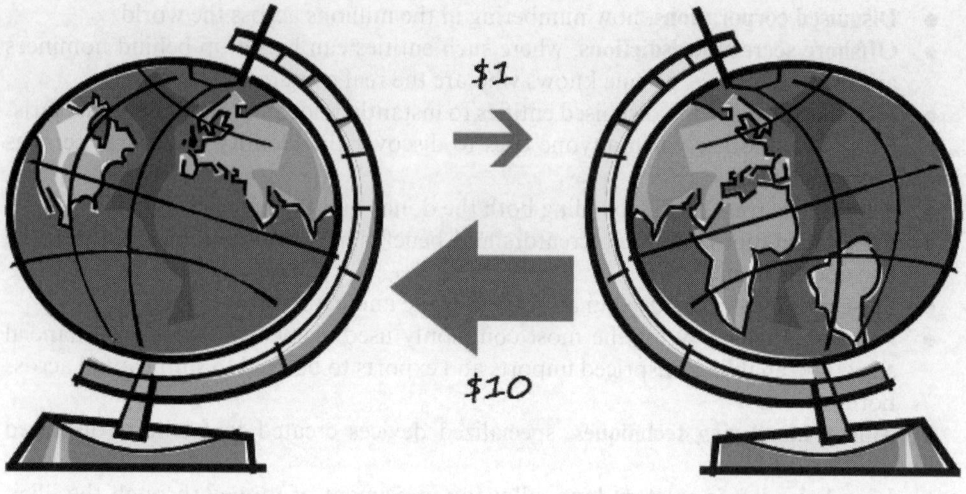

Figure 15.1 $10 in illicit money draining out of poor countries for every $1 of development assistance going in

- It makes the drug problem insoluble in producing, transiting, and consuming countries.
- It explains the explosion in cross-border crime over the past quarter century, one of the fastest growing activities in the world.
- An estimated $300 million passed through the illicit financial structure into Al Qaeda's hands in the decade prior to 9/11.
- It is the way that Saddam Hussein rearmed after the first Persian Gulf War, with an estimated $10 billion passing through this structure into his coffers.
- Pakistani nuclear scientist A.Q. Khan operated his nuclear network utilizing the global shadow financial system, buying and selling nuclear components and materials across the continents.
- Billions of dollars in drug money and stolen cash pour out of Afghanistan, further impoverishing the struggling nation.
- This structure and the money it moves has contributed to a number of failed states.

The question is sometimes asked whether or not wealth data can be used to estimate global money laundering? Wealth data has several problems:

1. The data is largely dependent on *World Development Indicators*, which attempt to make estimations of country income distributions in quintiles or in some cases smaller divisions. Such quintile distributions do not even begin to record satisfactorily the offshore asset accumulations of the rich and the income earned thereon. Assets of the rich held offshore, often in disguised entities in which nationalities of beneficial owners are unknown, are substantially underestimated in wealth data and therefore that portion of income which is illicitly generated or resulting from money laundering is likewise substantially underestimated.
2. The Bank for International Settlements generates data on holdings of non-banks

in foreign bank accounts. However this data only records end-of-period balances in personal or commercial accounts. It does not record throughput, and it does not record money that is shifted into custodial accounts.

3. Analysis of market capitalizations and holdings of high net-worth individuals include a portion arising from stockholdings. Share values of multinational corporations include a portion generated through abusive transfer pricing, which in almost all cases violates the VAT laws, customs duty regulations, or income tax statutes of countries out of which tax evading money is taken. But, again, it is very difficult to disaggregate the legal component of capital gains from gains accumulated on illicitly generated holdings.

Much further research needs to be done to improve estimates of global illicit financial flows and money laundering. Sources of data include the Bank for International Settlements, the US Treasury International Capital reporting system, Capgemini RBC World Wealth Reports, Organisation of Economic Co-operation and Development, Financial Action Task Force, World Bank governance data bases, International Monetary Fund assessments, International Money Laundering Information Network, and many more. Estimates of criminal flows are available from many organizations researching and analyzing particular types of criminal activities. Customs data from major trading nations would be an invaluable contribution to analyzing trade-based money laundering, but such data is closely guarded by the governments of nations into which laundered money traditionally flows.

The key fallacy in global anti-money laundering efforts is the idea that we can hold on to our use of the global shadow financial system for moving commercially tax evading money, while making others give up their use of the same system for moving corrupt and criminal money. This is not possible. All three parts of the illicit financial flows problem – corrupt, criminal and commercial – must be addressed if we are to succeed in curtailing any significant part of the problem.

In which direction is the trend line? Quite clearly, global money laundering is growing every year.

16. Efforts of the UN to find out about major routes of drugs and drug money

*Thomas Pietschmann**

16.1 CONTEXT

One of the key challenges for an international institution dealing with a problem is to identify its scale and to monitor the underlying trends. This should help policy makers at the national, regional and global level to identify successes and failures in their efforts to deal with the problem. The non-availability of such monitoring mechanisms is like major corporations trying to do business without any financial and cost accounting systems in place. Most people nowadays would find it difficult to imagine that large corporations could develop and follow strategies without basing their policies – *inter alia* – on functioning accounting systems; yet this has been the situation for decades for the authorities in most countries and for the international community at large when it came to drug control and efforts to fight money laundering. Attempts to remedy this situation at the level of the United Nations are rather new, dating back just some fifteen years when it comes to baseline drug data or some fifteen months when it comes to estimates regarding the amounts available for laundering.

International drug control started with the 1909 Shanghai Opium Conference and the 1912 Opium Convention of the Hague. Following the de facto inclusion of The Hague Convention in the peace treaties following World War I (Versailles, St. Germain en Laye, Trianon, etc.), drug control emerged as a global issue and became one of the key mandates of the League of Nations (1920). The mandate and the related tasks were then taken over by the then newly founded United Nations after World War II (Pietschmann 2007). Seizure statistics were collected right from the beginning of the work of the League of Nations, but it took until the late 1990s that serious efforts were undertaken by the then United Nations International Drug Control Program (UNDCP), the predecessor organization of the United Nations Office on Drugs and Crime (UNODC) to come up with global estimates on the area under cultivation, the production of illicit drugs as well as the number of drug users worldwide – which since then have been regularly published in the World Drug Reports (1997–2011) (UNODC 2011a). Estimates on the value of the global drug industry were first published in 1998 (US$359 billion) (UNDCP 1998) and again – based on a different methodological approach – in 2005 (US$ 322 billion) (UNODC 2005).

With the 1988 United Nations Convention against Illicit Traffic in Narcotic Drugs and Psychotropic Substances (UN 1988) the mandate was extended to also cover activities in the fight against drug related money laundering. The mandate was further extended to the overall fight against money laundering – irrespective of the predicate offence – with the Political Declaration[1] and the Measures for Countering Money-Laundering[2] adopted by the General Assembly at its twentieth Special Session in June 1998, the

United Nations Convention against Transnational Organized Crime,[3] signed in Palermo in December 2000, and the United Nations Convention against Corruption,[4] approved in 2003. All of the work aiming at drug control and fighting transnational organized crime and money laundering is now concentrated within the United Nations in the United Nations Office on Drugs and Crime (UNODC). Efforts so far have consisted mainly in assisting Member States to implement the conventions and in providing technical assistance. In 2011 UNODC also started to analyze the scope of the problem – summarized in its publication *Estimating Illicit Financial Flows resulting from Drug Trafficking and other Transnational Organized Crimes*, which consisted of a meta analysis of existing estimates provided in the literature (showing an average turnover of crime of 3.6 percent of global GDP, equivalent to US$2.1 trillion in 2009, of which 2.7 percent of GDP or some US$1.6 trillion may have been available for laundering), a detailed analysis of the financial funds generated and laundered in one specific transnational organized crime sector (trafficking in cocaine), an analysis of the socio-economic impact on money laundering, and a review of the existing legal instruments at the global level which deal with the problem (UNODC 2011b).

16.2 ESTIMATING MAJOR DRUGS ROUTES

As part of the drug control mandate, the conventions stipulate that Member States have to furnish the Secretary General (i.e. UNODC), on an annual basis, with detailed information on the supply and demand of illicit drugs, as laid out in the UNODC Annual Reports Questionnaire,[5] passed by the Commission on Narcotic Drugs (CND). Information to be provided includes, *inter alia*, estimates of illegal drug production,[6] drug seizures, information on the origin, transit and destination of the drugs trafficked, retail and wholesale prices and purities, as well as estimates on the number of drug users, available drug treatment and drug related mortality. In addition, Member States – in conformity with the 1961 Single Convention[7] – have to supply UNODC with detailed information on their individual drug seizures (amount seized, date, location of seizure, country of origin, country where the drugs were obtained, country of destination, nationality of traffickers, etc.). All of this information assists in the identification of the main drug routes, and thus in the physical flow of drugs from the production countries to the main consumption areas.

In the case of cocaine, the situation is facilitated by the fact that the coca leaf production – and subsequently also the illicit manufacture of cocaine – is largely limited to three countries: Colombia, Peru and Bolivia. Close to 100 percent of global coca leaf is produced in these three countries and, in most years (including in 2009) some 99 percent of all coca processing labs are dismantled in these countries, including more than 80 percent of all dismantled clandestine cocaine HCl manufacturing laboratories in 2009 (UNODC 2011a, p. 104). The main markets for cocaine are in North America followed by West and Central Europe as well as – in volume terms – in South America. UNODC's best estimates for 2009 suggested that some 179 tons of (pure) cocaine were consumed in North America (41% of the world total of 440 tons of pure cocaine in 2009), 123 tons (28%) in West and Central Europe, and 85 tons in South America (19% of the world total) (Table 16.1).

Table 16.1 Estimates of the amounts of cocaine (purity adjusted) consumed in 2009

Region / Subregion	Best estimates				
	Users		Per capita use grams per year	Consumption	
	in million	in % of total		in metric tons	in % of total
Americas	8.4	54%	32.6	275	63%
of which					
South America	2.4	15%	35	85	19%
Central America	0.1	1%	35	5	1%
Caribbean	0.1	1%	35	6	1%
North America	5.7	36%	31.5	179	41%
Europe	4.5	29%	28.4	129	29%
of which					
West and Central Europe	4.1	26%	30.3	123	28%
East and South-East Europe	0.5	3%	12.3	6	1%
Africa	1.7	11%	12	21	5%
of which					
West and Central Africa	1.1	7%	12	13	3%
Southern Africa	0.3	2%	12	4	1%
North Africa	<0.1	<1%	12	<1	<1%
East Africa	0.2	1%	12	3	<1%
Asia	0.7	4%	20	14	3%
Oceania	0.3	2%	7.3	2	<1%
Total	15.6	100%	28.1	440	100%

Source: UNODC (2011a, p. 120).

Based on this information and taking information from the ARQs (seizures, origin, destinations, purities) and information from the individual drug seizures (origin, destination) into account, the main flows could be identified (see Table 16.2), and are shown in Figure 16.1.

16.3 ESTIMATING FINANCIAL FLOWS

The subsequent discussion draws heavily on the approach taken in UNODC's study on *Estimating Illicit Financial Flows resulting from Drug Trafficking and Other Transnational Organized Crimes* (UDODC 2011b) with regard to the financial funds generated and laundered in the area of cocaine trafficking. Based on the information mentioned above, the drug flows were established and subsequently the value of the drugs sold and the 'gross profits' (sales less cost of drugs) generated by drug traffickers. The next step was to establish the proportion of funds actually available for laundering. The last two steps are to identify the amounts laundered that are actually leaving the jurisdictions where the profits were generated and to identify the likely destinations of such flows. Such

Table 16.2 Flows of cocaine (purity adjusted) to major consumer markets (in metric tons) in 2009*

Production**			1,111
Less seizures in Andean countries			−254
Less domestic consumption in Andean region			−13
Potential amounts available for export out of the Andean countries			844
Less losses in production and/or losses in global trafficking which cannot be attributed to specific regions			−56
Actual exports out of Andean countries			788
	West and Central Europe	North America	Non-Andean South America, Central America, Africa, Asia, Oceania
Amounts of cocaine leaving the Andean countries	217	378	193
Less amounts seized in non-Andean South America, Caribbean and Central America linked to trafficking flows	−59	−98	−64
Less domestic consumption in non-Andean South America / Caribbean / Central America			−83
Amounts leaving South America, Caribbean and Central America	158 (inc. 21 via West Africa)	280	46
Less amounts seized in consumer countries outside South America / Central America / Caribbean	−35	−101	−3
Amounts of cocaine consumed in countries outside South America / Central America / Caribbean	123	179 (incl. 157 in the USA)	43 (incl. 21 Africa, 14 Asia, 6 East and South-Eastern Europe; 2 Oceania)

Notes:

* Purity levels tend to decline along the trafficking chain. All numbers in this table have been adjusted to pure cocaine equivalents. Seizure data were adjusted based on reported wholesale purity data.

** The global cocaine production in 2009 was estimated to amount to between 842 mt and 1,111 mt. Actual cocaine consumption for 2009 was estimated at 440 mt. Seizures, not adjusted for purity, amounted to 732 mt in 2009. Considering purity-adjusted seizures of cocaine (unweighted average of all purities at retail and wholesale level reported by Member States in 2009), some 481 mt would be available for consumption and losses if the lower cocaine production estimate were used. If the higher cocaine production estimate were used, deducting seizures adjusted for whole purity (based on 2009 purity data or the latest year available), some 496 mt would be left for consumption and losses. The upper and lower production estimates could be thus sufficient to cover consumption (440 mt). For the calculation shown above, the higher production estimates and seizures adjusted at wholesale purities were used. This reflects the observation that wholesale seizures account for the bulk of seizures in volume terms and would support the higher production estimates. However, one cannot exclude the possibility that seizures may be over-estimated due to possible double-counting once several law enforcement agencies within or across countries have been involved in cocaine interceptions.

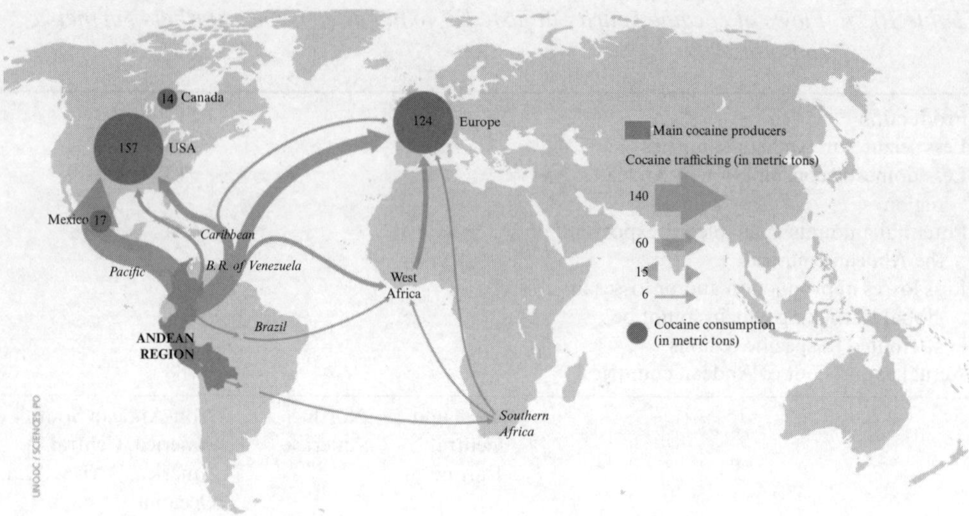

Source: UNODC (2011, p. 123).

Figure 16.1 Main global cocaine flows, 2009

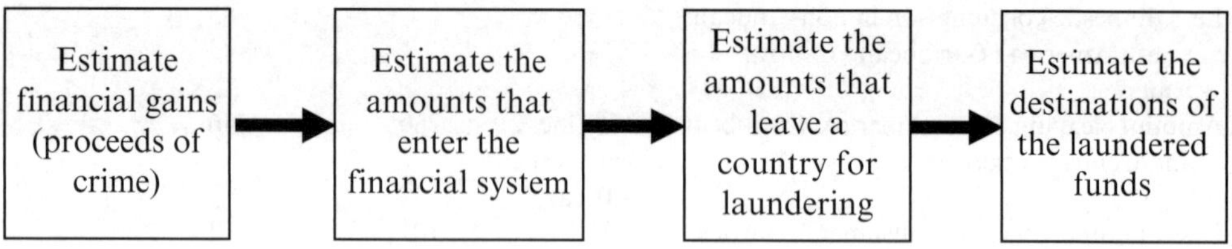

Figure 16.2

estimates can be generated with the help of a 'gravity model', as discussed in more detail in Chapter 13 of this book.

In order to estimate the financial gains or gross profits generated at country level, regional level and global level, a supply-based or a demand-based approach can be chosen.

The initial model used in 1998 by the United Nations International Drug Control Program (UNDCP) was a 'supply-based approach' to estimate the retail value of the global drug markets for the mid 1990s, including the global cocaine market. Starting from global production estimates (some 813 tons of cocaine in 1995) and deducting seizures (taking purity into account) and local consumption (of coca) in the main coca producing countries (where prices are extremely low so that sales figures can be ignored) and adding adulterations, estimates of overall consumption in the main consumer countries was established. This figure was then multiplied with average prices reported in the main cocaine consuming countries. The calculations resulted in a likely turnover of cocaine sales of around US$117 bn (range: US$20–US$196 bn) at the retail level for the year 1995 (UNDCP 1998). Taking inflation into account, this would have been equivalent to some US$165 bn if expressed in 2009 US$ (UNODC 2011a).

Based on a '*demand-based approach*' (number of users in each country multiplied with per capita consumption rates, resulting in consumption estimates per country – totaling some 440 tons at the global level – which were then multiplied with typical purity adjusted cocaine prices in each country to arrive at the retail value of cocaine sales), UNODC estimated global cocaine sales in 2009 at around US$85 billion (range: US$75–US$100 bn), slightly down from US$88 billion (US$80–US$100 bn) in 2008 (using a similar methodological approach). Given a total income of coca farmers of around US$1 billion, the gross profits[8] out of the cocaine trade can be estimated to have amounted to some US$84 billion in 2009. Given differences in the amounts potentially available for laundering (and thus for entering the financial system) depending on the countries concerned and on whether profits were generated at the retail or the wholesale level, a more detailed breakdown of these profits had to be established.

The analysis of the world's single largest cocaine market (United States) revealed that identified seizures and purchases by undercover agents were particularly frequent (i) at the gram level, reflecting retail sales, (ii) at the ounce level (28.3495 grams), reflecting sales of mid-level dealers to retailers, and (iii) at the kilogram level, reflecting purchases by wholesalers within the country (USA) (Anthony and Fries 2004). Still larger quantities – sometimes amounting up to a few tons – at far lower prices are purchased by importers from their counterparts abroad. This entails that typical cocaine retail profits are generated by purchasing cocaine at the ounce level from mid-level dealers – and selling it at the gram level to retailers while typical cocaine wholesale profits at the national level are generated by purchasing cocaine at the kilogram level and selling it at the ounce level. A mere comparison of such prices would, however, under-estimate the profits. Drug traffickers typically raise their profits by adding adulterants to the drugs that they sell. Calculations of profits must be thus always based on purity adjusted prices. The structure revealed by a first analysis of the cocaine markets is shown in Table 16.3. The calculations are basically correct for arriving at the amounts of gross retail profits. They underestimate, however, the additional wholesale profits made in transit countries

Drug traffickers in consumers' countries must purchase more drugs than they are able to sell due to seizures. These losses are, however, to the benefit of trraffickers in producer and transit countries who thus are able to sell more cocaine, thus creating additional profits for them. The calculations used in this model assume that half of the losses resulting from seizures are to be borne by importers and the other half by exporters.

Another issue are the tansit profits. Transit profits per sub-region were determined based on the drug flow. Such profits were subsequently allocated to individual countries based on average seizures over a three-year period. Taking seizures and transit profits into account, calculations show that a far higher proportion of global wholesale profits are in fact generated in the producing and transit countries. Still, the bulk of the global cocaine related gross profits are made at the retail level in North America (US$34 bn) and in West and Central Europe (US$20 bn). The largest wholesale profits, in contrast, are made in South America (US$15 bn incl. Central America and the Caribbean), more than in North America (US$7 bn) or West and Central Europe (US$6 bn) (see Table 16.4).

After having established the likely gross profits per region, attempts have been made to estimate the likely proportions available for entering the financial system. Typical

Table 16.3 Cocaine-related gross profits in million US$ generated at the global level – and their distribution (unadjusted for seizures and transit profits), 2009

	Retail profits (from ounce to gram price)	Wholesale profits			Profits from country of origin to transit countries
		Total wholesale profits (from import price to ounce price)	Of which: National wholesale profits (from kg to ounce price)	Of which: International wholesale profits (from import to kg price)	
Europe	20,985	9,744	3,687	6,056	4,857
West and Central Europe	19,692	9,203	3,475	5,728	4,437
South-East Europe	807	209	142	209	242
East Europe	397	120	70	120	178
North America	33,545	9,442	5,815	3,627	2,485
South and Central America and Caribbean	3,154	854	473	381	115
Asia	1,049	999	185	813	347
Oceania	997	636	176	460	80
Africa	909	618	160	458	254
TOTAL	54,262	22,293	10,497	11,797	8,138

Source: UNODC, calculations based on replies to the Annual Reports Questionnaire (ARQ) and other information sources.

estimates found in the literature 'assumed' that some two-thirds or around 70 percent of the profits were available for laundering (range of estimates: 39%–83%). However, the researchers, in general, did not provide indications of how they arrived at their 'assumptions'. Only in one case did the author indicate that the proportions were derived from a survey conducted among experts in one country (Australia).

Against this background, a deliberate attempt was made by UNODC to establish a new methodological approach to determine the likely proportions of the illicit income available for laundering.

A 'simple' model would have been to divide the size of the respective retail and wholesale market per country by the respective number of retail and wholesale traffickers. Separate models were developed to estimate the number of traffickers.[9] Income above a certain threshold level, needed for personal consumption (defined here as per capita GDP less proportion of gross savings in GDP) was assumed to be the money available for laundering.

Applying such a 'simple' model to the cocaine retail markets of the United States showed, however, odd results. There would not have been a single dollar available for laundering. Per capita income of retail traffickers would have been below the amounts needed by drug traffickers for covering their basic consumption needs.

Thus, a more sophisticated model was required, taking the market structure into

Table 16.4 Cocaine-related gross profits in million US$ generated at the global level after adjustments for seizures and transit profits

	Retail profits	Wholesale profits		
		Total wholesale profits	of which: National wholesale profits (from kg to ounce price)	of which international wholesale profits
Europe	20,985	6,594	3,687	2,906
West and Central Europe	19,692	6,272	3,475	2,797
South-East Europe	807	212	142	70
East Europe	397	110	70	40
North America	33,545	7,095	5,815	1,280
South and Central America and Caribbean	3,154	15,077	473	14,604
Asia	1,049	460	185	275
Oceania	997	308	176	132
Africa	909	706	160	546
TOTAL	54,262	30,239	10,497	19,742

Source: UNODC, calculations based on replies to the Annual Reports Questionnaire (ARQ) and other information sources.

account. Research done by the US Institute for Defense Analyses (IDA) suggested that the cocaine market was characterized by a 'power law' distribution (Anthony and Fries, 2004), also known as 'Pareto distribution'.[10] Cocaine seizures are following such a 'power law' distribution. Assuming that the distribution of seizures reflects rather well the underlying market structure (i.e. more small-scale than large-scale seizures take place because there are more small-scale (a few grams) than large-scale transactions (several tons) of cocaine taking place, existing national markets can be modeled accordingly, showing that a few traffickers make large profits – and have thus huge sums available that need to be laundered – while a large number of small-scale traffickers make hardly sufficient profits to survive, and thus need additional sources of income – for example, from unemployment and other social security benefits, from other family members or from various other forms of criminal income.

Applying such a model to the specific situation in the USA suggested that around 51 percent of gross retail profits (or 50% for North America, see Table 16.5) and 83 percent of gross wholesale profits (see Table 16.6) were available for laundering. Extending the analysis to other key markets suggested that around 46 percent of gross retail profits and 92 percent of gross wholesale profits (see Table 16.6) may have been available for laundering, that is, together some US$53 bn or 62 percent of total gross cocaine-related profits (US$84 bn) (see Table 16.7).

Thus, efforts have been made at the international level to identify drug trafficking flows as well as the extent of such flows in monetary terms, and the extent to which such flows are entering the financial system for money laundering purposes. Does this mean

Table 16.5 Tentative estimates of regional distribution of amounts available for laundering out of cocaine retail sales in 2009, in billion US$

	Gross retail profits (in bn US)	Proportion laundered	Amounts available for laundering (in bn US$)
Europe	20.9	44%	9.1
West and Central Europe	19.7	44%	8.7
South-East Europe	0.8	40%	0.3
East Europe	0.4	40%	0.2
North America	27.7	50%	13.8
South America (incl. Central America and Caribbean)	2.7	32%	0.9
Asia	1.0	40%	0.4
Oceania	1.0	48%	0.5
Africa	0.9	40%	0.4
TOTAL	54.3	46%	25.1

Sources: UNODC calculations based on UNODC, Individual Seizures Database and UNODC, Annual Reports Questionnaire data.

that we know now everything we need to know about the problem? Unfortunately, the answer to this question cannot be answered positively. We are still just at the very beginning of understanding the problem. So, what are the next steps?

The results obtained so far have aimed at providing policy makers with an idea of the *likely orders of magnitude of the problem and of the various parameters involved.* There can be, however, no doubt that improvements are still needed to arrive at results that could provide policy makers with answers to whether measures taken are leading to the desired outcomes.

The methodological approach required to provide such answers has been basically elaborated. The most tedious but still most promising approach is to quantify the various crimes involved (such as trafficking in cocaine, heroin, cannabis, ATS etc.) and to then measure the various flows in monetary terms on a country-by-country basis.

Having a reasonable approach in place is a necessary but not a sufficient condition for arriving at reliable results. There is still an urgent need to *improve availability of data as well as data quality*. The problems have been handled so far, by using a large number of assumptions to cope with missing data. Such assumptions will have to be eventually replaced with actual empirical findings.

Progress has been made in recent years in improving the accuracy of *drug production* estimates, notably for opium (and thus heroin) and for the coca leaf (and thus cocaine). Far less, in contrast, is still known about global cannabis production, as this substance is basically grown in each country and existing remote sensing technology is still too expensive to cover the whole world, and very little is actually known about the extent of the production of synthetic drugs. While the wider availability of cheap satellite photos might eventually remedy the situation on the cannabis side, sound methodological approaches to estimate the extent of synthetic drug production are still missing.

Countries are also asked to provide information on the *sources and the destinations*

Table 16.6 Tentative estimates of amounts available for laundering out of cocaine wholesale trafficking, 2009

Countries where gross cocaine profits (retail and wholesale) were estimated to exceed US$1 billion	Gross wholesale profits, adjusted for seizures and transit profits (in million US$)	Proportions laundered at the wholesale level		Amounts available for laundering (in million US$)
		'Simple model'	Model taking market structure into account	
Colombia	9,439	96%	97%	9,146
Mexico*	3,456	89%	92%	3,191
USA	3,441	9%	83%	2,868
UK	1,383	47%	89%	1,237
Italy	1,327	46%	90%	1,188
Spain	1,278	81%	93%	1,190
Germany	524	40%	89%	467
Brazil	479	74%	92%	442
France	471	25%	88%	415
Argentina	309	63%	91%	281
Australia	281	62%	91%	255
Canada	198	0%	85%	168
Unweighted average		53%	**90%**	
Confidence interval (95%)			88%–92%	
Subtotal	22,586			20,848
Other countries	7,653		90% (88%–92%)	6,892 (6,735–7,021)
Global (confidence interval, 95%)	**30,239**		**92%** (91%–92%)	**27,740** (27,583–27,869)

Note: * gross profits made by the Mexican cartels operating in the wholesale and retail trade within the United States are not included in these figures.

Sources: UNODC calculations based on UNODC, Individual Seizures Database and UNODC, Annual Reports Questionnaire data.

of drugs trafficked on their territory. Such information, however, is still mainly based on perceptions of law enforcement rather than actual data. The systematic collection of individual drug seizures and their subsequent analysis could provide a more reliable method. Moreover, drug signature programs could serve as a means to identify – in a more systematic way – the origin of seized drugs.

Some progress has been made on the demand side. A number of countries in the Americas, Europe and the Oceania region are now implementing *drug use surveys* at regular intervals. At the same time, it must be noted that such information is still widely missing from a majority of countries in Africa and in Asia. The methodology to implement such surveys is available. What would be needed here are basically the financial means to implement surveys.

Another area of interest is the *average drug consumption per user*. In fact, very little – so far – is known about this question. This does not only apply to developing countries but

Table 16.7 Tentative estimates of all cocaine-related profits laundered in 2009, in billion US$

	Gross profits* in billion US$			Profits available for laundering, from			**Overall proportion laun-dered******
	Whole-sale	Retail	**Total**	Whole-sale**	Retail***	**Total**	
Europe	6.6	20.9	**27.5**	5.9	9.1	**15.1**	**55%**
West and Central Europe	6.3	19.7	**26.0**	5.7	8.7	**14.3**	**55%**
South-East Europe	0.2	0.8	**1.0**	0.2	0.3	**0.5**	**50%**
East Europe	0.1	0.4	**0.5**	0.1	0.2	**0.3**	**51%**
North America	7.1	27.7	**34.8**	6.2	13.8	**20.0**	**57%**
South America (incl. Central America and Caribbean)	15.1	2.7	**17.8**	14.2	0.9	**15.1**	**85%**
Asia	0.5	1.0	**1.5**	0.4	0.4	**0.8**	**55%**
Oceania	0.3	1.0	**1.3**	0.3	0.5	**0.8**	**58%**
Africa	0.7	0.9	**1.6**	0.6	0.4	**1.0**	**62%**
TOTAL	30.2	54.3	**84.5**	27.7	25.1	**52.8**	**62%**

Sources:
UNODC calculations based on UNODC, Individual Seizures Database and UNODC, Annual Reports Questionnaire data.
* As shown in the table 'Cocaine-related gross profits in million US$ generated at the global level after adjustments for seizures and transit profits.'
** Based on the proportions shown in the table 'Tentative estimates of regional distribution of amounts available for laundering out of cocaine wholesale trafficking in 2009, in billion US$'.
*** Based on the proportions shown in the table 'Tentative estimates of regional distribution of amounts available for laundering out of cocaine retail sales in 2009, in billion US$'.
**** 'Total profits available for laundering' / 'Total of gross profits.'

also to the majority of developed countries. This information – together with information on the number of users – is, however, crucial to effectively measure the size of any market in volume terms. One possible way of obtaining such data – apart from surveys – would be the analysis of waste-water which is currently already under way in a number of countries. Establishing the amounts of drugs consumed in a certain area, in combination with information on the number of users, could help with the identification of average per capita use figures, which could then be applied to wider sections of drug users in a country.

Another area where data collection needs improvement are *price and purity data*. The challenge with regard to price data is simply to collect them in a systematic way from key informants, in the case of arrests as well as via under-cover purchases. In most countries, such comprehensive price data collection still does not take place. Similarly, drug purity is often identified by forensic laboratories, but this information is then not systematically shared and collected.

In all of these areas, efforts undertaken by UNODC are underway to help Member States. However – given current resource constraints – it will be many years, if not decades, until these efforts can be expected to translate into improved data availability and data quality. Once such data are available, a far more accurate and reliable determination of the individual drug flows and their related financial flows will be available.

The last question relates to the proportion of money that is actually laundered out of the drug proceeds. One model, based on the distribution of seizures, has been presented here. However, there would still be a need to validate the results. A number of case studies, based on actually dismantled drug trafficking networks could help to shed some light onto this question. This could be done, for instance, via interviews of persons imprisoned for drug trafficking. Moreover, courts could be asked to establish in a more systematic form the amounts generated out of the drug business and the amounts subsequently laundered.

All of this is not just of academic interest. As the UNODC study revealed, far less than 1 percent (probably just around 0.2%) of the illicit funds laundered worldwide are actually detected by the authorities (UNODC, 2011b). A close monitoring of the success rates of the law enforcement bodies of each country could act as an incentive to improve their efforts and to adjust the legislation and banking rules accordingly, as well as help to increase the funding and the effectiveness of the various financial intelligence units (FIUs).

No big corporation would dare to run multi-billion business activities without any financial or cost accounting systems in place; no country in the world would dare to undertake major economic policy interventions without any information on GDP or unemployment data. Yet, in the area of fighting money laundering, measures are still largely being taken and proposed without any appropriate feedback mechanism in place that would tell policy makers if they are on the right track. It is clearly time to change this. The results so far (with a less than 1% detection rate) clearly underline the need to become more serious about these problems.

NOTES

* The views expressed herein are those of the author and do not necessarily reflect the views of the United Nations.

1. United Nations General Assembly, S-20/2. Resolutions adopted by the General Assembly, *Political Declaration*, A/RES/S-20/2, 1998, http://daccess-dds-ny.un.org/doc/UNDOC/GEN/N98/775/09/PDF/N9877509.pdf?OpenElement
2. United Nations, General Assembly, Resolutions adopted by the General Assembly – S-20/4. *Measures to enhance international cooperation to counter the world drug problem* – Countering Money Laundering, A/RES/S=2-/4*, 1998, http://daccess-dds-ny.un.org/doc/UNDOC/GEN/N98/775/15/PDF/N9877515.pdf?OpenElement
3. United Nations Office on Drugs and Crime, *United Nations Convention against Transnational Organized Crime and the Protocols Thereto*, Vienna, 2004, http://www.unodc.org/documents/treaties/UNTOC/Publications/TOC%20Convention/TOCebook-e.pdf
4. United Nations Office on Drugs and Crime, *United Nations Convention against Corruption*, New York, 2004, http://www.unodc.org/documents/treaties/UNCAC/Publications/Convention/08-50026_E.pdf
5. UNODC, Annual Reports Questionnaire, http://www.unodc.org/unodc/en/commissions/CND/10-GlobalData.html
6. As part of UNODC's Illicit Crop Monitoring Programme (ICMP) UNODC supports main drug producing countries with overall coordination as well as direct technical support and supervision in conducting illicit crop surveys at the country level, usually using remote sensing technologies (analysis of satellite photos) to estimate the areas under cultivation, in combination with yield surveys in order to come up with overall production estimates. Regular annual surveys, supported by UNODC, are currently being

conducted in Afghanistan, Myanmar and the Lao PDR for opium, as well as in Colombia, Peru and Bolivia for coca. Cannabis surveys have taken place in Morocco and in Afghanistan.

7. Art. 18. The Parties shall furnish to the Secretary-General [UNODC] . . . 1 c) 'Such particulars as the Commission shall determine concerning cases of illicit traffic, including particulars of each case of illicit traffic discovered which may be of importance, because of the light thrown on the source from which drugs are obtained for the illicit traffic, or because of quantities involved or the method employed by illicit traffickers', UNODC, *Single Convention on Narcotic Drugs*, 1961, http://www.unodc.org/unodc/en/treaties/single-convention.html
8. '*Gross profits*' are defined here as the difference between the value of the drugs sold and the value of the drugs purchased. In order to arrive at '*net profits*' a number of expenditures would still have to be deducted such as 'wages' or 'salaries' for employed drug traffickers, transport costs and other logistics costs (such as renting warehouses to deposit the drugs), purchases of adulterants and laboratory know-how, various costs related to camouflaging the trafficking activities (such as running import-export or transport companies), bribes for police and customs officials, purchases of weapons to defend the interests of the organized crime group against assaults by other organized crime groups, etc.
9. The estimates were derived from, *inter alia*, the proportion of consumers arrested among the total number of past month users; assuming that the likelihood of arrest would be similar for drug traffickers, the arrest rate was applied to the number of persons arrested. This allowed for the calculation of an estimate of the total number of traffickers. Estimates on the number of traffickers could also be deduced from various capture-recapture models in combination with truncated Poisson models and the Chao and Zelterman estimators. The data requirement here is a distribution of the number of times a drug trafficker was arrested in the past. The minimum requirement is a distribution of the number of persons arrested for drug trafficking (i) for the first time, and (ii) arrested before.
10. A power law, also known as Pareto distribution, is a special kind of mathematical relationship between a data series and its frequency distribution, which in common language is often known as the 80–20 rule (e.g. 20% of the population earn 80% of the income in a country; 20% of the cocaine-using population account for 80% of the total cocaine consumption, etc.). There is evidence that the power law distribution is found for a wide variety of physical, biological and social phenomena, including such diverse phenomena as Pareto's law of income distribution, the impact and frequency of earthquakes (Gutenberg-Richter law for earthquake sizes), craters on the moon, solar flares, size and activity of neuronal populations (Stevens's power law of psychophysics), distribution of family names, sizes of power outages, scaling laws in biological systems, and frequency and impact of wars.

REFERENCES

Anthony, R. and A. Fries (2004), 'Empirical modelling of narcotics trafficking from farm gate to street', *Bulletin on Narcotics*, 'Illicit Drug Markets', **LVI** (1&2), 1–48.

Pietschmann, T. (2007), 'A century of international drug control', *Bulletin on Narcotics*, **LIX** (1&2), 1–167.

UNDCP (1998), *Economic and Social Consequences of Drug Abuse and Illicit Trafficking*, UNDCP, Technical Series, No. 6.

United Nations (1988), *United Nations Convention against Illicit Traffic in Narcotic Drugs and Psychotropic Substances*, http://www.unodc.org/pdf/convention_1988_en.pdf

UNODC (2005), *World Drug Report 2005*, Vienna: UNODC.

UNODC (2011a), *World Drug Report 2011*, Vienna: UNODC.

UNODC (2011b), *Estimating Illicit Financial Flows Resulting from Drug Trafficking and Other Transnational Organized Crimes*, Vienna: UNODC, http://www.unodc.org/documents/data-and-analysis/Studies/Illicit_financial_flows_2011_web.pdf

17. Using dynamic macroeconomics for estimating money laundering: a simulation for the EU, Italy and the United States

Michele Bagella, Francesco Busato and Amedeo Argentiero

17.1 INTRODUCTION: THE MEASUREMENT OF MONEY LAUNDERING

Money laundering (ML) is a by-product of the criminal economy, which has a size of approximately 5 percent of upon the world GDP (Napoleoni 2005). An efficient (and realistic) measure of this phenomenon may help authorities discover the actual origin of the resources that are laundered, and through this the right size of criminal economy. In this sense, ML is located downstream with respect to illegal acts from which dirty money is derived.

In 1996, the International Monetary Fund (IMF) stated that the aggregate size of ML in the world could be somewhere between 2 and 5 percent of the world's Gross Domestic Product (GDP). In the previous ten years (1997–2006), ML discovered in Italy consisted of 0.1 percent of 2006 GDP.[1] The dataset from which these results are extracted is constructed by considering the kinds of goods used to launder money, the class of penal violations contested, and for each transgression indicates the amount of money laundered.[2] Nevertheless, this figure hardly corresponds to the actual value of ML. In Italy, as well as in the majority of developed countries, Judicial authorities find it very hard both to detect ML transactions and to sentence definitively convicted guilty subjects.[3]

The key problem in measuring ML rests with its non-observational character, as is the case for some other economic variables such as the underground economy and home production.

Zizza (2002) surveyed all the methods used in the empirical literature to give a measure of the underground economy; these techniques can be also applied, with the relevant modifications,[4] to the criminal economy. Two sets of methods can be distinguished: the *direct* approaches and the *indirect* approaches.

The direct approaches are based on surveys among (supposed) suppliers and customers of informal services and activities, or they rely on the auditing of tax returns undertaken by tax collection and social security administrations. The indirect approaches share the assumption that informal transactions are paid in cash in order to make detection more unlikely. The size of the illegal economy is reflected in the amount of cash used in a country, beyond that used for official transactions.

The empirical estimates employed in the literature for the measure of unobserved economy (Frey et al. 1984; Bhattacharyya 1999; Tanzi 1999; Thomas 1999, among others) cover a short time span and are based on low frequency data.

Recently, Barone and Masciandaro (2011) developed a dynamic partial equilibrium model able to underline the connections between organized crime, money laundering and legal investment. Their framework is employed to simulate the total amount of legal wealth generated by organized crime through drug trafficking in different regions of the world, with particular attention given to Europe.

Our methodology, detailed in two published papers,[5] is an attempt to analyze ML by supplying a measure to this phenomenon over a large sample and with high frequency data. Moreover, we use a theoretical model that exploits firms' and households' optimality conditions to measure ML for the Italian economy, following the idea that unobserved series may be derived from a well-behaved theoretical model first implemented by Ingram et al. (1997) to measure the household production sector, and by Busato et al. (2006) for measuring the underground economy.

The analysis applies to Italy, EU-15 and the US and has a short-run perspective; for this reason, we discuss the stochastic properties of the Hodrick-Prescott filtered series. Here is an overview of the results: the model generates series for ML in Italy for 21 years (84 quarters), over the sample 1981:01–2001:04. According to our analysis, ML accounts for approximately 12 percent of aggregate GDP, is more volatile than aggregate GDP and is negatively correlated with it.

For the US and the EU-15 the sample analyzed covers the period 2000:01–2007:04: the simulations show that ML accounts for approximately 19 percent of the GDP measured for the EU-15, while it accounts for 13 percent in the US economy. Furthermore, the simulated ML appears less volatile both for the US and the EU-15 than the corresponding GDP, whereas ML is negatively correlated with respect to GDP for the EU-15, while it appears to be positively correlated in the US economy.

17.2 AN ALTERNATIVE METHODOLOGY OF MEASUREMENT: COMBINING THEORY AND TIME SERIES

The dynamic general equilibrium model, from which we derive the equilibrium time series for ML contains two sectors (the regular and the criminal sectors), each one with two agents: firms and households. Moreover, there are two classes of firms, producing two commodities. The former represents the regular good, whereas the latter is the one from which the money to be laundered is generated and whose main objective is the violation of Penal Law

A household operating in the regular and the criminal sector is subjected to a transaction cost that is proportional to the real consumptions of goods produced. Furthermore, workers in the criminal sector have to pay a cost that is the disutility of violating the penal code whenever they are found to be supplying labor illegally. Firms and households use the criminal sector to carry out criminal offenses and the regular economy to hide the revenues of these activities through ML.

17.2.1 The Households

The economy is populated by a large number of identical households with the same preferences defined over consumption and leisure on a period-by-period basis. Then, we assume that aggregate labor supply is constant and normalized to unity $N = 1$ and that each household allocates labor services in the regular sector (N_t) and in the informal sector ($1 - N_t$).[6] Whenever the household is not detected supplying labor to the irregular sector, it is not fined. This happens with probability $1 - p$. In this case, the utility stream is:

$$U_t^{ND} = \eta\frac{C_{1,t}^{1-q1}}{1-q_1} + (1-\eta)\frac{C_{2,t}^{1-q2}}{1-q_2} - z(C_{1,t} + C_{2,t}) \sim (1-p)$$

where C_1 is the private consumption of regular goods (with relative weight η) and $C_{2,t}$ is the private consumption of criminal goods (with relative weight $(1 - \eta)$ and both are subjected to a constant proportional transaction cost $Z(C_{1,t}+C_{2,t})$.

On the other hand, when the household is detected, with probability p, it is penalized $\Omega > 0$. In this case, the utility reads:

$$U_t^D = \eta\frac{C_{1,t}^{1-q1}}{1-q_1} + (1-\eta)\frac{C_{2,t}^{1-q2}}{1-q_2} - \Omega\frac{(1-N_t)^{1+\Psi}}{1+\Psi} - Z(C_{1,t} + C_{2,t}) \sim p$$

Now, under a Von Neumann-Morgensten formulation, the expected utility reads:

$$\tilde{U}_t = \eta\frac{C_{1,t}^{1-q1}}{1-q_1} + (1-\eta)\frac{C_{2,t}^{1-q2}}{1-q_2} - \Omega p\frac{(1-N_t)^{1+\Psi}}{1+\Psi} - Z(C_{1,t} + C_{2,t})$$

The quantity $Z(C_{1,t} + C_{2,t})$ represents the disutility of the time spent in transactions according to Wen and Love (1998), who identify the time spent in transactions as a specific factor able to lower the time, and hence the household's utility. Instead, the term $\Omega p\frac{(1-N_t)^{1+\Psi}}{1+\Psi}$ represents the expected idiosyncratic cost of working in the criminal economy. It denotes the specific expected disutility from violating the penal code. In short, the consumption of criminal goods is penalized by two factors: the former associated with the time spent in seeking a partner for the exchange, while the latter reflects the associated risk. This cost is, of course, idiosyncratic to the criminal sector.

The household can hold either cash, M, or capital, while facing the budget constraint and a customary capital accumulation constraint.

$$p_{1,t}(K_{t+1} + C_{1,t}) + p_{2,t}C_{2,t} + M_{t+1} = \overline{w}_{1,t}N_t + R_tK_t + \overline{w}_{2,t}(1-N_t) + M_t$$

$$I_t = K_{t+1},$$

where the latter assumes that capital fully depreciates on a period-by-period basis; $p_{1,t}(p_{2,t})$ is the nominal price of $C_1(C_2)$ at t.

A possible way to model ML in a micro-founded general dynamic general equilibrium model is to define a cash constraint before considering ML, with the inequality sign. In particular, let us assume that cash is needed to purchase both commodities (legal goods and criminal goods), but that the money supplied by the central bank M_t is insufficient to buy regular goods $C_{1,t}$ because of an endogenous money rationing linked to asymmetric information of the central bank. In other words, the central bank does not consider the criminal sector when it decides how much money to supply to the economy

$$\overline{M}_t - p_{2,t}C_{2,t} < p_{1,t}C_{1,t}$$

Next, consistently with empirical evidence (e.g. Tuck 1996; Galì 1999) and a large strand of theoretical literature, let us assume that prices are sticky in the short run, so that the cash constraint dynamically binds (see e.g. Clower (1967) for stickiness in the cash constraint and Calvo (1983), among others). In this case, the sale revenues of regular commodities cannot be used to buy both commodities in a period different from the one in which the legal goods have been produced. To satisfy cash constraint with the equality sign, 'new money' is created through the irregular sector, that is money laundered from the previous period:

$$\overline{M}_t - p_{2,t}C_{2,t} + \gamma_t(p_{2,t-1}C_{2,t-1}) = p_{1,t}C_{1,t}$$

where γ_t indicates the portion of revenues of criminal goods generated in the previous period, that is, *used to buy the legal goods*. Instead, the quantity $1 - \gamma_t$ indicates the fraction of revenues of criminal goods that is *used to buy criminal goods together with money supply provided by the central bank*.

$$(1-\gamma_t)(p_{2,t-1}C_{2,t-1}) + \overline{M}_t = p_{2,t}C_{2,t}$$

In the long term, prices that are supposedly fully flexible, together with an implicit learning process undertaken by the central bank (e.g. Carlstrom and Fuerst 2004; Lim and McNelis 2007, among others) are able to restore equality in the relationship characterized by the inequality sign. This means that money laundering activity described here arises as a short-run phenomenon, which supposedly vanishes in the absence of any sort of price rigidity as well as in the presence of a central bank that issues the amount of cash required from the regular goods sector.[7] This assumption is consistent with the methodology that this chapter utilizes, that is, a cyclical analysis of money laundering filterivng out the low frequencies of the generated series. This means that the focus of the analysis is on the short run.[8]

To conclude the households' presentation, we assume that the initial capital stock is positive, $K_0 > 0$ and given, and that the following inequality constraints hold $C_{1,t} > 0$, $C_{2,t} > 0, p_{1,t} > 0, p_{2,t} > 0, N_t \in (0,1)$.

17.2.2 The Firms

The economy is populated by two classes of firms, producing two commodities. Regular goods, C_1, are produced by a constant-return-to-scale technology using regular labor, N, and physical capital stock, K, which completely depreciates. Produced output can be either consumed or added to the existing capital stock. Defining Λ as the total factor productivity, the regular production function formally reads:

$$Y_{1,t} = N_t^{\alpha} K_t^{1-\alpha} \Lambda_{1,t}$$

Irregular goods, C_2, are produced by a technology using labor and fixed-quantity land, $\bar{l}$, with a constant rent, Q, and the produced output, Y_2, can only be consumed, that is, $Y_2 = C_2$. We can consider $\bar{l}$ as a physical space where illicit activities take place. Subsequently, normalizing the land input $\overline{L} = 1$ for the sake of simplicity, the production function reads:

$$Y_{2,t} = (1 - N_t)\, \Lambda_{2,t}$$

Note that this technology specification is equivalent to a more general set-up where both production functions use capital and labor, for example, $Y_{1,t} = N_t^{\alpha} K_t^{1-\alpha} \Lambda_{1,t}$ and $Y_{2,t} = N_t^{\xi} K^{1-\varepsilon\xi}_t \Lambda_{2,t}$. From Uzawa (1965) and Lucas (1988) if $\xi < \alpha$, we can set the smaller elasticity to zero without loss of any generality. Being irregular activities that are typically labor intensive, we can simplify the model and preserve the main economic intuition by assuming that the illegal sector produces by means of labor only.

Finally, we assume that the stochastic structure of the economy evolves according to the Markov process A:

$$A_{t+1} = dF(A_{t+1}; A_t)$$

where $A_t[\Lambda_{1,t}, \Lambda_{2,t}]$ is a stochastic disturbance vector that evolves according the following law of motion:

$$A'_{t+1} = \sum A'_t + v_t$$

where v_t is a vector including shocks' innovations, and the autocorrelation coefficient matrix Σ and the covariance matrix Ξ are defined below:

$$\Sigma = \begin{bmatrix} \varphi\Lambda_1 & 0 \\ 0 & \varphi\Lambda_2 \end{bmatrix} \text{ and } \Xi = \begin{bmatrix} \sigma\Lambda_1 & 0 \\ 0 & \sigma\Lambda_2 \end{bmatrix}$$

17.2.3 The Solution of the Decentralized Economy

17.2.3.1 Household first order conditions

We are interested in measuring thc fraction γ_t, that is, the fraction of money laundered which results from the optimization process. The household's problem, eliminating the capital accumulation constraint, is the following:

$$\max_{\substack{\{C_{1,t},\, C_{2,t}\}_{t=0}^{\infty} \\ \{N_t,\, K_{t+1}\}_{t=0}^{\infty} \\ \{M_{t+1},\, \gamma_t\}_{t=0}^{\infty}}} \mathcal{L}_0 = E_0 \sum_{t=0}^{\infty} \beta^t \left\{ \eta \frac{C_{1,t}^{1-q1}}{1-q_1} + (1-\eta)\frac{C_{2,t}^{1-q2}}{1-q_2} - \Omega p \frac{(1-N_t)^{1+\psi}}{1+\Psi} - Z(C_{1,t} + C_{2,t}) \right.$$

$$+\phi_{1,t}(w_{1,t}N_t+R_tK_t+M_t+\overline{w}_{2,t}(1-N_t)-p_{1,t}(K_{t+1}+C_{1,t})-p_{2,t}C_{2,t}$$

$$-M_{t+1})+\phi_{2,t}[\overline{M}_t-p_{1,t}C_{1,t}-p_{2,t}C_{2,t}+\gamma_t(p_{2,t-1}C_{2,t-1})]$$

$$+\phi_{3,t}[-p_{2,t}C_{2,t}+(1-\gamma_t)(p_{2,t-1}C_{2,t-1})+\overline{M}_t]$$

The first-order conditions for an interior optimal path for the households are given by:

$$C_{1,t}:\eta C_{1,t}^{-q1}-Z=\phi_{1,t}p_{1,t}+\phi_{2,t}p_{1,t}$$

$$C_{2,t}:(1-\eta)C_{2,t}^{-q2}-Z=\phi_{1,t}p_{2,t}+\phi_{2,t}p_{2,t}\phi_{3,t}p_{2,t}$$

$$N_t:\Omega\text{p}(1-N_t)^{\Psi}+\phi_{1,t}w_{1,t}=\phi_{1,t}\overline{w}_{2,t}$$

$$K_{t+1}:p_{1,t}\phi_{1,t}=\beta^tE_t\phi_{1,t+1}R_{t+1}$$

$$M_{t+1}:\phi_{1,t}=\beta^tE_t(\phi_{1,t+1})$$

$$\gamma_t:\phi_{3,t}=\phi_{2,t}$$

and the two transversal conditions are the following:

$$\lim_{T\to\infty}\beta^T\phi_{1,t}K_T=0\text{ and }\lim_{T\to\infty}\beta^T\phi_{2,t}M_T=0$$

17.2.3.2 Legal firm first order conditions

Note that only the firm producing legal goods, marginally prices its production factors; the firm producing illegal goods has a constant labor demand function, which in each period is equal to $1-N_t$. Consequently, only legal labor is paid at a nominal wage w_1 and capital is paid at an interest rate R_t, both equal to their nominal productivities in equilibrium, whereas criminal labor is remunerated at a fixed nominal wage $\overline{w}_2$, which will be properly calibrated from the data. The legal firm maximizes its profits, denoted as: $\Pi_{1,t}=p_{1,t}N_t^{\alpha}K_t^{1-\alpha}\Lambda_t-w_{1,t}N_t-R_tK_t$, and the first-order conditions for the legal firm are summarized in the next two relationships:

$$w_{1,t}=p_{1,t}\alpha N_t^{\alpha-1}K_t^{1-\alpha}\Lambda_t$$

$$R_t=(1-\alpha)N_t^{\alpha}K_t^{-\alpha}\Lambda_t$$

17.2.3.3 Money laundering

After some algebra, we obtain the following expression for the quantity γ_t which represents the equilibrium of money laundered, normalizing the price of the criminal commodity, that is, $p_{2,t}=1$:

$$\gamma_t^*=\frac{1}{2}\left(\frac{p_{1,t}C_{1,t}}{\left[\frac{\Omega\text{p}(1-N_{t-1}^*)\psi}{(w_{1,t-1}^*-\overline{w}_{2,t-1})(1-\eta)}+\left(2\frac{(\eta(C_{1,t-1}^*)^{-q1}Z)}{p_{1,t-1}}\right)\frac{1}{1-\eta}+\frac{Z}{w_{1,t-1}-\overline{w}_{2,t-1}(1-\eta)}\right]^{-\frac{1}{q2}}}+1\right)$$

where $$w_{1,t-1} = p_{1,t-1}\alpha N_{t-1}^{\alpha-1} K_{t-1}^{1-\alpha}\Lambda_t$$

The previous equations show that the optimal money laundered depends on the labor services allocated to sector 1, on the labor services allocated to sector 2 and on the prices and quantities of both goods.

17.2.4 Parametrization

The model is then parameterized for Italy, the US economy and for the EU-15. The system of equations we use to compute the dynamic equilibria of the model depends on the parameters shown in Table 17.1.

Parameter $q1$ is set to 0.17. for the US, to 0.99 for Italy and to 0.15 for the EU-15, while the elasticity of inter-temporal substitution for the informal consumption $q2$ is calibrated to 0.83, to 0.01 and 0.85.

The capital share α is set to match volatility between actual and simulated GDP, while the regular consumption weight η is set to match the share between actual regular consumption and GDP. The calibrated value of 0.90 implies that the representative household gives a weight of 90 percent to regular consumption flow. The parameter Ω represents the disutility of supplying labor specifically to criminal activities. This is intended to be typically risky and therefore provide a sufficiently large disutility to consumers. Technically, this can be seen as a free parameter and is calibrated to 300. Note, however, that the model is quite robust to a sensitivity analysis performed over this parameter.

The criminal consumption elasticity $q2$ is set in order to provide a stable solution for the model, following Argentiero, Bagella and Busato (2008).

The probability of being detected, p, is calibrated using data for the Italian economy, in accordance with Busato and Chiarini (2004). They calibrate this parameter by estimating the unconditional mean of the ratio of number of inspected firms to their total number, that is, $\widetilde{p}_t = \frac{\textit{Inspected firms at } t}{\textit{Total Number of firms at } t}$.[9] For Italy, as well as for the majority of countries,

Table 17.1 Parameters and calibrated values

Parameter	Calibrated value		
	US macro area	EU-15 macro area	Italy
q_1	0.17	0.15	0.99
q_2	0.83	0.85	0.01
η	0.9	0.9	0.9
Ω	300	300	300
p	0.03	0.03	0.03
α	0.5	0.11	0.17
Z	0	0.2	0.2
ψ	9	9	1.6

Notes: q_1: regular consumption elasticity; q_2: irregular consumption elasticity; η regular consumption weight; Ω: disutility of supplying labor for money laundering; p: probability of being detected; α: capital share; Z: transaction cost; ψ: inverse Frisch elasticity of labor supplied to ML.

only a portion of this data is publicly available. For the Italian economy, the Ministry of Labor reports that the number of inspected firms was 118,119 in 2000, 106,307 in 1999 and 95,676 in 1998. The overall number of firms in the Italian economy was 4,639,393 in 2000, 4,472,375 in 1999 and 4,311,369 in 1998. As suggested above, we first compute the probability of being detected in each year, $\tilde{p}_t$, and then we estimate the aggregate probability as $p^* = \frac{1}{T}\Sigma_{t=1}^{T}\tilde{p}_t$. For the Italian economy $p^* = 0.03$. Even though this is not a precise estimate and focuses simply on a single country, we believe that it represents the best possible calibration for this parameter, given the available data.

The specific value of the inverse Frisch labor supply elasticity for labor services supplied to the criminal sector is calibrated to 9, which is three times more than the standard value (Kydland and Prescott 1982; Cooley and Prescott 1995; Prescott 2004). The calibrated value of $\Psi = 9$ implies that the equilibrium share of labor services supplied to the regular sector equals 0.83. The calibrated value is qualitatively consistent with Domeij and Floden (2006), Kniesner and Ziliak (2005) (who estimate a Frisch labor supply elasticity of 0.5), Chari, Kehoe and McGrattan (2000) (who find an elasticity of 0.8) and Kimball and Shapiro (2003) who obtain a Frisch elasticity close to 1.

As regards to parameter Z, it is worth noting that transaction costs are typically represented by registration costs (fees and taxes incurred in registering the property with the competent land registry; these include registration fees, stamp duties, and notary fees) and transfer taxes imposed by local and national governments on the sale and purchase (they include deed taxes, transfer taxes and value-added tax (VAT)). For this reason, the transaction cost is calibrated to the value added tax rate. Hence, we set this value to 0.2 for Italy and the EU-15 and to 0 for the US.

Because the model does not provide a description of the trends in the series, we focus on the cyclical component by using the Hodrick and Prescott filter. The model generates time series at a quarterly frequency; after log linear transformation of the series, the trend is computed by setting the smoothing parameter to 1600, as the standard value in literature. The cyclical component is obtained as the difference between the actual (raw) series and the computed trend component.

Finally, the Table 17.2 includes the time series used in the calibration and simulations.

17.3 THE NUMERICAL RESULTS AND POLICY IMPLICATIONS

The model is simulated for Italy over the sample 1981:Q1–2001:Q4, for the EU-15 and the US over 2000:Q2–2007:Q4 to generate equilibrium allocations (i.e. equilibrium time series) for GDP, regular labor services, labor services allocated to the criminal sector, and to this end, equilibrium ML. In order to ensure that the model and the simulated time series are qualitatively consistent with the actual economy, we constantly check that the simulated GDP is qualitatively consistent with the actual series, as a control statistic.

Table 17.3 presents selected statistics computed for the Hodrick-Prescott (HP) filtered series as generated by the model presented and calibrated in the previous section. The table reports volatility measures for HP-filtered simulated series for ML and GDP. The third row presents the contemporaneous correlation between the two, while the last row reports the volatility ratio between ML and GDP.

Table 17.2 Times series used in calibration and simulations

ML/GDP ITALY*		ML/GDP USA**	ML/GDP EMU***
Q2-1981	6.015%		
Q3-1981	5.774%		
Q4-1981	5.982%		
Q1-1982	5.991%		
Q2-1982	6.263%		
Q3-1982	7.039%		
Q4-1982	7.076%		
Q1-1983	7.220%		
Q2-1983	7.074%		
Q3-1983	7.022%		
Q4-1983	7.536%		
Q1-1984	7.529%		
Q2-1984	7.149%		
Q3-1984	7.260%		
Q4-1984	7.574%		
Q1-1985	7.870%		
Q2-1985	7.931%		
Q3-1985	8.258%		
Q4-1985	8.478%		
Q1-1986	8.199%		
Q2-1986	8.204%		
Q3-1986	8.243%		
Q4-1986	8.644%		
Q1-1987	8.102%		
Q2-1987	8.093%		
Q3-1987	8.024%		
Q4-1987	8.062%		
Q1-1988	7.827%		
Q2-1988	7.919%		
Q3-1988	8.078%		
Q4-1988	8.498%		
Q1-1989	8.559%		
Q2-1989	8.632%		
Q3-1989	8.809%		
Q4-1989	8.833%		
Q1-1990	9.101%		
Q2-1990	9.112%		
Q3-1990	9.920%		
Q4-1990	9.890%		
Q1-1991	10.333%		
Q2-1991	10.781%		
Q3-1991	11.389%		
Q4-1991	11.604%		
Q1-1992	11.699%		
Q2-1992	11.955%		
Q3-1992	12.818%		

Table 17.2 (continued)

	ML/GDP ITALY*	ML/GDP USA**	ML/GDP EMU***
Q4-1992	12.313%		
Q1-1993	16.385%		
Q2-1993	17.813%		
Q3-1993	16.838%		
Q4-1993	16.899%		
Q1-1994	16.354%		
Q2-1994	16.213%		
Q3-1994	16.565%		
Q4-1994	16.790%		
Q1-1995	15.782%		
Q2-1995	15.134%		
Q3-1995	15.681%		
Q4-1995	14.801%		
Q1-1996	15.290%		
Q2-1996	15.624%		
Q3-1996	15.433%		
Q4-1996	15.697%		
Q1-1997	16.128%		
Q2-1997	16.465%		
Q3-1997	16.560%		
Q4-1997	16.573%		
Q1-1998	16.141%		
Q2-1998	16.731%		
Q3-1998	16.387%		
Q4-1998	16.669%		
Q1-1999	16.551%		
Q2-1999	16.984%		
Q3-1999	17.507%		
Q4-1999	17.504%		
Q1-2000	17.533%		
Q2-2000	17.180%	10.662%	18.537%
Q3-2000	18.269%	10.878%	18.451%
Q4-2000	19.158%	11.058%	18.567%
Q1-2001	19.943%	11.348%	18.543%
Q2-2001	19.855%	11.588%	18.753%
Q3-2001	21.202%	11.782%	18.879%
Q4-2001	21.098%	12.076%	19.017%
Q1-2002		12.486%	19.158%
Q2-2002		12.750%	19.583%
Q3-2002		12.922%	19.457%
Q4-2002		13.099%	19.384%
Q1-2003		13.334%	19.503%
Q2-2003		13.377%	19.583%
Q3-2003		13.481%	19.476%
Q4-2003		13.601%	19.420%
Q1-2004		13.917%	19.489%

Table 17.2 (continued)

ML/GDP ITALY*	ML/GDP USA**	ML/GDP EMU***
Q2-2004	14.079%	19.576%
Q3-2004	14.135%	19.492%
Q4-2004	14.317%	19.599%
Q1-2005	14.464%	19.450%
Q2-2005	14.653%	19.376%
Q3-2005	14.920%	19.140%
Q4-2005	15.037%	19.042%
Q1-2006	15.169%	19.011%
Q2-2006	15.648%	18.619%
Q3-2006	15.932%	18.487%
Q4-2006	16.096%	18.315%
Q1-2007	16.580%	18.083%
Q2-2007	16.978%	18.259%
Q3-2007	17.139%	18.099%
Q4-2007	17.472%	18.055%

Notes:
* Ratio between money laundering and GDP for Italian economy.
** Ratio between money laundering and GDP for US economy.
*** Ratio between money laundering and GDP for EU-IS economy.

Table 17.3 Statistics for simulated filtered series

EU-15		US		Italy	
σ_ML	0.003	σ_ML	0.006	σ_ML	4.376
σ_GDP	0.013	σ_GDP	0.016	σ_GDP	1.484
ρ{GDP,ML}	−0.252	ρ{GDP,ML}	0.583	ρ{GDP,ML}	−0.171
σ_ML/σ_GDP	0.228	σ_ML/σ_GDP	0.384	σ_ML/σ_GDP	2.95

Notes: σ_ML denotes the standard deviation for ML, σ_GDP: denotes the standard deviation for GDP; ρ_{GDP,ML}: denotes a contemporaneous correlation between ML and GDP. Statistics are computed over the sample 2000:Q2–2007:Q4.

The table shows that the cyclical behavior of money laundering significantly differs among the EU-15, Italy and the US economy. The ML simulated for the EU-15 is less volatile (relative standard deviation to GDP is 0.228 compared to a figure of almost 0.384 for the US), and negatively correlated with respect to GDP. The latter statistic is positive for the US economy. For Italy, ML is much more volatile than aggregate GDP (its relative standard deviation is on average almost three times larger than that of aggregate GDP), and it is negatively correlated with the latter quantity.

Indeed *a priori* it is not possible to establish the sign of correlation between ML and aggregate GDP. ML is a criminal way of hiding the revenues of a crime in a regular sector. The same definition of ML would suggest that when production in the regular sector increases (i.e. regular GDP increases), so does ML. Hence, this interpretation

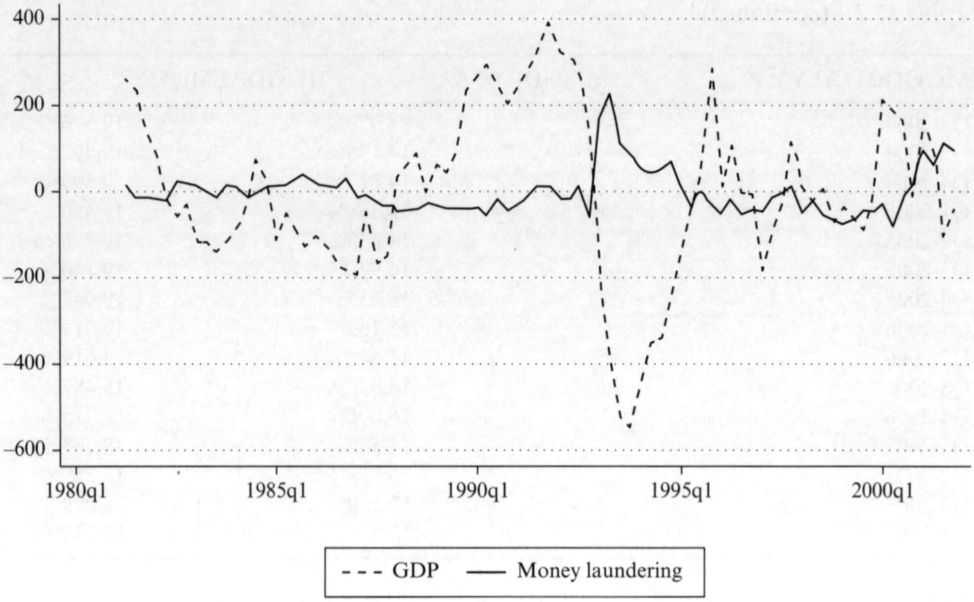

Figure 17.1 Italian money laundering and GDP

would support a *positive correlation* between the two quantities, because an increase of GDP would enhance the destination of ML. However, we believe there might be an alternative interpretation for this result. More precisely, we think that a relatively larger GDP could mean greater opportunities, better living conditions and hence form a deterrent to being a member of the criminal sector. In this respect, criminal activities would be seen as a 'buffer' that economic agents use in 'bad times'. Therefore, this reasoning would suggest a *negative correlation* between GDP and ML, because the increase of GDP could weaken the origin of ML. The simulations presented for the two economies suggest that the EU-15 economy uses ML according to the latter interpretation, while the US economy follows the former one.

Finally, the numerical predictions and the above economic intuition are also confirmed by a casual inspection of the parallel dynamic behavior of ML and regular GDP generated by the model.

Figures 17.1, 17.2 and 17.3 presents the Hodrick-Prescott filtered series for ML and the GDP (as a comparison time series) for Italian, the US and the EU-15 economies.

Figures 17.4, 17.5 and 17.6 show ML expressed as a percentage of the simulated GDP for Italy, the US and the EU-15.

The different results within Europe (in this case represented by the EU-15 and Italy) are able to provide important messages in terms of anti-ML policies.

In fact, in the US anti-ML controls should be more intense whenever the business cycle has a peak, in Europe an opposite scenario holds: more frequent controls should be realized in the contexts of negative growth of GDP.

Figure 17.2 US money laundering and GDP

Figure 17.3 EU-15 money laundering and GDP

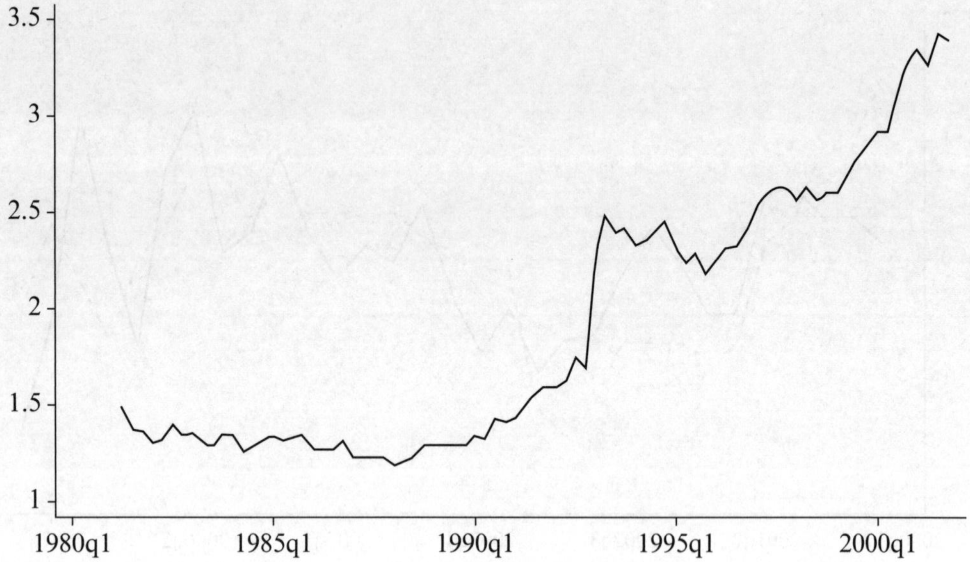

Figure 17.4 Italian money laundering (% GDP)

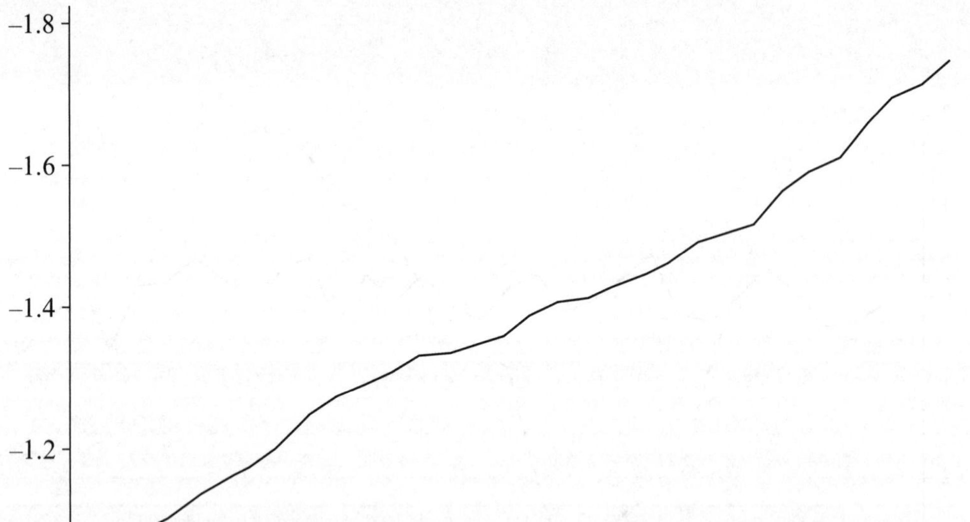

Figure 17.5 US money laundering (% GDP)

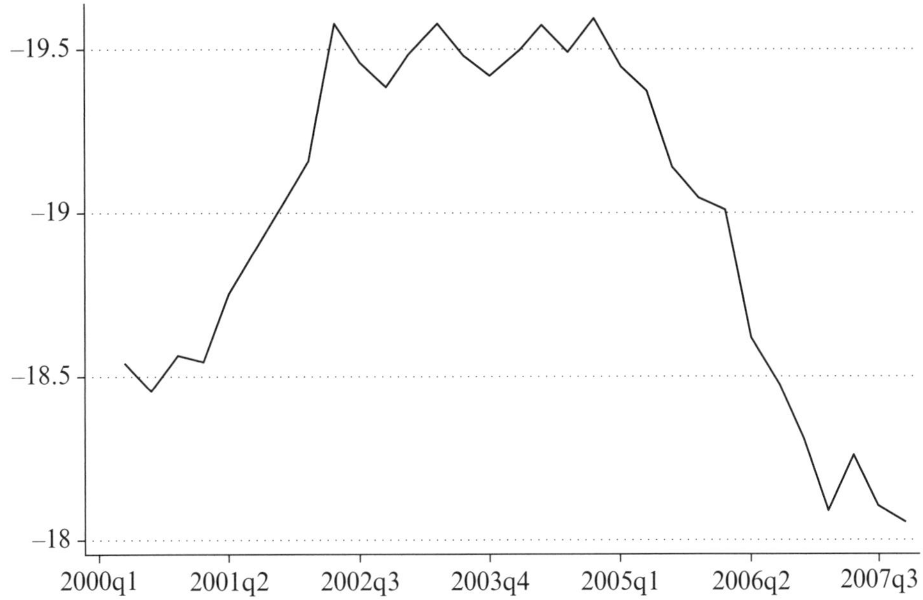

Figure 17.6 EU-15 money laundering (% GDP)

17.4 CONCLUSIONS

The methodology used to measure ML offers a tool to give a macroeconomic dimension to this criminal phenomenon, composed of many items, among which are tax evasion, corruption, drugs trade, etc. To try to measure a single source of money laundering, more data are needed, but if they are available, the methodology used here can be adopted.

Our approach is *top down* in the sense that the macro perspective does not use specific details, and is willing to give ML a percentage of the GDP consistent with the considered structure of the economy. In the literature, ML measures are based on data coming from particular surveys – a *bottom up* approach that generally speaking is not always well founded because of a scarcity of data. The key point is that institutions, economists and lawyers need to know more about ML than a traditional methodology may offer, considering the hidden nature of the activities involved. We think that the value added of this method is to provide a deep data set, potentially useful for undertaking long-run analysis and policy interventions.

Simulating a calibrated model to replicate the stationary properties at the steady state of a given country, we can generate a sufficiently large and deep data set, which could be used to perform econometric exercises.

But there is more: the approach is capable of offering to the econometricians high frequency data; that is because the model can be simulated over quarterly, yearly and/or monthly data. Theoretically, we could even perform weekly-based simulations, though it would be difficult because of the (non-)availability of statistics at this frequency.

After the 'pros', we cannot forget the 'cons'. The price we pay in our approach, common with other *top down* models, is to abstract from the descriptions of some details linked to the unobserved variable. In other words, we do not examine the different techniques and the channels for laundering money, but we intend to give a picture of this phenomenon consistent with macroeconomic data, relying on a fully-fledged microfoundation.

We would like to conclude this chapter by saying that it is hard to claim the existence of 'the perfect model' to measure ML. What we offer is an alternative, limited to the macro view, which can be used as the base for more detailed analysis.

NOTES

1. This figure is extracted from a reserved dataset kindly provided to us by the Guardia di Finanza, Nucleo Polizia Valutaria.
2. In Italy there are two articles of Penal Law that deal with the crime of money laundering: 648-bis and 648-ter. The former targets the subjects who substitute money or goods coming from criminal actions with other money or goods, whereas the latter legislates against the subjects who employ money or goods coming from criminal actions in economic activities.
3. In Italy only 5% of the total detected money-laundering transactions are successfully prosecuted (source: Guardia di Finanza).
4. The criminal economy represents the particular subset of the unobserved economy whose activities are in conflict with Penal Law, whereas the underground economy generally refers to those cases in conflict with civil laws (typically the evasion of social security contributions).
5. Argentiero et al. 2008 and Bagella et al. 2009.
6. Indeed the strong assumption implied in this construction is that all the unemployed households are 'criminal': we make this choice to simplify the model's structure, but, without a loss of generality, we could admit a third part of workers who do not work either in the regular sector or in the criminal one.
7. The transition from the short-run equilibrium to the long-term one goes beyond the purpose of this paper, that is, to give a theoretical explanation of *money laundering* and its measurement through a two-sector dynamic general equilibrium model.
8. An analysis of the long run (i.e. the study of the relationships between money laundering and the growth performance of the economy) would be the object of another work.
9. Note that an inspected firm is not necessarily convicted of evasion and therefore fined. Since inspections are based either on private information about institutions, or randomly, the conduct of a perfectly honest firm could possibly be inspected.

REFERENCES

Argentiero, A., M. Bagella and F. Busato (2008), 'Money laundering in a two-sector model: using theory for measurement', *European Journal of Law and Economics,* **26**(3), 341–59.

Bagella, M., L. Becchetti and M. Lo Cicero (2004), 'Regional externalities and direct effects of legislation against money laundering: a test on excess money balances in the five Andean countries', *Journal of Money Laundering Control*, **7**(4), 347–66.

Bagella, M., F. Busato and A. Argentiero (2009), 'Money laundering in a microfounded dynamic model: simulations for the U.S. and the EU-15 economies', *Review of Law & Economics, Berkeley Electronic Press*, **5**(2).

Barone, R. and D. Masciandaro (2011), 'Organized crime, money laundering and legal economy: theory and simulations', *European Journal of Law and Economics*, **32**(1), 115–42.

Bhattacharyya, D.K. (1999), 'On the economic national of estimating the hidden economy', *Economic Journal*, **109**, 348–59.

Busato, F. and B. Chiarini (2004), 'Market and underground activities in a two sector dynamic equilibrium model', *Economic Theory*, **23**, 831–61.

Busato, F., B. Chiarini and V. Di Maro (2006), 'Using theory for measurement: an analysis of the behaviour of the underground economy', working paper, Aarhus University.

Calvo, G. (1983), 'Staggered prices in a utility maximizing framework', *Journal of Monetary Economics*, **12**, 383–98.
Carlstrom, C.T. and T.S. Fuerst (2004), 'Learning and the central bank', *Journal of Monetary Economics*, **51**(2), 327–38.
Chari, V.V., P.J. Kehoe and E.R. McGrattan (2000), 'Sticky price models of the business cycle: can the contract multiplier solve the persistence problem?', *Econometrica*, **68**, 1151–80.
Clower, R.W. (1967), 'A reconsideration of the microfoundations of monetary theory', *Western Economic Journal* **6**, 1–9.
Cooley, T.F. and E.C. Prescott (1995), 'Economic growth and business cycles', in T.F. Cooley (ed.), *Frontiers of Business Cycle Research*, Princeton, NJ: Princeton University Press, 1–38.
Domeij, D. and M. Floden (2006), 'The labor-supply elasticity and borrowing constraints: why estimates are biased', *Review of Economic Dynamics*, **9**, 242–62.
Frey, B.S. and H. Weck-Hanneman (1984), 'The hidden economy as an unobserved variable', *Europeon Economic Review*, **26**, 33–53.
Galì, J. (1999), 'Technology, employment and the business cycle: do technology shocks explain aggregate fluctuations?', *American Economic Review*, **89**(1), 249–71.
Ingram, B.F., N.R. Kocherlakota and N.E. Savin (1997), 'Using theory for measurement: an analysis of the cyclical behavior of home production', *Journal of Monetary Economics*, **40**, 435–56.
International Monetary Fund (2005), 'The IMF and the fight against money laundering and the financing of terrorism', http://www.imf.org/external/np/exr/facts/aml.htm.
Kimball, M.S. and M.D. Shapiro (2003), 'Labor supply: are the income and substitution effects both large or both small?', manuscript.
Kniesner, T.J. and J.P. Ziliak (2005), 'The effect of income taxation on consumption and labor supply', manuscript.
Kydland, F.E. and E.C. Prescott (1982), 'Time to build and aggregate fluctuations', *Econometrica*, **50**(6), 1345–70.
Lim, G.C. and P.D. McNelis (2007), 'Central bank learning, terms of trade shocks and currency risk: should only inflation matter for monetary policy?', *Journal of International Money and Finance*, **26**(6), 865–86.
Lucas, R.E. (1988), 'On the mechanics of economic development', *Journal of Monetary Economics*, **22**, 3–42.
Masciandaro, D. (1993), 'Analisi economica della criminalità, teoria della regolamentazione e riciclaggio finanziario', in S. Zamagni (ed.), *Mercati illegali e mafie*, Bologna: Il Mulino, 243–97.
Masciandaro, D. (1999), 'Money laundering: the economics of regulation', *European Journal of Law and Economics*, **3**, 245–40.
Masciandaro, D. (2005), 'Combating black money: international cooperation and the G8's role', in M. Fratianni, J. Kirton and A. Rugman, *New Perspectives on Global Governance*, Aldershot: Ashgate, pp. 169–92.
Napoleoni, L. (2005), *Terror incorporated: Tracing the Dollars Behind the Terror Networks*, New York: Seven Stones Press.
Prescott, E.C. (2004), 'Why do Americans work so much more than Europeans?', *Quarterly Review Federal Reserve Bank of Minneapolis*, **28**, 2–13.
Tanzi, V. (1999), 'Uses and abuse of estimates of the underground economy', *Economic Journal*, **109**, 338–47.
Thomas, J.J. (1999), 'Quantifying the black economy: "Measurement without theory" yet again?', *Economic Journal*, **109**, 381–9.
Tuck, Y. (1996), 'Nominal price rigidity, money supply endogeneity, and business cycles', *Journal of Monetary Economics*, **37**, 345–70.
Uzawa, H. (1965), 'Optimally technical change in aggregative model of economic growth', *International Economic Review*, **6**, 18–31.
Wen, J.F. and D.R.F. Love (1998), 'Evaluating tax reforms in a monetary economy', *Journal of Macroeconomics*, **20**(3), 487–508.
Zizza, R. (2002), 'Metodologie di stima dell'economia sommersa: un'applicazione al caso italiano', Tema di discussione 463, servizio studi Banca d'Italia.

18. Are estimates of the volume of money laundering either feasible or useful?*

Peter Reuter

18.1 INTRODUCTION

In 1998 Michel Camdessus, Managing Director of the IMF, stated that money laundering might amount to about 2–5 percent of global GDP. He was not in fact announcing an IMF study but explicitly stating what he thought was expert opinion.[1] The number lives on, because people do want to have some number and nothing else seemingly as authoritative has appeared since.

My view is that knowing how much money is laundered serves no important policy purpose. It is simply one of those adornments for conversations about the phenomenon. That is very fortunate, since we have no methodology that plausibly would produce credible numbers. In these comments I use John Walker's model for estimating money laundering in Australia, to illustrate the frailties (Walker 2007; Walker and Unger 2009). What I hope to persuade you of is that there is no prospect, either in surveys of experts or in studies of crimes themselves as reflected in criminal justice statistics, for developing persuasive estimates.

18.2 THE MARGINALITY OF VOLUME MEASURES

What is the value of knowing how much money is laundered? The principal answer is because money laundering is believed to cause some harm. There are four mechanisms by which money laundering, as opposed to the underlying crimes themselves, might adversely affect society. First, money laundering poses a threat to the integrity of the financial system because at least some of the criminals who purchase or provide the service may attempt to acquire control of institutions. Second, it is believed that those who launder money are more likely to move money in and out of the system, in response to non-economic events; that potentially creates fiscal instability. Third, the investment patterns chosen by the criminals will not be optimal because they have concerns other than maximizing income. Fourth, once an AML system has been created, then discovery of money laundering at a bank or in a country creates a problem for that bank or country because of the AML response itself.[2]

All four mechanisms may be important but there is little evidence that any of them have turned out to have macroeconomic significance. There are two well-known instances in which money laundering may have reached such a scale that it caused macro-instability for a country. These involve Latvia in the 1990s and the Dominican Republic in 2002; these are referenced in IMF (2011). No other instances were identified in a review conducted by the IMF (2011). Moreover, in each of the two cases it may have been the underlying crimes rather than the laundering which caused the problem. It is striking how little evidence there is that money laundering has been a major problem in any country, even small ones. That is not to deny that there have been major money laundering scandals that have caused harm to many individuals, such as the scandal involving BCCI (the Bank for Commerce and Credit International) in the 1990s (Kerry 1993). However the question remains whether money laundering itself results in any significant harms.

18.3 THE GOALS OF MONEY LAUNDERING CONTROLS

The rationale for money laundering controls is not a concern that money is being laundered but a belief that these controls may turn out to be a good way of reducing certain kinds of crimes, and also of dealing with terrorism (Reuter and Truman 2004). It is conventional wisdom that in order to be able to use criminal revenues with tranquillity, offenders need to launder them through the financial system. Controls on those transactions may help society catch and punish the offenders. From this perspective, which is consistent with political statements around the creation of the controls (Cuéllar 2003, 374–80), they constitute a device for crime control.

For terrorism the logic is reversed. Much of the money for terrorist activities comes from legal sources. These sources are not 'black', indeed they are often whiter than white, since a lot comes from charitable giving. Society is not served by discouraging charitable giving. What is to be discouraged is the use of that money for terrorism purposes. Again, money laundering controls constitute a device to control terrorism and authorities may rather seek to pursue the money to the potential terrorist act rather than keep money from being laundered in the financial system.

Anti-money laundering controls thus can be thought of as a means to diverse ends. There are at least two primary goals:

(1) reducing predicate crimes, particularly those associated with high per participant revenues; and
(2) combating 'global bads', namely terrorism and kleptocracy.

There are also at least four secondary goals:

(1) protecting the integrity of the core financial system;
(2) sanctioning felons who would otherwise escape justice, such as high-level drug dealers who do not handle drugs but only the profits from dealing;
(3) providing just deserts, since there may be particular social satisfaction in seizing the assets of rich offenders; and
(4) simply inconveniencing felons by making it more difficult and nerve racking to get access to their own funds.

Which goals are primary and which are secondary is a matter of judgment. For a central banker, protecting the integrity of the core financial system is a primary goal. For those interested in drug control, which initiated the whole international system, the critical issue is the ability to reduce drug trafficking and the power of its most powerful participants.

Would knowing the volume of money laundering help achieve these goals? This raises the question of definition. In some countries, any expenditure, from any use of funds generated by predicate crimes, constitutes a money laundering offence. Under those terms, estimating the volume of money laundering is equivalent to estimating the revenues from crime. There are reasons to be interested in the latter but it is deceptive to call that the volume of money laundering. What is policy relevant is the amount of money processed through the financial systems (broadly defined), in order to evade detection of its criminal origins, so that it can be used for other purposes.

If that is the correct view of money laundering controls, how important is a decline in the volume of money laundering? Does it constitute evidence that the anti-money laundering system has worked? The money laundering volume matches very poorly with the goals of the money laundering control system as a performance measure. In fact, no agency offers money laundering volume reduction as one of its outcome measures. Even the recent spate of national Money Laundering Control Strategies has not included such figures.

One reason may be that money laundering is a highly differentiated activity. Reuter and Truman (2004) offer a typology of predicate activities that distinguished five types of predicate crimes, according to four dimensions; cash intensity, scale of individual operations, the severity of harms and the distribution of those harms (Table 18.1). The judgments about severity are just that, judgments; others may disagree for example that white collar crime has modest consequences per dollar. There is probably not much disagreement that terrorism is most severe in terms of its social harm per dollar. Nor is there likely to be disagreement that crimes differ in the intensity of harms per dollar laundered, which is the principal point here.

Consider a system in which money laundering volumes is one of the targets of AML controls. Assume for a moment that anti-money laundering controls can actually affect money laundering volume. This is a strong assumption, but one necessary for assessment purposes. Consider the incentives for an agency of this performance measure. The agency may go after low-hanging fruit, namely crimes that generate a high money laundering per unit of investigative resources. Thus an AML agency may target white collar crime,

Table 18.1 Taxonomy of predicate crimes for money laundering

Crime	Cash	Scale of operations	Severity of harm	Most affected population
Drug dealing	Exclusively	Very large	Severe	Urban minority groups
Other blue-collar	Mostly	Small to medium	Low to modest	?
White-collar	Mix	Mix	Low to modest	Broad
Bribery and corruption	Sometimes	Large	Severe	Developing countries
Terrorism	Mix	Small	Most severe	Broad

Source: Reuter and Truman (2004).

even though that generates very modest gains for society, as measured by reductions in criminal harms. Elevating money laundering volume as an important construct threatens to distort the functioning of the system from its true purpose, which is reduction of the most serious crimes and global bads.

18.4 HOW GOOD ARE THE ESTIMATES?

The existing estimates have an enormous range. None of them are well documented. Numbers are casually thrown around by public figures, ranging from hundreds of billions to trillions of dollars (e.g. UNODC 2011). One set of estimates have their origins in the work of Friedrich Schneider who has long labored at estimating the size of the underground economy in different countries (Schneider and Enste 2000; Schneider et al. 2010).[3] The second approach is what is represented by John Walker's estimates for Australia. I will focus here on Walker's approach as it has been used in a number of recent studies, such as UNODC (2011).

Walker builds estimates of money laundering from examining the individual criminal activities that might generate that money. A critique then must examine those components. Consider fraud and drug sales, generally the two leading contenders for first place in terms of the volume of money laundering generated. Another reason to highlight fraud is because the estimates are so weak. For example, in the US, where research on crime is relatively well developed, the most cited estimate comes from the Association of Certified Fraud Examiners (2002). The ACFE surveyed its membership, and achieved a 10 percent response rate. Using a survey with a 10 percent response rate requires careful examination of non-response characteristics, a topic totally absent from the study. The central question in the survey was 'what is the percentage of revenues that your firm lost in 2002 as a result of occupational fraud and abuse'. Why would a fraud examiner at General Motors be able to answer that question? At best, an individual might know all the instances in which fraud was detected, which is clearly an underestimate of the total amount. Nonetheless if asked a question in a survey, respondents often will try to provide an answer, regardless of their actual knowledge. The answer provided by the small fraction who did so was about 6 percent of the corporation's revenues. Thus the study estimated that 6 percent of GDP, roughly six hundred billion dollars was stolen by way of fraud.

It is hardly necessary to describe all the ways in which this estimating process is implausible. Nonetheless, it has produced the most widely cited estimate of fraud in the United States.

There is much more work on estimating drug market revenues. One general problem here is that those who use expensive addictive drugs, such as heroin, cocaine and methamphetamine in the US, are very hard to reach through population surveys. For example, the National Survey on Drug Use and Health in 2003 estimated only about 200,000 individuals had used heroin in the previous week in the US (U.S. Department of Health and Human Services 2004), whereas a survey of arrestees which included a question about use of heroin in the previous 48 hours (accompanied by a urine test) found that the number was likely four times as large (National Institute of Justice, 2004). A central problem for estimating quantities is that users can't report how much they've

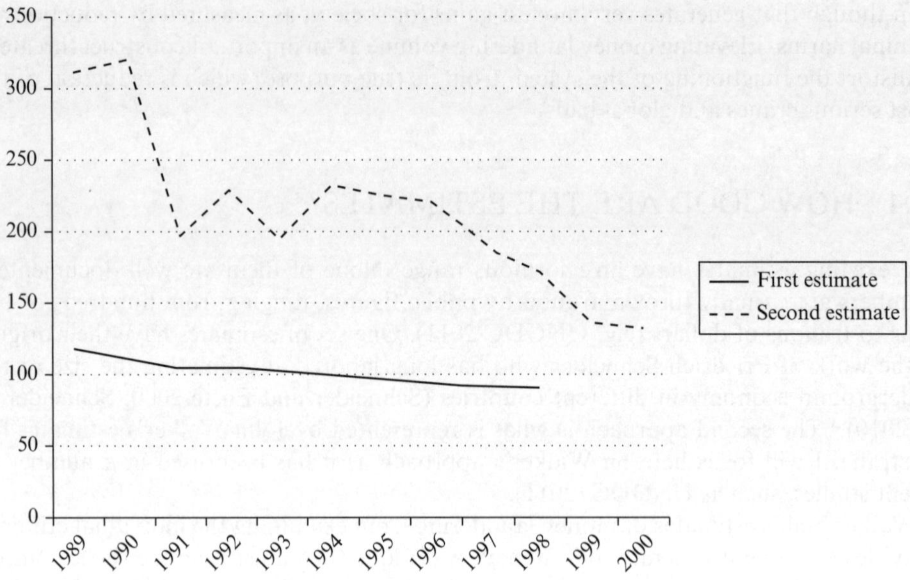

Source: US office of National Drug Control Policy (2000, 2001).

Figure 18.1 Two estimates of weekly methamphetamine expenditures

purchased but only how much they have spent, because packages simply consist of white powder; how much of that white powder is actually heroin is something that the user knows only roughly, even after consuming it.

The results of these surveys are highly sensitive to technical specifications. For example, two researchers in New York looked at the data from surveys of arrestees in Manhattan. Respondents in the early years of the survey were asked 'how much did you spend at your last transaction?' The question was later changed to 'how much do you spend in your typical transaction?' The change halved the estimated expenditures by drug users (Golub and Johnson 2004). More generally, quite small changes in methodology can lead to big changes in estimates.

Figure 18.1 gives estimates from the most well documented and systematic study of expenditures on drugs in the US. Two versions of the study were published; one in 2000, with estimates through 1998, and in 2001, with estimates through 2000 (U.S. Office of National Drug Control Policy 2000, 2001). In the 2000 estimate, the 1998 weekly expenditure estimates for people who are frequent users of methamphetamine, was estimated at about 100 dollars a week, a figure that had been fairly stable over the 1990s. In the 2001 version, that figure was much higher (173 dollars), and had fallen substantially over the prior ten years. It is difficult to have faith in series that can be revised so rapidly in a short period of time.

John Walker, in his recent study, examined two sources of estimates for criminal earnings and money laundering in Australia. One was official statistics, the other a survey of experts. Neither is convincing. Consider the figures for drug markets from the 2007 study, given in Table 18.2.

Table 18.2 Estimated Net Income to Drug Retailers in Australia

Drug type	Estimated number of users	Estimated retail price (AUD/pure gm)	Average consumption per user (pure gms/yr)	Total income drug retailers (AUD millions)	Wholesale price as % of retail price	Net income to drug retailers (AUD millions)
Opiates	80,000	560	56.5	2,531	25%	1,898
Cocaine	200,000	380	35	2,660	37%	1,680
Cannabis resin	20,000	24	150	72	27%	52
Herbal Cannabis	2,000,000	9	200	3,600	34%	2,364
ATS	500,000	84	13	546	52%	260
Ecstasy	450,000	298	10	1,341	48%	698
			Total	10,750	Total	6,952

Source: Walker (2007).

Herbal cannabis is the largest single item; the second one is opiates, which is almost exclusively heroin. In both cases the figures here are extraordinarily high. For cannabis the study estimates that users consume 200 grams per annum on average. A recent review found that across a number of studies 100 grams per user per annum was a reasonable estimate (Kilmer et al. 2011). For heroin, Walker used 56 grams per annum which is far above the 15 grams used in US studies and those now used in the UK (Paoli et al. 2009; Appendix D). These other figures are not necessarily right, but they point to the fragility of Walker's estimates. There simply is not a basis for providing more than very crude estimates of many of the critical crime bases in these estimations.

Walker also includes an estimate of the percentage of revenues that are laundered from drug sales, 83 percent. That is implausibly high. In drug sales, certainly for heroin, cocaine, and to a lesser extent for marihuana, most of the revenues go to sellers at the bottom of the system (Kilmer and Reuter 2009). If there is a 50 percent mark-up in each of the last two transactions, a conservative estimate, then about 60 percent of the money goes to the retailer and to the low-level wholesalers. The many studies of low-level dealers all show that retailers and low-level wholesalers make very small incomes from drug dealing (e.g. Levitt and Venkatesh, 2000). It is very unlikely that a substantial part of their earnings are laundered in the sense that there is an effort to conceal the origins through some transaction within the financial system. It is simply spent.

Separately, Walker reported estimates based on surveys of experts. Petrus van Duyne and others (e.g. van Duyne and Soudjin 2010) have raised valid questions about how plausible is it that experts would know much about aggregates. What intelligence agency activities would enable them to do so much better than social scientists at estimating these aggregates and their composition? Investigation is not science but an effort to obtain information from a specifically targeted set of actions. It is not an attempt to sample all offenders. Intelligence based on investigation does not permit development of an estimate of an average when the information comes from outliers. There is no reason to trust experts for purposes of aggregates. Kilmer et al. (2010), provide a critique of intelligence agency efforts to estimate US drug markets.

This is not a challenge to intelligence agencies' expertise in the job they are tasked to do. An agency is asking intelligence officers to use information in ways that enable the agency to improve investigative activities. They may do that well. But for aggregation they have neither the information base nor the skills to produce those figures.

Again, like fraud examiners, if asked a question, some intelligence analysts will give an answer. In fact only 40 percent of those approached by Walker responded. The figures they produced are much different from those Walker developed from standard statistical sources. For example, drug markets were estimated from the expert survey to produce only 382 million Australian dollars as compared to 6 billion dollars from the statistical sources. It is plausible that the true number lies between these two values but the band is so wide as to be useless.

It is not that I think that John Walker has done his work poorly. Rather I believe that this methodology is fundamentally flawed. Fortunately the number is not very important for policy purposes. This is not a challenge to the anti-money laundering system, or to the notion that we need to get a better understanding of both money laundering and how AML affects it. It's just that estimating the total volume is a diversion of attention.

NOTES

* Based on comments originally delivered at Utrecht University School of Economics symposium on money laundering, November, 2007.

1. 'I hardly need say that the IMF regards the anti-money laundering actions advocated by the FATF as crucial for the smooth functioning of the financial markets. While we cannot guarantee the accuracy of our figures – and you have certainly a better evaluation than us – the estimates of the present scale of money laundering transactions are almost beyond imagination – 2 to 5 percent of global GDP would probably be a consensus range . . . '(Camdessus 1998).
2. Once a money laundering problem is exposed in a nation, the banks of the principal financial centers such as London, New York and Zurich may withdraw respondent account privileges or in other ways make it difficult to process international financial transactions. That may precipitate macroeconomic instability.
3. Schneider's estimates use a sophisticated modeling technique with a latent dependent variable. It is difficult to assess the soundness of the estimates.

REFERENCES

Association of Certified Fraud Examiners (2002), *2002 Report to the Nation on Occupational Fraud and Abuse*, Austin, TX: ACFE.

Camdessus, M. (1998), 'Money laundering: the importance of international countermeasures', Speech to the Financial Action Task Force, at the Plenary Meeting of the Financial Action Task Force on Money Laundering on February 10, 1998, Paris (http://www.imf.org/external/np/speeches/1998/021098.htm).

Cuéllar, Mariano-Florentino (2003), 'The tenuous relationship between the fight against money laundering and the disruption of criminal finance', *Journal of Criminal Law and Criminology*, **93**, 312–466.

Duyne, P.C. van and M.R.J. Soudijn (2010), 'Crime-money in the financial system: what we fear and what we know', in M. Herzog-Evans (ed.), *Transnational Criminology Manual, Volume 2*, Nijmegen: Wolf Legal Publishers.

Golub, A. and B. Johnson (2004), 'How much do Manhattan-arrestees spend on drugs?', Final report to the National Institute of Justice Regarding Monitoring Drug Markets in Manhattan with ADAM (2003-IJ-CX-1028).

IMF (2011), *Anti-Money Laundering and Combating the Financing of Terrorism (AML/CFT) – Report on the Review of the Effectiveness of the Program*, Washington, DC: IMF.
Kerry, J. (1993), *The BCCI Affair: a Report to the Committee on Foreign Relations*, United States Senate, Washington, DC.
Kilmer, B. and P. Reuter (2009), 'Prime numbers: doped', *Foreign Policy*, November/December, 34–5 (http://www.foreignpolicy.com/articles/2009/10/19/prime_numbers_doped).
Kilmer, B., J.P., Caulkins B. Bond and P. Reuter (2010), *Reducing Drug Trafficking Revenues and Violence in Mexico: Would Legalizing Marijuana in California Help?* RAND Occasional Paper (http://www.rand.org/pubs/occasional_papers/2010/RAND_OP325.pdf).
Kilmer, B., J.P. Caulkins R.L. Pacula and P. Reuter (2011), 'Bringing perspective to illicit markets: estimating the size of the U.S. marijuana market', *Drug and Alcohol Dependence*, **119**, 153–60.
Levitt, S. and S.A. Venkatesh (2000), 'An economic analysis of a drug-selling gang's finances', *Quarterly Journal of Economics*, **115** (3), 755–89.
National Institute of Justice (2004), *Drug and Alcohol Use and Related Matters among Arrestees 2003*. By Zhiwei Zhang (https://www.ncjrs.gov/nij/adam/adam2003.pdf).
Paoli, L., V. Greenfield and P. Reuter (2009), *The World Heroin Market: Can Supply be Cut?* New York: Oxford University Press.
Reuter, P. and E.M. Truman (2004), *Chasing Dirty Money: The Fight against Money Laundering*, Washington, DC: Peterson Institute for International Economics.
Schneider, F. and D. Enste (2000), 'Shadow economies: size, causes, and consequences', *The Journal of Economic Literature*, **38** (1), 77–114.
Schneider, F., A. Buehn and C.E. Montenegro (2010), 'New estimates for the shadow economies all over the world', *International Economic Journal*, **24** (4), 443–61.
UN Office on Drugs and Crime (2011), *Estimating Illicit Financial Flows Resulting from Drug Trafficking and Other Transnational Organized Crimes*, Vienna: United Nations.
U.S. Department of Health and Human Services (2004), *Results from the 2003 National Survey on Drug Use and Health: National Findings*. NSDUH Series H-25, DHHS publication no. SMA 04-3964. Rockville, MD: U.S. Department of Health and Human Services, Substance Abuse and Mental Health Services Administration.
U.S. Office of National Drug Control Policy (2000), *What America's Users Spend on Illicit Drugs 1988–1998*. By William Rhodes, Mark Layne, Patrick Johnston and Lynne Hozick. Washington, DC: Executive Office of the President.
U.S. Office of National Drug Control Policy (2001), *What America's Users Spend on Illicit Drugs 1988–2000*. By William Rhodes, Mark Layne, Ann-Marie Bruen, Patrick Johnston and Lisa Bechetti. Washington, DC: Executive Office of the President.
Walker, J. (1995), *Estimates of the Extent of Money Laundering in and through Australia*. Paper prepared for the Australian Transaction Reports and Analysis Centre, John Walker Consulting Services, Queanbeyan, Australia.
Walker, J. (2007), *The Extent of Money Laundering in and through Australia in 2004*, RMIT University.
Walker, J. and B. Unger (2009), 'Measuring global money laundering: the Walker Gravity Model', *Review of Law and Economics*, **5** (2), 821–53.

19. Crime-money and financial conduct

Petrus C. van Duyne

Erst das Fressen, dann die Moral
Berthold Brecht

19.1 A BEHAVIOURAL LOOK AT CRIME-MONEY

The financial crisis has since 2007/8 affected virtually all countries around the globe, and taught us an (old) lesson: there is much psychology and sociology to money. Expectations, beliefs combined with the psychological variable of 'trust', seem to be more important than economic models. One can call this perspective the behavioural 'soft side' of money, but with 'hard effects': the credit crisis has to a large extent been attributed to such behavioural factors: the greed and bonus craving by bankers given too much leeway by their cosily buttered up supervisors (Dorn 2010). If it is proper to approach normal financial issues from a behavioural perspective, it is equally justified to address the criminal variation from this angle: the socio-psychology of crime and money.

This approach differs substantially from the usual macro-economic way of addressing crime-money and laundering traditionally furthered by organisations such as the OECD, IMF (Tanzi 1996; Quirk 1996) and World Bank. The latter approach uses broad economic models and invariably presents laundering as a grave threat illustrated with huge figures, endorsed by sponsored researchers. There is nothing wrong with model building, if it heeds basic principles of methodology and philosophy of science: a clear operationalisation of basic concepts and the principle of falsification (Popper 1963). The basic concepts, such as crime-money and laundering are still ill-defined, while the realisation of the assumed laundering threat has not been rigorously tested. I refer to earlier analyses and research findings (Van Duyne et al. 2009, 2010; Van Duyne 2003, 2007; Gelemerova 2011; Levi 2007; Reuter 2007). However, for some inscrutable reason this never entered into the economists' debate or that of the IMF, World Bank or FATF. Measured by absent references to preceding (deviating) research one cannot speak of a debate.

In contrast to the economists' approach, the socio-psychological research angle focuses on '*who does what*'. This implies a target population and the targeted conduct of individuals. This seems straightforward, however, it is beset with many methodological problems, not all of them were clear when at the outset of the Tilburg University projects there were yet no predecessors to learn from (Van Eekelen 2000). Penetrating the underlying criminal conduct and the resulting profits is difficult. Asking criminals about their ill-gotten profits and how they came by these is a delicate approach with uncertain findings. Vruggink (2001) interviewed imprisoned convicted criminals against whom also a recovery order had been served. However, his target group did not consist of high-earning criminals, while his research did not concern criminal economic conduct.

Given the dearth of data, such a behavioural approach has to start with looking at the outward conduct: the observable handling of crime-money (a shorthand for criminal profits), from spending to investment. This does not directly generate a 'socio-psychology of criminal finances', but rather a survey of economic choices made: statistics about the amount, ways and nature of spending crime-money combined with other variables.

In line with the behavioural approach we have to change and rename the central concepts of *money laundering*. This phrase, first mentioned within the context of the Watergate scandal, has developed into a *legal* term which is also used, however, to denote a certain criminal *conduct*. Semantically that concept denotes '*cleaning*' dirty money: in French, German or Dutch it is more appropriately called, 'blanchissement', 'Geldwäscherei' or 'geld witwassen' (Gelemerova 2011).

For this reason, I will sometimes use the literal translation from these languages, namely 'white washing'. In the course of time the meaning of the concept has broadened, mixing legal and behavioural notions. In the end its breadth of application is so broad that virtually no aspect of the handling of proceeds after a predicate crime is excluded. As this broadened concept has become almost tautological with the built-in conclusion of 'laundering soon after criminal profits have been acquired' (Van Duyne et al. 2005), it is useless for research. With a built-in conclusion it proves what still has to be proven: this is a researcher's mortal sin. The fuzzy way in which this concept is used in economic publications does not deserve following (see: Unger 2007; Unger and Ferwerda 2011, part 1). For this reason, it is preferable to speak of handling or managing the proceeds of crime: '*criminal money management*' and reserve the concept of *money laundering* for law enforcement and policy making. This basic concept encompasses the same range of behaviour: from simple (often carefree) spending, through straight forward hiding to elaborate accountancy smoke screens. But it abstracts from the outcome variable (the 'whitening' of crime-money) or other value-laden threat associations. I leave these aspects to the interested policy makers and economic researchers.

Hence, from this perspective the research focus will be at a behavioural level, looking at what criminals do with crime-money. This is still very broad. The focus will soon be narrowed to money management and two economic sectors.

19.2 WHAT DO CRIMINALS DO WITH THEIR MONEY?

Surveying the literature which abounds in warnings against the *threat* of the crime-money it is remarkable that this question has not been addressed systematically. The 'conventional wisdom' seems to be that criminals do bad things with 'bad money' or at least that 'bad money' has bad effects. However, these are not behavioural observations, but moral assumptions, which rarely lead to intriguing follow-up questions, let alone to good research. The present question: 'What do criminals do with their ill-gotten money?' is not a moral but a factual one – paraphrasing Bertold Brecht's adage about the order of eating and morality: 'First facts, then morals'.

Having said that, how to shed light on this question? In the first place we have a twofold problem of dark numbers. In the first place, there are criminals with criminal revenues who are not detected. In the second place, there are criminals who are caught, but of whom there are insufficient data about their criminal financial household. This is not compensated by anecdotal, mainly journalistic, evidence, while only a few research projects have explicitly addressed this question.

Since the beginning of the 1990s, the recovery of proceeds from crime has become a standard law enforcement approach, at least in most industrialised countries. To make this effective, suspects' assets used to be seized and/or frozen in an early phase of the investigation, often in the context of a house search. This means that all the belongings of the suspect (and his family) must be described and listed in a register. Such lists are informative: they read as a kind of 'family wealth still' at the moment of seizure. But they are not a pure measurement of criminal wealth: assets may not be detected and part of the assets may be acquired legally.

A number of research projects carried out in the Netherlands have aimed to obtain insight into this aggregate criminal wealth picture of (convicted) offenders. The underlying philosophy of these projects was: if there is so much crime-money around, it will not remain floating in the 'financial air', but must eventually come down somewhere into the economy to be converted into something meaningful for the owners. This led to a series of research projects directed at what crime-entrepreneurs earn, what they do with it and how they handle their crime-money.

This resulted in four related research projects, based on two related, but different sources:

- the analysis of criminal files of finalised cases (two projects on spending and criminal money management); and
- the analysis of the seizures/confiscation databases of the Dutch Public Prosecution Service and the Recovery Agency resulting in two projects on (a) the real estate sector and (b) banks and cash.

The following sections will first describe the file analysis on spending and managing crime-money.

19.3 EARNING, SPENDING AND MANAGING CRIME-MONEY

19.3.1 Scouting the Unknown Territory

During the organised crime research carried out in the Netherlands from 1988 onwards (Van Duyne et al. 1990; Van Duyne 1995; Van de Bunt and Kleemans 2007), the question about the criminal wealth forced itself upon the researchers: everybody in the field assumed a staggering wealth, but there was no empirically grounded knowledge. There were some financial 'pictures' which provided a few glimpses of the handling and spending of wealthy criminals. Some of these pictures were based on hunches of CID officers, which often proved to be gross overestimations, but were believed nevertheless. In some cases there were reports composed by the financial investigators of the detective squad. However, this was no guarantee of accuracy. My recalculation of the same data of some criminal files revealed lower figures due to various inaccuracies (Van Duyne, 1997). For example, investments were added to the assessment list even if they were not realised eventually; losses caused by loss-making enterprises were not included in the assessment; real estate was listed, but the mortgage (at a regular bank) was not mentioned. In short, the inaccuracies led to over-sizing the assumed wealth. It showed the need for a systematic independent research of the profits and money-management of serious crime-for-profit.

In the absence of previous studies, some pioneering had to be undertaken. Hence it was decided to start a project within the framework of a masters degree programme, carried out by John van Eekelen graduating at Tilburg University in 2000. Though it was a reconnaissance, it did not take place in a fully *terra incognita*. Earlier research on suspicious transaction reports had already provided some indications of a very skewed distribution of criminal wealth: 'Many move little and few move much' concluded Van Duyne and De Miranda (1999). Based on earlier experience in the field, we assumed that at the lower ranges of the criminal income distribution most of the money is spent on daily expenses and lifestyle with little surplus saving for other economic activities. Therefore, as a selection criterion of criminal cases to be analysed we set a minimum threshold of €45,000 (100,000 guilders at that time) criminal income *as determined by the Courts* to be recovered.

This approach implied that the cases had to be finalised such that no new information was to surface. In addition, we applied another selection criterion: the cases had to contain a financial report with an asset seizure list. Using the database of the Dutch Asset Recovery Agency, we obtained 19 criminal files.

The analysis was carried out by means of a code book for the standard variables concerning offenders' characteristics, type of offence, the assets categories and ways of managing the money. In addition, short summaries of the remarkable details were added.

Categorised according to determined illegal profits, 14 cases were in the range of €45,000 – €125,000, one case in the range of €125,000 – €250,000 and two above €450,000, reaffirming the skewed distribution found earlier. Thirteen cases concerned drug trafficking and the others fraud, embezzlement and other types of property crime.

In all cases there were more offenders who cooperated, though only eight cases were qualified by the Courts as 'participating in a criminal organisation'. These organisations were not necessarily big: only two of them had nine or more participants. The modal number of co-offending for the whole set was between three and six members, which reconfirms the general finding in organised crime research: most criminal cooperatives are small.

What was the economic conduct of the offenders? The first phenomenon the researcher looked for was 'real' laundering: the attempts to *clean* the crime-money by means of constructions intending to pretend a licit origin. In only one case – with the highest criminal revenue of €4 million – an elaborate loan-back construction was identified, together with money exportation, the establishment of legal persons abroad, nominate directors and the flow-back in the form of a loan. Otherwise, the money management consisted of putting assets in the name of another person or obtaining a fake labour contract. Or there was no specific 'whitewash' construction at all: the money was spent, hoarded or deposited in a bank (abroad, in four of the five cases).

Of special interest was the question of investment in offenders' own criminal enterprises or in the licit upperworld. The latter category is of interest because it relates to the fear of crime-money 'penetrating' or 'infecting' the licit economy. Indeed, there was evidence of both: crime-entrepreneurs also have business expenses, and, naturally, many such expenses occur and are paid for in the upperworld. This can be qualified as reinvestment in the crime-enterprise. Most of these expenses concern payment to staff or outside aid, often for hauling and storage. Some of these expenses were considered as normal business costs and declared by the Court as deductable from the 'gross criminal profits'.[1] In two cases a real investment in legal companies could be identified: the establishment of a Turkish enterprise for foreign currencies and precious metal, and a wholesale hashish smuggling enterprise (with the highest criminal income of €4 million) which established a network of legal front companies for investment (loans) in catering, gambling machines, a chain of Italian food stores and a public relations firm. This was also the only crime-enterprise which grew so big that it needed a professional financial advisor: at present qualified as 'facilitator'. However, the upperworld investments in this case concerned small and medium size enterprises and may be qualified as modest. The researcher could not deduce any strategic economic added value such as acquiring a leverage for social or economic 'higher-up' purposes. The Turkish exchange shop could be used for criminal money management, but no trace of such strategic use could be identified. The author wondered whether his findings really represented the dreaded 'torrent' of crime-money pouring down on society.

Naturally, the scale of this pioneer research was too small to be conclusive about the nature of criminal money management. Nevertheless, it demonstrated an approach which brought the focus to a basic behavioural level by raising the question: 'If crime-money is threatening, what do the owners do to realise such a threat?' Though little of significance was found, the findings were considered sufficiently promising to initiate a broader follow-up research project.

19.3.2 Broadening the Search: 'Million-plus' Crime-entrepreneurs

After this pioneer project the research department of the Dutch National Police obtained a grant to continue and broaden the research. In essence the same methodology was used but with a wider access to automated national databases.

The experience of the Tilburg pioneer research project showed that even at 'moderate' levels of criminal income (€50,000 – €500,000), the data about economic conduct tend to reflect mainly expensive lifestyles and reveal little about criminal money management. Therefore the threshold for case selection was increased to €450,000 (1 million Dutch guilder). From the accessible 159 recovery cases meeting this threshold since 1993, 52 cases were selected. In order not to be biased by major drug cases, which the police tend to put forward, also cases of fraud and other profit-oriented cases were selected. Altogether the sample consisted of:

- 26 drug cases (nine soft drug, 14 hard drugs, one managing drug money and two laundering cases in combination with fraud);
- 22 fraud/economic crime cases (six VAT carousels, five excise fraud schemes six embezzlement/deceit/receiving, three mortgage and two corporate fraud schemes)
- four cases of miscellaneous profit-oriented crimes: women trafficking; swindle with 'green' agricultural products; theft of trucks and cargo.

Crime-enterprises with revenues on or above this level are usually multi-offender businesses as was the case in this sample: the total number of offenders was 176, of which 45 per cent had an ethnic minority origin, though only 8 per cent actually lived abroad. The ethnic groups were mainly involved in (hard) drug traffic. A comparison of this sample with the Criminal Justice Database on other features such as sex, type of crime or verdict showed no statistically significant difference. This finding justifies the assumption that this sample was representative for the higher-income-class of crime-entrepreneurs. There are a few caveats which have to be mentioned. These concern particularly the potential extrapolation from the findings.

19.3.3 Some Caveats

In the first place, this sample concerns '€450,000 +' *cases* with multiple offenders: 176. But not all offenders involved had an individually assessed illegal income of this amount. This was the case with 59 per cent (82) of the offenders, while 30 per cent were assessed within the range of €45,000 to €450,000. For 15 offenders no revenue data were available.

In the second place, the selection criterion of €450,000 concerns *police* and *prosecution* assessments. During the trial (in first instance and/or appeal), the amount of illegal revenues appeared to be significantly reduced: in the first instance only 50 per cent of the illegal income assessments were sustained by the Courts; in appeal procedures another 29 per cent reduction could be observed. This makes us aware of the risks of extrapolating criminal income figures from police data.

In the third place, the sample covers about a decade. This raises the question of what we should select as a time standard: what does an income estimate mean if we cannot relate it to a time unit? The majority of the criminal activities were committed in 1995 and 1996. But some crime-enterprises were active over a much longer period, while for other cases the offending period was tailored to the available (strong) evidence. Depending on the case, the revenues were sometimes lumped together over time, but in other cases calculated per transaction and year. For example, in drug cases in which a regular selling was observed, the police/prosecutor used a linear extrapolation: weeks/months X turnover minus expenses, irrespective of less active periods like sickness, holidays, arrested providers, etc. These comments imply that the total criminal revenues of this sample are not suitable for assessment purposes going beyond this sample.

Given these caveats, the findings of the project are nonetheless suitable for shedding light on two important behavioural aspects: how crime-moneys are (a) being managed and (b) used in the upperworld economy.

To describe and categorise this criminal money management, the FATF description of the laundering phases of placement, layering and integration is often used. However, this is a crude typology which does no justice to the important aspects of the *justification* of proceeds and the ways these can become embedded. Another shortcoming in this approach is that it stems from the concern about the *cash*-based drug economy, which is not the sector in which most of the crime-money is being generated (Reuter and Truman 2004, ch. 2; Van Duyne 2007, pp. 75–6). This is the sector of economic crime and fraud. Most fraud schemes and economic crimes, however, do not start with cash, but with money wired through bank accounts. This implies that from the beginning the criminal

Table 19.1 Types of criminal money management, differentiated by type of crime

Ways of handling proceeds*	Categories of crime			Total
	Drug trade	Fraud and economy	Other crimes for profit	
Export of cash	31	9	2	42
Ownership disguise	10	5	4	19
Justification				
Loan back	3	3	–	6
Payroll	2	–	–	2
Speculation	–	–	–	–
Accounting	7	4	2	13
'Untraceable'	4	8	2	14

Note: * Per case the categories are not mutually excluding as in each case more ways of handling the crime-money can occur. For this reasons the figures in the columns are not added.

money management in fraud and economic crime usually starts in a different, non-cash phase.

For this reason, it is appropriate to classify the criminal money management by looking at its functional aspects. Obviously, the overriding function is to keep money out of sight of law enforcement agencies. In the cash-based crime economy this is physical: keeping money out of sight, often by smuggling it out of the country. Conversion of money into valuables of an *observable* value or valuables which are registered, implies an identifiable ownership. Lacking a justifiable income to account for the acquisition, the ownership must be disguised, which implies putting it in the name of another (legal) person. Subsequently, or parallel to that there is the problem of justification, if not of the acquired assets, then at least of the expenses of one's lifestyle. So there are various types of criminal money management: their occurrence in our sample is presented in Table 19.1.

As can be deduced from Table 19.1 simple *cash export* is the most frequent (detected) way of handling (tangible) crime-money. For the ethnic minorities, Moroccans and Turks engaged in drug trafficking, this appears to be an obvious choice, given the social and economic ties with their home countries. It is interesting to observe that also in about a third of the cases of economic crime and fraud the money was taken out of the country.

Disguise of ownership is the second large category also mainly observed with drug traffickers. This form of hiding or disguising proceeds can take various sophisticated forms by using (front) firms. However, this was observed in three cases only. The most prevalent way of disguising ownership was by putting the assets in the name of someone else: a friend or a relative. Obviously, this is a shallow method as the problem of justification is shifted to the nominal owner. Sometimes the nominal owner was unemployed or was not even aware of his nominal ownership. For example, the criminal's mother living on social security support learned retrospectively that her son made her the owner of a large villa. She lost her social allowance and got a visit from the tax inspector.

When it comes to the *justification*, the observations become less frequent and are spread over various categories. The range of sophistication varied widely. There were two elaborate constructions for loaning back the money. One international loan-back construction with a money flow of about €15 million being invested in real estate in the UK. The blocks of flats were used for justifying drug revenues by artificially increasing the rent of 200 residencies. Part of the proceeds was also used to support a rugby club to which end another loan-back construction was designed. Surprisingly, this construction was shallow, inserting a non-existing front firm with fake bookkeeping. It worked as long as it was not scrutinised. In the second loan-back case the offenders used a series of off-shore companies of which they were the hidden ultimate beneficiaries. They could buy shares with a loan of €600,000 for which they placed a collateral in another off-shore company. The third loan back was technically a botched affair, without collateral or terms of repayment.

Management in the sense of whitewashing/justification, pretending a licit income through a regular salary as employee was observed only twice. Of course, the firms which 'hired' the offenders got the salary compensated by a loan from which the salaries were paid. The amounts were modest, as were the salaries, but sufficient to explain one's 'economic existence' to the Tax Service.

It was surprising to observe that false justification by means of tampering with the paperwork was observed more frequently with the drug entrepreneurs than with the fraudsters and economic criminals. This may be due to the difference in victim awareness between these two categories of crime. An effectively operating drug enterprise is only successful as long as it remains underground and unobserved. Victimisation by violence would break this silence. When the turnover reaches substantial amounts of cash which are becoming awkward to handle, such as smuggling out of the country, the entrepreneur is in need of upperworld financial constructions to avoid attracting attention. In contrast, a fraudster operates visibly in the upperworld where he makes victims by deceitfully copying the normal business routines, including normal banking. Before (or during) detection, his prime concern is to take his money out of his firm which will go bankrupt, which does not require a money laundering construction. However, business criminals who intend maintaining their firm, operate with an on-going system of a fraudulent accountancy routine. For example, in cases of labour fraud (illegal labour, withholding taxes) most of the illegal profits are covered by routinely fraudulent accountancy and laundering at the same time. The fact that such entrepreneurs intended to continue their firm with the crime-money did not, however, imply that they recycled all of it: part of the 'black till' disappeared and was saved as a 'nest egg'.

This short survey reveals the large range of forms of criminal money management, from clumsy (most often) to most sophisticated. The most common concern appears to be hiding money from sight and disguising income and ownership.

19.4 WHAT TO DO ECONOMICALLY IN THE UPPERWORLD?

Naturally, criminal money management is an instrument for what follows: what will the crime-entrepreneur do next with his acquired wealth? There are various 'fear scenarios' listed in the literature, but none of them are supported by systematic research. Do criminals use their crime-money to corrupt their way upward to higher social levels, approaching perhaps even the 'control rooms' of power? Do they distort fair competition with cheap prices due to their illicit funds?

In order to create some order in this multitude of possibilities and hypothetical threats I designed a typology (Van Duyne 2003, pp. 76–7), which can be interpreted as an ordinal scale of 'seriousness'.

- *Corruptive permeation*: strategic penetration of politics, trade and industry at levels which allow taking influence on decision making;
- *Criminal upperworld subsidy*: investment in legal firms which would otherwise have no viability;
- *Once-only money influx*: investing in companies only once, after which the business has to operate legally on its own;
- *Reinvestment in crime-enterprise*: money ploughed back to the offender's own crime-enterprise for continuous operation;
- *Rainy day provision*: some kind of 'criminal pension fund' for later;
- *Lifestyle*: daily-life expenses encompassing also leisure events, luxury as well as living expenses.

It should be remarked that these categories are not fully mutually exclusive: money saved for a 'rainy day' may later be used for initiating a new criminal undertaking, while luxurious cars or boats as an element of lifestyle can also be used for smuggling operations. Also, analysing criminal files from the angle of these categories implies some interpretation, even if one sticks as close as possible to the text of the criminal files. This means that if there are no indications that the car or boat has been used or is intended to be used as a smuggling vehicle, it should be classified as a 'lifestyle' expense. Similarly, an investment of crime-money in a loss-making firm without more data is 'criminal subsidy'. Given this limitation and also uncertainty we consider it a justified approximation.

Table 19.2 provides the results of this interpretation. 'Corruptive permeation' was observed in six cases, equally divided over drug traffickers as well as economic criminals. None got very high-up in society or realised a more respectable investment except for one crime-entrepreneur – list the following examples:

- A Dutch cocaine wholesale importer tried to obtain an interest of €450,000 in a large car dealer firm. The offer was declined. Two days later the man was arrested.
- An entrepreneur withholding tax (social security contributions) paid handsome

Table 19.2 Typology of using crime-money

Levels of penetration	Drugs	Fraud and economic crime	Other crime for profit	Total
Corruptive permeation	3	3	–	6
Criminal subsidy	6	3	–	9
Once-only infusion	8	2	–	10
Investment in crime-enterprise	9	4	1	14
Rainy day provision	20	9	1	30
Lifestyle	9	6	2	17

bribes to firms in exchange for false invoices. He also provided soft loans to various befriended small firms, though without a recognisable strategy.
- A mid-level cocaine dealer established an exchange bureau, servicing his own needs as well as fellow criminals. It was closed when a dead body was found on the doorstep.
- An notorious UK drug entrepreneur, stranded in the Netherlands, invested not only in blocks of flats for generating licit income, but also in a rugby club.
- Investment fraudsters bought shares in a supermarket chain, which could be qualified as a 'penetration', though it was possibly only a silent investment.

The most common way of dealing with crime-money is storing it away as a 'saving', which was interpreted as the 'rainy day' provision. This is more frequently observed with drug entrepreneurs than with economic criminals. Compared to economic criminals and fraudsters, drug entrepreneurs were also more active investors in either their own criminal enterprises or by providing a criminal subsidy by means of once-only infusion or more permanently in a non-viable firm. These investment outlets used to be socially and economically 'next door': aligned with the criminal enterprises or socially within the trusted circle of relatives and friends. Hence, we find that drug wholesalers acquire coffee shops (good outlets), restaurants and gyms (attractive for social reasons), transport firms and real estate. Ethnic Turkish and Moroccan drug entrepreneurs often invested (or were rumoured to do so) in Turkey and Morocco. However, from these countries there was not reliable feedback information, except for concerning one large investment of four Turkish brothers who bought a hotel which went bankrupt.

Economic criminals and fraudsters also remained usually 'next door' in their investments, though the direct investment in their own (legal, but defrauding) enterprises occurred less than one would expect. This depended on the nature of the firm and the fraud scheme. Fraud schemes, like VAT carousels which naturally accumulate huge fiscal deficits, are bound to result in a bankruptcy, precluding further investments. In these cases a dispersal of investment outlets could be observed, of which the economic value was difficult to determine. Some investments, like a chain of supermarkets, may also have been instrumental for justification (whitewashing) purposes; other legal persons were used to siphon off money; a few firms were clearly family 'hobby businesses': a son's moto-crossing business or a wife's cosmetics shop.

Altogether the investment in their own or other firms, including loans, amounted to €8.5 million, to which should be added another €700,000 intended for the renovation of a hotel (not materialised) and a €500,000 proposal to a car dealer (declined). The profits made from some investments, like the rent from the letting of the premises of pubs, restaurants, a sex shop or a currency exchange bureau are difficult to calculate as some are listed as 'per month' or 'per year' without mentioning the whole time span. Nevertheless, a rounding off to approximately €10 million would be a plausible estimate.

A proper assessment of the upperworld economic 'weight' of these high-income cases remains difficult. The picture is fragmentary. Even if seven investments of more than €1 million look substantial, these were widely spread over time and place. The biggest investments were the result of fraudulent accountancy in the oil businesses: the money remained as a kind of criminal (fiscal) saving within the firms and did not move around in off-shore jurisdictions. To attribute to these crime-entrepreneurs a power position based on their criminal affluence remains highly speculative.

19.5 PROPERTY, BANKS AND CASH

The sample of the research discussed in the previous sections is part of the Prosecution Confiscation Database. It is a large database of some 34,000 records. Given its assumed wealth of information, Van Duyne and Soudijn (2010) decided to analyse this database in more detail. However, while inspecting the database line by line the researchers learned a hard methodological lesson: do not trust official databases. The database proved to be seriously corrupted since 1994, which had remained unnoticed because of a grave neglect of information management. Most errors led to an inflation of the amount of crime-money, supposedly the basis of policy making. In addition, there were many missing values.

Hence, the initial plan of a total analysis of confiscated criminal wealth had to be abandoned. Instead, the researchers narrowed their focus to crime-money in the *real estate sector* and the criminal funds, whether in *banks* or as *cash* elsewhere. Their basic question was: What is the role of crime-money in the real estate and the financial sector?

Could such a defective database tell us something about the role of crime-money within these (allegedly endangered) sectors? Against the background of what 'experts' cited as a 'threat', the authors thought it meaningful to survey these records under the assumption that if a (financial) phenomenon is so prevalent, it must surface statistically in a recognisable way. If that is not the case, the original threat assumption has to be re-examined. This issue was already raised in Van Duyne and Levi (2005), though on a much narrower empirical basis. Rejecting the 'never detected clever criminal' argument they asked: 'One cunning elusive "Scarlet Pimpernel" may dodge the law, but a supposed host of Pimpernels?'

What does the much broader, though imperfect asset confiscation database reveal statistically? We will first look at the real estate and then at the monies.

19.5.1 Property

The concern about criminals owning real estate is not unfounded: not only morally ('crime should not pay'), but because property is more than mere ownership of something of value (Unger and Ferwerda 2011). There are many legal aspects connected with property: for example, mortgages and environmental planning. Therefore, it is indeed important to know what kind of property criminals own. In terms of upperworld economy we also have a 'scale of importance': the ownership of a villa may hurt our moral feelings, but this may be of less importance than a criminal owning an office building or a shopping mall. For this reason we differentiated between the various categories of property and compared these with the confiscation database, as represented in Table 19.3.

The range of the type of property, in this database recorded as 'registered goods', as well its attributed value is large. We find house boats next to villas, a part of pond (for fishery rights) and building lots or offices (without recorded value). The value ranges

Table 19.3 Categories of seized property and known values

Category	Number of premises	Value known	Total value	Average value
Dwelling + garden etc.	354	109	23,415,638	214,822
Shop building*	17	7	593,138	84,734
Flat	32	6	683,908	113,985
Recreation house/boat	20	2	19,076	9,538
Garage	23	1	12,590	12,590
Parking place	10	1	2,500	2,500
Building lot	13	2	31,395	15,698
Agricultural land	19	1	124,200	124,200
Office	12	0	0	0
Pub, restaurant, hotel	8	3	639,812	213,271
Business building	24	12	946,973	78,914
Shed/barn	8	5	344,893	68,979
Garden/yard	8	0	0	0
Other registered objects	169	21	4,328,735	206,130
Total	**717**	**170**	**31,142,858**	**183,193**
				Median: **90,765**

Note: * Six shop buildings consist of a shop on the ground floor and a dwelling upstairs.

from €3,200,000 to €170 (both for a dwelling) with a *median* of €90,765 and an average of €183,193, indicating a left-skewed distribution. Most property was used as a dwelling, though a shop and a dwelling could constitute a combined property. The prevalence of dwelling was later also found by Unger and Ferwerda (2011), though the authors were not aware of our preceding findings (Van Duyne and Soudijn 2009; Van Duyne et al. 2009).

According to the case descriptions, property for *business* purposes also varied broadly. We find sheds, restaurants, pubs, shops, but also meadows and building lots. The highest valued pieces of business property were: a café with a flat on the upper floor (€330,500), a hotel (€263,934) and a shed (€192,857).

Another important aspect concerns the relative concentration of ownership: how much is in the hands of whom? when we raised this question before we concluded that the division of criminal wealth is very skewed, as in the upperworld (Van Duyne and De Miranda, 1999). This skewed division was also found here (see Table 19.4).

Indeed, many own little and few own much. Among these few multiple owners were criminals whose property was an economic asset in its own right, besides their crime-enterprise. One offender owned seven premises in the same street; another four office units with connected parking lots; a third offender owned six flats in the same block; and a fourth 17 garages, a dwelling and office premises.

Naturally, one should also look for contradictory evidence: property could have been acquired before the offending started or (partly) bought with a normal mortgage from a bank. In the course of the investigation we got access to another more accurate database, namely that of the Asset Recovery Agency concerning fully finalised recovery cases. From this database the authors selected again the higher-level criminal earners, but with

Table 19.4 Distribution of property over offenders

N persons	%	N possessions	Total	N value mentioned	€ value mentioned
269	*69*	1	269	96	20,990,487
65	*17*	2	130	36	2,791,077
18	*5*	3	54	13	4,829,714
12	*3*	4	48	7	385,248
10	*3*	5	50	6	463,829
5	*1.3*	6	30	6	406,500
1	*0.3*	7	7	0	0
3	*0.8*	8	24	6	1,275,000
1	*0.3*	9	9	0	0
3	*0.8*	10	30	0	0
1	*0.3*	11	11	0	0
2	*0.5*	15	30	0	0
1	*0.3*	25	25	0	0
391		total	717	170	31,141,855

Table 19.5 Recovery cases with property, buying prices and mortgage, 1991–2006 (Recovery threshold: > € 100,000)

Offences	N cases	Total known price €	Objects price known	Average €	Mortgage known: €	N
Cannabis growing	15	2,629,546	23	114,328	1,301,898	9
Other drugs trafficking	26	3,460,860	24	144,203	2,693,080	11
Fraud and ML	9	563,389	4	140,847	996,954	6
Other offences	5	1,313,376	5	262,675	54,454	1
Total	55	7,967,171	56	142,271	5,046,386	26

Source: CJIB database 'Serious crime unit'.

a somewhat lower recovery sum of €100,000 or more.[2] Analysing the acquisition and mortgage data we obtained the mortgage picture set out in Table 19.5.

Of course, this finding is (again) not without caveats, if only because of demonstrations of frivolous data management by the recording lower Prosecution Offices. Sometimes the mortgage was known, but not the buying price, or the other way round. It is also not known whether the mortgage was an element of a justification scheme. In some cases the mortgage was certainly not the result of a solid 'Triple A' banking transaction. Nevertheless, the findings showed a sizable total mortgage sum related to the total buying price in a ratio of about 5:8. This certainly warrants a better recording and in-depth investigation to filter out the real criminal part of the total wealth.

The other question concerns the acquisition dates of the confiscated property: is all this property really paid for with criminal revenues earned during the time of offending? Not necessarily, as the Table 19.6 suggests.

Again we have to be careful: the beginning offending date in the criminal files is not necessarily the real starting date: the recorded date is often determined on evidential and

Table 19.6 Property, known to be acquired before and after first year of offending

	Cannabis growers	Drug traders	Fraud and deceit	Other	Total
After	6	12	2	5	25
Before	4	10	4	1	19

Source: CJIB database 'Serious crime unit'.

procedural grounds. The *real* period of offending may be much longer. However, we must be strict and should not take that which is still to be proven as fact. A substantial part of this sub-section of the population did own property before their recorded offending period: three of them more than ten years before the first recorded offence. In eight cases the property was bought by means of a mortgage to the amount of €3,128,495.

Granted, these are tentative data, but they make clear that wealth and ownership need to be investigated with a keen eye for contradictory evidence. The research project of Unger and Ferwerda (2011) addresses this issue to a certain extent while applying criminological tests for the 'red flags' which indicate the risks of suspicious transactions. As the authors could have deduced from our earlier findings, not all hypotheses could be maintained, for example concerning the presence of off-shore legal persons and loan-back constructions, or the level of sophistication of 'whitewashing' in real estate.

All we can conclude is that on the dependent variable 'real estate' we have again a large variation of findings, and that not everything a criminal owns is illegal.

The discussion about a potential threat is deferred because first we must take a closer look at the 'victim' of 'money laundering': the financial industry.

19.5.2 Crime-money and the Financial Industry

Crime-money and related money laundering is also considered a special threat to the financial industry if not to the economy as a whole (Tanzi 1996). The financial system is supposed to be undermined by criminals attempting to place their ill-gotten profits in banks and other forms of criminal money management. For this reason Van Duyne and Soudijn (2010) made a separate analysis of all records containing information about money and banks, a summary of which is presented here.

As this database covered a period of more than ten years, it was assumed that its findings would be at least be indicative of the 'weight' of the crime-money, either within the financial system or outside in the form of cash money, part of which will eventually flow into the financial system too, whether directly or in the form of spending. The results of the analysis are presented in Table 19.7.

The total volume of €225 million looks substantial but, as remarked, it represents a confiscation period of more than ten years within a financial sector handling multiple billions of Euro deposits and savings per year. Assuming that these 'criminal bank accounts' represent technically normal deposits and savings they are an insignificant part of the total Dutch savings in the banks: €1,196,522 million (De Nederlandsche Bank: 1998–2004). The €121 million crime-money deposits, covering a longer period, are just a tiny slice of a very large cake.

Table 19.7 The confiscated bank accounts (1994–2006), cash and both (Mean, median, maximum value and the high range owners)

	Bank accounts	Cash money	Bank accounts & cash
	N = 460 (one empty account)	N = 3027	N = 3266
Total	€121,031,834	€104,640,741	€225,667,575
Mean	€263,113	€34,481	€69,076
Median	€20,000	€3,910	€4,695
Maximum value	€60,749,111	€12,600,374	€60,749,111
> €100,000	N = 90	N = 165	N = 250
> €1,000,000	N = 11	N = 12	N = 25

Also, here we observe a skewed frequency distribution: many assets in the hands of a (happy) few, while most have just a small savings account. In the subset of the subjects with only a confiscated bank account, the median was €20,000. However, if we put all the known money (bank and cash) and even the real estate values together, the median sinks to €4,725. The many small cash holders (25% had no more than €1,305) shifted the distribution heavily to the left. Only 3 per cent of the convicted offenders had more than €100,000 in their bank accounts.

A counter argument against this finding could be that these criminals are too smart to leave their crime-money in Dutch banks: really smart ones are operating *globally* and off-shore. With the proverbial one-click-of-the-mouse they allegedly shift their assets all over the globe. But what do we observe?

With 38 convicted offenders (1.2 %) one or more foreign bank accounts were observed with a total value of €16,209,704 spread over numerous jurisdictions, though without reflecting the dreaded financial criminal globalisation. Indeed, Table 19.8 does not lend support to this concern.

Again, the distribution is biased: one convict accounted for 38 per cent of the total of this subset: his foreign bank assets amounted to €6,099,616, spread over banks in Germany, Belgium, Luxembourg, Switzerland and one bank in Spain.

It seems that most offenders in this subset do not go very far to deposit and hold their assets: there is a clear preference for the surrounding countries. Naturally, the category 'elsewhere' contains more remote countries, stretching from Morocco to Hong Kong. However, the choice of a certain country looks to be determined rather by the national

Table 19.8 Foreign bank accounts

Country	Total assets in banks €	N
Luxembourg	4,964,321	11
Belgium	3,699,597	4
Germany	692,106	7
Elsewhere	6,853,680	16
Total	16,209,704	38

origin of the convicted persons and their social relationships than by 'laundering sophistication'.

We also note a further methodological flaw. At the time of the research the registration of off-shore banking was still in a pre-digital state – just a pencil-and-paper database (now perhaps in a transition state to a proper electronic database) – while few efforts have been devoted to tracing and seizing foreign assets. On the other hand, the details of the research of Meloen et al. (2003) do not deviate from these findings. In their 52 cases European banks were the most common institutions for depositing money, followed by banks in the home countries or where the crime-entrepreneurs had social ties (Meloen et al 2003, ch. 12.3). The Turkish crime-entrepreneurs deposited their money in Turkey, the Moroccans in Morocco, etc. In the few cases of 'exotic' off-shore banking (Panama, Thailand) existing social relationships could be identified. There may be quite a lot of ordinary psychology involved in finding the 'right' (= 'safe feeling') bank: not too far and staffed by people you can understand if not of your own nationality.

19.6 CONCLUSION

Does this series of research projects provide a conclusive answer to the question of what profit-making criminals do with their money, as managers of criminal money or within the upperworld? Given all the caveats mentioned, there is no conclusive answer. However, together with observations from other research, and against the threat image presented by interested bodies such as the IMF or FATF, supported by associated economists, a preliminary answer can be given. There is a small layer of affluent criminals, and some of them do penetrate the upperworld, but despite occasional successes, it usually remains a shallow penetration. The examples given in the Meloen et al., (2003) research do not differ very much from those given for Germany by Suendorff (2001). In the sectors of finance and real estate we find the same 'flat' pattern with a few peaks. Indeed, a few crime-entrepreneurs rise above the surface level, but they are in the small high-end tail of the distribution. And even then their economic exploits are not impressive. This is not a unique finding. Compare our real estate findings with those of the survey carried out by FinCen (2006), the US anti-laundering agency: FinCen found 190 Suspicious Activity Reports-with-potential-laundering in the commercial real estate sector during ten years in the whole of the US (2.2%). A new survey by FinCen (2008) of SAR filings, now concerning residential real estate, yielded more suspicions of structuring or laundering: 20.2 per cent or 151. Nevertheless, FinCen thought it a low return, explaining it by indicating that 'money-launderers' have no interest in victimising the lending institution and pay interest and instalments in a timely manner. This is a sharp observation: who cuts the branch on which he is sitting? Certainly not a smart launderer. But then: where is the threat?

We are still left with the question: If there is so much, why do we find so little? If the answer remains forthcoming, we may have to think of a counter-hypothesis: 'We find so little because there is not much; and what is find is the result of a criminal hustlers' economy'.

Of course, such a bold (and unpopular) hypothesis begs for refutation. But before putting this hypothesis to the test, first some spring-cleaning has to be carried out, to begin with the conceptual and legal backgrounds which function like a kind of general 'stage curtain' of the global money laundering stage play. Its 'laundering design' is the product of US-driven international policy making in the 1980s (Van Duyne and Nelemans 2011). In terms of conceptual coherence and consistency, it is a poorly woven fabric. There are not only many definitions (Gelemerova 2011, ch. 3.2; Unger 2007, ch. 2), most are of a wall-to-wall breadth which raises the (not ironically meant) question of the existence of *un*laundered crime-money. The FATF speaks of crime-money 'available' for laundering. As no authority has ever contradicted the FATF, yes: the very existence of unlaundered crime-money is taken as a fact. However, this applies only if that money is *not* disguised or hidden, because that is laundering. Assuming that criminal owners of proceeds will at least hide or disguise their criminal origin, how much unlaundered money will there be available? Actually nothing. This is not a sophism because many jurisdictions have moved to an actual 100 per cent coverage, like the UK (Fleming 2009, p.24: 'doing *anything* with criminal proceeds') and the Netherlands (almost an all-inclusive tautological definition: see Van Duyne and Nelemans, 2010).

This brings us to the concept of *threat* posed by crime-money and laundering as this is woven into the stage curtain. Within the already problematic conceptual framework it creates additional problems. Apart from moral considerations, is crime-money really a threat? Not if it has undergone a proper 'whitewashing programme': the *justification*. In that case it has become part of the GDP and a taxable asset. If not, it is still spent in daily life, becoming 'white' as soon as it is exchanged for taxable articles: generating VAT or sales tax plus income tax for the seller. Only *unspent*, hoarded or exported money remains invisible, outside the GDP. However, what threat does unspent money pose: the money buried in the ground or put into the mattress? To answer that question, we must also take into account of the hidden *licit* (the 'black savings' from licit work) and illicit money and measure whether they differ in their effects.

This approach would undermine the conventional wisdom of the stage curtain viewpoint, which is anyhow too moth-eaten to be useful for a behavioural research approach.

Lacking a sign of debate, it seems that these annotations are cast aside by economic research. Authors like Walker and Unger (2009) do not even mention them, though they have been brought to their attention. More serious is the neglect of the persistent quantitative finding of the skewed distribution of criminal wealth and the related *money-flows*. In any research which used the individual offender and his proceeds as a unit of observation, the median is far below the average. Whether one looks at the level of suspicious transactions (Van Duyne and De Miranda 1999), money transfers abroad (Van Duyne 2007; table 10), real estate, cash or bank accounts, the distribution is invariably skewed. Given this repeated finding, using averages as a central index distorts reality by inflating it.

To conclude: What do we have? We have a money-laundering play on a mainstream stage with a moth-eaten, badly woven and politically determined conceptual stage curtain, and a scenario with unrealistic assumptions. I think the best we can do is to discard this politically motivated stage curtain. We need a rigorous multiple source data collection system, pertaining to the observation units that matter: the law breakers, what they do and how they deal with their ill-gotten profits. Then comes the filtering, sifting, breaking down and ordering of facts to put hypotheses to the test by falsification.

And then, after the facts, come the morals.

NOTES

1. The Netherlands have a net confiscation regime: 'normal' business expenses such as transport and storage can be deduced. Expenses for 'requirements' like the purchase of weapons are not deductable, as these are prohibited in the first place.
2. This was the threshold used by the Serious Crime Unit of the Asset Recovery Agency.

REFERENCES

Bunt, H.G. van de and E.R. Kleemans (2007), *Georganiseerde criminaliteit in Nederland. Derde rapportage op grond van de Monitor Georganiseerde Criminaliteit*, Meppel, Boom Juridische Uitgevers.

Dorn, N. (2010), 'Ponzi finance and state capture: the crisis of the financial market regulation', in P.C. van Duyne et al. (eds), *Cross-border Crime Inroads on Integrity in Europe*, Nijmegen: Wolf Legal Publishers.

Duyne, P.C. van (1995), *Het spook en de dreiging van de georganiseerde misdaad*, 's-Gravenhage, SDU-uitgeverij.

Duyne, P.C. van (1997), 'Organized crime, corruption and power', *Crime, Law and Social Change*, **26**, 201–38.

Duyne, P.C. van (2003), 'Money laundering policy: fears and facts', in P.C. van Duyne, K. Von Lampe and J.L. Newell (eds), *Criminal Finances and Organising Crime in Europe*, Nijmegen: Wolf Legal Publishers.

Duyne, P.C. van (2007), 'Criminal finances and state of the art: case for concern?', in P.C. van Duyne, A. Maljevic, M. van Dijck, K. von Lampe and J. Harvey (eds), *Crime Business and Crime Money in Europe: The Dirty Linen of Illicit Enterprise*, Nijmegen: Wolf Legal Publishers.

Duyne, P.C. van and H. De Miranda (1999), 'The emperor's clothes of disclosure: hot money and suspect disclosures', *Crime, Law and Social change*, **3**, 245–7.

Duyne, P.C. van and M. Levi (2005), *Drugs and Money: Managing the Drug Trade and Crime-Money in Europe*, London: Routledge.

Duyne, P.C. van and M.D.H. Nelemans (2010), 'De lat van Aristoteles: formele logica en redeneren', in R.S.T. Gaarthuis, T. Kooijmans and Th.A. de Roos (eds), *Vertrouwen in de strafrechtspleging*, Deventer: Kluwer.

Duyne, P.C. van and M.D.H. Nelemans (2011), 'Transnational organised crime: thinking in and out of Plato's cave', in F. Allum and S. Gilmow (eds), *Routledge Handbook of Transnational Organized Crime*, Abingdon and New York: Routledge.

Duyne, P.C. van and M.R.J. Soudijn (2009), 'Gebakken stenen en gebakken lucht', *Tijdschrift voor Compliance*, **9** (3).

Duyne, P.C. van and M.R.J. Soudijn, (2010), 'Crime-money in the financial system: what we fear and what we know', in M. Herzog-Evans (ed.), *Transnational Criminology Manual, Volume 2*, Nijmegen: Wolf Legal Publishers.

Duyne, P.C., M.S. Groenhuijsen and A.A.P. Schudelaro (2005), 'Balancing financial threats and legal interests in money-laundering policy', *Crime, Law and Social Change*, **43** (2–3), 117–47.

Duyne, P.C. van, R. Kouwenberg and G. Romeijn (1990), *Misdaadondernemingen. Ondernemende misdadigers in Nederland*, Arnhem: Gouda-Quint.

Duyne, P.C. van, M.R.J. Soudijn and T. Kint (2009), 'Bricks Don't Talk: Searching for Crime Money in Real Estate', in P.C. van Duyne, S. Donati, J. Harvey, A. Maljevic and K. von Lampe (eds), *Crime, Money and Criminal Mobility in Europe*, Nijmegen: Wolf Legal Publishers.

Duyne, P.C. van et al. (2010), *Cross-border Crime Inroads on Integrity in Europe*, Nijmegen: Wolf Legal Publishers.

Eekelen, J. van (2000), *De neerslag van het misdaadgeld. Motregen, onweersbui of zondvloed*, Tilburg University.

Financial Crimes Enforcement Network (FinCen) (2006), *Money Laundering in the Commercial Real Estate Industry: Assessment based on Suspicious Activity Report Filing Analysis*, Washington: FinCen.

Financial Crimes Enforcement Network (FinCen) (2008), *Money Laundering in the Residential Real Estate Industry: Assessment based on Suspicious Activity Report Filing Analysis*, Washington: FinCen.

Fleming, M.H. (2009), *FSA's Scale & Impact of Financial Crime Project. Project (Phase One): Critical Analysis*. FSA Occasional Paper Series.

Gelemerova, L. (2011), *The Anti-Money Laundering System in the Context of Globalization: A Panopticon Built on Quicksand*? Nijmegen: Wolf Legal Publishers.

Levi, M. (2007), 'Pecunia non olet. The control of money laundering revisited', in F. Bovenkerk and M. Levi (eds), *The Organised Crime Community*, New York: Springer.

Meloen, J., R. Landman, H. de Miranda, J. van Eekelen and S. van Soest (2003), *Buit en besteding*, 's-Gravenhage: Elsevier Overheid.

Popper, K.R. (1963), *Conjectures and Refutations: The Growth of Scientific Knowledge*, London: Routledge and Kegal Paul.

Quirk, J. (1996), *Macro-economic Implications of Money Laundering*, IMF Working Paper, Washington.

Reuter, P. (2007), 'Are estimates of the volume of money laundering either feasible or useful? Comments on the presentation by John Walker', paper presented at the conference Tackling Money Laundering, University of Utrecht, Utrecht (The Netherlands), November 2–3.

Reuter, P. and E.M. Truman (2004), *Chasing Dirty Money. The Fight against Money Laundering*, Massachusetts, Institute for International Economics.

Suendorff, S. (2001), *Geldwäsche: eine kriminologische Untersuchung*, Neuwied: Luchterhand.

Tanzi, V. (1996), *Money Laundering and the International Financial System*, IMF Working Paper, Washington.

Unger, B. (ed.) (2007), *The Scale and Impacts of Money Laundering*. Cheltenham, UK and Northampton, MA, USA: Edward Elgar Publishing.

Unger, B. and J. Ferwerda (2011), *Money Laundering in the Real Estate Sector*. Cheltenham, UK and Northampton, MA, USA: Edward Elgar Publishing.

Vruggink, J. (2001), *Gepakt en gezakt. Invloed van de ontnemingsmaatregel op daders*, Universiteit Leiden.

Walker, J. (1995), 'Estimates of the extent of money laundering in and through Australia', John Walker Consultancy Services, September.

Walker, J. (1999), 'How big is global money laundering?', *Journal of Money Laundering Control*, **3** (1), 25–37.

Walker, J. and B. Unger (2009), 'Measuring global money laundering: "The Walker gravity model"', *Review of Law and Economics*, **5** (2), 822–53.

PART VI

WAYS TO LAUNDER

20. International trade mispricing: trade-based money laundering and tax evasion*

John S. Zdanowicz

20.1 INTRODUCTION

This chapter contributes to the literature on trade-based money laundering, tax evasion and terrorist financing by providing an analysis of previously unused statistical techniques and methodologies as a means of monitoring, detecting and prosecuting criminal money laundering activities. The chapter describes how new statistical profiling methodologies that evaluate transactions contained in a country's international trade database can mitigate the risks associated with trade-based money laundering. It discusses the application of four new trade-based money laundering profiling techniques which focus on country, product and transaction price risk characteristics.

For years, individuals who study international trade pricing patterns have reported on the evidence that abnormal pricing in trade was being used to move money across borders, undetected by governments and law enforcement agencies. It was argued that abnormal trade pricing may be motivated by attempts to evade income taxes or import duties, or it may be related to moving 'dirty' money earned from criminal activities. More recently, the concern is that false trade invoicing is being used as a source of money to support terrorist activities. Empirical evidence of trade-based money laundering has been published in both academic and professional publications (Bhagwati 1964; Cuddington 1987; De Boyrie, et al. 2005b; De Wulf 1981; Gulati 1987; Pak et al. 2003; Zdanowicz 2004a; Zdanowicz et al. 1999). Recently, three major events have revealed that there is a new focus on trade-based money laundering and tax evasion.

Trade Transparency Units: The US State Department and the US Treasury Department supported the Immigration and Customs Enforcement Bureau (ICE) of Homeland Security with the funding necessary to establish Trade Transparency Units (TTUs) with Brazil, Argentina and Paraguay. This funding resulted in a US/Brazilian transnational investigation called 'Operation Deluge'. Operation Deluge has shown that an investment in analyzing and detecting trade-based money laundering has a significant positive return on investment.

FATF: Trade-Based Money Laundering Report: In June 2006, the Financial Action Task Force (FATF), a Paris-Based multinational agency, released the first comprehensive report on Trade-Based Money Laundering which stated that 'the international trade system is clearly subject to a wide range of risks and vulnerabilities that can be exploited by criminal organizations and terrorist financiers' (Financial Action Task Force 2006).

One of the key findings of the FATF report was that trade data analysis is a useful tool for identifying trade anomalies, which may lead to the investigation and prosecution of trade-based money laundering cases. The study concludes, 'trade-based money laundering represents an important channel of criminal activity and, given the growth of world trade, an increasingly important money laundering and terrorist financing vulnerability. Moreover, as the standards applied to other money laundering techniques become increasingly effective, the use of trade-based money laundering can be expected to become increasingly attractive'.

FFIEC Bank Secrecy Act Anti-Money Laundering Examination Manual: The Federal Financial Institutions Examination Council (FFIEC) released its first Bank Secrecy Act Anti-Money Laundering Examination Manual in 2005 and revised the manual in 2006 and 2007 (Federal Financial Institutions Examination Council 2007, p. 273). Some key points in the FFIEC BSA/AML Examination Manual include:

> Objective: Bank examinations will 'assess the adequacy of the bank's systems to manage the risks associated with trade financing activities, and management's ability to implement effective due diligence, monitoring, and reporting systems'.
> Risk Factors: 'While banks should be alert to transactions involving higher risk goods, they need to be aware that goods may be over- or under-valued in an effort to evade AML or customs regulations.' One technique that can assist financial institutions in determining normal price ranges is through the statistical analysis of the US trade data base.

20.2 TRADE-BASED MONEY LAUNDERING

Money may be moved out of the United States to a foreign country by under-valuing US exports or over-valuing US imports. Money may be moved into the United States from a foreign country by over-valuing US exports or under-valuing US imports.

Example – Overvalued US Imports:

Assume a terrorist or criminal wants to launder $1 million to a foreign country. He would need to have a foreign exporter to collude on the transaction. The set of transactions used to launder the money would include:

1. Foreign exporter purchases 10,000 razor blades for $0.10 per blade ($1,000.00).
2. Foreign exporter exports 10,000 razor blades to a domestic importer for $100.00 per razor blade (total invoice $1,000,000.00).
3. Domestic importer receives 10,000 razor blades worth $1,000.00 but pays the foreign exporter $1,000,000.00.
4. Outcome: The domestic importer has moved $1 million to the foreign country less the $1,000.00 transactions cost of the razor blades.

Example – Undervalued US Exports:

Assume a terrorist or criminal wants to launder $1 million to a foreign country. He would need to have a foreign importer to collude on the transaction. The set of transactions used to launder the money would include:

1. Domestic criminal or terrorist uses his $1 million to purchase 200 gold watches for $5,000.00 per watch ($1,000,000.00). The watches would be purchased for cash.
2. Domestic exporter sells the 200 gold watches to a foreign importer for $5.00 per watch ($1,000.00).

3. Foreign importer receives the 200 gold watches and is presented with an invoice for $1,000.00 which he pays to the domestic exporter.
4. Foreign importer sells the gold watches at the market price of $5,000.00 per watch and converts the 200 gold watches into $1,000,000.00.
5. Outcome: The domestic exporter has moved $1 million to the foreign country less the $1,000.00 transaction cost of the invoice payment

The motivations and impact of trade price manipulation include:

Under-Invoiced Exports
- Money laundering from illegal activities
- Terrorist financing
- Income tax avoidance/evasion
- Capital flight
- Avoid export surcharges
- Conceal illegal commissions

Over-Invoiced Exports
- Increase export subsidies
- Increase value added tax rebates

Over-Invoiced Imports
- Money laundering from illegal activities
- Terrorist financing
- Income tax avoidance/evasion
- Capital flight
- Justify high domestic prices under price controls
- Conceal illegal commissions

Under-Invoiced Imports
- Evade/reduce import duties
- Dumping at below market prices

20.3 DATABASE

This research on determining abnormal international trade pricing is based on the analysis of the monthly data contained in the United States Merchandise Trade Data Base. This database is produced by the United States Department of Commerce, Bureau of Census and is used to determine the United States balance of trade. The database contains information at the transaction level and is reported to the US Census Bureau from the Shipper's Export Declarations and the US Customs Service Entry Summary forms, the legal documents required by US Customs to be filed for any export or import. All transactions with a value of more than $2,500 for exports and $1,250 for imports are recorded, with exclusions for shipments involving the US Armed Forces and diplomatic missions and for in-transit shipments through the United States. On average more than 10 million records per year are analyzed, with each record identifying the item, quantity and dollar value, along with the mode of transportation, the US customs district through which the goods passed and the foreign country involved in the trade. Products are classified using the international standard Harmonized Commodity Code System which contains over 17,000 categories of imports and over 9,000 categories of exports. All of the Census Bureau price data are converted to dollar terms. If the original documents were stated in foreign currency terms, then the exchange rate at the beginning of the quarter in which the transaction occurred is used to convert to dollars, except if the exchange rate had changed by more than 5 percent over the quarter. In the latter case, the rate used is the end of the quarter rate. For each year analyzed, all individual transaction records on the 12-monthly United States import databases and the 12-monthly United States export databases are combined. The total data set is segmented and entered into a country/product table containing the price data for all combinations of countries and products. In this country/product table, over 232 columns represent every country and the world, while every import harmonized code and every export harmonized code are represented by over 26,000 rows. The resulting table contains over 6 million cells. Each cell in the table contains the data on the population of transactions related to the United States import or United States export of a particular commodity from or to a specific country, as well as from or to the world. Some cells are empty if no transactions existed between the United States and a country for a particular commodity.

20.4 RESEARCH METHODOLOGIES

During the past 16 years, various methodologies have been employed to analyze abnormal international trade pricing:

Country Average Price vs. World Average Price: In January 1992, *Money Laundering Alert* published the first article with results of an empirical analysis of trade-based money laundering. In that pioneering work, the average country price was compared to the average world price for every product (Money Laundering Alert 1992). One of the criticisms of comparing country average prices with world average prices was that the analysis did not account for country/product heterogeneity. It was pointed out that the imported dresses from Haiti were different from imported dresses from France. This led to modifying the data analysis methodology to take into account country/product differences.

Prices 50 Percent Above or Below Average Country Price: The initial objective of this research methodology was to estimate the impact of over-invoiced imports and under-invoiced exports on the amount of money moved out of the United States during 1993. This methodology recognized that the characteristics of import and export transactions may vary among countries. Therefore, this methodology analyzed import and export transactions relative to historical US/Country trade. The analysis determined the dollar amount of over-invoiced imports for every import transaction, for every commodity, for every country, and determined the total dollar amount of over-invoiced imports for every country. The analysis also determined the dollar amount under-invoiced exports for every export transaction, for every commodity, for every country, and determined the total dollar amount of under-invoiced exports for every country. This analysis determined the total amount of money moved out of the United States in 1993 due to transactions at import prices greater than 50 percent of the average US/country commodity price and export prices less than 50 percent of the average US/country export commodity price. This analysis was extended employing the same methodology for 1994 and 1995. The following are the estimates of money moved out of the United States:

Money moved out of the United States due to:
Import Prices >150% of Average Country Import Price
Export Prices < 50% of Average Country Export Price

Table 20.1

Year	Money Moved Out of US
1993	$97.35 billion
1994	$116.18 billion
1995	$136.76 billion

The following are some examples of abnormally priced imports and exports detected by this methodology.

Table 20.2 Abnormally high US import prices

Product	Country	Price
Telephone answering machines	Mexico	$255.00/unit
Erythromycin	Japan	$1,693.83/gram
Dot matrix printers	Sweden	$5,493.26/unit
Toothbrushes	France	$18.00/unit
Safety pins	Canada	$29.65/unit
Cassette tape players	Denmark	$17,314.25/unit
Telephones (no features)	Japan	$270.43/unit

Table 20.3 Abnormally low US export prices

Product	Country	Price
Telephone answering machines	Mexico	$27.09/unit
Erythromycin	Japan	$0.08/gram
Men's bathrobes	Saudi Arabia	$4.81/dozen
Generators (int. combustion)	France	$9.56/unit
Electric cooking stoves	Mexico	$30.55/unit
Refrigerators (household)	Japan	$40.43/unit
TV Receivers (color)	Canada	$31.40/unit

Inter-Quartile Range Price Analysis: One of the main criticisms of the 50 percent deviation analysis was that the use of a 50 percent filter was arbitrary. This criticism was valid. In some cases the 50 percent filter may have been too low and in other cases it might have been too high.

In 1994, the United States Internal Revenue Service issued its 482 transfer pricing regulations and stipulated that the inter-quartile price range should be used to determine the validity of transfer prices in international trade. The IRS defines suspicious prices as those import prices that exceed the upper quartile import prices and those export prices that are less than the lower quartile export price. Based on the IRS definition of arms-length pricing norms, the research methodology shifted to using the product/country inter-quartile price ranges as statistical filters. The median price, lower quartile export price and upper quartile import price for every commodity exported and imported to and from every country were determined. Every import record was evaluated and compared to the country-specific import upper quartile price to determine if it was over-valued. The dollar amount of over-valuation for every import transaction was determined. Similarly, every export record was evaluated and compared to the country specific export lower quartile price to determine if it was under-valued. The dollar amount of under-valuation for every export transaction was determined. The dollar amounts of all under-valued export transactions and all over-valued import transactions for every commodity, for every country, were aggregated. The following table contains the total estimated money moved out of the US for 2004, 2005 and 2006 due to abnormal pricing based on the inter-quartile range analysis (International Trade Alert, 2005).

Money moved out of the US due to:

Import Prices > Upper Quartile Country Import Prices

Export Prices < Lower Quartile Country Export Prices

Table 20.4

Year	Money Moved Out of US
2004	$167.76 billion
2005	$191.95 billion
2006	$189.05 billion

The following are some examples of abnormally priced imports and exports detected by this methodology:

Table 20.5 Abnormally high US import prices

Product	Country	Price
Toilet/facial tissue	China	$4,121.81/kg
Threaded nuts	Belgium	$2,426.70/kg
Tweezers – base metal	Japan	$4,896.00/unit
Lawnmower blades	Australia	$2,326.75/unit
Razors	UK	$113.20/unit
Used clothing	Haiti	$260.00/kg
Women's cotton briefs	Venezuela	$50.00/unit

Table 20.6 Abnormally low US export prices

Product	Country	Price
Diamonds – not industrial	India	$13.45/carat
Forklift trucks – self propelled	Jamaica	$384.14/unit
Bulldozers – self-propelled	Colombia	$1,741.92/unit
Video projectors – color	Brazil	$33.95/unit
Missile and rocket launchers	Israel	$52.03/unit
Forklift trucks – self propelled	Haiti	$555.73/unit
New automobile tires	Russia	$3.97/unit

20.5 APPLICATIONS OF INTER-QUARTILE RANGE STATISTICAL ANALYSIS

The 1994 Internal Revenue Service's specification that the inter-quartile price range is the relevant arms-length definition of normal pricing gave researchers a statistical benchmark for the analysis of international trade pricing. Thus, many additional international trade pricing studies were conducted based on the US government's Merchandise Trade Data Base and the US Government's definition of abnormal international trade pricing. The following are summaries of some of these studies.

Money Moved Out of and Into the United States: In addition to estimating the amount of money being moved out of the United States using the inter-quartile range analysis, the estimate of the amount of money moved into the United States was also determined. Money can be moved into the United States through over-valued exports and undervalued imports. The analysis indicates that during 2004, $55.5 billion was the net capital flow into the United States.

Impact of New Banking Regulations on Money Moved Out of Switzerland: When central banking authorities enact legislation that only focuses on financial institutions, criminals and terrorists will find alternative techniques and channels to launder their

Table 20.7 Total money moved out of the United States by country dollar value (through under-valued exports and over-valued imports). Year: 2004

Under-valued exports	Over-valued imports	Total moved out of the US	Share of trade
$111,593,487,257	$56,167,170,400	$167,760,657,657	7.34%

Table 20.8 Total money moved into the United States by country dollar value (through over-valued exports and under-valued imports). Year: 2004

Over-valued exports	Under-valued imports	Total moved into the US	Share of trade
$48,066,362,572	$175,219,246,010	$223,285,608,582	9.77%

Table 20.9 Average monthly outflows – before vs. after new law

Time Period	Dollar Amount	% of Trade Volume
Before the law	$252,863,571	28.93%
After the law	$628,437,709	57.76%
Percent increase	149%	100%

money. The conclusion of a study based on the inter-quartile range analysis supports the argument that money launderers and terrorists will shift their money laundering activities to false invoicing in international trade. In 1998, the Swiss Federal Government broadened the reach of its money laundering regulations to include not only banks but its entire financial service sector. The law, known as the Federal Act on the Prevention of Money Laundering in the Financial Sector – Money Laundering Act (MLA), requires all financial institutions to report suspicious transactions to Switzerland's Federal Reporting Office for Money Laundering. The Act went into effect on April 1, 1998 (De Boyrie et al. 2005a).

The study measured the dollar amount of money moved from Switzerland to the United States through false invoicing before (1995 to1997) and after (1998 to 2000) the date the money laundering law was enacted. In order to evaluate the possible impact of other economic factors that might increase Swiss capital outflows, a detailed statistical analysis was conducted. Other economic variables considered in the analysis included differences in US/Swiss interest rates, exchange rates, consumer price indices and producer price indices. The results of the statistical analysis indicated that the new law was the only factor that could explain the increase in capital outflows from Switzerland to the United States. The results of the research study determined that the dollar amount of money moved from Switzerland to the United States increased significantly after the law was enacted. The average monthly amount of money moved increased from $253 million per month before the law to $628 million per month after the law. There was also a significant increase in money moved as a percentage of Swiss/US trade. The average monthly amount of money moved as a percentage of Swiss/US trade increased from 29 percent to 58 percent. Subsequent to the passage of the law, the monthly average dollar amount of money moved increased by 149 percent and the money moved as a percentage of Swiss/US trade increased by 100 percent.

20.6 TRADE FINANCING

The US government created the Federal Financial Institutions Examination Council which adopted a common examination manual in an attempt to eliminate inconsistent bank examinations. The examination, first published in June 2005 resulted from the collaboration of the Federal Reserve Board, Office of the Comptroller of the Currency, Federal Deposit Insurance Corporation, National Credit Union Administration and the Office of Thrift and Supervision. The examination manual was revised in 2006 and 2007 based on input from the industry. A significant addition to the manual was the inclusion of trade financing as an area for bank risk monitoring and examination.

FFIEC Manual: The 2007 FFIEC Examination Manual states that financial institutions engaged in trade financing activities should give greater scrutiny to:

1. Items shipped that are inconsistent with the nature of the customers' business (e.g. a steel company that starts dealing in paper products, or an information technology company that starts dealing in bulk pharmaceuticals).
2. **Customers conducting business in high-risk jurisdictions.**
3. **Customers shipping items through high-risk jurisdictions, including transit through non-cooperative countries.**
4. **Customers involved in potentially high-risk activities, including activities that may be subject to export/import restrictions (e.g. equipment for military or police organizations of foreign governments, weapons, ammunition, chemical mixtures, classified defense articles, sensitive technical data, nuclear materials, precious gems, or certain natural resources such as metals, ore, or crude oil).**
5. **Obvious over- or under-pricing of goods and services.**
6. **Obvious misrepresentation of quantity or type of goods imported or exported.**
7. Transaction structure appears unnecessarily complex and designed to obscure the true nature of the transaction.
8. Customer directs payment of proceeds to an unrelated third party.
9. Shipment locations or description of goods not consistent with letter of credit.
10. **Documentation showing a higher or lower value or cost of merchandise than that which was declared to customs or paid by the importer.**
11. Significantly amended letters of credit without reasonable justification or changes to the beneficiary or location of payment. Any changes in the names of parties also should prompt additional OFAC review. (FFIEC 2007, p. 244)

Before conducting the complex price analysis of the letter of credit transaction, financial institutions should conduct character-based analysis to determine if further and more extensive analysis is warranted. According to the FFIEC, 'Unless customer behavior or transaction documentation appears unusual, the bank should not be expected to spend undue time or effort reviewing all information' (FFIEC 2007, p. 245). The analysis of trade data will provide filters to determine suspicious transactions that should be evaluated in more detail (Zdanowicz 2007; *Money Laundering Alert* 2008).

Character-based analysis requires a financial institution to evaluate the non-price characteristics of the financing transaction such as: the risk of the country of import or export; the risk of the product; the client's appearance on PEP lists; or the results of OFAC filtering. Many of the existing 'Know Your Customer' policies can be applied to international trade financing activities. The FFIEC provides guidance to assess the appropriateness and comprehensiveness of a bank's customer due diligence (CDD) policies, procedures and processes.

Character Based Analysis – Country, Product and Customs District Risk Profiles: The analysis of the US trade data base will assist financial institutions with identifying trade financing transactions that should be investigated in more detail. The analysis of the US trade database may assist in evaluating six of the eleven red flags listed in the FFIEC Examination Manual (**2, 3, 4, 5, 6** and **10**). Various risk profiles can be determined by evaluating recent US international trade transactions such as:

- **Country Risk Index**: A risk profile of every country in the world, based on the most recent 12-month abnormal pricing history in the country's international trade.
- **Product Risk Index**: A risk profile of every product classification, based on the most recent 12-month abnormal pricing history of that product.

Each risk index is based on the analysis of every US import and export transaction, for all products and countries. The analysis is based on the Internal Revenue Service's 482 Transfer Pricing Regulations which defines the inter-quartile range as the arms-length pricing range in international trade. The risk indices can be updated every month as new US trade data is released to the public. The three character-based profiling risk indices discussed in this section are new statistical methodologies and will assist law enforcement and financial institutions with mitigating risk.

The risk indices are determined by calculating the dollar amount of money moved out of the United States as a percentage of the total trade for a country or product. This may result in shares of trade that exceed 100 percent. For example, assume that the median export price for a product is $100.00 and that the lower price filter (lower quartile price) is $50.00. A reported export transaction for $10.00 would result in an estimated undervalued export transaction of $40.00. Thus, the percentage undervaluation for this transaction would be 400 percent ($40.00/$10.00 = 400%)

Country Risk Index: An analysis of the total dollar value of abnormal international trade pricing by country is detailed in Table 20.10. This table contains a sample of the dollar amount of money moved out of the US in 2004 through undervalued exports and overvalued imports for the top ten countries (out of 218 countries) that trade with the US. This analysis shows that the largest amount of money being moved out of the US corresponds to the largest US trading partners. This analysis may not be useful in identifying high-risk countries.

However, Table 20.11 contains a sample (top ten out of 218 countries) of the Country Risk Index for 2004 which measures the money moved from the US to all countries in the world as a percentage of their trade with the US This type of character-based analysis

Table 20.10 Total money moved out of the United States by country dollar value (through under-valued exports and over-valued imports). Year: 2004

Rank	Country	Under-valued exports	Over-valued imports	Total moved out of the US	Share of trade
1	Canada	$11,039,683,286	$7,256,738,049	$18,296,421,335	4.12%
2	Japan	$8,151,814,635	$5,974,212,167	$14,126,026,802	7.68%
3	China	$6,007,716,795	$7,800,914,990	$13,808,631,785	5.97%
4	Mexico	$8,785,360,653	$4,192,936,064	$12,978,296,718	4.87%
5	Germany	$6,407,989,714	$5,433,984,370	$11,841,974,084	10.90%
6	UK	$7,594,995,153	$2,484,349,794	$10,079,344,947	12.24%
7	Republic of Korea	$5,816,253,001	$1,425,414,117	$7,241,667,118	9.99%
8	France	$3,897,833,867	$1,625,064,324	$5,522,898,191	10.41%
9	Taiwan	$3,094,430,949	$1,698,479,949	$4,792,910,898	8.51%
10	Singapore	$3,636,170,934	$713,527,417	$4,349,698,351	12.46%

Table 20.11 Country Risk Index – 1/1/2004 to 12/31/2004. Total money moved out of the United States by country (through under-valued exports and over-valued imports)

Rank*	Country	Under-valued exports	Over-valued imports	Total moved out of the US	Share of trade
1	Azerbaijan	$528,389,802	$157,416	$528,547,218	268.54%
2	Yugoslavia	$169,598,049	$741,061	$170,339,110	72.49%
3	Iran	$152,952,617	$12,628,410	$165,581,027	70.03%
4	Cuba	$247,970,745	–	$247,970,745	61.91%
5	Kazakhstan	$291,952,547	$7,378,273	$299,330,820	34.90%
6	Bulgaria	$214,509,017	$14,467,039	$228,976,056	33.72%
7	Estonia	$156,854,211	$9,510,139	$166,364,350	31.52%
8	Denmark	$1,451,172,673	$432,241,119	$1,883,413,791	31.26%
9	Barbados	$99,437,204	$820,250	$100,257,454	26.08%
10	Philippines	$3,398,036,934	$512,074,712	$3,910,111,646	24.11%

Note: * Rank ordered by percent of trade, by country.

will provide the bank with an indication that a more detailed analysis is warranted. An analysis of the Product Risk Index will provide additional evidence regarding the risk of financing the transaction.

Product Risk Index: A similar analysis was conducted to determine a product risk index. First, the amount of money moved out of the United States by under-invoicing exports and over-invoicing imports for products defined by the six-digit harmonized codes were calculated. The Product Risk Index was calculated by finding and ranking the products that had the highest percentage of trade related to money moved out of the United States. The Table 20.12 is a sample of the Product Risk Index that ranks the products based on this metric. There are 4,758 six-digit product codes.

Table 20.12 Product risk index – 2006. Money moved out of the United States by product

Rank*	Product	Money Moved out of US ($)	Percent of trade
1	Cartridges for riveting	416,426,777	2,756.98%
2	Iodides and iodides oxides	529,245,774	1,500.75%
3	Photo plates and film	165,778,813	747.94%
4	Mechanisms for music boxes	6,653,673	694.50%
5	Optical fibers	1,956,532,697	627.56%
6	Rare earth metals	79,794,777	605.30%
7	Cadmium and articles thereof	13,184,553	459.90%
8	Radioactive elements & isotopes	1,617,767,386	416.36%
9	Recorded media sound or image	1,567,385,322	388.22%
10	Unrecorded cards with magnetic stripe	213,685,706	384.93%

Note: * Rank ordered by percent of trade.

International Price Profiling System – IPPS: The FFIEC BSA/AML Examination Manual stipulates that financial institutions engaged in trade financing conduct both character-based and transaction-based analysis. Transaction-based analysis is the evaluation of import or export prices to determine 'obvious over- or under-pricing of goods and services'. Analysis of the US Merchandise Trade Data Base can produce statistical price filters to assist financial institutions with detecting abnormally priced products. This analysis is defined as the International Price Profiling System.

The International Price Profiling System (IPPS) is a new risk-based analysis system that evaluates the risk characteristics of prices related to international trade transactions (For more details see http://www.internationaltradealert.com). The details of this methodology have not been published in the academic literature. The IPPS may be employed to evaluate transactions that have a risk of being related to money laundering, terrorist financing, income tax evasion, and import duty fraud. This new International Price Profiling System is currently being used by some financial institutions as a means of mitigating trade financing risk. It has also been reported that some European countries are evaluating their international trade transactions with similar methodologies.

Money is moved across borders through false invoicing of import or export transactions. Money is moved out of a country by under-invoicing exports or over-invoicing imports. Money is moved into a country by over-invoicing exports or under-invoicing imports.

The IPPS evaluates an international trade price based on four (4) different filters.

- World 5th and 95th percentile
- Country 5th and 95th percentile
- World Mean (−) and (+) 2 standard deviations
- Country Mean (−) and (+) 2 standard deviations

The statistical filters are calculated from 12 months of international trade transaction data as reported by the United States Department of Commerce. The IPPS analysis evaluates an international trade price and produces a 'Risk Index' that may range between '−4' and '+4'. A negative 'Risk Index' reflects the potential of money being moved out of the United States to a foreign country. A positive 'Risk Index' reflects the potential of money being moved into the United States from a foreign country. The magnitude of the 'Risk Index' reflects probability or likelihood that a price is over-valued or under-valued, and is determined as shown in Table 20.13.

The International Price Profiling System is based on statistical analysis and indicates suspicious prices in international trade. It does not prove that the suspicious transactions are related to money laundering, terrorist financing, or other illegal activities. There is some probability that the IPPS will generate false positives. It is the responsibility of the governmental agencies, or financial institutions to conduct further investigations as to the nature of the suspicious transactions. The investigations can only lead to three mutually exclusive outcomes: (1) the suspicious price is 'right' – there may be some unique characteristic that is reflected in the price; (2) the suspicious price is 'wrong' – it may be due to a clerical error; and (3) the suspicious price is 'abnormal' and indicates a criminal activity. The IPPS is meant to be a dynamic analytical tool. Institutions should modify

Table 20.13

Risk Index	Analysis	Interpretation of price abnormality
−4	Violates 4 filter prices	$ Moved out – very extreme indication
−3	Violates 3 filter prices	$ Moved out – extreme indication
−2	Violates 2 filter prices	$ Moved out – moderate indication
−1	Violates 1 filter price	$ Moved out – slight indication
0	Violates 0 filter prices	No risk of $ moved out or in
+1	Violates 1 filter price	$ Moved in – slight indication
+2	Violates 2 filter prices	$ Moved in – moderate indication
+3	Violates 3 filter prices	$ Moved in – extreme indication
+4	Violates 4 filter prices	$ Moved in – very extreme indication

the price filters based on the outcomes of using the system. Some products may require wider or narrower price filters. This can only be determined by evaluating the results of the price profiling.

The following presentation demonstrates the application of the IPPS.

Example 1–1 Export of Tomato Ketchup to Kuwait

The following is an example of the International Price Profiling System for the export of tomato ketchup to Kuwait at a price of $0.14 per kilogram. This price is below the lower bounds as calculated by all four risk measures. Therefore it indicates a risk index of −4.

Table 20.14

World		Kuwait	
Transactions:	2,378	Transactions:	26
95th Percentile:	$1.28	95th Percentile:	$2.53
Median:	$0.81	Median:	$0.58
5th Percentile:	$0.55	5th Percentile:	$0.51
Mean + 2SD:	$2.20	Mean + 2SD:	$3.55
Mean:	$0.81	Mean:	$0.76
Mean – 2SD:	$0.30	Mean – 2SD:	$0.16
	Risk Index = −4		

Example 1–1 Import of Soccer Balls from Pakistan

The following is an example of the International Price Profiling System for the Import of soccer balls from Pakistan at a price of $30.00 per unit. This price is above the upper bounds as calculated by all four risk measures. Therefore it indicates a risk index of −4.

Table 20.15

World		Pakistan	
Transactions:	3,014	Transactions:	966
95th Percentile:	$7.14	95th Percentile:	$7.02
Median:	$2.79	Median:	$3.54
5th Percentile:	$1.35	5th Percentile:	$2.19
Mean + 2SD:	$27.40	Mean + 2SD:	$20.61
Mean:	$2.96	Mean:	$3.73
Mean – 2SD:	$0.32	Mean – 2SD:	$0.67
	Risk Index = −4		

20.7 CONCLUSION

This chapter provides new information that will contribute to the attempt to minimize trade-based money laundering, tax evasion and terrorist financing. It provides an analysis of previously unused statistical techniques and methodologies as a means of monitoring, detecting and prosecuting criminal money laundering and terrorist financing activities through international trade. The chapter describes how new statistical profiling methodologies that evaluate transactions contained in a country's international trade database can mitigate the risks associated with trade-based money laundering. It discusses the application of four new money laundering profiling techniques which focus on country risk profiles, customs district risk profiles, product risk profiles, and transaction price risk characteristics. The practice of profiling as a means of detecting suspicious individuals and activities is controversial and frowned on by many. However, the statistical analysis of information and statistical profiling is crucial in the fight against money laundering and the financing of terrorist activities.

The analysis of the US Merchandise Trade Data Base (and other countries' trade databases) provides a vast amount of information to assist financial institutions, and law enforcement and governmental agencies to detect and minimize trade-based money laundering. The inclusion of other countries' databases would make the analysis even more robust. The events of September 11, 2001 have made the analysis of trade-based terrorist financing even more compelling

NOTE

* This chapter is a condensed version of an article published in J.S. Zdanowicz (2009), 'Trade-based money laundering and terrorist financing', *Review of Law and Economics*, **5** (2), 855–78.

REFERENCES

Bhagwati, J.N. (1964), 'On the underinvoicing of imports', *Bulletin of the Oxford University Institute of Economics and Statistics*, **26**, 389–97.

Coleman, R. (2006), 'U.S. and Brazilian stings nab trade-based laundering ring', *Money Laundering Alert*, August.
Cuddington, J.T. (1987), 'Capital flight', *European Economic Review*, **31**, 387–98.
De Boyrie, M., S. Pak and J.S. Zdanowicz (2005a), 'The impact of Switzerland's money laundering law on capital flows through abnormal pricing in international trade', *Applied Financial Economics*, **15**, 217–30.
De Boyrie, M., S. Pak and J.S. Zdanowicz (2005b), 'Estimating the magnitude of capital flight due to abnormal pricing in international trade: the Russia-USA case', *Accounting Forum*, **29**, 1–22.
De Wulf, L. (1981), 'Statistical analysis of under-and overinvoicing of imports', *Journal of Development Economics*, **8** (3), 303–23.
Federal Financial Institutions Examination Council (2007), *Bank Secrecy Act Anti Money laundering Examination Manual*, August 24.
Financial Action Task Force (2006), 'Trade based money laundering', June 23, available at http://www.fatf-gafi.org
Freer, J. (2001), 'Honey trade launders Al Qaeda cash', *South Florida Business Journal*, October 26.
Gulati, S.K. (1987), 'A note on trade misinvoicing', Institute of International Economics, October.
International Trade Alert – Working Paper (2005), 'International trade pricing analysis – 2004: money moved out of the U.S. and into the U.S.', June available at http://www.internationaltradealert.com
Money Laundering Alert (1992), 'Exports, imports cover flight of U.S. drug proceeds', January.
Money Laundering Alert (2008), 'Mitigating trade-based money laundering risk', March.
Pak, S., S. Zanakis and J.S. Zdanowicz (2003), 'Detecting abnormal pricing in international trade: the Greece-USA case', *Interfaces*, **33** (2), 54–64.
Pak, S. and J.S. Zdanowicz (1994), 'U.S. trade with the World: an estimate of 1993 lost U.S. federal income tax revenues due to over-invoiced imports and under-invoiced exports', Trade Research Institute Working Paper #9404-01, available from john.zdanowicz@fiu.edu, April 1, 1994.
Zdanowicz, J.S. (2003), 'Movie inspires new research into suspicious import weights', *Money Laundering Alert*, May.
Zdanowicz, J.S. (2004a), 'Detecting money laundering and terrorist financing via data mining', *Communications of the Association of Computing Machinery*, **47** (5), 53–5.
Zdanowicz, J.S. (2004b), 'Who's watching our back door?', *Business Accents Magazine*, **1** (1), Florida International University.
Zdanowicz, J.S. (2005), 'Trade-based terrorist financing analysis: suspicious trade with Al Qaeda countries', International Trade Alert Working Paper, June 16, available at http://www.internationaltradealert.com.
Zdanowicz, J.S. (2007), 'Mitigate trade financing risks with proper documentation, analysis', *Money Laundering Alert*, April.
Zdanowicz, J.S. (2008), 'Trade finance: mitigating trade-based money laundering risks', *Money Laundering Alert*, March.
Zdanowicz, J.S. (2009), 'Trade-based money laundering and terrorist financing',. *Review of Law and Economics*, **5** (2), 855–78.
Zdanowicz, J.S., S. Pak and M. Sullivan (1999), 'Brazil-United States Trade: capital flight through abnormal pricing', *The International Trade Journal*, **XIII** (4), 423–43.

21. Detecting money laundering in the real estate sector

*Joras Ferwerda and Brigitte Unger**

21.1 INTRODUCTION

Estimations of the level of money laundering reach up to 2 to 5 per cent of world GDP,[1] raising the question where does all this money go. A potential answer lies within the real estate sector, which is large enough to absorb a large part of this money and prone to money laundering because of features such as the heterogeneity of buildings, the non-transparency in the market and possibilities for hiding the true owner. So far, however, no systematic study has been conducted on the importance and frequency of money laundering in the real estate sector. This study tries to use the information known to authorities to systematically identify and analyse money laundering in this sector. Though the data refer to the Netherlands only, the method can be used for other countries as well.

This chapter is organized as follows: After describing why the real estate sector is prone to money laundering, we explain our research method and present a list of seventeen indicators that we use to find the real estate objects that are most likely related to money laundering. Subsequently, we describe how criminologists analyse 200 of these objects on a case-by-case basis. The results of this criminological research are used in the last part of this chapter to find out, through use of econometrics, which indicators can detect conspicuous real estate and which fail to do so. In the conclusion we present a draft magic formula which can help to find money laundering objects in the real estate sector.

21.2 THE POTENTIAL ABUSE OF THE REAL ESTATE SECTOR

The real estate sector has certain characteristics that make it prone to money laundering. It has a very high value, which makes it attractive for both legal and illegal investments (Eichholtz 2006). Therefore, this sector has quite a potential to absorb a substantial volume of money laundering activities. The real estate sector displays the following characteristics that make it susceptible to money laundering (see Nelen 2008):

Real estate

- is a safe investment
- is a prestigious investment
- has an objective value that is difficult to assess
- is a sector in which speculation is tradition

- allows a distinction between legal and economic ownership (the buyer and seller in the papers are not necessarily the person who provides or gets the money)
- allows the realization of 'white' returns (e.g. apartment rents)
- can be used to conduct criminal activities (e.g. a chemical drugs lab)

The OECD (2006) identifies that the real estate sector is used to facilitate tax fraud and money laundering in most of the countries they survey. There is a general concern that the construction industry is used to generate unreported income and to invest unreported income coming from other industries, including illegal activities (OECD 2006).

The study of Meloen et al. (2003, p. 246) also shows that real estate is a popular sector for criminals to invest in. Meloen et al. analysed 52 Dutch criminal cases in which property with unlawful advantages was confiscated. They found that in 30–40 per cent of money laundering cases, money was invested in immovable property. The study points to the importance of the real estate sector for laundering. However, given the limited number of cases studied, conclusions cannot be drawn regarding the overall size of the problem.

The Dutch Scientific Research Documentation Centre WODC (Kleemans et al. 2002, p. 132) also finds, from analysing 80 cases, that investment in real estate is an efficient method of dealing with large amounts of money. The price increases of real estate make it profitable and the profits in the real estate sector create a legal basis for income.

Real estate objects can be used for criminal purposes in a number of ways. In the literature a distinction is made between criminal exploitation and criminal speculation. Money laundering belongs to the latter category and is defined as a series of activities meant to disguise the origin of illicit funds. It can refer to the first phase of laundering, where one tries to place the illegal money into a real estate construction (e.g. giving cash to a real estate agent in order to buy a house), to the second phase of laundering, where one tries to pump the money around the world (e.g. a foreign bank giving a loan to a person buying a house, with the loan in reality being the hidden money of the person buying the house), and on to the third phase of laundering, in which case the criminal parks the money in the real estate sector and is not interested in trading real estate, but in investing.

However, real estate can also be used for criminal investment without the intention of laundering money. For example, an ecstasy producer who buys a house in order to use it for ecstasy pill production might not do this with the intention of hiding the illicit origin of his money, but just to do criminal business. In this study, we did not (and could not) distinguish between money laundering and criminal investment without the intention of hiding the illicit origin of money.

21.3 RESEARCH METHOD

Although 'it is often extremely difficult to identify real estate transactions associated with money laundering' (FATF 2007, p. 5), the aim of this research is to develop a data research method that enables its user to filter out suspicious real estate transactions and distinguish them from all the ordinary ones. We are looking for the transactions of real estate objects with a motive other than the normal transactions: the outliers. According

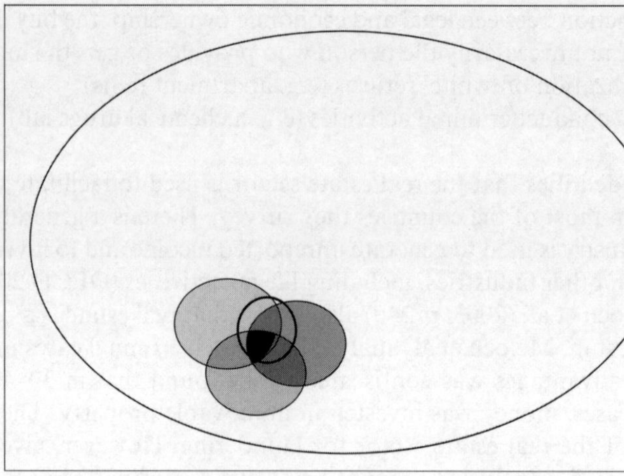

Note: The outer circle shows all the real estate objects. The grey circles are three indicators. The black open circle represents the criminal investments in this sector.

Figure 21.1 Visual explanation of the method used for this research

to the definition, an outlier in general is an observation that deviates so much from other observations as to arouse suspicion that it was generated by a different mechanism (Hawkins 1980). To find the criminal investments amidst all the usual real estate transactions, we developed a list of characteristics that are associated with criminal investments in the real estate sector: the 'red flags'.[2] This is in line with the remark by Nelen et al. (2007, p. 75) that illogical and unusual behaviour in the real estate sector indicates an increased risk of criminal behaviour. Although a single characteristic in itself is not enough to arouse suspicion of a criminal investment, we believe that a combination of these characteristics might be. To give an example: although it is often mentioned in the literature that many criminal investments in the real estate sector are financed with money from abroad, we cannot, of course, conclude that all real estate transactions financed from abroad are suspicious. However, we can label them unusual[3] and conclude that the more unusual characteristics a transaction has, the more it should arouse suspicion (this is in line with the vision of Belastingdienst/FIOD-ECD 2008, p. 28).

For a visual representation of this research method, we refer to Figure 21.1. The outer circle represents all the investigated real estate objects and the grey circles are the subgroups found with the indicators. The black surface is the congruent of real estate objects that have the characteristics of all three indicators. The small open circle represents the criminal investments in this sector (the subgroup we are looking for). We assume that by using more and more indicators this circle will be filled more and more with darker surfaces.

When using such an indicator-based approach, one is always confronted with the trade-off between false positives and false negatives, or the so-called type I and type II errors, respectively. A false positive in this specific research occurs when an object is marked as (potentially) criminal while it actually is not. A false negative occurs when a

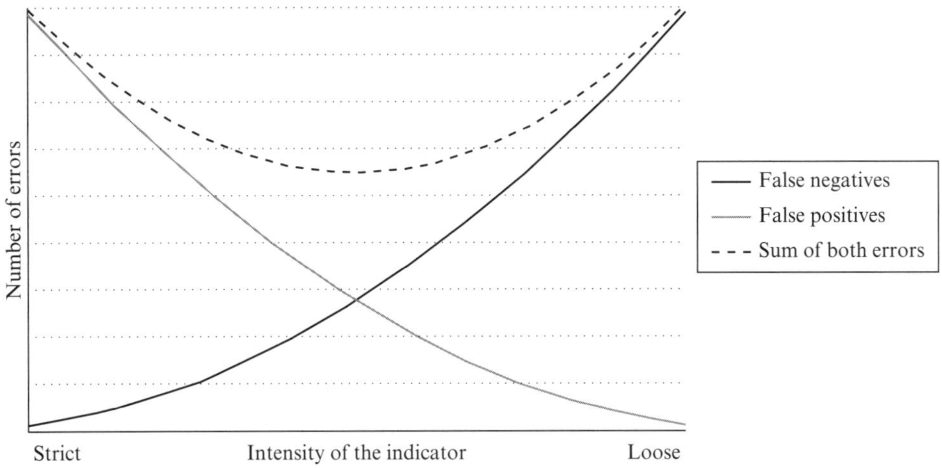

Figure 21.2 Trade-off between false positives and false negatives

criminal investment is not detected by our research method. The trade-off between these two errors is visualized in Figure 21.2.

Figure 21.2 is best explained by discussing the two extremes: a very strict indicator and a very broad indicator. When one chooses a very broad indicator (right end of the graph), almost all objects are marked as unusual. Therefore, there will be very few false negatives (the downward sloping line), at the expense of a lot of false positives (the upward sloping line). When one chooses a very strict indicator (left side of the graph), hardly any object will be marked as unusual. Therefore there will be almost no false positives, at the expense of a large amount of false negatives. The optimum can be found at the minimum of the sum of these two errors (the parabola), if one attaches equal importance to both errors. Since we do not know the amount and types of errors we make, we circumvent this dilemma by choosing a different research method. We will not mark any object unusual based on just one indicator, but will do so based strictly on the combination of several indicators. Since we assume that real criminal activities have an increased chance of receiving more red flags than normal activities, we can conclude that the number of false positives will diminish quickly once we start looking at the combination of several indicators. Therefore, we focus more on the false negatives of a single indicator than on the false positives. This means that we will use relatively broad indicators (and therefore accept an increased degree of false positives).

21.4 THE INDICATORS

Based on an extensive literature research, we developed a list of 17 indicators that we can operationalize[4] for our dataset. We mainly use Dutch publications (like the reports of the Dutch Financial Expertise Centre (FEC) and the Dutch Financial Intelligence and Investigation Unit (FIOD)) because our analysis is on the Dutch real estate sector, but we also include some international publications (like the reports of the Financial Action Task Force (FATF) and the OECD).

Indicator 1: Financier is from Abroad

The misuse of a foreign legal party as a financier is the prototype of disguising the fact that you invest your ill-gotten gains into the real estate sector (van de Bunt et al. 2007, p. 67). The idea is that it becomes harder to discover the origin of the money when a (preferably anonymous) foreign company is used to finance the investment. The Dutch Tax Administration and the Dutch financial intelligence and investigation unit in their report also warn about the use of foreign companies for the financing of real estate (Belastingdienst/FIOD-ECD 2008, pp. 12, 20, 23, 32 and 33). The literature mentions many cases in which foreign companies played an important role in money laundering constructions. For instance, case 1.1 in FATF (2007), where money was invested in the Dutch real estate sector with loans from several foreign companies that were actually controlled by the person receiving the loan.[5] The idea behind this is that one can invest their own (dirty) money by first transferring it to a foreign country and then lending it back to themselves. This disguises the origin of the money, which is exactly the aim of money laundering. The use of foreign companies for this loan-back method is also described, among others, in Nelen et al. (2007, pp. 54–5), Trouw and Knobbout (2007, p. 10) and Belastingdienst/FIOD-ECD (2008, pp. 13).

Indicator 2: Financier is a Person, not a Company

When banks provide a mortgage to finance the purchase of real estate, there are certain control mechanisms in place, like comparing the necessary income with the applicant's wage. When people provide a mortgage, this control is unclear, which can be an indication that this way of financing is used for dubious purposes. The Belastingdienst/FIOD-ECD (2008, p. 33) states that a mortgage not provided by a financial institution can point in the direction of money laundering. See also van de Bunt et al. (2007, chapter 6) and FEC (2008), who mention that a mortgage by a non-business party, especially a foreign one, must raise suspicion.

Indicator 3: Financing is Unusual Compared to Appraised Value

An indication for a fictitious mortgage is when the mortgage is significantly higher than the appraised value of the object, since a bank will normally not provide a mortgage above the actual value of the property (Belastingdienst/FIOD-ECD 2008, p. 24). The FATF (2007, p. 36) also mentions in its report that buyers taking on a debt that is significant in relation to the value of the property should arouse suspicion. A significantly high mortgage is found especially in cases where a 'straw man construction' is used.

Indicator 4: Financing is Not Used (No Mortgage)

Real estate is the most expensive property most people will ever buy and not many buyers are wealthy enough to pay the whole purchase amount without the use of a mortgage. The absence of a mortgage should raise the suspicion of the notary (FEC, 2008, p. 19) and can indicate the misuse of foreign legal persons (van de Bunt et al. 2007, p. 114). A study on real estate in Amsterdam (PEO 1995) specifically focused on objects that were bought without the use of a mortgage, because it considered this a helpful indication of money laundering (Trouw and Knobbout 2007, interview 3). This indicator is also apparent in case study 3.5 described by FATF (2007), in which two high-value properties (of more than €20 million) were bought in France with a single payment (not a loan). Later it became clear that this concerned an investment of dirty capital, disguised by offshore companies.

Indicator 5: Financing is Provided by the Owner (Same Person)

The use of transactions with oneself is mentioned as a characteristic of money laundering in the real estate sector (Belastingdienst/FIOD-ECD, 2008, p. 10). According to the Belastingdienst/FIOD-ECD (2008, p. 28) and the FATF (2007, p. 35), the use of illogical and unnecessarily complex financial constructions should arouse suspicion. We consider providing a mortgage to oneself dubious. This indicator is often mentioned in connection to the loan-back construction, which is described in many publications on money laundering methods, see for example OECD (2006), Ferwerda et al. (2007), Nelen et al. (2007, p. 55), Belastingdienst/FIOD-ECD (2008, pp. 12–13) and FATF (2007, pp. 7–8).

Indicator 6: Owner is from Abroad

Purchasing real estate abroad adds a layer of disguise, because one is not known by the local authorities. In the back-to-back loan construction especially, the purchase of real estate is done from abroad. Although it is often mentioned that this is done by offshore companies only (like in FATF 2007, pp. 12–13 and p. 35, and van de Bunt et al. 2007), others mention that it is done by foreigners in general (Nelen et al. 2007, p. 54).

Indicators 7 and 8: Owner is a Person with an Unusual Number of Objects or Transactions

The FEC (2008, pp. 20) and FATF (2007, pp. 34; 2006, pp. 8) mention that a red flag should be raised when a person performs several transactions. The Belastingdienst/FIOD-ECD (2008, p. 29) mentions that a sudden increase in someone's real estate portfolio can indicate a wish to launder a large amount of money within a short period of time (see also FEC 2008, p. 23).

Indicator 9: Owner is a Company with a Particular Exploitation

The FEC (2008, p. 16) and Trouw and Knobbout (2007) suggest that money launderers invest in and with companies that they have knowledge of. Also Belastindienst/FIOD-ECD (2008, p. 5 and p. 37) cautions against business sectors with an increased risk for criminal investment. The FATF (2007, p. 27) mentions that within the real estate sector some areas are more attractive for criminal investment than others. Which sectors are specifically suspicious and have an increased risk or are more important for money laundering? While the FEC (2008) does not mention any sectors, Belastingdienst/FIOD-ECD (2008, pp. 5 and 37) mentions illegal exploitation (such as illegal pensions, cannabis nursery, human trafficking, illegal gambling and illegal prostitution) and risky legal sectors (such as hotels, restaurants, 'coffeeshops',[6] prostitution, gambling and transport). Trouw and Knobbout (2007) mention catering services, prostitution and transportation. The FATF (2007, p. 27) cites the hotel business, construction firms, development of public or tourist infrastructure (especially luxury resorts) and the catering business.

Indicator 10: Owner is a Company just Established

The FEC (2008) suggests that a company that has just been established and is immediately buying up real estate is likely to be part of a construction of companies designed to conceal the ultimate beneficial owner and to launder money. Also, Belastingdienst/FIOD-ECD (2008, p. 28) and the FATF (2007, p. 35) warn about transactions by certain companies that have just been founded.

Indicator 11: Owner is a Company without Employees

According to the FEC (2008), real estate companies that do not have employees are very likely to be part of some sort of money laundering construction (see also van de Bunt et al. 2007, chapter 4). The use of empty companies in money laundering constructions is described by the FATF (2007, p. 14), which calls these companies 'shell companies'; the company only consists of a shell, without any contents.

Indicator 12: Owner is a 'World Citizen' (Unknown to the Tax Administration)

When a foreigner purchases real estate in the Netherlands, this leads to a tax payment duty abroad. A problem occurs with this payment obligation when it is unknown where the purchaser pays his taxes, that is, when the purchaser is unknown to the national Tax Administration. According to the FEC (2008, p. 16), investors who have no tax payment duty, or at least not in the Netherlands, should raise a red flag. Also Belastingdienst/FIOD-ECD (2008, pp. 4 and 28) mentions these kinds of foreign real estate owners as an indicator for money laundering.

Indicator 13: Real Estate Object is Involved in Multiple Transactions

When an object is bought and sold multiple times, this can indicate a swindle to push the price above the property's actual worth. FEC (2008), Ferwerda et al. (2007, chapter 4) and Belastingdienst/FIOD-ECD (2008, p. 17) all mention that this occurs and that it can be a major part of a money laundering process, especially with the use of the ABC construction and carousel fraud (driving up the price by successive sales and purchases within the same organization with the eventual goal of making the object appear to be worth more (or less) than it actually is). The FATF (2007) explains that the method of successive sales and purchases, which is in line with the above-mentioned methods, has the specific characteristic that the property is (fictitiously) sold in a series of subsequent transactions, each time at a higher (or lower) price.

Indicators 14 and 15: Real Estate Object is in a Very Bad or Very Good Neighbourhood

The FATF (2007, p. 37) sees transactions in high-risk urban areas as an indicator for money laundering in the real estate sector. Also van Gestel et al. (2008, pp. 35–36) mention the link between criminal activities in this sector and the liveability in the corresponding district. Nelen and Huisman (2008) find the relationship between bad neighbourhoods and organized crime not undisputed, and mention that there is hardly any evidence that deprived areas and marginalized business activities are breeding grounds for organized crime. Areas and sectors that, as a result of governmental policies, have been uplifted seem to be just as vulnerable. It could be that criminals want to show off their purchases and show the rest of the world that they are (or were) successful in business. This consideration might result in investments in very good, fashionable and expensive neighbourhoods. Therefore both extremes (very bad and very good neighbourhoods) are used as separate indicators in this study.

Indicators 16 and 17: Purchase Amount is Unusual Compared to Appraised Value or Previous Purchase Amount

A purchase amount that is too high or too low can indicate a swindle to drive up the price, like an ABC construction or the fraud carousel, or play a role in tax fraud. This is one of the most visible indicators of criminal investments in real estate, since the purchase prices are transparent, at least in the Netherlands. This might be the reason that, as so often mentioned in the literature, a too high or too low purchase price is suspicious (see e.g. Nelen et al. (2007, pp. 47 and 56), FATF (2007, p. 24 and 21) and Ferwerda et al. (2007, chapter 4)). The comparison of the appraised value with the purchase amount using Dutch data was suggested by Eichholtz (2006, p. 67) and done by Siegman (2006). Although Siegman (2006) was able to depict strange price increases of real estate in Amsterdam, he did not continue his efforts to estimate the amount of money laundering in the real estate sector, simply because there was no way he could differentiate between the price increases caused by money laundering and those caused by the speculation of real estate agents. This study tackles this issue, at least partly, by using many more indicators, by cooperating with criminologists and by the use of closed data in addition to publicly available information.

21.5 THE APPLICATION OF THE INDICATORS TO OUR DATASET

To be able to apply all the above-mentioned indicators, we compiled a database of 11,895 real estate objects, which comprises all real estate objects in Utrecht and Maastricht (two cities in the Netherlands with respectively about 310,000 and 120,000 inhabitants) that were sold at least once within the period 2002–2006.[7] This database consists of data from the Dutch Offices of Land Registry (information from the deed of conveyance, object number, purchase amount, name and date of birth of purchaser and seller, gender for natural persons, business form for legal persons, mortgage amount, the provider of the mortgage, etc.) and from the Dutch Tax Administration (like income of the subject,

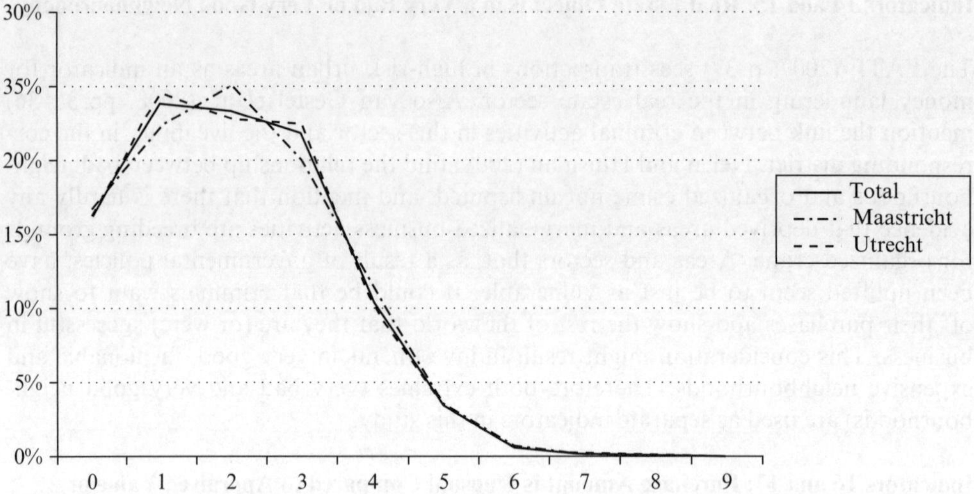

Source: Compiled by the authors. The percentage refers to the percentage of objects with an X (0 through 9) number of red flags relative to the number of objects in the group (Utrecht, Maastricht or the two cities combined).

Figure 21.3 Distribution of red flags for Utrecht and Maastricht

establishment date of legal persons, appraisal value, some tax information, etc.). Once we apply all the 17 indicators to our dataset,[8] we can see (as depicted in Figure 21.3) that many real estate object have a couple of red flags,[9] but that finding more than five red flags for one object is quite exceptional. The 150 real estate objects with the most red flags receive a criminological case-by-case analysis. To increase the impartiality of the criminological research we add 50 real estate objects with less than five red flags to the list as a control group, without signalling this to the criminologists.[10]

21.6 CRIMINOLOGICAL ANALYSIS

The criminological research is done independently from the application of red flags and by criminologists that do not know how many red flags each object received. For the impartiality of this study we have to stress that the criminologists try to focus as much as possible on different indicators than those mentioned above. This is mainly possible because the case-by-case basis of the criminological research provides the possibility of using many more sources of information and applying a whole different range of indicators. For example, the 200 cases are supplemented with open-source information (like the name of the notary, the use of the notary account during the transaction, anything that might show up on Google) and closed source information (e.g. whether the persons involved have antecedents, whether the persons involved performed any unusual or suspicious transactions[11] and the tax declarations of the persons involved). The case-by-case analysis also gives an opportunity to perform more extensive analyses, like a network analysis to detect natural and legal persons that work together in an organized fashion or an individual analysis to detect whether the persons involved can play the role that they play (e.g. do they have enough capital/income to get that mortgage, or is there some kind of straw men construction?).

The method of analysis is based on describing two possible scenarios – a licit and an illicit one – and the evaluation of which of the two is best supported by the facts that showed up during the analysis. Eventually, the criminological analysis indicates that 36 of the 200 objects should be labelled as 'conspicuous'. We do not use the term 'suspicious', because we are only able to analyse what we see on paper and cannot go as far as actual police investigation. Of the 36 conspicuous objects, five are linked with drugs, 27 with fraud and four with renting irregularities. While nine of the 36 cases are strongly conspicuous, eight are moderately conspicuous and 19 have only a weak indication that something is wrong.

In addition to this criminological research, the criminologists also asked stakeholders at the ground level (such as local police officers) which subjects and objects have raised their awareness in the two cities. Overall, this survey resulted in a list of 356 subjects and 32 objects deduced from various sources. Comparing this list with the list of 1130 subjects identified in the 200 cases gives only two hits, which concern the same strongly conspicuous case. The meagre results of this so-called bottom-up analysis can indicate that the application of red flags is not very effective to find the relevant objects and subjects, but can also indicate that our method points to subjects and objects that are not yet known to the local authorities.

We now use the results of the criminological analysis (36 conspicuous cases) to estimate which indicators can identify the relevant real estate objects and which indicators fail to do so.

21.7 STATISTICAL AND ECONOMETRICAL ANALYSIS

If red flags are a good indication for conspicuous cases, we would expect that the conspicuous cases have more red flags on average than the objects that are not marked as conspicuous by the criminologists. The conspicuous objects have, on average, 5.4 red flags, while the 200 selected objects have, on average, 4.8 red flags. So, red flags seem more frequent for the conspicuous objects than for the sample of 200. More disappointing at first glance it seems that when we remove the 50 objects of the control group, the 150 unusual objects identified in the economic analysis have on average 5.7 red flags, that is more red flags than the 36 conspicuous objects identified by the criminological analysis. This disappointing finding changes, however, when we take into account the degree of conspicuousness, which shows that more red flags indeed do point at more strongly conspicuous objects: the weakly conspicuous objects have 5.1 flags on average, the moderately conspicuous objects have 5.5 red flags on average, and the strongly conspicuous objects have 6.1 red flags on average. The average, median and mode amount of red flags of all 11,895 analysed objects lie around two. This result seems to confirm the idea behind this study that a real estate object with more red flags has an increased chance of being related to money laundering or other criminal investments.

In our econometrical analysis the dependent variable (whether the object is conspicuous or not) is a binary variable. We will therefore use a specific econometric estimation

Table 21.1 Econometrical estimation results

Dependent variable:	(1)	(2)	(3)	(4)	(5)
Conspicuous (or not)	probit	Logit	cloglog	OLS	dprobit
2 Financier is a natural person and	0.73	1.12	0.80	0.16	0.23
5 Mortgage to self (same surname)	(0.56)	(1.02)	(0.87)	(0.14)	(0.21)
3 Unusual mortgage compared to	0.03	0.20	0.29	0.03	0.01
appraised value	(0.37)	(0.67)	(0.60)	(0.09)	(0.09)
4 Absence of mortgage	0.32	0.60	0.56	0.08	0.08
	(0.30)	(0.54)	(0.47)	(0.07)	(0.07)
6 Foreign owner	0.53*	0.95*	0.81*	0.14*	0.15
	(0.30)	(0.52)	(0.44)	(0.08)	(0.09)
7 Owner has unusual number of objects and	0.31	0.64	0.61	0.07	0.07
8 Owner does unusual number of transactions	(0.29)	(0.53)	(0.45)	(0.07)	(0.06)
9 Risky exploitation	0.36	0.57	0.45	0.08	0.10
	(0.30)	(0.52)	(0.45)	(0.08)	(0.09)
10 Owner is a just-established	0.78**	1.36**	1.17**	0.21**	0.24*
company	(0.36)	(0.62)	(0.52)	(0.09)	(0.13)
11 Owner is a company without	−0.17	−0.27	−0.19	−0.05	−0.04
employees	(0.26)	(0.46)	(0.40)	(0.07)	(0.07)
12 Owner is a 'global citizen'	0.22	0.42	0.43	0.05	0.06
	(0.35)	(0.62)	(0.53)	(0.09)	(0.10)
13 Object involved in multiple	0.02	0.03	−0.04	0.00	0.01
transactions	(0.33)	(0.58)	(0.53)	(0.08)	(0.08)
15 Object in good neighbourhood	0.08	−0.06	−0.29	0.01	0.02
	(0.34)	(0.64)	(0.56)	(0.08)	(0.09)
16 Unusual purchase amount	−0.37	−0.67	−0.55	−0.12	−0.08
compared to appraised value	(0.33)	(0.61)	(0.54)	(0.08)	(0.06)
17 Unusual price fluctuation	0.84***	1.44***	1.20***	0.23***	0.25**
	(0.30)	(0.52)	(0.44)	(0.08)	(0.10)
Constant	−1.67***	−2.93***	−2.89***	0.03	
	(0.37)	(0.72)	(0.65)	(0.08)	
Observations	200	200	200	200	200
Pseudo R^2	0.103	0.103			0.103
Adjusted R^2				0.0364	

Note: Standard errors are given in parentheses. P-values (chance of a coincidental relationship) are shown with superscripts: *** = $p<0.01$, ** = $p<0.05$, * = $p<0.1$. The (adjusted or pseudo) R^2 (coefficient of determination) of cloglog cannot be calculated, but regarding the comparable values of the log likelihood it is most likely comparable to the probit model (in column 1) and the logit model (in column 2).

model that takes this into account: the so-called Probit model. To show the robustness of the results of this specification, we present the results of two other estimation models: OLS and Logit.[12] Since the number of conspicuous objects is quite low (less than 20%), we add the results of the complementary log-log model,[13] which is particularly useful for cases where one of the outcomes (conspicuous in this case) is rare. Since the Probit model does not assume linearity and therefore cannot be interpreted directly, we calculate the marginal effect[14] of each indicator and show this with the other estimation results. The results of the econometric analysis are shown in Table 21.1.[15] Practically, the primary focus is on the results (significant or not) in column 1. Columns 2, 3 and 4 are a check on the robustness of the results and column 5 is used to interpret the significant results.

All the significant effects in Table 21.1 are positive, which means that these indicators can be used to 'detect' conspicuous objects. The most significant effect found in the econometric analysis is that objects with an unusual price fluctuation (indicator 17) are associated with an increased chance of 25 percentage points to be conspicuous. Objects owned by a company that was just established (indicator 10) are associated with an increased chance of 24 percentage points to be conspicuous. Finally, objects with a foreign owner (indicator 6) are associated with an increased chance of 15 percentage points to be conspicuous. For the rest of the indicators there is no significant effect on the probability to be conspicuous.

21.8 CONCLUSION

This study can be seen as a pioneer and pilot study for detecting money laundering in the real estate sector by using the skills of both economists and criminologists. The study consists of three main steps. We start with an outlier detection model based on 17 indicators derived from the literature. In the second step a criminological analysis is conducted on the 150 objects with the most indications for money laundering, mixed with 50 seemingly normal objects. Once we determine that 36 objects can be labelled conspicuous, we use an econometrical analysis in the last step to find out which of the 17 indicators can detect these conspicuous objects.

Our hope for this study was to end up with a magic formula that allows the identification of suspicious objects from objective data. At this stage of research we can only provide a first draft formula for such a magic detection tool, which could be refined and improved in the future (Box. 21.1).[16]

Figure 21.4 shows the objects with five or more red flags and which are labelled as conspicuous on the map of both cities. As one can see, there is no clear concentration in one neighbourhood, as the objects are rather evenly spread on the map.

BOX 21.1

The draft magic formula that can 'detect' conspicuous objects:
Chance to be conspicuous = 15% * foreign owner + 24% * just-established company + 25% * unusual price fluctuation

21.9 RESEARCH LIMITATIONS AND POSSIBLE FURTHER RESEARCH

Note that the significant relationships are not causal per se; a characteristic could lead to criminal activity, but criminal activity could also lead to a certain characteristic. Also

Source: The authors, graphic made by Arjen Siegman. The five black bars are the objects from the control group of 50 objects that are nevertheless identified as conspicuous, while the 31 dark grey bars are the conspicuous objects that are not in the control group of 50. The other 119 bars light grey are the objects that have five or more red flags, but are not labelled conspicuous in the criminological analysis. The bars are moved slightly to protect the privacy of the analysed objects and subjects.

Figure 21.4 Objects Identified in Utrecht (left) and Maastricht (right)

note that it is not clear to what extent we can generalize the results, since the sample is fairly small (200 objects) compared to the whole sector (11,895 objects), and not random and therefore normally not representative. We hope, however, to have demonstrated that using a multidisciplinary approach including outlier detection, criminology and econometrics is a promising method to create a detection tool for criminal investments in the real estate sector. However, it needs further refinement. Refinement can be achieved by focusing on more narrow concepts of criminal behaviour (e.g. specific forms of fraud or drugs), specific real estate sub-sectors (e.g. housing or commercial market) and by the mere use of behaviour-specific indicators.

NOTES

* This chapter is the shortened version of a study financed by the Dutch Ministries of Finance, Interior Affairs and Justice, which has been published as B. Unger and J. Ferwerda (2011) *Money Laundering in the Real Estate Sector, Suspicious Properties*, (with a contribution from H. Nelen and L. Ritzen), Edward Elgar, Cheltenham, UK. We would like to thank criminologists Hans Nelen and Luuk Ritzen from Maastricht University for their cooperation in this research project.

1. This was a first estimate of money laundering by the managing director of the IMF, Michel Camdessus, in 1998. Figures within that range were later found by Walker (1999) and Unger (2007).
2. With respect to the use of red flags, we follow the phrasing and research method of FATF (2007) and FEC (2008).
3. By using the word 'unusual', we follow the phrasing of the Dutch FIUs that make a distinction between unusual transactions and suspicious transactions.
4. Although the literature mentions more indicators, here we only present the indicators that we can actually apply to our dataset. See Unger and Ferwerda (2011) for a more complete list of indicators and a more extensive explanation of these indicators. The indicators might not all be directly related to money laundering, but could also indicate other forms of criminal investments or exploitation.
5. See also, for example, case 4.1 in FATF (2007) and case 18 in FATF (2006)
6. In the Netherlands the selling of marihuana is tolerated in so-called coffeeshops.

7. We did not select any one part of the real estate sector, which means that all kinds of real estate are included, ranging from houses and offices to churches and undeveloped land.
8. The application of these indicators is sometimes quite cumbersome and has led to some limitations for the research. For example, the nationality of the owners is not available in the dataset and therefore we use the former addresses of the owners as a rough indication of the nationality. Another example is that some indicators need threshold levels to indicate what is unusual and what is not, while this is not specified in the literature. We describe the limitations and (sometimes arbitrary) decisions for the application of the indicators in Unger and Ferwerda (2011), chapters 4.2 and 5.3.
9. This is a logical consequence of the use of relatively broad indicators, as explained earlier.
10. The selection of only 200 objects for criminological research is due to the limited criminological research capacities in the project.
11. In the Netherlands obliged entities (like banks, notaries, car dealers, etc.) report all unusual transactions to the FIU-Netherlands. The FIU-Netherlands then starts to analyse these reports and decides which of them can be classified as suspicious.
12. The standard OLS estimation with Y as the dependent variable and X as the independent variable is: $Y = \beta_0 + \beta_1 X$. The Logit model (with Pr as the probability) estimates: $p_i = \Pr[y_i = 1|x_i] = \frac{\exp(\beta_0 + \beta_i x_i)}{1 + \exp(\beta_0 + \beta_i x_i)}$, which clearly ensures that $0 < p_i < 1$. The Probit model, on the other hand, estimates: $p_i = \Pr[y_i = 1|x_i] = \Phi(\beta_0 + \beta_i x_i)$, where $\Phi(.)$is the cumulative distribution function for the standard normal distribution, which means that $p_i = \int_{-\infty}^{\beta_0+\beta_1 x_i} (2\pi)^{-1/2} e^{-z^2/2} dz$ and thus that $0 < p_i < 1$ (Cameron and Trivedi 2005, pp. 464–5).
13. The coefficients in the complementary log-log model are also probabilities, estimated by $p_i = 1 - \exp(-\exp(\beta_0 + \beta_i x_i))$ (Cameron & Trivedi 2005, p. 466–7).
14. The marginal effect of the probit model is: $\partial p/\partial x_i = \phi(X\beta)\beta_i$ with $\phi(.)$ as the probability density function for the standard normal distribution (Cameron & Trivedi 2005, p. 467).
15. Since indicators 2 and 5 and indicators 7 and 8 are strongly correlated, these indicators measure more or less the same. We combine the indicators to prevent potential multi-collinearity and to require fewer independent variables and therefore have more degrees of freedom. The results when these indicators are used separately are more or less similar, except that 7 and 8 both become significant, one positive (7) and one negative (8). These effects seem to counter each other when combined (as an interaction term). The multiplication of indicators 2 and 5 is the same as just indicator 5. Indicator 1 and 14 are dropped due to insufficient variation (not enough conspicuous cases have this characteristic, respectively 1 and 0).
16. How could this formula be used? If we have a case where a foreigner sells a real estate object to a just-established company, which then sells the object a couple of months later for a significantly higher or lower price, there is a 64% chance that this case is conspicuous. Because it has all three characteristics the calculation is: 15% * 1 + 24% * 1 + 25% * 1 = 64%. Now let us consider a case where a just-established company buys real estate from a foreigner for a normal price: then the chance that this real estate is conspicuous is 39%. Because it has two of the above characteristics, the calculation is: 15% * 1 + 24% * 1 + 25% * 0 = 39%.

REFERENCES

Belastingdienst/FIOD-ECD (2008), *Witwassen en Vastgoed. Over Methoden om Criminele Gelden Wit Te Wassen Via Vastgoed (Money Laundering and Real Estate. On Methods to Launder Criminal Money Using Real Estate)*, Coördinatiepunt Witwassen.

Bunt, H. van de, T. van Koningsveld, M. Kroeze, B. van der Vorm, J. Wezeman, C. van Wingerde and A. Zonneberg (2007), *Misbruik van Buitenlandse Rechtspersonen. Een Verkennend Onderzoek Naar de Aard, Omvang en Ernst van Misbruik van Buitenlandse Rechtspersonen in Nederland (Abuse of Foreign Legal Entities. An Exploratory Investigation into the Nature, Extent and Gravity of Abuse of Foreign Legal Entities)*, Rotterdam: Erasmus Universiteit Rotterdam.

Cameron, A.C. and P.K. Trivendi (2005), *Micro-econometrics, Methods and Applications*, Cambridge: Cambridge University Press.

Eichholtz, P. (2006), 'Een AFM voor de vastgoedmarkt (A Supervising Authority for the real estate sector)', *Justitiële Verkenningen*, **32**(2), 67–75.

Ferwerda, H., R. Staring, E. de Vries Robbé and J. van de Bunt (2007), *Malafide Activiteiten in de Vastgoedsector (Mala Fide Activities within the Real Estate Sector)*, Amsterdam: B.V. Uitgeverij SWP.

Financial Action Task Force/Groupe d'action Financière (FATF/GAFI) (2006), *The Misuse of Corporate Vehicles, Including Trust and Company Service Providers*, Financial Action Task Force/Groupe d'action Financière.

Financial Action Task Force/Groupe d'action Financière (FATF/GAFI) (2007), *Money Laundering and Terrorist Financing through the Real Estate Sector*, Financial Action Task Force/Groupe d'action Financière.

Financieel Expertise Centrum (FEC) (2008), *Reportage Project Vastgoed (Report Project Real Estate)*, Amsterdam: Financieel Expertise Centrum.

Gestel, B. van, R.F. Kouwenberg, M.A. Verhoeven and M.W. Verkuylen (2008), *Vastgoed & Fout. Een Analyse van Twaalf Strafrechtelijke Opsporingsonderzoeken Naar Illegale en Criminele Praktijken in de Woningsector (Real Estate Right and Wrong. An Analysis of Twelve Criminal Investigations into Illegal and Criminal Practices in the Housing Sector)*, Meppel: Boom Juridische Uitgevers.

Hawkins, D.M. (1980), *Identifications of Outliers*, Monograph on Applied Probability and Statistics, Reading and London: Chapman and Hall.

Kleemans, E.R., M.E.I. Brienen, H.G. van de Bunt, R.F. Kouwenberg, G. Paulides and J. Barensen (2002), *Organized Crime in the Netherlands*, The Hague: BJu/WODC.

Meloen, J., R. Landman, H. de Miranda, J. van Eekelen and S. van Soest (2003), *Buit en Besteding: Een Empirisch Onderzoek Naar de Omvang, de Kenmerken en de Besteding van Misdaadgeld*, Den Haag: Reed Business Information.

Nelen, H. (2008), 'Real estate and serious forms of crime', *International Journal of Social Economics*, **35**(10), 751–61.

Nelen H. and W. Huisman (2008), 'Breaking the power of organized crime? The administrative approach to organized crime in Amsterdam', in D. Siegel and H. Nelen (eds), *Organized Crime: Culture, Markets and Policies*, New York: Springer, 207–18.

Nelen, H., B. ter Luun and A. de Bruin (2007), *De Omgeving van de Rijksgebouwendienst; Integriteitsrisico's Bij de Koop en Huur van Vastgoed (The Environment of the Government Buildings Agency; Integrity Risks When Buying and Renting Real Estate)*, Maastricht University and Vrije Universiteit Amsterdam.

OECD (2006), *Report on Tax Fraud and Money Laundering Vulnerabilities Involving the Real Estate Sector*, Centre for Tax Policy and Administration, Paris: OECD.

Parlementaire Enquêtecommissie Opsporingsmethoden (Parliamentary Inquiry Committee on Investigation Methods) (PEO) (1995), *Inzake Opsporing (On Investigating)*, Den Haag, Sdu, http://www.burojansen.nl/traa/

Siegman, A. (2006), Cadastre prices of real Estate objects in the city of Amsterdam', unpublished graph, University of Amsterdam, UvA.

Trouw, J. and B. Knobbout (2007), *Witwassen in de Vastgoedmarkt (Money Laundering in the Real Estate Sector)*, thesis written at the Utrecht School of Economics.

Unger, B. (2007), *The Scale and Impacts of Money Laundering*, Cheltenham, UK and Northampton, MA, USA: Edward Elgar Publishing.

Unger B. and J. Ferwerda (2011), *Money Laundering in the Real Estate Sector, Suspicious Properties* (with a contribution from H. Nelen and L. Ritzen), Cheltenham, UK and Northampton, MA, USA: Edward Elgar Publishing.

Walker, J. (1999), 'How big is global money laundering?', *Journal of Money Laundering Control*, **3**(1), 25–37.

22. Cash economy, measuring the tax gap from the tax administrative perspective*

Victor van Kommer

22.1 INTRODUCTION

Lately, the US and the FATF have made a large effort to include tax evasion as a predicate crime for money laundering. Tax evasion in Europe is a predicate crime only in some countries, such as Greece, where the anti-money laundering (AML) policy concern is mainly to hunt out corruption and tax evasion, or in the Netherlands, where tax fraud is fought by a specific police-like authority, FIOD. Tax evasion is, however, not a predicate crime for money laundering in other countries, such as in Austria, where hunting drug dealers is the major concern of AML authorities. When it turned out that the German government had offered several million euros to a Liechtenstein bank employee for a list of potential German tax evaders holding an account in Liechtenstein (see the contribution of Prince Michael von and zu Liechtenstein in this volume, Chapter 11), it became quite clear that hunting tax evaders will become more important in the future. In particular, governments in need of financing their public debt will become more eager to hunt tax evaders, as the German government demonstrated.

Whether European Union member states will follow the US strategy with regard to broadening the money laundering definition, and will include tax evasion in the list of predicate crimes, or whether Europe will follow the suggestion of Prince Michael von and zu Liechtenstein, and make tax laws more transparent so that banks can identify tax evaders more easily and tax evaders feel less compelled to bring their money abroad, only time will tell. The goal of this contribution is to help both identifying tax evasion and monitoring tax compliance.

22.2 THE ROLE OF THE TAX ADMINISTRATION

Tax Administrations have a responsibility to report on their performance and achievements related to their organizational objectives. This includes a responsibility to monitor and report on taxpayers' compliance and the impact of the Administration's efforts to improve taxpayer compliance. The need to monitor taxpayers' compliance in any form is obvious: it is a direct consequence of the primary goal of Tax Administrations to improve overall compliance with tax laws. Understanding and monitoring taxpayers' compliance is, however, a complex challenge. Tax Administrations should therefore develop and apply tools and indicators to measure levels and trends in taxpayers' compliance in order to report on the health of the tax system to their stakeholders from a tax compliance viewpoint and show the impact of compliance improvement strategies on the levels of taxpayers' compliance, evaluating the impact of specific strategies on taxpayers' behaviour.

22.2.1 Trends in Public Sector Accountability Reporting

The need for measures of the compliance-related performance outcomes achieved by Tax Administrations is fully in line with the directions of public sector reform being witnessed in many countries, as these selected quotes from an OECD publication by Curristine (2005) show:

> Over the past two decades, enhancing public sector performance has taken on a new urgency in OECD member countries as governments face mounting demands on public expenditure, calls for higher quality services and, in some countries, a public increasingly unwilling to pay higher taxes. (p. 128)
>
> Currently, the strongest trend in performance across OECD member countries is the introduction of performance-oriented budgeting and performance management. Many governments have sought to adopt an approach to both management and budgeting which seeks to shift the emphasis of budgeting, management and accountability away from controlling inputs towards achieving results. – In theory – input controls are relaxed and managers and/or organisations are given flexibility to improve performance. In return they are held accountable for results measured in the form of outputs and/or outcomes. (p. 130)
>
> The design of measures is made difficult by finding measures for specific activities, and by relating what an agency or programme actually contributes towards achieving specific outcomes. Output and outcome measures each present a different set of challenges (OECD, 2002b). Outcomes are technically more difficult to measure; they are complex and involve the interaction of many factors, planned and unplanned. Also, there are problems with time lag issues and in some cases the results are not within the control of the government. Outcomes, however, have a strong appeal for the public and politicians. Most countries appear to have adopted a combination of outputs and outcomes. (p. 146)

Monitoring of taxpayers' compliance behaviour and assessing their compliance level may include measuring or estimating the overall tax gap. The tax gap is the difference between the tax that would have been assessed and paid if all taxable citizens and businesses had registered with the tax authority, had they reported all their activities, transactions, assets and liabilities correctly and had they paid all taxes due, and the tax assessed and paid in practice. Theoretically, measuring changes in the size and nature of the tax gap over time is the most appropriate measure of tax administration effectiveness; however, measuring the tax gap is quite controversial and in practice rarely done by Tax Administrations. The tax gap is frequently associated with the phenomenon of the cash economy, but the overall tax gap is evidently a much wider concept, including uncollected taxes resulting from all possible forms of non-compliance and the collection of surplus taxes not legally due from all forms of *over*compliance.

We have to keep in mind that the tax gap estimation is calculated from the tax administration's perspective and is in several studies seen to be correlated with the size of a country's shadow economy. An existent shadow economy of course has a direct impact on missing tax revenues, and we can summarize different elements of this correlation between the shadow economy and the tax gap.

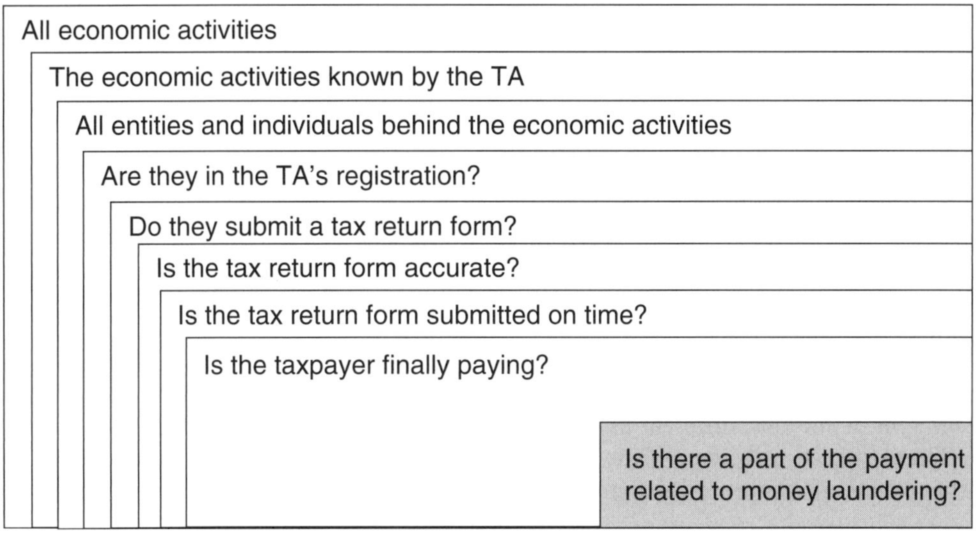

Figure 22.1 Elements important for taxing the economy

The tax administration needs to have an overview of the following elements in taxing the economy, shown in Figure 22.1.

In this image we see the whole playing field of tax administration; what is finally paid is of course always a smaller part than the potential revenues that could have been collected in an ideal world without a shadow economy, tax avoidance and tax evasion. The modern Tax Administration in developed countries is more effective in diminishing the tax gap thanks to the support of sophisticated information systems, exchange of information with third parties and, most importantly, more compliant taxpayers who witness the 'return on their investment' in a society with widely available public services.

In this image, also the collected revenues related to money laundering are mentioned, yet here we see one of the difficulties of many Tax Administrations: their focus is on combating tax evasion, but Tax Administrations can also be *used* by criminal organizations for money laundering. Collected taxes may be wrongly labelled, as in many countries these criminal activities are not subject to taxation, as they are not recognized as normal and legitimate activities in the official economy. The seizure of goods and money by the public prosecution has to be the preferred procedure, and not the channel of the Tax Administration, where only a part of transactions are being monitored, and even a smaller amount will be collected as taxes. Therefore, we can safely state that probably every Tax Administration has once in a while collected too much taxes and thereby delivered a warmly welcomed service to organized crime.

22.3 THE CASH ECONOMY

The cash economy is a significant and complex problem for Tax Administrations in many countries. The cash or underground economy consists of economic activity not accounted for as required by the law. For many years policy-makers, academia and Tax Administrations have been trying to assess the size of the cash economy. Estimates by academics show a consistent upward trend. There are serious doubts, however, whether accurate estimates of the underground economy can be made realistically.

A growing cash economy challenges governance in a number of ways. It reduces tax revenue and requires honest taxpayers to pay more taxes, increases the national deficit (which further increases taxes), reduces the level and quality of public services, and, overall, reduces the legitimacy of the taxation system. In addition, it distorts macroeconomic policy and threatens the social contract between government and its community.

Although many efforts have been made to measure the size of the cash economy, researchers and governments face significant difficulties in undertaking this work. Different definitions, different assumptions and different calculation methods produce different results in the size of the cash economy. It is therefore highly questionable to what extent an accurate measurement of the entire tax gap is realistically attainable.

22.4 DEFINITION OF CASH ECONOMY

There is no commonly agreed or used definition of the underground or cash economy. Terms such as 'underground', 'grey', 'hidden', 'shadow' and 'cash' economy are often used as if representing the same thing; however, their definitions generally include or exclude different activities.

Schneider and Enste (2000) define the cash economy as 'all economic activities that contribute to the officially calculated (or observed) gross national product but are currently unregistered' (p. 78). Schneider (2007) also provided a more detailed description of the shadow economy:

> [A]ll market-based legal production of goods and services that are deliberately concealed from public authorities for the following reasons: i) to avoid payment of income, value added and other taxes; ii) to avoid payment of social security contributions; iii) to avoid having to meet certain legal labour market standards, such as minimum wages, maximum working hours, safety standards, etc.; and iv) to avoid complying with certain administrative procedures such as completing statistical questionnaires or other administrative forms. (p. 5)

Lafleche (1994) uses the definition 'all production, both legal and illegal, that is hidden from income tax'. Restricting the concept to production excludes such activities as theft and extortion, which produce no added value in the economy and may be regarded as transfers.

Bajada (2003) and Tanzi (1983, 1999) provide a narrower definition from a tax evasion perspective. In their view, the underground economy consists of activities which would normally be measured in the national accounts, but because of the failure to report income in whole or in part are neither measured nor taxed. Their definition excludes all forms of criminal activities, such as theft, drug trafficking and prostitution, and also all types of do-it-yourself activities, such as household repairs and maintenance by the homeowner, as well as non-market activities.

Academic researchers use different terminology when indicating the cash economy. However, these different terms often have a different meaning. Examples of the different terminologies used include:

- The *unreported economy*, standing for tax evasion and benefit fraud;
- The *unrecorded economy*, representing hidden income-producing activities that are not included in national income accounts; accounting conventions are violated;
- The *illegal economy*, including corruption, extortion, illegal work (without permission), financial fraud, smuggling, (organized) crime and theft; and
- *The informal economy*, an often used term for activities that are not recognized, regulated or protected by existing legal or regulatory framework, that circumvent government regulation, taxation and observation, and are excluded from the benefits and rights incorporated in the laws and regulations covering property relationships, commercial licensing, labour contracts, financial credit and social security systems.

22.5 MEASURING THE TAX GAP

From a Tax Administrator's perspective, the most practical terminology is the 'overall tax gap'. This is the total amount of tax not collected resulting from all forms of non-compliance for all taxes administered by a Tax Administration or, more precisely, the difference between the theoretical amount of tax to be collected and the actual amount of tax collected, which also includes elements of overcompliance.

Researchers use a number of different methodologies to measure the size of the cash economy. Basically, there are three main methods to estimate the tax gap:

1. *Direct* or *micro-approaches*, such as random auditing methods and survey methods;
2. *Indirect or macro-approaches*, based on national accounts (measuring the discrepancy between legitimate income and expenditure, the relationship between the volume of transactions and the official GNP, assessing the participation rate on the labour market) and (most popular among academics) monetary methods monitoring variations on currency demand;
3. *Model approaches* with multiple indicators.

Theoretically, measuring the tax gap and, in particular, changes in the size and nature of the tax gap over time is the most appropriate measure of tax administration effectiveness. Detailed analyses and understanding of the different elements composing the tax gap are highly instrumental in improving the effectiveness of the operations of the Tax Administration, enabling it to improve the quality of risk assessment and treatment strategies. Only a few Tax Administrations have published estimates of their tax gap or non-compliance level. The methodologies used by these Tax Administrations vary from pure macroeconomic analyses to the uses of random audit techniques, while a few Tax Administrations combine micro- and macro-analyses. Tax Administrations actually measuring the tax gap recognize that their methods are imperfect and that the outcomes are incomplete, but they consider the research findings as useful information helping them to improve overall compliance levels. Many Tax Administrations strongly question the extent to which accurate measurements of the entire tax gap are realistically attainable, given that a substantial amount of income goes unrecorded and remains unreported, and is very difficult to quantify through traditional tax verification processes.

Global integral figures on the size of the tax gap do not really help Tax Administrations to identify the major specific compliance risk areas to be addressed by them. Another factor is that Tax Administrations which undertake research to assess the rate of non-compliance are also quite reluctant to publish their results.

22.6 USE OF RANDOM AUDIT PROGRAMMES

Provided they are conducted properly, random audit programmes can identify important elements of non-compliance. Execution of random audit programmes on a broad scale, however, is very expensive in terms of use of (human) resources. Random audit programmes also place an extra compliance burden on taxpayers, many of whom are compliant taxpayers. Although these programmes can identify important elements of non-compliance, they do not fully measure the entire tax gap accurately. On the other hand, neither will any other tax gap measurement method.

22.6.1 Published Tax Gap Estimates by Tax Administrations

- Sweden has published an overall estimate of its tax gap at around 9 per cent of the theoretical revenue base (consisting of 60% informal sector, 15% international transactions, 15% large companies and 10% others).
- The UK has measured and published its compliance rate for VAT (87%). HMRC has also done research on the income tax gap but has not published the results of its research.
- The US has also published estimates of compliance levels. Most recent estimates suggest an initial compliance rate of 84 per cent (86% after the results of various enforcement efforts are included).

A distinction is made in the US research between the 'gross tax gap' and the 'net tax gap'. The gross tax gap is defined as the difference between the taxes that taxpayers should pay and the taxes they actually pay before IRS enforcement actions are taken. The net tax gap stands for the difference between the taxes that taxpayers should pay and the taxes they actually pay after enforcement actions undertaken by the IRS.

The gross tax gap includes three different components:

1. non-filing (failure to file a return) accounts for 8 per cent of the total gross tax gap;
2. under-reporting (understating income, overstating deductions) represents 82 per cent of the gross tax gap; and
3. underpayment (failure to fully pay reported taxes owed) accounts for the remaining 10 per cent of the gross tax gap.

Swedish research in the form of in-depth analysis of its tax audits indicates that:

- established self-employed business owners compared with employees in the same sector have considerably lower declared income;
- other living standard indicators, including home size and value and car ownership show that entrepreneurs have a standard of living that is proportionate with a considerable higher income than is declared; and
- an estimate of the real income in a business household, compared with that for a wage-earner based on consumption, provides strong indications of under-declaration among business owners.

Monitoring tax compliance in the form of measuring the total tax gap is very complex, likely impossible and apparently very controversial. Methods of taxpayers' monitoring developed and presented by Tax Administrations generally suffer from limited satisfactory empirical evidence about the liability of the applied research methods and thus on the benefits of these methods.

Currently, it seems quite irresponsible to blankly recommend Tax Administrations implement a method of tax compliance monitoring in the form of tax gap measuring. More research is needed to evaluate the applied research methods as well as the results and perceived benefits of such methods.

One of the instruments used to measure non-compliance is the use of random audit programmes. This method clearly has value. However, the frequently expressed perception that the use of extensive random audit programmes would produce the most adequate and comprehensive picture of overall taxpayers' compliance is hardly justified. Without any doubt, random audit programmes (like other instruments) can form a useful tool to detect elements of non-compliance. For this reason, the use of random audit programmes might be justified even where the costs of such programmes are very high and the extra burden put on compliant taxpayers can cause a very serious negative effect on the future compliance behaviour of taxpayers. However, it is probably an illusion to believe that random audit programmes would provide a full compliance picture; at least there is no evidence for that and there is also no evidence either that this method is superior to other methods in detecting compliance risks. Statements about the comparative value of different methods of compliance measurement cannot be made without proper (long-term) comparative evaluation.

For monitoring purposes, the tax gap is usually defined in a simple and schematic way. The overall tax gap is then the total amount of tax not collected resulting from all forms of non-compliance for all taxes administered by a Tax Administration. This definition is understandable and attractive for measurement purposes, but does not fully represent the difference between theoretical and actual tax revenue. It is therefore important when using this definition to be aware that reality is much more complex.

First of all, it is quite obvious that the tax gap is not fully knowable. The total tax potential is not knowable by its very nature for several reasons. Tax liabilities are not absolute and constant but subject to ongoing changes in tax law interpretation and jurisdiction. Moreover, tax laws include large numbers of subjective elements (valuations, depreciations, etc.) with the consequence of a variety of different possible and defensible outcomes. Values and principles of higher rank such as equal treatment of taxpayers may require Tax Administrations to accept an interpretation of the law against their own interpretation. However, the most serious barrier to obtaining full knowledge of the total tax liabilities is of course the impossibility for a Tax Administration or a scientific researcher to detect all relevant facts and to fully assess the meaning of these facts.

Secondly, it should be noted that the total tax gap consists of positive and negative elements. Some taxpayers declare and pay too little and others declare and pay too much, and even within the tax liability of a single taxpayer, positive and negative tax gap elements can exist at the same time. The task of a Tax Administration is not to collect as much tax as possible. It is not that simple. The task of a Tax Administration is to collect the right amount of tax, no more and no less. Tax Administrations should be equally concerned about positive and negative elements of the tax gap. As an example of the negative elements of the tax gap, according to a report by the National Audit Office (NAO 2009), 1.5 million older people in the UK as of March 2009 had overpaid tax as a result of discrepancies between HMRC's records and the tax deducted by employers and pension providers. In addition to that, the NAO (2009) estimates that some 3.2 million older people in the UK do not claim the additional allowances that they could, mainly because they do not realize they are entitled to them.

A careful and balanced approach and presentation on the issue of the nature of the tax gap and its measurement is not only desirable for logical and conceptual reasons, but also for strategic and political reasons. We should be clearly aware that focusing strictly on tax gap measurement/enforcement methods might encourage tax administrations and their political principals – especially in developing countries that face relatively low compliance levels – to go all out for revenue maximization strategies, leaving all nuances aside, including respecting taxpayers' rights, which is quite undesirable in general, and definitely in contradiction with developments such as the call for enhanced relationships with taxpayers.

Another concern about currently used tax gap measurement methods relates to the concept used by Tax Administrations of gross tax gap and net tax gap in relation to the monitoring of the outcomes of the enforcement activities of Tax Administrations. The distinction between compliance programmes or enforcement activities on the one hand and service delivery programmes on the other is highly artificial. Reality is more complex. Ongoing enforcement actions are supposed to have a strong preventive function and include elements of service provision and law interpretation. The value of evaluating the outcome of enforcement activities plainly by measuring the difference between gross and net tax gap seems to be limited and is hardly convincing.

A serious concern related to the methodology, where the net tax gap is compared to the gross tax gap to measure the effectiveness of the enforcement efforts of the Tax Administration, is that this method also strongly stimulates Tax Administrations to put their resources mainly on enforcement activities targeted at those taxpayers who are significantly responsible for the tax gap; in other words, to allocate their resources according to the distribution of the tax gap. These enforcement activities targeted at the most serious non-compliers need very substantial resources, and the effectiveness in terms of overall improvement of taxpayers compliance is likely limited and probably not in proportion with the efforts undertaken.

There are also other methodological concerns. An example of a method of monitoring taxpayers' compliance often used by researchers is a method that compares the data of the Tax Administration with the data of the statistics body. It is important to be aware of the fact that in many countries gross statistics on economic data are collected by the Tax Administration itself and subsequently provided to the statistics body. Comparison of such data will then be meaningless. This phenomenon is likely to become more important where more advanced governments tend to create single portals to receive information from citizens and to reuse this information to reduce the administrative burden for businesses and citizens. But even in countries where data are collected separately by statistics bodies, there should be awareness that there is not always evidence that such data are fully reliable.

As mentioned earlier, most Tax Administrations do not measure or estimate the total tax gap and, if they do, they do not publish the results of their research. A more useful approach, recommended by the OECD, includes the following elements:

- a well-developed compliance risk management processes for identification, assessment and treatment of major compliance risks for each of the major groupings of taxpayers;
- a risk assessment approach which entails an element of estimating the revenue potential of a particular risk (e.g. undeclared business income of self-employed persons and overclaimed employee work-related expenses; and
- once the major risk areas are assessed and prioritized, the development of treatment strategies.

By using this methodology it should also be clear that the ultimate purpose of compliance risk management is not only to select individual cases of taxpayers for enforcement activities to reassess the tax obligations of these taxpayers to reduce the tax gap, but that the purpose of compliance risk management should serve the overall objective of the Tax Administration, that is improving the overall tax compliance of taxpayers.

Tax Administrations should develop instruments and methods enabling them to report more on the outcomes of their compliance activities, rather than reporting about the activities themselves. A key outcome of compliance programmes should be improvement of the behaviour of taxpayers. Compliance monitoring programmes should thus primarily focus on this important factor. Several Tax Administrations are doing this by monitoring trends in norms and values related to tax compliance.

NOTE

* This article is partly based on a section in M. Alink and V. van Kommer (2011), *Handbook on Tax Administration*, Amsterdam: IBFD.

REFERENCES

Bajada, C. (2003), *Australia's Cash Economy: A Troubling Issue for Policymakers*, Aldershot: Ashgate.

Curristine, T. (2005), 'Government performance: lessons and challenges', *OECD Journal on Budgeting*, **5** (1), 127–51.

Lafleche, T. (1994), 'The demand for currency and underground economy', *Bank of Canada Review*.

National Audit Office (NAO) (2009), *National Audit Office Annual Report 2009*, June.
Schneider, F. and D.H. Enste (2000), 'Shadow economies: size, causes, and consequences', *Journal of Economic Literature*, **XXXVIII**, 77–114.
Schneider, F. (2007), 'Shadow economies and corruption all over the world: new estimates for 145 countries', *Economics – The Open-Access, Open-Assessment E-Journal*, Kiel Institute for the World Economy, **1** (9), 1–66.
Schneider, F. and D.H. Enste (2002), *the Shadow Economy: An International Survey*, Cambridge: Cambridge University Press.
Tanzi, V. (1983), 'The underground economy in the United States: Annual estimates, 1930–1980', *IMF papers*, **30**.
Tanzi, V. (1999), 'Uses and abuses of estimates of the underground economy', *The Economic Journal*, **109** (456), Features (June) F338–F347.

23. Is the Netherlands a tax h(e)aven?

Lotte Tromp, Iris van Rossum, Andreas Buehn and Victor van Kommer

Oh, a storm is threat'ning
My very life today
If I don't get some shelter
Oh yeah, I'm gonna fade away
('Gimme Shelter', The Rolling Stones)

23.1 INTRODUCTION

Every now and then newspaper reports naming the Netherlands as a tax haven pop up as brands like Ikea, Prada, Microsoft or The Rolling Stones are all seen to be located in the Netherlands, partly to take advantage of the Dutch fiscal regime. On May 4, 2009, President Obama called the Netherlands a low tax country because one third of US companies' profits from abroad come from just three jurisdictions: Bermuda, Ireland and the Netherlands (The White House 2009). The media later replaced this phrase by the term 'tax haven' (*De Volkskrant* 2009; *NRC Handelsblad* 2009). Afraid of the consequences, this statement resulted in immediate protests by the Dutch government, claiming the Netherlands should not be mentioned together with preferential regimes or even true tax havens. As a result, the entire sentence was retroactively removed from the press release the next day and a few weeks later no one was talking or writing about it anymore.[1]

This, however, seems to be a general taxonomy: as soon as such statements pop up they disappear from the media attention and the political agenda, only to come back as shocking news just a few months later. Indeed, in October 2009 the Dutch TV program *Zembla* had been broadcast on national television under the heading 'Obama was right. The Netherlands is a tax haven', requiring an explanation from the State Secretary of Finance J. K. De Jager (to the members of the parliament). *Zembla* claimed that the Netherlands is a tax haven for both foreign and Dutch multinationals because the Dutch tax treaty network offers advantageous legal opportunities and protection to foreign multinationals, while Dutch multinationals can make use of special fiscal constructions to reduce their effective tax burden. This of course gave rise to a fierce political debate. Eventually, De Jager cleared the air by making a statement that Dutch multinationals are taxed 25.5 per cent of their profits, and foreign headquarters are established in the Netherlands, not because of the low tax burden, but because of the certainty about the amount of taxes to be paid (the so-called rulings). However, he also admitted that there *are* possibilities for tax avoidance and there *is* a tax leakage of several billion dollars, and promised to implement counter-measures (Bakker 2009; Grotenhuis 2009a; Kamerstukken II 2009–2010). This satisfied politicians and the media in the Netherlands for a while.

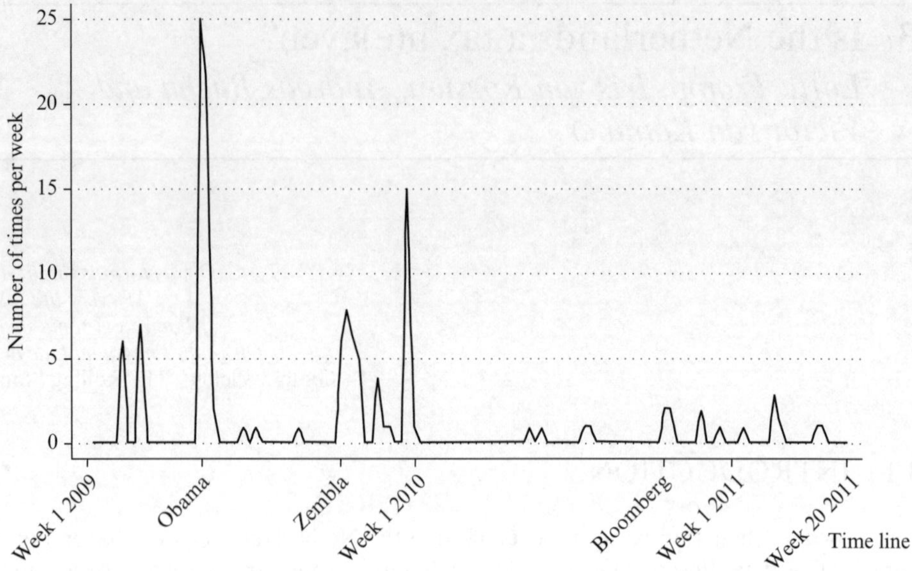

Figure 23.1 Occurrences of 'The Netherlands is a tax haven' in Dutch newspapers (01.01.2009–22.05.2011)

But as it is with mushrooms, so it is with the question of whether the Netherlands is a tax haven: it keeps popping up in Dutch newspapers. Using the national databases LexisNexis and searching for 'Belastingparadijs Nederland' (in English: 'tax haven the Netherlands') across all Dutch newspapers, we counted the number of times this issue had been mentioned in a newspaper report per week between the first week in 2009 and week 20 in 2011. Figure 23.1 shows that the issue of being a tax haven is a recurring topic in the Netherlands.

When newspapers report that the Netherlands is a tax haven, politicians systematically deny it. Sometimes they simply state that the Netherlands cannot be considered a tax haven because it has no bank secrecy. On the other hand, statements like: 'The Netherlands is a tax haven; just look at the thousands of Dutch letterbox companies' is too simplistic. It may be an indication for a jurisdiction being a tax haven, but it is certainly not evidence on its own.

But what exactly is a tax haven and why are the Netherlands sometimes considered to be one? Mostly, tax havens are defined as jurisdictions offering low tax rates and favorable regulatory policies to foreign investors. Often, these are small islands with populations below one million and above-average incomes, which are also known as 'offshore financial centers' or 'international financial centers', phrases that are mostly used interchangeably with 'tax havens' (see e.g. Hines 2010).[2] What is the reason that the Netherlands – a highly developed country in the heart of Europe – is called a tax haven? Can it be that the lack of agreement on a proper definition of a tax haven in the literature blurs evidence brought forward to establish jurisdictions as a tax haven while opening wiggle room for interpretations? For example, a report of the Internal Revenue Service (IRS) in 1981 explicitly defines tax havens in a way that excludes large, rich countries.

The OECD, employs a definition favorable for them and participating rich countries (Sharman 2006).

In order to shed more light on that debate, this chapter reviews the circulating definitions and tax haven lists, since such a summary is truly missing in the literature. Moreover, we aim to develop an easily applicable definition of a tax haven by means of a checkbox. This is a valuable contribution to the literature for a couple of reasons: first, to be able to answer the question whether the Netherlands is a tax haven or not and; second, and similarly important, for empirical research about tax havens in general, because an improper definition may lead to different if not incorrect tax haven lists that potentially produce biased estimates in empirical research. Finally, clearing the air about which jurisdictions are tax havens may also improve the analysis of money laundering. Clearly, whether tax havens can be directly linked to money laundering or not depends on the money laundering definition. When tax evasion is a predicate crime for money laundering, tax havens are very likely to facilitate laundering. At the moment the role of tax evasion for money laundering is still under debate and differs across countries. Some countries are definitely more attractive for avoidance and/or evasion than others. Here we want to focus on corporations and their possibilities to shift both legal and criminal money around the globe. Is it possible to identify tax havens that are more attractive for placing corporate money than other places, or more concretely: is the Netherlands a tax haven?

This chapter is structured as follows. Section 23.2 reviews circulating tax haven definitions from various sources. Section 23.3 presents an overview of the (international) tax policies in the Netherlands for corporations to clarify the main reasons why the Netherlands is sometimes seen as a tax haven. Section 23.4 develops an easily applicable tax haven definition by means of a checkbox and tests the Netherlands according to that definition. Section 23.5 finally summarizes and concludes.

23.2 TAX HAVEN DEFINITIONS

23.2.1 The Academic Literature

In the economic literature there is no standard definition of what a tax haven is, leaving room for some degree of subjectivity in classifying jurisdictions as tax havens (Dharmapala 2008). Not surprisingly, different authors use different definitions of a tax haven and therefore use different lists in their empirical research. However, economists do agree that tax havens are jurisdictions that offer favorable tax[3] regimes to foreign investors. But which other criteria are used depends to a large extent on the author. Thus, according to the economic literature, a tax haven is a place with at least a low tax rate. All authors expand on this definition, mostly by using bank secrecy (e.g. Schwarz 2011a) or favorable regulatory policies to foreign investors (e.g. Hines and Rice 1994; Gordon and Hines 2002; Desai et al. 2006; Dharmapala and Hines 2006; Dharmapala and Hines 2009; Hines 2010) as criteria. The number of jurisdictions seen as tax havens range from 18 to 69, although most lists are based on two sources (or their definition), namely the list in Hines and Rice (1994) and the list of the OECD. According to most of these lists, one can conclude that the Netherlands in general is not considered a tax haven. However, there are some exceptions. Hines and Rice explicitly exclude the Netherlands from their tax haven list in 1994, but then in a later paper put it back on the list when checking for robustness, revealing the uncertain tax haven status of the Netherlands (Dharmapala and Hines 2009). Also, Palan (2002), Sullivan (2004) and Shaxson (2011) count the Netherlands as a tax haven.

Before discussing the law literature it is important to emphasize that the Dutch law does not have a legal definition of a tax haven and, as in the economic literature, there is no clear cut definition used in the law literature either (Evers et al. 2011). Evers, de Graaf and Stevens (2011) present the most detailed overview of the criteria used for defining a tax haven from a law perspective. They base their definition on definitions given by the Dutch government and several institutions, including the OECD and the EU. They conclude that common features are: '(1) (consciously or not) gives residence to entities who by that avoid tax, (2) has no or almost no taxation, (3) hosts corporations with a lack of substance in the jurisdiction, and (4) has a lack of transparency or willingness to exchange information' (translation by authors, Evers et al. 2011, p. 65). According to Evers et al. (2011) the Netherlands has the appearance of a tax haven, as it has several beneficial tax regimes and is home to a great many US corporations. From the academic law literature it appears that several authors use different tax haven definitions and no consensus exists on whether the Netherlands can be qualified as a tax haven or not.

23.2.2 International Organizations

23.2.2.1 OECD

Beside the academic literature about tax havens many reports concerning tax havens or harmful tax practices by different institutions have been published, of which the OECD report is the most cited and evaluated report. The OECD uses four key factors to identify tax havens: '(i) no or only nominal tax rates, (ii) lack of effective exchange of information (i.e. very strict secrecy laws), (iii) lack of transparency and (iv) no substantial activities requirement' (OECD 1998, p. 23). The first key factor is the starting point, since this factor is seen as a necessary condition to be fulfilled. According to the OECD, it can even be a sufficient condition. The second and third key factors are seen as particularly harmful characteristics of tax havens and preferential tax regimes since they facilitate money laundering and tax evasion. The last key factor is included because this factor in particular shows the motivation of a jurisdiction to attract mobile activities solely for tax reasons (OECD 1998). In 2001, the OECD revised these criteria, dropping the substantial activities requirement criterion as their focus shifted from tax avoidance and evasion to tax evasion only. Based on these revised criteria, the Forum on Harmful Tax Practices pointed out 41 cooperative jurisdictions or uncooperative tax havens, not including any OECD member state.

Besides identifying tax havens, the OECD took a look at her own member states' tax practices as well.[4] The starting point for identifying harmful preferential tax regimes is the criterion of no or low *effective* tax rates. Taken together with at least one of the three other criteria a regime is considered to be harmful: the 'ring fencing' of regimes (i.e. meaning that some tax regimes are only available to foreign corporations), lack of transparency, and a lack of effective exchange of information. In their 2000 report the Forum identified 47 potentially harmful tax regimes (i.e. preferential regimes). While some jurisdictions had two or three, the Netherlands, with seven preferential regimes, had by far the most preferential regimes (followed by Belgium (5) and Greece (4)). Among the seven Dutch preferential regimes were three rulings. These practices will be explained in more detail in section 23.3, where the Dutch tax practices are examined. It is rather difficult to see how this coincides with the Dutch explanation of rulings (i.e. given certainty beforehand about how to interpret the tax rules). Apparently more is going on than just giving certainty.

23.2.2.2 European Union

Another major international institution frequently raising concerns about tax havens and harmful tax practices is the European Union (EU), although the EU does not have an official definition of a tax haven. The EU has a different approach from the OECD to combatting harmful tax practices. While the OECD focuses more on tax evasion (i.e. the tax haven criteria: transparency and exchange of information) and on non-member practices, the EU instead focuses more on tax competition in and between member states, in line with tax avoidance (i.e. on harmful tax practices affecting business locations) (Code of Conduct Group 1999; ECOFIN 1997; OECD 1998).

According to the EU the basis criterion for harmful tax practices is the following: '. . . tax measures which provide for a significantly lower effective level of taxation, including zero taxation, than those levels which generally apply in the Member state in question are to be regarded as potentially harmful . . .' (ECOFIN 1997, p. 3).

In addition to this, other criteria for measuring harmful tax practices are:

> When assessing whether such measures are harmful, account should be taken of, *inter alia*:
> 1. whether advantages are accorded only to non-residents or in respect of transactions carried out with non-residents, or
> 2. whether advantages are ring-fenced from the domestic market, so they do not affect the national tax base, or
> 3. whether advantages are granted even without any real economic activity and substantial economic presence within the Member State offering such tax advantages, or
> 4. whether the rules for profit determination in respect of activities within a multinational group of companies departs from internationally accepted principles, notably the rules agreed upon with the OECD, or
> 5. whether the tax measures lack transparency, including where legal provisions are relaxed at administrative level in a non-transparent way. (ECOFIN, 1997, p. 3)

The Primarolo Report tested these criteria and found 66 tax measures with harmful features, of which 10 come from the Netherlands. Five out of the ten measures were rulings (ECOFIN 1997; Code of Conduct Group 1999).

From the criteria used by the EU to identify harmful tax practices an important difference with the OECD becomes clear. While the OECD considers the absolute effective level of taxation, the EU considers this level *with regard to* the general level of taxation in the particular member state (i.e. taking the level of taxation that generally applies in the member state as a benchmark). This means that if a jurisdiction has for example an overall tax rate of 8 percent, a tax rate of 7 percent is not considered to be harmful by the EU, but can be seen as harmful by the OECD if considered a low level.

23.2.2.3 The Dutch government

The first questions as to whether the Netherlands is a tax haven were asked in 1979 in a meeting about the avoidance and evasion of taxes. Over the next 22 years the Dutch government mentioned four different characteristics of a tax haven: '(1) a jurisdiction must strive to be a tax haven; (2) a jurisdiction must treat national and foreign corporations unequally; (3) a tax haven has no or relatively low taxes; and (4) a tax haven lacks transparency' (Aanhangsel van de Handelingen 2006–2007; Aanhangsel van de Handelingen 2010-2011; Kamerstukken II 1979–1980; Kamerstukken II 1980–1981). According to its government, the Netherlands has none of these four characteristics.

23.2.2.4 Other institutions

The Tax Justice Network (TJN), a non-governmental organization, is heavily involved in identifying and fighting tax havens (Shaxson 2011). The TJN has a clear-cut definition for a tax haven. According to this definition a tax haven has four aspects (quoted in Murphy n.d., p. 7):

1. Non-residents undertaking activities in the tax haven pay no or little tax.
2. It has no effective exchange of taxation information with other countries.
3. Its activities and those of the organizations based there lack transparency.
4. It seeks to attract investment which requires no substantial commercial activity to take place.

Using this definition the TJN highlights a total of 72 tax havens, including the Netherlands. According to the Dutch representative of the TJN, Albert Hollander, some multinationals pay far less than the Dutch standard 25.5 percent on taxes. This is (seen as) unacceptable when a corporation does not perform substantial commercial activity.

The Stichting Onderzoek Multinationale Ondernemingen (SOMO, in English: 'Centre for Research on Multinational Corporations') is a Dutch non-profit research center that investigates the consequences of multinational corporations' policies. The SOMO tax haven definition is based on both the OECD and the EU and defines a tax haven as 'any country or territory whose laws may be used to avoid or evade taxes which may be due in another country under that other country's laws' (Weyzig and Van Dijk 2007, p. 7). But SOMO does something striking; it divides tax havens into two categories. The first category includes the so-called 'pure' tax havens:

> 'Pure' tax havens correspond with the standard image of the offshore island with palm lined beaches and numerous 'brass plate' companies whose whole existence is of little greater substance than the contents of a filing cabinet drawer. The main source of income of such places is in the assistance of tax avoidance or evasion by operating under a veil of secrecy. Consequently, any standard form of income or corporate taxation is absent. Such havens exist. Examples are the Bahamas, Cayman Islands and Bermuda . . .
>
> The second group of tax havens consists of countries with a diversified economy and industrial base which have a normal tax system but with certain, often very lucrative, exceptions for certain activities or types of corporation. In addition, such countries are commonly characterized by the presence of specialized lawyers and accountants who assist companies with their tax planning and a large number of tax treaties which make it possible to minimize taxation. (Van Dijk et al. 2006, p. 13)

In their 2006 report, SOMO includes a tax haven list, however the list does not distinguish between the two different tax haven categories. The list is based on the TJN list and a tax haven list of the Offshore Business Magazine and includes 72 jurisdictions (Van Dijk et al., 2006). According to SOMO, the Netherlands is a tax haven of the second category, because the Netherlands has a diversified economic and industrial base as well as lucrative tax arrangements which cause corporations to establish in the Netherlands for merely tax reasons.

The United States' Governmental Accountability Office (GAO) describes tax havens as jurisdictions with low taxes[5] and a general lack of transparency. After a review of a variety of governmental, international and academic sources the GAO came up with a combined tax haven list, not including the Netherlands (U.S. GAO, 2008).

Beside the GAO, other US institutions investigate tax havens too. The Congressional Research Service (CRS) does not develop its own definition of tax havens, but has its own tax haven list. The list is however, except for Tonga, exactly the same as the GAO list. In addition the CRS notices some other jurisdictions which are often overlooked as tax havens. One in particular is mentioned: the Netherlands. The Netherlands is considered a tax haven because of the various possibilities for reducing taxes, due to the existence of the Dutch-wide treaty network and the allowance for reducing taxes on dividends and capital gains from subsidiaries, and this is illustrated by the famous examples of Bono and U2 (Gravelle 2010). Finally, the Internal Revenue Service (IRS) defines tax havens as jurisdictions offering financial secrecy laws and imposing little or no tax on foreign income sources. According to the IRS at least forty jurisdictions actively promote themselves as tax havens, although the IRS does not specify which (IRS website 2011).

The International Monetary Fund (IMF) does not give a definition of tax havens, but of Offshore Financial Centers (OFCs). The definition of an offshore financial center is the following:

> (i) Jurisdictions that have financial institutions engaged primarily in business with non-residents;
> (ii) Financial systems with external assets and liabilities out of proportion to domestic financial intermediation designed to finance domestic economies;
> (iii) and centers which provide some or all of the following services: low or zero taxation; moderate or light financial regulation; banking secrecy and anonymity. (IMF 2000, n.p.)

Initially the IMF identified 42 jurisdictions as OFCs, but later they stopped maintaining this list due to the fact that no objective criteria for defining OFCs existed and because the globalization process blurs the distinction between OFCs and other financially active jurisdictions (Government Commission on Capital Flight from Poor Countries 2009; IMF 2006; IMF website 2011).

Finally, the government of Norway takes the view 'that the combination of secrecy and virtually zero tax terms characterize such jurisdictions' (Government Commission on Capital Flight from Poor Countries 2009, p. 15). The report uses two lists in their analysis, based on a narrow and a broader definition. Although the report recognizes the fact that the Netherlands falls outside a number of tax haven definitions, the Netherlands is included in the broad definition: 'The Netherlands is probably the largest and most popular pass-through state in the world today' (Government Commission on Capital Flight from Poor Countries 2009, p. 17).

23.2.2.5 Summary of the results from literature review

If something has become clear from the literature overview, it is the following:

- There is no agreed upon definition of a tax haven.
- There is no agreed upon tax-haven list.
- It is far from clear whether the Netherlands is a tax haven or not.

For certain, one similarity in the tax haven definition is the appearance of the *tax rate criterion*, present in all sources. Although different sources use different words to explain this criterion, the intention is always the same: describing a tax rate system that gives rise to tax rates that are significantly lower than a certain amount (absolute evaluation) or significantly lower than in other jurisdictions (relative evaluation).[6] Beside the tax rate criterion, two additional criteria are often used, namely the criteria about *transparency* and *information exchange*. Transparency means that governmental authorities have set clear rules and have access to all relevant bank or other financial or ownership information to control these rules. Effective information exchange means the availability of such information for other jurisdictions if they need this information for civil or criminal tax matters. Again, different words are used, ranging from simply 'a lack of effective exchange of (taxation) information and a lack of transparency' to a more specific choices of words, like 'offering low regulation standards', '(strict) bank secrecy (laws)' 'legislation that supports banking and business secrecy', 'an inappropriately high level of client confidentiality based on impenetrable secrecy laws' or 'banking secrecy and anonymity'. Some definitions in the academic literature, the OECD, the EU (although only for harmful tax practices), the Dutch government, the TJN definition, the GAO, the IRS, the IMF and the government of Norway use one or both criteria. Thus, before a jurisdiction is considered a tax haven it has to satisfy (besides the tax rate criterion) the information exchange and/or transparency criterion.

An additional criterion commonly used is the *different treatment* of domestic and foreign corporations in favor of the latter. This is also described as 'favorable regulatory policies to foreign investors', 'promoting tax evasion to attract and increase foreign capital' or as ' treating national and foreign corporations not equal'. A second additional criterion is the *no substance criterion*. Being a tax haven or having a harmful tax practices depends in some definitions on this criterion. It appears in one academic economic article, one academic law article, in the TJN and in the OECD definition. In the economic literature only Addison (2009) uses this criterion in his definition ('jurisdictions that do not seek to attract real investment'). Evers et al. (2011) talk about 'a lack of substance'. The 1998 OECD report talks about 'no substantial activities requirement' (although in practice the OECD dropped this criterion in 2001 because of the difficulty of proving it[7]).The TJN talks about 'attracting investment which requires no substantial commercial activity to take place'.

A third additional criterion sometimes used is that a jurisdiction is a tax haven when *several other sources* establish the jurisdiction as a tax haven. Hence, this is a kind of a reputation test. The different sources using this criterion are: some economists (e.g. Hines and Rice (1994): 'identification as a tax haven by multiple authoritative sources') and the 1987 OECD report ('when the country was recognized as a tax haven in general'). Beside the fact that such a criterion is very controversial due to the subjectivity involved (Who are the others? How many times should the jurisdiction be listed as a tax haven before it is mentioned by several others?), it can act as a kind of 'virus'. If one author uses a certain jurisdiction in a tax haven list and someone else then replicates this list, the third person then notices it has been used by several others and is therefore counting the jurisdiction as a tax haven too. Instead of investigating the characteristics of the jurisdiction itself, one judgment can spread like a 'virus' to others.

An additional criterion which sometimes appears is about *the motivation* of a jurisdiction to become a tax haven. Remember the defense strategy against the tax haven establishment of the Netherlands by the Dutch government: 'we are not a tax haven, because we do not strive to be one'. However, this criterion is even more subject to subjectivity than the identification by several other sources criterion. After all, how is one going to find out about the intrinsic motivation of a jurisdiction? Sometimes even *other additional criteria* in definitions emerge. The IMF, for instance, uses the criterion of 'moderate or light financial regulation'. Also the academic economic literature sometimes uses additional criteria and describes tax havens by their characteristics. For example the fact that most tax havens are small islands is often mentioned. Table 23.1 summarizes the criteria used and a check indicates that the respective criterion is used in the 'official' definition of that source.

The EU and the CRS are excluded from Table 23.1 since they do not have an official tax haven definition. Regarding SOMO only the criteria in their 'pure' tax haven definition are shown, since the description used for defining jurisdictions under the second category cannot be specified into different criteria. From Table 23.1 it becomes clear that there are a lot of criteria besides the tax rate criterion, resulting in a wide variety of jurisdictions listed as tax havens. After investigating and looking to the different tax

Table 23.1 Quick overview of all the criteria used

Criterion	OECD > 1998	Dutch government	TJN	SOMO 'pure'	GAO	IRS	IMF	Government of Norway
Absolute tax rate	X[a]		X					
Relative tax rate		X						
Nominal tax rate	X[a]			X	X	X	X	X
Effective tax rate[c]		X	X					
Lack of exchange of information	X		X	X		X	X	X
Lack of transparency	X	X	X	X	X	X	X	X
Different treatment		X	X[b]			X		
No substance criteria	X[a]		X					
Motivation/ self-promotion		X						
Flexible regulations							X	

Notes:
a. The OECD dropped these criteria in 2001.
b. This criterion can be implicitly seen in the tax rate criterion.
c. If a source does not explicitly mention the word effective in their tax rate criterion it is assumed it uses a nominal tax rate criterion.

haven lists, it is clear that the Netherlands is certainly not the only borderline case. While some sources will classify the Netherlands as a tax haven under a more narrow definition (e.g. SOMO, the government of Norway), we conclude (on the basis of the investigated sources) that the Netherlands is not a tax haven in the 'traditional' sense since it does not have a lack of effective exchange of information and transparency. The next section discusses the tax policies in the Netherlands.

23.3 TAX POLICIES FOR CORPORATIONS IN THE NETHERLANDS

In this section, the Dutch tax system will be explained in more detail. The topics that are discussed in this chapter are often evoked as the main reasons the Netherlands is used for tax avoidance (Evers et al. 2011).

Wet Vpb 1969 The Wet op de Vennootschapsbelasting 1969 (in English: 'The corporate income tax act 1969', from now on: Wet Vpb 1969) requires corporations to pay a tax on (a part of) their profits. Currently, the nominal corporate tax rate in the Netherlands is 20 percent on the first 200,000 euros profit and 25.5 percent on the remaining profits above 200,000 euros (art. 22 Wet Vpb 1969).

Participation exemption rules The Wet Vpb 1969 makes a distinction between domestic and foreign corporations. Domestic corporations are basically taxed on all their profits, regardless of the place where the profits come from. Foreign corporations only have to pay tax on the profits they have achieved in the Netherlands (Chapter II, Wet Vpb 1969; Van de Streek 2010). This distinction was seen as a disadvantage for domestic international operating corporations. These corporations create profits abroad and are being taxed on those profits in the foreign jurisdiction. However, they are officially Dutch corporations and are therefore being taxed on all their profits in the Netherlands, including the profits obtained abroad on which they have already paid taxes. Those profits are then being taxed twice. The Netherlands confirmed the participation exemption (in Dutch 'deelnemingsvrijstelling') rules (updated in 1969 and now known as Article 13 Wet Vpb 1969)[8] and concluded tax treaties with several jurisdictions to eliminate this problem (Van den Berg et al. 2008). Besides, the costs of having the foreign subsidiary are deductible from taxable profit. The discovery and use of advantages due to these policies has almost become a separate profession: tax planning. It must be emphasized that tax planning most of the time deals with tax avoidance, which is not illegal. Tax evasion is illegal. However, one has to keep in mind that what is legal is not necessarily right (Van de Streek, 2010).

Ruling practice In the Netherlands every taxpayer, both an individual and a corporation, has the right to obtain information about their possible future tax situation from the Tax Administration. This certainty in advance about taxes is called 'ruling'. Certainty about the possible future tax situation can be favorable to internationally operating corporations in determining the costs of doing business in a jurisdiction. In providing this information one could argue that the Dutch tax authorities were actively participating in determining the most favorable business structure and therefore actively participating in the avoidance of taxes.

Tax treaties From April 1, 2011 onwards, the Netherlands had Double Tax Agreements with 90 jurisdictions (Ministerie van Financiën 2011). Historically these treaties were set up to exchange information between two jurisdictions, but nowadays are used to avoid double taxation (Van Weeghel 1997). Not only does the Netherlands have a large network of treaties, they are mostly relatively favorable towards the taxation of dividends, interest and royalties (Evers et al. 2011). The treaties not only create advantages for Dutch corporations, foreign international corporations have an opportunity to use them too as the following example demonstrates. If a company pays interests directly to the investor, it may face a tax liability of 10 percent, given the tax treaty between the two countries. Using a holding in a third state however, the tax liability can be reduced to zero percent, due to the tax treaties between the third state and both countries. (Evers et al. 2011, p. 65). Corporations can thus avoid the treaties and corresponding rules of their home country with other jurisdictions by making use of the treaty between their home country and the Netherlands and the treaty network of the Netherlands.

Withholding taxes on dividends, interest and royalties The Dutch withholding taxes on dividends, interest and royalties system, sometimes in combination with tax treaties, could also be favorable for multinational corporations. On dividends paid by Dutch resident corporations to Dutch shareholders, one has to pay a dividend withholding tax of 15 percent.[9] However, if the dividend falls under the participation exemption rules the dividend is exempted of this dividend withholding tax. The withholding taxes on interest and royalties are even easier to understand; on both one has to pay no taxes.[10]

Combination of arrangements Even though the previous subsections have explained and treated the different Dutch arrangements on different taxes as separate arrangements, in practice these arrangements might overlap or be used in combination with others. Every tax avoider is a special case and needs a particular kind of tax haven or combination of arrangements.

23.4 IS THE NETHERLANDS A TAX HAVEN?

The list of criteria listed in Table 23.1 suggests that three criteria may be considered in a sound tax haven definition.[11] One criterion that must be definitely considered is the tax rate criterion, since it is the most often mentioned and important one. In the end the main reason why corporations use tax havens is to lower their tax burden and the main reason why most jurisdictions are against tax havens is because they erode their tax base. The lack of transparency criterion should be included in a potential tax haven definition because not satisfying this criterion will probably result in corrupt and/or discriminatory behavior.[12] Jurisdictions should be clear about corporate rules and tax conditions, such that every corporation is treated fairly according to these rules and regulations and tax authorities can be supervised. Without clear rules and regulations room will be given for individual negotiations with (tax) authorities, leading to an unequal treatment in similar situations, which may stimulate discriminatory behavior and create incentives for corruption. A lack of transparency will probably lead to a lower effective tax rate for corporations in a jurisdiction, which facilitates tax evasion and avoidance. The lack of exchange of information criterion should be included as well because not participating in the exchange of tax information can result in avoidance of taxes. A jurisdiction with no exchange of information can be beneficial for a corporation because the investor's home jurisdiction cannot calculate the appropriate tax base (in the case of a worldwide tax system) or taxes to be paid (in the case of a territorial system) by this corporation. One can argue that this process leads to lower effective tax rates; however, this only applies if the source jurisdiction has a lower nominal tax rate than the residence jurisdiction. In addition, not fulfilling the exchange of information criterion can also lead to tax evasion, which cannot necessarily be seen in a lower effective tax rate.[13]

23.4.1 Three Tax Haven Categories

Having identified three useful criteria, it is time to distinguish several categories of tax havens. In the end, being established as a tax haven does not mean that all jurisdictions are to the same extent usable for tax avoidance and/or evasion.

Three different categories of tax havens will be introduced, which allow us to make a distinction between tax havens for normal tax avoidance, and tax havens for tax evasion and tax avoidance that requires secrecy. Corporations seeking tax avoidance will establish themselves in a jurisdiction that gives them the lowest effective tax rate, irrespective of the other characteristics of that jurisdiction. Corporations seeking tax evasion will establish themselves in a jurisdiction that has a low standard of exchange of information and/or transparency. However, between tax avoidance (legal) and tax evasion (illegal) lies a whole grey area; multinationals operating in this area often require court cases to establish on which side their behavior/the shelter lies (Shaxson 2011). It is assumed that tax practices, like transfer (mis)pricing, in this area are intended to be legal but require secrecy due to their controversy. Hence the term 'tax avoidance that requires secrecy'. Corporations seeking tax avoidance requiring secrecy are treated in our definition as equal to corporations seeking tax evasion.[14] Testing whether a jurisdiction is a tax haven for tax avoidance that requires secrecy and (or) for tax evasion depends in essence on the criteria of information exchange and transparency. These distinctions give rise to the structure shown in Figure 23.2.

23.4.1.1 Low tax category: tax havens for 'normal' tax avoidance

The tax haven definition for 'normal' tax avoidance includes the tax rate criterion only as argued above. Hence, the name: low tax category. As the nominal tax rate is not a good indicator of what corporations in the end effectively pay in taxes, the effective tax rate is a natural choice. In particular, the taxes to be paid depend on two features: the nominal tax rate and the tax base. Therefore, a high (or low) tax rate does not necessarily imply high taxes, since taxes to be paid depend on the tax base too, which can lead to significantly different tax payments than the nominal tax rate suggests. As Clausing (2003) points out, the effective tax rate quite often differs from the nominal rate.[15] In addition,

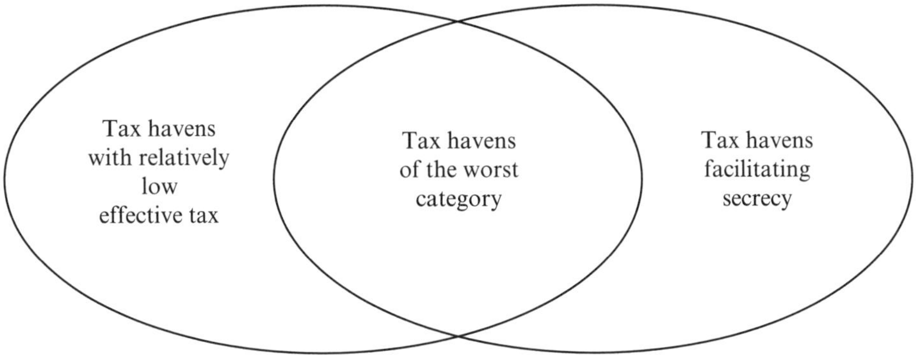

Figure 23.2 Two co-existing tax haven lists

a choice has to be made between using an absolute or a relative tax rate. We opt for the latter, since in this way value judgments about the desired level of taxes are avoided. Moreover, it also takes into account the fact that a jurisdiction with a high absolute rate but relatively low effective tax rate is attractive for tax avoidance. This suggests that jurisdictions are attractive for tax avoidance that offer a *relatively lower* effective tax rate compared to other jurisdictions. As a result, the test is the following: 'A jurisdiction is a tax haven for "normal" tax avoidance for corporations if the jurisdiction has a relatively low effective tax rate.'

23.4.1.2 Secrecy category: tax havens for tax avoidance requiring secrecy and tax evasion

The paragraphs above already explained why the lack of effective exchange of information and transparency facilitates tax avoidance requiring secrecy and/or tax evasion. Thus: 'A jurisdiction is a tax haven for tax avoidance requiring secrecy and tax evasion for corporations if it facilitates secrecy through not effectively exchanging information or by having a lack of transparency.'

Testing transparency or the lack thereof requires knowledge about how laws and rules are applied in practice. Bank secrecy is one of the possible indicators to test the level of transparency. Having bank secrecy, for example, will be seen as having a lack of transparency. Other indicators are, for example, the access of authorities to bank information for information exchange purposes and the existence of an up-to-date public trust and foundations registry, accessible to authorities and the public for a reasonable price (TJN 2009b).

Whether jurisdictions exchange information with other jurisdictions depends to a great extent on the agreements regarding tax information exchange matters, usually called Tax Information Exchange Agreements[16] between jurisdictions. For example, France has 120 of such agreements and will therefore establish all of these 120 jurisdictions as 'an exchange of information jurisdiction'. Argentina has 21 of such agreements and will therefore establish only 21 jurisdictions as an 'exchange of information jurisdiction' (OECD 2009). Hence, the level of exchange of information for the same jurisdiction can be different from the perspective of other jurisdictions. Since a jurisdiction falls into the secrecy category if it has either a lack of transparency *or* has a lack of exchange of information, this means that if there are jurisdictions which are transparent but not exchanging information with some other jurisdictions, these jurisdictions are only tax havens for the jurisdictions which do not get the relevant tax information. Hence, every jurisdiction maintains its own tax haven list. We therefore propose another approach.

For identifying non-exchanging information jurisdictions we use an approach similar to the OECD and TJN. The OECD and the TJN, for their Financial Secrecy Index, both set a minimum level of agreements regarding tax information exchange matters in advance and then test which jurisdictions falls below that boundary. The OECD uses a minimum threshold of 12 of such agreements, which leads to 53 out of 86 jurisdictions having a status of 'effectively exchanging information' (OECD 2009; TJN 2009a). The more agreements a jurisdiction has, the bigger the chance the jurisdiction does not only have meaningless agreements.[17] To tackle the problem of meaningless agreements, which may be a problem with the low OECD boundary according to TJN, TJN has set its boundary quite high at 60 agreements. This boundary was chosen since it is the mean of agreements in the G20. TJN tested this boundary for those jurisdictions considered to be secrecy jurisdictions, 60 in total. Out of these 60 jurisdictions only five jurisdictions (the Netherlands, Belgium, the United Kingdom, the Virgin Islands and the United States) do not have a lack of information exchange. This is quite harsh. Looking at all jurisdictions the OECD included in its report, 26 (out of the 86) jurisdictions satisfy the TJN exchange of information criterion (OECD 2009; TJN 2009a). Both boundaries, the one set by the OECD and the one set by TJN seem to be either too low or too high given the actual allocation of the amount of agreements per jurisdiction as shown in Figure 23.3.

Based on Figure 23.3 we opt for a boundary of 34 of such agreements, since this is the 2009 median. This is to some extent a flexible boundary, since the median will differ per year.[18] Thus, the criteria of having a lack of exchange of information means that a jurisdiction has less than 34 tax information exchange agreements.[19]

23.4.1.3 Worst order category: tax havens for 'normal' tax avoidance and tax avoidance requiring secrecy and tax evasion

A tax haven falls under this category if it passes the following test: 'A jurisdiction is called a tax haven for corporations if it has a relatively low effective tax rate and facilitates secrecy through not effectively exchanging information or by having a lack of transparency.'

The three categories and their corresponding criteria can be summarized in Table 23.2.[20] A jurisdiction will qualify as a tax haven if it falls into one of the three categories of tax havens as specified in Table 23.2, that is, if it satisfies one of the specified tests. A jurisdiction is thus a tax haven falling into the low tax category if it has a relatively low effective tax rate; a jurisdiction is a tax haven falling into the secrecy category if it has a lack of exchange of information and/or a lack of transparency; and a jurisdiction is a tax haven of the worst order if it has a relatively low effective tax rate and facilitates secrecy through not effectively exchanging information or by having a lack of transparency.

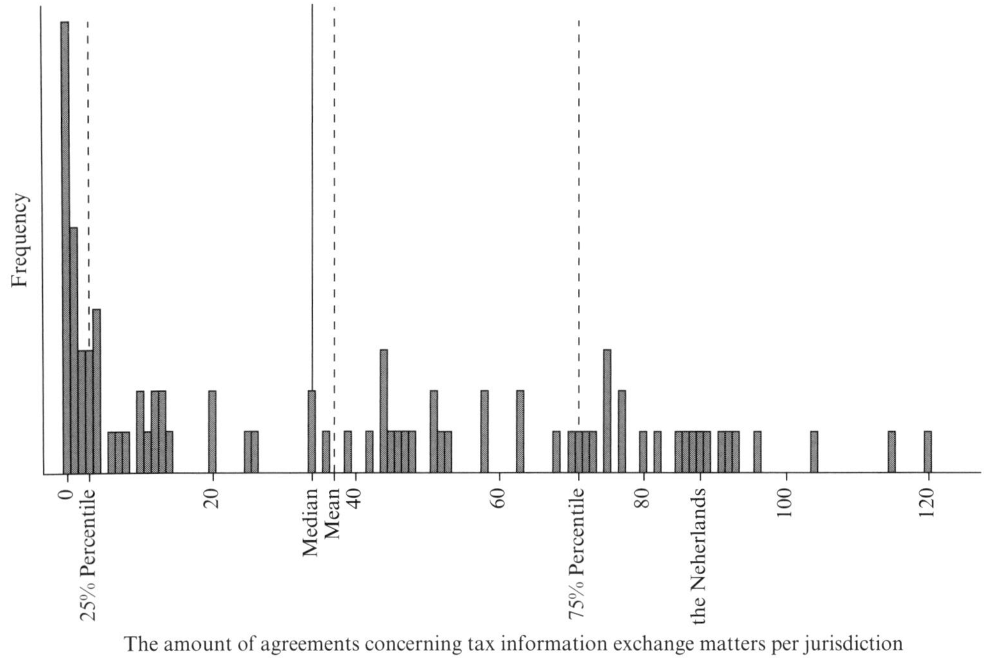

Note: Each bar stands for a jurisdiction for which we had information available. The frequency on the y-axis refers to the amount of agreements in place concerning tax information exchange each jurisdiction had as of 1 January 2009 (OECD 2009, p. 130). The median line indicates our boundary of the lack of exchange of information.

Source: OECD, (2009, p. 130).

Figure 23.3 The amount of agreements regarding tax information exchange matters for 86 jurisdictions

23.4.2 Testing the Netherlands

Testing the low tax category for the Netherlands Since data suitable to calculate the effective tax rate and to test tax havens is hardly available, we were not able to calculate accurate effective tax rates. Therefore, we have to refrain from concluding whether the Netherlands (and other jurisdictions) is a tax haven falling into this category.

Testing the lack of transparency for the Netherlands The Netherlands has a good practice with respect to transparency. Some relevant laws are:

- *Wet ter voorkoming van witwassen en financieren van terrorisme* (in English: 'Act to prevent money laundering and terrorist financing'), requiring financial institutions to know the identity of the client before providing services and requiring anybody who provides professional or business services to report unusual transactions;
- *Wet Financieel Toezicht* (in English: 'Act on financial supervision') requiring financial institutions to have a license, banks to have a 'know-your-customer'

Table 23.2 Checkbox

Criterion \ Tax haven category	Low tax category	Secrecy category[a]	Worst order category
Relatively low effective tax rate	X		X
Lack of transparency		(X)	X
Lack of exchange of information		(X)	X

Note: a. Satisfying either one or both of these two criteria make a jurisdiction fall in the secrecy category.

policy and the De Nederlandse Bank (in English: 'Dutch Central Bank') to have the right to be a supervisor for these financial institutions;

- *Wet Toezicht Trustkantoren* (in English: 'Act on the supervision of trust companies') lays down all the obligations for the trust companies and their policy makers including the obligation to have a license and the fact that trust companies are under the supervision of the De Nederlandse Bank;
- *Sanctiewet 1977* (in English: 'Sanction law 1977') which prohibits corporations to do business with corporations or persons on which national or EU sanctions rest;
- *Wet Financiële Betrekkingen Buitenland 1994* (in English: 'External financial relations Act') requiring financial institutions to be registered by the De Nederlandsche Bank and to provide information to the Bank which the Bank needs for establishing the Dutch balance of payments.

All of these laws are well maintained. Besides, the Netherlands has no bank secrecy and maintains a public trust and foundations registry ('Kamer van Koophandel'), which is up-to-date and accessible to authorities and the public for a reasonable price (Aanhangsel van de Handelingen 2006–2007; De Nederlandsche Bank 2007; TJN 2009b; Van den Berg et al. 2008). In other words, we conclude that the Netherlands does not have a lack of transparency.

Testing the lack of exchange of information for the Netherlands The Netherlands has 88 agreements regarding tax information agreements (OECD 2009), by far exceeding our boundary of 34 agreements. Note that both the OECD and the TJN threshold are satisfied.

Conclusion about the Netherlands So, the Netherlands does not have a lack of transparency and does not have a lack of exchange of information. It can thus be concluded that the Netherlands does not satisfy the test for being a tax haven for tax avoidance requiring secrecy and tax evasion. Hence, the Netherlands does not fall into the secrecy category for tax havens.

Testing the worst order category for the Netherlands Since the Netherlands did not fall into the secrecy category, it fails this test. Hence, the Netherlands is not a tax haven of the worst order.

23.4.3 Results

The results section can be very short: the Netherlands may or may not be a tax haven falling into the low tax category, that is the Netherlands may or may not be a tax haven for 'normal' tax avoidance. With certainty it can be said that the Netherlands is not a tax haven falling into the secrecy or worst order category. Hence, the Netherlands is not facilitating tax avoidance requiring secrecy or tax evasion.

23.5 SUMMARY AND CONCLUSION

This chapter answers the question 'Is the Netherlands a tax haven?' by first presenting a workable definition and then testing the Netherlands according to this definition. Using most of the criteria appearing in the literature we created a checkbox for three different types of tax havens, that is, the low tax category for 'normal' tax avoidance, the high secrecy category for tax avoidance and tax evasion, and the worst order category for a combination of both low taxes and high secrecy. We apply a simple test for each category. After establishing the checkbox and testing the Netherlands against this list, we concluded that the Netherlands is not a tax haven falling into the secrecy or worst order category. Hence, the Netherlands is not facilitating tax avoidance requiring secrecy or tax evasion; the Netherlands might be a tax haven falling into the low tax category, that is, the Netherlands might be a tax haven for 'normal' tax avoidance. In particular, so-called Special Purpose Entities (SPE) (Bijzondere Financiele Instellingen (BFI) in Dutch) are frequently used by multinationals to transfer internal funds between subsidiaries with the purpose of reducing their tax bill: it was estimated that subsidiaries of US multinationals in Bermuda, Ireland, Luxemburg and the Netherlands were assigned almost one-third of all foreign profits of US enterprises, although they contributed only as little as 5 percent to production in 2001 (Sullivan 2004, p. 590). These figures suggest that the Netherlands is very likely used for tax avoidance. Unger and Busuioc (2007) conclude that if only a very small proportion of all transactions via SPEs had an illegal background such as tax evasion or money laundering, the amount of criminal money flowing into the Netherlands would be huge. Although their view is that the Netherlands is an attractive destination for the money launderer, more in-depth investigations are necessary to provide evidence for these presumptions.

To come back to our title 'Is the Netherlands a tax h(e)aven?' a little more explanation is needed. Looking up haven in the dictionary gives the following definition: 'a place, of safety or refuge'. Overall, we cannot conclude that the Netherlands provides such a place for corporations. However, as explained in section 23.3, the Netherlands has some very favorable regimes, which all together lead to a place where corporations can experience the 'shelter' of low taxes. Whether this will lead to the qualification of a tax haven in the low tax category is left open for discussion in future research. Another promising avenue of research in the tax haven literature would be to calculate effective tax rates on a broad basis. This is however a hard task due to the lack of appropriate micro data on the firm level.

NOTES

1. We have to keep in mind that the Netherlands, represented by assurance companies and pension funds, plays a considerable role at the US financial market and much criticism followed by the retroactively reaction by the Obama administration has to be seen in this light.
2. Of course, small jurisdictions such as islands are special. In the past, small islands were able to finance themselves to a large degree by customs duties. Due to trade liberalization they lost a substantial amount of revenues and the mechanisms for a corporate income tax system or a value added tax were hardly available. Limited internal capacity for an appropriate income tax system is also one of the reasons why small jurisdictions choose the easy path of becoming an offshore financial center (Kommer 2011; Baunsgaard and Keen 2005).
3. In this chapter when taxes are discussed corporate income tax is meant, unless stated otherwise.
4. Some authors claim that this is a 'double standard', since some harmful tax practices are in fact the same as some practices in tax havens. See for example Addison (2009) or Hishikawa (2002).
5. Low tax is a very subjective criterion and depends of course on the domestic level of taxation. We already mentioned the difference between the OECD that considers the absolute effective level of taxation and the EU that considers this level *with regard to* the general level of taxation in the particular member state. The EU is increasingly recognizing the sovereignty of the national legislator in this regard instead of using an international standard. It is maybe peculiar to address the Luxembourg tax provision: For the purposes of the participation exemption regime, a tax haven company can be defined as a company which is not fully liable to a tax corresponding to Luxembourg Corporate Income tax, that is, is not subject to a mandatory effective tax burden of at least 10.5% calculated under similar rules to those existing in Luxembourg.
6. However, opinions about how to calculate this vary widely.
7. This is a weak argument. If the criterion is right then the fact of proving it is another dimension. The opposite is even more worrying if only criteria are recognized as relevant if the evidence can easily be found. The problem with money laundering and tax evasion is probably always the fact that the difficulty of finding the evidence creates a bottleneck.
8. The participation exemption has existed in Dutch tax legislation since 1914.
9. Which is relatively low compared to Germany (25%), Belgium (25%) and France (25%), but not to the United Kingdom (0%) (IBFD 2011).
10. Which is low compared to Germany (interest: 25%, royalties: 15%), Belgium (interest: 15%, royalties: 15%), France (interest: 0%, royalties: 33.33%) or, for example, the United Kingdom (interest: 20%, royalties: 20%) (IBFD 2011).
11. The other criteria listed may be not taken into consideration as they overlap with the three main criteria, are too weak or vulnerable for subjectivity.
12. Of course, countries support and protect their major industries through tax policy and firms try to extract rents eagerly influencing national tax policies. A jurisdiction is however seen to be transparent if – once the rules are set – governmental authorities have access to all relevant banks and other financial institutions or ownership information to control and enforce these rules.
13. Of course, the exchange of information is not always easy to organize, as data in one country do not necessarily match with data in another jurisdiction. For that reason, effective information exchange refers to the availability of such information for other jurisdictions (for tax matters) only.
14. Although this distinction does not matter for the definition presented here, it does for corporations, as tax avoidance is legal, while tax evasion is not.
15. See also Schwarz (2011b) for the possible mismatch between the nominal tax rate and the effective tax rate.
16. The purpose of these agreements is to promote international co-operation in tax matters through exchange of information. It was developed by the OECD Global Forum Working Group on Effective Exchange of Information. The Agreement grew out of the work undertaken by the OECD to address harmful tax practices. The lack of effective exchange of information is one of the key criteria in determining harmful tax practices. The mandate of the Working Group was to develop a legal instrument that could be used to establish effective exchange of information. The Agreement represents the standard of effective exchange of information for the purposes of the OECD's initiative on harmful tax practices (see: http://www.oecd.org/document/7/0,3746,en_2649_33767_38312839_1_1_1_1,00.html).
17. For the real importance of TIEAs we have to put them in a framework of inbound and outbound investments. When there is hardly any economic relation between two countries, meaning no substantial foreign (direct) investment, the existence of a TIEA is also irrelevant.
18. Over the last years the overall amount of exchange of information agreements has been rising.
19. A critical footnote has to be made: tax information exchange agreements are an important step forward

to fight against harmful tax practices, and the number of TIEAs is an indicator of a country's willingness to cooperate in combating tax evasion; more important, however, is the effectiveness of the agreement, meaning whether the countries involved are able to provide the required information in the context of taxpayer identification and risk detection.
20. Remember that a jurisdiction is a tax haven if it, consciously or unconsciously, facilitates tax avoidance or evasion.

REFERENCES

Aanhangsel van de Handelingen, 2006–2007 (January, 2007), *Vragen gesteld door de leden der Kamer, met daarop de door de regering gegeven antwoorden*. Nr. 539. Retrieved on 28 April 2011 from https://zoek.officielebekendmakingen.nl/ah-tk-20062007-539.html

Aanhangsel van de Handelingen, 2010–2011 (November 16, 2010), *Vragen van het lid Bashir (SP) aan de staatssecretaris van Financiën over constructies waarbij bedrijven zoals Google via Nederland massaal belasting ontwijken (ingezonden 26 October 2010). Antwoord van minister De Jager (Financiën) (ontvangen 16 november 2010)*, nr. 492. Retrieved on 28 April 2011 from https://zoek.officielebekendmakingen.nl/ah-tk-20102011-492.html

Addison, T. V. (2009), 'Shooting blanks: the war on tax havens', *Indiana Journal of Global Legal Studies*, **16** (2), 703–27.

Bakker, M. (December 9, 2009), 'Nederland snoeit in fiscale voordelen. Brievenbusfirma's en opkoopfondsen geviseerd.', *De Tijd*, 10.

Bartelsman, E. J. and R. M. W. J. Beetsma (2003), 'Why pay more? Corporate tax avoidance through transfer pricing in OECD countries', *Journal of Public Economics*, **87**, 2225–52.

Baunsgaard, T and M. Keen (2005), 'Tax revenue and (or?) trade liberalisation', *IMF Working Paper*, WP/05/112.

Bloemen, R. (November 2, 2009), 'Nederland vijftiende belastingparadijs', *Algemeen Nederlands Persbureau*. Retrieved on 6 May 2011 from http://www.elsevier.nl/web/Artikel/249734/Nederland-vijftiende-belastingparadijs.htm

Bloomberg (October 21, 2010), '*Google 2.4% rate shows how $60 billion lost to tax loopholes*' [video]. USA: Bloomberg.

Blum, R. H. (1984), *Offshore Haven Banks, Trusts, and Companies: the Business of Crime in the Euromarket*. New York: Praeger.

Christian Aid (2008), *The Morning After the Night Before: The Impact of the Financial Crisis on the Developing World*. Retrieved on 28 May 2011 from http://www.christianaid.org.uk/Images/The-morning-after-the-night-before.pdf

Clausing, K. A. (2003), 'Tax-motivated transfer pricing and US intrafirm trade prices', *Journal of Public Economics*, **87**, 2207–23.

Code of Conduct Group (1999), *Code of Conduct (Business Taxation)*. Retrieved on 28 April 2011 from http://ec.europa.eu/taxation_customs/resources/documents/primarolo_en.pdf

Commission of the European Commission (2009), *Promoting Good Governance in Tax Matters*. Retrieved on 20 May 2011 from http://ec.europa.eu/development/icenter/repository/COMM_ De Telegraaf (2009) COM_2010_0163_TAX_DEVELOPMENT_EN.PDF

De Telegraaf (2009), 'Nederland paradijs voor multinationals', *De Telegraaf*, 18 October, 4.

De Nederlandsche Bank (2007), *Bijzondere financiële instellingen – integriteitrisico bij grote geldstromen*. De Nederlandsche Bank, Kwartaalbericht maart.

De Volkskrant (2009), 'Nederland van lijst belastingparadijzen', *De Volkskrant*, 6 May, 1.

De Waard, P. (May 18, 2010), 'Belastingconflict Antillen', *De Volkskrant*. Retrieved on 7 May 2011 from http://www.volkskrant.nl/vk/nl/2680/Economie/archief/article/detail/997083/2010/05/18/Belastingconflict-Antillen.dhtml

Desai, M. A., C. F. Foley and J. R. Hines Jr. (2006), 'The demand for tax haven operations', *Journal of Public Economics*, **90**, 513–31.

Devereux, M. P. and R. Griffith (1999), 'The taxation of discrete investment choices', *Institute for Fiscal Studies Working Paper*, W98/16.

Devereux, M. P. and P. B. Sørensen. (2006), *The Corporate Income Tax: International Trends and Options for Fundamental Reform*. Retrieved on 3 June 2011 from http://ec.europa.eu/economy_finance/index_en.htm

DFA website (2011), Dutch Fiduciary Association. Retrieved on 10 May 2011 from http://www.dutchfiduciaryassociation.nl/

Dharmapala, D. (2008), 'What problems and opportunities are created by tax havens?', *Oxford Review of Economic Policy*, **24** (4), 661–79.
Dharmapala, D. and J. R Hines Jr. (2006), 'Which countries become tax havens?', NBER working paper series, 12802.
Dharmapala, D. and J. R Hines Jr. (2009), 'Which countries become tax havens?', *Journal of Public Economics*, 93, 1058–68.
Doggart, C. (1975), *Tax Havens and their Uses*. London: Economist Intelligence Unit.
Drucker, J. (October 21, 2010), 'Google 2.4% rate shows how $60 billion lost to tax loopholes'. Retrieved on 4 May 2011 from http://www.bloomberg.com/news/2010-10-21/google-2-4-rate-shows-how-60-billion-u-s-revenue-lost-to-tax-loopholes.html
ECOFIN (1997), 'Conclusions of the ECOFIN council meeting on 1 December 1997 concerning taxation policy'. Retrieved on 28 April 2011from http://ec.europa.eu/taxation_customs/resources/documents/coc_en.pdf
Eden, L. and R. T. Kudrle. (2005), 'Tax havens: renegade states in the international tax regime?', *Law & Policy*, **7** (1), 100–127.
EU website (European Union website) (2011), European Union and the G8 & G20. Retrieved on 29 May 2011 from http://www.deljpn.ec.europa.eu/modules/world/g8/?ml_lang=en
Evers, M., A. C. G. A. C. De Graaf and A. J. A. Stevens (2011), 'Zembla-uitzending "Nederland belastingparadijs" nader beschouwd', *Maandblad Belasting Beschouwingen*, **2**, 59–75.
FSF (Financial Stability Forum) (2000), *Report of the Working Group on Offshore Financial Centres*.Retrieved on 29 May 2011 from http://www.financialstabilityboard.org/publications/r_0004b.pdf
Global Forum website (2011), *Global Forum on Transparency and Exchange of Information for Tax Purposes*. Retrieved on 29 May 2011 from http://www.oecd.org/site/0,3407,en_21571361_43854757_1_1_1_1_1,00.html
Gordon, R. H. and J. R. Hines Jr. (2002), 'International taxation'. Retrieved on May 12 2011 from http://www.bus.umich.edu/OTPR//WP2002-2paper.pdf
Government Commission on Capital Flight from Poor Countries (2009), *Tax Havens and Development: Status, Analyses and Measures*, Oslo: Gruppen AS.
Gravelle, J. G. (2010), *Tax Havens: International Tax avoidance and Evasion*. Retrieved on 29 May 2011 from http://info.publicintelligence.net/R40623.pdf
Grotenhuis, A. L. J. (December 7, 2009a), *Kabinet: multinational zwaarder belasten*. Retrieved 6 May 2011 from http://vorige.nrc.nl/economie/article2431636.ece/Kabinet_multinational zwaarder_belasten
Grotenhuis, A. L. J. (2009b), Verslag symposium: Tax Justice. WFR 2009 (6821), 926–931.
Harris, D., R. Morck and J. B. Slemrod (1993), Chapter 8: 'Income shifting in U.S. multinational corporations', *Studies in International Taxation*, Chicago: University of Chicago Press.
Hines Jr., J. R. (2010), 'Treasury islands', *Journal of Economic Perspectives*, **24** (4), 103–26.
Hines Jr., J. R. and E. M. Rice (1994), 'Fiscal paradise: foreign tax havens and American business', *The Quarterly Journal of Economics*, **109** (1), 149–82.
Hishikawa, A. (2002), 'The death of tax havens?', *Boston College International and Comparative Law Review*, **25** (2), 388–417.
IBFD (International Bureau of Fiscal Documentation) (2011), *Netherlands – Corporate Taxation*. Retrieved on 28 May 2011 from http://online.ibfd.org/kbase/
IMF (International Monetary Fund) (2000), *Offshore Financial Centers. IMF Background Paper*. Retrieved on 29 May 2011 from http://www.imf.org/external/np/mae/oshore/2000/eng/back.htm
IMF (2006), *Offshore Financial Centers. The Assessment Program – A Progress Report*. Retrieved on 29 May 2011 from http://www.imf.org/external/np/pp/eng/2006/020806.pdf
IMF website (2011), *International Monetary Fund*. Retrieved on 28 May 2011 from http://www.imf.org/external/np/ofca/ofca.asp
IRS website (Internal Revenue Service website) (2011), *Internal Revenue Service*. Retrieved on 26 May 2011 from http://www.irs.gov/businesses/small/article/0,,id=106568,00.html
Jongsma, M. (April 20, 2011), '"Fiscus spekt vooral Zuidas"; GroenLinks zet vraagtekens bij miljardenstromen door belastingparadijs Nederland', *Het Financieele Dagblad*, 4.
Kamerstukken II, 1979–1980 (December, 1979), 'Verslag van schriftelijk en mondeling overleg', *Ontgaan en ontduiken van belasting*, 15 975, nr. 1. Retrieved on 28 April 2011 from http://resourcessgd.kb.nl/SGD/19791980/PDF/SGD_19791980_0006163.pdf
Kamerstukken II, 1980–1981 (April, 1981), 'Eerste tussentijds verslag' *Onderzoek gedragscodes multinationale ondernemingen*, 16830, nr. 1. Retrieved 28 April 2011 from http://resourcessgd.kb.nl/SGD/19801981/PDF/SGD_19801981_0007287.pdf
Kamerstukken II, 2008–2009 (December 15, 2008), 'Brief van de staatssecretaris en minister van Financiën', *Winstbelasting multinationals*, 31 369, nr. 5. Retrieved on 28 April 2011 from https://zoek.officielebekendmakingen.nl/kst-31369-5. html

Kamerstukken II, 2009–2010 (October 26, 2009), 'Brief staatssecretaris over "Nederland als belastingparadijs"', *Winstbelasting multinationals*, 31 369, nr. 8. Retrieved on 28 April 2011 from https://zoek.officielebekendmakingen.nl/kst-31369-8.html?zoekcriteria=%3fzkt%3dUitgebreid%26pst%3dParlementaireDocumenten%26dpr%3dAlle%26dosnr%3d31369%26kmr%3dEersteKamerderStatenGeneraal%257cTweedeKamerderStatenGeneraal%257cVerenigdeVergaderingderStatenGeneraal%26sdt%3dKen&resultIndex=3&sorttype=1&sortorder=4

Keuning, W. (October 19, 2009), 'Multinationals omzeilen belasting; Fiscus liep in 2007 voor 16 miljard euro aan vennootschapsbelasting mis door gaten in wet', *De Volkskrant*, 6.

Klaar voor de toekomst. Verkiezingsprogramma 2010 GroenLinks (2010), Retrieved on 28 April 2011, from http://tweedekamer.groenlinks.nl/files/VerkiezingsprogrammaGroenLinks2010.pdf

KPMG (2010), *Japanese Tax Haven (CFC) Rules*. Retrieved on 28 May 2011 from http://www.us.kpmg.com/microsite/tnf-asiapacific/2010/Japan_August24.pdf

Kommer, van V. (2011), 'Small and less-developed jurisdictions and their struggle to comply to international standards', *Asia-Pacific tax Bulletin*, **17** (1).

Langereis, Ch. J. (1992), 'Richtige heffing is dood, lang leve fraus legis?', WFR 1992 (6020), 1097–8.

Martinez-Serrano, A. and B. Patterson (January 2003), *Taxation in Europe: Recent Developments* (Economic Affairs Series Working Paper ECON 131 EN). Retrieved on 15 May 2011 from http://ec.europa.eu/taxation_customs/resources/documents/recent_dev.pdf

Meeus, J. (November 12, 2008), 'Een markt van 8.000 miljard', *NRC Handelsblad*, 13.

Michielse, G. M. M. (2009), 'Gemiste vennootschapsbelasting?', *NTFR* 2009 (44), 2257.

Ministerie van Financiën (2011), *Verdragen op het gebied van directe belastingen per 1 april 2011*. Retrieved on 9 May 2011 from http://www.rijksoverheid.nl/onderwerpen/belastingen-internationaal/documenten-en-publicaties/circulaires/2011/04/01/verdragenoverzicht-per-1-april-2011.html

Mulder, W. F. (1987), Nederland, aantrekkelijke vestigingsplaats of belastingparadijs. *WFR* 1987 (5782), 848–54.

Mulder, T. (October 28, 2009), 'De Jager: Nederland geen belastingparadijs', *Het Financieele DagblaMurphy, R. (n.d.). Fiscal Paradise or Tax on Development?* Retrieved on 28 April 2011 from http://www.taxjustice.net/cms/upload/pdf/Fiscal_paradise.pdf

Musalem, A. and L. Errico (1999), Offshore banking: an analysis of micro- and macro-prudential issues', *IMF Working Paper, WP/99/5*.

Nicodème, G. (2001), 'Computing effective corporate tax rates: comparisons and results', *MPRA Paper no. 3808*.

Nicodème, G. (2007), 'Comparing effective corporate tax rates', *Frontiers in Finance and Economics*, December, 4 (2).

Niessen, R. E. C. M. and L. Pieterse (2009), 'Internationale belastingconcurrentie', *SEW* 2009 (4), 155–61.

Niessen, R. E. C. M. and R. M. P. G. Niessen-Cobben (2009), *Wegwijs in de Fiscaliteit*. Amersfoort: Sdu Uitgevers.

NRC Handelsblad (2009), 'Nederland is één dag een fiscaal paradijs', *NRC Handelsblad*, 6 May, 1

OECD (Organisation for Economic Co-operation and Development) (1998), *Harmful Tax Competition. An Emerging Global Issue*. Retrieved on 28 April 2011 from http://www.oecd.tax/transparency/44430243.pdf.

OECD (2000), *Towards Global Tax Co-operation*. Retrieved on 28 April 2011 fromhttp://www.oecd.org/dataoecd/9/61/2090192.pdf

OECD (2001), *The OECD's Project on Harmful Tax Practices: the 2001 Progress Report*. Retrieved on 28 April 2011 from http://www.oecd.org/dataoecd/60/5/2664450.pdf

OECD (2004), *The OECD's Project on Harmful Tax Practices: the 2004 Progress Report*. Retrieved on 28 April 2011 from http://www.oecd.org/dataoecd/60/33/30901115.pdf

OECD (2006), *The OECD's Project on Harmful Tax Practices: 2006 Update on Progress in Member States*. Retrieved on 28 April 2011 from http://www.oecd.org/dataoecd/1/17/37446434.pdf

OECD (2009), *Tax Co-operation 2009. Towards a Level Playing Field*. Retrieved on 27 June 2011 from http://dx.doi.org/10.1787/taxcoop-2010-en

OECD website (2011), *Organisation for Economic Co-operation and Development*. Retrieved on 2 May 2011 from http://www.oecd.org/document/19/0,3343,en_2649_33745_1903251_1_1_1_ 37427,00.html

Oxfam (n.d.), *Tax Havens: Releasing the Hidden Billions for Poverty Eradication*. Retrieved on 29 May 2011 from http://www.taxjustice.net/cms/upload/pdf/oxfam_paper_-_final_version__06_00.pdf

Palan, R. (2002), 'Tax havens and the commercialization of state sovereignty', *International Organization*, **56** (1), 151–76.

'Rekensom belastingparadijs deugt niet.' (October 28, 2009), *Het Parool*, 22.

Roin, J. (2007), 'Can income from capital be taxed? An international perspective', *Brookings Draft, 9/20/05*.

Schwarz, P. (2011a), 'Estimating tax-elasticities of foreign direct investment: the importance of tax havens', *Economics Bulletin*, **31** (1), 218–32.

Schwarz, P. (2011b), 'Money launderers and tax havens: two sides of the same coin?', *International Review of Law and Economics*, **31**, 37–47.

SEO (Stichting Economisch Onderzoek) (2008), *De Nederlandse trustsector: 'Groeimarkt met uniek karakter'*. Retrieved on 28 April 2011 from http://www.seo.nl/fileadmin/site/overige-publicaties/topics/Topics-juni-2008.pdf

Sharman, J. C. (2006), *Havens in a Storm: the Struggle for Global Tax Regulation*. Ithaca: Cornell University Press.

Shaxson, N. (2011), *Treasure Islands: Tax Havens and the Men who Stole the World*. London: The Bodley Head.

Slemrod, J. (2008), 'Why is Elvis on Burkina Faso postage stamps? Cross-country evidence on the commercialization of state sovereignty', *Journal of Empirical Legal Studies*, **5** (4), 683–712.

Slemrod, J. and J. D. Wilson (2009), 'Tax competition with parasitic tax havens', *Journal of Public Economics*, **93**, 1261–70.

SOMO (Stichting Onderzoek Multinationale Ondernemingen) (2007b), *The Global Problem of Tax Havens: The Case of the Netherlands*. Retrieved on 28 April 2011 from http://somo.nl/publications-nl/Publication_3464-nl/?searchterm=tax%20haven

Sullivan, M. A. (2004), 'Data show dramatic shift of profits to tax havens', *Tax Analysts 2004, Tax Notes 2004*, 1190–1200.

The White House (2009), 'Leveling the playing field: curbing tax havens and removing tax incentives for shifting jobs overseas', 4 May, *The White House, Office of the Press Secretary*. Retrieved on 30 April 2011 from http://www.whitehouse.gov/the_press_office/LEVELING-THE-PLAYING-FIELD-CURBING-TAX-HAVENS-AND-REMOVING-TAX-INCENTIVES-FOR-SHIFTING-JOBS-OVERSEAS/

TJN (Tax Justice Network) (2005), *Tax Us If You Can*. Retrieved on 28 April 2011 from http://www.taxjustice.net/cms/upload/pdf/tuiyc_-_eng_-_web_file.pdf

TJN (2007), *Closing the Floodgates: Collecting Tax to Pay for Development*. Retrieved on 28 May 2011 from http://www.taxjustice.net/cms/upload/pdf/Closing_the_Floodgates_-_1-FEB-2007.pdf

TJN (2009a), *Key Financial Secrecy Indicators 9: Number of Bilateral Treaties*. Retrieved on 23 June 2011 from http://www.secrecyjurisdictions.com/Archive2009/KFSI/BilateralTreaties.pdf

TJN (2009b), *The Methodoloy of the Financial Secrecy Index*. Retrieved on 23 June 2011 from http://www.secrecyjurisdictions.com/Archive2009/FSI-2009/FSI%20-%20Methodology.pdf

TJN (n.d.), *Nederland belasting-paradijs, een misverstand?* Retrieved on 29 April 2011 from http://www.taxjustice.nl/?nid=30000&oid=2947fa4f-14e1-4a4e-b984-c6a0cbd7b78c

Unger, B. and M. Busuioc (2007), 'How money is being laundered', in B. Unger, *The Scale and Impacts of Money Laundering* Cheltenham, UK and Northampton, MA, USA: Edward Elgar Publishing, pp. 89–108.

U.S. GAO (United States Government Accountability Office). (2008). International taxation: large U.S. corporations and federal contractors with subsidiaries in jurisdictions listed as tax havens or financial privacy jurisdictions', *GAO-09-157*. Retrieved on 28 April 2011 from http://www.gao.gov/new.items/d09157.pdf

Van de Streek, J. L. (2010), 'Vennootschapsbelasting', in R. L. R. Hennuin (ed.), *Hoofdzaken Belastingrecht*, Den Haag: Boom fiscale uitgevers, 237–70.

Van Dijk, M., F.Weyzig and R. Murphy (2006), *The Netherlands: a Tax Haven?* Retrieved on 28 April 2011 from http://somo.nl/publications-nl/Publication_1397-nl/? searchterm=tax%20haven

Van Dongen, J. (Producer) (October 18, 2009), *Zembla* [video]. Netherlands: Vara/NPS.

Van den Berg, M., K.,Van Buiren T. Van Giffen and P. Risseeuw (2008). *The Dutch Trust Industry – facts & figures*. Retrieved on 28 April 2011 from http://www.hollandfinancialcenter.com/publications//The%20Dutch%20Trust%20Industry.pdf

Van der Geld, J. A. G. (2004), 'De wetswijziging naar aanleiding van het Bosalarrest', *Maandblad voor Accountancy en Bedrijfshuishoudkunde*, **6** (78), 310–315.

Van der Geld, J. A. G. (2006), 'Het wetsvoorstel Werken aan winst', *Dossier VPB 2007*, **1** (1), 1–12.

Van Uffelen, X. (May 27, 2010), 'Oost-Europa ontdekt Nederland als gunstige vestigingsplaats', *De Volkskrant*.

Van Weeghel, S. (1997), *Improper Use of Tax Treaties*. Amsterdam: Kluwer Law International.

VIMS website (2011), *Vereniging International Management Services*. Retrieved on 10 May 2011 from http://www.vims.nl/

Warburton, R. F. E. D. and P. Hendy (2006), *International Comparison of Australia's Taxes*. Canberra: CanPrint Communications Pty Ltd.

Weyzig, F. and M. Van Dijk (2007), *Tax Haven and Development Partner: Incoherence in Dutch Government Policies?* Retrieved on 28 April 2011 from http://somo.nl/publications.nl/Publication_2088-nl/?searchterm=tax%20haven

Wisselink, M. A. (1977), 'Vennootschappen in goedkope belastinglanden (tax havens). Toepassing regels van Nederlands belastingrecht', WFR 1977 (5336), 993–1010.

APPENDIX A. TAX HAVEN LIST OF THE ECONOMIC LITERATURE SECTION

Table A.1 Tax haven lists of various academic economic sources

Jurisdiction \ Author	Hines & Rice (1994)[i]	Updated version Hines & Rice (1994)[ii]	Basis list of Hines (2010) in 'Treasury Islands'[iii]	Musalem & Errico (1999)[iv]	Eden & Kudrle (2005)[v]	Harris, Morck and Slemrod (1993)[vi]	Sullivan (2004)[vi]
Number of jurisdictions	42	49	52	69	59	18	18
Andorra	X	X	X	X	X	X	
Anguilla	X	X	X	X	X		
Antigua (& Barbuda)	X	X	X	X	X	X	
Aland Islands							
Alderney (part of Guernsey)							
Aruba		X	X	X	X		
Australia				X			
Austria				X			
Bahamas	X	X	X	X	X	X	
Bahrain	X	X	X	X	X		
Barbados	X	X	X	X	X	X	X
Belgium							X
Belize	X	X	X	X	X		
Bermuda	X	X	X	X	X	X	X
British Virgin Islands	X	X	X	X	X	X	
Campione (d'Italia)				X			
Canary Islands					X		
Cayman Islands	X	X	X	X	X	X	X
China							X
City of London							
Cook Islands	X	X	X	X	X		
Costa Rica			X	X	X		
Cyprus	X	X	X	X	X	X	
Denmark							X
Djibouti			X	X	X		
Domini							
Dominica	X	X	X	X	X		
Dominican Republic							X
Dubai				X			
Frankfurt							
Gibraltar	X	X	X	X	X	X	
Grenada	X	X	X	X	X	X	
Guam				X			
Guernsey	X	X	X	X	X	X	
Hong Kong	X	X	X	X	X		X
Hungary				X			
Iceland							
Ingushetia							
Ireland (Dublin)	X	X	X	X	X		X
Israel				X			

Table A.1 (continued)

Author / Jurisdiction	Hines & Rice (1994)[i]	Updated version Hines & Rice (1994)[ii]	Basis list of Hines (2010) in 'Treasury Islands'[iii]	Musalem & Errico (1999)[iv]	Eden & Kudrle (2005)[v]	Harris, Morck and Slemrod (1993)[vi]	Sullivan (2004)[vi]
Isle of Man (& Sark)	X	X	X	X	X		
Japan (Japanese Offshore Market)				X			
Jersey	X	X	X	X	X	X	
Jordan	X	X	X		X		
Kiribati						X	
Kuwait				X			
Labuan					X		
Latvia							
Lebanon	X	X	X	X	X		
Liberia	X	X	X	X	X		
Liechtenstein	X	X	X	X	X	X	
Luxembourg	X	X	X	X	X		X
Macau	X	X	X	X	X		
Madeira				X	X		
Malaysia (Labuan)				X			X
Maldives	X	X	X		X		
Malta	X	X	X	X	X		
Marianas				X			
Marshall Islands	X	X	X	X	X		
Mauritius		X	X	X	X		
Micronesia			X	X			
Monaco	X	X	X	X	X		
Montserrat	X	X	X	X	X		
Nauru		X	X	X	X		
Netherlands				X			X
Netherlands Antilles	X	X	X	X	X	X	
New York							
New Zealand							X
Niue		X	X	X	X		
Oman				X			
Panama	X	X	X	X	X		
Philippines				X			
Portugal							X
Puerto Rico				X	X		
Russia				X			
Samoa (Western)		X	X	X	X		
San Marino		X	X		X		
São Tomé e Príncipe							
Sark (mentioned apart from Isle of Man) (Part of Guernsey)							
Seychelles		X	X	X	X		
Singapore (Asian Currency Units)	X	X	X	X	X		X

Table A.1 (continued)

Jurisdiction \ Author	Hines & Rice (1994)[i]	Updated version Hines & Rice (1994)[ii]	Basis list of Hines (2010) in 'Treasury Islands'[iii]	Musalem & Errico (1999)[iv]	Eden & Kudrle (2005)[v]	Harris, Morck and Slemrod (1993)[vi]	Sullivan (2004)[vi]
Somalia							
Solomon Islands					X		
South Africa							
Spain							X
St. Kitts (and Nevis)	X	X	X	X	X	X	
St. Lucia	X	X	X	X	X		
St. Martin	X		X				
St. Vincent (& the Grenadines)	X	X	X	X	X	X	
Sweden							X
Switzerland	X	X	X	X	X		X
Taipei							
Tangier				X			
Tel Aviv							
Thailand (Bangkok international Banking Facilities)				X			
Tonga (Islands)		X	X		X		
Trieste							
Tunisia					X		
Turks & Caicos Islands	X	X	X	X	X		
Turkish Republic of Northern Cyprus							
United Arab Emirates					X		
United Kingdom (London)				X			
United Kingdom Caribbean Islands	X						
United States of America (some states)				X			
Uruguay				X	X		
Vanuatu	X	X	X	X	X	X	
Virgin Islands (US)		X			X		

Sources:

i. *Source:* Hines & Rice (1994), p. 178. Their sources: IRS-identified: Glautier and Bassinger (1987); Beauchamp (1983); Doggart (1983).

ii. *Source:* Dharmapala & Hines (2006), p. 32.

iii. *Source:* Hines, (2010), p. 104.

iv. *Source:* Musalem & Errico (1999), p. 11. Their sources: Bank of International Settlements; IMF staff; Ghosh and Ortiz (1994); Cassard (1994); *Far Eastern Economic Review* (March 1992); Doggart (1993), and U.N. Office for Drug Control and Crime Prevention (1998).

v. *Source:* Eden & Kudrle (2005), pp. 111–12.

vi. *Source:* Harris, Morck and Slemrod (1993), p. 284. Their list also includes 'other Caribbean'.

vii. *Source:* Sullivan (2004), p. 1190.

APPENDIX B. TAX HAVEN LIST OF THE OECD, TJN, SOMO AND THE US GAO

Table A.2 Tax haven list of the OECD, TJN, SOMO and the US GA0

Jurisdiction \ Source	OECD (uncooperative and cooperative list)[i]	TJN[ii]	SOMO[iii]	U.S. GAO[iv]
Number of jurisdictions	41	72	72	50
Andorra	X	X	X	X
Anguilla	X[d]	X	X	X
Antigua (& Barbuda)	X[d]	X*	X	X
Aland Islands		X*		
Alderney (part of Guernsey)		X*	X	
Aruba	X[b]	X*	X	X
Australia				
Austria				
Bahamas	X[d]	X	X	X
Bahrain	X[b]	X	X	X
Barbados	X[e]	X	X	X
Belgium		X	X	
Belize	X[d]	X	X	X
Bermuda	X[a]	X	X	X
British Virgin Islands	X[d]	X	X	X
Campione (d'Italia)		X*	X	
Canary Islands				
Cayman Islands	X[a]	X	X	X
China				
City of London		X	X	
Cook Islands	X[d]	X	X	X
Costa Rica		X	X	X
Cyprus	X[a]	X	X	X
Denmark				
Djibouti				
Domini			X	
Dominica	X[d]	X*		X
Dominican Republic				
Dubai		X*	X	
Frankfurt			X	
Gibraltar	X[d]	X*	X	X
Grenada	X[d]	X	X	X
Guam				
Guernsey	X[d]	X	X	X
Hong Kong		X	X	X
Hungary		X*	X	
Iceland		X*	X	
Ingushetia		X*	X	
Ireland (Dublin)		X*	X	X
Israel				
Isle of Man (& Sark)	X[b]	X	X	X

Table A.2 (continued)

Jurisdiction \ Source	OECD (uncooperative and cooperative list)[i]	TJN[ii]	SOMO[iii]	U.S. GAO[iv]
Japan (Japanese Offshore Market)				
Jersey	X[d]	X	X	X
Jordan				X
Kiribati				
Kuwait				
Labuan		X	X	
Latvia				X
Lebanon		X	X	X
Liberia	X	X	X	X
Liechtenstein	X	X	X	X
Luxembourg		X	X	X
Macau		X*	X	X
Madeira		X*	X	
Malaysia (Labuan)				
Maldives	X[e]	X*	X	X
Malta	X[a]	X*	X	X
Marianas		X	X	
Marshall Islands	X	X	X	X
Mauritius	X[a]	X	X	X
Melilla		X*	X	
Micronesia				
Monaco	X	X	X	X
Montserrat	X[d]	X*	X	X
Nauru	X	X*	X	X
Netherlands		X	X	
Netherlands Antilles	X[b]	X	X	X
New York		X	X	
New Zealand				
Niue	X[d]	X*	X	X
Oman				
Panama	X[d]	X	X	X
Philippines				
Portugal				
Puerto Rico				
Russia				
Samoa (Western)	X[d]	X*	X	X
San Marino	X[a]			X
São Tomé e Príncipe		X*	X	
Sark (mentioned apart from Isle of Man) (Part of Guernsey)		X	X	
Seychelles	X[b]	X*	X	X
Singapore (Asian Currency Units)		X	X	X
Somalia		X*	X	

Table A.2 (continued)

Jurisdiction \ Source	OECD (uncooperative and cooperative list)[i]	TJN[ii]	SOMO[iii]	U.S. GAO[iv]
Solomon Islands				
South Africa		X*	X	
Spain				
St. Kitts (and Nevis)	X[d]	X*	X	X
St. Lucia	X[d]	X*	X	X
St. Martin				
St. Vincent (& the Grenadines)	X[d]	X*	X	X
Sweden				
Switzerland		X	X	X
Taipei		X*	X	
Tangier				
Tel Aviv		X*	X	
Thailand (Bangkok international Banking Facilities)				
Tonga (Islands)	X[c]	X*	X	
Trieste		X*	X	
Tunisia				
Turks & Caicos Islands	X[d]	X	X	X
Turkish Republic of Northern Cyprus		X*	X	
United Arab Emirates				
United Kingdom (London)				
United Kingdom Caribbean Islands				
United States of America (Some states)				
Uruguay		X*	X	
Vanuatu	X[d]	X	X	X
Virgin Islands (U.S.)	X[d]	X*	X	X

Sources:

i. *Source:* OECD (2000), page 17; OECD (2001), p. 8; OECD (2004), p. 11; OECD website (2011).
   a. Committed jurisdictions before 2000 report publication.
   b. Additional committed jurisdictions before 2001 progress report publication.
   c. Excluded from tax haven list by 2001 progress report.
   d. Additional committed jurisdictions before 2004 progress report publication.
   e. Excluded from tax haven list as of 2011.

ii. *Source:* Murphy (n.d., p. 21). Note: The official title of the table: 'The tax havens of the world (some of whom would rather be called offshore financial centers)'.
Note: This list of 72 countries and territories excludes some territories which have some tax haven features but are not commonly used as such e.g. New Zealand.
Those 35 territories marked with an asterisk have developed their activities in the last 25 years according to Christensen and Hampton, representing an almost doubling in the number of tax haven territories in that period.

iii. *Source:* Van Dijk et al. (2006), p. 81. Their source: *Offshore Business Magazine,* http://www.magverlag.com/offshore_magazine09.pdf (20 Sep. 2006), pp. 66–7 and TJN, 'Tax us if you can', ibid.

iv. *Source:* U.S. GAO (2008), pp. 12–13.

24. Dirty complexity: money laundering through derivatives

*John Biggins**

24.1 INTRODUCTION

Trading in financial derivatives has increased exponentially in recent decades. This is especially true with respect to over-the-counter (OTC) derivatives. Given the relative opacity, complexity and size of the derivatives markets (particularly the OTC segments) they may be hospitable breeding grounds for money laundering.[1] From the turn of the twenty-first century up to the global financial crisis (GFC) originating in 2007, trading in OTC derivatives between sophisticated market participants in some of the largest markets was not substantially directly regulated.[2] Amongst other things, this generated concerns with respect to the integrity of audit trails in these markets (FATF 1999, p. 13; hereinafter 1999 FATF Report). In the wake of the GFC, proposals for regulatory reform in OTC derivatives market infrastructure have been forthcoming in many jurisdictions. Amongst developed economies, the US, in particular, has made notable progress at time of writing.[3] These proposals primarily seek to reduce risks in OTC derivatives trading and are not principally concerned with money laundering issues. This is mainly because most major OTC derivatives jurisdictions already have pre-existing anti-money laundering/financing of terrorism (AML/FT) regulations which typically encompass money laundering through financial instruments such as derivatives.[4] Nevertheless, it is possible that if proposed market infrastructure reforms for OTC derivatives are implemented in full they could, in principle, further mitigate the potential for money laundering through these instruments, or at least through particular types of OTC derivatives. At the same time, it is equally conceivable that infrastructure reforms may shift OTC-based money laundering to less regulated jurisdictions and/or generate new types of money laundering opportunities.

In order to provide necessary context in relation to how derivatives might be used to launder money, this chapter commences with a primer on derivatives and a description of the main differences between the OTC and exchange-traded segments of the markets. The respective sizes of these markets as well as the actors which operate within them and typical uses of derivatives will then be outlined. Subsequently, this chapter will attempt to flesh out some of the ways in which derivatives might be invoked to engage in money laundering in support of, for example, organised crime and terrorist finance. The nature of forthcoming market infrastructure reforms for OTC derivatives will then be briefly considered. Finally, this chapter will attempt to draw some conclusions.

24.2 A PRIMER ON DERIVATIVES MARKETS

Derivatives are not recent inventions.[5] The association of derivatives with market losses, crises and scandals, including rogue trading, is also nothing new.[6] It is not necessary to be a mathematician in order to understand and explain derivatives either. Derivatives have been described as nothing more than 'probabilistic bets on future events' (Stout 2011, p. 304). It is thus possible to conceptualise derivatives as 'aleatory contracts', meaning 'the payoffs to and from each counterparty depend on the outcome of one or more extrinsic, future, uncertain events or metrics' (Lynch 2011, p.10).

Financial derivative instruments proliferate in form but share at least one factor in common in so far as they embody a value which is intrinsically linked or contingent upon some external item of worth, hence they 'derive' their value from something else. This 'something else' is known as the 'underlying', which, depending on the type of derivative, can be attributable to the price movements of a broad range of instruments or indictors. These include stocks, bonds, currencies, interest rates, energy, third party or instrument credit quality, commodities, the weather, macroeconomic data and mortality rates, for example.

A derivative position enables market participants to trade on 'leverage', also known as 'gearing' (Gerding 2011). In other words, a derivative position can facilitate a market participant to gain or lose an amount of money in excess of the 'margin' (collateral) which may have been posted to secure the contract.

In an option transaction,[7] one party (option writer) receives a premium for granting another party (option holder) the *right, but not the obligation* to buy (call option) a quantity of a particular 'underlying', for example a security, currency or commodity, at a specified price termed the 'strike price' on a specified future date termed the 'strike date'. If the 'spot price' (i.e. the prevailing market price) is less than the strike price, the option holder is considered to be *in the money*. For instance, if a bond option holder is in the money and the option is cash-settled, the option holder is entitled to receive a cash payment based on the difference between the strike price and the market value of the reference bond, multiplied by a notional amount (Feder 2002, 696–7).

Forwards differ from options in the key respect that they represent *both the right and the obligation* either to physically deliver the 'underlying' security or commodity in return for pre-agreed payment or, alternatively, to exchange a 'difference payment' at a specified date in the future. Forwards can be illustrated with reference to two basic examples. For example, a physically settled commodity forward contract might stipulate that an airline will pay a certain amount in a particular currency at some future specified date in return for delivery of an agreed quantity of fuel from a supplier at a specified location. A forward foreign exchange contract (FX) may stipulate that two banks will exchange a given amount of a particular currency for a given amount of different currency at a settlement rate on a settlement date in the future (Feder 2002, p. 700).

Swaps could be considered a species of forward contract and typically involve cash flow exchanges, ultimately dependent upon the performance of some other financial instrument or entity. Perhaps the most notable example of a swap is the credit default swap (CDS). In a CDS a 'protection buyer' makes periodic payments to a 'protection seller' who agrees to compensate the protection buyer in the event that some stipulated 'credit event' occurs with respect to a third party reference entity or instrument not a party to the CDS contract (Shadab 2010, pp. 431–2). For example, a CDS contract referencing particular sovereign bonds could be triggered by a failure of that sovereign to pay out on those bonds at the time and terms stipulated within the bond contracts.[8]

While these are intended as basic examples of common options, forwards and swaps, it should be noted that there exist an array of hybrid and exotic derivative instruments within and between types (Feder 2002, pp. 701–16). In general, derivatives contracts are entered into in order to 'hedge',[9] 'speculate'[10] and/or engage in 'regulatory arbitrage'.[11]

Exchange-traded derivatives are executed through central trading venues or platforms, known as 'derivatives exchanges'. Derivative instruments traded through exchanges are usually subject to limitations in terms of their structures and delivery conditions. There are also some differences in terminology. For example, standardised forward contracts traded through exchanges are called 'futures'. Derivatives exchanges are often self regulatory organisations (SROs) with internal rules. Over the last few decades, the main derivatives exchanges, as well as other alternative trading facilities, along with the instruments traded upon them, have also been subject to at least some degree of direct public regulatory oversight.[12]

24.2.1 OTC Derivatives

OTC derivatives are usually traded 'off-exchange' bi-laterally on the basis of individually negotiated and tailored agreements using standard form contracts, such as derivatives 'Master Agreements' promulgated by the International Swaps and Derivatives Association (ISDA).[13] OTC derivative instruments are typically more tailored or 'bespoke' than those traded on exchanges. In contrast to most exchange-traded instruments, in OTC transactions both parties typically bear the relevant trading risks[14] directly against one another. Collateral (for example in the form of cash) is often deployed to secure OTC derivatives contracts and mitigate the fallout in the event that one of the parties fails to meet their obligations.[15] 'Purely speculative' OTC derivatives contracts[16] present a particular public policy challenge, especially in light of the insufficiency of collateral alone to govern such OTC derivatives trading in the midst of the GFC.[17]

Public regulatory proposals at the time of writing are thus substantially occupied with dampening the potential for negative externalities arising from purely speculative OTC derivatives transactions. Policy makers in the largest markets are hopeful that this objective can be at least partly achieved through the increased use of central clearing counterparties (CCPs). The use of CCPs has historically been less common in the OTC derivatives markets, though they are familiar to the exchange-traded derivatives markets.

24.2.2 CCPs

A CCP is usually a corporation in its own right and may be commercially related to an exchange (Markham and Harty 2008, pp. 882–83). A CCP interposes itself between the sell and buy side of a derivatives trade, thus acting as the purchaser to every seller and vice versa, managing each trade and associated collateral.[18] The benefits of CCPs include their capacity to ensure streamlined payment and settlement mechanisms (Ledrut and Upper 2007, p. 91; Ceccheti et al. 2009, pp. 49–50). Ideally, CCPS should dampen the potential for 'systemic risk'[19] in derivatives markets, though can be systemically important in their own right[20] (Duffie et al 2010, p. 7).

24.2.3 Market Actors

Both the exchange-traded and OTC derivatives markets are dominated by 'end users', 'dealers' and intermediaries, such as 'brokers'. End users or 'buy side' participants mostly consist of corporations, governmental entities, financial institutions, institutional investors, such as hedge funds,[21] and, to a limited extent, high net worth individuals. Exchange-trading venues may also be accessible to retail investors to some degree, in contrast to the OTC markets. Certain companies also offer in-house trading platforms which facilitate, for example, spread betting through derivatives and these are particularly accessible to retail investors. The 'sell side' in derivatives markets is dominated by 'dealers'. The largest global dealers are known as the 'G16'. At time of writing the G16 consists of Bank of America-Merrill Lynch, Barclays, BNP Paribas, Citigroup, Crédit Agricole, Credit Suisse, Deutsche Bank, Goldman Sachs, HSBC, JPMorgan Chase, Morgan Stanley, Nomura Group, Royal Bank of Scotland, Sociéte Générale, Union Bank of Switzerland (UBS) and Wells Fargo.

With respect to OTC derivatives, dealers essentially 'make the market', by developing products and acting as intermediaries in OTC derivatives trades. Brokers are involved in intermediating derivatives exchange-trading and are usually exchange members themselves, thereby subject to certain obligations in accordance with the exchange rules. However, it is also increasingly possible for market participants to access 'exchange-like' alternative trading venues without the heavy involvement of intermediaries and with a more noticeable level of anonymity (FATF 2009, p. 22; hereinafter 2009 FATF Report).

Dealers also simultaneously operate as end users in the markets, engaging in proprietary trading (prop trading) for the benefit of their own accounts (Waldman 1994, p. 1037). Other important actors in the derivatives markets include CCPs and Trade Repositories (TRs). A TR is 'a centralised registry that maintains an electronic database of the records of open OTC derivatives transactions. The primary public policy benefit of a TR stems from the improved market transparency facilitated by its record keeping function' (CPSS and IOSCO 2010, p. 1). Aside from this, other relevant derivatives market actors are information and trade services providers, as well as law and accountancy firms.

24.2.4 Size of the Derivatives Markets

Semi-annual OTC derivatives statistics indicating notional amounts of derivatives contracts outstanding, issued by the Bank for International Settlements, illustrate the largesse of these markets. Notional amounts of derivatives contracts outstanding are 'the gross nominal or notional value of all deals concluded and not yet settled on the reporting date' (Bank for International Settlements 2012). This data portrays the combined size of the OTC derivatives markets of certain reporting jurisdictions, based on information submitted to their central banks by leading global derivatives dealers.

The reporting jurisdictions are Australia, Belgium, Canada, France, Germany, Italy,

Japan, the Netherlands, Spain, Sweden, Switzerland, the United Kingdom (UK) and the US. The outstanding notional value of all OTC derivatives contracts in these jurisdictions as of December 2011 was put at approximately US$648 trillion (Bank for International Settlements 2012). This figure dwarfs the size of the exchange-traded derivatives market which, according to information available at time of writing, was put at approximately US$30 trillion as of June 2011 (Bank for International Settlements 2011). However, it is important to highlight the fact that notional measurements of derivatives contracts are subject to limitations. In particular, notional measurements do not reflect the risk-mitigating effects of, for instance, collateralisation and 'netting'.[22]

Aside from the reporting advanced derivatives jurisdictions, it is also important to highlight that both OTC and exchange-traded derivatives are of increasing in prominence in emerging derivatives markets (EDMs). Reporting on derivatives activity in EDMs is generally less systematic, though many of these jurisdictions do participate in a *Bank for International Settlements Triennial Central Bank Survey of OTC FX and Interest Rate Derivatives Market Activity*[23] What can be gleaned from the information available is that EDMs are generally of a different complexion to advanced economies (Mihalijek and Packer 2010, p. 44). South Korea, Hong Kong, Singapore and Brazil are amongst the largest and most mature EDMs (Mihalijek and Packer 2010, p. 51).

In light of the context offered by the foregoing analyses, the next section will consider the possible ways in which derivatives, including of the OTC variety, might be invoked to engage in money laundering. The following analysis does not purport to provide an exhaustive account of all of the possible ways through which derivatives could conceivably be used to launder money. Rather, this account should only be considered as indicative of some of the ways in which such outcomes could be achieved.

24.3 MONEY LAUNDERING THROUGH DERIVATIVES

In general, international money laundering consists of roughly three stages. In principle, these stages can also apply to money laundering conducted through derivatives. These stages are: (1) the placement stage, where cash proceeds from crime or terrorist related activities are deposited into the financial system; (2) the layering or 'asset cloaking' (Simser 2008) stage, usually involving a number of transactions aimed at distancing the money from its origins; and (3) the integration stage, whereby the money actually gets invested, for example in derivatives, and mixes with legitimate funds (Sharma 2001, p. 311). When considering the potential for money laundering to occur through derivatives, it is important to highlight not only the derivative related strategies themselves, but also the existence of, for example, sham companies and other arrangements, such as the complicity of professionals involved in the derivatives markets. These factors can be crucial, providing necessary infrastructural support in the initiation of the money laundering strategy and results flowing from it.

The first example is so-called 'mirror trading'. This strategy would be relatively easier to execute in liquid exchange-traded derivatives and could be assisted by a complicit derivatives broker. Here two trading accounts are opened, one to receive the funds which are to be laundered and the other to receive the 'washed' funds. The broker enters the market and, for example, simultaneously buys and sells some quantity of futures contracts. Later in the day, the broker re-enters the market and repeats this process. The broker has thus, in effect, created four trades. The broker makes it appear as though the account set up for the funds to be laundered has made a loss while the account set up to receive the 'washed' funds has recorded a profit (Sharma 2001). Put simply, 'framework conditions must be manipulated in such a way that the dirty money is lost on the bet, while winnings are clean money' (Hetzer 2003, p. 275).

The difference in the profit and loss between the two accounts may constitute part or whole of the payment from the criminal organisation to the broker for engaging in the laundering (FATF 1999, p. 29). If a complicit broker cannot be found, it would be possible instead to instruct an offshore lawyer to open two accounts with two brokers and instruct both to execute the same positions (Sharma 2001, pp. 316–17).

A similar process can be engaged in the OTC markets, for example through 'offsetting positions'. Here a complicit broker simultaneously buys and sells a forward contract. One contract records a gain and the other records a loss. The launderer liquidates the winning contract and cancels the losing contract, compensating the broker for the loss amount. The complicit broker proceeds to destroy any record of the losing transaction and a gain accrues to the launderer. The cost of laundering the money may be the commission on both transactions, as well as any extra money to buy the silence of a complicit broker (Bedi 2006, pp. 2–3).

There are other ways in which money laundering through derivatives can be achieved, including on a more sustained and/or lower level scale. These strategies do not necessarily require the complicity of a rogue broker. An example of this would be where a launderer engages in otherwise legitimate long-term derivative transactions, such as swaps, facilitated through, for instance, offshore front companies (Schneider 2008, p. 19). Swaps contracts usually necessitate payment exchanges and could be useful mechanisms for laundering (Bedi 2006, p. 3). Additionally or alternatively, a launderer may engage in frequent derivative transactions with limited volatility, for example through options. Options could be particularly useful where parties wish to avoid direct fund transfers (FATF 2009, pp. 21–2).

Given the increasing popularity of online spread betting and instruments, such as contracts for differences (CfDs), it has also become relatively easier for individuals posing as retail customers to launder money through accounts set up with firms which host their own trading platforms. CfDs are derivative contracts which typically stipulate that an investor will either pay or receive monies to or from a CfD seller when the CfD is closed, depending on the price movement of an underlying security or other instrument. For example, the direction of the payment in equity CfDs will be determined with reference to the price shifts of underlying shares from the date the CfD was opened to its closure (Faulkner 2005).

In a recent report the Financial Action Task Force (FATF) offered an indicative example, highlighted by Australian authorities, regarding the vulnerability of online CfD trading firms to the activities of money launderers. In the case highlighted by the FATF, a launderer opened an online CfD trading account using false identification. Over a period of eight days a substantial amount of money was deposited into the account in amounts which individually fell below the relevant money laundering reporting thresholds. The funds were subsequently utilised to engage in CfD trading. The manner in which the amounts were deposited raised suspicions and, following an investigation, the fraudulent account was exposed and found to have been trading at a profit, with gains deposited into an Australian bank account (FATF 2009, pp. 26–7).

Certain derivative products available in EDMs also present a significant money laundering threat. A prime example of this is the use of 'participatory notes' (PNotes). PNotes are offshore derivative instruments (ODIs), intermediated by brokerage houses, and issued by registered foreign institutional investors (FIIs) in EDMs such as India and China. FIIs dealing in these products include the subsidiaries of some of the largest derivatives dealers. Notably, controversy has surrounded the use of these instruments in the Indian financial market in recent years (Singh 2007). Taking the Indian example, FIIs registered in India undertake to invest in securities or derivatives on behalf of overseas clients who themselves are not necessarily registered, or interested in going through relatively onerous procedures, to trade on the Indian stock market (Mathur 2008, p. 43). These transactions appear to proceed roughly as follows. An investor deposits funds with a US or European operation of an FII based in India or Mauritius. The Indian or Mauritian office of the FII then uses its account to purchase stocks or derivatives in India, issuing a PNote to the overseas client. The client then enjoys dividends or other benefits accruing from the securities or derivatives underlying the PNote. However, beneficial ownership of PNotes may be particularly obscure, given that these instruments may subsequently be traded by the overseas client with some other third party.

These instruments have been popular because the holders of PNotes can effectively take positions on stocks and derivatives without having to formally register with the Securities Exchange Board of India (SEBI) (Kapoor 2012, pp. 44–6). However, given their structure, PNotes can also evidently facilitate potentially deleterious activities such as money laundering (Kapoor 2012, pp. 44–6). Because of the money laundering threat as well as other 'hidden ownership'[24] related concerns, in recent years SEBI has issued more restrictive requirements with respect to these instruments.[25] In particular, SEBI now requires that beneficial owners of shares through PNote instruments be identified by FIIs and has taken enforcement actions, including against at least two large derivatives dealers, in relation to alleged inadequate ownership disclosure with respect to PNotes.[26]

24.4 FORTHCOMING OTC DERIVATIVES MARKET INFRASTRUCTURE REFORMS IN BRIEF

Public regulatory reforms in the wake of the GFC, especially in the US[27] and EU,[28] aim to push a greater volume of OTC derivative instruments through CCPs and to increase the volume of derivatives traded on regulated exchanges (Morgan 2012). The reforms also demand notification of most OTC derivatives transactions to trade (swap data) repositories (TRs) or public regulatory authorities. These market infrastructure reform proposals ultimately seek to alter the regulatory situation prevailing in the years immediately prior to the GFC when trading in OTC derivatives between sophisticated market participants in the largest markets was not substantially directly regulated.[29] However, at the time of writing, many technical aspects of market infrastructure reforms in OTC derivatives markets, both within and across jurisdictions, are debateable and are yet to be fully elaborated.[30] Consequently, there are clear signals at the time of writing that a potentially significant divergence in the substantive implementation of reform across jurisdictions may materialise.[31]

In so far as market infrastructure reforms are finally implemented, they could, in principle, conceivably reinforce existing anti-money laundering regulations across jurisdictions and thereby mitigate certain types of laundering through derivatives. However, there are at the same time other reasons to suspect that OTC derivatives market infrastructure amendments may not necessarily exert a significant mitigating effect on money laundering and/or may open up new opportunities for laundering. This is because, as illustrated, it has historically been possible to engage in laundering through the traditionally more heavily regulated exchange-traded derivatives markets. Given that OTC derivative market infrastructure reforms seek to emulate trading structures in the exchange-traded markets, there is no guarantee that the implementation of market infrastructure reforms, in themselves, will necessarily mitigate money laundering in the OTC derivative markets.

Furthermore, even if OTC derivatives market infrastructure reforms are fairly consistently implemented in the more advanced derivatives markets, it is apparent that implementation could differ across jurisdictions. In practice, this could operate to increasingly export OTC derivatives-related money laundering activities to emerging derivatives markets (EDMs).

24.5 CONCLUSIONS

This chapter has sought to set out a general overview of derivatives markets and their regulation, as well as their size and the main actors which populate them. This was followed by an indication of some of the ways in which derivatives could be invoked to engage in money laundering. It must be stressed that the methods outlined in this chapter are indicative and there could conceivably be a multitude of ways in which money laundering through derivatives could occur; especially as these markets, and the regulations governing them, evolve over time.

NOTES

* The substantive content of this chapter was largely completed in October 2011, with minor revisions in August 2012 and February 2013. This chapter emanated from a larger research initiative entitled Regulating OTC Derivatives for Better Corporate Governance, conducted under the umbrella of a transnational research collaboration titled Transnational Private Regulation: Constitutional Foundations and Governance Design. That broader research initiative was funded by The Hague Institute for the Internationalization of Law (HiiL) http://www.privateregulation.eu. I am grateful to Colin Scott and Blanaid Clarke for their guidance on the broader research initiative. Any views expressed in this chapter are the personal views of the author alone and do not necessarily represent the views of any other individual or organisation to which the author is affiliated. Errors and omissions are also the author's alone.

1. See, e.g., B. Unger and J. den Hertog, 'Water Always Finds its Way: Identifying New Forms of Money Laundering' (2012) 7 *Crime, Law and Social Change* 287, at 297.
2. See, e.g., Commodity Futures Modernization Act, Pub. Law No. 106 – 554, 114 Stat. 2763 (2000) (US). Although OTC derivatives have been regulated to some degree indirectly through usage constraints, documentation and suitability standards, and so forth. See, e.g., Directive 2009/65/EC of the European Parliament and of the Council of 13 July 2009 on the coordination of laws, regulations and administra-

tive provisions relating to undertakings for collective investment in transferable securities [2009] OJ L 302; Directive 2004/39/EC of the European Parliament and of the Council of 21 April 2004 on markets in financial instruments amending Council Directives 85/611/EEC and 93/6/EEC and Directive 2000/12/EC of the European Parliament and of the Council and Repealing Council Directive 93/22/EEC [2004] OJ L 145.

3. Financial Stability Board, *OTC Derivatives Market Reforms: Fourth Progress Report on Implementation* (31 October 2012) [http://www.financialstabilityboard.org/publications/r_121031a.pdf].
4. See, e.g., Directive 2005/60/EC of the European Parliament and of the Council of 26 October 2005 on the prevention of the use of the financial system for the purpose of money laundering and terrorist financing [2005] OJ L 309/15; European Commission, *Financial Crime* [http://ec.europa.eu/internal_market/company/financial-crime/index_en.htm]. See also, generally, C. Proctor, *The Law and Finance of International Banking* (Oxford: OUP, 2010).
5. Though the explosion of financial, rather than commodity, derivatives trading since the 1980s may warrant analytical segregation. See, e.g., D. Bryan and M. Rafferty, *Capitalism with Derivatives: A Political Economy of Financial Derivatives, Capital and Class* (New York: Palgrave macMillan 2006); E.J. Swan, *Building the Global Market: A 4000 Year History of Derivatives* (London: Kluwer 2000).
6. L.L. Jacque, *Global Derivative Debacles: From Theory to Malpractice* (Singapore: World Scientific 2010); J. Kim, 'Can Risks be Reduced in the Derivatives Market? Lessons from the Deal Structure Analysis of Modern Financial Engineering Debacles' (2007) 6 *DePaul Business and Commercial Law Journal* 29; A. Tickle, 'Creative Finance and the Local State: The Hammersmith and Fulham Swaps Affair' (1998) 17 *Political Geography* 865; N. Leeson, *Rogue Trader: How I Brought Down Barings Bank and Shook the Financial World* (London: Time Warner 1997); P.M. Garber, 'Famous First Bubbles' (1990) 4 *Journal of Economic Perspectives* 35.
7. For further discussion see, e.g., F. Partnoy, *Infectious Greed: How Deceit and Risk Corrupted the Financial Markets* (Philadelphia: PublicAffairs 2009) pp. 11–12.
8. For further discussion of CDS, including sovereign CDS in the context of the Eurozone sovereign debt crisis see, e.g., A. Gelpern and M. Gulati, 'CDS Zombies' (2012) 13 *European Business Organization Law Review* 347; A. Chander and R. Costa, 'Clearing Credit Default Swaps: A Case Study in Global Legal Convergence' (2010) 10 *Chicago Journal of International Law* 639.
9. A counterparty is exposed to a particular risk and seeks to shift that risk to another party better placed or willing to bear it. R.M. Stulz, 'Should We Fear Derivatives?' (2004) 18 *Journal of Economic Perspectives* 173, at 182; K.D. Krawiec, 'Derivatives, Corporate Hedging and Shareholder Wealth: Motigliani-Miller Forty Years Later' (1998) *University of Illinois Law Review* 1039; H.T.C. Hu, 'Hedging Expectations: "Derivative Reality" and the Law and Finance of the Corporate Objective' (1995) 21 *Journal of Corporation Law* 3.
10. A counterparty is in a position to assume a risk and/or seeks to capitalise on superior information regarding price movements. On the contested concept of speculation see, e.g., A.S. Kyle, 'Informed Speculation with Imperfect Competition' (1989) 56 *Review of Economic Studies* 317; O.D. Hart and D.M. Kreps, 'Price Destabilizing Speculation' (1986) 94 *Journal of Political Economy* 927; S. Grossman and J. Stiglitz, 'On the Impossibility of Informationally Efficient Markets' (1980) 70 *American Economic Review* 393.
11. The exploitation of a 'gap between the economic substance of a transaction and its legal or regulatory treatment, taking advantage of the legal system's intrinsically limited ability to attach formal labels that track the economics of transactions with sufficient precision', V. Fleischer, 'Regulatory Arbitrage' (2011) 89 *Texas Law Review* 227, at 229; F. Partnoy, 'Financial Derivatives and the Costs of Regulatory Arbitrage' (1997) 22 *Journal of Corporation Law* 211.
12. Geoffrey Poitras, 'From Antwerp to Chicago: The History of Exchange Traded Derivative Security Contracts', (2009) 20 *Journal for the History of the Social Sciences* 11.
13. [http://www2.isda.org/]. For discussion see, e.g., J. Biggins and C. Scott, 'Public-Private Relations in a Transnational Private Regulatory Regime: ISDA, the State and OTC Derivatives Market Reform' (2012) 13 *European Business Organization Law Review* 309.
14. These include market, credit, liquidity, operational and legal risk. See, e.g., K.D. Krawiec, 'More Than Just New "Financial Bingo": A Risk Based Approach to Understanding Derivatives' (1997) 23 *Journal of Corporation Law* 1.
15. ISDA, *ISDA Margin Survey 2012* [http://www2.isda.org/functional-areas/research/surveys/margin-surveys/].
16. For further discussion of these types of transactions and their potentially negative side effects see, e.g., T.E. Lynch, *Gambling By Another Name? The Challenge of Purely Speculative Derivatives* (Indiana University Maurer School of Law-Bloomington Legal Research Paper Series No. 188, March 2011) p. 14 [http://ssrn.com/abstract=1788219]; L.A. Stout, 'Why the Law Hates Speculators: Regulation and Private Ordering in the Market for OTC Derivatives' (1999) 48 *Duke Law Journal* 701.
17. See, e.g., M.J. Roe, 'The Derivatives Market's Payment Priorities as Financial Crisis Accelerator' (2011)

63 *Stanford Law Review* 539; W.K. Sjostrum Jr., 'The AIG Bailout' (2009) 66 *Washington & Lee Law Review* 943.

18. For a description of CCPs see, e.g., C. Pirrong, *The Economics of Central Clearing: Theory and Practice* (ISDA Discussion Papers No. 1, May 2011) [http://www2.isda.org/functional-areas/research/discussion-papers/].
19. For a definition of systemic risk see, e.g., S.L. Schwarcz, 'Systemic Risk' (2008) 97 *Georgetown Law Journal* 194, at 204.
20. See, e.g., C. Pirrong, *The Economics of Central Clearing: Theory and Practice* (ISDA Discussion Papers Series No.1 May 2011) [http://www.2isda.org/functional-areas/research/discussion-papers/].
21. Hedge funds can be defined as entities which 'capture private pools of capital for collective investment by sophisticated professional qualified investors, with no or limited regulatory constraints on what the vehicle invests in, allowing short selling in addition to or instead of classic long only investments, using leverage to finance securities positions and magnify funds' return to investors, the use of derivatives to take on or hedge out risks, and generally much more active trading than long-only mutual funds', W.V. Eechoud, W. Hamersma, A. Sieling and D. Young, 'Future Regulation of Hedge Funds: A Systemic Risk Perspective' (2010) 19 *Financial Markets, Institutions and Instruments* 269, at 274.
22. See, e.g., C.A. Johnson, Regulatory Arbitrage, Extraterritorial Jurisdiction and Dodd-Frank: The Implications of US Global OTC Derivative Regulation (Working Paper, 30 Ooctober 2012) [http://papers.ssrn.com/sol3/papers.cfm?abstract_id=2169401]; D. Mengle, *The Importance of Close-Out Netting* (ISDA Research Notes, 2010) [http://www.isda.org/researchnotes/pdf/Netting-ISDAResearchNotes-1–2010.pdf].
23. See, e.g., Bank for International Settlements, *Triennial Central Bank Survey of Foreign Exchange and OTC Derivatives Market Activity in April 2010* (1 September 2010) [http://www.bis.org/publ/rpfx10.pdf].
24. See, e.g., H.T.C. Hu and B. Black, 'Equity and Debt Decoupling and Empty Voting II: Importance and Extensions' (2008) 156 *University of Pennsylvania Law Review* 625.
25. See, e.g., SEBI, *Reporting of Offshore Derivative Instruments (ODIs)/Participatory Notes (PNs) Activity* (Circular, 7 June 2012) [http://www.sebi.gov.in/cms/sebi_data/attachdocs/1339064295331.pdf]; U. Varottil, 'Strategies for Host-Country Regulation of Hedge Funds: Lessons from India's Approach' (2009) 11 *Australian Journal of Asian Law* 113.
26. See, e.g., J. Leahy, 'India Suspends SocGen from Trading' *Financial Times* (15 January 2010); J. Leahy, 'Indian Regulator Acts Against Barclays' *Financial Times* (10 December 2009).
27. Title VII *Dodd-Frank Wall Street Reform and Consumer Protection Act 2010*, Pub. L. 111–203, H.R. 4173.
28. Regulation (EU) No 648/2012 of the european Parliament and of the Council of 4 July 2012 on OTC derivatives, central counterparties and trade repositories [2012] OJ L 201/1; European Commission, *Proposal for a Regulation on markets in financial instruments and amending Regulation [EMIR] on OTC derivatives, central counterparties and trade repositories* (20 October 2011) [http://eur-lex.europa.eu/LexUriServ/LexUriServ.do?uri=COM:2011:0652:FIN:EN:PDF].
29. See, e.g., D. Awrey, 'The FSA, Integrated Regulation and the Curious Case of OTC Derivatives' (2010) 13 *University of Pennsylvania Journal of Business Law* 1; T.L. Hazen, 'Disparate Regulatory Regimes for Parallel Activities: Securities Regulation, Derivatives Regulation, Gambling and Insurance' (2005) 24 *Annual Review of Banking and Financial Law* 375.
30. See, e.g., J.P. Braithwaite, 'The Inherent Limits of "Legal Devices": Lessons for the Public Sector's Central Counterparty Prescription for OTC Derivatives Markets' (2011) 12 *European Business Organization Law Review* 87.
31. See, e.g., FSB, *OTC Derivatives Market Reforms: Third Progress Report on Implementation* (15 June 2012) [http://www.financialstabilityboard.org/publications/r_120615.pdf].

REFERENCES

Bank for International Settlements (2011), 'Derivative Financial Instruments Traded on Organized Exchanges' (September 2011) [http://www.bis.org/publ/qtrpdf/r_qa1109.pdf#page=136].

Bank for International Settlements (2012), 'OTC Derivatives Statistics at End-December 2011' (May 2012) [http://www.bis.org/publ/otc_hy1205.pdf].

Bedi, R. (2006), 'Dirty Derivatives' (June 2006) AsiaRisk, 2–3 [http://www.rohanbedi.com/Dirty_Derivatives.pdf].

Ceccheti, S.G., J. Gyntelberg and M. Hollanders (2009), 'Central Counterparties for Over-the-Counter Derivatives,' *Bank for International Settlements Quarterly Review*, 45, 45–58.

CPSS and IOSCO (2010), *Considerations for Trade Repositories in OTC Derivatives Markets*, Bank for International Settlements: May.
Duffie, D., A.Li and T. Lubke (2010), 'Policy Perspectives on OTC Derivatives Market Reforms', *Federal Reserve Bank of New York Staff Report*, 424.
Faulkner, R. (2005), 'Contracts for Differences: The Case for Disclosure', *International Financial Law Review*, 15.
Feder, N.M (2002), 'Deconstructing Over-the-Counter Derivatives', *Columbia Business Law Review*, 677.
Financial Action Task Force [FATF] (1999), *1998–1999 Report on Money Laundering Typologies* (10 February 1999) http://www.apgml.org/frameworks/docs/5/FATF%20Typologies%20rpt%201998–99.pdf.
Financial Action Task Force [FATF] (2009), *Report on Money Laundering and Terrorist Financing in the Securities Sector* (October 2009) [http://www.fatf-gafi.org/media/fatf/documents/reports/ML%20and%20TF%20in%20the%20Securities%20Sector.pdf].
Gerding, E.F. (2011), 'Credit Derivatives, Leverage and Financial Regulation's Missing Macroeconomic Dimension', *Berkeley Business Law Journal*, 8.
Hetzer, W. (2003), 'Money Laundering and Financial Markets', *European Journal of Crime, Criminal Law and Criminal Justice*, 264.
Ledrut, E. and C. Upper (2007), 'Changing Post-Trading Arrangements for OTC Derivatives', *Bank for International Settlements Quarterly Review*, 83.
Kapoor, K. (2012), 'FII Taxes in India: Clear as Mud', *Financial Times* (30 March).
Lynch, T.E. (2011), 'Derivatives: A Twenty First Century Understanding', *Indiana University School of Law – Bloomington Legal Studies Research Paper Series*, Research Paper No. 187, March 2011.
Markham, J.W. and D.J. Harty (2008), 'For Whom the Bell Tolls: The Demise of Exchange Trading Floors and the Growth of ECNs', *Journal of Corporation Law*, 865.
Mathur, H. (2008), 'Indian Securities Market and Participatory Notes: A Corporate Quandry', *VIDHIGYA: The Journal of Legal Awareness*, 42.
Mengle, D. (2010), 'Concentration of OTC Derivatives Among Major Dealers', *ISDA: Research Notes*, 4.
Mihalijek, D. and F. Packer (2010), 'Derivatives in Emerging Markets', *Bank for International Settlements Quarterly Review*, 43.
Morgan, G. (2012), 'Reforming OTC Markets: The Politics and Economics of Technical Fixes', *European Business Organization Law Review*, 391.
Schneider, F. (2008), 'Money Laundering and Financial Means of Organized Crime: Some Preliminary Empirical Findings,' *Paolo Baffi Centre Research Paper Series*, 2008–16.
Shadab, H.B. (2010), 'Guilty By Association? Regulating Credit Default Swaps', *Entrepreneurial Business Law Journal*, 407.
Sharma, S.K. (2001), 'Dirty Money: How the UK Securities and Derivatives Markets Are Used to Launder Money', *Journal of Money Laundering Control*, 309.
Simser, J. (2008), 'Money Laundering and Asset Cloaking Techniques', *Journal of Money Laundering Control*, 15.
Singh, M. (2007), 'Use of Participatory Notes in Indian Equity Markets and Recent Regulatory Challenges', *IMF Working Paper* WP/07/291, December 2007.
Stout, L.A. (2011), 'Derivatives and the Legal Origin of the 2008 Credit Crisis', *Harvard Business Law Review*, 302.
Waldman, A.P. (1994), 'OTC Derivatives and Systemic Risk: Innovative Finance or Dance Into the Abyss?', *American University Law Review*, 1023.

25. E-gaming, money laundering and the problem of risk assessment*

Michael Levi

25.1 INTRODUCTION

Criminal risk levels are a combination of criminal motivations, existing/developing criminal capacities, and situational opportunities for crimes offered by the way control is organised. Gambling is an area of considerable moral controversy and legislative/judicial change within and outside the European Union (EU). There is scope for improvement in controls over fraud and laundering and regulators need to be vigilant about the resourcing levels of anti-fraud/Anti-Money Laundering (AML) efforts in the private sector, as well as being internationally consistent in their requirements, following deliberation between different regulators and consultation with the industry. There is much mythology about e-gaming laundering risks, fed by: (a) the self-interest of monopolistic and other state lotteries;[1] (b) inadequate information (though it is not obvious what levels of information would count as 'adequate'); and (c) a tendency to project a dislike of gaming – and/or private sector involvement in it – into alarm about e-crime in general and the role of gaming in e-crime in particular. This is a review of e-gaming in the EU and the money-laundering risks that can arise, and are known to arise, from it (see also the recent discussion in European Commission 2011; 2012).

People use the term 'money laundering' in two quite distinct ways, though the difference may not always be apparent to themselves or to others. The first is to mean the hiding of the illicit origins of funds in order to make tainted wealth look legitimate. This, we suspect, is what most people who encounter the term would expect money laundering to mean. The second – acquiring, possessing or using the proceeds of crime – comprises all acts that fall within the laws and regulations against money laundering. These terms are intentionally framed broadly by legislators in order to stimulate business, finance, and the professions to make it harder for criminals to legitimate their wealth in the first sense above. This penalises broadly defined self-laundering by those who commit the primary money-generating crimes ('predicate crimes'), to the extent that almost anything they do with the proceeds constitutes laundering (Van Duyne 2003; Van Duyne et al. 2005). Thus, any euro spent in (illegal) gambling is laundering, irrespective of whether the criminal is winning or losing the game.

25.2 RISKS AND THREATS IN MONEY LAUNDERING AND E-GAMING

There has been a slow evolution in the understanding (and/or misunderstanding) of money laundering and responses to risk, and in the construct of proportionality of those losses. In the first phase, during and after the international criminalisation recommendations in the 1988 Vienna Convention, analysts examined what they took to be the most common forms of money laundering in the cases of which they had knowledge – mostly proceeds of cash-generating crimes like illegal drug sales. In the second phase – which existed in inchoate form in the 1980s – some conceptual work was done to identify the ways in which criminals might be able to launder money. This accompanied the growth of the range of predicate offences and of the number of areas of commerce regulated by AML (from the initial exclusive focus on financial services businesses). Nevertheless, there was curiously little effort to examine how commonly these vulnerabilities were actually exploited or, indeed, what the impact of such exploitation might be on society or on levels of different crimes.[2] Such cost–benefit efforts are implicit in the concept of proportionality of responses to risk, which is important since 'risk' is so omnipresent in our daily lives. Along with other activities traditionally associated with criminals, gambling has come under scrutiny by AML bodies (FATF 2008a, 2009), but this chapter will focus on e-gaming, which, like many on-line activities, is seen by some as carrying especial risks.

25.2.1 E-gaming Risks

In 2010, global revenue for on-line gambling was nearly $30 billion, and less than 15 per cent came from the US (H2 2011). As of 30 June 2010, Spectrum Gaming (2011) found 2,679 Internet gambling sites owned by 665 companies. These included:

- 865 on-line casinos
- 616 on-line poker rooms
- 516 sports betting sites
- 426 on-line bingo sites
- 187 lottery and other sites.

The aim of this review is to contribute to more developed thinking in one particular area of money laundering risk: that related to e-gaming or remote gambling.[3] These include the following areas of activity (s. 4, UK Gambling Act 2005):

- remote wagering on horse races;
- remote lottery play;
- on-line telephone race and sports books;
- multi-player on-line poker through interactive poker rooms;
- on-line casinos offering on-line gambling through games such as blackjack;
- betting exchanges – peer-to-peer betting exchanges by which individual bettors can place wagers against one another on opposing outcomes of a future event;
- interactive gambling – including wagering forms as diverse as traditional betting to fixed-odds gambling, live and interactive bingo betting, and interactive betting on live sporting events.

It will be argued that e-gaming *does* present money laundering risks, but that – despite the evocations of alarm and evil (see Bauer 2008) that often accompany the 'e' word attached to crime (Levi 2008, 2009) – in a *regulated* environment, the risks are lower than in land-based gaming and in cash-based businesses. This is due to: (a) the high traceability of transactions, (b) betting limits, and (c) customer identification controls in the regulated sector. If e-gaming firms themselves were illegal and unregulated (in the formal sense), AML would be wholly dependent on controls exercised by card issuers and merchant acquirers.

There are very few areas of social and commercial life that present no crime risks.[4] However, there remain problems of how we judge risks to individual countries or groups of countries, such as the EU. There are three sorts of criminal situations in which businesses are involved that are relevant to threats against e-gaming firms and the public:

1. perpetrators who use businesses as tools to victimise others (like fake gaming websites to collect card and other personal details which can then be used fraudulently, on-line or off-line);
2. perpetrators who utilise businesses to facilitate other crimes (e.g. wholly or partly as money laundering vehicles); and
3. perpetrators who use their positions inside businesses to commit substantive crimes (from duplicating customer identity details to defrauding the companies for which they work).

The key points that require analysis are: (a) what money laundering harms theoretically *could* follow from e-gaming; (b) what do we know about how commonly these are *actually* exploited; (c) how (if at all) would we know if these opportunities were exploited at a significantly greater rate than at present; (d) and why would offenders (in general, or particular sorts of offenders) choose to launder funds through e-gaming rather than through other mechanisms?

There is much dispute about the total volume of proceeds from crime, and little evidence about how this varies between different sectors of the wholly illicit and partly illicit economy. The often-quoted International Monetary Fund estimate is based upon very little evidence (Levi and Reuter 2006), and mere repetition does not compensate for its lack of underlying validity. UK government economists have 'estimated' an annual mid-point figure of £30 billion for trafficking in drugs and people, fraud and financial crime generated in the UK (Cabinet Office/Home Office 2009). However, even on the heroic assumption that this is acceptable as a very rough order-of-magnitude figure, this tells us nothing about what proportion of these proceeds is spent on daily expenses or laundered (in the narrower sense of saved and/or re-invested in the licit economy). There are no equivalent defensible estimates for the EU as a whole, but the total sum would obviously be very large. One key question is how plausible it is that a significant amount of this total laundering would occur via e-gaming.

The financing of terrorism presents different issues; because direct operational costs[5] of the London and Madrid bombings were under €10,000, very small amounts of laundering may be critical to terrorists' success. But since terrorism can be funded by both licit and illicit activities, the range of behaviours that could generate such sums is so vast that it is almost impossible to monitor without sophisticated aggregate models and/or listing individuals and institutions believed to constitute such a threat. Thus, e-gaming is

Table 25.1 Volume and value of payment card expenditure on gaming in the UK

	Volume (000s)	Value (m)	Average transaction Value
2004	65,234	£1,975	£30.29
2005	86,945	£2,641	£30.38
2006	113,193	£3,312	£29.26
2007	128,117	£3,511	£27.40
2008	130,155	£3,562	£27.36

only one potential source of terrorist finance among many others. And even if it was connected with terrorist plots (as some newspaper sources have claimed and as is evidenced in one UK case), terrorists would not have found it difficult to find another source of funding or 'value transfers'.[6]

25.2.1.1 E-gaming in Europe: the economic context

Let us look at the money laundering risks within the perspective of the size of the on-line betting and gaming industry. On-line gambling accounts for some 5 per cent of global Gross Gaming Revenues (stakes minus winnings). European players constitute around half the global market for on-line gaming (excluding lotteries). In 2009, H2 Gambling Capital estimated Gross Gaming Revenues in the European gaming market at €85 billion for 2008, of which €6.5 billion (7.65 per cent of the total) was from on-line gaming. Three quarters of this (€4.8 billion) went to private operators, the rest going to state monopolies. On-line gambling volumes were projected to rise significantly by 2012, but the public/private sector ratios are not expected to change. Gambling (a wider category than just e-gaming) accounts for 2.2 per cent (by volume) and 1.2 per cent (by value) of total plastic card spending at UK acquired merchants. According to UK Payments, the trends for plastic spending on gaming in the UK were fairly stable, as shown in Table 25.1.

25.2.1.2 Review of money laundering data in e-gaming

E-gaming (as contrasted with land-based forms of gambling) does not feature significantly, or indeed at all, in the recent published threat assessments of Europol (2011)[7] and other European policing organisations, or in the policing priorities that accompany or develop out of these threat assessments. The expressions of concern about possible risks of the Internet are often wrapped up with the trade in child pornography (itself a very broad category) but do not evidence laundering via e-gaming.[8] Historically, e-gaming risks have often been placed in the same category as two other areas of commerce: (1) gaming/gambling generally[9] and (2) e-gold and other forms of e-wallet/prepaid cards that are designed to transfer funds, and that have been the arena of choice among some cyber-criminals for their inter-criminal transfers (Glenny 2011).

It is important to understand the basis for some of the risk statements made, and how these can vary over time and place, a variation not always appreciated in some critiques of on-line gaming risks (Bauer 2008). There is an enormous difference between the limitations imposed on prepaid cards in a European and in the, typically much less constrained, American context. Europe places low limits on payments into prepaid cards and imposes some customer identification on them. The American prepaid cards that generated FATF concern had high limits and no significant customer identification or post-purchase monitoring. (For a discussion of risks arising from Stored Value Cards, see Choo 2008.)

Prior to the Fourth Money Laundering Directive proposed in 2013, there have been no AML regulations designed with a specific focus on e-gaming. Thus the FATF risk-based review of casinos (2008a) treated Internet casinos as a special case of casino, noting the lower risks normally attached to the former than the latter. The FATF (2008b) report on Internet payments noted (para. 4):

> The financial transactions that are initiated from a bank account or a credit card (which is the majority of online payments) already involve a customer identification process as well as transaction record keeping and reporting obligations. While low value transactions do not necessarily equate to low risk, these transactions are subject to the regulatory controls already applicable to the financial sector and may be consequently less risky. Regarding the risks associated with the non-face-to-face registration and the possible anonymity of the users, the study highlights the need for online identity verification solutions (the electronic identity card used in certain countries for instance) to help commercial websites and Internet payment service providers mitigate the risk of criminal activity. . . If Internet payment service providers adequately monitor the financial transactions of their customers, monitoring for and acting on deviations from the customer transaction profile, the lack of face-to-face contact at the beginning of the relationship with the commercial website and Internet payment service provider may not constitute a problem. Online and offline retail merchants and payment services should have comparable AML/CFT obligations.

However, it is important to disentangle the levels of risk from different products. One important distinction arises out of the legality or illegality of e-gaming itself. Where e-gaming offered by private operators is per se illegal, as is currently the situation in the US and some European countries, the knowing use of such funds by e-gaming businesses arguably[10] becomes money laundering because under the 'all crimes' laundering model mandated by FATF, illegal e-gaming is a predicate act. Consequently, all subsequent acts, like concealment, disposal, and assisting in the disposal of funds etc. obtained from e-gamers, become money laundering. Thus, in the US and in some EU countries, e-gaming offered by private operators presents a 'serious' problem of money laundering because (*and only because*) unlicensed e-gaming is criminal and because many people like to bet, both on-line and off-line with private operators. By contrast, the identical behaviour engaged in within the UK presents very little money-laundering risk because the gambling is not a predicate crime. So from an overall EU perspective, it is problematic to include within a crime-threat framework activities such as e-gaming itself that are legal in parts of the EU.[11]

What is more significant and worthwhile is to examine the use of e-gaming to launder the proceeds of crimes other than (where the gaming is prohibited by criminal law) the activity of e-gaming itself. Financial institutions have primary responsibility for Know Your Customer (KYC) on their account-holders. As the FATF (2008a, b) concedes, the fact that e-gaming requires funds from a financial institution suggests that these risks are not high (or, one might add, are, at worst, no higher than any activity perpetrated via an account with a licit savings institution).

25.2.2 Areas of Money-Laundering Risk

Risks from (and to) offenders are also a function of controls. One area of risk relates to the possibility that e-gaming firms can credit winnings or unused funds back to an account other than the one on which the original bet was made: an issue which gaming firms share with other business areas. Payment card firms normally do not allow winnings and cash-ins to be credited to card accounts other than those used in the original gaming transactions,[12] though they may be obliged to do so if the customer insists. But then they have the option to report this as a suspicious activity to the appropriate financial intelligence unit. They may also pay the customer by cheque or other means of payment, even if the original payment in was made by card. To the extent that they do, and especially if they reimburse to cards in names other than that of the original gamer, this is a control weakness. If detected after the fact, e-gaming on stolen cards/card numbers imposes charge-back costs on gaming firms, and it also imposes (mainly) non-economic costs on cardholders (who – as in all fraud and overcharging cases – have to go to the trouble of complaining and getting the costs reversed). The funds credited to the other account will be proceeds of crime, and therefore money laundering, even where the misused cardholder loses nothing financially.

However, for the assessment of the *general* risks posed by e-gaming, what is crucial is the *scale* of the repayments to other cards or forms of funds that is allowed, and the time over which this is possible without controls kicking in. For card fraudsters, such 'windows of opportunity' are fairly crucial, since elapsed time enhances the risk of reporting and discovery, though, even if discovered, the actual and perceived risk to offenders of criminal action being taken against payment card fraudsters of all kinds is modest, because of criminal justice resource constraints and priorities in many EU Member States. Concerning the scale of repayments, offenders would have to work quite hard to move significant quantities of funds via e-gaming. It is not obvious why they would bother with this process at all. The fact that losses from card fraud related charge-backs (for rejected card transactions made on counterfeit or stolen cards/card numbers) are less than 1 per cent of total funds deposited – below the industry average – suggests that the level of card fraud used for e-gaming is under control. Hence, this component of the risk is not severe, though the total euro value of sums charged back (and therefore obtained/transmitted by criminals) may be large. Charge-backs may not reflect laundering (moving funds to obscure the illegality of the source) as much as the gambling appetite of risk-taking criminals, enjoying gaming at what is, in the end, the expense of the gaming firms themselves, since cardholders and merchant acquirers are reimbursed for their losses. So to that extent, a focus on charge-backs overstates the e-laundering component, ignoring the fact that many criminals are risk-takers who simply enjoy gambling.

Some of the gaming is stopped by the e-gaming firms themselves because it does not correspond to the risk profile of cardholders. Far more data are available for e-gaming firms to develop such profiles than in almost all off-line environments.

A second area of risk arises from the possibility of using 'front people' – i.e. nominees acting for undisclosed principals – through whom to run gaming transactions. This can be done in any area of financial services, as in the case of students being paid as 'mules'[13] to allow their personal accounts to be used as conduits for transfers from overseas. At a more serious level, launderers can pay business people (or covertly act as beneficial owners themselves) to merge proceeds of crime with their normal takings. This is a risk that is heightened at times of economic pressure. They can also purchase lottery and other winning bets from the real winners (at what marginal laundering cost mark-up is unknown) so that they get a cheque/electronic payment from a legitimate-source agency, which should disarm bankers' suspicions of money laundering. However, there is a limit to how many such wins – especially lottery wins – anyone can plausibly get to defeat the suspicions of bankers, and/or any criminal investigator, if they do not accept these explanations of wealth at face value. So, although people prohibited from gaming in their own names (because they are too successful and lose gaming firms money) can use front people to conduct their gaming covertly, one might question why *launderers* of crime proceeds would do so when there are so many other avenues for concealment of beneficial ownership.

A third area of risk arises in the context of peer-to-peer games, where value transfers can occur between players as a result of deliberate losses. Such losses do not generate any direct financial risks for the e-gaming firms themselves – indeed they benefit from their share of the bets – and, therefore, their only motive for intervention is the avoidance of reputational or regulatory/penal damage.[14] However, in addition to widely available poker manuals on probabilities of winning for different hands that generate 'expected data', they have expert players observing such games, whose judgment that players are losing deliberately can lead to the freezing of transactions and accounts, and perhaps to suspicious activity reports (SARs).

A fourth area of risk arises from the possibility of paying via other financial intermediaries, which are regulated for AML purposes but where KYC is of modest or variable quality (as is also the case in the mainstream financial sector). Funds used to purchase e-money can come from legal sources, licit but tax-evading sources, or wholly criminal sources. It is obviously possible for criminals to use the proceeds of crime to purchase e-wallets or vouchers, which can be spent on e-gaming and on more tangible commodities. Persons using these more anonymous media are still, however, subject to the customer identification and trading pattern checks of the e-gaming firms themselves, which include bans on multiple identities playing from the same geo-location/IP address. Thus, even the leisure expenditure by criminals on e-gaming would be subject to controls if they are using fraudulent cards or multiple addresses.

The final area of risk to be mentioned here is different from the others, but arises from the FATF (2009) review of *Money-Laundering Through the Football Sector*. The report states that separate attention should be paid to laundering via legal and illegal betting but this is a 'huge and increasing problem' (p. 8, para. 26), though the empirical grounds for this view remain obscure. It adds (pp. 24–25):

> **Betting activities**
>
> 79. There is an ambiguous relationship between betting and sport. On the one hand, betting has historically been an important revenue source for sport in many countries. On the other hand, betting has also been associated with attempts to fix matches and alter the results of sporting competitions. Betting can be used both for the generation of illegal proceeds from game fixing and for pure money laundering purposes.
>
> 80. The FIFA Task Force 'for the Good of the Game' has observed that 'due to its particular structure, as well as the considerable need to finance the system at short notice, football offers a tempting platform for irregular betting activities. As the media and the public eye focus on fixtures in top competitions and top leagues, irregular betting activities can

frequently be observed in less important fixtures (including lower divisions of domestic championships), where the environment can be manipulated more easily. Recent scandals in which betting has resulted in the manipulation of matches have brought the game into serious disrepute'.

81. While problems linked to betting are not new, it appears that betting in sport has reached new levels of sophistication with various operators involved across several countries and continents and new offshore betting companies being established. Moreover, the use of the Internet for online betting further increases the risk of money laundering.

. . .

84. Due to the fact that most countries have different gambling regulations, the gambling market is non-transparent and is a heterogeneous market with a mix of private and state companies acting both nationally and internationally. Providers are often established in countries which allow the organisation of gambling activities or in countries that do not regulate or supervise gambling. It is however not easy to take legal action against providers who offer their services online and are established abroad. This in combination with the non-transparency of the gambling market makes betting an interesting money laundering vehicle for criminals.

This mixes up legal and illegal betting in a way that is unhelpful for the purposes of assessing risks. Moreover, it does not separate out cases where the operating companies (and sometimes the clubs or horse owners, and other bettors) are the victims – as in corrupt fixing of overall or spread-betting results in order to ensure success – from those in which operating companies do not have a particular interest or risk of loss. 'The Internet' does indeed change the nature of most forms of social risk, but, though the criminal courts may have difficulty dealing with data-driven cases, the large amount of data available in the *regulated* e-gaming sector makes it difficult to comprehend the nature of the extra risks attributed to e-laundering through the football sector as compared with other sorts of crime risks, especially match or spot-fixing. In some respects, this makes an argument for the regulation rather than prohibition of Internet gambling, but it is not self-evident that state-owned e-gaming generates few (or no) risks compared with private sector e-gaming. Nor does the FATF report make it clear in an e-gaming context whether the extra laundering risks result from fraud and corruption in the *betting* process, or from the laundering of the proceeds of crimes other than from fraud and corruption. It is clear that the purchase and management of football clubs (and inadequacies in the identification of beneficial owners thereof) offer opportunities for placement, layering, and integration; however, there is little risk analysis.

Choo and Smith (2008: 50–51) discuss the variety of risks arising in on-line gaming, of which the most relevant to this study are:

- Creating special programs to gain unfair advantages by modifying game software and data, by exploiting bugs and design flaws, and reverse engineering the gaming program. The perpetrators then have a better chance of winning in competitions and tournaments that award winners with prizes (e.g. unlocking new car components or car models). These acquired virtual assets can subsequently be traded or sold.
- Designing cloned websites with the aim of gaining the login credentials of legitimate players and committing other crimes including identity theft.
- Choo and Smith argue that the future will see the continued development of

malicious code by organised cyber-criminal groups targeting the on-line gaming community. However, these risks are aimed more at 'domestic' gaming, Second Life and its virtual currencies, than at the sort of e-gaming conducted via the regulated e-gaming sector. It is also possible to programme electronic bets to offer bets at unusual times which are taken up by other bets (both on 2-player tables or on 6-player poker tables, which are unlikely to be occupied at those times) who then win. Done occasionally, so that the easy bet is not taken on by another player who is not in the conspiracy, or is not identified as a suspicious pattern of play by the gaming firm, this can be used to transfer value. However, as a large-scale laundering mechanism, it is unlikely to be successful.

- Since there continues to be debate about the risks from prepaid cards, it should be noted that *reloadable* prepaid cards in the UK, from Member Banks of the Card schemes (i.e. open loop) require the same KYC checks as is required for opening a UK Basic Bank Account without a credit facility. There do not appear to be different legal limits on *reloadable* prepaid cards; the card is seen as merely the access device to the customer's account. However:
  - As there is no on-going banking relationship, *non-reloadable* prepaid cards (fixed value) e.g. gift cards, do not require KYC.
  - The maximum value on a non-reloadable card is circa $750 in Europe. These cards are issued anonymously (no personalisation) and therefore do not have ATM (cash) access. General controls on them are more modest but some of the same analytical techniques used to control e-gaming fraud and money-laundering risks (geo-location, IP addresses, etc.) can be used here also.

The 2009 E-money Directive (EMD) makes significant changes across the European Community regarding jurisdiction and access rights to who can offer e-money on a prepaid card.[15]

There has been a significant rise in Card-Not-Present (on-line) payment card fraud generally, largely reflecting the enhanced controls over off-line and card/cardholder present risks generated by the spread of Chip and PIN in the Single European Payments Area (SEPA). In the UK, for example, phone, Internet and mail order fraud rose 13 per cent to £328.4 million in 2008 (a rise of 350 per cent since 2000), though it has subsequently fallen. Looking at Internet fraud alone, £181.7 million of card fraud took place over the Internet in 2008, an increase of 2 per cent since 2007. Internet fraud now accounts for over half of card-not present losses. No information is available on the extent of such card fraud usage in the e-gaming sector, but industry sources confirm that this sector does not account for a significant proportion of fraud losses.

25.3 EFFORTS TO COMBAT MONEY LAUNDERING

On-line gaming companies licensed and regulated in the EU have chosen to comply with the Third EU Directive[16] for the prevention of money-laundering, which – strictly speaking – applies only to casinos within the gaming sector. In addition, the regulated sector also subscribes to codes of conduct such as that of the European Gaming and Betting Association[17] and the Remote Gambling Association.[18]

On-line gaming companies collect a significant amount of data on the IP addresses, gaming, and gaming finance patterns of their customers, which are used to build up profiles against which to assess the risks posed by particular customers. E-gaming firms vary in the extent to which they impose spending limits and in general business sectors and financial services this would be regarded as a purely business decision. Greater diligence is (and should be) exercised where gaming limits are higher, since this generates greater laundering opportunities.

All the businesses interviewed by this author in 2008 have different business models, and consequently implement different risk-based solutions to mitigate the potential for anti-money laundering and crime risks. The operators interviewed acknowledge that there is no single magic bullet to combat crime, but that a cocktail of tools – which may vary over time – is required to combat any risks in a proportionate manner. Consequently, they employ a hybrid anti-fraud model using a combination of techniques, including, but not limited to, manual external data checks, internal business rules, and statistical profiling. In addition, some businesses are utilising, or intend to utilise, advanced machine learning techniques. Analytically, these may be split into categories as follows:

- *Manual*
    - agents flag cases they consider to be 'suspicious' based on risk alerts, customer tip-offs, and unusual betting and or wagering play by customers.
- *Third Party Data*
    - age verification lists sourced from firms in the market;
    - hotlists, including the sorts of data sources used by banks to identify terrorists and public officials (entitled 'Politically Exposed Persons') who require 'Enhanced Due Diligence';
    - telematching;
    - the European Sports Security Association watch list.
- *Rules Based*
    - pre-defined rules based on business knowledge and past experiences. For example limitation on the number of credit cards that can be used; device reputation models.
- *Statistical Profiling*
    - outliers of transactional behaviour determined through regression analysis;
    - risk scoring models.
- *Advanced Analytics – Artificial Intelligence*
    - creating predictive modelling techniques;
    - implementation of neural networks to assist the human thought process in detecting fraudulent trends.

Compared to methods of customer identification and monitoring in the off-line gaming and financial services sector, the scope for substantial abuse of e-gaming for laundering purposes is modest, both for those crimes that generate cash and for those that generate benefits in forms other than cash. This is partly a result of the greater recording of transactions in this industry than in most others, and partly the consequence of legitimate firms being subject to regulation (though it is possible for criminals to take control of e-gambling firms, as can be the case with any business, even regulated ones).

The industry does make efforts to identify and report suspicious activities by customers, though – as in every area of commerce – firms have different approaches to this. However, the research by Levi (2009) did not have the opportunity of evaluating operationally how different firms operated this scrutiny in practice. *In itself, the number of SARs is neither a success nor a failure indicator of AML effectiveness.* The more effective that front-line KYC controls are, and the less inherently exploitable an industry is to large post account-opening expansion of trading (enabling more funds to be laundered), the smaller the overall laundering problem that is posed. Subject to their skills and contacts, offenders typically will search for easier ways to launder. Thus, if money laundering controls are tight and are perceived by offenders to be tight – or if e-gaming is not contemplated at all by them as a laundering route – one might expect few SARs to be made.

In the UK in 2010 to 2011, 671 out of 247,601 SARs were made by the gaming sector, plus 207 from the spread-betting sector. (One from each sector was forwarded for terrorist financing investigation.) The total for gaming was down from the previous year but up from 403 in 2007 to 2008 and 299 in 2006 to 2007 (SOCA 2011). However, there is no breakdown for e-gaming compared with land-based gaming.

25.4 CONCLUSIONS

Legislation on Internet gambling is changing, not just in Europe, but elsewhere in the world, as countries struggle between trying to enforce moral attitudes and the practicalities of controlling behaviour. While taking account of businesses that offer both land-based and Internet gaming, it is desirable to have separate AML regulations for *e*-gaming, since opportunities for monitoring are so different. E-gaming using Stored Value Cards and even newer financial media, such as payment-enabled mobile phones, that have *not* been through significant KYC controls may present different orders of risk. Not all laundering via e-gaming can be eliminated, but because of the controls over the number of cards used per account-holder and the electronic monitoring of location and IP addresses, there is no evidence that the *general* risks posed by e-gaming are serious compared with other methods of laundering the proceeds of crimes. One must return to offender rationalities and ask why, among the set of laundering opportunities open to them, those who profit from crimes would choose e-gaming as a route to transfer funds that they have not spent on their lifestyles?

NOTES

* An earlier version of this chapter was presented at the Cross-border Crime Inroads on Integrity in Europe conference at the University of Ghent in 2009. I am grateful to the anonymous reviewers for their comments on that paper, and to the European Gaming and Betting Association for their assistance with the study. The chapter is based on research carried out under the ESRC Professorial Fellowship RES-051–27–0208.

1. Though it is arguable that since the *profits* (net of expenses) from such lotteries go to the public sector, this self-interest is also 'public interest'; by contrast with the benefits accruing primarily in low-tax jurisdictions to private sector gaming operators.
2. The level of current exploitation is not definitive here, since this is an indication of past activity, not of

future threats. It is quite reasonable to examine vulnerability independent of actual misuse, provided one does not represent that as a fully developed risk analysis. For one discussion of this issue, see Dorn and Levi (2006).

3. Gaming is defined in the Oxford English Dictionary on-line as: 'The action or habit of playing at games of chance for stakes; gambling'. Gaming is often understood as legal gambling: to gamble is defined as: 'To play games of chance for money, *esp.* for unduly high stakes; to stake money (*esp.* to an extravagant amount) on some fortuitous event. As the word is (at least in serious use) essentially a term of reproach, it would not ordinarily be applied to the action of playing for stakes of trifling amount, except by those who condemn playing for money altogether.'
4. This is not to accept or reject more general arguments about the positive and negative consequences of e-gaming: it is rather that these are not germane to the present project on money laundering risks.
5. This excludes the broader costs of creating a climate in which support for terrorist acts is stimulated, and of the indoctrination, recruitment, and preparation of potential attackers.
6. As the report for the Remote Gambling Association by consultants MHA (2009: 32) notes, the only publicly identified case is that of Tsouli and Al-Daour in July 2007. To elaborate on their account, the defendants had together purchased websites using stolen identities and credit card details on which were then published the extreme propaganda and recruiting material produced by al-Qaeda in Iraq. The material was crafted to incite and recruit suicide bombers accessing the websites and forums internationally, comprising as it did graphic and emotive media. It included daily statements and films of the murder of coalition forces, police, officials, and civilians, together with footage of the beheading of hostages (http://www.cps.gov.uk/publications/prosecution/ctd.html#_10). Al-Daour allegedly laundered money through on-line gambling sites, using accounts set up with stolen credit card numbers (http://news.bbc.co.uk/1/shared/bsp/hi/pdfs/03_06_08_fo4_terror.pdf). He and other members of the group conducted 350 transactions at 43 different on-line gambling sites, using more than 130 compromised credit card accounts. Winnings were withdrawn and transferred to on-line bank accounts that the men controlled, with the help of insiders. The media portrayed the case as the world's first cyber-terrorism trial. The media did *not* report that a number of attempts to launder through a remote gambling site were unsuccessful (and incompetent) and were identified, Suspicious Activity Reports were submitted to the authorities, and the accounts were closed. Thus, the AML system did its work as well as it could and as, it is hoped, it will in the future.
7. An older Europol (2005) report, compiled under the now outdated model rather than the post-2006 Organised Crime Threat Assessment (OCTA), stated (p. 17): 'In some Member States legal gambling schemes are quite a widespread modus operandi to launder money. It is estimated that the above-mentioned trend will continue and increase in the future. OC groups also make their way directly into the gambling world by buying companies in this field.' The owners and directors of regulated gaming firms are required to pass 'fit and proper person' tests, so, depending on the quality of regulation, we may assume that the older Europol comments are irrelevant to this study and that the allegation is of a highly general nature. Some later threat assessments and situation reports mention risks from gambling, but not e-gaming.
8. Among the sources that provide no explicit evidence to suggest that e-gaming is a significant source of money laundering risk are: United States General Accounting Office, *Internet Gambling – An overview of the issues*, 2002, p. 34 et seq., available at: http://www.gao.gov/new.items/d0389.pdf; the 2007 report of the German Financial Intelligence Unit at the Bundeskriminalamt, available at: http://www.bka.de/nn_192960/EN/Publications/AnnualReportsAndSituationAssessments/FinancialIntelligenceUnitFiuGermany/financialIntelligenceUnitFiuGermany__node.html?__nnn=true, the relevant section of which repeats the wording from the Europol report of 2005; the report for the French Parliament presented by Blessig and Myard (2008: 89–90), available at: http://www.assemblee-nationale.fr/13/pdf/europe/rap-info/i0693.pdf; the French Lexsi report, *Cybercriminalité des Jeux en Ligne*, available at: http://www.lexsi.fr/sites/default/files/publications/livre_blanc_-_cert_lexsi_-_jeux_en_ligne.pdf.
9. There are signs of a more sophisticated and nuanced approach emerging. The FATF/APG Report on Vulnerabilities of Casinos and Gaming Sector notes (2009: 56): '197. While this study has not included online gaming/online casinos in its scope of enquiry, it is clear that there are a number of related risks and vulnerabilities from online casinos. A number of jurisdictions license physical casinos and online casinos under a similar process. This report notes a significant gap with understanding regional money laundering risks and vulnerabilities from online casinos and online gaming. There is a need for further study in this area and for sharing case studies and regulatory models.'
10. There is a difference between the US and the EU, not just because of differences in the AML regime, but because there is a genuine dispute over the constitutionality of prohibitions against a free market in private sector e-gaming within the Single European Market.
11. Of course, it could be argued that just as all crimes are artefacts of the criminal law, by definition, *all* money-laundering risks are an artefact of criminalisation of their predicates. However, we mean

something more than this truism here. The distinction we are making is between acts that are universally regarded as harmful and acts such as e-gaming, where there is substantial disagreement both about how harmful the behaviour is and whether those harms should be dealt with by the criminal law or by the more subtle controls that accompany money-laundering regulation. Overall net benefits/dis-benefits of e-gaming are out of the scope of this review.

12. Payment into what is termed 'non-originator' cards is forbidden by the scheme rules of Visa and MasterCard, while American Express does not permit expenditure on Internet gaming. In Australia, it is legal to use credit cards for e-gaming, but it is not permitted to credit winnings to such cards, the object presumably being to make gamblers think harder about playing. There, they cash in winnings by bank transfer, cheque or other mechanisms.
13. So called because they are allowing themselves to serve as transporters of other people's property.
14. If there are parties other than the conspirators playing the game, they may become annoyed if they think that one party is cheating, and therefore cease playing with the site on which the suspected cheating occurs. This would constitute an economic opportunity cost for the gaming site.
15. Directive of the European Parliament and of the Council on the taking up, pursuit and prudential supervision of the business of electronic money institutions amending Directives 2005/60/EC and 2006/48/EC and repealing Directive 2000/46/EC. PE-CO_S 3666/09, 16 July 2009, available at: http://register.consilium.europa.eu/pdf/en/09/st03/st03666.en09.pdf.
16. Directive 2005/60/EC of the European Parliament and of the Council of 26 October 2005 on The Prevention of the Use of the Financial System for the Purpose of Money Laundering and Terrorist Financing.
17. See http://www.egba.eu/pdf/EGBA_Standards_March_2009_EN.pdf.
18. See http://www.rga.eu.com/data/files/rga_sr_code___final_final_14_11_07.pdf.

REFERENCES

Bauer, A. (2008), *Jeux En Ligne et Menaces Criminelles*, Report for the Ministre du Budget, des Comptes publics et de la Fonction publique, Paris: Institut de Criminologie de Paris, Université de Paris II.

Blessig, E. and Myard, J. (2008), Rapport d'Information Déposé par la Délégation de l'Assemblée Nationale pour l'Union Européenne (1), Sur le Monopole des Jeux au Regard des Règles Communautaires. Assemblee Nationale, N° 693, available at: http://www.assemblee-nationale.fr/13/pdf/europe/rap-info/i0693.pdf.

Cabinet Office/Home Office (2009), *Extending Our Reach: A Comprehensive Approach to Tackling Serious Organised Crime*, London: Home Office.

Choo, R. (2008), 'Money laundering risks of prepaid stored value cards', *Trends and Issues in Crime and Criminal Justice No 363*, Canberra: Australian Institute of Criminology.

Choo, R. and Smith, R. (2008), 'Criminal Exploitation of Online Systems by Organised Crime Groups', *Asian Journal of Criminology*, 3: 37–59.

Dorn, N. and Levi, M. (2006), 'From Delphi to Brussels, the policy context: prophecy, crime proofing, impact assessment', *European Journal on Criminal Policy and Research*, 12: 213–20.

European Commission (2011), *GREEN PAPER on On-line Gambling in the Internal Market*, SEC(2011) 321 final.

European Commission (2012), *COMMUNICATION FROM THE COMMISSION TO THE EUROPEAN PARLIAMENT, THE COUNCIL, THE ECONOMIC AND SOCIAL COMMITTEE AND THE COMMITTEE OF THE REGIONS: Towards a Comprehensive European Framework for Online Gambling*, COM(2012) 596 final.

Europol (2005), *2005 EU Organised Crime Report – public version*, 13788/1/05 REV 1 Crimeorg 117, The Hague: Europol.

Europol (2011), *EU Organised Crime Threat Assessment 2011*, The Hague: Europol.

FATF [Financial Action Task Force] (2008a), *RBA Guidance for Casinos*, Paris: FATF.

FATF (2008b), *Money Laundering & Terrorist Financing Vulnerabilities of Commercial Websites and Internet Payment Systems*, Paris: FATF.

FATF (2009), *Money-Laundering Through the Football Sector*, Paris: FATF.

FATF/APG (2009), *Vulnerabilities of Casinos and Gaming Sector*, Paris: FATF and Sydney: APG.

Glenny, M. (2011), *DarkMarket: CyberThieves, CyberCops and You*, London: Bodley Head.

H2 Gambling Capital (2011), 'Quarterly Interactive Gambling' (April), available at: http://www.americangaming.org/sites/default/files/uploads/docs/final_online_gambling_white_paper_5-18-11.pdf.

Levi, M. (2008), 'White-collar, organised and cyber crimes in the media: some contrasts and similarities', *Crime, Law and Social Change*, 49: 365–77.

Levi, M. (2009), *Money-Laundering Risks and E-gaming: A European Overview and Assessment*, available at: http://www.egba.eu/pdf/Levi_Final_Money_Laundering_Risks_egaming%20280909.pdf.

Levi, M. and Reuter, P. (2006), 'Money laundering', in M. Tonry (ed.), *Crime and Justice: A Review of Research*, Vol. 34: 289–375, Chicago: Chicago University Press.

MHA (2009), *The Threat of Money Laundering and Terrorist Financing through the Online Gambling Industry*, London: Remote Gambling Association.

SOCA (2011), *Suspicious Activity Reports Regime: Annual Report 2011*, London: Serious and Organised Crime Agency.

Spectrum Gaming (2011), *White Paper for National Indian Gaming Association*, Linwood, NJ: Spectrum Gaming Group.

Van Duyne, P. (2003), *Money Laundering Policy – Fear and Facts*, available at: http://www.petrusvanduyne.nl/files/Witwassen%20Fears%20and%20Facts.pdf.

Van Duyne, P. and Soudijn, M. (2009), *Crime Money in the Financial System – What We Fear and What We Know*, available at: http://www.petrusvanduyne.nl/files/Hoofdstuk%20Van%20duyne%20-%20soudijn.pdf.

PART VII

LEGISLATION OF MONEY LAUNDERING

26. The risk-based approach to anti-money laundering and counter-terrorist financing in international and EU standards: what it is, what it entails

*Paolo Costanzo**

26.1 INTRODUCTION

The 'rule-based' and the 'risk-based' are two approaches to the implementation of Anti-Money Laundering and Counter-Financing of Terrorism (AML/CFT) systems. They affect areas like the scope of AML/CFT legislation (for example, in relation to the identification of obliged entities and of the measures they should apply), the type and intensity of the preventive measures (this is typically the case for customer due diligence (CDD) obligations), and the extent and nature of controls performed by competent authorities. It is important to stress, on the other hand, that other components of the AML/CFT system like, for example the criminalization of money laundering and terrorist financing and the obligation to report suspicious transactions or confiscation measures are not risk-sensitive and therefore do not in principle vary depending on whether a risk-or rule-based approach has been followed.[1]

Both approaches have been adopted in individual countries' legislation and have confronted each other on the international scene over the last 15–20 years. While the risk-based approach requires that existing risks are well understood and that relevant measures are calibrated accordingly, the rule-based approach rests on the *ex ante* indication of pre-defined measures resulting from a general evaluation of risks. In this chapter, it is argued that risk-based systems may be more effective, as they take into account particular circumstances in a more granular and targeted manner; however, they may be relatively complex, costly and difficult to implement. On the other hand, rule-based systems are normally simpler to implement and less costly, as obligations and measures to put in place are determined in advance and do not vary depending on the circumstances; these systems can however be less flexible and, by providing similar responses to different situations, less effective.

After a brief description of their main features, this contribution argues that an assessment of what approach is best in terms of its cost-effectiveness is difficult to perform. Nonetheless, international and European Union standards have clearly endorsed a risk-based approach, although rule-based components are not ruled out and countries and obliged subjects retain some flexibility. Against this background, based on available evidence, the chapter also emphasizes that, while the question of what system is more appropriate may still be open, the implementation of a new risk-based approach in many EU countries entails costs and burdens which, in the transition phase, are likely to increase more than the effectiveness of the AML/CFT systems.

The essential implications of the risk-based approach are then discussed in light of the third EU AML Directive (2005/60/EC). I focus separately on risk-sensitive elements in the AML/CFT regulation, on how the risk assessment affects compliance by obliged subjects, on supervision, and conclude with a reference to expected developments on the risk-based approach to AML/CFT, particularly as a consequence of the revision of the standards of the Financial Action Task Force (FATF).

26.2 FEATURES OF THE RULE-BASED APPROACH

The essential feature of rule-based AML/CFT systems is that applicable measures and due behaviours are pre-determined by rules. The AML rulebook is fully populated by provisions that, at least in principle, are intended to cover all instances in which measures have to be applied and determine the content of such measures. This detailed rulebook is composed of provisions of law or other regulatory means. The most appropriate combination between legislation, regulation and other enforceable means varies across systems and, within each system, over time depending on the level of detail which is deemed appropriate.

Regardless of how this regulatory mix is configured, however, there is no or little room for obliged entities or persons to apply different measures or to lift measures that are mandated by the enforceable provisions, even though these measures may prove inadequate or even ineffective in a particular case. Some room for discretion can be left in the implementation, depending on how detailed the regulation is. Nonetheless, covered entities and persons face a set of obligations which are, at the same time, exhaustive (no further measures are due) and prescriptive (the measures provided for must be applied in all relevant circumstances).

Since all AML measures and obligations have to be precisely indicated and spelt out in the regulation, it is no surprise that in rule-based systems the rules are numerous and often particularly detailed. The objective is to cover all possible circumstances and limit as much as possible the room for interpretation (which is often associated with uncertainty) and the need for covered entities and persons to exercise discretion in order to identify which behaviour should be put in place in a particular circumstance that is not fully and specifically envisaged in the law. As a consequence, rule-based systems normally rely on well-developed rulebooks based on hard-law provisions, with little room for 'soft' instruments like guidance or instructions or 'best practices' documents.[2] As we will see, the opposite is often true in risk-based AML systems.

The rulebook underpinning rule-based systems is intended as a complete set of rules; in principle all relevant circumstances should be covered and all possible measures should be envisaged. Ideally, no loopholes should exist. Obviously, not everything can be regulated and, therefore, new rules are added over time to take account of the experience in implementation as well as of the evolving interpretation of existing provisions. For these reasons, in rule-based systems the rulebook tends to grow in size and complexity, in a continuous search for clarity and completeness. New provisions and changes to the existing provisions have to be introduced through the appropriate procedures, depending on the type of regulatory means. This can bring an element of rigidity in rule-based systems which can also translate into delayed updates to the rulebook.

Another feature of the rule-based approach is that, as applicable measures are established in the law, given the same 'triggering event' the same behaviour is required in all relevant situations with in principle little or no variation. For example, when a business relationship is opened or a transaction above the relevant threshold is requested an identification obligation has to be fulfilled by obtaining certain data as indicated in a valid identity document (in case of natural persons) or in appropriate corporate documents (for companies or other entities). These measures are to be applied in all circumstances, where the identification obligation is triggered, regardless of any other considerations which might suggest the application of different or additional measures (for example, in light of the degree of the risk, the characteristics of the counterpart or its opacity). In this framework, even when the risk is higher and the counterpart particularly opaque, obtaining the prescribed data from a valid document may still be enough to ensure compliance. On the other hand, also when the customer is well known (the risk of anonymity being therefore low) the same procedure must be activated and the official document has to be shown and acquired.

All this, of course, has implications on what precisely 'compliance' means in a rule-based system. In fact, in a rule-based scenario, compliance is ensured by obliged entities and persons when the pre-determined behaviours *ex ante* mandated by the law for the case at hand are adopted, regardless of their suitability to that particular situation and regardless also of the capacity of these behaviours to achieve the objective which the regulator had in mind when drafting the relevant provisions.

In other words, in a rule-based environment compliance is in principle achieved by enacting the behaviour as prescribed by the law with essentially no further concerns as to its actual adequacy and effectiveness. In fact, the suitability of the prescribed behaviour is evaluated by the legislator once and for all when the provision is crafted (not by the obliged party when the provision is applied) and essentially no room for further judgement is left to the obliged subject in the implementation phase. This subject, therefore, when that particular obligation is triggered, has to fulfil the prescribed behaviour and, by this, proper compliance is ensured. In this respect, the rule-based approach results in a formal, simple and basically certain framework, with limited responsibility for the obliged subjects (apart from that of putting in place a behaviour that corresponds to the description in the law).

Of course, this overview focuses on abstract features of an ideal rule-based approach and, therefore, is intentionally general and necessarily omits several important details. For example, precisely in order to take account of varying factual circumstances, impossible to envisage in a fully comprehensive and detailed legal framework, the law ordinarily allows for some flexibility and consequent adaptation of the measures based on the circumstances. In this context, obliged entities or persons necessarily need to exercise some judgement, keeping in mind the purpose pursued by the provision that is being applied. Nonetheless – and this is the essential feature of the rule-based system – this provision, and the steps which should be taken, have been established by the law itself on an *ex ante* basis (with more or fewer details) for all the cases which fall under its scope of application; the obliged subject, though he may exercise some discretion in implementation, cannot depart from the prescription and, for example, apply a different measure that appears (and might actually be) more appropriate and effective to achieve the relevant objective (for example, a reliable verification of the identity of a customer or of the beneficial owner). Therefore, compliance under a rule-based approach means simply enacting the measures described in the law; it has, in this perspective, an intrinsic formal element which makes it unnecessary, in principle, to adapt to the substance of the case at hand.

Though this may look simple (and rule-based systems are indeed intended to achieve as much clarity and certainty as possible for covered subjects and competent authorities), difficulties, even significant ones, often arise from the interpretation of the provisions (which can lend themselves to different understandings as to the cases they intend to address or the measures they prescribe) and from the translation of abstract provisions into concrete case-specific behaviours. Also, the regulatory framework itself can be particularly intricate; the more so, as it tends to accrue over time, with additional provisions aimed at taking account of circumstances not originally foreseen or to better specify particular measures.

The above considerations highlight another feature of rule-based approaches: given the tight and detailed regulatory framework, there is little or no discretion in adapting measures that have to be taken in concrete cases. This is true, by the way, for both covered subjects and competent authorities; the latter have a duty to conduct checks and controls in the same way vis-à-vis all obliged entities and persons, although cases of non-compliance as well as outright money laundering or terrorist financing risks may be more concentrated in certain sectors or areas. As a consequence, under a rule-based approach different situations may receive equal, or at least similar treatments and available resources may not be deployed in the most efficient way (more resources where they are most needed, for compliance or controls, in light of the risks).

26.3 FEATURES OF THE RISK-BASED APPROACH

We focus now on the risk-based approach. It relies on the general assumption that the components (although not necessarily all of them) of the AML system (especially regulation, compliance and controls) should be shaped taking account of the risks they are intended to face and mitigate. This apparently easy and straightforward assumption brings with it a number of particularly important consequences, even more noticeable if considered in comparison with the implications of the somehow opposite rule-based philosophy, as outlined above.

The regulatory framework in risk-based systems is usually based on high-level legislation which sets out the main objectives to be pursued through compliance and essential measures to apply for these purposes. Specific rules of conduct applicable in particular cases are not always found in the law; in fact, those rules need in many instances to be determined by the obliged parties themselves in light of concrete circumstances and the inherent risks.

This approach clearly reverses that of rule-based systems. While in a rule-based framework the rule of conduct is laid out *ex ante* in the law or in the implementing regulations, under a risk-based approach, on the contrary, the law indicates to obliged subjects what the pursued objective is and how these subjects must themselves determine the appropriate behaviour. The measures which should be applied, therefore, result *ex post* from the judgemental determination taken by the obliged subjects, based on the factual circumstances and the appreciation of risks.

As legislation tends to be simple and generally high-level, AML/CFT risk-based systems need to be fuelled by means of frequent and widespread guidance, instructions, and best practices indications. These 'soft' instruments (as opposed to the extensive hard-law provisions typical of rule-based systems) may be particularly extensive and need to be updated and improved in an ongoing manner to take account of changing circumstances (e.g. in relevant markets, market participants, products, etc.) and evolving vulnerabilities and risks. Guidance and instructions on how to assess the risk and pursue the mandated objectives through appropriate compliance are neither exhaustive nor mandatory, but can reach significant extent and complexity. The 'Guidance for the UK Financial Sector' adopted in the UK by the Joint Money Laundering Steering Group (and approved by the Minister of the Treasury), for example, is thicker than many rulebooks enacted in rule-based jurisdictions.

In this peculiar regulatory framework, where the rules of conduct must be found *ex post* by each obliged party depending on contingent factors, behaviours may well differ from case to case, even in similar circumstances. They actually should differ, reflecting different risk patterns. There is not a one-size-fits-all response to compliance (there is not even a predetermined response in the law) and measures adopted vary consequently.

It is interesting to note that variance in compliance, therefore, is not an undesired consequence but rather is a built-in feature of a risk-based framework: measures must be tailored to existing risks and, precisely because these risks vary depending on particular circumstances, the measures adopted to tackle them must vary accordingly. Under the risk-based philosophy, it is the capacity of the measures to mitigate the risks (that is, their effectiveness) which must remain equal, not the measures themselves. More specifically, the latter have to change precisely in order to ensure that the former is kept constant while the risks change and evolve. Therefore, variance is associated with flexibility and proportionality more than with uncertainty.

Clearly, this is an approach opposite to that underpinning the rule-based systems, whose fundamental tenet is that measures must be predetermined by the rules, thus being essentially the same in all relevant circumstances, and discrepancies in the application of the same obligations are to be avoided. Should these discrepancies occur, this would be seen as a potential sign of wrong application by at least some of the involved obliged subjects, unless some room for discretion is explicitly left open in the legislation.[3]

26.3.1 The Nature of Guidance in Risk-Based Systems: Implications on Compliance and Controls

The need to determine the most appropriate measures to apply in light of circumstances and risks in risk-based systems requires obliged parties to exercise their judgement. As there is not one pre-established solution, applicable measures must be identified on a case-by-case basis, taking into account available information, guidance and experience. This is precisely the reason why guidance is needed in risk-based systems; but this also sets very clear limitations to its relevance.

Guidance assists obliged parties in exercising their discretion by indicating how risks should be identified and assessed and provides examples of measures that may be taken.[4]

It encourages convergence towards common practices that have proven effective in tackling particular risks in specific circumstances;[5] the more so, when there are sufficiently long track records of experience.

Over time, guidance and best practices can be consolidated in a comprehensive 'rulebook'. This 'rulebook', however, is intrinsically and profoundly different in nature and effects from rulebooks developed in rule-based systems. First of all, this book does not set out proper rules but, consistent with the nature of the risk-based approach, simple guidelines or practices that can be followed. That is, the indications therein are not mandatory but offer examples of measures which, based on the available knowledge and experience, could be taken and are likely to produce effective risk-mitigation. Or they simply provide instructions on how applicable measures can be determined and on the risk assessment process for this purpose.

When measures are set out in the guidance under a risk-based approach there is not a straightforward obligation to apply them as they are described. Also, if obliged subjects decide to adhere to the guidance and precisely apply indicated measures, this would not excuse them where these measures proved to be inappropriate in light of circumstances as they unfold in reality, or if an appropriate assessment of risks and the required response has not been performed.

It is also important to stress that not only the 'soft' indications set out in the guidance are not compulsory, they are not even exhaustive. Nothing, in fact, prevents, nor exempts, obliged parties from reverting to other, non-listed, measures if these are more appropriate in light of the circumstances.

Therefore, to sum up, concrete measures to adopt depend on the risk situation, are not predetermined in a book, and must be established *ex post* on a case-by-case basis: we have recalled these as the essential features of the risk-based approach. As a consequence of the non-prescriptiveness of the guidance, sticking to it is *per se* not enough to ensure compliance. Against a charge of lack of compliance, arguing that the measures taken are those described in a guidance is not, *per se*, a sufficient defence: this top-down argument needs to be complemented by a demonstration that those measures are indeed appropriate, taking account, in a bottom-up logic, of the factual circumstances at hand.[6]

The risk-based approach puts a considerable emphasis on the obliged parties' judgement in determining applicable measures with the attached responsibility. This, as we have already mentioned, implies some inevitable level of variance in the outcome of compliance. It is now necessary to note that discretion and variance in compliance, as essential features of the risk-based approach, go together with an assumption of the possibility of failure of the measures taken to properly achieve the objectives they are intended to. Risk-based obligations incorporate the assumption that the objectives pursued may not be achieved in particular cases despite all reasonable measures being put in place according to applicable prescriptions. Indeed, the risk-based approach is not a zero-failure regime and this is another fundamental feature that it has.

We have seen that, under a risk-based approach, there are no one-size-fits-all circumstances and that, as a consequence, the rules of conduct must be determined on a case-by-case basis through a risk assessment. Under this approach, what is imposed on obliged subjects is that they collect information about the risks, judge the type and the extent of such risks, devise and apply the measures that appear adequate in light of the circumstances, taking due account of any available guidance. Despite all these tasks and efforts being properly conducted, it may well happen that the measures adopted, though reasonable and proportionate, do not meet their objectives.[7] For example, the person whose identity has been verified as accurately as the situation required may not be the actual beneficial owner of a counterpart (that is, according to the definition under the FATF and EU standards, the natural person who ultimately owns or controls the client entity). Or a customer may actually qualify as a 'Politically Exposed Person' although the due diligence process, duly conducted in accordance with any relevant guidance and taking account of any appreciable risks, did not highlight that circumstance.[8] In the risk-based approach, the obligation is more to follow an appropriate process than to reach a specific objective.

Of course, as in risk-based systems, also in rule-based ones the possibility exists that the measures adopted do not achieve their objectives. However, due to the more formalistic nature of the latter, where the focus is more on the achievement of specific objectives, there may not be any assumption of tolerable failures in achieving them and, when these inevitably occur, infringements may be recognised and sanctions levied, regardless of the adequacy of the measures adopted and of the efforts put into performing the obligations.[9] Given the complexity of many AML obligations, and the multiplicity of factors to consider in discharging them, this may appear unrealistic and disproportionate:[10] failures do happen but, while in a risk-based approach they can go without sanctions if the charged entity or person shows that all reasonable measures have been taken in light of circumstances and risks, this may not be a valid defence in a different rule-based legal environment.

This conclusion can also be seen from a different angle. Risk-based obligations are centred on the duty to properly assess the circumstances and the inherent risks and on the adoption of measures which are adequate in light of this assessment. The focus is on the means, or the process, rather than on its results. The question of how the obliged entity has organized itself (in terms, *inter alia*, of information gathering, policies and procedures for assessing the risk) is particularly relevant in this context. By contrast, under a rule-based approach it is the final outcome that counts most in determining if a particular obligation has been fulfilled: has the customer or the beneficial owner been properly identified and its identity verified? Has the customer's political exposure been duly established?

Clearly, these differences between the two approaches have essential implications, not only on compliance by obliged subjects, but also on controls performed by competent authorities to verify this compliance. In rule-based systems, as compliance consists of enacting predetermined measures, controls are aimed at verifying that such measures have been put in place or that the prescribed objectives have been properly achieved. In general, these are frequently 'yes or no' types of checks which, though it would be too simplistic to qualify this as a box-ticking exercise, certainly may not imply the exercise of particular discretion in evaluating the behaviour of obliged parties. Difficulties in determining if this or that provision has been applied and complied with may arise from the interpretation of these provisions, with a view to establishing if they are indeed relevant in particular circumstances and how they should be understood and implemented.

Controls may be more complex in risk-based systems. Obliged entities need to exercise their judgement in gathering information, assessing the risk and determining which measures suit the situation best. Supervisors have to establish if these measures are appropriate and if the underlying reasoning which underpins them is well grounded. They need therefore to re-think the compliance process and review (or second-guess) the risk assessment done by the obliged entity and evaluate its judgement with regard to adopted measures, with the aim of identifying possible loopholes or inconsistencies. Controls, like compliance, also have an essential judgemental component and require that competent authorities focus on the whole compliance process and on the logic behind it.

Also, in checking compliance in risk-based systems, competent authorities should be able to understand in which cases the failure of the measures adopted does not depend on poor compliance and, at the opposite end, in which cases the compliance with the duty to acquire information and assess risks cannot be considered satisfactory although the measures taken have luckily turned out to be adequate in that particular instance. As for compliance, also in the case of controls much of the focus is on the organization, the policies and the procedures in place to properly apply risk-based measures.

26.4 THE CHANGE-OVER TO THE RISK-BASED APPROACH: ARE EFFICIENCY AND EFFECTIVENESS ENHANCED?

While national AML/CFT systems, as a consequence of the evolution of international standards, have to be risk-based in some of their essential features, the rule-based approach is not entirely ruled out. There are areas where the risk-based approach is not mandated (record keeping is an example) and, for matters where the risk-based approach is indeed prescribed, its scope can often vary to a large extent and countries can choose to keep this extent to a minimum by injecting rules setting out pre-defined measures that have to be applied in all cases on a non-risk sensitive basis. Most significant examples in this respect come from the provisions on customer due diligence.

With this caveat, however, international and EU AML/CFT standards, moving from a purely rule-based to a more risk-based approach, require countries to follow this direction and adjust their systems accordingly. A new risk-based system has been deemed appropriate, or even necessary, to enhance effectiveness and ensure a higher harmonization of national solutions, at the same time allowing for a considerable flexibility, which is naturally embedded in the risk-based approach, to preserve domestic specificities and the capacity to adapt to different circumstances.

Clearly, the assumption underpinning the adoption of a risk-based approach in the international and EU AML/CFT standards is that, while effectiveness will be enhanced, costs will increase less than proportionally, so that the additional benefits will not be entirely set-off. However, it is true that, as a consequence of these new standards, a number of countries have been somehow forced to introduce significantly different or completely new risk-based AML systems. This has been the case particularly for EU countries, where in many cases the AML systems had to be reconfigured rather than simply adjusted,[11] to ensure the implementation of the Directive 2005/60/EC which in turn transposed the 2003 FATF Recommendations which first endorsed a risk-based approach.

In this context, while the increase in effectiveness remains to be seen in those systems that had to change from a previous rule-based approach,[12] available evidence shows that costs have certainly increased, especially in the 'transition' period. The investments that have to be made, in terms of organization, procedures, staff, training, IT tools, etc. have been, and still are, considerable.

The study contracted by the European Commission to estimate the cost of compliance for financial institutions (especially banks) with six key EU Directives in the financial services area provides some revealing evidence in this respect.[13] The study estimates separately 'one-off' costs, that is, costs incurred specifically in the transition to the new system, and 'ongoing' costs, that is, recurring after the implementation as a consequence of the new rules. As to the one-off costs associated with the transition to the new AML system by banks, financial conglomerates and investment banks, these roughly account for 10 per cent of all regulatory costs related to the six Directives included in the survey.[14]

The AML Directive ranks third in terms of one-off costs for banks and financial conglomerates, behind the Capital Requirements Directive and the MiFID.[15] While the fact that the compliance costs for the changeover to the new AML system are the third highest in the financial sector is already quite surprising in itself, further interesting elements come from the breakdown of these costs.[16] IT is the main source of expense in the setting-up of the new AML system, followed by training and consultancy. IT spending is particularly related to: meeting the 'know your customer' requirements, especially as regards the additional information needed for customer due diligence purposes;[17] facilitating increased monitoring of suspicious transactions through increased automation of processes;[18] facilitating Politically Exposed Persons screening;[19] and assisting in risk assessment.

Turning now to ongoing costs of compliance with the newly established AML requirements, the study indicates that, for banks, these costs account for roughly 13 per cent of all their regulatory costs related to financial services regulation.[20] The third AML Directive ranks third again, preceded only by the Capital Requirements Directive and MiFID.

The most important drivers for ongoing expenditures or investment for compliance with the AML Directive are those related to IT and additional staff costs (as a consequence of recruitment and training).[21] As to the IT costs, the study highlights that 'whilst some firms (generally larger banks) see automation as the only way to provide the necessary evidence of an audit trail to the regulatory authorities . . ., a number of firms have retained significant (or total) human oversight in this area'. Indeed, as we have indicated, the human judgemental element, combined with, and supported by, appropriate data processing capacity, is an essential underpinning of the risk-based approach.[22]

These costs, both one-off and ongoing, are of course related to the transposition and the application of the whole new set of measures introduced by the third AML Directive; those measures include, but stretch beyond, the risk-based approach. However, as highlighted above, the breakdown of cost drivers suggests that most of the expenditures are related to the implementation of the new risk-sensitive requirements.

The perception by the AML/CFT community of increased complexity and higher costs brought about by the new system, not yet compensated for by a comparable improvement on the efficiency and effectiveness sides, together with a still weak sense of ownership by the obliged entities (also due to traditional deficiencies in vertical feedback on results by competent authorities),[23] are further elements which add to the difficulties of implementation. While the deadline for the transposition of the third EU AML Directive by Members States was 15 December 2007, country evaluations conducted by the FATF and MONEYVAL have clearly shown that long after that deadline expired EU Member States were not yet in full compliance with the risk-based features of the new system.

In this context, the expectation is that the changeover to the risk-based approach will see an evolution in two main steps. In the transitional period, the costs for compliance increase, as indicated by the evidence available on one-off costs associated with the start-up of the new system. On the other hand, it is reasonable to assume that the lack of previous specific experience and track records, as well as the need to become familiar with the new framework (as witnessed by the significant costs borne for training and consultancy), are likely to prevent effectiveness from increasing to the same extent. As a result, in this stage of the changeover to a risk-based framework, the system seems to be (or has been, in the countries that have completed this phase) less well-off in terms of its cost-effectiveness balance.

In the longer run, when the new system will be well established and all the stakeholders adequately acquainted with its functioning, it is expected that costs will decrease, as the initial investments will produce their return and the new expenditures will be less onerous. At the same time, the enhanced granularity allowed by the risk-based approach, as compared with the rule-based one, due to its capacity to shape and adjust the measures in a more tailored fashion and allocate resources accordingly, is likely to foster efficiency and effectiveness. Although this remains to be seen, and will need to be estimated, the assumption underlying the risk-based approach is that, when this system will be up and running, the cost-effectiveness ratio will be higher than what was possible under the previous rule-based system.

This conclusion, however, rests on a fundamental assumption which also needs to be verified in practice, that is, countries should be able to implement the new complex risk-based approach properly, eventually getting rid of the rigidities (but also of the certainties) of the rule-based approach. This may be difficult for countries where the risk-based approach was not previously applied and the rule-based approach is deeply rooted in the legal system. The risk-based approach cannot function properly without significant adaptations, not only to compliance by obliged parties but also to the way in which regulation is conceived and drafted, controls and supervision are conducted, sanctions are calibrated, and responsibilities are distributed between the public and the private sectors – not to mention the need to set up systems to assess the risk, having regard for multiple layers, to monitor the application of relevant measures and to estimate the effectiveness of the measures applied.

26.5 'MICRO' AND 'MACRO' RISK ASSESSMENTS

We have seen that the risk-based approach endorsed by the international standards and the EU Directive requires many different actors to evaluate the risks of money laundering and terrorist financing for a number of different purposes and involves several different areas, ranging from the setting of the regulatory framework to the identification of appropriate applicable measures, to the enforcement and supervisory stage.

The first type of risk assessment at the 'micro' level is typically performed by obliged subjects when, in complying with their CDD obligations, they need to evaluate particular circumstances where, for example, a customer is requesting the opening of a business relationship or is carrying out a certain activity. This is precisely the risk assessment which underpins the decisions concerning the choice of the appropriate CDD procedure and of the due diligence measures which can best tackle the identified risks.

Clearly, depending on the objectives pursued, there are different kinds of risk assessments. A basic distinction can be drawn between the assessment that is done to determine the extent of the risk in specific circumstances (e.g. in relation to a customer or a particular transaction) and the assessment conducted with a view to understanding general risk factors affecting an entire system or its parts (e.g. a firm in its area of business, a sector of the market, a region or a country overall).

Supervisors also need to perform risk assessments of this 'micro' nature, that is focused on particular situations and individual activities, when they verify the compliance with risk-based obligations. More precisely, supervisors in this role have to review the risk assessment done by the obliged subjects, that is, second-guess their judgement to see if it takes account of all relevant circumstances and properly reflects the actual risk conditions; based on this assessment, supervisors can then determine if the measures adopted in a particular case were adequate in light of the existing risks. Therefore, supervisors need to conduct 'micro' risk assessments as a means to establishing if risk-based measures have been duly complied with by obliged subjects.

The 'macro' type of risk assessment, on the other hand, focuses on systemic risk factors beyond specific circumstances and is necessary with a view to devising regulatory and policy options. In fact, in order to appropriately shape AML/CFT defences through regulation and policy, regard must be given to risk factors in the overall context, as opposed to those related to specific situations. Relevant elements in this respect include: the extent of money laundering and terrorist financing taking place in the interested jurisdiction, the forms in which they are realized, the tools and channels that are most commonly used for such illegal purposes, main sources of illicit funds, types of predicate offences, exposures to foreign criminality, most recurrent criminal practices and features of the domestic system which appear particularly exposed to misuse.

The 'macro' risk assessment is performed by competent authorities to ensure that the risk-based approach is properly implemented, in line with the EU and international provisions. The understanding of relevant risk factors of a systemic importance assists competent authorities in shaping the scope of application of AML/CFT measures (by identifying categories of subjects respectively with lower exposure, which could be exempted, and with higher exposure, which should be included), calibrating CDD measures (e.g. by indicating additional instances of enhanced CDD or specific measures for particular circumstances) and defining the sanction regime.[24] The outcome of the macro risk assessment is also used by supervisors: the consideration of general risk factors underpins the planning and the conduct of the risk-based supervision.

This type of general risk assessment of a macro nature has received increased attention at the international level, especially by the FATF. In 2008 a 'Strategic Surveillance Initiative' was launched by the FATF with the aim of identifying and monitoring criminal and terrorist threats at the global level. Specific objectives of this initiative are to: '(1) detect and share information on the types of criminal or terrorist activities that pose an emerging threat to the financial system, and (2) develop a more strategic and longer-term view of these threats'.[25] Based on the 2008 and 2009 Strategic Surveillance exercises and on the experience gained through the ongoing work that the FATF conducts for the identification of typologies of money laundering and terrorist financing, a *Global Money Laundering and Terrorist Financing Threat Assessment* has been developed by the FATF in order to provide an overview of systemic risks. One of the purposes of this initiative is 'to assist jurisdictions in the identification of specific threats and their associated vulnerabilities and the application of specific measures to those threats and associated vulnerabilities'.[26]

As of course threats and vulnerabilities change depending on local circumstances, countries are encouraged to conduct 'their own national ML/FT assessments' using the FATF Global Threat Assessment as a common reference framework. Precisely with a view to defining a common approach and a shared methodology to the assessment of systemic risks at the country level (which would also allow comparability across different systems), the FATF also indicates the need to conduct national threat assessments as 'an organised and systematic effort to identify and evaluate the sources and methods of money laundering and terrorist financing and weakness in the AML/CFT systems and other vulnerabilities that have an impact, either direct or indirect, on the country conducting the assessment'.[27] The need for a risk assessment at the country level is now explicitly recognized in the revised FATF Recommendations, issued in February 2012.

26.6 TOOLS FOR THE RISK ASSESSMENT

Different kinds of risk assessments obviously require different sets of tools or risk indicators.

Micro risk assessments mainly rely on guidance from competent authorities. In this respect, art. 35(2) of the Directive specifies that obliged subjects should 'have access to up-to-date information on the practices of money launderers and terrorist financers and on indications leading to the recognition of suspicious transactions'. Indeed, indicators designed to assist obliged entities in detecting suspicious transactions can also provide useful indications on risk factors. The same can be said of feedback provided on the outcome of suspicious transaction reports: the results of the analysis performed by the FIU and of subsequent investigations and prosecutions can help identify areas of activities or criminal behaviours that have proven particularly risky. Through feedback the experience gained is used to enhance the assessment of risks and to refine the measures taken to tackle them. An obligation to provide (wherever practicable) 'timely feedback on the effectiveness of and follow-up to reports of suspected money laundering or terrorist financing' is set out in art. 35(3) of the Directive.[28]

The definition of guidance and tools aimed at assisting obliged subjects in their micro risk assessments is a well-established practice in many countries. Indications on risk factors such as products risks, counterpart risks and geographical risks are often widely available and regularly updated. These tools or indicators, although they may take also account of general risk factors, are however designed for the evaluation of specific instances or situations (customers, transactions) with a view to applying particular measures in individual cases.

The macro risk assessment, being focused on the consideration of general risk factors of a systemic nature cannot be adequately supported by such 'micro' indicators; it needs more appropriate tools, specifically tailored for this purpose. Such 'macro' tools for the assessment of systemic risks of money laundering and terrorist financing are often less developed. In the remaining part of this section we make an attempt to outline a few elements which could be taken into account for such purpose.

Indicators for the macro risk assessment may be of a 'quantitative' or a 'qualitative' nature. The former should ideally include an estimation of the volume of resources of illegal origin being laundered (or susceptible to being laundered), that is the overall extent of the problem which needs to be tackled. Based on this measurement, indications on, *inter alia*, the origin and destination of illicit funds, the most common types of predicate offences generating them, and the sectors of the economy which are most vulnerable would be particularly important.

While the estimation of the size of funds produced through illicit activities together with the analysis of relevant 'qualitative' aspects is of critical importance, attempts to conduct such assessments have encountered several problems, both as far as the sources of data are concerned and the methodology applicable for these kinds of quantitative studies. In the 1990s, the FATF made an attempt to identify a method to estimate the magnitude of money laundering at the global level. However, this has proved too ambitious a goal. Although it is clear that illegal economic activities, at least those of major relevance, have trans-national dimension and exploit the best opportunities at the global level, 'regional' approaches to the estimation of quantitative aspects of money laundering look more promising.[29]

Depending also on the rate of domestic criminality, the money which is laundered internally can derive either from offences committed within the country or from crimes which have occurred in other jurisdictions (being therefore imported). On the other hand, illicit profits produced by national criminals can be exported in order for them to be laundered in other jurisdictions (and possibly repatriated at a later stage). As the pattern of risk is different in these situations, the dynamic of the flows of illicit money should be considered as a part of the macro risk assessment.

Still on the qualitative side of the overall risk assessment, the consideration of most common types of profit-generating crimes, as predicate offences for money laundering, can offer valuable insights into the nature of the problem, especially with a view to better focusing the preventive and repressive efforts (by, for instance, targeting appropriate CDD measures or providing suitable indicators for the detection of suspicious transactions). With regard to the way in which illicit funds are generated, the practices which are most commonly realized should be identified in the form of 'typologies'.

As criminals tend to exploit the sectors which are most vulnerable to the introduction of illegal money, affected or exposed sectors should be identified, so that defences can be targeted and resources for prevention and repression can be allocated appropriately.

Also, the most common instruments used to transfer funds in money laundering schemes (e.g. wire transfers, alternative remittance channels, payment cards, cash, trade-based schemes) should be identified. This kind of sectoral assessment can help preparing (cost-)effective countermeasures.

Another area in which systemic risks can originate is represented by regulatory shortcomings capable of creating loopholes or discrepancies which criminals are ready to exploit. Contrary to the objectives of harmonization, regulatory weaknesses at the national level can create room for regulatory arbitrage put in place by criminals; risks are more significant, especially considering how fast and easily economic resources can be transferred and transformed. Since compliance with AML/CFT measures is a component of costs for covered institutions, those discrepancies can also trigger forms of competition among legal systems or sectors of legal markets. These 'regulatory risks' must also be carefully assessed.

26.7 RISK ASSESSMENT AND EVALUATION OF THE EFFECTIVENESS

Risk-based systems need ongoing maintenance efforts to make sure that the understanding of the risks (at both the macro and the micro levels) is always up-to-date and that the measures adopted to tackle these risks are adequate and properly evolving to reflect the changing patterns of risks. This means that an essential component of a sound risk-based approach is a system to estimate the effectiveness of the measures in place, in terms of their adequacy to properly deal with the identified risks, taking due account of the results achieved in their application.

This essential effectiveness component of the risk-based AML/CFT system is well captured by the FATF Recommendations and the EU Directive: they both include provisions mandating countries 'to review the effectiveness of their systems to combat money laundering and terrorist financing by maintaining comprehensive statistics on matters relevant to the effectiveness of such systems';[30] under the same standards, these statistics notably include, at a minimum, 'the number of suspicious transaction reports made to the FIU, the follow-up given to these reports' as well as 'the number of persons prosecuted, the number of persons convicted for money laundering or terrorist financing offences and how much property has been frozen, seized or confiscated' (art.33(2) of the Directive).

The challenges posed by such a task of measuring the effectiveness of the AML/CFT system, or of its parts, are very significant. First of all, difficulties lie in the identification of reliable sources of information on the application of AML/CFT measures and in the collection of data of sufficient quality.

In this context, one important element is that while measures aimed at repression are relatively easy to 'calculate' (through, for example, the number and amounts of suspicious transaction reports, of convictions, confiscations, etc.), measures of a more preventive nature are difficult to appraise. In fact, in so far as these measures are effective they prevent specific facts (i.e. money laundering or terrorist financing operations) from occurring. For this reason, it is particularly difficult to conceive, let alone compile, statistics on the application of preventive measures and the results thereby achieved. For example, the issue arises of how, and based on what information, the effectiveness of preventive CDD measures can be appreciated. In this respect, an overall estimation of the systemic exposure to money laundering or terrorist financing, especially based on amounts of illegal flows being channelled through the legal system and most relevant types of criminal behaviours could provide a particularly helpful benchmark to gauge the appropriateness of preventive measures on more qualitative grounds. However, such an *ex ante* approach (as opposed to the *ex post* approach based on the specific results achieved) is also particularly challenging.

A second problem is that of defining a methodology which allows one to infer from raw data and statistics concerning the application of specific measures a sensible assessment on the outcome of those measures in terms of their effectiveness (that is, their capacity to achieve the objectives underlying each of them). One instructive example is that of the effectiveness of the measures concerning the disclosure, the analysis and the investigation of suspicious transactions.

As allowed by the international and EU provisions, national arrangements can vary to a large extent as to the scope and content of the duty to report and of the analytical function of the FIUs: there are countries where hundreds of thousands of reports are filed each year and countries where only a few hundred disclosures are made to the FIU, with a number of intermediate situations in between, depending on, *inter alia*, the expected content of the reports and the level of scrutiny requested of reporting subjects.[31] In order to evaluate the effectiveness of such diverse systems (also taking costs into account), it is of course not enough to consider these figures *per se*; it is necessary, for example, to compare the number of reports with the number of cases set aside by the FIU as not relevant and the number of cases disseminated to competent law enforcement agencies for investigation. But this is also not enough to come to sensible conclusions on the effectiveness of these systems, because the divide between 'analysis' done by the FIU and 'investigation' performed by law enforcement bodies may vary in each system, and so the capacity of the FIU to filter the disclosures received may also vary. An FIU that disseminates 90 per cent of the disclosures received is not necessarily working less effectively than another FIU disseminating 70 per cent of the cases analysed. Further complexities arise when it comes to considering the judicial follow-up in terms of prosecutions, convictions (or acquittals) and confiscations.

Following the adoption in 2012 of its revised standards, which put greater emphasis on the Risk-Based Approach, the FATF has set out to include the assessment of the effectiveness of AML/CFT measures in the scope of countries' mutual Evaluations. In view of the start of the fourth round of the Evaluations, due to begin by the end of 2013, an ad-hoc methodology has been defined for measuring effectiveness,[32] alongside the more traditional assessment of the compliance of the measures adopted with the standards.

What is important to highlight here is that the measurement of the effectiveness of risk-based measures is essential for calibrating and adjusting these measures, taking account of their demonstrated capacity to tackle the risks they have been conceived to face. Ultimately, the effectiveness test serves the purpose of assisting and facilitating the implementation of a well-functioning risk-based approach. Seen in a more dynamic perspective, the risk assessment and the evaluation of effectiveness can be seen as integrated components of an overall cycle: *ex ante*, each country should assess its own overall risk-profile, so that the AML/CFT system can be shaped in an appropriately tailored fashion, with a view to mitigating those risks and counter relevant threats; *ex post*, the effectiveness of the system has to be measured, taking account of all relevant factors – including rate of convictions, costs of compliance, deterrence and prevention mechanisms.[33]

These two complementary evaluations are to be performed on a continuous basis, so that a virtuous circle can be activated, whereby the risk-based system is adapted over time taking account of evolving patterns of threats and its results are constantly monitored.

26.8 CONCLUSIONS AND RECENT DEVELOPMENTS IN THE RISK-BASED APPROACH

Based on the consideration of main characteristics of the two approaches, we have argued that there is no simple way to determine what is the most suitable one. This evaluation depends on a number of factors, among which are the level of maturity of the AML/CFT system and the resources available. Nonetheless, international and EU standards have opted for a risk-based approach to AML/CFT, though allowing considerable room for retaining or introducing rule-based elements. As shown by the available evidence, the need to change over to risk-based systems has had (and is still having) a considerable impact, especially in countries with traditionally rule-based systems. An evaluation of whether this change has been successful, in terms of the results achieved compared to the costs borne, has yet to be made. In the meanwhile, a proposal for a fourth EU AML/CFT directive has been issued by the European Commission; the proposed directive aims at implementing the revised FATF standards in the EU and strongly promotes the Risk-Based Approach.

Against this background, this chapter has provided an overview of what the risk-based approach entails in the EU AML regulation. The main implications have been highlighted for regulators, obliged subjects and competent authorities. In this framework, different types of risk assessment have been identified; also their general features and the tools needed in each case for their conduct have been described. Finally, it has been stressed that a risk-based approach requires, for its proper functioning, systems for the evaluation of the effectiveness of the measures applied, which, combined with the ongoing assessment of evolving risks, are necessary to ensure that the AML/CFT system can be properly maintained and developed. However, appropriate information is difficult to collect for this purpose and a suitable and robust methodology to gauge effectiveness is particularly needed.

Initiatives are underway at the international level addressing the configuration and functioning of the risk-based approach to AML/CFT. The FATF has recently finalized a revision of its Recommendations and in this context work has been done to better specify and clarify the risk-based approach and its implications for all involved stakeholders.[34] An ad-hoc Interpretative Note now outlines, in the FATF standards, the main features of the risk-based approach, grouping together, in a comprehensive overview, implications stemming from different Recommendations. At the same time, the risk-based CDD measures have been further clarified with a view to providing more certainty while keeping the necessary flexibility in regulation and compliance. The risk-based approach to controls and supervision is another area where additional indications have been provided, in line with existing guidance from the Basel Committee of Banking Supervisors.

Another important stream of work concerns effectiveness. We have argued that the evaluation of the results achieved through the application of risk-based measures is essential to the implementation and development of the risk-based approach; we have also indicated that a comprehensive Methodology to perform this task has been developed by the FATF for its fourth round of countries' Mutual Evaluations and this work will certainly help fill this gap.

NOTES

* The views expressed in this chapter are those of the author and do not necessarily represent those of the Bank of Italy or of the Egmont Group.

1. For an overview of the AML/CFT legal framework at the international and EU level, see Van den Broek and Addink, Chapter 27 of this volume.
2. Useful indications for compliance may derive from feedback from competent authorities, opinions issued about the interpretation of specific provisions, and the 'jurisprudence' developed in issuing sanctions.

   Guidance can obviously be provided, and normally is in rule-based AML/CFT systems, to assist covered entities and persons in detecting and reporting suspicious transactions. The need for competent authorities to issue guidelines in this respect, as well as to provide feedback on the outcome and investigation of STRs, is explicitly prescribed in EU and FATF provisions: see, for example, art. 35(2) and (3) of Directive 2005/60/EC (third EU AML/CFT Directive), which does not make any distinction between rule-based and risk-based systems.

   This, however, makes no exception to the consideration that the rule-based approach is essentially based on hard-law instruments, with relatively little room for soft guidance: in fact, the obligation to make suspicious transactions reports is based on suspicion, and neither on rigid law prescription (nobody can prescribe what should certainly be suspicious, or mandate someone to suspect, without altering the nature of the obligation to report suspicions), nor on the consideration of risk (what is risky may not indicate money laundering or terrorist financing, and vice versa). Based on international and EU standards, this suspicion-based nature of the duty to file STRs does not change depending on whether a rule-based or a risk-based approach to AML/CFT is in place.
3. Incidentally, this consideration has important implications when the issue of 'harmonization' is considered, particularly in an international or supranational approach to regulation, as for the FATF Recommendations and the European Union Directives. 'Harmonization' in a rule-based mentality is intended as the result of establishing similar rules to cover the same circumstances in all the jurisdictions involved, leaving little or no room for contingent adaptations. In this perspective, the bigger the room for country-specific divergence, the less the scope of harmonization. On the contrary, risk-based approach supporters would assume that harmonization among different national AML/CFT systems is achieved when the measures can vary (that is, are allowed to vary according to the law) in the same way in different countries to properly follow the risk patterns: measures must not be forced into conformity but, rather, must be proportionate to the risks and must change across local systems to keep this proportionality constant in each of them.

   In other words, in rule-based systems it is the rules that are harmonized and the harmonization consists precisely in having uniform rules across different systems. In contrast, under a risk-based approach, rules must vary to take account of the different risks, and what must be maintained constant (that is, harmonized) is the mechanism which determines local adaptations (that is, the sensitivity to the risk) and, as a consequence of this, the equal capacity of different measures across different systems to tackle AML risks.
4. Examples of guidance for the implementation of risk-based systems are the FATF 'Guidance on the Risk-Based Approach' adopted between 2007 and 2010 for the different industry sectors covered by the Recommendations (they are all available at http://www.fatf-gafi.org).
5. This may be seen as a bottom-up approach, moving from the experience up to the identification of applicable measures, as opposed to the top-down approach inherent in rule-based systems, where applicable measures are a given and normally apply regardless of specific circumstances and past experience.
6. Of course, though it may not be enough, showing that the applied measures are in line with the indications given in official guidance provides a strong initial argument against charges of non compliance; the more this is the case, the more the 'rulebook' is complete and well consolidated (this may be particularly the case for guidance developed in partnership by the competent regulators and the private sector, as in the guidance issued by the Joint Money Laundering Steering Group in the UK). Interestingly, by ending up with detailed guidance which resembles hard-law provisions, and are accepted as a consolidated set of instructions to follow, the risk-based approach can become significantly similar to the rule-based one, at least as far as its practical application is concerned.
7. These concepts are well summarized in a 2004 letter from the UK Financial Services Authority published on the FSA website at http://www.fsa.gov.uk/pubs/other/money_laundering/jmlsg.pdf.
8. These two examples have not been chosen randomly. In fact, the obligations to verify the identity of the beneficial owner and to ascertain the political exposure of a customer (or of a beneficial owner) are typically risk-based in the FATF and EU standards. These standards specifically mandate that 'risk-based and adequate measures' be taken (see, for example, art. 8(1)(b) of the EU third AML/CFT Directive 2005/60/EC on beneficial ownership).

Therefore, the obligation is focused on taking adequate measures (the means), rather than on the outright verification of the identity of the beneficial owner or on determining the political exposure (the result). If, in the majority of cases, 'adequate measures' means achieving the intended results (in fact, 'adequate' means capable of getting there), this is not necessarily so in all circumstances. Clearly, what is important under these risk-based obligations, is that obliged subjects take reasonable measures, based on a sound judgement about the circumstances and the risks. If they do, and to the extent that they do, no violation can be charged against them even if the results (e.g. the verification of who is the beneficial owner or the political exposure of a counterpart) are not achieved in a particular case.

9. For example, while under a risk-based approach the obligation about beneficial owner's verification is to adopt adequate measures to establish who this is, the corresponding rule-based obligation can consist in a straightforward duty to identify the beneficial owner and verify their identity with certainty. If this is not done, this may amount to an infringement.
10. Or even unfair, particularly when the impossibility to comply is due to causes outside of the control of the obliged subject
11. The risk-based approach was already in place and well rooted in common-Law countries.
12. And, as we will see in section 26.7, the estimation of effectiveness in a risk-based environment is a complicated task.
13. Europe Economics, *Study on the Cost of Compliance with Selected FSAP Measures*, January 2009 (see http://ec.europa.eu/internal_market/finances/docs/actionplan/index/090707_cost_of_compliance_en.pdf). The survey embraces banks and financial conglomerates, asset managers, investment banks and financial markets and focuses on the cost of compliance with measures stemming from the Prospectus Directive (2003/71/EC), the Financial Conglomerates Directive (2002/87/EC), the Capital Requirements Directive (2006/48/EC), the Transparency Directive (2004/109/EC), the Markets in Financial Instruments Directive – MiFID (2004/39/EC), and the AML/CFT Directive (2005/60/EC).
14. See paragraphs 4.4 ff. of the *Study* and relevant tables.
15. The European Commission Staff Working Paper *Compliance with the Anti-money Laundering Directive by Cross-Border Banking Groups*, 2009 (http://ec.europa.eu/internal_market/company/docs/financial-crime/compli_cbb_en.pdf), p. 54, notes on this point that 'these two other Directives represented the most important regulatory changes in this area in recent times and their compliance costs are significantly higher'.
16. See paragraphs 4.26 ff., 4.57 ff. of the *Study* and relevant tables.
17. The customer due diligence requirements introduced by the third EU AML Directive are typically one area where the risk-based approach is applied extensively.
18. STR related monitoring and detection are, similarly to the risk-based measures, requirements which rely on the scrutiny of massive quantities of data and, based also on objective criteria and the application of automated processes, on the exercise of judgement.
    Interestingly, the European Commission Staff Working Paper notes that 'a different survey carried out in 2007 found that transaction monitoring is the single greatest area of AML expenditure for banks'. At that time, before the implementation of the third Directive, the know-your-customer requirements were not risk-based in the EU regulation (with a limited exception for non face-to-face transactions) and did not imply complex tasks of information gathering and assessing.
19. This is also an area where the risk-based approach applies extensively, as already noted above (see art. 13(4) of Directive 2005/60/EC and the considerations in paragraph 6.2.3).
20. See paragraphs 5 ff. of the *Study*.
21. See paragraphs 5.18 ff. of the *Study* and relevant tables.
22. In Deloitte, *Final Study on the Application of the Anti-Money Laundering Directive*, 2011, also contracted by the European Commission (published at http://ec.europa.eu/internal_market/company/docs/financial-crime/20110124_study_amld_en.pdf), in fact, it is noted that, to better meet their risk-based obligations, 'most financial institutions have implemented electronic compliance and client data management systems which can also perform automated customers profiling. . . . These systems, however, can come at a significant development and implementation cost' (p. 48). The *Study* also highlights on this point that one issue raised by the financial sector is 'the compliance cost attached to IT systems or to the manual work that comes with the risk assessment' (p. 49).
23. 'The lack of guidance from the competent authorities or FIU regarding the risk-based approach' is again noted in the *Study on the Application of the Anti-Money Laundering Directive* (p. 49). The scarce feedback provided by competent authorities to obliged subjects about the outcome of the measures adopted is a legacy of the previous system and, in the new framework, is likely to produce even more negative consequences: as we have seen, in fact, the risk-based approach needs to be fuelled by appropriate guidance and feedback is a valuable source of guidance.
24. This is now well reflected in FATF Recommendation 1, as resulting from the revision concluded in February 2012: 'Countries should identify, assess, and understand the money laundering and terrorist

financing risks for the country, and should take action, including designating an authority or mechanism to coordinate actions to assess risks, and apply resources, aimed at ensuring the risks are mitigated effectively. Based on that assessment, countries should apply a risk-based approach (RBA) to ensure that measures to prevent or mitigate money laundering and terrorist financing are commensurate with the risks identified. . . . Where countries identify higher risks, they should ensure that their AML/CFT regime adequately addresses such risks. Where countries identify lower risks, they may decide to allow simplified measures for some of the FATF Recommendations under certain conditions'.

25. See FATF, *Global Money Laundering and Terrorist Financing Threat Assessment*, 2010 (http://www.fatf.gafi.org/media/fatf/documents/reports/Global%20 Threat %20 assessment.pdf).
26. Ibid., see pages 10 and 62 ff.
27. See, for example, FATF, *Money Laundering and Terrorist Financing Risk Assessment Strategies*, 2008 (http://www.fatf-gafi.org/dataoecd/46/24/40978997.pdf). The quoted text is at page 5 of this document.
28. Feedback can be both specific, in relation to the outcome of particular cases, and general, that is referred to general trends and patterns. This latter type of feedback can also fulfil the duty to provide obliged subjects with indications on the 'practices of money launderers and terrorist financers', mentioned in art. 35(2).
29. An example in this perspective is offered by B. Unger, *The Amounts and the Effects of Money Laundering* (Utrecht School of Economics 2006). Further considerations on a methodology capable of supporting an estimate of the magnitude of money laundering can be found in B. Unger, *The Scale and Impacts of Money Laundering* (Edward Elgar Publishing 2007).
30. The text is quoted from art. 33(1) of the Directive. FATF Recommendation 33 contains similar language.
31. It is worth recalling that the available evidence shows that the application of the duty to report suspicious transactions by lawyers is not as effective as was expected when relevant provisions were first introduced in FATF and EU standards. On the complex issues surrounding the application of AML/CFT measures to lawyers and the interplay with the right to defense and the related professional privilege see, *inter alia*, European Commission, *Report to the European Parliament and the Council on the application of Directive 2005/60/EC on the prevention of the use of the financial system for the purpose of money laundering and terrorist financing*, 11 April 2012, esp. pp. 15 ff.. See also Stouten and Tilleman, Chapter 30 of this volume.
32. The revised FATF 'Methodology for Assessing Technical Compliance with the FATF Recommendations and the Effectiveness of AML/CFT Systems' can be consulted at www.fatf-gafi.org/media/fatf/documents/methodology/FATF%20Methodology%2022%20Feb%202013 pdf.
33. It is important to stress that this mechanism based on the interaction between risk assessment and evaluation of effectiveness can be replicated also at the micro level, that is at a firm-specific level: obliged subjects, with a view to implementing and maintaining an appropriate risk-based approach, should perform *ex ante* risk assessments for the configuration of tailored measures; this should be corroborated, *ex post*, by an evaluation of the effectiveness of the measures applied, with the aim of reviewing these measures and adjusting the resources' allocation whenever needed or possible, in light of the risks.
34. See, in particular, Recommendations 1 and 2, respectively, about 'Assessing risks and applying a risk-based approach' and 'National cooperation and coordination', together with the detailed provisions in the Interpretative Note to Recommendation 1, where the overall risk-based approach is broken down into discrete measures and obligations for countries, supervisors, covered entities; additional, more specific indications on the risk-based approach are set out in the Recommendations dedicated to customer due diligence measures (10–16) and to regulation and supervision (26–28).

27. Prevention of money laundering and terrorist financing from a good governance perspective

Melissa van den Broek and Henk Addink

27.1 INTRODUCTION

Since the start of the 1990s, when the first initiatives to combat money laundering began to bite, criminal law has been at the forefront of the fight against money laundering and terrorist financing.[1] Ever since, however, important developments at the international, European and national level have taken place, which have led to a more prominent role for administrative law in anti-money laundering and combating terrorist financing (hereafter: AML/CTF) policy.

Currently the fight against money laundering and terrorist financing follows a so-called 'twin-track approach' (Stessens 2000). On the one hand this twin-track approach consists of a preventive policy, which aims at the prevention of money laundering through setting identification and reporting obligations for financial institutions, certain non-financial institutions and legal professionals such as lawyers and notaries. The main objective of the preventive policy is to prevent the misuse of institutions by criminals, aiming to launder their proceeds through these institutions. In the words of Levi and Reuter, the preventive policy aims 'to deter criminals from using institutions to launder the proceeds of their crimes and to create sufficient transparency to deter institutions from being willing to launder' (Levi and Reuter 2006, p.297). Administrative law plays a very important (though not exclusive) role in this track. On the other hand the twin-track approach consists of a repressive policy, of which the objective is to punish the money launderer, usually through the use of criminal law and by the freezing, seizure and confiscation of assets.

The increased relevance of administrative law in the fight against money laundering and terrorist financing makes it desirable to shed light on the policy from an administrative law perspective. This chapter focuses on the preventive AML/CTF policy. After having described the legal framework and key elements of the preventive policy (section 27.2), we introduce the notion of good governance as an adequate administrative law approach in section 27.3 and apply it. From this perspective, we have a look at the preventive AML/CTF policy and point out some underlying tensions within the policy (section 27.4). This chapter ends with some concluding remarks.

27.2 THE PREVENTIVE POLICY: LEGAL FRAMEWORK AND KEY ELEMENTS

27.2.1 Legal Framework

The prevention of money laundering and terrorist financing is regulated at the international, regional and national level. The most authoritative norms that stem from the international level are the forty Recommendations on Combating Money Laundering and the Financing of Terrorism & Proliferation from the Financial Action Task Force.[2] The FATF Recommendations focus both on preventive and on repressive elements. At the regional, or European, level there are two EU directives in place with the objective of preventing the use of the financial system for the purpose of money laundering and terrorist financing.[3] Furthermore, the Council of Europe has developed an important legal standard: the 2005 Convention on Laundering, Search, Seizure and Confiscation of the Proceeds from Crime and on the Financing of Terrorism.[4] The legal norms stemming from both levels are transposed in the national legal norms, while the national legislature can opt for additional norms or can regulate matters in more detail or more stringently.[5]

27.2.2 Key Elements

It can be said that the current preventive AML/CTF policy consists of four key elements:[6] customer due diligence; the reporting obligation; the record keeping obligation; and the enforcement (supervision and sanctioning) of those obligations.[7] We will now shortly describe these key elements below.

27.2.2.1 Customer due diligence

Customer due diligence measures ensure that institutions know whom they are dealing with and try to prevent institutions from having business relationships with unknown customers or businesses they do not fully understand. The customer due diligence measures include the identification of customers and the verification of their identity, identification of the identity of the beneficial owner and verification of this identity, and obtaining information on and understanding the purpose and intended nature of the business relationship and on-going due diligence. Customer due diligence procedures need to be undertaken when establishing a business relationship, or carrying out an occasional transaction when there are doubts about the veracity or adequacy of previously obtained documents used for identification, or when there is a suspicion of money laundering or terrorist financing.[8]

Customer due diligence measures should be applied to new and existing customers. In order to be more effective, institutions are allowed to perform customer due diligence measures on the basis of a risk-based approach. The essence of this approach is that resources should be directed in such a manner that the highest risks receive most attention.[9] The levels of customer due diligence are simplified when there is a low risk and enhanced when there is a high risk.[10] It is up to the institutions to decide under which category they place their customers, but additional measures are at least required in the case of politically exposed persons, correspondent banking relationships, money or value transfer services, new technologies and wire transfers.[11] Furthermore, the FATF

Recommendations stipulate that enhanced customer due diligence requirements are required in cases where a higher risk exists. The higher risk can relate to customers (e.g. cash intensive businesses, non-resident customers), countries (in which the FATF Recommendations are insufficiently applied or which are subject to UN sanctions or embargos) or products (private banking or non-face-to-face transactions).[12]

Customer due diligence measures should be conducted before or during the course of establishing a business relationship or conducting transactions for occasional customers.[13] If the measures cannot be concluded, the institution may not open the account, start the business relation or perform a transaction or it should terminate the business relationship. Furthermore, it should give consideration to filing a suspicion report to the competent authorities. Customer due diligence measures may – under certain conditions – be performed by third parties. The ultimate responsibility for reliance on third parties remains with the relying institution.[14]

27.2.2.2 Reporting obligation

The second key element, and maybe the most important one, is the obligation for institutions to report on their own initiative (reasonable) suspicions of money laundering or terrorist financing to the competent authority, the Financial Intelligence Unit (FIU).[15,16] Suspicious circumstances are, for example, cases where the transaction serves no apparent purpose, the nature of the transaction does not match the customer's business needs or the transaction structure is unnecessarily complicated (Blöcker 2002).

The national legislature is free in deciding what form the report should take. One can think of suspicious transaction reports, unusual transaction reports, cash transaction reports, threshold reports, and so on. Three factors have influenced the way in which national legislatures have implemented the reporting obligation: the choice between administrative and criminal law; the scope of the predicate offences and, hence, the reporting obligation; and the fact that there is no one agreed upon definition of suspicion or one set of criteria for determining the suspicious nature (Stessens 2000). When one takes a look at the European Member States' current reporting systems, one will notice there are a lot of differences among them (Ferwerda et al. 2011).

The reporting obligation is not an uncontested obligation. The legal and financial service providers particularly, most notably lawyers, consider the reporting obligation to be an infringement on their legal professional privilege. Legal professional privilege is a legal norm that protects the confidentiality of communications made between a lawyer and his or her client. It is a fundamental right and cannot be easily be overridden by other interests (i.e. it can only be limited by 'overriding requirements in the public interest in certain specific circumstances',[17]) yet not all communications fall under this privilege. Only communications categorized as 'legal advice' or in relation to 'litigation' fall under the privilege (Itzikowitz 2006). In Europe there is some case law on the relationship between the reporting obligation and this fundamental notion of legal privilege (Komárek 2008). The European Court of Justice decided in the Ordre des Barreaux-case that the reporting obligation does not infringe the right to a fair trail.[18] In their contribution in this volume (see Chapter 30), Stouten and Tilleman delve deeper into the relationship between the reporting obligation and the principle of legal privilege.

27.2.2.3 Record keeping obligation

The record keeping obligation entails the obligation for institutions to keep the identification documents and all transaction data stored for a period of at least five years following the carrying out of the transactions or the end of the business relationship.[19] One needs to think of copies of identity cards or passports, driving licenses, but also account files and business correspondence.

The purpose of this requirement is twofold: on the one hand it enables supervisory authorities to check compliance with the preventive AML/CTF norms, while on the other hand record keeping enables the competent authorities to gather evidence in case of criminal prosecution. Stessens has formulated the relevance of the record keeping obligation as follows:

> [b]y keeping customer identification records and records of financial transactions, financial institutions are in fact keeping a database of information which can be tapped by law enforcement authorities in their investigations into money laundering. In their efforts to trace the proceeds of crime, law enforcement authorities need to reconstruct the paper trail left by the movement of those proceeds. (Stessens 2000, p. 164)

27.2.2.4 Enforcement

Enforcement in the preventive AML/CTF policy includes the supervision by authorities on the compliance with the preventive obligations, as well as the sanctioning in the case of non-compliance. Where the enforcement runs through criminal law, it entails the stages of investigation, prosecution and effectuation of sanctions. In most EU Member States, the enforcement of the preventive AML/CTF norms is of an administrative law nature.

For quite some time the international and regional norms paid only little attention to the enforcement of the policy. The norms regarding enforcement were mostly left to the national legislatures. As a result, there is now a patchwork of enforcement systems in the preventive AML/CTF policies of countries (Van den Broek 2011). There are, however, careful attempts to harmonize enforcement in the preventive policy.[20] For example, on the matter of supervision, the Third Money Laundering Directive stipulates that Member States shall require the competent authorities at least to effectively monitor and to take the necessary measures with a view to ensuring compliance with the requirements by the Directive by all institutions and persons covered.[21] In order to achieve this goal, the Directive stipulates that supervisory authorities must at least have the power to compel the production of any information that is relevant to monitoring compliance and perform checks.[22] Both the FATF Recommendations and the Directive stipulate that there must be 'effective, proportionate and dissuasive sanctions' to deal with non-compliance by institutions.[23] The international and European norms of enforcement provide minimum conditions, but the design of the enforcement system is still left to the countries' procedural autonomy.[24]

27.3 THE ADMINISTRATIVE LAW CONCEPT OF GOOD GOVERNANCE

In the foregoing we have seen that administrative law is more and more embedded in the fight against money laundering and terrorist financing. In the preventive AML/CTF policy the instruments show this, as well as the enforcement of this policy, which – as explained above – is usually of an administrative law nature.

An obvious question that accompanies this development is whether or not the norms in the preventive AML/CTF policy and the application or enforcement of those norms fulfill the requirements that administrative law sets. In the first place we tend to look at the classic principles of proper administration that the public administration has to abide by (Addink 1999). But in European[25] and international[26] administrative law there is a tendency to focus more on the requirements that follow from the concept of good governance. Particularly noteworthy is the right to good administration, as codified in the EU Charter of Fundamental Rights (Addink 2008; Millet 2002; Wakefield 2007). Besides, in the literature, attention is requested for (the protection) of public values, whereby the prevalent view is that public values are being put under pressure (Stout 2007). At the national level, we also see that the principles of good governance are put into practice (Statskontoret 2005; for the Netherlands specifically: Addink 2010).

The concept of good governance is a meta-concept, which means that it builds on other concepts. In short, it encompasses the duty to pay attention to everything that is necessary for government to serve a community well. Aspects of good governance have been presented as constitutional principles (Endicott 2009). Its development can be seen as comprising three phases. The first is the group of requirements that follow from the concept of 'Rechtsstaat' (loosely translated: rule of law), that form the basis of the current government models as we can find them today. The second phase – in addition to the first – is formed by the democratic demands, which become increasingly important in a developing society. The third phase focuses more on the functioning and quality of government as such, the set of instruments that the public institutions have at their disposal and the legal norms that have to be observed in this context. Within each of the three phases two elements can be distinguished. In phase I, these are the principles of proper administration and the (protection of) fundamental rights, in phase II transparency and participation and in phase III effectiveness and accountability.

These elements can be considered together as the principles of good governance (Addink et al. 2010). The principles can be used in a good governance framework in which they are interpreted and function as demands for a good functioning of public institutions and government (Curtin and Dekker 2005). The set of principles is broad and it could be that in some circumstances a selection of the most relevant principles has to be made. The principles can strengthen one another, but can also lead to tensions. This will be shown in the next section. What is important is that a proper balance between the principles is found.

We will now focus on the principles themselves (Addink et al. 2010). What do they mean? We have seen above that on the basis of the three phases of good governance, there are six (groups of) principles of good governance.

The first group is the principles of proper administration. Within that group, eight principles can be distinguished: the principle of the prohibition of misuse of power; the principle of the prohibition of arbitrariness; the principle of legal certainty; the principle of legitimate expectation; the principle of equality; the principle of proportionality; the principle of carefulness; and the principle of reasoning (Addink 1999). Together they provide the minimum requirements that the government must adhere to in its relationship with citizens and institutions. Hence, the government must, *inter alia*, use its powers for no other purpose than that for which the power was conferred upon it (prohibition of misuse of power); it must act proportionately to the aims pursued (principle of proportionality); it must not discriminate (principle of equality); and the government must state reasons when it takes a decision to increase rational decision-making by the administration and to provide citizens with an explanation (principle of reasoning), etc.

The second principle is the principle of transparency. It ensures that the government employs a certain degree of openness in its actions, by ensuring citizens and institutions access to all kinds of information, for example information on meetings, on policy and on administrative acts. A new aspect is transparency in the context of public procurement, in which case publication demonstrate the competitive effects of the economic market. There are more examples in the field of (European) economic public law (Buijze and Widdershoven 2010; Zoellner 2006).[27]

The third principle is the principle of participation. In a representative democracy not all the activities of the government are controlled by the representatives of the people: the Parliament. For that reason there is an additional need for participation by the citizens. It is important that in all the government's activities which have direct consequences for people, the directly affected persons are involved in the decision-making process. Examples are the popular initiative, citizens' panel, referendum and community-level participation (Addink 2009). The principle of participation requires that a choice has to be made whether or not to involve citizens or institutions. This decision is to be based on the issue concerned and on the desired degree of participation of citizens.

The fourth principle is the principle of effectiveness. Its development started in the non-legal context, but nowadays it is also being studied in the legal context; especially in relation to the enforcement of law. Effectiveness can be found at all levels of law: international, European and national (Addink et al. 2010). Generally it requires that policies are effective; that is, that they deliver what is needed on the basis of clear objectives. Accordingly, legal norms must not impede the reaching of those objectives.

The fifth principle is accountability. It concerns 'a relationship between an actor and a forum, in which the actor has the obligation to explain and justify his or her conduct, the forum can pose questions and pass judgment, and the actor might face consequences' (Bovens 2007, p.450). Accountability enhances the public legitimacy of government's actions. Good governance requires that there is a certain level of public accountability. Three forms of public accountability are traditionally distinguished: civil, criminal and political (Burkens et al. 2006).

The last principle concerns fundamental (human) rights. The activities of government should respect, protect and fulfill fundamental rights. The government should, for instance, respect the right of citizens (and institutions) to a fair trial as enshrined in article 6 of the European Convention on Human Rights (ECHR). The other principles of good governance closely interact with this last principle of fundamental rights. For example, the transparency and the participation principles can be found in several international human rights treaties.

27.4 GOOD GOVERNANCE TENSIONS IN THE PREVENTIVE AML/CTF POLICY

In the foregoing we have briefly explained the concept of good governance and the accompanying principles. We will now turn to two tensions that strike the eye when we look at the preventive AML/CTF policy from this good governance perspective. The questions that are posed in this section serve as an illustration of the tensions.The first tension that we see concerns the tension between effectiveness and the protection of fundamental rights, in particular the tension between the reporting obligation and the principle of legal privilege (which forms part of the right to a fair trial). Because of the fact that financial and legal service providers ran a high-risk of being used in money laundering schemes, it was decided to include them under the scope of the preventive AML/CTF policy (Ping 2006). Behind this, one can identify a meta-objective which is to effectively prevent and combat money laundering and terrorist financing. However, lawyers have fiercely objected to their inclusion in the preventive AML/CTF policy. They have argued that due to legal privilege they cannot be subjected to the reporting obligation, for this would infringe citizens' fundamental right to speak openly with their lawyers, and thus to a fair trial.[28] The question that arises from a good governance perspective is: how to balance the values of effectiveness and protection of fundamental rights properly? For now, international and European norms have come with the solution that legal professional privilege can constitute an exception to the reporting obligation – namely when information is obtained before, during or after judicial proceedings or in the course of ascertaining the legal position for a client. Yet, as Stouten and Tilleman show in their contribution in this volume (Chapter 30), such an approach is not as clear-cut as it seems at first sight.

A second tension comes to light when we consider the risk-based approach for customer due diligence in the preventive policy. As explained above, there is an important role for the private sector. After all, institutions have to calibrate their AML/CTF policies on risk. They have to determine which risk factors play a role and how to deal with those risks in terms of their customer due diligence obligations; government only provides the preconditions. The risk-based approach has replaced the former rule-based approach in the preventive policy, and 'has opened up for changed roles for private actors in the public sector' (Bergström et al. 2011, p. 1044). Several advantages of the risk-based approach were outlined when the approach was first introduced: it would allow for more flexibility, a reduction of costs for the private sector and more high quality suspicion reports (Van den Broek 2011; Ross and Hannan 2007; Unger and Van Waarden 2009). Altogether this shows that the introduction of the risk-based approach was pervaded with effectiveness considerations.

However, in terms of (democratic) accountability the change in approach implied a shift from the public to the private realm. The problem is that while 'public actors are accountable within the democratic system of command and control', the private actors are not (Bergström et al. 2011, p. 1060). Under the rule-based approach it was obviously the government who was responsible for the design and functioning of the applicable rules, but with the risk-based approach a far more active behaviour is required from the institutions. In an empirical study performed in the United Kingdom and Sweden, Bergström and colleagues conclude that the risk-based approach with respect to customer due diligence in the prevention of money laundering and terrorist financing has diluted the boundaries between the public and private sector and that the strong involvement of private actors in the process could jeopardize the classic understanding of accountability. The question is: who can be held accountable for a proper functioning of the preventive policy, and how? The above shows us that there is a tension between the principles of effectiveness and accountability, and that in the current system the emphasis seems to lie with the former to the detriment of the latter.

27.5 CONCLUDING REMARKS

In this contribution we have explained the increased relevance of administrative law in the overall fight against money laundering and terrorist financing and the concept of good governance. Administrative law is in particular prominent in the preventive AML/CTF policy. For this reason we have first explained the legislative framework and key elements of the preventive AML/CTF policy. It has become clear that legal norms regarding the prevention of money laundering come from the international level (most notably the FATF), the regional level (in Europe: European Union and the Council of Europe) and the national level. The key elements are customer due diligence, the reporting obligation, the record-keeping obligation and enforcement. We argued that because of the increased importance of administrative law, it has become more and more important that the norms and application of those norms meet the requirements that follow from administrative law. We subsequently showed that good governance is an adequate framework to specify those administrative law requirements. Finally, we have looked at the preventive AML/CTF policy from a good governance perspective and identified two underlying tensions, where effectiveness clashed with the protection of fundamental rights and accountability. Though we realize that an effective preventive AML/CTF policy is of utmost importance in the overall fight against money laundering and terrorist financing, good governance requires a proper balance with the other values as well. This is something that the policy-makers in this field, whether at the international, regional or national level, should keep in the back of their minds.

NOTES

1. For example: UN Convention Against Illicit Traffic in Narcotic Drugs and Psychotropic Substances, December 19, 1988 (Vienna Convention) and Convention on Laundering, Search, Seizure and Confiscation of the Proceeds from Crime, November 8, 1990 (Strasbourg Convention).
2. In February 2012 the FATF revised and adopted new Recommendations. See for a thorough analysis of global responses to money laundering and on more information on the FATF Recommendations: Gilmore (2004) and Damais (2007).
3. Directive 2005/60/EC of the European Parliament and of the Council of 26 October 2005 on the prevention of the use of the financial system for the purpose of money laundering and terrorist financing, OJ L 309, November, p.15 and Commission Directive 2006/70/EC, of 1 August 2006 laying down implementing measures for Directive 2005/60/EC of the European Parliament and of the Council as regards the definition of 'politically exposed person' and the technical criteria for simplified customer

due diligence procedures and for exemption on grounds of a financial activity conducted on an occasional or very limited basis, OJ L 214, August, p. 29. With the adoption of the new and revised FATF Recommendations, the Third Directive will be repealed by a Fourth Directive that takes into account the amendments and innovations from the new FATF Recommendations. Useful literature on the current European legal framework with respect to AML/CTF: Mitsilegas and Gilmore (2007) and Rietrae (2007).

4. CETS No.: 198. Its relevance for the preventive policy is limited, only articles 12–14 deal with preventive instruments.
5. Article 5 of the Third Directive stipulates that Member States may adopt or retain in force stricter provisions in the field covered by this Directive to prevent money laundering and terrorist financing. See for an inventory of national AML/CTF policies: Muller, Kalin and Goldsworth (2007).
6. See for a different categorization Levi and Reuter (2006) at 297–8.
7. A supportive element is the obligation to establish internal procedures and provide training to employees. See: FATF Recommendations 18 and 23; article 34, first paragraph, and article 35 Third Money Laundering Directive.
8. FATF Recommendations 10 and 22; articles 7 and 8 of EU 'Third Money Laundering Directive'.
9. FATF(2007), *Guidance on the Risk-based Approach to Combating Money Laundering and Terrorist Financing: High Level Principles and Procedures*, Paris.
10. For more information on the risk-based approach see the contributions of Costanzo (Chapter 25) and Unger and Van Waarden (Chapter 29) in this volume. Also useful is: Ross and Hannan (2007).
11. FATF Recommendations 12–16; article 13 Third Money Laundering Directive.
12. Interpretative Note to FATF Recommendation 10; article 13 Third Money Laundering Directive. In this Interpretative Note, the FATF provides a lot of examples of lower and higher risk situations. These examples are not mandatory elements of the FATF Standards, and are meant as guidance only.
13. However, FATF Recommendation 10 and article 9, second paragraph, of the Third Money Laundering Directive allow countries to decide that institutions may complete the verification at a later moment where the money laundering risks are low and where this is essential not to interrupt the normal conduct of business.
14. FATF Recommendation 17; articles 14–19 Third Money Laundering Directive.
15. FATF Recommendation 20; articles 21 and 22 Third Money Laundering Directive.
16. An FIU should serve as a national center responsible for receiving and analyzing suspicious transactions reports and other information relevant to money laundering, associated predicate offences and terrorist financing, and for the dissemination of the results of that analysis (FATF Recommendation 29). Pursuant to the FATF Recommendations and EU Third Money Laundering Directive, Member States are required to establish an FIU. See for more information about the types and core tasks and functions of FIU: IMF (2004).
17. Opinion of AG Maduro of 14 December 2006 in case C-305/05, *Ordre des barreaux francophones et germanophone e.a.* v *Council*, [2007] ECR I-5305, paragraph 47.
18. ECJ, Case C-305/05, *Ordre des barreaux francophones et germanophones and Others v Conseil des ministres*, [2007] I-5305; Luchtman and Van der Hoeven (2009).
19. FATF Recommendation 11; article 30 Third Money Laundering Directive.
20. Chapter IV, sections 2 and 4, Third Money Laundering Directive; FATF Recommendations 26–28 and 35. The Interpretative Notes to the new FATF Recommendations provide more detailed guidance and information than before on how to design a risk-based approach to supervision, which powers supervisors must have and on the adequacy of supervisors' resources.
21. Article 37, first paragraph, Third Money Laundering Directive.
22. Article 37, second paragraph, Third Money Laundering Directive.
23. FATF Recommendation 35; article 39, first paragraph, Third Money Laundering Directive.
24. European Commission (2012). Here the European Commission states that in the drafting of the Fourth Money Laundering Directive consideration could be given to a greater harmonization of the sanctioning regime by proposing a set of minimum common rules to be applied.
25. In the context of the European Union we can point to the Commission of the European Communities (2001) & European Ombudsman (2005). In the context of the Council of Europe we can point to the Recommendation of the Committee of Ministers to Member States on good administration, 20 June 2007, CM/Rec (2007).
26. World Bank 1989, 1997; IMF 1997; OECD 2001; Office of the United Nations High Commissioner for Human Rights 2007. Useful literature: Esty 2007; Wouters and Ryngeart 2005.
27. See more generally on the transparency principle: Prechal and De Leeuw (2007) and for the application of this principle: Addink (2003).
28. See the earlier cited *Ordre des Barreaux* case, note no. 18 above.

REFERENCES

Addink, G.H. (1999), *Algemene beginselen van behoorlijk bestuur*, Deventer: Kluwer.

Addink, G.H. (2003), 'The transparency principle in the framework of the WTO from an administrative law perspective', *Merkourios, The Utrecht Journal of International and European Law*, **67**, 21–30.

Addink,G.H. (2008), 'Goed bestuur: een norm voor het bestur of het recht van een burger ?', in G.H. Addink, G. Jurgens, Ph.M. Langbroek and R.J.G.M. Widdershoven, *Grensverleggend Bestuursrecht*, Deventer: Kluwer, 3–25.

Addink, G.H. (2009), *Local and Regional Level Participation in Europe: a comparative exploratory study on the application of the participation principle at local and regional level within the framework of the Council of Europe*, report drafted at request of the Province of Utrecht (NL), November 2009, available at: http://ec.europa.eu/dgs/secretariat_general/citizens_initiative/docs/provincie_utrecht_2_en.pdf.

Addink, G.H. (2010), *Goed bestuur*, Deventer: Kluwer.

Addink, H., G., Anthony A. Buyse and C. Flinterman (2010), *Sourcebook: Human Rights & Good Governance*, Utrecht University: SIM special 34 available at: http://www.uu.nl/faculty/leg/NL/organisatie/departementen/departementrechtsgeleerdheid/organisatie/onderdelen/studieeninformatiecentrummensenrechten/publicaties/simspecials/Documents/SIM_Special_34.pdf

Auburn, J. (2000), *Legal Professional Privilege: Law and Theory*, Oxford: Hart.

Bergström, M., K. Svedberg Helgesson and U. Mörth (2011), 'A new role for for-profit actors? The case of anti-money laundering and risk management', *Journal of Common Market Studies*, **49**(5), 1043–64.

Blöcker, K. (2002), 'Reporting suspicions of money laundering and whistle blowing under German law', *Journal of Money Laundering Control*, **6**(1), 52–6.

Bovens, M. (2007), 'Analysing and assessing accountability: a conceptual framework', *European Law Journal*, **13**, (4), 447–68.

Broek, Van den M. (2011), 'The EU's preventive AML/CTF policy: asymmetrical harmonisation', *Journal of Money Laundering Control*, **14**(2) 170–82.

Buijze, A.W.J.G. and Widdershoven, R.J.G.M. (2010), 'De Awb en EU-recht: het transparantiebeginsel', in T. Barkhuyzen W. den Ouden and J.E.M. Polak *Bestuursrecht harmoniseren: 15 jaar Awb*, Den Haag: Boom Juridische Uitgevers, 589–607.

Burkens, M.C. et. al (2006), *Beginselen van de democratische rechtsstaat*, Alphen aan den Rijn: Kluwer.

Commission of the European Communities, *European Governance: A White Paper*, COM(2001) 428 final.

Curtin, D.M. and I. Dekker (2005), 'Good governance: the concept and its application by the European Union', in D.M. Curtin and R.A. Wessels, *Good Governance and the European Union: Reflections on Concepts, Institutions and Substance* Antwerp: Intersentia, 3–20.

Damais, A. (2007), 'The Financial Action Task Force', in W.H., Muller C.H. Kalin and J.G., Goldsworth, *Anti-money Laundering: International Law and Practice*, New York: Wiley, 69–83.

Endicott, T. (2009), *Administrative Law*, Oxford: Oxford University Press.

Esty, D.C. (2007) 'Good governance at the World Trade Organization: building a foundation of administrative law', *Journal of International Economic Law*, **10**(3), 509–27.

European Commission (2012), *Report from the Commission to the European Parliament and Council on the application of Directive 2005/60/EC on the prevention of the use of the financial system for the purpose of money laundering and terrorist financing*, COM (2012) 168 final, 14.

European Ombudsman (2005), *The European Code of Good Administrative Behaviour*.

Ferwerda, J., I. Deleanu M. Van den Broek and B. Unger (2011), *Comparing the Incomparable. The principal agent problem of the FATF in assessing countries' anti money laundering policy performance*, paper presented at the conference 'The Shadow Economy, Tax Evasion and Money Laundering', July 28–31, 2011 in Muenster (not yet published).

Gilmore, B. (2004), *Dirty Money: the evolution of international measures to counter money laundering and the financing of terrorism*, 3rd edn, Strasburg: Council of Europe Publishing.

IMF (1997), *Good Governance: the IMF's Role*, Washington DC: IMF.

IMF (2004), *Financial Intelligence Units: An Overview*, Washington DC: IMF.

Itzikowitz, A. (2006), 'Legal professional privilege/intermediary confidentiality: the challenge for anti-money laundering measures', in C. Goredema *Money Laundering Experiences, ISS Monograph Series*, 73–90.

Komárek, J. (2008), 'Legal professional privilege and the EU's fight against money laundering', *Civil Justice Quarterly*, **27** (1), 13–22.

Levi, M. and P. Reuter (2006), 'Money laundering', *Public Policy*, 289–375.

Luchtman, M. and R. van der Hoeven (2009), 'Case comment to Case C-305/05, Ordre des barreaux francophones and germanophones & Others v. Conseil des Ministres', *Common Market Law Review*, **46**(1), 301–18.

Millet, P. (2002) 'The right to good administration in European law', *Public Law*, **47**, 309–22.

Mitsilegas, V. and B. Gilmore (2007), 'The EU legislative framework against money laundering and terrorist finance: a critical analysis in the light of evolving global standards', *International and Comparative Law Quarterly*, **56**(1), 119–40.

Muller,W.H., C.H. Kalin and J.G. Goldsworth (2007), *Anti-money Laundering: International Law and Practice*, New York: Wiley.

OECD (2001), *Governance in the 21st Century*, Paris: OECD.

Office of the United Nations High Commissioner for Human Rights (2007), *Good Governance Practices for the Protection of Human Rights*, New York: UN.

Pennarts, H.T.F. (2008), *Beginselen van behoorlijk bestuur*, Antwerpen: Maklu.

Ping, H. (2006), 'Lawyers, notaries, accountants and money laundering', *Journal of Money Laundering Control*, **9**, (1), 62–70.

Prechal, S. and M. De Leeuw (2007), 'Dimensions of transparency: the building blocks for a new legal principle?', *Review of European Administrative Law*, **1**(1), 51–61.

Rietrae, J. (2007), 'The 3rd EU Anti-money Laundering Directive: main issues and intriguing details', in P.C. Van Duyne et al., *Crime Business and Crime Money in Europe: The Dirty Linen of Illicit Enterprise*, Nijmegen: Wolf Legal Publishers.

Ross, S. and M. Hannan (2007), 'Money laundering regulation and risk-based decision making', *Journal of Money Laundering Control*, **10**(1), 106–15.

Statskontoret (2005), *Principles of Good Administration in the Member States of the European Union*, available at: http://www.statskontoret.se/upload/Publikationer/2005/200504.pdf (last visited August 2011).

Stessens, G. (2000), *Money Laundering: A New International Law Enforcement Model*, Cambridge: Cambridge University Press.

Stout, H.D. (2007), *Weerbare waarden – borging van publieke belangen in nutssectoren*, Den Haag: Boom Juridische Uitgevers.

Unger, B. and F. Van Waarden (2009), 'How to dodge drowning in data? Rule- and risk-based anti money laundering policies compared', *Review of Law & Economics*, **5**(2), 953–85.

Wakefield, J. (2007), *The Right to Good Administration*, Deventer: Kluwer.

World Bank (1989), *Sub-Saharan Africa: From Crisis to Sustainable Growth*, Washington DC: World Bank.

World Bank (1997), *Corruption and Good Governance*, Washington DC: World Bank.

Wouters, J. and Ryngaert, C. (2005) 'Good governance: lessons from international organizations', in D.M. Curtin and R.A. Wessels, *Good Governance and the European Union: Reflections on Concepts, Institutions and Substance*, Antwerp: Intersentia, 69–104.

Zoellner, C.S. (2006), 'Transparency: An analysis of an evolving fundamental principle in international economic law', *Michigan Journal of International Law*, **27**, 579–628.

28. Economic crimes and money laundering: a new paradigm for the criminal justice system?*

John Vervaele

28.1 INTRODUCTION: PHENOMENOLOGY

Money laundering is a complex issue, not only as a result of the development of the processes of internationalization and globalization, but also because of its transverse nature and its relationship to criminal law, criminal procedure, administrative – both substantive and process – law, financial, and international public law.

To become familiar with the concepts of money laundering, let us begin with the phenomenology from a criminological perspective. Afterwards, we shall revise a little of the history in order to discover where these concepts have their origin and how they have been legally drawn together, and in this way place ourselves in the history of the criminal policy connected with this new regulatory offense. Subsequently, we shall deal with certain aspects of criminal law, such as specific problems connected to the substantial elements of the offense and certain relevant matters of criminal procedure. Finally, we shall deal with the human rights framework and the question of international cooperation in the criminal law domain, related to this phenomenon.

The first case of criminal conviction can be traced back to 1988 and comes from the United States. The BCCI bank (Bank of Credit and Commerce International), by that time quite well known and active in many countries, with over 500 affiliates, was convicted of money laundering. Unfortunately, a section of this bank specialized in the laundering of assets from the Pablo Escobar cartel, especially its affiliates from Florida. This demonstrated the structure of the crime of money laundering, which today is considered financial engineering. It basically develops in three well known stages. The initial stage is receiving the money. Subsequently, the money was displaced in a series of operations through financial companies located in France, the United Kingdom, Luxembourg, the Bahamas and Panama, and also in somc banks in South America. The purpose of this was to hide the money and search for ways of protecting or shielding it. Some countries offer this protection more than others, and are even allowed to apply bank secrecy, while others are denominated as *tax havens*. Finally the money is recovered for consumption or reinvestment purposes.

At the beginning of the 1990s, the Slavenburg bank – an important bank in the Netherlands at that time – was convicted of money laundering; it had five affiliates and its headquarters were located in Amsterdam. Knowingly, the Board of the bank specialized in the laundering of assets of a series of activities of groups trafficking marihuana. We are referring to the so-called Dutch *coffee-shops*, where the consumption of this plant was legal, but not its trafficking or the laundering of assets. The latter activities were by that time already included as criminal offenses under Dutch law. The bank was submitted to an in-depth judicial investigation, resulting in the cancellation of its license and the closure of its activities. The management of the bank was personally convicted either for the perpetration of the laundering of assets or for the omission of related duties of due care or diligence. The same fate befell the management of the affiliate, its employees, and the executive. Also, its legal capacity was cancelled.

Another recent case covered in the media, less complex and less institutional than those from the banking sector, is that of Mr Roldán, head of the Spanish Civil Guard (one of the major national police forces). He was convicted of money laundering and corruption. Mr Roldán was the first civil – not military – authority in charge of the police force, but benefited from the construction contracts of military premises. He charged rather high commissions on the contracts, which in Spain is held to be a crime. With the obtained assets he carried out a series of financial operations to launder the money and later purchased properties in different European countries.

There are two more cases that can be included here because they illustrate, firstly, the global nature of the crime and, secondly, the substantial legal elements of the crime. The first case is rather recent, and was also covered in the media. It refers to a conspiracy to launder assets perpetrated by Alfonso Portillo, former president of Guatemala. Portillo was extradited from Mexico to Guatemala for having appointed personal friends in a number of ministries – *figureheads* who quickly emptied the coffers of the state, specifically those of the Ministry of Defense, the Ministry of Public Works, the Ministry of Development, and other public funds for development granted by foreign countries such as Taiwan.

When it comes to laundering money, the same scheme is always applied. In the case of Portillo, a series of companies were established – the issue of legal capacity is here very important – and by their means various financial operations were performed with the money from the Guatemalan state. This money circulates through the banks concealed as investment and ends up as illicit earnings in the hands of companies controlled by the head of state through his relatives. Guatemala was initially incapable of finding evidence against Portillo, given the particular capacity and quality of the Guatemalan judicial system. In this context it is not strange that in this country a transnational prosecutor has been established. In agreement with the United Nations (UN), a special Prosecutor's Office has been put in place called CICIG, the International Commission Against Impunity in Guatemala (*Comisión Internacional Contra la Impunidad en Guatemala*). Thanks to this organization, sufficient evidence against Portillo was found and two lawsuits requesting his extradition were brought forward: one in the United States, the other in France. Both countries have jurisdiction in the case since the operations were performed through their banks. When a case like this is investigated, jurisdiction can extend to twenty or more countries. This adds complexity to the investigation, but especially to the prosecution. The United States applies an extended concept of jurisdiction (long arm jurisdiction) in this regard.

The second case, perhaps less notorious, unravels the complex legal nature of these crimes. The Wachovia Bank, one of the five biggest and most important in the United States, specialized in money transfers (remittances) and currency exchange in some parts of Latin America, especially in connection to the drug cartels of both Mexico and Guatemala. The remittances and currency exchanges were used to launder the assets. There are legal decisions from the American judiciary against the bank. One of these imposes civil fines, but criminal investigations are underway. In the countries belonging to the civil law tradition, this civil way is considered as a minor evil for the firms, but in the United States it is regarded as a serious problem as it can also lead to the confiscation or deprivation of property under a civil forfeiture scheme.

On the criminal side, the bank has not yet been accused of money laundering, but its further failure to establish an administrative system oriented to the prevention of the laundering of assets (compliance program) will be prosecuted as money laundering. This is because such failure is regulated as a criminal offense. In this case, the Prosecutor can opt for charging the bank with a fine if the latter accepts its responsibility. Otherwise, the record is sent to the criminal court, and is granted with one year to improve and adopt measures. This ensures that not only predicate offenses such as corruption, trafficking of women, etc. which create illicit assets, are taken into account for the criminal charge; today the criminal offense of the laundering of assets also exists as an autonomous criminal offense, as well as the lack of compliance with the preventive measures.

At this point it is appropriate to concretely define the concept of money laundering. It is a process through which the assets of criminal origin are integrated into the legal system with the appearance of being legally obtained. These illicit assets are put somewhere else because the perpetrator, criminal associations, physical or legal persons must get rid of the earnings materially, by means of a series of operations of financial engineering. In the second phase it is important to disguise the origin of the illicit products by means of numerous financial transactions, all of which require even more financial engineering. The third phase consists in the integration of these illegally obtained assets into the legal economy without raising suspicions, and thus masking them with an appearance of legitimacy in their origins to later utilize them legally as an investment or for consumption. These three phases reinforce the art behind this financial engineering.

Through these cases we can conclude that the concept of laundering of assets is more coherent than the mere concept of money laundering, because it is not only capital that can be laundered. It can also refer to real estate investment or buying and selling of works of antique art. I will, however, use the concept of money laundering, as it is the standard term in English. To those who are interested in deepening the phenomenology and the methods necessary to launder assets and launder capitals, see the report of the Workgroup of the Units of Financial Intelligence entitled GAFISUD.[1]

This report contains a description of the regional criminal concepts of money laundering in Latin America, although they are also to a large extent typical for Europe, and for other continents. The transactions between the official market and the monetary black market, or the transactions intended to take advantage of the differences between levels of tariffs or taxes are specifically addressed. Along with the report, a detailed explanation of several operations is explained: fictitious expenditures; fictitious export of services; fictitious exportation or import of goods under a scheme of false invoicing; foreign investment in a local company, etc. One quite well known case concerns soccer clubs on the verge of bankruptcy and the *savior* who invests in them. When an important amount of money is offered to save a club, we are talking about fractioned transfers of illicit money through credit transfers, checks, or by means of dummy companies.

Less well known are the cases of insurance companies. By means of insurance contracts, large sums of money can be transferred, hidden and laundered. Similar cases involve lottery prizes, when the winner is offered a higher amount than the amount won in order to legalize the money. Currently, such types of prizes are submitted to stricter levels of control. Another example is the physical transportation (cash transfers) of illicit money.

Unfortunately, a growing number of non-governmental, non-profit organizations of a humanitarian character are also used for or are using money laundering schemes. Given the high flow of money, through these organizations, they can either be established for this purpose or abused. It seems rather strange to us that the FATF document does not stipulate all types of money transfer systems, since in reality many limited transfers are made through interbank systems. Besides, certain money transfers among Muslims or indigenous ethnic groups, do not transfer the money physically, but as a loan among themselves, known as the system of the *Hawala*; we should consider the likelihood of the abuse of this system.[2]

28.2 CRIME AND CRIME ASSETS

Until the 1970s and the 1980, criminal law and even criminal procedure did not have that much interest in the financial aspects of crime. It was perfectly possible to secure criminal punishment on the basis of fines or imprisonment but, in the end, the offender was able to make use of the earnings from the offense. Seizure and confiscation are classic tools in the criminal justice system, but they had specific functions and related limited functions. Seizure and related confiscation or forfeiture had a double function: seizure of evidence (instruments of the crime) and seizure of dangerous goods such as arms, drugs, etc. However, there was no direct connection with the illicit earning – *the assets* – because it was the actions of the perpetrator that took a central role within the criminal system. In other words, the measures in relation to the personal assets were regarded as an accessory to the investigation and the main sanction. As far as they existed, in many countries they were conceived as security measures (to secure evidence or to secure dangerous goods).

28.3 HISTORY OF MONEY LAUNDERING

We said that up until the 1970s there was no emphasis on the illegal earnings from crime, at least not as an autonomous object, since it was viewed only as an accessory. The first experiences of money laundering in the 1920s until the 1930s were attributed to the European mafia in connection to heroin trafficking. Al Capone and his gang used laundries as dummy companies in order to launder the earnings obtained from the trafficking of narcotic drugs, mostly heroin. Their business became very fruitful because of the complete prohibition of drugs and alcohol in the US at that time. This shows the degree of intervention of the state into the economy from that time onwards. With the Wall Street crash, or 1929 Great Depression, the state intervened in order to protect property, including socio-legal or socio-economic interests. However, it is astonishing that the US government did not criminalize money laundering at that point, but elaborated a long list of regulatory offenses, as for instance the use of privileged information at the stock exchange.

From the criminal law perspective, the first capital laundering cases to ever take place in the United States dated from the 1960s. At that time, tax crimes were considered the first predicate offenses for money laundering. The chief historical case of this period was that of H.M. Klein accused of laundering assets in relation to the smuggling of whisky in Canada.[3] It is very curious to note that the only predicate offence at that time was tax fraud. Already at that time tax fraud was a very serious offense in the US. It still is today, judging by the many US judicial investigations into tax offenses, including those in off-shore centers or in tax havens such as Switzerland. The major Swiss Banks have been struggling with orders to unveil their US clients suspected of having committed tax fraud. As this concerns a serious judicial matter, the effectiveness of the judicial system justifies extra-territorial jurisdiction.

In the 1970s, preventive administrative financial law was developed. In this way that the United States imposed a whole series of obligations upon the financial sector, such as that of having to identify its clients, and to inform the Financial Intelligence Unit (FIU) of the suspicious operations, all actions which were developed outside the ambit of the criminal justice system. We could state that this was the first wave of financial regulation directed towards the administrative and preventive phase of money laundering in banking laws and financial regulations, as well as the one related to bank secrecy. After the bankruptcy of the financial holding Lehman Brothers in 2008, we entered a second wave.

Nevertheless, the real establishment of money laundering as a criminal autonomous definition, including an open amount of predicate offenses, will have to wait until the 1980s, when the legal definition of money laundering was launched as a criminal concept. More specifically, this took place in 1986. In 1983, Reagan's government established a National Commission against Organized Crime under this new paradigm: *War on Organized Crime* – following the *War on Drugs* – through which a legal autonomous definition for the laundering of money arose. Nevertheless, the first legal definition of the laundering of money in the world would arise in Italy in the 1970s, out of the close relation that existed between the crime and the earnings of the mafia.

This paradigmatic shift of the 1980s not only takes place within the United States, but also extends and develops internationally in an important way. This seems to occur not only through the influence the United States, but also because of the shift expenenced in the very concept of financial markets. Financial services, especially from the banking sector and insurance companies were obliged in the first place to adopt rules imposed by self-regulation. Central banks or self-regulators created the Basel Committee on Banking supervision in Basel, Switzerland. Their self-regulation is binding for both banks and insurers. The first package of measures: *Basel I*, from 1986 to 1987, coincides with the very rigid intervention of the United States in the financial sector. We could claim that Basel I made a belated appearance with respeet to the definition of all these interbank obligations, and it was ultimately superseded by state-public intervention into the financial sector, which demanded the adoption of criminal sanctions.

From 1988, the development of international treaties in this regard has been impressive. The first international convention, designated as the Vienna International Convention on Drug Trafficking, obliged member states to make money laundering a criminal offense when associated with drug trafficking. This took place two years after the designation of money laundering as a criminal offense in the United States. In this case money laundering is only related to drug trafficking as a predicate offense.

In 1990, a new treaty on search, seizure and confiscation was approved at the Council of Europe, imposing the duty to criminalize money laundering as an autonomous offense. This time though, an important change related to serious crimes in the context of organized criminality takes place: the range and reach of the predicate offenses for money laundering are enlarged from drugs trafficking to all serious crimes and criminal associations of organized crime. Despite being a European treaty, it also opened the way to its ratification by Non-European states such as the United States and Canada, amongst others.

Again in 1990, globalization and internationalization have an increasing impact. This not only expresses itself in a proliferation of international treaties, but it also results in the creation of a body and procedures for international monitoring, something never before seen in criminal affairs. The G7, an organization of a non-public nature, comprised of the heads of state of the seven most developed countries in the world – which afterwards would become the G8, and currently is the G20 – organized events related to these matters and further declared them as having prime political importance. Later, they established a group called the Financial Action Task Force (FATF) in order to put forward general recommendations, based on international conventions, whether ratified or not by the states. These general recommendations – *soft law* – impose very detailed duties on the states, both with regard to the implementation of the law, and in connection to its practice in the field of administrative law, criminal law, criminal procedure, and mutual legal assistance (MLA), among other areas.

With these recommendations, FATF – afterwards with the support of G20 – established a constant system of monitoring states. That is to say, they monitor each member state in relation to the legal framework and to its implementation and practice (law in action). They hold rounds of meetings every four or five years, and later, experts from FATF visit each country and elaborate an official report on the performance of the recommendations. If the state does not perform satisfactorily, which usually happens, a negative report is sent to the G20, which publishes it. Depending on the degree of performance of the recommendations there are white, grey and black lists of countries. In the last FATF round, three European states were put in the grey list, principally due to the existence of bank secrecy. For a European state to be in the grey list is regarded as prejudicial, and it brings severe financial consequences. As we see, the influence of FATF over states, legislative and judicial practice is enormous. Currently, FAFT is preparing the fourth round of mutual evaluations. It can be consulted on the internet. For Latin-America there is a Sub-Committee of evaluation called GAFISUD.

Back to history, an event took place in 1999 that deserves our attention because of the complexity that it adds. The UN adopted a new convention called the International Convention for the Suppression of the Financing of Terrorism. This convention imposes upon states to duty to criminalize money laundering in relation to terrorism as a predicate offense and with respeet to the financing of terrorism in particular. There are, of course, cases in which crimes are committed to obtain money to finance terrorism, such as in the case of kidnapping performed with the purpose of committing acts of terrorism. But we are also aware that for the classic terrorist – and here we enter into the third paradigm: *War on Terror* – the ideological element is more important: these acts of terrorism are not performed with the purpose of earning money. That is not the main goal, but only its instrument, and it is also relevant to consider that a high share of terrorist acts do not cost that much. Moreover, assets to finance terrorism are not always from an illegal or criminal source. However, the International Convention for the Suppression of the Financing of Terrorism obliges member states to regard terrorism, its acts and associations created for that purpose as a criminal offense. Likewise, it stipulates that states should treat its financing as a criminal offense, independently of its legal or illegal source. It refers then to all funds that are used to commit terrorist crimes. For instance, in the United States, there are non-governmental bodies which collect funds to re-build hospitals in Palestine because of the conflicts with Israel. These funds could be seen as illegal by some, but they are not. Also, we could wonder whether it is illegal if there is terrorist financing for these hospitals, in the case where the flow of money depends on the political and military Islamic resistance movement *Hamas*. Although Hamas has been democratically elected, it is classified as a terrorist organization both in the United States and by the United Nations. In other words, terrorism and the financing of terrorism as predicate offenses for money laundering are referring to an open definition of terrorism. Rather than money laundering from convicted predicate offenses, in this case we are speaking about the financing of offenses yet to be committed (which can be preparatory offenses or preparatory acts of the main offense). The UN Conventions against terrorism do not contain a substantial definition. The 1999 Convention, just like FATF and the G20 recommendations, oblige member states to apply the same money laundering monitoring scheme, including all preventive administrative obligations, to the financing of terrorism. And it is there, in 1999, where both conceptions are mixed; just before 2001, when the attack on the twin towers took place in New York. The FATF elaborated a series of eight (later expanded to nine) special recommendations, besides the 40 on money laundering, aimed at the financing of terrorism.

After 2001, the United Nations went beyond their conventional approach to terrorism and put forward Security Council resolutions that further complicated the legal framework. Initially, the Security Council of the United Nations decided that the fight against terrorism is the number one political goal and that the United Nations member states are expected to comply with the obligations of the conventions on matters of terrorism, without taking into account whether they have ratified them or not. This is because the resolution adopts the form of binding law for the member states. It is then that the United Nations installed a system of monitoring by means of a committee which controls whether the states are applying the content of all the conventions on matters of terrorism, which include the financing of terrorism. The monitoring refers to the law in the statute books and the laws in practice. This system of monitoring was copied from the one created by FATF on matters related to the money laundering.

Subsequently, the Security Council decided to blacklist terrorists and terrorist organizations at the UN level. By doing so, the UN is copy-pasting a system created under the Clinton Administration and still in force under the Obama Administration. This system consists of elaborating a list of terrorist persons and organizations to which so called *smart sanctions* are applied.

In practice there is a link between the criminalization of terrorism and the blacklisting of terrorism. This means that the executive branch of government de facto decides on the substantial reach of terrorism. From the point of view of criminal law this is a very substantial paradigm change to pro-active prevention. This list is of an executive – not judicial – nature. The persons and the organizations included on the list do not need to be convicted or suspected of acts of terrorism or under judicial investigation. The mere inclusion on the list represents a danger as defined by the Executive, which is based on information provided by the intelligence services. The smart sanctions are in fact provisional, precautionary measures, such as freezing orders of assets, monitoring and freezing of financial transactions, visa bans, etc.

The Clinton list was copied worldwide by means of a Security Council resolution. From 2001 onwards, similar lists have existed in the UN, the European Union, and in countries like England. This situation is peculiar as the dangerousness is not necessarily criminalized, because it is a concept of social dangerousness, to which financial measures apply. The measures imposed on those who are registered on these lists are limited in time and have a precautionary nature. Nevertheless, they can result in the freezing of the entire personal or organization's assets, which in the end is very different from confiscation, as the former does not have a definitive nature. These persons cannot travel, nor perform any financial transaction, and this situation can last many years. In other words, these are precautionary measures which severely limit the public freedoms and liberties of the people and organizations affected by them.

Finally, in 2000, the renowned Convention against Transnational Organized Crime was signed. The convention includes as a criminal offense all the crimes with features of transnational organized crime – corruption, arms trafficking, trafficking of women, terrorism, etc. – and assesses these offenses as predicate offenses for money laundering and in the case of terrorism for the financing of terrorism. This Convention can be considered as the final result of an evolution begun in the 1980s, at least with regard to money laundering. Beside the obligation for the Party Stated to criminalize the predicate offenses and the related money laundering and financing of terrorism offenses, it also obliges member states to introduce special techniques of investigation into their criminal procedure (such as wiretapping of telecommunications, controlled deliveries, infiltration, etc.), and to establish efficient mechanisms of mutual legal assistance (MLA), such as extradition, letters rogatory, transnational freezing of assets, seizure and confiscation, and expiration of ownership.

28.4 INTERMEDIATE CONCLUSIONS

Firstly, it is clear that the underlying circle of predicate offences is no longer limited to drug trafficking but it extends to a large circle of serious crimes and organized crime and terrorism. Indeed, in many countries criminal prosecution for money laundering has become an ordinary procedure. Secondly, with the expansion of money laundering to the financing of terrorism, the focus has not been limited to the illicit money of criminality; it also extends to the legal and illegal funds, in case they are related to the act of committing terrorism. With this change of focus a new important paradigm is introduced, as the criminal justice systems is now also used as a control mechanism *ante delictum*, and as a preventive tool of policy. A new preventive and proactive criminal justice system has been born, which can be called criminal security law.

28.5 THE FATF RECOMMENDATIONS

The FATF recommendations, including the original ones of 1990 and the 2001 ones on financing terrorism, have been constantly revised and actualized. The 2012 FATF recommendations can be easily consulted on the internet.[4] They are the international standards on combating money laundering (AML) and countering the financing of terrorism (CFT) and the financing of the proliferation of weapons of mass destruction.[5] They consist of 40 consolidated recommendations that contain various obligations, including preventive administrative and financial measures, measures of substantive criminal law and measures of criminal procedure. The recommendations on AML/CFT are endorsed by over 180 countries. The FATF Standards comprise the Recommendations themselves and their Interpretive Notes, together with the applicable definitions in the Glossary. The measures set out in the FATF Standards should be implemented by all members of the FATF.

In summary, these obligations concern the inclusion as criminal offenses of predicate offenses for money laundering. The circle of predicate offenses is wide and includes all serious offenses, organized crime and terrorism. Recommendation 3 clearly stipulates that countries should criminalize money laundering on the basis of the Vienna Convention and the Palermo Convention and that they should apply the crime of money laundering to all serious offenses, with a view to including the widest range of predicate offenses.

Recommendation 5 is enlarging this obligation to terrorist financing (CFT) and the financing of proliferation. Countries should criminalize terrorist financing on the basis of the Terrorist Financing Convention, and should criminalize not only the financing of terrorist acts but also the financing of terrorist organizations and individual terrorists even in the absence of a link to a specific terrorist act or acts. Countries should ensure that such offenses are designated as money laundering predicate offenses. This obligation clearly includes the proactive, preventive approach of the blacklisting. Recommendations 5 and 6 indeed prescribe the duty to impose the smart sanctions (targeted financial sanctions). It also contains the obligations of administrative preventive supervision intended for ethnic systems of informal banking such as the *Hawala*, and it enforces obligations to the funds of non-governmental organizations (NGO) that could be used for money laundering schemes or the financing of terrorism.

A series of recommendations is detailed on the preventive-administrative obligations that are demanded from a group of persons and institutions. These recommendations are dealing with customer due diligence and record keeping, bank secrecy and reporting of suspicious transactions. They are not directed only at financial institutions – banks, insurance companies, etc. – but also at casinos, companies of direct sale and purchase of real estate assets, art, antiquities, precious metals, and also at notaries, accountants, and lawyers, whose first obligation is to get to know the identity of their clients and to communicate suspicious transactions. Any person or institution related with flows of assets shall have to register the real identity of their clients. In this regard, European countries faced problems not only because of the existence of bank secrecy, but especially because of the related codified bank accounts without name or surname; an act which is now totally forbidden. It also does not matter if the transaction begins in the United States and is later transferred to another place or if it ends up in a country in Latin America;

in every place the client must be known. If he or she is suspected of suspicious transactions, it is obligatory to communicate this to a body of financial intelligence called the Financial Information Unit (FIU). Every country must have such a body.

Yet, suspicious transactions are defined neither in the international conventions nor in the recommendations. Countries use different criteria to define suspicious transactions larger than ten thousand dollars. Depending on the definition of 'suspicious transactions' the reporting can involve small or enormous amounts of daily reports, particularly in the light of the great movements of capital around the world today. FINCEN, which is the FIU of the United States, receives an amount of reports per second that requires a continuously growing capacity of analysis. In other countries, like the Netherlands, there are objective and subjective criteria to define a suspicious transaction. If a person is a client of a bank, the bank must be aware of the monthly amount that the person earns, and in the case that an individual transfers higher amounts than permitted, there is grounds for suspicion. Also, if somebody appears in a bank in which he or she is not a client, bringing with them a considerable amount of cash money to open an account, that will be rendered as grounds for suspicion. In this way we encounter different criteria, both objective and subjective, as defined in the guidelines of the Prosecutor General's Office.

The FATF provide that every country must have an FIU. Recommendations 26 and following deal with the powers and responsibilities of the authorities. However, the regulation of FIUs vary depending on the country. In some cases it is an administrative independent body, in others it forms a part of the Central Bank, of the Ministry of Finance, or the judicial police, etc. The FIU is obliged to analyze and to investigate the suspicious transaction reports – this being exactly where the trouble begins. When receiving the report, they need to access the information regarding this person, be it a natural or legal person. What are the investigative powers of the FIU? Can they send out compulsory (subpoena) production orders and/or can they access the files of the natural and/or legal persons? It can be that the administrative authority needs to carry out certain investigative actions which require access to the administrative records of the company. In this case, the capacity to investigate requires a specialized staff in financial auditing and investigation, because if it is concluded that there is suspicion that money laundering could have been committed, the file is transferred to the Prosecutor. Not identifying clients or not reporting to the FIU, when appropriate, or the fact that the company does not have a policy of prevention, are in almost every country defined as illegal acts, be it under punitive administrative law, or be it as a criminal offense, in the case of intentional commission or grave omissions. The recommendations (31 and following) also deal with the law enforcement capacity (in law and in practice) of the judicial investigative bodies.

The group of persons that must inform the FIU is ample because there is a group of professions that traditionally deals with large sums of money. Those who deal with the purchasing and selling of precious metals and antiques generally perform a large amount of transactions with cash, unofficially. The duty is problematic for notaries and lawyers. In the case of notaries, many of them carry out real estate transactions, and handle the accounts of their clients, all of which depend on the regulation of each country, but they do this in many countries as part of a public or semi-public profession. In the case of lawyers, it is perhaps surprising that they are included in the recommendations, and in Europe political problems with lawyers have occurred in connection to these obligations.

The lawyer establishes a confidential relationship with his or her clients – *legal privilege* – which, in many countries, is stipulated in criminal procedure and in some countries even in the Constitution. However, both the recommendations and international regulations compel lawyers to inform the FIU of suspicious conduct.

An example can illustrate the kind of obligations to which lawyers are held. The Netherlands is considered a *tax haven* for transnational companies attempting to avoid double taxation, based upon international or bilateral tax treaties. For this reason, if we consider global money transfers and transnational money investment, the Netherlands is usually at the top of the list; it could be thought that this is strange since the Netherlands is such a small country, but of course this takes place with regard to flows of capital that are coming from other countries. These flows run under the tax planning strategies of multinationals, which in the Netherlands are assisted by thousands of tax lawyers who have never defended cases in courts, and who advice these so-called *letter-box* companies, to which all the money is transferred. But these lawyers have obligations just like notaries or real estate brokers. They defend their clients in tribunals by providing legal advice in relation to the financial plans of these companies and in converting their assets from illegal into legal assets through financial-legal engineering. Recently, several notaries and bar lawyers have been investigated, prosecuted and even convicted and given prison sentences in the Netherlands for participation in or perpetration of money laundering. These professions are regarded as being positions of high risk and some of their members are found to collaborate with certain groups of organized crime for the laundering of their assets.

The FATF recommendations also include judicial obligations related to the criminal justice system. Efficient measures of investigation, freezing of assets, confiscation and extinction of ownership are imposed. Additionally, states must adopt effective international cooperation measures in the criminal field (recommendation 36 and following) – mutual legal assistance requests for the taking of evidence, extradition, penalty execution, decisions of confiscation or extinction of ownership.

As mentioned before, both FATF and MONEYVAL for Europe and GAFISUD for Latin America perform continuous monitoring of evaluation. Each six years, experts visit countries and publish a report.

The reports on Latin American countries are very illustrative of the reach and impact of this monitoring process. Here a couple of examples are given as illustration. The last report on Colombia dates back to 2004, a year in which it received good evaluations for their administrative preventive policies, both from the financial institutions and the Colombian FIU (UIAF). However, the performance was very low considering the excessively restricted number of predicate crimes for money laundering, which did not include financing terrorism, smuggling, or fiscal fraud. Also, the excessively restricted circle of people compelled to report the suspicious transactions did not include notaries, accountants, or lawyers. Further, the country was criticized for the low efficiency of its criminal justice system, and the extremely small number of convictions. In 2006, the Colombian government implemented a series of reforms, which involved the inclusion of the financing of terrorism as a criminal offense. Other obligations, such as fiscal fraud, laundering of assets, or the obligation of lawyers and accountants to report suspicious conduct are still in a preparatory phase.

Another interesting country to look at is Argentina. The situation there is delicate because the second report of evaluation and monitoring from GAFISUD took almost a year to be delivered. In Argentina, a strong internal political struggle is currently taking place. The 2006 report, which was the first one on Argentina was not very positive about the implementation of the recommendations. Afterwards, Argentina published a national agenda against money laundering with the goal of accomplishing the recommendations between 2007 and 2009 – so it should currently be fulfilled.

This national agenda is ambitious because it includes matters such as identifying money laundering and the financing of terrorism as criminal offences, provisional measures, confiscation, special procedural measures, regulations on investment funds which can also be utilized for laundering, mutual funds, measures on international transfers or transnational cash transactions, special measures on vulnerable legal persons based on their position close to ministries through which large sums of money are flowing, special measures on NGOs, etc. All that is stipulated; nevertheless, the problems mentioned in the 2006 report still seem to persist, and from this national agenda little or nothing has been done.

Argentina has not secured any convictions for money laundering, which has caused a great deal of concern in the 2006 report. Currently, only one conviction and only one fine have been imposed by the administrative authorities. Congress had not included as a legal offense the case of *self-laundering*, which means that when there is no self-laundering, the perpetrator can only commit the crime through third parties.

In the majority of the countries, self-laundering has to be included as a legal offense, and this is also an obligation imposed by FATF. It seems that in Argentina there are serious problems with the FUI for several reasons, including lack of money and lack of a capable, independent and permanent staff of civil servants, among other factors. Advances when comparing recent actions with the tendings of the 2006 report, are the inclusion of the financing of terrorism as a legal offense and the existence of a specialized unit for money laundering within the Office of the Public Prosecutor. However, the people who work at the specialized unit complain about the lack of resources because cases are not reported and about the difficulties linked to the investigations. This picture raises concern over Argentina in light of the recommendations.

The report on Brazil is very recent, dating from 2010. It includes a favorable assessment, but it has also made a number of some critiques. Financing terrorism is not yet included as a legal offense. Lawyers are not obligated to report financing terrorism. There are few criminal convictions, and the system of international cooperation is complex and slow.

28.6 CRIMINALIZATION OF MONEY LAUNDERING

The inclusion of money laundering as a criminal offense is complex, since it demands to be autonomous, that is to say, disconnected from the predicate offense. The predicate offense must be criminalized too. In other words, the earnings coming from the money laundering or the financing of terrorism must be an autonomous criminal offense. Problems emerge in criminalizing the three phases of money laundering – the disposal of the assets, disguising the assets, and returning the assets as a whole into the process – or in making each element an autonomous criminal offense (*actus reus* element of the offence). There are different strategies which can make the work of the Prosecutor easier when it comes to prosecuting the case, filing the charge and submitting the relevant evidence. The most important question regarding money laundering is, first, whether it is made a criminal offense based on intent or based on negligence (the *mens rea* element of the offence), and second, whether the omission is sufficient for negligence. In these cases we see great differences from one country to another. This is because some criminal procedures are only acquainted with the intentional variant and leave negligence and omission to the administrative law or do not declare them illegal at all.

When it comes to money laundering, both the legal person and private companies are very important in their application. If criminal responsibility is not possible in the case of legal persons, there will be a problem. Perhaps there is a well structured punitive administrative law for this, but then not all coercive measures shall be at the disposal of the investigative bodies. The last complex element is the causal relationship between the offence and the result (the laundering). Depending on the financial engineering, it can be very complex to prove this causal relationship, in other words, to prove the strict causality between the criminal earning of the assets and the laundering of the same assets. Normally, if there is causality between the commission or omission of the crime and the result, there should be causality between the crime produced by the predicate offence, and the reintegration at the end of the process of the laundering of the assets, obtained by the commission of the predicate offence. In the formulation of the criminalization, a one-to-one equivalence must exist between the product – the earnings of the offence – and the final laundering. This could be established in a very rigid way, with the consequence that it would be very difficult for the Prosecutor to prove a one-to-one equivalence; but it could also be established easily if other criteria were utilized, as assets by analogy. This means that the Prosecutor only has to prove that the laundered assets arise from similar illegal acts. This can be very useful in a case in which some assets have disappeared or are hidden.

Finally, the criminalization is not only about the money laundering itself, but also about the compliance with the administrative obligations (record keeping, reporting, etc.). Noncompliance must be defined as serious administrative breaches of criminal offences. Sanctions must be in any case effective, proportionate and dissuasive (recommendation 35).

28.7 MONEY LAUNDERING AND CRIMINAL PROCEDURE

We shall limit ourselves here to revising the most important elements. Since the increasing shift to organized crime and terrorism, the historically classical measures of judicial investigation are no longer sufficient. We can observe that the change of paradigm in criminal law has gone hand in hand with the change in paradigm in criminal procedure, which, in many countries has been structured within the process of the criminal system as a second way. Besides the classic judicial investigation, a second separate track of financial investigation has been created as a special judicial tool under criminal procedure. The classic judicial interrogation of witnesses, of search and seizure, etc., has been widened by financial investigation into illicit earning with the purpose of knowing the sources, the investment schemes and the final outcome. Asset tracing has become a very important tool, both with the aim of finding and preserving evidence, but also with the aim of freezing, seizing and confiscating illegal assets. Freezing of assets, seizure, confiscation, extinction of ownership are applied as an outcome of these financial investigations. The financial investigation cannot be done by classic judicial authorities. It requires specialized branches of financial auditing within the Prosecutor's office, with highly specialized personnel.

In many countries, within the criminal procedure, alongside judicial investigation, a special track of financial investigation has been created, with measures aimed at identifying, following, freezing, seizing and confiscating the assets of the suspect and/or convicted. The monitoring and freezing of bank transactions has become common and bank secrecy has lost much of its shielding capacity in criminal matters. For financial investigations, the thresholds are flexible and most of the measures can be executed by the prosecutor and/or financial experts in the police, without any prior or *a posteriori* judicial authorization. To use the classic judicial investigative measures, such as search and interception of communications, there must be a reasonable ground for suspicion. Moreover, to use these coercive measures, the judicial police or the Prosecutor cannot act on their own; they need the previous authorization of a judge, because such measures interfere with civil rights and freedoms. However, within the financial investigation, it can be observed that such investigations are fully under the supervision of the Prosecutors and generally do not need judicial authorizations or court orders. As long as a natural or legal person cannot prove the legal origin of suspicious assets considered illegal, they are deemed to be illegally obtained. There is thus also a shift in the burden of proof, as the suspect has to prove the legal origin of the assets. A further consequence of this paradigmatic shift in the criminal justice system is that it is possible to impose seizure and final confiscation through a separate proceeding from the conviction. It becomes an autonomous proceeding with a strong civil law character within the criminal justice system. This is an evolution that becomes even worse with the financing of terrorism and, overall, when it is applied – based on FATF recommendations – to black lists. There is a duty to apply the smart sanctions and a duty to investigate and freeze the assets of the listed persons and organizations. However, it is not necessary that they are suspects or convicted. It is enough that they are considered dangerous by the executive branch of government and therefore listed. The financial investigation as an autonomous path within our judicial systems expresses, in our opinion, an interesting development with regard to efficiency, but runs the risk of conflicting with classic legal guarantees and the rule of law.

Beside the new judicial track on financial investigations, criminal procedure has recently also included so-called special *investigation techniques*. The Palermo Convention against Transnational Organized Crime obliges states to introduce special techniques of investigation in their criminal procedure for the purpose of establishing a global, common standard. Many states are already applying it. The Netherlands has been applying such techniques since the 1980s. They consist in the fact that beyond the classic coercive measure of judicial investigation, new special legal provisions such as controlled delivery, undercover agents, infiltration in criminal organizations, and every kind of interception of telecommunications have become part of the tools of judicial investigation, at least for organized crime, terrorism and serious offences.

Moreover, the fight against organized crime and terrorism seems to justify relaxing thresholds and guarantees; that is, the more coercive the measures, the fewer the guarantees. These measures were installed under a very broad definition of serious criminality. In practice, the special measures of investigation are applied to all serious criminality based on the Palermo Covenant, which stipulates a maximum penalty of two years' imprisonment. This explains why the special investigative measure have become common, and the list of serious crimes which justifies special measures keeps growing.

28.8 HUMAN RIGHTS AND COOPERATION

When we refer to human rights and cooperation, we are referring to the norms of International Human Rights Law (IHRL): The UN Covenant on Civil and Political Rights, the Inter-American Convention of Human Rights, and the European Convention of Human Rights, amongst others.

With regard to terrorism, or at least, with regard to organized crime, the issue is more complex as 'human rights' define a whole series of protections for the citizen against the state, such as freedom of expression, the right to private life, the right to due process of law, and the rights to an impartial and independent criminal court. It is always about a protection against the state, which cannot violate these norms, the negative duty of the state which has to refrain from violating IHRL. In the last years, however, we have observed an evolution away from this. In other words, there is an increasing positive duty of the state to guarantee the human rights of citizens, especially the right to life, where unfortunately Latin America still shows serious and massive violations. To guarantee the life of persons, the state has the duty to investigate, prosecute, adjudicate and punish these crimes.

With regard to terrorism, the same reasoning should be applied: the state has the duty to protect the life of citizens and to offer security. With this reasoning, the right to security – which does not exist in human rights, but which is invented – has primacy over public freedoms. Then, the right to security guaranteed by the state becomes more important than due process of law. There, a conceptual abuse exists, because when speaking of the financing of terrorism and secret information utilized to register persons on black lists, or to ensure the criminal conviction of a person, it is *security* and not the *due process of law* that prevails.

In the inclusion of terrorist association as a criminal offense, several important questions can be raised on how to deal with secret information coming from intelligence services, and whether it is criminal evidence. In the Netherlands, for instance, there is a clear shift towards special features in criminal justice when it comes to terrorism and terrorist financing, creating a series of problems: the rights of the defense in relation to secret evidence, or how the judiciary can check the legitimacy and legality of the secretly obtained evidence. There are a series of doubts that are raised as a result of the rivalry between security and justice, and security versus human rights.

More concretely, we find very specific problems in this field, such as shifts in the burden of proof with regard to seizure. This is problematic, as the presumption of innocence, the obligations of lawyers, and the right to confidentiality in the lawyer–client relationship (legal privilege), could all end up endangered. Unfortunately, when it comes to terrorism we all know that human rights are not absolute, but susceptible to limitations for specific purposes of general interest. The exceptions are the right to life, which cannot be restricted and the prohibition of torture (at least in Europe this cannot be restricted). Other rights can however be restricted, as they protect other human rights.

In certain countries, in relation to the crime of financing terrorism, lawyers are no longer free to choose their clients, but are state appointed, mostly based on a security screened list. These are state sanctioned professionals and as such they can access secret information of the state with the approval of intelligence services. These are policies labeled under the fight against terrorism, which, at this point, the European Court of Human Rights has declared in conformity with the European Convention of Human Rights.

Finally we shall deal with the issue of cooperation. The source of a crime can be in one country, but very rapidly covers the world and forms part of the scheme of concealment. Many operations and a smokescreens are essential to describe the elements of the crime. Once an investigation takes place, it becomes extremely difficult to bring to light what has happened with money or earnings, and to transform this obtained information into evidence. For this reason, if talking of the laundering of assets, the investigation is more complex and requires cooperation, not only between the border countries, but globally. We find financial centers and small countries which specialize in the laundering of assets counting on the protection of their authorities, making it very difficult to investigate, especially in the case of bank secrecy rules or special tax heaven regimes.

Cooperation, and all the instruments we indicated from the Vienna Convention up to the Palermo Convention, which deal with the financing of terrorism, stipulate many clauses and measures on administrative cooperation between the FIUs and judicial cooperation in the criminal domain.

Within the administrative domain, the situation is more complex because administrative preventive bodies such as FIUs have statutes in every country, which depend on many different bodies at the same time. If there are problems of access to information in individual countries, we can already imagine what these are at the international level. The FATF and the European Union have often intervened with specific regulations in order to oblige these FIUs and their states to change legislation so information can be shared, and countries can assist in the administrative investigation. Now, at the international level, there is the Egmont group, which regularly meets as a regulatory and enforcement body to facilitate the cooperation of the participating cooperation states. There is also a digital network to send and receive requests of cooperation.

Criminal and judicial cooperation is also complex, as it has to deal with new tools in criminal procedure: financial investigation, special investigation techniques and use of criminal procedure for freezing, seizing and confiscation of assets.

To develop cooperation, we not only need specific instruments, regulated in the international conventions, but also effective implementation of the domestic legal orders (in law and in practice). This means that whether they want it or not, member states of the European Union, and the United Nations must incorporate measures of financial investigation, special techniques of investigation, seizure, confiscation and practical capacity of cooperation in this regard. The Palermo Convention is developed to the point that it can now stipulate states that have joint investigation teams in place.

It must be stressed that in financial matters, the current measures of investigations not only accommodate new techniques and rules of cooperation, they also embrace the classic forms of mutual legal assistance (letters rogatory, extradition, execution of sanctions).

28.9 CONCLUSION

After what has been discussed, there is a series of questions that we could raise from the point of view of criminal policies and criminal theory. One of them being whether socio-economic interests can and should deserve criminal law protection. If we belong to the Frankfurt School of Hassemer, the response would be that this cannot be accepted, and that therefore even money laundering should not be criminalized, but should be regulated by administrative law. But if we abide by the Tiedemann School, we would affirm the necessity of regulatory offences and justify the inclusion of money laundering as a criminal offense.

Far more complex are the following questions: Are we at the forefront of a new paradigm? Is it only a symbolic legal development? Are we faced with moral panic which justifies all kinds of measures and changes of our criminal justice systems? Is this preventive and proactive criminal justice paradigm a form of criminal law of the enemy? Or, in other words, are we leaving aside the classic concepts of criminal theory such as the principle of *nullum crimen sine injuria*, or the harm principle? The responses would depend on the autonomous character of money laundering and the financing of terrorism in relation to the predicate offences. Nevertheless, when we relate money laundering to the financing of terrorism and black lists, it is clear that we enter into the field of criminal law for the enemy, and that the key concepts of criminal law are set aside.

We can conclude that the concept of money laundering does involve a change of paradigm in the criminal justice system from several points of view. The classic AML approach of the FATF has resulted in several substantial changes: the elaboration of an autonomous offence; the elaboration of asset-freezing, asset-seizure and asset-confiscation into an autonomous control and sanctioning mechanism. The real paradigmatic chance has however been established by enlarging the AML-approach to CTF. This change entails the evolution of criminal law into a proactive law, of a preventive kind. We see an evolution from a judicial criminal law to a criminal law with a strong power of the executive branch of government. We also see an evolution from a criminal law based on the violation of a legally protected interest into a criminal law of dangerousness of a person.

We hope to have offered a cricital overview of the issue with a historical perspective, to see how it articulates or, according to some, how it fragments the classic system of criminal investigation, of criminal definitions, and the functioning of the criminal system as a whole. In our opinion, there is a paradigm shift with certain perils that must be studied in an in-depth manner, both by academia and by legal practitioners.

NOTES

* Based on a paper delivered at a conference celebrating the thirty years anniversary the University of Ibagué, Colombia on July 21st, 2010 and published in Spanish in J.A.E. Vervaele (2011), 'Delincuencia

Económica y lavado de activos. 'Un nuevo paradigma del sistema penal' *en Cuadernos de Derecho Penal Económico, Lavado de activos y delitos afines* Universidad de Ibagué, Ibagué, Colombia, **5**, 27–52.

1. FATF, *Money Laundering Typologies 2002–2003*, http://www.fatf-gafi.org/documents/documents/moneylaunderingtypologies2002–2003.html and GAFISUD. *Informe de tipologias regionales*, http://www.gafisud.info/documents/esp/doc_interes/gafi-tipologies/001-informe%20de%20Tiolog%EDas%20Regionales%20de%20GAFISUD%202005.pdf
2. The Hawala system has been used for hundreds of years to move money among countries. It started in the Middle East and in the south of Asia. It was installed by the Arab traders of the Silk Road in order to avoid being robbed. In actuality, millions of Pakistanis, Indians and many other migrant workers use this system to send money to their families.
3. H.H. Klein set up a selling scheme to avoid paying taxes. Whisky was bought by a New York based distributor, a Cuban subsidiary which falsified the records and returned excess profits to Klein and his employees through secret banks. See http://bulk.resource.org/courts.gov/c/F2/247/247.F2d.908.374.23905_1.html
4. http://www.fatf-gafi.org/media/fatf/documents/recommendations/pdfs/FATF_Recommendations.pdf
5. The financing of the proliferation of weapons of mass destruction was added recently.

PART VIII

IMPLEMENTATION AND EFFECTIVENESS OF AML

29. How to dodge drowning in data? Rule- and risk-based anti-money laundering policies compared*

Brigitte Unger and Frans van Waarden

In the past decade, anti-money laundering policy has switched both in the US and in Europe from a rule- to a risk-based reporting system in order to avoid over-reporting by the private sector. However, reporting instead increased in most countries, while the quality of information decreased. Governments were drowned in data because private agents feared sanctions for not reporting. However, unlike in other countries, this 'crying wolf problem' (Takats 2007) did not happen in the Netherlands, where the number of reports diminished, but the information quality improved. The reasons for this can be found in differences in legal institutions and legal culture, notably the contrast between US adversarial legalism and Dutch cooperative informalism. The established legal systems also provide for resistance to change. Thus, lowering sanctions in order to reduce over-reporting may not be a realistic option in a legal system which traditionally uses deterrence by fierce criminal and private legal sanctions. Furthermore, a risk-based approach may not be sustainable in the long run, as litigation may eventually replace a risk-based approach again by a rule-based one, now with precise rules set by the courts.

29.1 INTRODUCTION

Awareness has grown that money laundering is harmful. It makes crime pay, changes the cost–benefit calculation of criminals (Becker 1968) and enhances their incentives to engage in criminal activities. Money laundering can also have negative effects on society, the economy and politics in other respects. Honest businesses may get crowded out. Financial markets may lose in integrity and that could have a serious impact on large financial centers and their reputation. Corruption may increase in some sectors and eventually in the whole economy. The underworld could become intertwined with the upperworld. Launderers and other criminals could undermine politics, which poses a threat to democracy. Terrorist financing is now also considered part of money laundering and poses additional threats to society.

Governments have therefore found it necessary to combat money laundering. In order to do so, money laundering risks, potential money launderers and laundering transactions have to be identified. For this, governments are dependent on information from the private sector. Financial institutions and transaction partners or intermediaries involved in businesses prone to money laundering, such as used car dealers, real estate agents, casinos and lawyers, encounter (potential) money laundering transactions in their daily business. They may or could see dubious transactions which they may suspect of money laundering. Governments need clues as to which transactions from which persons or companies seem dubious. Private businesses must be willing to give such information and if necessary actively search for it. They must filter their transactions for possible cases of money laundering. Private businesses are not likely to submit such information voluntarily, as it could threaten their reputation and relations with their clients. They would have to be forced to do so. The government has the authority to do so, but it has to follow the rule of law, that is, enact formal legislation. In the interest of legal security it has to make explicit what information the private sector has to provide, what negative or positive incentives back up this obligation, and under which conditions the sticks and/or carrots will be applied.

In the following, several regulatory approaches to money laundering reporting will be discussed and evaluated, notably rule-based and risk-based regulation. The rule-based approach implies that governments enact regulations imposing rather precise norms for private business to adhere to, in this case precise norms as to what transactions to report to public authorities. By contrast, the risk-based approach gives private actors more discretion as to what to report. The regulations instruct private business to report transactions that *they* consider suspicious of possible money laundering, that is, it gives them vaguer criteria as to what transactions to report. The risk-based approach means not only that private actors have to estimate the risks of a transaction being suspect in terms of money laundering; it also means that they themselves run the risks of being accused of false reporting, or more generally of being held responsible for whether they did a good job or not. In section 29.2 we will elaborate on the differences between rule- and risk-based regulations, and discuss some of their advantages and disadvantages. A rule-based approach provides precise rules and hence legal certainty, but it also encourages formalistic over-reporting. This is why many countries switched to a risk-based approach, in the hope of reducing over-reporting. Yet it often had the opposite effect, and encouraged even more relatively useless over-reporting, also called the 'crying wolf problem' (Takats 2007; Dalla Pellegrina and Masciandaro 2009). In section 29.3 we will then compare the reporting systems of two countries, the United States and the Netherlands. Both countries moved from rule- to risk-based regulation. Yet, the consequences were rather different, almost the opposite, as we will show in section 29.4. Under the new risk-based approach, the amount of reporting in the US increased (and as Dalla Pellegrina and Masciandaro (2009) show, also in many other countries), whereas it decreased in the Netherlands. However, the quality of information provided by the private sector to the government in the US declined, whereas there is no indication that it worsened in the Netherlands. On the contrary, it seems to have improved, judging by the relative number of convictions for money laundering which in recent years were much higher in the Netherlands than in the US. In section 29.5 we try to find an explanation for this puzzle: More or less similar regulatory measures have different policy outcomes as they are conditioned by intermediary variables, notably the differences in legal systems, that is, in legal institutions and legal cultures. Section 29.6 then draws conclusions and discusses some alternative regulatory measures and the future fate of risk-based regulation.

29.2 ON RULE- AND RISK-BASED REGULATION

29.2.1 The Long-Term Historical Trend: From Broad and Vague Standards to Detailed and Precise Rules

Governments can be more or less precise in the legal obligations which they impose upon citizens and business. In the law and economics literature, it is customary to call precise norms *rules* and less precise ones *standards* (Ehrlich and Posner 1974; Diver 1983 Kaplow 1992; Schäfer 2002).[1] Rules are clear and straightforward and draw precise boundaries between legal and illegal behavior. Standards, however, 'are general legal criteria which are unclear and fuzzy and require complicated judiciary decision making' (Schäfer 2002, p. 1). Typical standards are found in English common law, such as the standard of 'due diligence'[2] or of 'reasonable care' in tort law, of 'duty of care' and of 'fiduciary duty' (Johnson et al. 2000), or the prohibition of behavior such as negligence, invasion of privacy, nuisance, fraud, deception, murder, restraint of trade, etc. Such broad terms require specification and that is done when courts apply them (or not) in concrete cases. Over the course of time such broad and vague standards have acquired rather precise meanings through judicial decisions.

The legislator can enact laws with either precise, detailed norms or with broader and vaguer standards. In the case of the latter, those implementing and enforcing the law, public administrators, inspectors, judges but also private actors, have a greater discretionary authority. That affects the costs involved. The formulation of a broad standard is easily done and hence cheap. It is usually also easier to get a parliamentary majority if not consensus over norms such as the right to freedom and privacy or a ban on discrimination and slander. Disagreement comes over the detail, over the operationalization, and over how to balance it against other standards, for example slander versus free speech. Therefore, broad standards entail significant costs in implementation and enforcement. Posner (1998) identified the following costs: of the specification of the norm, of the process of adjudication, and of the legal uncertainty due to the large discretionary authority of the bureaucrats and judges, which could force subjects to take possibly unnecessary preventive measures.

Historically, there has been a trend to reduce the legal uncertainty stemming from the discretion of judges. In English common law this was based on the principle of the force of precedent of earlier judicial decisions. In order to inform judges about those earlier decisions, treatises containing collections of common law decisions were compiled, and they were somewhat generalized in the famous 'Commentaries on the Laws of England' by William Blackstone in the later eighteenth century, which was easier to carry around. In civil law countries the codification movement of the eighteenth and nineteenth centuries deduced more general but still concrete rules out of customary law in those countries, and using Roman law as a basis. These general rules were collected in codices such as the Code Napoleon or the Algemeines Landrecht of Prussia, both from around 1800 (Koselleck 1967), which were quite detailed. Schäfer (2002, p. 5) mentions that the Prussian code 'had more than 19,000 articles, four times more than the modern civil code and the criminal code of Germany taken together'. These law books gave precise guidance to citizens, administrators, and judges, as they defined in detail what was lawful and what unlawful. Their freedom was limited, but so was their freedom from arbitrariness.

This legality and consistency increased certainty and predictability, thus also facilitating economic transactions by reducing their risks and uncertainties. It became easier to conclude economically efficient contracts, as costs could be calculated more easily ahead of time.

Given this tradition of increasing precision in regulation, it was not surprising that the first Anti-Money Laundering laws in most countries, including the Netherlands and the US, were so-called *rule-based* laws. They contained clear formal criteria given by the state to business. Whether a transaction could be called unusual or suspicious was decided by the regulator. He set the criteria for identification of a potential money laundering case. For example every transaction above a certain threshold amount was considered suspect or unusual and had to be reported. Governments wanted to minimize the discretion of the private actors whose information it wanted. On the one hand, to be sure that any possible money laundering transaction would be reported, on the other hand to keep the risk and uncertainty for business low.

The rules were clear and transparent, thus providing legal certainty and legal equality, as all subjects of the regulation were confronted with the same precise norms. But this approach also had disadvantages. Criminals could manipulate their transactions so that they would be just below the threshold. The formal rule could lead to over-reporting and high reporting costs for the private sector. It was rigid, formalistic, bureaucratic, and entailed high administrative burdens and hence was considered ineffective and inefficient.

29.2.2 Now Back Again from Precise to Vaguer Norms with the Move from Rule- to Risk-Based Regulation

Frustration over this formalism and rigidity led countries to replace rule-based AML regulation in the early 2000s (and in the US already by 1996) by what is called *risk-based* regulation, leaving more discretion to the subjects of regulation with reporting duties. This change happened at a time when everywhere governments introduced supposedly less bureaucratic, more subject-friendly, more responsive regulations (Ayres and Braithwaite 1992; Hutter 2005, 2006). In the new AML-regulation, business got some freedom to judge whether a case was 'risky', whether it could be a money laundering case, and whether it should be reported. This change marked a turn-around from the long-term historical trend from vague to more precise regulations, namely a move back again from precise to vaguer norms.

Risk-based regulation has become popular as it promises to have many attractions over rule-based regulation. It offers the prospect of less obedience merely for the sake of obedience, less formalism, less administrative burdens both for the subjects of regulation and its enforcers, in short, less ('unnecessary') bureaucracy. That is, it would also be cheaper. It aims to achieve this by simplifying and focusing on critical points, on those parts in a system or process – such as the enforcement of regulations – where things could go wrong, where the risks are greatest. This requires first an identification of possible risks and subsequently an estimation and assessment of both the probability and the seriousness or impact of these risks. This is also done in Risk-Based Auditing or in HACCP (Hazard Analysis and Critical Control Point) methodology. Assessing risks seems best done by those best placed to do so, the experts. These can include those concerned, the 'locals' of regulation: in the first place the regulators, supervisors, inspectors, enforcers, but often also the subjects of the regulation.

Hence risk-based regulation requires that one leaves some room for maneuver, for appraisal, for sound judgment to those closely involved. And those subsequently use the experiences and knowledge they have gained in the process of regulatory enforcement to improve and focus the regulations further. This is another attraction of the risk-based approach. It befits democracy, where citizens are both the authors of regulations and their subjects. Risk-based regulation offers to respect these subjects, to make use of their experience and knowledge, to take their judgments seriously, as useful contributions to rule development and application. Citizens and companies, subjects of the law, are treated as resourceful actors, rather than ignorant children who have to be taught a lesson. As a consequence, it is hoped that rule observation could be realized by intrinsic rule internalization, rather than by extrinsic threats with carrots and/or sticks. Thus it promises to enhance not only the effectiveness and efficiency of regulations, but also their legitimacy. Who would not like freedom, less bureaucracy, more legitimacy and still social order?

Risk estimation can be done both by the subjects and by the enforcers. Risk estimation by these different actors differs however also in kind and differs also from the rule-based approach where the regulator assesses the risk. Let us clarify this with the example of a simple traffic rule: pedestrians have to stop for a red pedestrian traffic light. Rule-based regulation would mean: any cross-over while the light is red is a transgression of the rule and ought to be punished. The assumption is that the regulatory authority knows what is good for its citizens, when it is safe to cross. And it does, because it also controls other traffic lights that tell others at the crossing to stop and when yet others can go. The command 'do not cross, otherwise you risk your life' is also given to others, though at different times. If everyone concerned around a crossing obeys the commands of the lights, traffic can flow safely.

Risk-based regulation could first of all mean that we give the pedestrian the discretion to decide whether crossing is risky or safe enough to do. Such discretion can be based on the assumption that he or she is capable of estimating the risk of crossing-over; and on the assumption that he or she has an interest in not being hit. Punishment for crossing-over would then only be justifiable in the case that the pedestrian is an obviously reckless jaywalker, for example because intoxication has reduced his capacity for sound judgment. A red pedestrian traffic light under risk-based regulation would no longer be a prohibition to cross, but a warning to be careful, just as the zebra crossing stripes are. Which is what is usually the case in actual practice.

Risk estimation can also be done by the enforcers. For them, it is impossible to enforce the rule perfectly, that is, to punish any disregard of a red pedestrian traffic light – short of installing cameras at every light (and fitting citizens with a 'license plate' on their back, or another more modern electronic identifier). The police cannot be present at every traffic light. They have limited resources, and, on top of that, enforcing pedestrian traffic lights has low priority. The enforcer has to make choices: whether, where, and when to control. If they do check, they have several options. First, spot checks, based on random selections of lights and times. Second, incidental or accidental enforcement, whenever a police(wo)man sees someone transgressing the rule while they are on the beat or just happen to pass by. Third, they can base enforcement on risk estimations and concentrate controls on known risky places and times: near blind curves; close to a senior citizens' home whose inhabitants cross slowly; when children leave school; when the pubs close.

After all, the concept of risk-based regulation is derived from older 'risk-based auditing'. Auditors cannot control all processes and all data when auditing a large corporation. Hence so-called system- or process-based auditing has gradually been replaced by risk-based auditing. Auditors focus on known risky or critical phases or elements rather than trying to follow all of the complete administrative processes. They focus on the points where experience has shown that 'things could go wrong', where there are chances are for mistakes, malpractice, or outright fraud to happen. The importance of such points is based on an estimation of both (a) the probability that something fishy could occur, and (b) the impact or the seriousness of its consequences. The aim of internal auditing controls is to manage risks to acceptable levels in the organization (Griffiths 2006).

Critical point concentration of inspections and enforcement requires that enforcers assess in turn the risk assessment of citizens, that is such risk-based regulation is based on double risk assessment. Enforcers have to estimate whether and when infants, teenagers, or the elderly can or care to oversee and evaluate the risks they run in crossing. Sound enforcement may also imply adjusting the disciplinary reaction to the conditions of transgression and categories of transgressors. It may not make much sense to fine infants. Better would be to give traffic lessons in school or to appoint volunteer 'lolly-pop (wo)men' (crossing guards), and equip them with a uniform and a fried-egg-shield, which should give them some authority, both over the children and the car drivers. That is, educate children to make sound judgments and protect them as long as necessary.

Such double risk assessment is what is done with risk-based AML-regulation. First, banks assess the risk or possibility that a transaction could be suspicious. Subsequently the risk that their estimation may be right or wrong is in turn assessed by state inspectors. In this way the knowledge, expertise and sound judgment of the lower-level employees at street- and shop floor level can be used. They may know the 'real world' of transactions, the tricks money launderers use. And in their daily work they are likely to have developed an intuitive feeling allowing them to identify possible money laundering cases. After all, commercial businesses are used to risk assessment and risk management, and have developed methods to guide them more systematically in that. By allowing them the freedom to develop their own explicit or implicit criteria for money laundering cases, the rules might be more effective. They might more easily separate the sheep from the goats. Such more focused information would be more useful. Furthermore, it could be expected that such a less rigidly bureaucratic procedure would produce less false alarms. Thus the private sector could save on reporting costs, and the administration on having to deal with redundant information from over-reporting.

29.2.3 The Risks of Risk-Based Regulation

Risk-based regulation is not without risks, for the regulator, as well as for the regulatees. Leaving the subjects some discretion to decide what to report entails the risk for the government that detection, assessment, and reporting is done sloppily and/or that it is done arbitrarily. There may be under-reporting or over-reporting, the government may get not enough, not the right, or too much information. As different businesses with a reporting duty may take this task more or less seriously, reporting might be erratic, and lack homogeneity and standardization.

The reporting businesses also run risks. They risk identifying a legal transaction as a potentially illegal one, and could get sued under private law by the accused. In order to reduce this risk, US federal law has tried to shield banks from such lawsuits from clients for reporting them. But banks of course still run the risk of losing customers. On the other side, banks run the risk of being fined for under-reporting. The uncertainty over whether or not one should report a certain case also means legal uncertainty; and as different banks are likely to make different reporting decisions or follow different strategies, this ambiguity could be further increased.

The risk of being held liable may induce businesses with a reporting duty to play it safe, by reporting as many cases as possible. Takats (2007) has called this the '*crying wolf*' problem. His model explores the principal–agent problem between government law enforcement agencies and banks. The government uses auditors and banks to obtain information about their clients. None of them like to give this information, which creates the agency problem. But most auditing models focus on the disclosure of verifiable information, while in the case of money laundering the information is unverifiable.

In this setup, harmful excessive reporting might be the result.

> Intuitively, if the bank identifies all transactions as suspicious, then it fails to identify any one of them – exactly as if it would not have identified a single one. Thus, 'crying wolf' can fully eliminate the information value of reports. 'Crying wolf' can arise because excessively high fines for false negatives force the uncertain bank to err on the safe side and also report transactions which are less suspicious. In the extreme case, the bank is forced to report all transactions, thereby fully diluting the information value of reports. (Takats 2007, p. 5)

Over-reporting has the added advantage that the bank can protect its customers by diluting their information in the mass and drowning the government in information. It might even be done intentionally. Banks have at least an incentive to do so. The government expects banks to reveal and accuse their own customers, but they are the ones who bring in money and profits. Reporting units, so Takats suggests, might behave strategically by purposely diluting information through over-reporting, and behaving like the little boy in the fairy tale and 'crying wolf' so often that when the wolf actually appears (when there is really a money laundering case) no one will take the cry seriously.

The seriousness of this risk for the bank depends of course on the administrative costs of over-reporting, the chance of being caught for intentional dilution, and the sanctions which that carries with it, monetary or otherwise, for example in terms of loss of reputation.

How these risks have affected the actual reporting behavior in the two countries that we focus on in this paper, the US and the Netherlands will be discussed below in section 29.4. However, first we will compare in section 29.3 their AML regulations and reporting duties. We have selected these two countries, because, though they face a similar regulatory change from a rule-based to a risk-based reporting system, they are almost each other's opposite in some dimensions of the legal system (see section 29.5) and, as we claim, as a consequence, in their performance.

29.3 COMPARING THE AMERICAN AND DUTCH AML REPORTING SYSTEMS

29.3.1 Differences in Regulation

According to Walker (1999) and Unger (2007), the US is the largest money launderer in the world. Half of the globally laundered funds are probably transferred through American banks, according to the estimates of some lawmakers. Hence it is not surprising that the US has been among the first countries to enact regulatory measures to counter the threat, and it has also developed some of the strictest anti-money laundering regulations.

The Banking Secrecy Act (1970) curbed banking secrecy in order to fight money laundering. It was followed by a series of laws, each of them further strengthening money laundering enforcement: The Money Laundering Control Act (1986), the Annunzio-Wylie Money Laundering Act (1992), the Money Laundering Suppression Act (1994), The Money Laundering and Financial Crimes Strategy Act (1998) and finally the USA Patriot Act (2001) (Takats 2007, fn.1).

The first specific AML act was enacted in 1986 (Title 18, US Code Sec. 1956), and already also had an extraterritorial reach. If the offense is committed by a US citizen or by a non-US citizen who conducts at least part of the offense in the United States, and if the transaction involves more than $10,000, such a person can be prosecuted. In addition to its heavy criminal penalties of up to 20 years in prison and $500,000 in fines, the law permits civil penalty lawsuits by the government for the value of the funds or property involved in the transaction.[3] After 9/11, terrorist financing has been included as a predicate crime in the money laundering definition in the Patriot Act. With this, preventing money laundering became a matter of national security.

Originally, the regulations were rule-based. Money laundering enforcement relied on the private sector reporting to public law enforcement agencies. Money transfer offices and banks had to provide two kinds of reports: rule-based and discretionary reports. Thus banks file a rule-based Currency Transaction Report (CTR) for cash transactions exceeding $10,000. Rule-based was less risky both for the private sector and the government. As there were explicit criteria for reporting, it was a standard disclosure problem. Bank reports were ex-post verifiable.

However, the precision of rule-based regulation also had disadvantages. Not only banks, but also money launderers were aware of the criteria for suspected money laundering and could circumvent them. Thus they could 'smurf', that is break down large cash deposits over the reporting threshold of $10,000 into smaller ones just below it (Takats 2007, p. 8).

The weaknesses of rule-based reports led the US in 1996 to introduce a discretionary report, the Suspicious Activity Report (SAR). This report is filed for any activity that the bank considers 'suspicious.' If a bank spots several transactions just below $10,000 it could identify them as suspicious because they hint at smurfing. The definition of suspicious was left vague on purpose, in order to keep both money launderers and banks in uncertainty. This made it difficult for money launderers to circumvent the rules. And it forced banks to keep on the alert, continually updating their understanding of how money laundering could be and was done. 'This intentional vagueness can be understood as another form of constructive ambiguity' (Takats 2007, p. 8). CTRs still co-exist next to SARs. There were more than 37 million CTRs filed between 2004 and 2006.[4] But according to experts, SARs are much more important for enforcement (Reuter and Truman 2004, Ch 5).

By changing from a rule- to a risk-based approach, the government tried to reduce the administrative burdens on business and introduced both a more pragmatic and more effective policy on business. However, by giving businesses strong incentives to take this task seriously – that is, by sanctioning neglect with serious fines – the unintended outcome was less effectiveness and efficiency. As Takats (2007) argued, this policy creates an incentive for businesses to over-report suspicious financial transactions, drowning government agencies in data and thus not really identifying potential money laundering transactions.

The Netherlands took a different approach. As a member of the European Union, the Dutch anti-money laundering policy is first and foremost shaped by the EU, which in turn is strongly influenced by the policies of the Financial Action Task Force on Money Laundering (FATF), an intergovernmental body established by the G-7 (now G-8) in 1989. The FATF has developed forty recommendations (plus nine on terrorism financing), which the EU has translated into several directives, which have to be transposed into national law by the member states.

The first EU directive 'for the prevention of the use of the financial system for the purpose of money laundering' (91/308/EEG) included an identification and a reporting duty of suspicious financial transactions for financial institutions. The Netherlands transposed this first Directive of 1991 with the Act on the Identification for Financial Services (*Wet identificatie bij financiële dienstverlening – Wif*) and the Act of Reporting Unusual Transactions (*Wet melding ongebruikelijke transacties – Wet Mot*).

The second EU Directive (2001/97/EG) on money laundering extended the reporting obligation beyond financial services to other economic sectors. Since 2001, car dealers, sellers of ships, art and antiques, and of gold, silver and jewellery, and, since June 2003, also lawyers, notaries public, tax consultants, accountants and real estate agents have been under reporting duty in the Netherlands. In 2001, money laundering was also included as an offense in the Dutch Penal Code (Nederlands Wetboek van Strafrecht, artikel 420bis, 420quater and 420ter 18 October 2004). According to this law, all serious offenses are predicate crimes for money laundering. In the Netherlands, laundering includes (as in the US) self-laundering (if a criminal launders his proceeds himself)[5] and can be punished by up to four years in prison (note the difference in severity with the US) in addition to the punishment for the underlying crime.

The third and most recent EU Directive on money laundering (2005/60/EG) replaced the first one and broadened the definition of money laundering to include terrorism financing. It was transposed into Dutch law with the 2008 Act on the Prevention of Money Laundering and Terrorism Financing. In order to use information more efficiently, a single reporting institution, the Financial Intelligence Unit FIU Nederland, was established and became part of the national police KLPD (Korps landelijke politiediensten) in 2006. The fourth Directive had still not been implemented by June 2013.

29.3.2 Differences in Reporting Duties

29.3.2.1 What?

In the US any transaction suspected of having criminal content has to be reported in a Suspicious Activity Report. 'If the financial institution knows, suspects, or has reason to suspect . . . any known or suspected Federal criminal violation, or pattern of criminal violations . . . ' it has to be reported.[6] SAR reporting duties clearly refer to suspicious transactions only. However, SAR is not only aimed at money laundering, but has a much broader field of application, as it regards any crime, including financial crimes such as insider abuse, computer abuse, and all sorts of criminal violations against financial institutions themselves.

In addition, all US businesses must fill out a Currency Transaction Report (CTR) for any cash transaction exceeding $10,000, no matter whether they are considered suspicious or not. These CTR-obligations are strictly rule based.

The Dutch government requires the reporting of *unusual* rather than *suspicious* transactions. Under the rule-based approach 'unusual' was just a different label for 'suspicious,' since strict and precise rules determined what had to be reported. The difference might have become more important under the risk-based approach, since 'unusual' is a much broader category than 'suspicious.' Grandma buying a car for €20,000 for her grandson with cash saved under her pillow is an 'unusual' transaction, however not 'suspicious' for money laundering. However, the more the risk-based approach was implemented in the Netherlands, the more the reporting duties for 'unusual transactions' became like the US reporting duties for 'suspicious transactions', so that the difference nowadays is rather one of labeling than of deeper meaning.

In 2005, in anticipation of the Third EU AML-Directive and a risk-based approach, the Netherlands developed an indicator list defining unusual transactions. This list consists of three objective indicators and a subjective one. The first one refers to transactions with specifically blacklisted *countries* (a blacklist which is currently empty though). The second objective indicator refers to *crimes* related to money laundering which have to be reported to the police anyway. The third one concerns the *type* of the transaction and the *amount* which has to be exceeded, and differs by each economic sector with a reporting duty. Fourthly, the list has a subjective criterion, namely 'a transaction where there is reason to assume that it is related to money laundering or terrorist financing' (FIU Nederland, 2007). Transactions are unusual if one or more of these four criteria is satisfied. The last indicator requires identification of transactions 'where there is reason to assume a relation to money laundering', which comes close to what the US labels suspicious transactions. As the Dutch reporting behavior analysis shows (see below), the subjective factor plays an increasing role in reporting (FIU Nederland 2008), especially for the transactions reported by financial institutions. What the Dutch kept calling unusual transactions became in actual fact suspicious transactions reporting. Thus the Dutch and the US reporting of transaction requirements are very similar under the risk-based approach.

29.3.2.2 How much?

In the Netherlands all transactions which are believed to be unusual *and* related to money laundering have to be reported to the FIU, regardless of the amount involved.

Transactions exceeding a certain threshold (in combination with changing the currency or other criteria), always have to be reported. In the US with regard to money laundering only suspicious transactions exceeding $5,000 have to be reported in the SAR, and transactions exceeding $10,000 must be filed in both reports. The main difference between the two countries is that transactions below a threshold of $5000 are not covered under the American reporting duties, while they are under the Dutch system. The threshold for mandatory reporting in the Netherlands is much higher than in the US (€15,000 for financial institutions, €25,000 for dealers in big values) compared to $10,000 in the United States (http://www.fincen.gov/forms/files/f9022-47_sar-di.pdfFIU, Nederland 2008).

29.3.2.3 Who?

The Dutch duty to report unusual transactions applies to more reporting units than in the US for the SAR. The US SAR has to be filled out by financial institutions, casinos, money services businesses, and by securities and futures industries, whereas the Dutch reporting obligation also applies to car and diamond dealers, real estate agents, notaries public, and accountants. However, the Dutch reporting system restricts itself to one reporting list only, whereas US firms may have to file both a SAR and a CTR for the same case.

The recipient of the SARs in the US is the Financial Crime Enforcement Network (FinCEN), which might forward them to law enforcement agencies for further investigation. In the Netherlands, unusual transactions are reported to the Financial Intelligence Unit (FIU) Nederland. This organization analyzes and classifies the filed reports as to whether they are suspicious or not. Thus in the Netherlands a government agency does the screening as to whether an unusual transaction is also a suspicious one, while in the US private business is supposed to have done that already. Thus the Dutch government is in principle less dependent on the private reporting agents and could, by doing the filtering itself, improve the quality of the information.

Figure 29.1 gives an overview of the change from the rule-based to the risk-based approach in both countries. In both countries the regulator intended to switch to the risk-based approach in order to reduce over-reporting, to improve the quality of information and to establish a more effective and efficient reporting system.

29.4 COMPARING THE AMERICAN AND DUTCH AML REPORTING PERFORMANCE

29.4.1 Differences in the Number of Transactions Reported

Considering these differences in regulation and reporting duties one would expect the Dutch private sector to report more cases under the rule-based approach, as the threshold for that is lower. Such is indeed the case. Before the introduction of the risk-based approach the Dutch reported about 3.5 times more per million inhabitants than the Americans (see Figure 29.2). Under the new risk-based approach this picture changes dramatically when correcting for structural changes.[7] Figure 29.2 compares American and Dutch reporting scores per million inhabitants, corrected for money transfers. In the

	Reporting in the US	Reporting in the Netherlands
Rule-based approach	Clear and transparent criteria for reporting US thru 1996 (only Currency Transaction Report CTR)	Netherlands 2001–2004
Risk-based approach	Vague and possibly subjective criteria for reporting *Intended: Less reporting, better quality and more efficiency* US since 1997 (Suspicious Activity Report SAR) (but still CTR required)	Netherlands since 2005 (objective and subjective indicator list)

Figure 29.1 Different AML-regulatory approaches and their use in the US and the Netherlands

Netherlands the latter account for 87 percent of unusual transactions reported in 2011 and for 86 percent of suspicious transactions classified by the FIU (FIU Nederland 2011; see also Table 29.1). This means that the money transfer agents report a lot of very small transactions and all transactions above €2000. Most of them would have fallen below the American threshold of $5000 for reporting duty.

Without such money transfers, unusual transaction reports per unit of population in the Netherlands fell drastically from 50,631 in 2005 to 25,093 in 2007 and to 21,572 in 2012. In 2007, they were only about half of what they had been two years before that (Figure 29.2). By contrast, the US saw a sharp increase in reporting. The February 2009 report from the US Government Accountability Office (GAO) noted that between the years 2000 and 2007 suspicious activity report (SAR) filings by depository institutions nearly quadrupled, from 163,000 to 649,000. In 2008 there were 733,000 SARs and in 2011 794,710 SARs reports filed by financial institutions. In Figure 29.2 they are included as related to unit of population. Thus in the Netherlands unusual transaction reporting per million inhabitants fell sharply from 3102 in 2005, to 1532 in 2007 and further to 1289 in 2012 – even below the US rate of suspicious reporting (2152 in 2007, 2400 in 2008 and 2550 in 2011).

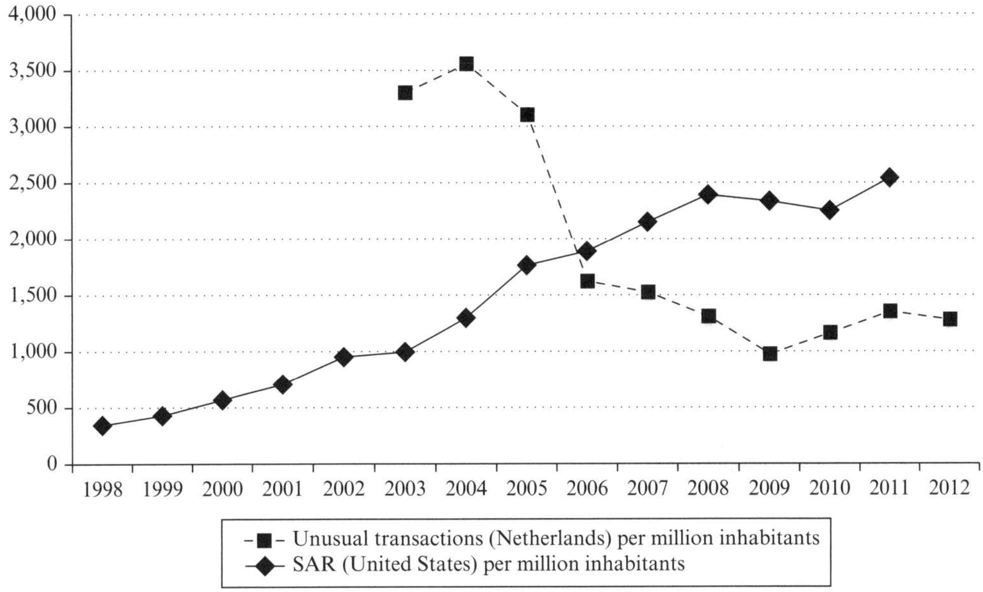

Sources: FinCen diverse years, http://www.fincen.gov and http://www.gao.gov; Nederland FIU Netherlands 2008, 2011 and own calculations. For the Netherlands: reports exclude money transfers.

Figure 29.2 Suspicious (US) and unusual (NL) transactions reported per million inhabitants

The sharp fall in reporting shown in the Netherlands, excluding money transfers, coincides with the introduction of the new indicator list for unusual transaction reporting in 2005. This list not only raised one of the objective criteria for unusual transactions from a minimum of €10,000 to €15,000 for banks, but it also introduced, in anticipation of the new European risk-based approach, the aforementioned fourth subjective criterion for 'unusual' transactions. As a consequence, reporting by banks went down and the administrative costs of banks fell by about 20 percent (= by €8 million). Ninety-four percent of bank reporting was based on the subjective criterion. Banks did a good job, as their auditor, the Dutch FIU, considered 26 percent of their reports also suspicious (Table 29.1).

Table 29.1 shows the number of unusual transactions reported by various private sector agents, the percentage from the total reports that each of these groups provided, and the number of reported cases that the Dutch Financial Intelligence Unit screened as suspicious transactions that could be forwarded to the public prosecutor. The last column (5) divides the amount of suspicious transactions as identified by the FIU by the amount of unusual transactions reported by the private sector, as an indicator for 'successful' reporting by the private sector.

Increased risk for the private sector, due to their new task of making risk assessments, led them to report less rather than more unusual – read suspicious – transactions. They apparently did not feel the need to play it safe and report any possible AML risk to the government, thus drowning it in data.

Table 29.1 Number of unusual transactions reported and number identified as 'suspicious' by the Dutch FIU, by reporting sector in 2011

Reporting sector	Unusual transactions	As percentage of total reports	Number of unusual cases identified by FIU as suspicious	Percent 'successful' private reports
Money Transfer Businesses	145,629	87.1	23,224	15.9
Casinos	1,734	1.0	354	20.4
Credit card companies	1,444	0.9	114	7.9
Money exchange offices	2,915	1.7	683	23.4
Banks	6,469	3.9	1,648	25.5
Traders of goods with high value (diamonds, cars, ships)	3,957	2.4	479	12.1
Government (customs, tax and supervising authorities)	4,287	2.6	86	2.0
Investment funds, other financial services	10	0	0	0
Liberal Professions of which:	794	0.5	289	36.4
• Accountants	325	0.2	66	20.3
• Lawyers	11	0	4	36.4
• Notaries-public	359	0.2	199	55.4
• Real estate agents	23	0	2	8.7
• Tax consultants	35	0	9	25.7
• Business advisors	15	0	6	40.0
• Trust companies	26	0	3	11.5
Total transactions excluding money transfers	**21,610**	12.9	3,653	16.9
Total transactions including money transfers	**167,239**	100	26,877	16.1

Source: FIU Nederland (2011).

This outcome is in sharp contrast with the model prediction of Takats (2007) and of Dalla Pellegrina and Masciandaro (2009), and with experiences of other European countries mentioned by them. They expected and found an increase in reporting, and they reasoned that an increased risk for the private sector induced it to play it safe by reporting more.

29.4.2 The Quality of Information

Takats (2007) and Dalla Pellegrina and Masciandaro (2009) also note that, in addition, the number of reports considered useful to starting investigations, and eventually to promoting money laundering prosecutions, has fallen or remained low in most countries. That speaks even more of an overflow of useless AML information. This problem was identified earlier by Pieth and Aiolfi (2003) for the US and by KPMG (2003) and Gold and Levi (1994) for the UK.

Not so in the Netherlands. The number of *unusual* transactions per head in that country was already below the number of *suspicious* ones per head in the US, as Figure 29.2 shows. But the percentage of suspicious cases that the Dutch Financial Intelligence Unit filtered out, was relatively high. Overall, 16 percent of the cases reported by the private sector were identified as suspicious (Table 29.1). That is an indication of the relatively high quality of the data provided by the private sector. They did not report much, but what they reported was relatively useful. The banks did a decent job. While they accounted for only 3.9 percent of the total unusual transactions reported, every fourth report of an unusual transaction was classified as suspicious by the FIU. Other sectors that provided good quality data were – percentage wise – money exchange offices (23%), casinos (20%) and the liberal professions (36%).

Relatively successful filtering was, on the one hand, the result of less but better quality information from the private sector. But on the other hand it was also because the Dutch public authority FIU had access to additional information, which helped it in identifying suspicious transactions. It could link the data on unusual transaction reports with data from police files, tax authorities, the Chamber of Commerce, social security authorities, its detailed access to all bank accounts, etc. A person who has an unusual transaction of, for example, buying jewels despite a very low income is classified as suspicious by the FIU. So is a company that appears repeatedly in unusual transactions and is located in areas prone to money laundering such as the Virgin or the Cayman Islands, or that has a police record. Thus the diluted information from the private sector can be more *purified* by the government's access to additional data. The Dutch found a different way than suggested by Dalla Pellegrina and Masciandaro (2009) to reduce the asymmetric information gap between the public principal and the private actors: not a supervisor who checks on the private sector's information quality, but an agency which has additional information to fill the information gap between principal and agent.

This comes of course at a price, namely less protection of a citizen's right to privacy. By giving the FIU legal authority to combine different databases which the government has at its disposal, it intrudes quite deeply into the privacy of citizens. This is, for a democratic country like the Netherlands, indicative of quite a high public trust in the government. Most other Western democratic populations would object to such a form of data combining and mining, especially countries like Germany and Austria, which have a recent authoritarian past. The latter, for example, still insists very much on bank secrecy.

29.4.3 Convictions

A good indicator of success is the number of convictions for money laundering. Between 2002 and 2007, a total of 2787 cases for money laundering reached the public prosecutor in the Netherlands. Of these about 70 percent were prosecuted further and in 1200 cases someone was convicted: 865 cases ended with a jail sentence (partly conditional), 288 in a work sanction, and 68 in a fine of between €140 and €1 million (Algemene Rekenkamer 2008, p. 79). While the number of unusual transactions declined after 2004, the number of convictions rose sharply, from 113 in 2004 to 427 in 2007 (FIU Nederland 2008, p. 26). The number of 1200 comes down to 15 per year and per million inhabitants. That is more than five times the rate in the US, which according to Takats (2007) and the Federal Justice Statistics hovered around three convictions per million inhabitants in 2005.[8] As

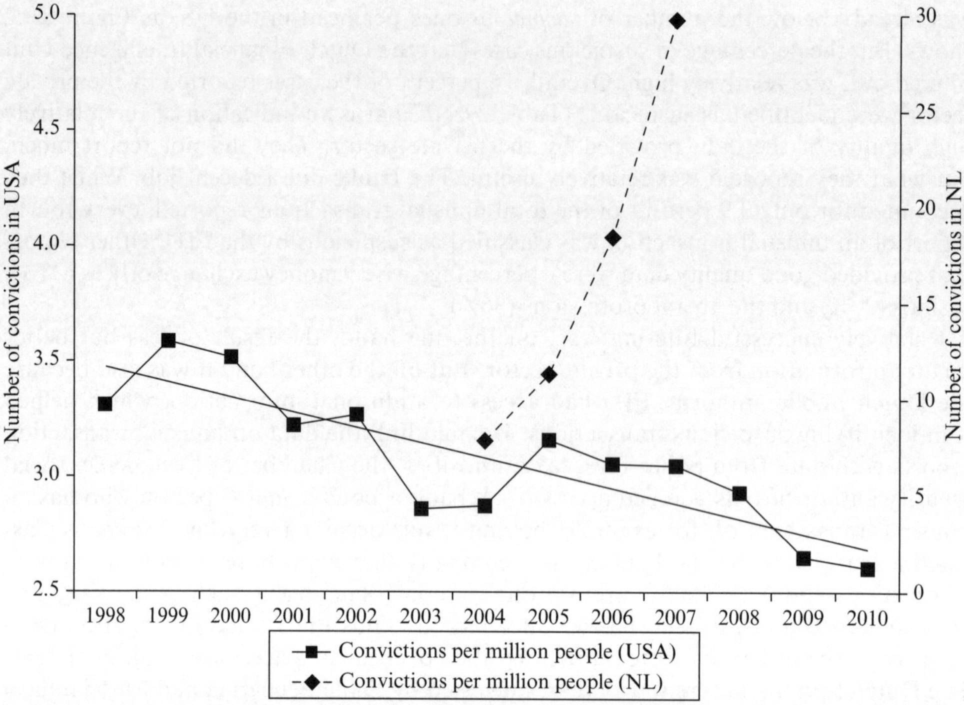

Source: Federal Justice Statistics Resource Center.

Figure 29.3 Dutch and US convictions form money laundering per million inhabitants

Figure 29.3 shows, while the conviction rate went up sharply in the Netherlands, in the US it declined.

29.5 EXPLAINING THE DIFFERENCES

How to explain this Dutch exceptionalism of low reporting rates but relatively high quality reports as indicated by high conviction rates? Exceptional, compared to the opposite in the US: very high reporting rates but low conviction rates.

The differences in sanctions are significant. The 'crying wolf' problem in the US is caused by private businesses wanting to play it safe. And they do so because under-reporting is risky for them, given the severe sanctions the government has placed on them. Fines have even increased since the Patriot Act. Failing to file SARs led to fines of $25 million for Riggs Bank, $24 million for Arab Bank, $50 million for AmSouth Bank and $80 million for ABN-AMRO Bank in the years following 9/11.

By contrast, non-reporting by Dutch banks and other actors involved in transactions has not been sanctioned much in the Netherlands. The maximum fine is €150,000 and the probability that someone will be fined for not fulfilling his reporting duty is almost nil. Between 2002 and 2007, 371 cases of non-reporting[9] were passed on to the public prosecutor (Algemene Rekenkamer 2008, p. 81). This is on average 75 offenses per year. In three-quarters of the cases the prosecutor himself set a fine between €175 and €11,250. The rest of the cases were forwarded to a judge, who imposed sanctions of between €150 and €150,000.

In order to reduce the 'crying wolf' problem in the US, Takats (2007, p. 8) has pleaded for a reduction in fines and an introduction of reporting fees, to give banks a cost incentive to internalize into their calculations the externality caused by their over-reporting. The Dutch case of low fines, low reporting, but relatively high convictions would support his argument.

However, it is not always so easy to turn back the use and severity of sanctions. There may be constraints both in the legal and the political system to raise or lower sanctions. The size of politically and legally legitimate sanctions differs between countries. The US legal system typically imposes heavy sanctions, under both criminal as well as civil law. Underlying that are some strongly ingrained cultural values, such as that individuals and organizations are free and independent, but as such they are also responsible for their deeds and deserve to be punished if they misbehave. In addition, there is also a strong belief that heavy sanctions can and will correct behavior, that they will affect the cost-benefit analysis of free rational calculating individuals in such a way as to deter misbehavior, as is also often assumed in the US law and economics approach.

By contrast, typical for the Dutch legal culture was that as far as enforcement is concerned, the emphasis has been less on punishment and immediate and harsh sanctions, and more on information, advising, and education of potential transgressors. That holds for businesses which have transgressed standards for product quality, health and safety at work, or environmental pollution, but also for individuals who do not abide by traffic rules, identification obligations, or who have committed crimes against the life, liberty and property of others. Many minor and business offenses are not transgressions of criminal but of administrative law. And wherever criminal law was invoked, sanctions were not heavy and were not immediately, without respect of persons, imposed.

The belief system behind this was that criminal behavior was considered less the free choice of an individual, but the consequences of circumstances beyond his control – a deprived childhood, poverty, mental disease, opportunity – and judges were willing to take account of that in their judgments. Society, rather than the criminal, was viewed as being to blame for crime. The criminal was actually the victim. Incarceration would only add to his problems, such as psychological problems, loss of social contacts, damaging social contacts, drug addiction, stigmatization, resulting in even less chances in the labor market. The emphasis was on resocialization, rehabilitation, reintegration, education, and prevention rather than on revenge. If punishment was unavoidable, alternative forms were preferred. Typical of the difference in approach are the incarceration rates. In 2004 the Netherlands had 101 prisoners per 100,000 inhabitants, while the US had 721 (CEPEJ 2006).

Tort law provides punishment in civil cases. Though under English law this has developed as an important deterrent for inflicting harm on others, and as such has been valued by law and economics scholars (e.g. Shavell 2007; De Geest and Dari-Mattiacci 2007), in the US it has expanded considerably – too much in the eyes of many (Kagan 2001; Van Waarden 2001). The frequency and size of demanded and awarded compensatory and punitive damages in the US are infamous. Fear of such liability has induced formalistic legalism in the US economy and society, such as detailed safety warning labels or extensive due diligence in economic transactions. Such tort litigation has been unimportant in the Netherlands. Victims have not started proceedings readily, because the rules on proof of causality have been rather strict and courts did not award high damages. Hence it did not pay to litigate, all the more so because there were alternative ways to get compensation, for example through the social security system and private insurance.

In addition, many comparative studies of regulatory enforcement in different countries have shown that European, and in particular Dutch, rule enforcers – policemen, labor and food inspectors, environmental controllers – followed a more consensual enforcement style, compared to American inspectors, who were known for a more rigid, strict and adversarial style, immediately imposing heavy sanctions (e.g. Bardach and Kagan 1982; Badaracco 1985; Brickman et al. 1985; Vogel 1986; Wilson 1985; Van Waarden 1995, 1999). Traditionally, state–industry relations in the US have also been much more adversarial and distrustful than in Europe (Fritschler and Ross 1980). The US early on had independent regulatory agencies, which had the task of closely supervising business. Thus, in the US, business met the government of old mostly as regulator, inspector, and controller, rather than as supporter and ally. In those cases where Dutch (or Swedish or British) policemen or inspectors did impose sanctions and such cases made it to an administrative or criminal court, judges often acquitted or reduced the sanctions in exchange for promises on the part of the accused to mend their ways. Typical of the cooperative relations between state and industry is also that the new norms for reporting unusual (read suspicious) transactions of 2005 were developed in close cooperation between government agencies and the various trade associations of the involved economic sectors, such as the banking association.

More generally, playing it safe and defensive reporting are likely to also be influenced by the broader legal system. And the Dutch and American legal systems differ substantially, not only and so much in the substance of the law, the criterion on which La Porta et al. (1998) distinguished common law and three varieties of civil law countries, but in form, that is, legal institutions and legal procedures, such as court procedures and the importance of judges versus lawyers (see also Damaska 1986), the importance of case law versus statutory law, and in the ease of and inclination towards litigation. A standard indicator for such procedural differences is the number of lawyers per 100,000 inhabitants. In 2005 the Netherlands had 84 lawyers per 100,000 inhabitants (up from 16 in 1970), compared to 373 lawyers per 100,000 inhabitants for the US (Van Waarden and Hildebrand 2009).[10]

US defensive reporting seems the logical thing to do in a legal system which Kagan (1997, 2001, 2007) among others has called 'adversarial legalism', and which he considered very fearsome as well as 'woefully inefficient and erratic'. He writes:

> The United States has a 'legal style' that remains distinctive. Its lawyers and judges are uniquely aggressive and creative – or, as critics would put it, presumptuous. In no other country do aggrieved citizens so often haul highway departments, prison wardens, and business corporations into court. Germans may file many tort suits, but nowhere is the tort law system so extravagantly costly, erratic, and fearsome as it is in the United States.
>
> A growing number of excellent socio-legal studies carefully compare different national approaches to a particular social problem – such as compensating injured people, regulating

⁄IARY AND CONCLUSION

he problem of drowning in data? How to increase the effectiveness and IL reporting by private actors? How to give them an incentive to report t they would consider suspicious, using their expert knowledge and intui- ring business from over-reporting? Is the shift from rule-based to risk- helpful in this respect?

d approach was developed because the rule-based approach did not in the US and in Europe, including the Netherlands. The rule-based over-reporting, as many of the reported transactions had nothing to do dering, but at least there were clear criteria about what to report and it government to control this reporting and to impose fines on banks that cording to these criteria.

a rule- to a risk-based approach implies that 'suspicious behavior' is l by the government in the form of fixed rules, but by many different perts on the ground of the financial services sectors. Private actors like ny countries notaries public, accountants, real estate agents, and public nd law enforcement actors such as customs agents, the police and the have to and can develop their own interpretation and definition of ior' in a client or a transaction. The new risk-based approach has led to iffering definitions and concepts of 'suspicious transactions'. In short, ncertainty for all the actors involved.

or can profit from this. A risk-based approach might leave more room he private sector to determine suspicious behavior, but it is also much he government to control the quality of the information and to impose reporting. Banks could try to protect their customers by drowning the a, by creating a 'crying wolf' problem, so that the real culprits cannot l. However, the marketing possibilities of this are limited. It is some- banks to openly advertise this to attract customers.

approach creates not only opportunities for the private sector to but also uncertainty. And that may be an additional motive for t playing it safe and reporting anything that could smell like money eporting could in principle be risky. Identifying a legal transaction al one may get banks into trouble with the accused, who might sue urt. In order to reduce this risk, US law has declared that banks their clients for reporting them. However, under-reporting is risky government. Banks may be heavily fined for it. As Takats (2007) onsequence, banks are likely to follow a risk-averse strategy and ve have seen that in many countries they do (Dalla Pellegrina and).

ults between the US and the Netherlands that we discussed in this whether or not over-reporting will take place under a risk-based on the legal system: its institutions and the cultural values of which e an expression. A legal system such as US adversarial legalism, with enforcement, fierce criminal and administrative sanctions and fear- ed a general attitude of private actors to play it safe. In such a legal

nursing homes, or cleaning up toxic waste du
distinctive characteristics of the American g

1. more complex bodies of legal rules;
2. more formal, adversarial procedures fo
3. more *costly* forms of legal contestation
4. more punitive legal sanctions;
5. more frequent judicial intervention int
6. more political controversy about legal
7. more legal uncertainty and malleabilit

Important is not only the severity of c
the importance of principles such as the
the uncertainty over whether one will b
tion of how heavy the sanction will be
uncertainty in outcomes, among them t
rather than judges de facto lead the p
the presence of jury adjudication, and,
contingency fees.

Adversarial legalism is not only leg
values such as the formal equality for
that its force should fall on all citizens
conflict, the often severe sanctions, a
play it safe, to be formalistic and choo

By contrast, the Netherlands has
consensual rather than adversarial, i
rigid, and pragmatic rather than pri
Waarden 2009; Van Waarden and H
Dutch style of regulatory enforcem
legal culture', Bruinsma (2005) spok
Hildebrand (2009) of 'consensual in
sarial legalism.

The formal legal institutions are
European countries use an inquisit
differences between adversarial and
a minor role and where the judge ste
state also has a rather simple and co
US federal states, which offers much
way, at least in some respects; and t

It is understandable that in a fear
(and their legal counsel) want to pla
than under-report. The Dutch legal
latter can afford to save on the adm
keeping this on a modest scale.

To sum up, if one wants to avo
of money laundering, it may not b
Takats (2007) wants. They are ve
they have come about and functio

29.6 SUMM

How to dodge t
efficiency of AM
transactions tha
tion, while deter
based regulation

The risk-base
work well, both
approach led to
with money laun
was easy for the
did not report ac

The shift from
no longer define
actors, mostly ex
banks, and in ma
implementation a
public prosecuto
'suspicious behav
a large range of d
it has increased u

The private sec
for maneuver to t
more difficult for
a fine for wrongfu
government in da
easily be identifie
what difficult for b

The risk-based
use its discretion,
over-reporting: jus
laundering. Over-
as a potential illeg
them in private c
cannot be sued by
in relation to the
has argued, as a c
over-report. And v
Masciandaro 2009

The different res
paper indicate tha
regime depends als
these institutions ar
its strict public rule
some tort law induc

system, over-reporting is much more likely than in a legal system like that of the Dutch, where regulatory enforcement is much more flexible and lenient, where sanctions are much lower, and where the threat of liability claims is minimal.

The eventual effect of new regulations depends also on the pre-existing legal-institutional framework of a country in which they are introduced, as La Porta et al. (1998, p. 1114) also indicated. That implies that if one wants to evaluate the actual deterrent effectiveness and efficiency of regulation versus tort liability, that is, of sanctions under public versus under civil law (De Geest and Dari-Mattiacci 2003, 2007), or of precise rules versus broader standards (Schäfer 2006), it might be wise to take the pre-existing legal context, for example the fierceness of tort law, into account. Schäfer differentiates between poor and rich countries. Similarly, one could differentiate between different (tort) law traditions.

Furthermore, such legal systems are not easily changed. They are the product of decades if not centuries of development of public policy, regulation and case law. Legal systems are particularly path dependent, given the importance of precedent in the interests of legal certainty and legal equality. Thus, modifying them is not an easy policy option, certainly not if done only to increase the effectiveness and efficiency of anti-money laundering policy.

Takats (2007) has argued for lower fines for wrongful money laundering reporting. It is questionable whether that is legally possible or has political legitimacy in a political and legal system such as that of the US, which expresses the belief that all vices can be rooted out by severe punishment. It might be easier in more flexible systems like that of the Netherlands, but there sanctions on wrongful AML reporting are already very low.

Dalla Pellegrina and Masciandaro (2009) build a theoretical model to reduce the asymmetric information problem by introducing a third player into Takats' principal agent problem: a supervisor, who can, through his skills and expertise, identify complicated money laundering constructions, thereby evaluating the risk of laundering and the effort made by the reporting unit. In this way, the supervisor reduces the asymmetric information between the public agencies and the private sector reporting units. The role of the supervisor in their model is to increase the incentive for correct reporting by increasing the risk for an untruthful private sector reporting unit of being detected.

However, it remains questionable whether this solves the problem. The uncertainty over what a suspicious transaction is may also hold for the supervisor, and he may also want to play it safe, by allowing or facilitating over-reporting. Furthermore, there will still be a problem of asymmetric information between the government and this supervisor, involving principal agent problems, irrespective of whether he or she is publicly or privately employed. Even publicly employed supervisors may eventually come to share interests with the subjects he is to supervise or develop so much understanding for the difficulties of the private sector that he may end up more on their side than on that of the public authorities, as the extensive 'capture' literature on US 'independent' regulatory agencies has taught us (Bernstein 1955; Mitnick 1980). The government will still have to 'trust' its supervisors. If not, the problem will only be displaced, and a new supervisor of the supervisor will have to be appointed. In principle the chain of supervisors of supervisors is endless. This will only add to the costs of the regulatory system, that is, make it increasingly less efficient.

Indeed, many economic sectors have seen the burgeoning of what could be called a veritable 'control industry' (Van Waarden 2006). Checks have been piled upon checks. A good example is provided by the American accounting scandal, which produced the Sarbanes-Oxley (SarbOx) Act in 2002. Suddenly it turned out that the supposedly 'independent' external supervisors, the accountants, could not be trusted anymore. The law created a new regulator, the Public Company Accounting Oversight Board (PCAOB). In line with the rigid and adversarial policy style that has characterized American regulators for decades (Van Waarden, 1999), it executes the new stricter rules very precisely and rigidly. The greater external controls have led to extra layers of internal control. 'At KPMG, the auditors are now reviewed not only by their boss, who focuses on business growth, but also by risk experts, who rate how well the accountant complied with the firm's rules' (Byrnes 2003, p. 68). Also in the companies checked by accountants, new levels of control have been built in. 'Companies have spent at least $1 billion adopting new Sarbanes-Oxley rules. Corporate audit committees are gathering more often for longer meetings and asking tougher questions' (Byrnes 2003, p. 68). So by now we have at least seven levels of control: PCAOB – top management of accountancy companies – their risk experts – the accountants – the management of the companies that will be checked – company accountants committees – company accountants – the final bookkeepers.

History teaches us that time and again the effectiveness of controls is questioned. And subsequently the costs of the control system increase, decreasing its efficiency.

But perhaps the problems posed by the uncertainty of risk-based regulation will disappear as risk-based regulation itself is likely to disappear eventually. The subjects of regulation will want to reduce that uncertainty. Risk-based regulation will in the beginning lead to an increase in misunderstandings and legal insecurity, reduced intelligibility, transparency and predictability. Clients might feel mistreated by wrongly being classified suspect, and appeal to the Courts. Banks might feel unfairly fined because of inaccurate monitoring of suspicious transactions and appeal to the Courts. In the long run the definition of suspicious transactions and the monitoring of these transactions will converge, if not by mutual agreement among the actors themselves, then by the actions of the Courts. Convergence through case law and the Courts will eventually change the risk-based approach back again into a new rule-based approach. However, in this new system the rules are no longer set by the legislators, but by the Courts in their case law. Politicians will not be ruling anymore, but lawyers. This will take time though, and will first lead to a period of legal insecurity, accompanied by trial and error, demonstrated by as a higher number of appeals, more police investigations, privacy violations, etc. In short, it will produce costs to private and public organizations and to society at large, and thus it is not efficient. But over time, precision, clarity, transparency, and predictability will eventually re-emerge as risk-based regulation regresses back to de facto rule-based regulation.

This could also be the fate of another supposed innovation in regulation: principle-based regulation. The British Financial Services Authority (FSA) has recently pushed this as another industry-friendly and efficient form of regulation. It has elaborated this in 11 basic principles, such as 'the financial firm must conduct business with integrity', 'with due skill, care and diligence', 'must maintain adequate financial resources', 'must observe proper standards of market conduct', 'must pay due regard to the interests of its customers and treat them fairly', and 'must arrange adequate protection of clients' assets'. Firms will want to play it safe and know what the FSA considers to be 'adequate', 'proper', or 'due regard', When are they indemnified against sanctions or liability claims? Legal systems have many such broad and hence vague principles – legality, opportunity, proportionality, equality, legal certainty, discrimination – but these have over time acquired rather precise meanings in the legal discourse. The aim of the FSA principles is to reduce red tape and to lower the costs of filling out forms and reporting. However, they could very well increase the costs of liability claims and litigation. Their operationalization will produce a lot of lawyering and new (and old) forms of bureaucracy.

This process can be illustrated by the 30-year history of the HACCP quality standards developed by the US FDA and USDA in food quality control. What started as risk-based regulation has developed into a set of detailed SOPs (standard operating procedures) for the identification of potential hazards and of critical points in processes where these hazards could occur, for preventive measures with critical limits for each control point, for procedures for monitoring critical control points, for required corrective actions when monitoring has shown that a critical limit has not been met, for procedures to verify that the system is working properly, and for keeping records to document the HACCP system. These SOPs, which are officially 'recommendations' but de facto mandatory standards as they are recognized and referred to by the judicial authorities, now make up 123 pages. The risk-based system has evolved into a rule-based one.

Whether or not risk- and principle-based regulation will regress again to rule-based regulation, and how soon, will depend on a number of factors. A major one is the likelihood and frequency of litigation over the regulation. Without litigation there is no case law. Whether or not citizens or firms litigate is in turn dependent on the degree of actual enforcement. With less enforcement there are less conflicts over interpretation of the regulations. Though the American federal government tried to protect reporting banks from litigation by those reported, it is not unimaginable that the complicated multi-layered US legal system will provide sufficient loopholes for inventive and aggressive lawyers or state public prosecutors to sue.

That means that a legal culture characterized by strict enforcement and frequent litigation, as that of the US, will sooner produce more specific operationalizations of broad and vague norms such as what 'suspicious' transactions are. Where the problems of over-reporting are greater, in the US, the solution will come from the gradual disappearance of risk-based regulation and the re-appearance of a new rule-based approach, with the precise rules now being set by courts and case law. Where the problems are fewer, as in the Netherlands, there will be less litigation, and it will take more time before risk-based regulation will revert back to a rule-based approach. Thus the legal system itself will provide the solution where it is most needed. Unless public authorities introduce once again another regulation 'innovation'.

NOTES

* This chapter is an updated version of B. Unger and F. van Waarden (2009), 'How to dodge drowning in data? Rule- and risk-based anti money laundering policies compared', *Review of Law & Economics*, **5**(2), 953–85.

1. It must be said that the term standards is also often used for the opposite, for detailed and precise norms, notably outside of the law and economics world, e.g. among socio-legal scholars and in general discourse on technical standards (among others Voelzkow 1996). Technical standards are highly specific norms that allow for 'standardization'. There, broad general norms are often referred to as 'principles' or 'doctrines'.
2. Made more concrete in the 'customer due diligence' standard in anti-money-laundering regulations.
3. http://www.altassets.net/casefor/countries/2002/nz2627.php
4. http://www.gao.gov/new.items/d08355.pdf
5. For the problems that occur within the EU due to different money laundering definitions, e.g. some countries excluding self-laundering, see Unger (2007).
6. http://www.fincen.gov/forms/files/f9022-47_sar-di.pdf
7. In 2011 the Dutch reported 167,239 unusual transactions (FIU Nederland 2011). The development over time in the Netherlands is obscured by structural changes – changes in the reporting criteria and enlargement of the number of reporting units – and especially by some incidental events. An important incidental event was that two major money transfer businesses, Western Union and MoneyGram, were licensed as money transaction offices in the Netherlands by the Dutch Central Bank and as such fell under the reporting duty. Such incidental events can have a substantial impact in a small country. It explains the strong increase from 172,873 to 214,040 in reported unusual transactions in 2007 (FIU Nederland 2008, p. 62).
8. These US data relate to federal court convictions. According to Reuter and Truman (2004, p. 108), there is some evidence from inmates in jail surveys that there are few convictions for money laundering by state courts.
9. Offenses against the Law of Reporting Unusual Transactions (Wet Mot), the Law of Identification services (Wid) and the Sanctiewet, 1977.
10. Barzilai (2007) arrives at somewhat different numbers because he seems to have used a different definition of lawyers (Van Waarden and Hildebrand (2009) used the official numbers of the American Bar Foundation). Barzilai's figure came to only 230 lawyers per 100,000 inhabitants. Yet the US also scored at the top in his ranking, while the Netherlands was the lowest-scoring western industrialized country. Below it were mostly East European and Asian countries.

REFERENCES

Algemene Rekenkamer (2008), *Bestrijden witwassen en terrorismefinanciering*, Tweede Kamer, vergaderjaar 2007–2008, 31477, nrs 1–2,'s Gravenhage, http://www.rekenkamer.nl/Publicaties/Onderzoeksrapporten/Introducties/2008/06/Bestrijden_witwassen_en_terrorismefinanciering

Annual Report FIU Netherlands (2007), *Jaaroverzicht 2006*. The Hague, http://www.fiu-nederland.nl/

Annual Report FIU Netherlands (2008), *Jaaroverzicht 2007*. The Hague, http://www.fiu-nederland.nl/

Ayres, Ian and John Braithwaite (1992). *Responsive Regulation: Transcending the Deregulation Debate*. Oxford: Oxford University Press.

Badaracco, Joseph L. (1985), *Loading the Dice: A Five-Country Study of Vinyl Chloride Regulation*, Cambridge: Harvard Business School Press.

Baker, Raymond (2005), *Capitalism's Achilles Heel*, Hoboken, NJ: John Wiley.

Bardach, Eugene and Robert A. Kagan (1982), *Going by the Book: The Problem of Regulatory Unreasonableness*, Philadelphia: Temple University Press.

Barzilai, Gad (2007), 'The ambivalent language of lawyers in Israel: liberal politics, economic liberalism, silence and dissent', in T.C. Halliday, L. Karpik and M.M. Feeley (eds), *Fighting for Political Freedom*, Portland: Hart Publishing, 247–79.

Becker, Gary S. (1968), 'Crime and punishment: an economic approach', 76 *Journal of Political Economy* 169–217.

Bernstein, Marver H. (1955), *Regulating Business by Independent Commission*, Westport, CT: Greenwood Press.

Blankenburg, Erhard (1997), 'Civil litigation rates as indicators for legal culture', in D. Nelken (ed), *Comparing Legal Cultures*, Aldershot: Dartmouth Publishing Co, 41–68.

Blankenburg, Erhard (1998), 'Patterns of legal culture: the Netherlands compared to neighboring Germany', 46 *American Journal of Comparative Law* 1–41.

Blankenburg, Erhard and Fred J. Bruinsma (1994), *Dutch Legal Culture*, Deventer and Boston: Kluwer.

Brickman, Ronald, Sheila Jasanoff and Thomas Ilgen (1985), *Controlling Chemicals: The Politics of Regulation in Europe and the United States*, Ithaca: Cornell University Press.

Bruinsma, Fred J. (2005), 'Judges and lawyers in the Netherlands – an overview from 1970 till 2000', in William L.F. Felstiner (ed), *Reorganization and Resistance: Legal Professions Confront a Changing World*, Portland: Hart Publishing, 67–92.

Byrnes, Nanette (2003), 'Governance reform: who's making the grade?', *Business Week*, 22 September, 64–8.

CEPEJ (European Commission for the Efficiency of Justice) (2006), *European Judicial Systems*. Strasbourg: Council of Europe.

Cioffi, John (2009), 'Adversarialism vs legalism: juridification and litigation in corporate governance reform', 3(3) *Regulation and Governance* 235 58.

Dalla Pellegrina, Lucia and Donato Masciandaro (2009), 'The risk-based approach in the new European anti-money laundering legislation: a law and economics view', 5(3) *Review of Law and Economics*, December.

Damaska, Mirjan (1986), *The Faces of Justice and State Authority: A Comparative Approach to the Legal Process*, New Haven: Yale University Press.

Diver, Carol S. (1983), 'The optimal precision of administrative rules', 93 *Yale Law Journal* 65–109.

Ehrlich, Isaac and Richard Allen Posner (1974), 'An economic analysis of legal rule-making', 3(1) *Journal of Legal Studies* 257–86.

Es, Peter C. van (2007), 'Informatieplicht en geheimhoudingsplicht van de notaris', in *Meer spreken, minder zwijgen?, Preadvies KNB 2007*, Den Haag, 56–61.

Ferwerda, Joras (2009), 'The economics of crime and money laundering: does anti-money laundering policy reduce crime?', 5(2) *Review of Law and Economics*.

FinCen (Financial Crimes Enforcement Network, U.S. Department of the Treasury) (2008), 'The SAR activity review–by the numbers', Issue 10 (May), http://www.fincen.gov/news_room/rp/files/sar_by_numb_11.pdf http://www.fincen.gov/news_room/rp/files/sar_by_numb_10.pdf

FIU (Financial Intelligence Unit) Nederland (2007) Jaaroverzicht 2006, KLPD-DNRI, Zoetermeer, October.

FIU (Financial Intelligence Unit) Nederland (2008), *Jaaroverzicht 2007*, http://www.fiu-nederland.nl/

FIU (Financial Intelligence Unit) Nederland (2011), FIU-Annual Report 2010, KLPD-IPOL Department Zoetermeer, September.

Fritschler, A. Lee and Bernard H. Ross (1980), *Business Regulation and Government Decision-Making*, Cambridge, MA: Winthrop.

Geest, Gerrit de and Guiseppe Dari-Mattiacci (2003), 'On the intrinsic superiority of regulation and insurance over tort law', 10th Joint Conference between the Geneva Association for the Study of Insurance Economics and the European Association of Law and Economics (EALE), Seminar.

Geest, Gerrit de and Guiseppe Dari-Mattiacci (2007), 'Soft regulators, tough judges', 15 *Supreme Court Economic Review* 119–40.

Gold, Michael and Michael Levi (1994), *Money Laundering in the UK: An Appraisal of Suspicion-Based Reporting*, London: Police Foundation.

Griffiths, David (2006), *Risk-Based Internal Auditing: An Introduction*, http://www.internalaudit.biz.

Hutter, Bridget M. (2005), *The Attractions of Risk-Based Regulation: Accounting for the Emergence of Risk Ideas in Regulation*, CARR Discussion paper, 33. Centre for Analysis of Risk and Regulation, London: London School of Economics and Political Science.

Hutter, Bridget M. (2006), 'Risk, regulation, and management', in Peter Taylor-Gooby and Jens O. Zinn (eds), *Risk in Social Science*, Oxford: Oxford University Press, 202–227.

IMF (International Monetary Fund) (2005), 'Technical review of the quality and consistency of the AML/CFT assessments', Report by an Independent panel of experts on behalf of the IMF and the World Bank, Washington DC.

Johnson, Simon, Rafael La Porta, Florencio Lopez-de-Silanes and Andrei Schleifer (2000), 'Tunneling', 90(2) *American Economic Review* 22–7.

Kagan, Robert A. (1997), 'Should Europe worry about adversarial legalism?', 17 *Oxford Journal of Legal Studies* 165–83.

Kagan, Robert A. (2001), *Adversarial Legalism: The American Way of Law*, Cambridge, MA: Harvard University Press.

Kagan, Robert A. (2007), 'Globalization and legal change: the "Americanization" of European Law?' 1(2) *Regulation and Governance* 99–120.

Kagan, Robert A. and Lee Axelrad (2000), *Regulatory Encounters: Multinational Corporations and American Adversarial Legalism*, Berkeley: University of California Press.

Kaplow, Louis (1992), 'Rules versus standards: an economic analysis', 42(3) *Duke Law Journal* 557–629.

Kaplow, Louis (2000), 'General characteristics of rules', in Boudewijn Bouckaert and Gerrit de Geest (eds), *Encyclopedia of Law and Economics*, Volume 5, *The Economics of Crime and Litigation*, Cheltenham UK and Northampton MA, USA Edward Elgar, 502–28.

Koselleck, Reinhard (1967), *Preussen zwischen Reform und Revolution: Algemeines Landrecht, Verwaltung und soziale Bewegung von 1791 bis 1848*, Stuttgart: Ernst Klett Verlag.

KPMG (2003), *Money Laundering: Review of the Regime for Handling Suspicious Activity Reports*. London: National Criminal Intelligence Service.
La Porta, Rafael, Florencio Lopez-de-Silanes, Andrei Shleifer and Robert W. Vishny. (1998), 'Law and finance', 106(6) *Journal of Political Economy*, 1113–55.
Laar, Marijke van, Guus Cruts, André van Gageldonk, Esther Croes, M. van Ooyen-Houben and Robert Meijer (2007), 'Drug situation 2006 – the Netherlands: report to the European Monitoring Center for Drugs and Drug Addiction', Trimbos Institute, Utrecht, http://www.wodc.nl/onderzoeksdatabase/national-report- 2006-emcdda.aspx
Levi, Michael and Peter Reuter (2006), 'Money laundering', 34 *Crime and Justice*, 289–375.
Masciandaro, Donato, Elod Takats and Brigitte Unger (2007), *Black Finance: The Economics of Money Laundering*, Cheltenham UK and Northampton, MA, USA: Edward Elgar.
Mitnick, Barry (1980), *The Political Economy of Regulation*, New York: Columbia University Press.
Pieth, Mark and Gemma Aiolfi (2003), 'Anti-money laundering: leveling the playing field', Basel Institute of Governance, Working Paper, n.1.
Posner, Richard Allen (1998), *Economic Analysis of Law*, New York: Wolters Kluwer.
Reuter, Peter and Victoria Greenfield (2001), 'Measuring global drug markets: how good are the numbers and why should we care about them?', 2(4) *World Economics*, 100–121.
Reuter, Peter and Edwin M. Truman (2004), *Chasing Dirty Money: The Fight Against Money Laundering*, Washington DC: Institute for International Economics.
Schäfer, Hans-Bernd (2002), 'Legal rules and standards', 2002 *German Working Papers in Law and Economics*, paper 2.
Schäfer, Hans-Bernd (2006), 'Rules versus standards in rich and poor countries: precise legal norms as substitutes for human capital in low-income countries', *Supreme Court Economic Review*, Vol. 14, Chicago: University of Chicago Press, 113–135.
Shavell, Steven (2007), 'Liability for accidents', in A. Mitchell Polinsky and Steven Shavell (eds), *Handbook of Law and Economics*, Vol. 1, Chapter 2, Amsterdam: North-Holland, 139–82.
Schoot, C.R.A, van der (2006), *Organised Crime Prevention in the Netherlands: Exposing the Effectiveness of Preventive Measures*, Amsterdam: Boom Juridische Uitgevers.
Takats, Elod (2007). 'A theory of "crying wolf": the economics of money laundering enforcement', IMF Working Paper No. 07/81, April, http://ssrn.com/abstract=979035.
United Nations Office on Drugs and Crime (UNODC) (2006), *World Drug Report 2006*, 2 volumes, http://www.unodc.org/pdf/WDR_2006/wdr2006_volume1.pdf
Unger, Brigitte (2007), *The Scale and Impacts of Money Laundering*, Cheltenham UK and Northampton, MA, USA: Edward Elgar.
Unger, Brigitte, Greg Rawlings, Madalina Busuioc, Joras Ferwerda, Melissa Siegel, Wouter de Kruijf and Kristen Wokke (2006), 'The amounts and the effects of money laundering: report for the Dutch Ministry of Finance', February, The Hague: Dutch Ministry of Finance, http://www.minfin.nl
Van Waarden, Frans (1995), 'Persistence of national policy styles: a study of their institutional foundations', in Brigitte Unger and Frans van Waarden (eds), *Convergence or Diversity? Internationalization and Economic Policy Response*, Aldershot: Avebury, 333–72.
Van Waarden, Frans (1999), 'European Harmonization of national regulatory styles?', in John Vervaele et al. (eds), *Compliance and Enforcement of European Community Law*. Deventer: Kluwer Law, 95–124.
Van Waarden, Frans (2001), 'Institutions and innovation: the legal environment of innovating firms', 22(5) *Organization Studies* 765–95.
Van Waarden, Frans (2002), 'Market institutions as communicating vessels: changes between economic coordination principles as a consequence of deregulation policies', in J. Rogers Hollingsworth, Karl H. Mueller, Ellen Jane Hollingsworth (eds), *Advancing Socio-Economics: An Institutionalist Perspective*, Lanham, Boulder, New York and Oxford: Rowman and Littlefield, 171–212.
Van Waarden, Frans (2006), 'Werk in een wantrouwende wereld. Omvang en oorzaken van een uitdijende controle-industrie' ('Work in a distrustful world: size and causes of an expanding control-industry'), 33(4) *Beleid en Maatschappij*, 232–51.
Van Waarden, Frans (2009), 'Power to the legal professionals. Is there an Americanization of European law?', 3(3) *Regulation and Governance*, 197–216.
Van Waarden, Frans and Youri Hildebrand (2009), 'From corporatism to lawyocracy. On liberalization and juridification', 3(3) *Regulation and Governance*, 259–86.
Voelzkow, Helmut (1996), *Private Regierungen in der Techniksteuerung, eine sozialwissenschaftliche Analyse der technischen Normung*, Frankfurt am Main: Campus Verlag.
Vogel, David (1986), *National Styles of Regulation: Environmental Policy in Great Britain and the United States*, Ithaca and London: Cornell University Press.
Walker, John (1995), 'Estimates of the extent of money laundering in and through Australia', paper prepared

for the Australian Transaction Reports and Analysis Center, September 1995, Queanbeyan: John Walker Consulting Services.
Walker, John (1999), 'How big is global money laundering?', 3(1) *Journal of Money Laundering Control* 25–37.
Walker, John (2005), 'Global illicit drugs trades', study done for UN, see UNODC (2006).
Wilson, Graham K. (1985), *The Politics of Safety and Health*, Oxford: Clarendon Press.
Zini & Associates (2002), *Money Laundering Prevention in the US*, 17 September, http://www.altassets.net/casefor/countries/2002/nz2627.php

30. Reporting duty for lawyers versus legal privilege – unresolved tension

*Maaike Stouten and André Tilleman**

The reporting duty pursuant to the EU AML/CTF legislation is precarious. Can lawyers who have a duty to secrecy be forced to report clients for money laundering or terrorist financing? Exceptions to the reporting duty in case of legal privilege are left, to some extent, to the EU Member States. This contribution shows that questions surrounding the AML/CTF reporting duty are not yet resolved, and seem to ask for a more harmonised approach of the legal privilege exemption in the Member States.

30.1 INTRODUCTION

The right to confidential communication between the client and the lawyer[1] is an important fundamental value in democratic societies.[2] It allows the client the opportunity to obtain access to expert legal advice in order to learn the contents of the client's legal position without the interference of any external party. This is important in today's complex society, in which it is difficult to know one's rights without the assistance of a professional legal adviser. This right of the client to confidentiality is combined with a duty of secrecy of the lawyer.[3] In this chapter we refer to this as 'legal privilege'.

'Legal privilege' is approached differently in various jurisdictions with regard to *inter alia* (i) the professionals that it applies to, and (ii) the scope of it. In most EU Member States it may apply both in contentious and non-contentious situations.[4] It may be applied to lawyers only, to lawyers and notaries, or to lawyers, notaries, tax advisers and also accountants. In this chapter we focus solely on the right to confidential communication with the lawyer, leaving aside the other mentioned professionals.[5]

With the adoption of the Second Directive, lawyers have been placed under the range of the anti-money laundering (AML) directive.[6] This directive entails two main obligations: on the one hand a duty to client due diligence,[7] and on the other hand a duty to report a suspicious transaction of money laundering to the competent authority.[8] For lawyers, this competent authority could be a Financial Intelligence Unit ('FIU') or a self-regulatory body.[9] The Second Directive was replaced by Directive 2005/60/EC ('Third Directive') whereby the reporting duty was extended to also cover suspicions of terrorist financing.[10] Notwithstanding the extension of the reporting duty, the scope of the reporting obligation and exceptions thereto remain the same.

The duty to report a suspicious transaction ('the reporting duty') contrasts with the confidential relationship that is supposed to exist between a lawyer and his client, and thus with the duty to secrecy underlying the legal privilege principle. In short: it contradicts 'legal privilege'.

In this chapter we will discuss the arguments underlying the conflict that exists between these two duties. We will commence by looking at the protection of the legal privilege principle by the European Court of Justice ('ECJ') and the European Court of Human Rights ('ECtHR'). This is followed by some remarks concerning the general international and European framework on anti-money laundering and combating of terrorist financing. This international framework consists of the so-called Forty (40) Recommendations of the Financial Action Task Force ('FATF'),[11] and the EU framework set up by the EU directives.[12] Thereafter, we will go into more detail with regard to the obligation of lawyers to make a report. Within this context, we will discuss a court case that evolved around this subject. We will conclude with some brief observations.

30.2 THE LEGAL PRIVILEGE PRINCIPLE PROTECTED BY THE ECJ AND THE ECtHR

As said before, we use the term 'legal privilege' to define the confidential relationship between the lawyer and his or her client. In most Member States it applies, whether or not the client consults his lawyer in a contentious or non-contentious situation. The legal privilege principle as such is uncodified; however, it is a principle of EU law where acknowledgement (i.e. protection) of legal privilege may, *inter alia*, be based on the EU Charter[13] and ECHR.[14]

The ECJ ruled for the first time on the concept of legal privilege in the AM&S case.[15] In this case, the ECJ had to decide whether and how legal professional privilege applied in EC law, and the extent of the client's right to confidential communication with his lawyer.[16] The ECJ concluded that (i) (written) communication between lawyer and client are protected in connection with the client's rights of defence and (ii) that such exchange of communication must be between the client and an independent lawyer; that is, any lawyer allowed to practise his profession in a Member State and not bound to the client by a relationship of employment. The ECJ reconfirmed these conditions in the Akzo Nobel case.[17] As such, legal privilege was determined solely in relation to the principle enshrined in Article 6 ECHR that allows individuals the right to a fair trial, including the right to defence.

In the meantime, legal privilege has also been dealt with by the 'ECtHR' in relation to Articles 6 and 8 of the European Convention on Human Rights ('ECHR'). Article 8 ECHR governs the right to confidential communication between a client and his lawyer, whatever the aim of such contact.[18] There are several cases in which the ECtHR ruled on infringements of legal privilege; however, for the scope of legal privilege the Campbell case is of great importance.[19] In *Campbell v. England* the ECtHR ruled:[20]

> It is clearly in the general interest that any person who wishes to consult a lawyer should be free to do so under conditions which favour full and uninhibited discussion. It is for this reason that the lawyer–client relationship, is in principle, privileged . . . [para 46] . . . Admittedly, . . . the borderline between mail concerning contemplated litigation and that of a general nature is especially difficult to draw and correspondence with a lawyer may concern matters which have little or nothing to do with litigation. Nevertheless, the Court sees no reason to distinguish between the different categories of correspondence with lawyers which, whatever their

> purposes, concern matters of a private and confidential character. In principle, such letters are privileged under Article 8 . . . [para 48]

We conclude on the basis of the foregoing, that legal privilege, as interpreted by the ECtHR, may extend to all types of contact between a lawyer and his client, whether or not this is in relation to litigation or legal advice.[21] In the case law of the ECJ, the protection seems less, as it relates only to the rights of defence. The starting point of protection in this regard should however be the ECHR, as interpreted by the ECtHR. This is based on the fact that the EU Charter refers to case law of the ECtHR, and the assumption that follows the principle 'not less, but rather more protection'.[22]

This being the case, what does legal privilege mean in relation to the reporting obligation pursuant to the FATF Recommendations and the Third Directive? Let us first explain these legal frameworks.

30.3 FATF – AND THE EUROPEAN AML/CTF FRAMEWORK

For the purposes of this chapter, it is worth looking at Recommendation 22 (previously 12) of the Forty (40) Recommendations, especially as it governs the applicability to lawyers. The EU directives are to a great extent inspired by these Recommendations and are an instrument to clarify the scope of the duties laid down in the Third Directive.[23]

There are differences between the FATF standards and the Third Directive.[24] An example concerns the fact that lawyers have a reporting obligation pursuant to Article 22 of the Third Directive that relates to all of the activities, whereas Recommendation 20 (previously 13) provides a reporting obligation in case it concerns funds that are the proceeds of a criminal activity.[25] A more noteworthy difference from a legal perspective is however, that the FATF standards are soft law, whereas the EU directives are binding on the Member States. We will not discuss these differences here, as they fall outside the scope of this contribution. A point of concern could, however, be differences in interpretation and harmonisation that may arise amongst Member States, as some of them may prove to be more willing to be influenced by 'obligations' following from the FATF standards than others.[26]

When looking at the type of lawyers' work involved, both sets of standards (generally and summarised) provide that lawyers are subject to the anti-money laundering/combating of terrorist financing rules when they perform assistance in the case of the following material subjects:

(i) buying or selling of real estate or business entities;
(ii) managing of client money, securities or other assets;
(iii) (opening or) management of bank, savings or securities accounts;
(iv) organisation of contributions (necessary) for the creation, operation or management of companies;
(v) creation, operation or management of trusts, companies or similar structures.[27]

Furthermore, both sets of standards generally determine that a reporting obligation applies in the case that any reason of suspicion occurs.[28]

In order to understand the extent of the standards that apply, it is also necessary to peruse any applicable exemptions. The Third Directive determines on the one hand that Member States are not obliged (a) to force lawyers *not to* carry out a transaction or terminate a business relationship, and consider making a report to the FIU, in case certain customer due diligence measures cannot be performed, and on the other hand (b) to apply the reporting obligations to lawyers, in case either of these two mentioned situations occur '*in the course of ascertaining the legal position for their client or performing their task of defending or representing that client in, or concerning judicial proceedings, including advice on instituting or avoiding proceedings*, whether such information is received or obtained before, during or after such proceedings'.[29]

Pursuant to the interpretive note to Recommendation 23 (previously 16), lawyers are not required to report a suspicious transaction if that information came to their knowledge in a situation covered by legal privilege. According to the Interpretative Note to this recommendation, it is up to each jurisdiction to determine what matters would fall under legal professional privilege or professional secrecy. The interpretative Note to Recommendation 23 second paragraph reads:

> It is for each jurisdiction to determine the matters that would fall under legal professional privilege or professional secrecy. This would normally cover information lawyers, notaries or other independent legal professionals receive from or obtain through one of their clients: (a) in the course of ascertaining the legal position of their client, or (b) in performing their task of defending or representing that client in, or concerning judicial, administrative, arbitration or mediation proceedings . . .[30]

Judging from the content and structure of this Interpretative Note (using points a and b separately), one may assume that a broad interpretation of legal privilege seems intended.

This being the case, it appears that the ground rule is that the Member States meet the obligations pursuant to the EU directive, but a facultative exception seems to be allowed, whereas it reads that Member States are not obliged to require that those obligations apply to lawyers in certain situations. It is however unclear, what should be understood by the exemption '*in the course of ascertaining the legal position for their client or performing their task of defending or representing that client in, or concerning judicial proceedings, including advice on instituting or avoiding proceedings*'. Does this mean that each Member State is at liberty to apply its own national legal privilege exception? Below we will endeavour to shed light on this by reference to an important ECJ judgment on the matter.

30.4 CASE C-305/05 *ORDRE DES BARREAUX ET AL. v. COUNCIL OF MINISTERS* ('BELGIUM CASE')[31]

The Belgian bar, supported by some other bar associations, initiated a court case seeking the annulment of certain articles of the Belgium law implementing the Second Directive.[32] The Belgian court sought a preliminary ruling from the ECJ on the legality of the reporting duty to lawyers pursuant to the Second Directive in relation to *inter alia* Article 6 ('Right to a fair trial') of the ECHR.[33]

In the *Ordre des Barreaux* case the ECJ determined:

> 33 As was pointed out in paragraph 22 above, it is clear from Article 2a(5) of Directive 91/308 that the obligations of information and cooperation apply to lawyers only in so far as they advise their client in the preparation or execution of certain transactions – essentially those of a financial nature or concerning real estate, as referred to in Article 2a(5)(a) of that directive – or when they act on behalf of and for their client in any financial or real estate transaction. As a rule, the nature of such activities is such that they take place in a context with no link to judicial proceedings and, consequently, those activities fall outside the scope of the right to a fair trial.
>
> 34 Moreover, as soon as the lawyer acting in connection with a transaction as referred to in Article 2a(5) of Directive 91/308 is called upon for assistance in defending the client or in representing him before the courts, or for advice as to the manner of instituting or avoiding judicial proceedings, that lawyer is exempt, by virtue of the second subparagraph of Article 6(3) of the directive, from the obligations laid down in Article 6(1),[34] regardless of whether the information has been received or obtained before, during or after the proceedings. An exemption of that kind safeguards the right of the client to a fair trial.
>
> 35 Given that the requirements implied by the right to a fair trial presuppose, by definition, a link with judicial proceedings, and in view of the fact that the second subparagraph of Article 6(3) of Directive 91/308 exempts lawyers, where their activities are characterised by such a link, from the obligations of information and cooperation laid down in Article 6(1) of the directive, those requirements are respected.
>
> 36 On the other hand, it must be recognised that the requirements relating to the right to a fair trial do not preclude the obligations of information and cooperation laid down in Article 6(1) of Directive 91/308 from being imposed on lawyers acting specifically in connection with the activities listed in Article 2a(5) of that directive, in cases where the second subparagraph of Article 6(3) of that directive does not apply, where those obligations are justified by the need . . . to combat money laundering effectively, in view of its evident influence on the rise of organised crime, which itself is a particular threat to society in the Member States.

The ECJ then concludes that the reporting obligation pursuant to Article 6(1) Second Directive and imposed on lawyers – and account being taken of the exception thereof laid down in subparagraph 2 of Art. 6(3) – does not infringe the right to a fair trial as guaranteed by Article 6 ECHR and Article 6(2) EU.

The ECJ decides such that the Second Directive provides an exemption to the whole area that Article 6 ECHR refers to. This exemption under the EU directives applies as soon as the lawyer is requested to provide assistance in 'defending the client or in representing him before the courts, or for advice as to the manner of instituting or avoiding judicial proceedings'.[35] The ECJ ruling makes clear that the facultative exception formulated in the Second Directive is obligatory in case the rights of defence are concerned. The case remains important after the entry into force of the Third Directive, as the reporting duty and the exception thereto in case of legal privilege circumstances are the same in these directives.

This being the outcome, the judgment received various reactions.[36] These mainly concern the limited basis that the ECJ takes into account in this situation by referring to Article 6 ECHR and not judging on the concept of legal privilege dealt with by the ECtHR on the basis of Articles 6 and 8 ECHR. Furthermore, what is to be understood by the exception 'ascertaining the legal position' – an important phrase to understand the exact scope of legal privilege – remains (also) unclear.

30.5 CONCLUSION – OBSERVATIONS

In the case of *Reporting Duty v. Legal Privilege*, the outcome remains fairly uncertain.

The *Ordre de Barreaux* case indicates that the EU directives that provide a reporting obligation to lawyers, are permissible as long as legal privilege remains protected in the situation where a link with judicial proceedings is present. This is, however, one area where legal privilege has its function. So far, the question has not been solved in non-contentious circumstances.

The *Ordre de Barreaux* case also reveals that the interpretation of 'ascertaining the legal position' is open to interpretation by national courts, as the judgment of the Belgian Constitutional Court (that followed after the ECJ's judgment) shows.[37] The Belgian court applied a broad interpretation of the ECJ's judgment. In a similar situation in France, the French court did the same.[38] On the contrary, the Polish, Finnish and Dutch legislation apply a narrow interpretation.[39]

If we now return and look at both the Recommendations and EU directives, one may conclude that a certain level of harmonisation may ensue in case the type of work of the lawyer falls under the ambit of EU AML/CTF legislation. It must, however, be noted that such harmonisation fails when exceptions under the definition 'ascertaining the legal position' may vary. The latter seems to be the case where the Recommendations, on the one hand, allow for each jurisdiction to determine itself what the contents of 'legal privilege' are and the European Union allows, on the other hand, a national interpretation of 'ascertaining the legal position'. In other words: what level playing field will arise if harmonised AML/CTF identification and reporting obligations – and all supplementary rules – see the light, but exceptions thereto remain for the national legislator to decide?

It appears that efficiency in combatting 'money laundering' and 'terrorist financing' is not reaching the level internationally aimed for. This problem is even bigger if one realises that a great variety exists amongst the professionals in the Member States that may invoke the legal privilege exception.

ABBREVIATIONS

AB	*Administratiefrechtelijke Beslissingen*
AG	*Advocate General*
AML	Anti-money laundering
CMLRev	*Common Market Law Review*
CTF	Combating of Terrorist Financing
ECJ	European Court of Justice, Luxembourg
ECHR	European Convention on Human Rights
ECtHR	European Court of Human Rights, Strasbourg
EU	European Union
FATF	Financial Action Task Force
First Directive	Council Directive 91/308/EEC of 10 June 1991 on prevention of the use of the financial system for the purpose of money laundering, OJ L 166/77, 28/06/1991
FIU	Financial Intelligence Unit

NJB	*Nederlands Juristenblad*
Second Directive	Directive 2001/97/EC of the European Parliament and of the Council of 4 December 2001 amending Council Directive 91/308/EEC on prevention of the use of the financial system for the purpose of money laundering, OJ L 344/76 28/12/2001
SEW	*Tijdschrift voor Europees en economisch recht*
Third Directive	Directive 2005/60/EC of the European Parliament and of the Council of 26 October 2005 on the prevention of the use of the financial system for the purpose of money laundering and terrorist financing, OJ L309/20, 25.11.2005

NOTES

* This contribution is on a personal title. The views expressed in this chapter are entirely personal.

1. We use the term 'lawyer', meaning the advocaat, advocate, avvocato, barrister/solicitor, member of a bar or law society and subject to professional rules of conduct and not subject to a relationship of employment with his or her client.
2. See nr. 1, 29 and especially part III Opinion AG Maduro in: ECJ 26 juni 2007, C-305/05, [2007] ECR I-5305 (*Ordre des barreaux*).
3. See also Tilleman (2007).
4. See also AG Slynn/Warner in: ECJ 18 May 1982, C-155/79, [1982] ECR, p. 1575; *NJ* 1983, 150 (*AM&S/Commissie*) and see also Edward (1976) and Ehlermann and Oldekop (1977). See also European Commission DG International Market and Services-Budget (2009, 247ff).
5. The problems we reveal in this chapter may, however, also be present in relation to these other professionals.
6. Article 2a Directive 2001/97/EC of the European Parliament and of the Council of 4 December 1991 amending [the First Directive:] Council Directive 91/308/EEC on prevention of the use of the financial system for the purpose of money laundering, OJ L 344/76, 28.12.2001 ('Second Directive').
7. Article 3 Second Directive. See also Chapter II Third Directive.
8. Articles 6–10 Second Directive. See also Chapter III Third Directive. Note that some Member States require the reporting of an unusual transaction. See for example: The Netherlands, Article 16 Money Laundering and Terrorist Financing Prevention Act. For a brief description of these duties, see Chapter 27, this volume, by Van den Broek and Addink, section 27.2.
9. Article 6 (3) Second Directive. See also Article 23 Third Directive.
10. Directive 2005/60/EC of the European Parliament and of the Council of 26 October 2005 on the prevention of the use of the financial system for the purpose of money laundering and terrorist financing, OJ L309/20, 25.11.2005 ('Third Directive').
11. Financial Action Task Force, see http://www.fatf-gafi.org
12. As mentioned in notes 6 and 10.
13. Articles 7, 41 paragraphs 1 and 2, 47 and 48 paragraph 2 Charter of fundamental rights of the European Union – 30–3–2010, OJ EU C 83/38.
14. Articles 6 and 8 ECHR. See also AG Slynn/Warner in: ECJ 18 May 1982, C-155/79, [1982] ECR, p. 1575; *NJ* 1983, 150 (*AM&S/Commissie*) and see also Edward (1976) and Ehlermann and Oldekop (1977). See also European Commission DG International Market and Services-Budget (2009, 247ff.).
15. ECJ 18 May 1982, C-155/79, [1982] ECR, p. 1575; *NJ* 1983, 150 (*AM&S/Commissie*).
16. See also Bo Vesterdorf (2005, 1184).
17. ECJ 14 September 2010, C-550/07P (*Akzo Nobel/Commission*), see § 40–41. From this case it is also clear that legal privilege does not apply to the 'in-house lawyer', as such a lawyer is presumed not to be (so) independent due to the existence of a relationship of employment with the entity that he or she acts for.
18. AG Maduro, nr. 43 in: ECJ 26 juni 2007, C-305/05, [2007] ECR I-5305 *(Ordre des barreaux)* as mentioned in Stouten 2012, Chapter 3.3.6).
19. For an overview of cases and remarks, Stouten 2012, Chapter 3.4).
20. ECtHR 25 March 1992, nr. 13590/88 (*Campbell v. England*) para. 46 and 48 – see Stouten 2012, Chapter 3.4.6).
21. See also Stouten 2012, subconclusion 3.4.8 and conclusion 3.6).

22. Article 52 (3) EU Charter.
23. See for example recital 5 Third Directive.
24. See Joeb Rietrae (2007). See also van den Broek (2011).
25. See Rietrae (2007), notes 52 and 53.
26. Note also the difference in wording (and presumably scope) in: 'lawyers . . . prepare for or carry out transactions (FATF) and 'lawyers . . . when they participate, whether by acting on behalf of and for their client in a financial or real estate transaction, or by assisting in the planning or execution of . . . ' (Third Directive).
27. Article 2a para 5 Second Directive. Article 2 para 1 under 3(b) Third Directive. Recommendation 22(d) in conjunction with 23(a) FATF.
28. See Article 22 Third Directive and Recommendation 23 (a) in conjunction with 20 FATF.
29. Article 9 para 5 part 2 and Article 23 para 2 Third Directive respectively. The words in italics are literally the same in articles 9 para 5 subpara 2 and article 23 para 2 Third Directive. Article 23 para 2 has the added wording 'whether such information is received or obtained before, during or after such proceedings'.
30. See also Stouten 2012 chapter 6.2.1. and Adrienne Margolis (2005) with also a reference to FATF President Professor Kader Asmal: 'The FATF adds that Recommendation 16 [old, see Recommendation 23 new + interpretative note] "takes full account of legal professional privilege or professional secrecy which may apply in many jurisdictions." Also, the way in which countries apply the recommendations is left to them, so they can maintain "the fundamental principles of their laws such as legal professional privilege". Despite these assurances, both the IBA and the CCBE report concerns over the effects of changes in money laundering rules from Bar Associations all over the world . . . '.
31. Case C-305/05, European Court of Justice, 26 June 2007 [2007] E.C.R. I-5305. See Stouten 2012 chapter 3.3.6 and Luchtman and van der Hoeven (2009).
32. As seen before: the Second Directive 2001/97 amends the First Directive 91/308.
33. Article 6 of the Convention for the Protection of Human Rights and Fundamental Freedoms ('ECHR').
34. Article 6 First Directive 91/308 (equivalent Article 22 Third Directive).
35. Para 34, Case C-305/05.
36. Luchtman and Van der Hoeven (2009) ibid Komárek (2008); CCBE (2007); Stouten 2012 chapter 3.3.6; Stouten (2007).
37. Belgian Constitutional Court 23 January 2008, nr. 10/2008, http://www.grondwettelijkhof.be
38. Conseil d'État 10 April 2008, Conseil national des barreaux et al. nr. 296845, 29690, http://www.conseil-etat.fr
39. See Stouten 2012, chapters 5.2.5, 5.6.3, 6.2 and 6.3; AG Maduro, nr. 57 referring to his note 48 in Case C-305/0

REFERENCES

Broek, M. Van den (2011), 'Gelijkwaardigheid in het anti-witwasbeleid: de FATF en de EU' [Equivalence in AML policy: the FATF and the EU], *SEW* 2011/10, 422–8.

CCBE (2007), CCBE press release 26 June – http://www.ccbe.eu

Edward, D.A.O. (1976), *The Professional Secret, Confidentiality and Legal Professional Privilege in the Nine Member States of the European Community*.

Ehlermann, C.D. and D. Oldekop (1977), *Due Process in Administrative Procedure*, 3 FIDE.

European Commission DG International Market and Services-Budget (2009), 'Final Study on the Application of the Anti-Money Laundering Directive' [ETD/2009/IM/F2/90] 'Deloitte Report'.

Komárek, J. (2008), 'Legal professional privilege and the EU's fight against money laundering', *Civil Justice Quarterly*, **27**, http://ssrn.com/abstract=1031721

Luchtman M.J.J.P. and R. van der Hoeven (2009), Case C-305/05, Ordre des barreaux francophones et germanophone et al. v. Conseil des Ministres, judgment of the Court of Justice of 26 June 2007, Grand Chamber; [2007] ECR I-5305, *CMLRev* 2009, nr 46, 301–18.

Margolis, A. (2005), 'Gatekeepers or policemen? Third Money Laundering Directive a step too far', *International Bar News*, October, 7.

Rietrae, J. (2007), 'The 3rd EU Anti-money Laundering Directive: main issues and intriguing details', in P.C. Van Duyne et al. (eds), *Crime Business and Crime Money in Europe: The Dirty Linen of Illicit Enterprise*,Nijmegen: Wolf Legal Publishers, 15–42.

Stouten, M. (2007), 'Meldplicht witwaspraktijken niet in strijd met artikel 6 EVRM. HvJ EG 26 juni 2007, C-305/05', *NJB* 2007, 1959, afl. 38, 2432–7, and *AB* 2007/45, 369.

Stouten, M. (2012), *De witwasmeldplicht. Omvang en handhaving van de Wwft-meldplicht voor juridische en fiscale dienstverleners* [The anti-money laundering reporting duty. Scope and enforcement of the Dutch reporting duty for legal and fiscal service providers], thesis, Den Haag: Boom Juridische uitgevers.
Tilleman, A.T.A. (2007), 'Money laundering and the professional sector – supervision of lawyers and civil-law notaries in the Netherlands – what about professional secrecy?' in P.C Van Duyne et al.(eds), *Crime Business and Crime Money in Europe: The Dirty Linen of Illicit Enterprise*, Nijmegen: Wolf Legal Publishers, 43–68.
Vesterdorf, B. (2005), 'Legal professional privilege and the privilege against self-incrimination in EC Law: recent developments and current issues', *Fordham International Law Journal*, **28**(4), 1179–215.

CASE LAW

ECtHR 25 March 1992, nr. 13590/88 (*Campbell v. England*)
ECJ 26 juni 2007, C-305/05, [2007] ECR I-5305; *AB* 2006/390, m.nt. Stouten (*Ordre des barreaux)*
ECJ 18 May 1982, C-155/79, [1982] ECR, p. 1575; *NJ* 1983, 150 (*AM&S/Commissie*)
ECJ 14 September 2010, C-550/07P, not yet published (*Akzo Nobel/Commission*)
Belgian Constitutional Court 23 January 2008, nr. 10/2008, http://www.grondwettelijkhof.be
Conseil d'État 10 April 2008, Conseil national des barreaux et al, nr. 296845, 29690, http://www.conseil-etat.fr

31. Money laundering – 'You don't see it, until you understand it': rethinking the stages of the money laundering process to make enforcement more effective

Jan van Koningsveld

31.1 INTRODUCTION

Money laundering is considered to be a serious threat to the financial system, both at a national and an international level. On a regular basis, media coverage directs its attention at fraud cases in which money laundering plays a major role. Given the relevance and seriousness of the problem, it is not surprising that policy makers have made quite some effort to tackle money laundering. However, several publications highlight that the approach to combating money laundering has numerous shortcomings and does not appear to be truly effective. The main reasons are a combination of a lack of (a) sufficient knowledge and skills, and (b) the capacity of law enforcement officers regarding the techniques and methods of money laundering (Algemene Rekenkamer 2008, p. 20).

In my opinion, the classic idea of money laundering as a three-phase process is not only incorrect and incomplete, but also antiquated (see Figure 31.1). My criticism does not concern the first two stages, but the third. I am of the opinion that this final stage should be subdivided into two separate parts, being *justification* and finally *investment* (integration), in order to avoid serious mistakes in legislation and investigation. The

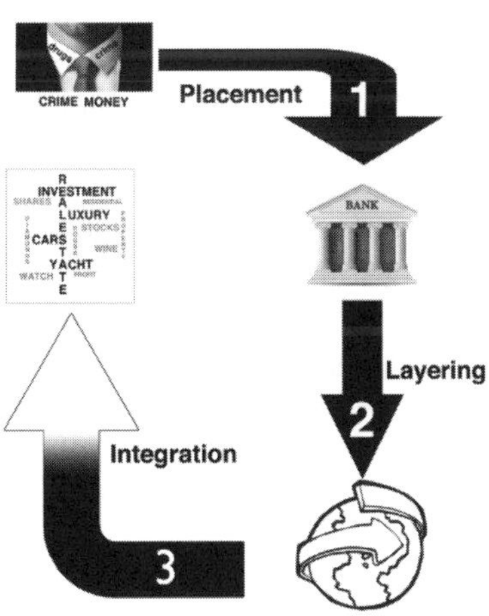

Source: Own graph 2012.

Figure 31.1 The classic 3-phase money laundering process

three-stage model is a misconception that has undesirable consequences, both legally (legislation and regulations) and practically (investigation, prosecution and transfer of knowledge) (see also Van Duyne 2003, p. 79).

The third EU directive[1] proposes a more risk-oriented approach which entails that financial institutions must identify money laundering risks themselves.[2] To aid in better identifying these risks, financial institutions should be able to: (a) identify potential laundering customers; (b) do research on risk assessment; (c) follow an effective customer due diligence (CDD) policy; and (d) if the customer is a foreign legal person, identify the ultimate beneficial owner (UBO) of the foreign entity or the transaction. Another measure taken is more and better money laundering training programmes for employees.[3]

An increase in both theoretical and practical knowledge is essential to successfully combat money laundering. This applies to the (private) supervisors of the financial system as well as to the competent authorities (law enforcement). Or, as Van Duyne so eloquently put it: the government should invest more in brain cells than in prison cells.[4] A key element responsible for misunderstandings and wrong practical guidance is the current theory regarding the multi-stage money laundering process. This theory forms the foundation for most aspects of practical training. In this chapter I would like to elaborate an alternative theory, to improve and avoid the defects of the current approach.

This theoretical improvement is particularly important when one takes into account that the third EU Directive urges Member States to properly train the staff of supervisors and law enforcement involved in reporting unusual transactions.[5] This training is seen as a salient step for the third Directive to become effective. The aim is that the existing knowledge will be updated regularly, leading to better risk-assessment skills, which should result in a more efficient reporting of unusual transactions. However, this training recommendation should also apply to the authorities themselves so that these reports will lead to more effective investigation and prosecution of money laundering offences.

Although still in its formative years, anti-money laundering (AML) policy and the connected confiscation policy go back almost 20 years. The fight against money laundering still draws attention. The question is whether our views have also developed with the passage of time. After all, there have been many publications on money laundering in specialist and scholarly journals, mainly supporting the present view on money laundering, apart from a few critical notes.

Due to this overwhelming consensus, little attention is paid to perceptions that may be incorrect. And, if inaccuracies are pointed out at all, there does not seem to be a real debate going on; criticism is merely taken note of before going on to business as usual.

Section 31.2 explains differences in the definition of money laundering, section 31.3 describes the incumbent three-stage system, followed by its consequences. The challenging four-stage system is then laid out in more detail and exemplified with a case study in section 31.6 before conclusions are drawn in section 31.7.

31.2 WHAT EXACTLY IS MONEY LAUNDERING?

When Unger (2006, pp. 30–35) conducted a literature research, she found no less than 18 different definitions of money laundering.[6] From these 18 however, in my opinion two core elements can be distinguished:

1. Concealing the actual origin of the money (actions that mainly take place in the 2nd stage);
2. Giving a legal origin to money, which was obtained from crime (actions that mainly take place in the 3rd stage).[7]

Chaikin (1992) stated this second core element aptly: 'Creating a justification for controlling or possessing assets is the essence of money laundering' (p. 63).

Therefore, the core of this action concept of money laundering is the conversion (on paper) of money originating from crime into legally obtained money. It should be regarded as a paper/digital transformation process which – by definition – concerns the creation of a false origin, other than the real origin of the money. Therefore, the mere spending or possession of criminal money does not fall under the *empirical* definition of money laundering even if in legal terms this is qualified as laundering too.

31.3 THE CLASSICAL THREE STAGES CONCEPT

Literature based within the incumbent three-stage framework divides the money laundering process into three stages: placement, layering and investment.[8] This has been the classic three stages theory since 1990. However, the question is whether this classification reflects actual practice. As previously mentioned, in my opinion the third stage must be subdivided into two separate stages: the *justification stage* and the *investment stage*.

Historically speaking, studying the stages of the money laundering process was based on the relatively simple problem that existed in the 1980s, which mainly concerned the transfer of large amounts of cash which originated in the drug trade and were deposited in cash in banks.[9] At that time, the US received a lot of cocaine from Colombia and the US government became more and more concerned about the large quantities of its currency leaving the country. Money laundering was put on the political agenda as an (international) problem when the US once more intensified the 'war against drugs'. This concerned the fight against a cash economy. This cash economy was characterised by profits in small denominations, obtained from the street trade in drugs. From this very traditional perspective the Financial Action Task Force on Money Laundering[10] (FATF) distinguished the above-mentioned money laundering stages that since became entrenched within AML theory. Schaap (2007) stated the following about the creation of the stages in the money laundering process:[11]

> This theory was created by the US investigation service DEA [Drug Enforcement Agency] in the late 1980s. This service tried to explain and simplify the current money laundering practice for its colleagues. It used the three-stage model. At the time the DEA was mainly conducting investigations into drug trafficking and had little experience with financial investigations.

Subsequently, in 1986 the three-stage model was introduced in the first US AML legislation: the Money Laundering Control Act. After this, the three-stage notion was embraced by the FATF who spread it over the rest of world like a virus through cutting and pasting. The same uncritical 'cut and paste jobs' remain nearly ubiquitous in the present literature.

Given the problem of the large quantities of cocaine money, the US DEA preference for three stages is understandable. In fact, the US DEA only saw large sums of money, literally bags full, being transported and deposited in banks or brought outside the country. As a result, the initial measures taken were aimed at these types of monetary transactions and at financial institutions in general (more specifically, banks). It was in this environment, dealing only with drug crimes, that the DEA developed the three stages of money laundering. Because the concept of money laundering has become more complicated, the classic three-stage model needs a refinement. In my opinion splitting up this stage is not only a refinement, but actually contributes to a correct understanding of the money laundering phenomenon through reinterpretation. This reinterpretation applies to a large number of divergent criminal offences that are not committed in the cash economy of the drug trade. Below, I will first describe the classic stages briefly and will then give my alternative ideas about the subdivision of the third stage.

31.3.1 The First Phase: Placement

The essence of the placement stage is that the cash proceeds of a crime are brought into the financial system and, therefore, are made transferable.[12] As a result, the money is easier to move around. This can be done in different ways but it nearly always involves financial institutions. In many cases the money is transferred or brought in cash from the country where it was earned to another country where it can be put into the financial system safely. Sometimes the money is first exchanged for larger denominations to help facilitate its transportation or conversion into other currencies, which is the first step to concealing the origin and ownership.

Recently, a new weapon against money laundering was deployed in the EU: the EU Regulation on liquid resources that came into force on 15 June 2007.[13] This regulation aims to increase the control on cash entering or leaving the EU.[14] In practice this means that a natural person who imports or exports more than €10,000 in cash is obliged to declare this to Customs.

For the owners of the cash proceeds of crime, this is a dangerous stage with many opportunities for the supervisory bodies and investigation services to detect transactions (or to have them reported by the financial institutions). Depositing the money also starts with what is known as an 'accounting trail'. This connects money transactions with their administrative records and plays an important role in the gathering of evidence in criminal investigations.

31.3.2 The Second Phase: Layering

In this second stage, the criminal money is brought into the legal financial system and can be used for different purposes. The main purpose is to further conceal the origin and ownership of the initial criminal money by transferring the same money several times (Schaap et al. 1992, p. 8). The initial sum of money is divided into smaller sums or 'layers': 'layering'. This often involves international structures of offshore companies consisting of legal entities in different countries, between which money is moved back and forth by means of transfers.[15] There usually is no logical economic reason for these money transactions.[16] In fact, they only give rise to transaction costs, a fixed amount for maintaining the structure of companies, costs of devising and setting up the structure and costs of managing the foreign legal entities.

The impression is given that it concerns transactions between independent parties, whereas in reality one and the same person controls everything. Business transactions are often purported to be the reason for the transfers, using false documents, for example contracts or invoices, usually with a vague description of non-material services such as 'management fee' or something similar, to suggest a legal origin.[17]

Concealing the initial origin differs from giving the criminal money a different origin (justification). Even if one could not prove its criminal origin, the owner of this money is not (yet) able to prove that he/she has obtained it lawfully. Therefore, he/she remains vulnerable.

31.3.3 The Third Phase: Integration

Available literature describes this third stage as the stage in which all the transactions are aimed at 'integrating' the money into the legitimate economy. In this last stage of the classic money laundering process, the capital, of which the criminal origin has already been concealed, is brought into the economy with a (supposed) legal origin.

This stage includes a very wide variety of economic transactions, ranging from the normal daily expenses to extremely professionally devised money laundering constructions. Therefore, the name of this stage is rather vague, although it does involve a series of actions that are very important for the investigation procedures. This is of particular concern to the justification actions. Most authors leave this problem out of consideration, others place these actions in the third stage (NIBESVV 2001, p. 2), whereas some regard these actions as a part of the second stage.[18] To put it briefly: vagueness rules.

31.4 THE ALTERNATIVE FOUR STAGES CONCEPT

The problems identified in section 31.3 have the potential to be alleviated by shifting to the four-stage model (see Figure 31.2). The essence of the four-stage model is that the third phase of the three-stage model is divided into two phases, being a third phase, called *justification*, and a fourth stage, called *investment*. The first and second phases in both models are the same. It is plausible to assume that in the future more specific justification typologies will be developed that can better aid in contributing to evidence. Finally, the four-stage model better reflects the current practice and the recent money laundering legislation.

31.4.1 The Third Phase: Justification

The *justification* of the criminal money is obviously the final act in the chain of fictitious transitions and financial movements, usually along different tax havens. It concerns a mixture of tried and tested methods and techniques as well as new examples of ingenuity.

The available methods and techniques are based on two basic principles; mainly creating fictitious income or profits or by borrowing back one's own money ('loan back construction').[19] In many cases money laundering involves 'reverse' tax fraud, in which

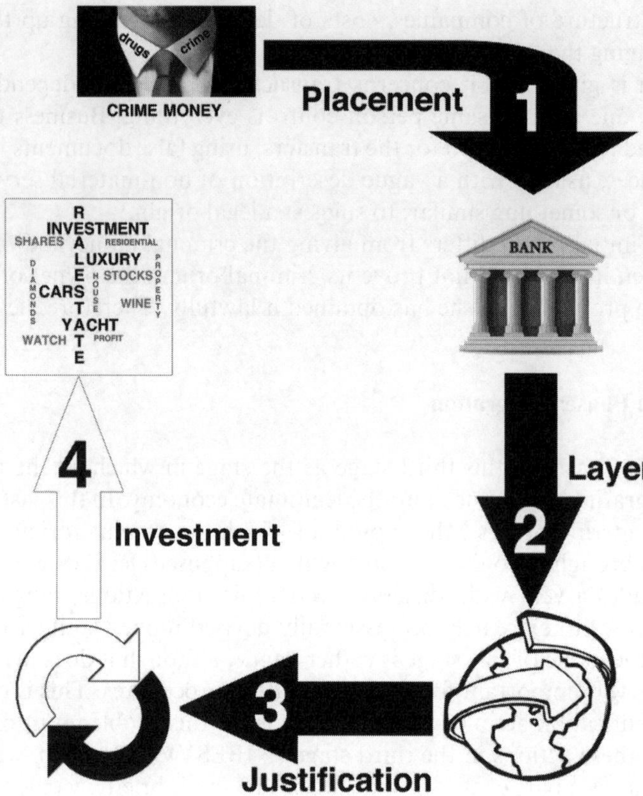

Source: Author's own graph. The colour of the arrows represent whether the money is still black or can be considered white. As one can see, it is not until after the justification phase that the money becomes white and therefore laundered.

Figure 31.2 The proposed new 4-phase money laundering process

some respective methods mirror each other. Money laundering intends to make illegally obtained income legally visible; tax fraud intends to conceal income from view.[20] Therefore, it is not strange that contrary to tax fraud, money laundering involves making paper or digital records in order to be able to demonstrate its intended legal origin. Therefore, it is important for money laundering fighters to have knowledge of fiscal constructions.

As it is a necessity to provide a legal origin, often false paper trails are set up in business accounts. After all, the financial transactions that suggest a legal origin must be expressed in the business accounts of natural persons/legal entities. This is the essence of money laundering.

The third stage, *justification*, is not always necessary. Money launderers can also decide to invest directly without arranging a justification, for instance by means of a foreign legal entity that acquires real estate directly. Money launderers are able to do this because it is difficult for the authorities to determine who is behind certain foreign legal entities and, therefore, there is little chance of being discovered. As a result, the motive for laundering criminal money no longer exists. Justification is sometimes arranged afterwards when the offender perceives that he might be discovered.

31.4.2 The Fourth Stage: Investment[21]

Investing criminal money is the final step in the series of money laundering actions and is also the aim of the whole process. After the justification, criminal money has reached its final destination and is now part of the formal economy. The ultimate goal of the money laundering process has now been reached.

It must be clear that this fourth stage involves *genuine* legal acts. If the money laundering process has gone well, not only is the origin of the money no longer traceable, but the owner of this money is also able to justify his possession of the money to the authorities. He has then converted his illegally obtained income into (registered) valuable goods, investments or production factors: an expensive car, a yacht, shares in companies quoted on the stock exchange, real estate or direct investment in companies.

31.5 CONSEQUENCES OF APPLYING AN INCORRECT THREE-STAGE MODEL

The difference of opinions regarding the various money laundering stages is not only an academic question, but is also of interest for practitioners. What follows is a list of the most important consequences of utilising a three-stage framework. These consequences are important for all the persons and institutions involved in the fight against money laundering.[22]

31.5.1 Investigation and Evidence Gathering

A criminal investigation into money laundering is often focused on the evidence that the money in question has a criminal origin.[23] The evidence can often be found in the business accounts of companies and financial institutions. This involves following (international) money movements.[24] These flows of money are recorded in the business records of companies and financial institutions such as banks and trust offices. They are money laundering's '*smoking gun*'. The money launderer attempts to justify the legality of his or her acquired criminal money. Some financial transactions will be concealed, however others must be recorded in the business accounts in order to make a legal origin plausible (on paper). In this respect it is essential that the *real* tracks are investigated and not the *false* ones. The aim is to see the 'underlying reality'.

Generally, the public prosecutor has to prove the act of money laundering. The criminal has the right to remain silent, unless the situation is calling for an explanation.[25]

31.5.2 Track Examination: Real and False Tracks or Origin and Destination/Expenditure?

In a criminal investigation it is often necessary to establish the acquisition of the capital.[26] This means that the financial track has to be followed up to the initial origin, in order to produce the evidence for 'money originating from crime'. In this respect it is important for the investigation services to know that the money laundering methods and techniques used in the third stage are intended to leave false tracks by definition, whereas the fourth stage involves real, or at least non-hidden acts. The third stage involves *bogus transactions* aimed at giving the untaxed money a *legal* origin on paper. The fourth stage involves giving the meanwhile laundered money a legal *destination/expenditure*. However, to be convicted of money laundering, a direct relationship between the object and the earlier crime must be proven.

The classical three-stage model makes no distinction between these real and fake tracks, essentially muddying the waters and further decreasing visibility. The consequence is that much time is lost following false tracks. Furthermore, it is of direct interest to the authorities to know what methods are used in the third phase, which by definition are designed and implemented to leave a false trace. In contrast to that, the fourth stage is real, where actions are intended to justify the authenticity of the money's source. The acts that make up the third stage of the four-stage model are directed to give the money from crime an apparent legal origin on paper; while in the fourth phase, money arrives at its apparent legal destination/use. This subdivision of the current model's third stage provides a distinction between the origin and destination/use of resources. In other words, the money's re-emergence into the formal economy is highlighted, better enabling one to answer the questions of where money comes from and what is its destination. These are two different flows and hence two different monetary tracks (false and real, respectively). By doing so, business economics is followed, which also distinguishes between the origin and the destination/expenditure of resources. The problem with the three-stage model is that it does not reflect the current practice of money laundering and thus erodes away the effectiveness of new AML legislation.

The investigation of a money laundering case often depends on circumstantial evidence. This is because the direct evidence that income is the result of crime is often difficult to find. It is important that facts or circumstances of notoriety do not need proof.[27]

31.5.3 Typologies and Characteristics of Money Laundering

In order to see through a money laundering process, the different acts and techniques within the various money laundering stages must be clear. Investigation officers and the public prosecutors can use the so-called money laundering 'typologies' as presented by the FATF.[28] Typologies are 'objective' characteristics of financial acts and accompanying observable phenomena that may suggest money laundering, requiring a degree of clairvoyance. Looking at these so-called typologies, one may notice hardly any attention is paid to acts that take place in the justification stage, which are all characterised by fraudulent paper work.

An addendum to the 'money laundering instruction' of the Dutch prosecutors general mentions applicable typologies. An analysis of this list shows that 18, that is almost 80 per cent of the 23 different typologies[29] relate to the first stage, the exchange and placement of money. The other five typologies (nos 4, 8, 14, 20 and 21) are difficult to categorise into a certain stage. Thus, there are no typologies mentioned that relate to the (false) justification stage. This omission results in great difficulties during the investigation process, when formulating a reasonable suspicion and when the public prosecutor decides on the acceptance and prosecution of a money laundering case.[30]

Another salient reason for having a comprehensive list of characteristics is the introduction of the third EU money laundering directive. This directive reveals a shift from a 'rule based' to a 'risk based' approach.[31] Reporting suspicious transactions on the basis of rules meant that the financial institutions started reporting everything that could somehow be reported. The result of the shift to a risk-based model was, however, that the number of reports decreased dramatically. The question is whether the quality of reports increased accordingly. With this rule- to risk-based shift, banks are advised to make a risk analysis: how likely is it that a certain monetary transaction relates to criminal money?

This dramatically increases the importance of effective risk indicators and typologies. As a result of this risk-oriented approach, more responsibility is shifted to the assessors for reporting suspicious transactions.

The analysis of ongoing and completed money laundering cases must reveal these signals, characteristics and typologies. In 2006, the FATF published a report named *Misuse of Corporate Vehicles, Trusts and Company Service Providers*[32] that proposed for the first time in 15 years that there may be four stages instead of the traditional three. Later the OECD report on taxes and money laundering also hinted at a four-stage money laundering model (OECD 2009, pp. 11, 21).

More attention is paid to money laundering in and by (foreign) legal entities, however attention is still predominantly focused on the first stage of the money laundering process. For instance, the police mainly investigate the predicate offences at the beginning of the money laundering process, that is, in the first and second stages. This is understandable from their traditional offender-oriented approach and their information position. However, as a result, less attention is being paid to intelligent and complex money laundering constructions, which often involve larger amounts of money and many transactions.

31.5.4 Knowledge and Understanding

For the effective combating of money laundering it is essential that all persons and institutions involved in AML enforcement have sufficient knowledge and understanding of the money laundering process. But as money laundering theory is still in its formative years, the literature shows that there is still insufficient knowledge of money laundering and the corresponding flows of money.[33]

The act of separating the money laundering into different phases is intended as a teaching tool to better understand the different actions and persons involved in the money laundering process. However, attention needs to be shifted more to the third and fourth phases, rather than the still dominant focus on the first phase of the money-laundering trail – particularly by police investigators, who mainly focus on the predicate offence at the start of the money laundering process. This is understandable in the light of the traditional offender-orientated approach of the police and their information position; however, this approach is not appropriate to intelligent and complex structures, which often involve larger amounts of money than in cash transactions cases.

As a result, there still is little understanding and knowledge of the money laundering methods used and the concealment instruments applied, such as offshore companies, offshore trusts, foundations, the use of nominees, etc.[34]

Considering the fact that the same old money laundering methods are still applied frequently, my conclusion is that the 'learning ability' within law enforcement agencies is not optimal and should therefore be improved.

31.6 CASE STUDIES

In this section I describe two cases which show the relevance of the four-stage model. The first case is an example of bad practice, because it resulted in an acquittal, which might have had a different outcome if the four-phase model had been applied. The second case is a best practice scenario where the criminal was caught and convicted.

31.6.1 Air Holland

The following real-life case clearly illustrates the four described stages (see Figure 31.3).[35] Although this case resulted in an acquittal it is still instructive, firstly due to the fact that all four stages of the money laundering process are apparent. The facts and circumstances regarding the cash transactions are not disputed. Secondly, it clearly illuminates that the core problem in convicting a money launderer relies on proving that the money originally comes from crime. This case shows how a court may be reluctant to convict someone even when the classic three stages are present.

31.6.1.1 Brief case description

This simplified money laundering case concerns a number of persons employed by the Dutch airline company Air Holland who were suspected of money laundering. Air Holland had been in serious financial problems for some time and urgently needed capital. At some point, Air Holland became acquainted with two brothers who most likely belonged to a criminal organisation (CO) that allegedly earned millions through the drugs trade. These brothers were prepared to invest tens of millions in the airline company. The problem was that the criminal investors only had cash money. The public prosecutor claimed that the financial director of Air Holland subsequently devised, set up and executed the international structure set out in Table 31.1, with the purpose of laundering said drug money. It is alleged that a total of approximately 25 million guilders (€11 million) was laundered in 2001 and 2002.

It is clear that the investors did not transfer the invested money directly to the bank account of Air Holland, but (from a normal business point of view) via an unnecessarily complex international route that appears to have no logical economic reason. Normally, a moneylender who invests or loans money would transfer the money to the bank account of Air Holland itself.

31.6.1.2 The legal dispute

The legal dispute concerns whether the offence is part of Article 420bis of the Dutch penal code, that states 'money derived from a crime', which has been legally and convincingly proven. The burden of proof lies in principle with the public prosecutor, however,

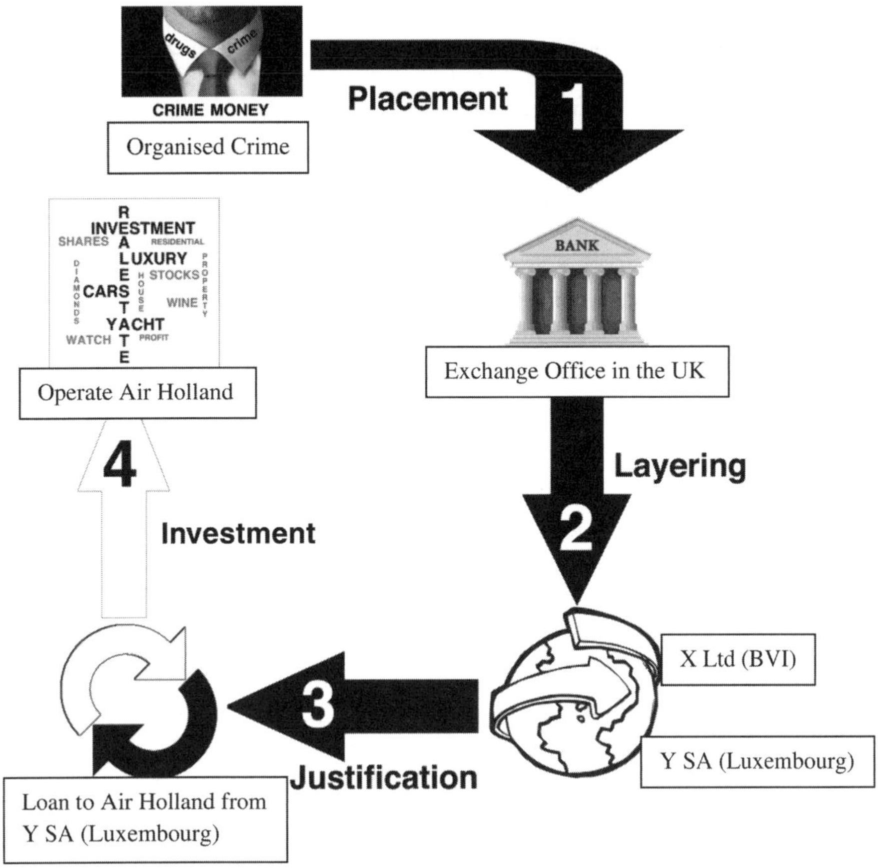

Figure 31.3 The new 4-phase money laundering process filled in for the Air Holland case

Table 31.1 Short overview of the Air Holland money laundering activities per stage

Stage	Short overview of the money laundering activities
1	The financial director transports the cash money to the UK in the trunk of his car and deposits the money with an exchange office.
2	The money is transferred in the name of the offshore company X Ltd, incorporated under the laws of the British Virgin Islands and after that the money is transferred to a bank account in the name of Y SA in Luxembourg.
3	This third stage (which is the essence of the case) concerns the justification actions. In this case the company Y SA provided a 'money loan' to the Dutch company Air Holland.
4	The 'fictitious loan' is booked in the business accounts and the acquired money is used to operate the Air Holland business. As a result of this routing the ready (drug) money was converted into money which was apparently legally borrowed from a company in Luxembourg. The initial origin is now difficult to trace.

given the specific facts and circumstances in this case, the Court considered that the suspect may be required to provide a statement about the origin of the money.[36] The suspect G. (the financial director of Air Holland) claimed that the money was derived from the sale of cambios (exchange bureaux) in Surinam, which he learned from the (criminal) investors.

31.6.1.3 Court decision

In the first instance, the court in Rotterdam convicted the suspects for money laundering and imposed a term of imprisonment of 18 to 36 months. The court found that the suspect's claim regarding the legal origin of the money had insufficient substantiation. The court stated that: 'The investigation and the prosecution show the following facts and circumstances, under which the court's view is that the money in question has a criminal origin.'

On 12 March 2008, the Court of Appeal in The Hague reached a different conclusion and acquitted three suspects. In its judgment the Court of Appeal considered that there was insufficient evidence in the criminal file that the money originated from crime. The Court considered that the statement as given by the suspect on the origin[37] of the money was *concrete, more or less verifiable and not unlikely*, and that the investigators should have examined this declaration and that they failed to do so in this case.

31.6.1.4 Conclusion

The Court made it clear in their decision that if there is a concrete, verifiable and substantiated proof of the legitimate origin of the money, the investigators have to examine the statement. In itself a legitimate and logical determination of the Court; however, the question is whether there is a concrete, verifiable and justified statement?

If this statement is not unlikely, as the Court states, it remains a mystery as to why such an illogical and costly route for the transport of the money was chosen. The situation, so to say, is calling for an explanation. The case has all the basic characteristics of money laundering; the transport of cash in plastic bags hidden in the trunk of a car, the deposit of cash in an exchange office abroad, using an offshore company located in the British Virgin Islands, and then 'borrowing back' the money via a company based in Luxembourg to the original owner – Air Holland in the Netherlands. Furthermore, it remains a mystery whether the outcome would have been different if the money launderers had been arrested during the transport or the exchange of large amounts of cash. After all, in that case all the known typologies are applicable. It seems that the importance of the aforementioned facts is hardly considered, if at all. Or would this also have to do with the relative lack of knowledge of the justification phase? It is possible that the discussion would differ if specific justification typologies existed. Nevertheless, the court of Appeal considers that there is a logical explanation. It is clear that the legal development of this offence is still in motion. It will be interesting to hear the judgment of the Supreme Court.

31.6.2 Case 2: Paarlberg

A Dutch court convicted Jan Dirk Paarlberg on 8 June 2010 of laundering more than €17 million, documentary fraud and tax fraud. This money was made by the Dutch criminal

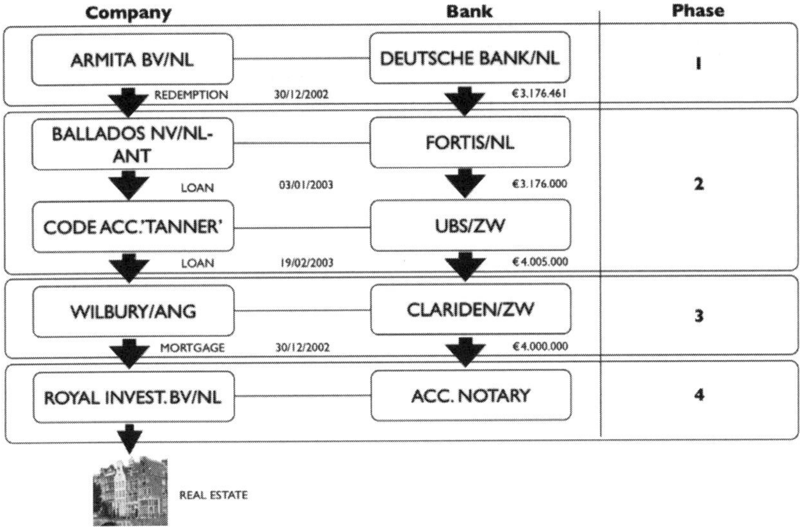

Source: Own figure, 2011.

Figure 31.4 Visual representation of the money flow in the Paarlberg case

Willem Holleeder by extorting real estate dealer Willem Endstra. Jan Dirk Paarlberg was hired by Willem Holleeder to launder the money by first making it disappear from the public eye and then later funnelling it back to the Netherlands to invest the money in real estate. In this case we focus on one of the money flows with the strange amount of €3,176,461.50, because it clearly shows the four stages of money laundering and because it is quite well documented.[38]

Figure 31.4 shows a visual representation of the money flow. The extortion money is not paid in cash, but is transferred directly from the bank account of Armita (a Dutch Company of Willem Endstra) at the Deutsche Bank to the bank account of Fortisbank in the Netherlands in the name of Ballados NV, an offshore company registered in the Dutch Antilles. This can be considered as the first phase of the money laundering process: the placement. Then the money starts its travels around the world, from the Netherlands via the Dutch Antilles (the company Ballados that is managed by a local trust company with a Dutch bank account at Fortis) to Switzerland, where the money is deposited in an anonymous code account of the Swiss bank UBS. The money is then transferred as a loan to a company (Wilbury Ltd) registered at a small island in the Caribbean (Anguilla), although the money does not actually cross any border, because the company Wilbury Ltd has its bank account at the Swiss bank Clariden. All these transactions are the second phase of money laundering: the layering. Now the actual money laundering starts. This Anguillan offshore company Wilbury Ltd is willing to provide a mortgage loan to Royal Invest, a Dutch company that wants to buy real estate in Amsterdam, the Netherlands. On paper, Royal Invest now has an apparent legitimate source of the money, being a mortgage from abroad. This is the third phase of money laundering: the justification. Consequently, the mortgage provided to Royal Invest is used to buy real estate in Amsterdam, the

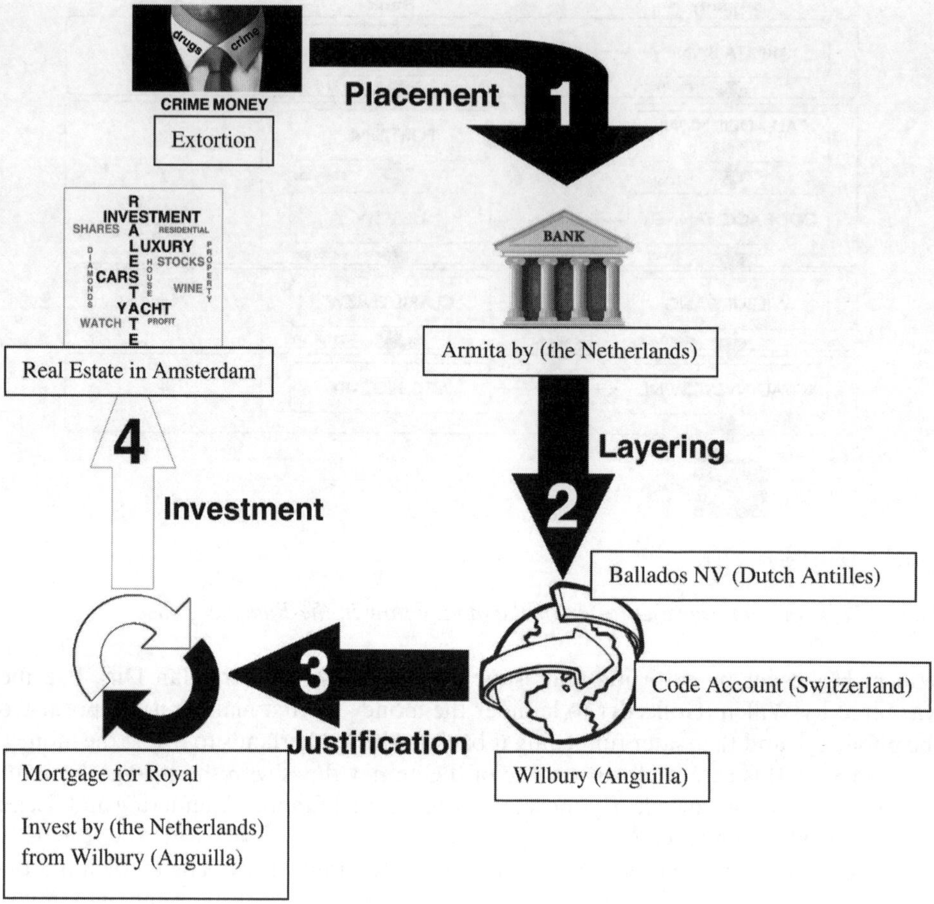

Figure 31.5 The new 4-phase money laundering process filled in for the Paarlberg case

Netherlands, which can now be enjoyed or resold. This investment is the final and fourth phase of money laundering.

We can now easily fill in the four phases of money laundering in this case, as depicted in Figure 31.5.

31.7 CONCLUSIONS

The primary aim of money laundering (in the strict sense of the word) is reintegrating criminal money into the legal economy, without arousing the authorities' suspicions as to the true origin of the money. In my opinion, consumer spending does not necessarily constitute money laundering (e.g. grocery shopping or visiting a cinema). Firstly, after all, nobody knows or can observe that the money originates from crime. Secondly, this (small) spending does not arouse direct suspicion with the authorities. Nor does it impair the integrity of the financial sector.

From a historical point of view, money laundering's main concern is to disguise the origin of and provide a justification for criminal money. In particular, the justification phase is essential to the laundering process, so the money launderer can remain in full view while the money originating from crime is put forward as legally earned. It is precisely this justification phase that is missing in the classic three-stage model.

In the literature, the current money laundering three-stage model (placement–layering–integration) is presented as universally applicable. The aim of the model is to make laundering easy to explain. This is based on the stereotype that arose in the 1980s of a drug organisation that placed large cash amounts in the legitimate economy via banks.

In this chapter, I argue that the three-stage model no longer corresponds with the present day reality of money laundering practice, laws and regulations. The result is that problems arise in the detection, collecting of evidence, developing typologies and the acquisition of knowledge and understanding. The four-stage model, however, is more in line with reality and gives the false justification its rightful place in tackling money laundering. This will result in a clearer and more intuitive exposition of the laundering process which will help improve the understanding of all actors involved in the AML process, effectively increasing the efficiency of the fight against money laundering. The introduction of a separate justification stage will also enable the development of future specific justification typologies, which may contribute to gathering evidence of money laundering

NOTES

1. Directive no. 2005/60 EC of 26 October 2005, to prevent the financial system being used for money laundering and the financing of terrorism, PbEU 2005, L 309.
2. The FATF referred to risks in several reports, e.g. FATF (2012).
3. See third money laundering directive 2005/60/EC of 26 October 2005, PbEU 2005, L309, article 35 (hereafter: third directive).
4. Professor of empirical penal law at the Tilburg University, the Netherlands, well known for his publications in the field of organised crime and money laundering.
5. Third directive, article 35; FATF 2007, 19.
6. Unger uses a broad definition of money laundering which partly explains the enormous amount of laundered money cited in her study.
7. See e.g. Kleemans et al. 2002, 127; Stessens 1997, 322–4; Doorenbos 1997, 2; Schaap 1995, 11 and P.C. van Duyne 1993, 15.
8. Different (international) organisations such as FATF, IMF, Interpol, FINCEN, the US service that deals with anti-money laundering, FIU-Nederland, formerly the Meldpunt Ongebruikelijke transacties (MOT), the Dutch Ministry of Finance, <www.minfin.nl> search query: combating money laundering: different authors and reports such as: Madinger and Zalopany 1999, 15; Unger of 2007, 89.
9. So the basis of money laundering was simple at that time: money was generated from one predicate crime: drugs. The method was in cash and the institution involved was a bank. Nowadays the world is more complicated.
10. An international organisation, established in 1989, which initially mainly dealt with making recommendations and studying and describing money laundering methods and typologies. The organisation also supervised the implementation of the recommendations in the Member States. Nowadays it also focuses on financing terrorism. See the website: http://www.fatf-gafi.org
11. Professor C. Schaap wrote a dissertation about money laundering in 1999.
12. However, in some cases the money is already within the financial system, like in tax or investment fraud cases.
13. It should be noted that this EU Regulation is not fully applied yet.

14. EC no. 1889/2005 of the European parliament and the Council of 26 October 2005 concerning the control on cash entering and leaving the Community.
15. An offshore company is an important tool for the concealment of the true beneficial owner (OECD 2009, 24. See also recommendation 33).
16. According to the Explanatory Memorandum, Parliamentary Papers II, 1999–2000, 27 159, no. 3, p. 10 this is a characteristic of many cases of money laundering and is cause for the suspicion of money laundering.
17. This technique of false invoices can also be found in the third stage of the four-stage model, namely the justification stage.
18. See e.g. Meloen et al. 2003, 257, in which the loan back construction is included in the layering stage (Unger 2007, 94).
19. See also Parliamentary Enquiry into Investigation methods, encl. X (The Hague: SDU, 1996), pp. 14–15; Kleemans 2002, 128; J.C. Westerweel and J.L.S.M. Hillen, 'Maatregelen tegen witwassen in Nederland', brochure issued by the Ministry of Finance in 1994; Akse 2003, 53–7; Van Duyne and Levi 2005, 156.
20. This mirror image does not always hold true: e.g., in the case of VAT fraud the fraudster tries to diddle a tax administration out of money.
21. See Schaap, Rozekrans and van Duyne 1992, 8 et seq.
22. Example: a bank employee, accountant or notary public who has to report unusual transactions, the investigator who gathers evidence, the public prosecutor who decides on the acceptance and prosecution of a money laundering case and the court that weighs the evidence and judges whether it is legal and convincing.
23. The wider the scope of predicate crimes, the easier it is to get enough evidence that the money comes from crime. In the Netherlands tax fraud is also a predicate crime, according to the decision of the High Court of 7 October 2008.
24. An empirical study from 1990 allegedly shows that approximately 80 per cent of all money laundering cases take place in an international context in which flows of money pass through several countries and in which financial institutions and/or companies from several countries are involved (Schaap 1999, 84).
25. Case Murray EHRM 8–2–1996.
26. The Air Holland case is a good example of this. I will discuss this case in section 31.6.
27. In the Netherlands this is made explicit in article 339 paragraph 2 of the Dutch penal code.
28. Several typology reports from the FATF, http://www.fatf-gafi.org/topics/methodsandtrends/.
29. The previous money laundering instruction of 18 October 2005 described 22 typologies. New is no. 16: 'the fact that the suspect refuses to make a statement about the origin of the money'.
30. Money laundering instruction from the Board of Procurators General, Government Gazette of 4 March 2008/45, p. 15. This instruction is addressed to all the heads of the public prosecutors' offices. The Public Prosecution Service intends to investigate and prosecute more money laundering offences.
31. Third EU money laundering directive, Directive no. 2005/60 EC of 26 October 2005, to prevent the financial system being used for money laundering and the financing of terrorism, PbEU 2005, L 309.
32. The author participated in the FATF working group that wrote this report.
33. See Unger (2006) and money laundering instruction of the Board of procurators general, Government Gazette of 4 March 2008, no. 45.
34. See also Money laundering instruction of 18 October 2005 which states – among other things – that there still is little understanding of flows of money and B. Hoogenboom, in his book review in *Justitiële verkenningen* (2006, volume 32, p. 82). He states that there is a disproportionate attention on financial transactions in the first and second money-laundering stage (Van Duyne et al. 2007, 69–98).
35. This case is described on the basis of the following information sources: four judgments of the Rotterdam Court of 7 December 2006, LJN AZ4404, AZ4394, AZ4159, AZ4397, several newspaper articles, the television programme *Profiel* of 19 April 2006 and the press release of the Public Prosecutor Service of 12 March 2008.
36. A situation that is 'calling for an explanation' (EHRM 8 February 1996, Murray-case).
37. Stating that the money came from the selling of cambios in Surinam.
38. This money flow is documented (in Dutch) in the verdict of the court in Haarlem, The Netherlands on 8 June 2010 at fact 1. The judgment was upheld in a court of appeal in Amsterdam on 16 May 2012.

REFERENCES

Algemene Rekenkamer (Dutch General Accounting Office) (2008), *Bestrijden witwassen en terrorismefinanciering* (combatting money laundering and terrorist financing).

Aske, T. (2003), *En de kleur is vuil*, Recherche themaboek, KLPD.
Chaikin, D.A. (1992), 'Money laundering as a supranational crime: an investigatory perspective', Jesus College Cambridge.
Doorenbos, D.R. (1997), *Witwassen en voordeelsontheming*, Kluwer.
Duyne, P.C. van (1993), 'Geld witwassen: omvangschatting in nevelsliesten', in J.M. Reijntjej (ed.), Misdaadgeld Arnhem, Gouda: Quint, 13–32.
Duyne, P.C. van (2003), 'Money laundering: fears and facts', in P.C. van Duyne, K. von Lampe and J.L. Newell (ed.), *Criminal Finances and Organizing Crime in Europe*, Nijmegen: Wolf Legal Publishers, 67–104.
Duyne, P.C. van and M. Levi (2005), *Drugs and Money: Managing the Drug Trade and Crime-Money in Europe*, Abingdon: Routledge.
Duyne, P.C. van, et al. (2007), *Crime Business and Crime Money in Europe: The Dirty Linen of Illegal Enterprise*, Nijmegen: Wolf Legal Publishers.
FATF (2006), 'The Misuse of Corporate Vehicles, Trust and Company Service Providers', 13 October, Paris: FATF/OECD.
FATF (2012), 'Specific Risk Factors in Laundering the Proceeds of Corruption Assistance to Reporting Institutions', June, Paris: FATF/OECD.
Kleemans, E.R. et al. (2002), *Georganiseerde criminaliteit in Nederland, onderzoek en beleid no. 198*, Den Haag: WODC.
Madinger, J. and S.A. Zalopany (1999), *Money Laundering: A Guide for Criminal Investigators*, CRC Press.
Meloen, J.D., R. Landman, H. De Miranda, J. van Hekelen, S. van Soest, P.C. van Duyne and W. van Tilburg (2003), *Buit en besteding. Een empirisch onderzoek naar de omvang, de kenmerken en de besteding van misdaadgeld*, Elsevier.
NIBESVV (2001), Handboek Bestrijding Money Laundering.
OECD (2009), *Money Laundering Awareness Handbook for Tax Examiners and Tax Auditors*, http://www.oecd.org/tax/exchangeofinformation/43841099.pdf
Schaap, C.D. (1995), 'Money laundering', NIBE section no. 30.
Schaap, C.D. (1999), *Heling getoest – Studie naar het witwassen van geld en de strafbaarstellng daarvan door middel van de helingbepalingen*, Sanders Instituut: Gouda Quint.
Schaap, C. (2007), Personal communications (10 August 2007).
Schaap, C., R. Rozekrans and P.C. van Duyne (1992), *Geld witwassen*, National Criminal Intelligence Division.
Stessens, G. (1997), *De nationale en internationale bestrijding van het witwassen*, Antwerp: Intersentia.
Unger, B., G. Rawlings, M. Siegel, J. Ferwerda, W. de Kruijf, M. Busuioc and K. Wokke (2006), *The Amounts and the Effects of Money Laundering*, Report for the Dutch Ministry of Finance.

32. Access by law enforcement agencies to financial data

Burkhard Mühl

32.1 INTRODUCTION

This chapter asks whether access by law enforcement to financial data is it effective, or (is) in fact the weak link in the investigation of financial crime and the tracing of criminal proceeds?

Successfully investigating financial crime relies heavily on the ability of law enforcement agencies to get access to financial data in order to follow suspicious financial flows and to trace the proceeds of crime. The aim of this chapter is to provide an insight into the issue of how law enforcement can access financial information. The article is based on the findings of research that has been carried out by the author amongst the members of the CARIN Network, which at the time surveyed 46 countries and jurisdictions, including all 27 countries of the European Union. The research provided general information on how the systems in the respective countries function, supplemented by five cases studies which focused in particular on the identification of bank accounts via central bank account registers, central credit referencing agencies and other means. The research examined procedures, practical questions and obstacles in the daily work of law enforcement in their attempts to obtain financial information.

The research findings indicate that two-thirds of the participating countries believe that the procedures they have in place to obtain financial information work well, whereas one-third is of the opinion that their system does not work well. An increase in the submission of electronically processed and standardised data by the financial institutions as well as shorter response times by financial institutions are commonly seen as areas where improvement is needed. Finally, the study makes it clear that the establishment of central bank account registers as a tool to identify bank accounts and to trace crime proceeds seems to be an important requirement for law enforcement. The research shows that law enforcement's access to financial information is not a weak link in financial investigations, but that there is some room for improving the system, in particular by introducing central bank account registers.

32.2 ASSET RECOVERY – AN EFFECTIVE TOOL TO FIGHT CRIME?

Crime generates money, a lot of money. According to the 2009/2010 UK Threat Assessment on Organised Crime, the revenue made by organised crime in the UK is £15 billion per year, and a significant amount of these proceeds is laundered abroad (UK Threat Assessment 2009).

The World Bank estimates the cross-border flow of the global proceeds from criminal activities, corruption and tax evasion to be between US $1 trillion and US$1.6 trillion per year. The estimations of the revenue of organised crime are sometimes questioned and seen as merely speculative (Nelen 2004, p. 523), or, as pointed out by Levi – 'numbers are frequently cited, with minimal documentation, becoming facts by repetition' (Levi and Reuter 2008, p. 6). It seems to be beyond any reasonable doubt that the profits generated by crime are huge, but 'whether that is 1 per cent or 10 per cent of GDP in developed economies is very much guesswork' (Levi and Reuter 2008, p. 20).

Even when assuming that the lowest figure of 1 per cent of GDP might be accurate, it is clear that crime revenues are immense, warranting the full attention of policy makers and law enforcement. To provide an example, the Austrian GDP for 2009 was US$376.8 billion (CIA World Factbook 2010), which would indicate, following Levi's lowest estimation, a minimum criminal revenue in Austria of US $3.8 billion (~ €2.8 billion) per year. To put this amount into perspective, the Austrian Ministry of the Interior, responsible for the entire Austrian Police with approximately 30,000 personnel, can serve as an example. In 2010 the Ministry had a budget of €2.4 billion (Austrian Ministry of the Interior 2010), thus having a smaller budget than the criminals.

The huge revenue generated by crime becomes more plausible when looking a little more closely at one of the main driving factors behind committing crimes. It is estimated that about 70 per cent of all crimes are acquisitive crimes (UK Cabinet Office 2000), and as a result the majority of cases investigated by law enforcement have one common denominator, that is a financial motive for committing the crime. The generated crime profits will leave traces, similar to fingerprints or DNA, which offer valuable leads to law enforcement. Money deriving from crime will most likely enter the financial sector at some stage, creating financial records which will be highly relevant for law enforcement in investigating and solving crimes.

Money, similar to energy, may transform from one level to another, from one country to another, but it does not vanish. There will be little doubt that the successful commission of an acquisitive crime generates money which ends up somewhere. The proceeds of crime might not always be traceable by law enforcement; however, it is highly likely that in the end somebody will benefit from this money.

Arguably, following the money offers great opportunities for law enforcement and judicial authorities. Following the money trail will provide leads to the person who committed the crime; it will disrupt associates of the perpetrator; and, finally, it enables the confiscation of crime proceeds. As observed by Bell (1999, pp. 371–84), confiscation might influence rational thinking about re-offending if an offender loses all financial benefits from his criminal activity, and confiscation attacks the economic base of criminal enterprises and renders illegal proceeds unavailable as working capital for re-investment in further criminal enterprise. Bell also argues that a justice system that is not effectively depriving criminals of their ill-gotten assets is not effectively deterring crime, and that to allow criminals to keep their ill-gotten gains and to spend them as they wish breaches fundamental notions of justice.

Following the money trail is a promising activity. However, it seems that following the money, in particular once it has left the country and found its way to other jurisdictions, still poses a serious challenge for investigators. New technologies like electronic wire transfers via the internet together with liberalised and globalised markets enable criminals to send their crime proceeds to almost any place in this world within minutes. As described by Blum et al., 'fuelled by advances in technology and communications, the financial infrastructure has developed into a perpetually operating global system in which "megabyte money" can move anywhere in the world with speed and ease' (Blum et al. 1998, p. 69). To investigate a single cross-country financial transaction usually requires quite cumbersome mutual legal assistance procedures and even under ideal conditions one can assume that it will still take at least a couple of weeks to get the requested information from the foreign country. As described in the preparatory Act regarding the European Investigation Order (Council of the European Union, 2010):

> Despite the progress generated by international instruments on mutual legal assistance, the provided mechanisms remain characterized by the principle of national sovereignty and as a consequence, the processing of a request for mutual legal assistance can be slow and inefficient. This statement can be justified by the many weaknesses of the co-operation mechanism: the channel for transmission of requests; the range of the facts giving rise to co-operation; the number of grounds for refusal; the lack of deadlines and the possibility given to the Member States to make reservations and declarations.

At international level, and also within the European Union, it has been recognised for more than three decades now that preventing money laundering and confiscating crime proceeds requires enhanced co-operation of law enforcement agencies. This has been addressed by a variety of international treaties and conventions, one of the earliest being the 1988 UN Convention against illicit traffic in narcotic drugs and psychotropic substances (UN 1988), which was the first international legal instrument criminalising money laundering and introduced the terms proceeds, freezing and confiscation.

It is certainly fair to say that substantial progress has been made since, and in particular within the European Union the concept of mutual recognition of court orders like the Council Framework Decision on freezing orders has contributed to speeding up international judicial co-operation in order to seize crime proceeds. This Framework Decision enables the judicial authorities of one Member State to send an order to another Member State to freeze assets with the aim of obtaining evidence or with a view to future confiscation of property. The order is executed very quickly and without further formality.

The best laws on international co-operation to fight money laundering and to freeze and seize crime proceeds are of no avail when the financial flows resulting from criminal activity cannot be followed up properly by law enforcement agencies at a domestic level. The question arises whether or not law enforcement's access to banking data is effective, or is in fact the weak link in investigating financial crime and tracing criminal proceeds. The answer to this will be relevant for investigating crime at the domestic level and is in particular relevant for international police and judicial co-operation. Mutual Legal Assistance (MLA) requests for the access to financial information held by the financial industry depend on the ability of law enforcement to get timely access to the requested information.

Several legal and procedural factors determine how law enforcement can access financial data, but 'soft' factors like resources, response time by the financial sector and response quality will also influence law enforcement's performance in this regard. Even when all legal and procedural steps provide for a swift access to financial data, in some cases the transmission of bank statements to law enforcement in hard copy can be a serious obstacle to processing the information properly. This might even influence law enforcement's readiness to obtain financial data because the resources might not be available to enter the data contained in the hard copies manually into an electronically readable format. On the other hand, even when procedures are cumbersome, well-established co-operation between law enforcement and the financial sector might provide for a well-performing system.

Inspiration for this research was drawn from a 2008 Communication of the European Commission (European Commission 2008) which encourages Member States to establish national registers in order to facilitate requests relating to the identification and tracing of criminal assets. Drawing on from this recommendation of the EU Commission, it seems to be the case that the lack of national centralised bank registers is an obstacle in identifying the bank accounts of suspects at national level. However, even when bank accounts can be located, access for law enforcement to financial data held by the financial sector still seems to be a lengthy and cumbersome procedure with an uncertain outcome.

32.3 SCOPE OF THE RESEARCH

The aim of the research was to provide an elaborated insight into the issue of how law enforcement accesses banking information within the European Union and in a broader context within the countries participating in the Camden Asset Recovery Inter Agency Network (CARIN), in order to establish whether gaps still exist and why, and, if this is the case, to show how this can affect international co-operation, in particular in tracing and identifying criminal proceeds.

CARIN is an informal network of judicial and law enforcement experts in the field of asset recovery. CARIN has, to date, 55 registered members (46 states and jurisdictions, including all 27 EU Member States and nine international organisations, as outlined in Appendix). Eurojust, an agency of the European Union dealing with judicial co-operation, is a permanent observer in the Steering Group and Europol holds the permanent secretariat of CARIN. One law enforcement and one judicial contact have been nominated from each state and jurisdiction to assist in cross-border co-operation in relation to tracing, freezing, seizing and confiscating assets. These English-speaking contacts are able to assist with general questions about asset recovery in their own jurisdictions, as well as providing operational support via available legal channels.

The research focused more on practical questions and did not attempt to produce a comparative legal study of the respective legislations within the Member States of the European Union and the CARIN countries.

The question was whether or not the very developed international legal regime in this area is mirrored by what law enforcement is able to achieve in daily practice at national level. One assumption was that access by law enforcement to financial data held by the financial sector is regulated very differently throughout the European Union and the CARIN Countries and that its effectiveness varies considerably. If this was the case, it of course would have a serious impact on international law enforcement co-operation and would also be detrimental to efficient judicial co-operation, following the simple argument – what law enforcement cannot identify and trace, the judiciary cannot freeze, seize and confiscate.

In general the survey tried to answer how law enforcement accesses financial information held by the financial sector. Furthermore the results were complemented by information on emerging technologies to identify bank accounts via national bank account registers or credit reference agencies. The study also considered how this can contribute to the effectiveness of law enforcement.

32.4 IS LAW ENFORCEMENT EFFECTIVE IN ACCESSING AND PROCESSING FINANCIAL DATA?

This chapter seeks to answer the question whether or not law enforcement's access to financial data is effective, a problem, or in fact the weak link in investigating financial crime and tracing criminal proceeds, based on the research findings and the case studies.

The first part of the survey tried to obtain information on legal issues and to clarify what the legal or procedural rules are that regulate access to financial information in the participating countries and jurisdictions. Not surprisingly, the results show a large variety of normative rules and procedures in place, the majority of them to be found in penal procedure acts. None of the replies indicate a firm wish for a change of the law and the regulation in place.

Banking secrecy regulations seem to be rather common. In 72 per cent of the countries and jurisdictions relevant laws can be found, again in a large variety of legal norms.

Against the expectation of the researcher, none of the respondents perceived banking secrecy as a hindrance in getting access to financial data at a national level. This came as a surprise, because on the basis of the quite frequently held public discussions on banking secrecy, one would assume that at least in a couple of countries banking secrecy may be seen critically, and possibly as a limitation for financial investigations. This clearly is not the case. This result raises the question whether banking secrecy is seen as a limitation in international judicial and law enforcement co-operation. This would require further research, taking into account not only the view of law enforcement, but also including the historical, political, social and economical parameters which influence banking secrecy regulations. Most likely research on the question of how banking secrecy impacts on international co-operation will lead to different results

With regard to the authorisation of law enforcement to get access to financial data, two main strands can be identified – authorisation by competent authorities, mainly judges and prosecutors, or direct access without prior contact, often limited to specialised services such as Financial Intelligence Units (FIUs) or Asset Recovery Offices (AROs), or to investigating certain crime phenomena such as money laundering and terrorist financing. The majority of FIUs (66%) can request financial information without prior authorisation from a judge or prosecutor, usually limited to a previously filed suspicious transaction report. Some countries even go further and enable their FIUs to request financial information actively in money laundering and terrorist financing cases. Likewise, some AROs are entitled to request financial information for the purpose of asset tracing and confiscation without the need for a court order. However, the majority of AROs do not have this possibility and need to apply for a court order to get access to financial information.

The need for authorisation of law enforcement by a competent authority does seem to present an obstacle for law enforcement in obtaining financial data. However, there seems to be a best practice of allocating certain powers to specialised services whose main purpose is to work with financial information, such as FIUs and AROs. In the vast majority of cases (79%), financial institutions are not entitled to inform their customers that law enforcement has accessed their accounts and the results do not indicate that this would actually pose a particular problem. The disclosure by financial institutions has to be distinguished from the disclosure by the competent authorities, such as prosecution services, which may be required to inform the account holder of the steps undertaken. Some countries and jurisdictions have rules which provide for the postponement of disclosure by judicial authorities if this would endanger the investigation. This approach seems to cover the needs of law enforcement to carry out investigations without fear that the target may be warned and hides money or destroy evidence, and it also ensures the right of the individual to a fair trial. A further interesting question was to find out whether or not appeal procedures against orders were in place which could actually jeopardise the collection of financial data. This is certainly not the case and even where appeal procedures exist, they are hardly used. Only three participants to the survey reported that appeal procedures can lead to sometimes serious delays. Where this is the case, this could have an impact by delaying the execution of a mutual legal assistance request for obtaining financial information. Where appeal procedures do exist, it seems that they do not present an obstacle when the appeal does not suspend the execution of the order. Also the type of information that is available for law enforcement after requesting access to financial information seems to be sufficient, covering the account holders, beneficial owners and the related financial transactions and records concerning the account relationships in general. There has been not a single report that law enforcement is limited to obtaining certain types of financial information.

One significant finding of the survey concerns the identification of bank accounts. The CARIN Network of asset recovery experts also regards this particular question as being important. Although international instruments such as the Protocol to the Convention on Mutual Assistance in Criminal Matters or the 2005 Council of Europe Convention on laundering, search, seizure and confiscation of the proceeds from crime and financing of terrorism require the identification of bank accounts at national level upon request from a third country, the measures in place do not seem sufficient to enable law enforcement agencies to identify bank accounts. For a proper assessment of this very issue, a part of the research questionnaire dealt with central bank account registers and the research has been supplemented by a couple of case studies. Only five of the 39 participating CARIN countries and jurisdictions can access central bank account registers. If bank accounts have to be identified, the majority of the countries need to find an alternative route, such as making requests to the tax authorities, contacting compliance officers from banks, obtaining information from utility service providers, and so on. Finally, five participants in the survey stated that they cannot identify bank accounts at a national level. In total 16 countries and jurisdictions stated that central bank account registers are very important, six regard it as important and only two think that they are not so important. Although there is no direct link between this fact and the recently adopted SWIFT agreement to exchange financial data between the USA and the EU, it might be interesting to contrast the concept of central bank account registers with the possibilities offered for law enforcement by the SWIFT agreement. Under this agreement, US law enforcement can access worldwide money transfers via SWIFT for counter-terrorism investigations. There is no need for prior authorisation by a judge or prosecutor. The possibilities offered under this agreement of obtaining financial data go much further than any procedures currently used by the CARIN members, including those already using central bank account registers. According to the survey results the majority of law enforcement agencies seem to have difficulties in identifying bank accounts at a national level in the course of criminal investigations. They sometimes even depend on their creativity to find bank accounts, for example using the dog tax register, as stated in one interview.

The cases studies gave an overview of best practice and made it clear that law enforcement agencies in these countries regard the central bank account registers as an important tool for identifying bank accounts. This approach in combination with judicial safeguards requiring an order of a competent authority to access the bank accounts that were identified via the central bank account register could be a model for other countries.

The research has identified a need to improve law enforcement's abilities to identify bank accounts, and the results also indicate that practitioners see a necessity for establishing central bank account registers. As this need of the practitioners is in line with international initiatives including best practice identified by the FATF, this question would merit further attention from decision makers and legislators. However, one interview made it clear that credit reference agencies could be a very useful alternative where central bank account registers are currently not feasible. To conclude from the case studies and the survey, credit reference agencies are used by 12 countries and jurisdictions and they seem to present an alternative in the absence of centralised bank account registers. One disadvantage of using these agencies might be the fact that they do not cover the entire set of financial information that is available at banks, such as savings accounts and bank safes. Furthermore, the agencies, which are privately run companies, depend on the voluntary contribution of data by the financial sector.

Another significant conclusion relates to the processing of financial data by law enforcement. Two aspects are of particular relevance in this regard, the response time of financial institutions to deliver the requested information and, even more importantly, the format of the data provided. Only six participants in the study reported that the requested information is generally provided within one week, 11 participants state that they get the information in less than two weeks. In ten cases the response time is as much as one month, in seven it is up to two months, four have to wait up to three months and in one case it takes up to six months and longer. The response times are of course dependent on the urgency and the amount of data requested. Nevertheless, the response times seem to be quite long and in some cases even excessive. This finding might be linked to the fact that the provision of electronic data by financial institutions is anything but routine. Financial data is provided in electronic format in only four cases, in 27 cases it depends on the bank and in eight cases data is only provided in hard copies. Furthermore, 28 countries and jurisdictions report that once data is provided in hard copies it needs to be processed manually, with a few exceptions where the data can be scanned and automatically imported into an electronically readable format. The response time of financial institutions along with cumbersome methods of processing financial data submitted in hard copies, is seen by law enforcement as a serious obstacle in accessing financial information. The overall satisfaction of law enforcement with their ability to access financial information is quite high. In total, two-thirds of the participating CARIN members were satisfied with the procedures and one-third thought that their system was not working well.

The areas of improvement which would be most likely to lead to a higher satisfaction rate for law enforcement would be the establishment of centralised bank account registers and the introduction of standardised or at least compatible electronic data formats of the transmitted financial data. In achieving this goal, the third concern regarding long response times would most likely also cease to exist. In attempting to answer the research question one can conclude from the research findings that law enforcement's access to financial data is not as effective as it could be and that there are areas where improvement is needed. However, the results also indicate that the procedures in place work fairly well and there is no reason why law enforcement's access to financial data should be seen as the weak link in financial investigations and asset tracing.

REFERENCES

Austrian Ministry of the Interior (2010), 'Mehr Geld für die Sicherheit'. Available at: http://www.bmi.gv.at/cms/BMI_OeffentlicheSicherheit/2009/05_06/files/Budget.pdf

Bell, R.E. (1999), 'Civil forfeiture of criminal assets', *The Journal of Criminal Law*, **63**, 371–84.

Blum, J.A., M. Levi, T. Naylor and P. Williams (1998), 'Financial havens, banking secrecy and money laundering', *UNDCP Technical Series*, **8**, 68–71.

CIA World Factbook (2010), 'Austria'. Available at: https://www.cia.gov/library/publications/the-world-factbook/geos/au.html

Council of the European Union (2010), 'Initiative of the Kingdom of Belgium, the Republic of Bulgaria, the Republic of Estonia, the Kingdom of Spain, the Republic of Austria, the Republic of Slovenia and the Kingdom of Sweden for a Directive of the European Parliament and of the Council regarding the European Investigation Order in criminal matter'. Available at: http://eur-lex.europa.eu/LexUriServ/LexUriServ.do?uri=OJ:C:2009:219:0007:0017:EN:PDF

European Commission (2008), '"Crime does not pay"'. Available at: http://europa.eu/legislation_summaries/justice_freedom_security/fight_against_organised_crime/jl0017_en.htm

Levi, M. and P. Reuter (2008), 'Money laundering', in M. Tony (ed.) *Handbook on Crime and Public Policy*, New York: Oxford University Press.

Nelen, H. (2004), 'Hit them where it hurts most: the proceeds-of-crime approach in the Netherlands', *Crime, Law & Social Change*, **41**, 517–34.

UK Cabinet Office (2000), 'Recovering the proceeds of crime'. Available at: http://webarchive.nationalarchives.gov.uk/+1 http://www.cabinetoffice.gov.uk/media/cabinetoffice/strategy/assets/crime.pdf

UK Threat Assessment (2009), 'Criminal finances'. Available at: http://www.soca.gov.uk/threats/money-laundering/criminal-finances

UN (1988), *United Nations Convention against Illicit Traffic in Narcotic Drugs and Psychotropic Substances*, New York: United Nations.

APPENDIX: CARIN NETWORK – HISTORY AND STATEMENT OF INTENT

In October 2002 a conference was held in Dublin co-hosted by the Criminal Assets Bureau Ireland and Europol. The conference was attended by representatives of all Member States of the European Union and some applicant states as well as with Europol and Eurojust. Participants were drawn from law enforcement agencies and judicial authorities within Member States. Workshops were held between practitioners and the objective was to present recommendations dealing with the subject of identifying, tracing and seizing the profits of crime.

One of the recommendations arising from the workshops was to look at the establishment of an informal network of contacts and a co-operative group in the area of criminal asset identification and recovery.

The name agreed for the group was the Camden Assets Recovery Inter-Agency Network (the Camden Court Hotel Dublin being the original location of the workshops where the initiative started).

The aim of the Camden Assets Recovery Inter-Agency Network is to enhance the effectiveness of efforts in depriving criminals of their illicit profits. This is now a major law enforcement tool in targeting organised crime gangs with particular reference to financial deprivation. There is added value in that membership of the group will improve cross-border and inter-agency cooperation as well as information exchange, within and outside the European Union.

The official launch of CARIN took place during the CARIN Establishment Congress in The Hague, 22–23 September 2004. The aim of this congress was the establishment of an informal network of practitioners and experts with the intention of improving mutual knowledge on methodologies and techniques in the area of cross-border identification, freezing, seizure and confiscation of the proceeds from crime. It is expected that this network will improve international co-operation amongst law enforcement and judicial agencies, which in turn will provide a more effective service.

The following states and jurisdictions attended the launch congress

Austria, Belgium, Cyprus, Czech Republic, Denmark, Estonia, Finland, France, Germany, Hungary, Ireland, Italy, Latvia, Liechtenstein, Lithuania, Luxembourg, Malta, Netherlands, Norway, Poland, Portugal, Romania, Slovak Republic, Slovenia, Spain, Sweden, Switzerland, UK (including the UK Crown Dependencies of the Isle of Man, Guernsey, Jersey and Gibraltar), USA.

1. Statement of Intent

1.1 Introduction

CARIN is an informal network of contacts and a co-operative group in all aspects of tackling the proceeds of crime.

1.2 Aim

The aim of CARIN is to increase the effectiveness of members' efforts, on a multi-agency basis, in depriving criminals of their illicit profits.

1.3 Key objectives

In seeking to meet its aim CARIN will:

- establish a network of contact points;
- focus on the proceeds of all crimes, within the scope of international obligations;
- establish itself as a centre of expertise on all aspects of tackling the proceeds of crime;
- promote the exchange of information and good practice;
- undertake to make recommendations to bodies such as the European Commission and the Council of the European Union, relating to all aspects of tackling the proceeds of crime;
- act as an advisory group to other appropriate authorities;
- facilitate, where possible, training in all aspects of tackling the proceeds of crime;
- emphasise the importance of co-operation with the private sector in achieving its aim;
- encourage members to establish national asset recovery offices.

The Europol Criminal Assets Bureau acts as the permanent Secretariat. The CARIN network currently has 60 members,[1] of which nine are international organisations. There are two CARIN-style regional networks: Asset Recovery Inter-Agency Network Southern Africa (ARINSA) and the Latin American Red de Recuperacion de Activos de GAFISUD (RRAG).

NOTE

1. Albania; Asset Recovery Inter-Agency Network Southern Africa (ARINSA); Australia; Austria; Belgium; Bulgaria; Canada; Croatia; Cyprus; Czech Republic; Denmark; Egmont Group; Estonia; Eurojust; Europol; Finland; France; Germany; Gibraltar; Greece; Guernsey; Hungary; Iceland; International Criminal Court (ICC); International Monetary Fund (IMF); Interpol; Ireland; Isle of Man; Israel; Italy; Jersey; Kosovo; Latvia; Liechtenstein; Lithuania; Luxembourg; Malta; Moldova; Monaco; Montenegro; Netherlands; Norway; European Anti-Fraud Office (OLAF); Poland; Portugal; Latin American Red de Recuperacion de Activos de GAFISUD (RRAG); Romania; Russia; Serbia; Slovak Republic; Slovenia; South Africa; Spain; Sweden; Switzerland; Turkey; United Kingdom; United Nations Office on Drugs and Crime (UNODC); United States of America; World Bank.

33. The role of information for successful AML policy

Ioana Deleanu

In order to effectively fight money laundering governments need to be able to distinguish healthy financial transactions from those transactions that hide a profitable criminal activity. Financial intelligence is therefore crucial for the law enforcement authorities. Financial intelligence is the result of an information collection and analysis process. We make use of information flow theories to analyze the process of intelligence gathering in the current AML frameworks. Further, we discuss several changes that could increase the efficiency of these information flow systems.

33.1 INTRODUCTION

Gathering relevant intelligence is crucial in any war. Intelligence gathering is therefore also crucial in the fight against money laundering. The current war on money laundering started some twenty years ago as an extension to the already ongoing war on drugs. For this purpose, anti-money laundering frameworks have since been developed, and with the formation of the FATF, these frameworks have converged and have become interconnected. In a global fight where differences among systems have been noted and are monitored through periodic evaluations, how has information gathering evolved? How does information become intelligence and what organizational measures can be taken to improve efficient information gathering?

33.1.1 Using Intelligence Gathering to Shift The Balance of Power

Economics information theory deals with the study of decisions that are taken in transactions where one party has more or better information than the other one. Imperfect information is widely thought to create power imbalances and distort markets that otherwise could be efficient (Wilson 2008). In the seminal paper 'The Market for "Lemons"', Akerlof (1970) observes that in a market where the buyer has imperfect information, sellers of high-quality goods suffer and are driven out of the market by sellers of low quality goods. This would entail that trade suffers because the relationships between the transacting parties would not only reflect the quality of the good but also the degree of uncertainty between them.

The anti-money laundering (hereafter AML) war illustrates a setting where one party – namely national governments – have imperfect information regarding the nature of the financial transactions they oversee nationally and internationally. The transacting parties that launder money can be considered the sellers in low quality goods. They have an incentive to hide this information from the law enforcement community. In a successful AML framework, therefore, the government could precisely spot the money-laundering-related transactions and could sanction them accordingly. Conversely, an AML system is completely inefficient when the law enforcement agencies cannot observe the nature of the financial transactions happening in the financial system. If that is the case, money laundering transactions yield more benefits that non-money laundering transactions; and assuming rational financial agents, the non-crime related transacting parties would be taken out of the market.

The current global AML system is characterized by asymmetric information. Intelligence gathering is therefore the key to reducing this asymmetry. In what follows we discuss the information systems that have been put in place for this purpose. Furthermore, using information flow theories and sociological theories of human behavior we discuss what has to further change in order to improve the efficiency of intelligence gathering.

33.2 THE EMERGENCE OF THE AML BATTLEGROUND

The last decades of the twentieth century have witnessed an unprecedented rise in international financial activity.[1] This increase in cross-border transactions worldwide as well as the upsurge of flows of capital to and from developing economies was thought to give drug lords a better chance of hiding their illegally obtained money (Simmons 2000). Nevertheless, despite recognizing the sizeable problem of money laundering (hereafter ML), consensus on a global AML policy has been hard to achieve. As Simmons so eloquently summarizes, the process of setting an AML policy has been the result of decade-long consultations and negotiations, driven mainly by the US, which revolved around the necessity to criminalize ML itself, around the question of whether the financial system should bear the costs of this fight, and around the possible ways to block ML-related transactions without detriment to the ever increasing international financial transactions (Simmons 2000). Diverging individual country incentives have had to be replaced with a common strategy and – in the absence of a common credible 'stick'– the process was lengthy and painful.

As a result, the Financial Action Task Force on Money Laundering (hereafter the FATF) was created by the major industrial countries at the G7 Summit in Paris in 1989. The FATF became the authority responsible for the detection of money laundering techniques and trends, setting the measures that need to be taken in the AML/CTF fight and evaluating countries' performances in this field as well as their compliance with international standards. This moment marks the establishment of the first coherent coercion mechanism to press for international cooperation in AML matters – the formation of a credible 'stick' (Simmons 2000).

Hereafter, the FATF created a set of Recommendations that formed the structure of a global action plan to combat ML. These Recommendations set out the main players in the AML combat: the reporting entities (REs), the Financial Intelligence Units (FIUs) and the law enforcement authorities (LEAs) (described below). At the EU level, these recommendations were updated and later implemented through the Directive 2005/60/EC and since then have been transposed into each Member State's national legislation in a way that best matched the 'spirit of the Directive'. Despite the fact that the Directive was implemented differently in the various EU Member States, convergence has been ensured through mutual evaluations performed either by the FATF or by Moneyval.

So who are the main players in the AML fight? At the foundation of the AML framework lie the Reporting Entities – a title that originally encompassed the classical financial institutions and that later grew to include casinos, brokerage and securities firms, notaries, lawyers, real estate agencies, auditors, and more. Given their proximity to the transacting parties, reporting entities (hereafter REs) were thought to be able to easily detect money laundering (2005/60/EC Directive, art. 20).

Furthermore, a Financial Intelligence Unit (FIU) was established with the purpose of collecting these suspicions and to pass what is relevant to the adequate law enforcement authorities (2005/60/EC Directive, art. 21). As its name suggests the FIU is a national unit that provides the law enforcement authorities with intelligence regarding possible money laundering activities, money launderers and possible criminal offenders. The FIU's role is therefore to transform information it receives from its sources into intelligence. Understanding the mechanisms that underline this transformation is crucial to judging the success of the AML framework.

33.3 THE DRIVE FOR CRIMINAL AND FINANCIAL INTELLIGENCE GATHERING

According to the Cornell University Law School Legal Information Institute, 'money laundering refers to a financial transaction scheme that aims to conceal the identity, source, and destination of illicitly-obtained money' (Money laundering: an overview, n.d.). For this purpose, gathering intelligence on a money laundering offense requires gathering information on the 'scheme' as well as on the 'illicit nature' of the funds used therein.

The LEAs were already gathering criminal intelligence, even before the emergence of an FIU. In this sense, the LEAs were collecting information on violent, financially profitable crimes. The difficulty lies, however, in collecting information on the non-violent financially profitable crimes and on the subsequent financial schemes intended at concealing them. The IMF (2004) reported that when developing their AML strategies, law enforcement agencies noticed a crucial difficulty in accessing relevant financial information. At that point whatever information was readily available to the reporting entities was not reaching the LEAs as intelligence (Thony 1996). Furthermore, the LEAs were not initially built to analyze complex financial information in such a way that this could help them start-up new investigations or support the ongoing ones. As a result, the FIU became an intermediary whose primary task was to filter financial information and transform it into intelligence for the LEAs.

So, what matters most – financial or criminal information? The discussion on what is more important – information on non-violent, financially profitable crimes or information on violent, financially profitable crimes – was picked up by the legislators when constructing the FIUs. The IMF (2004) report suggests that in the formation of national FIUs some legislators placed more importance on obtaining financial information on the non–violent, profitable crimes and on the means of consealing these white collar crimes, whereas others emphasized collecting criminal intelligence to combat the violent, finan-

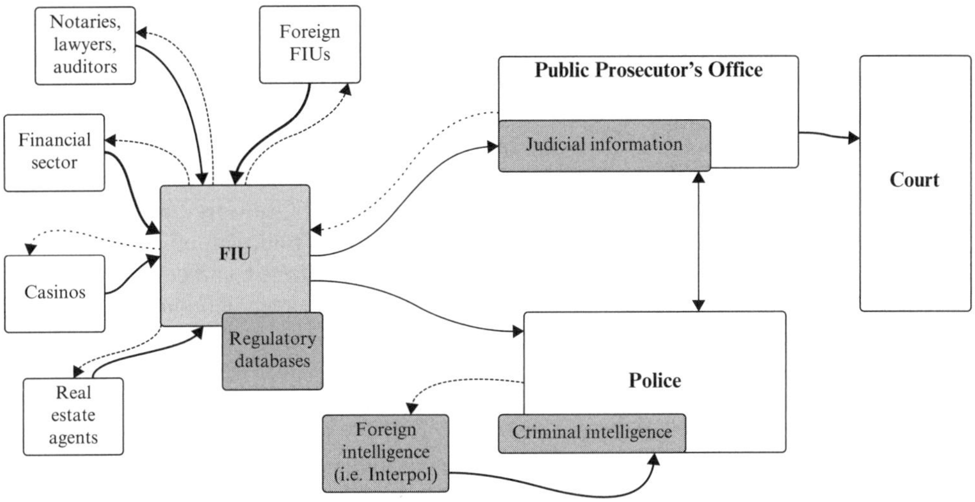

Note: In the figure above the continuous arrows show the ML/TF flows of information; dotted arrows represent the feedback given and received by the FIU; the thickness of the arrows reflects the intensity of the information flows – both in terms of quantity and quality; the dark grey boxes designate the databases relevant to the discovery, investigation and prosecution of ML.

Figure 33.1 Information flows in the AML framework when the FIU is an administrative type

cially profitable crimes – such as drugs trading and human trafficking. This bias was reflected in the design of the AML systems which at first were highly different but which I argue will converge into a unique model.

A simple way to trace who knows what and how much in the AML setting is to look at each country's flow of information. Information flow charts are virtual maps that reflect the communication that takes place between different agents within a system. They are used in understanding the nature and frequency of the interactions between the different agents, and they allow a better understanding of what type of information is mostly used in the particular AML setting.

The administrative FIU model: According to the FATF recommendations, the financial system has a duty to report to the FIU once they suspect that one of their clients might be committing money laundering. Figure 33.1 depicts the main groups of reporting entities that transmit information to the FIU in the left side of the graph. Some – and this is in particular the financial sector – disclose more information than others, and, moreover, some have to be encouraged by the FIU into reporting. In Figure 33.1 the continuous lines mark the flow of information through the system towards the end-user who is the prosecuting authority; whereas the dotted arrows depict the feedback that the law enforcement agencies as well as the FIU give to their respective sources of information (see the ECOLEF project).

Reporting entities can attempt to distinguish between sound transactions and transactions concealing illicit funds, and they are trained by the FIU to do so. The FIU, however, can scan as it gathers all suspicious reports and cross checks them with all the

FIU available financial and criminal databases. The reporting entities do not have such oversight. The FIU has therefore better oversight and knowledge on what kinds of crime these transactions could conceal and on whether investigating the transaction could lead to a successful prosecution.

Administrative types of FIUs are generally either autonomous entities or are located within another regulatory body (IMF 2004). They have easy access to regulatory databases (i.e. administrative databases belonging to state institutions and supervisory authorities) and relatively less access to criminal records, police intelligence, judicial databases and other classified information (Verhelst 2002). Some EU member states that have adopted this informational flow system are Belgium, France, Romania and Italy.[2]

The suspicions of the reporting entities are centralized at a national level in the database of the FIU and thereafter financial investigators select what is relevant to the LEAs. This information is transmitted further, depending on the protocol, directly to the Public Prosecutor's Office (PPO) or to the police. Thereafter, the financial information is checked with the criminal databases and eventually discarded or used in prosecutions. Finally, the financial information is transformed into evidence presented in court to obtain a conviction of the criminals and/solidus or confiscation of the proceeds of crime.

From an intelligence gathering point of view, in this system, a large amount of information from criminal sources circumvents the screening of the FIU. Furthermore, there is little interaction between the prosecution and the FIU, and hence the end-user might lose sight of what the FIU is or should be doing.

The law enforcement FIU model: Other legislators have chosen to set up the FIU as a new unit within their national police force (see Figure 33.2). The advantage of such a construction is given in the relatively easy and secure access that the FIU has to criminal intelligence, both at a national and international level. The disadvantage of such a construction relates to the fact that financial information and especially regulatory information is harder to obtain as the reporting institutions can be reluctant to disclose all suspicions directly to an LEA (IMF 2004).

Furthermore, Member States report a relatively difficult interaction of the FIU with the financial sector in the sense that not enough resources would be allocated to support the REs in developing their detection systems (i.e. that the feedback given by the FIU would be minimal). The law enforcement types of FIUs are present, for instance, in Portugal, Ireland and Germany.

From an intelligence gathering point of view, in this system a large source of information from administrative sources circumvents the screening of the FIU. Furthermore, since the interaction between the reporting entities and the FIU is reduced the end-user can lose sight of how the FIU is managing its sources.

The judicial type of FIU: Some legislators have opted to include the FIU within the prosecutor's office. This was generally thought to have been a good solution in countries where financial information was reluctantly given by the REs (IMF 2004). Some of the stated advantages of such a system were the possibility that the FIU has access to, and can immediately cross-check financial information with, judicial information and that the FIU is well aware of the next steps that are taken upon its disclosure to the prosecutors.

Another advantage of the judicial FIU is that the FIU does not need that much

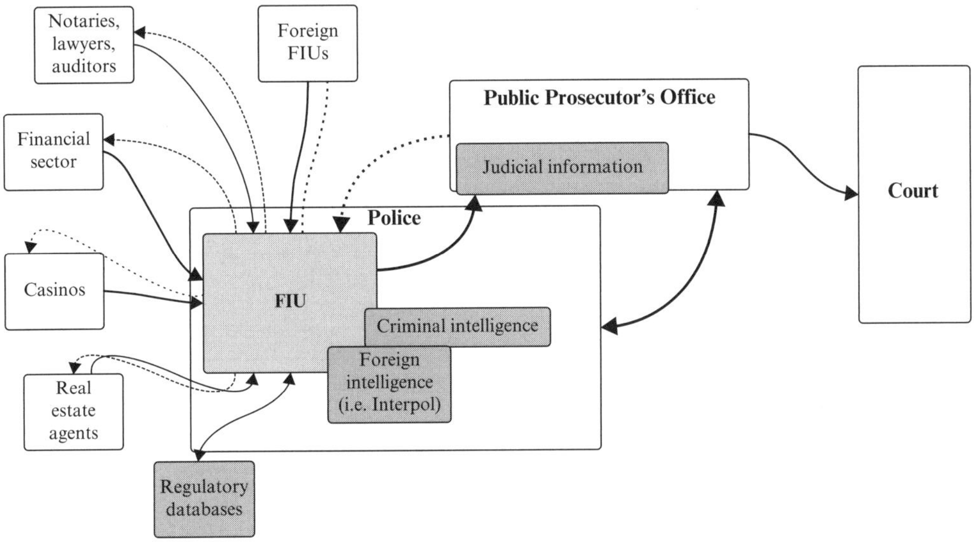

Note: In the figure above the continuous arrows show the ML/TF flows of information; dotted arrows represent the feedback given and received by the FIU; the thickness of the arrows reflects the intensity of the information flows – both in terms of quantity and quality; the dark grey boxes designate the databases relevant to the discovery, investigation and prosecution of ML.

Figure 33.2 Information flows in the AML framework when the FIU is a law enforcement type

feedback from the LEAs, as the FIU is part of the end-user. This means that fewer resources need to be put into giving feedback. One of the downsides of this informational flow system, also presented in Figure 33.3, is the relative distance between the FIU and both the regulatory databases and towards the criminal intelligence available to the police. This system has most notably been implemented in Luxembourg and in Denmark.

FIUs are being constantly compared to each other. FIUs have been included in the methodology used to assess countries' AML frameworks since 2001 according to the IMF (2004) report. The FATF has recently focused more on the role and functioning of the FIUs and the LEAs. Their evaluation have begun to emphasize the implementations of Recommendations R.26–R.29 (see ECOLEF project). This pressure imposed by FATF cross-country verifications has materialized in a procedural convergence concerning the work of the FIUs and their interaction with the LEAs. This means in effect that countries learn from each other (i.e. they copy each other's strategy) and that the winning FIU model will become a hybrid one – fine tuned to the national realities but in effect conducting more or less the same activities as any of its counterparts. Moreover, nowadays, steps are taken further to harmonize prosecution of money launderers, among others – see the proposal for the establishment of an EPPO (European Public Prosecutor's Office, n.d.). So, what we see at a macro level is that this soft law has successfully reached its goals and that countries have converged to a rather similar model of fighting ML.

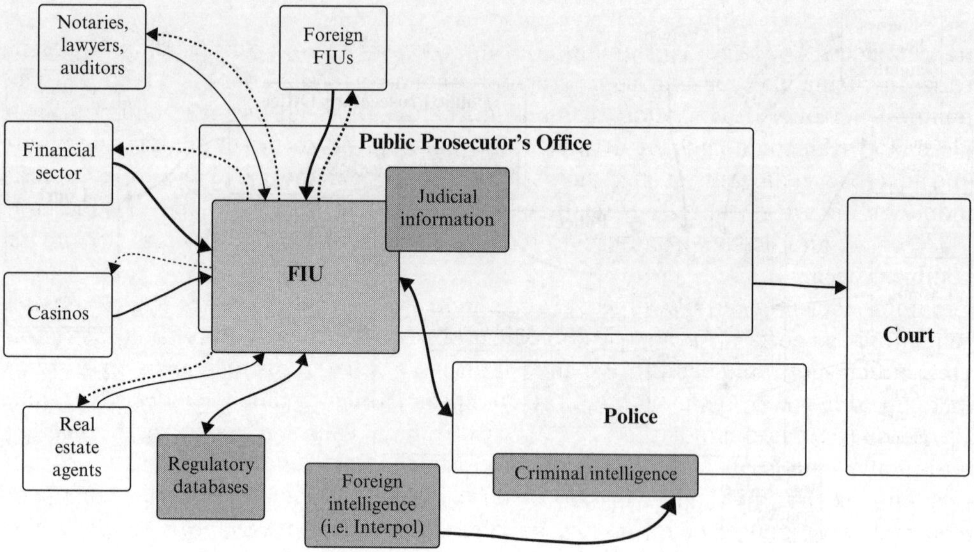

Note: In the figure above the continuous arrows show the ML/TF flows of information; dotted arrows represent the feedback given and received by the FIU; the thickness of the arrows reflects the intensity of the information flows – both in terms of quantity and quality; the dark grey boxes designate the databases relevant to the discovery, investigation and prosecution of ML.

Figure 33.3 Information flows in the AML framework when the FIU is a judicial type

33.4 THEORETICAL BACKGROUND

The growth of openly available sources has made it much more difficult to effectively extract useful information from all the available information. When faced with an overwhelming amount of data, one needs a mechanism that can efficiently reduce this information to what is essential. All information systems are based on selecting the most relevant information for the end-user. For this purpose, information systems have two functions that could at first sight seem opposing: they reduce the information overload – by filtering they only provide relevant results – and they add items to the information flowing towards a user – by making recommendations they increase relevance (Hanani et al. 2001).

If filters take away redundant information, recommenders add relevant information. The former helps reduce the resources consumed to absorb and use information. The latter are learning systems that aim to expand the knowledge of the end-user in his field of interest by predicting what else falls in this area of relevancy that the user has not yet received (Ricci et al. 2011). Combining the two and allowing them to perfect themselves automatically is seen as the future of information systems (Hanani et al. 2001).The future is therefore considered to be creating information filters and recommenders that adapt to past (i.e. Bayesian learning) and present experience. To allow for this learning to happen, the system needs to have positive and negative examples and it needs to be 'taught', by experts and ordinary end-users, how to differentiate between them.

Collaborative filtering is a state of the art recommender system. It uses several viewpoints (expert viewpoints) and sociological rules of thumb on human behavior to make recommendations on possibly relevant additional information (Linden et al. 1998). Furthermore, collaborative filtering systems allow for the development of these rules of thumb by the experts.

One of the most widely used sociological theories suggests that people get the best recommendations from the peers they share most in common with. The underlying assumption of the collaborative filtering approach is that if a person A has the same opinion as a person B on an issue 'X', A is more likely to share B's opinion than another random person's opinion on issue 'Y'. It is therefore believed that if individuals A and B have something in common, they are more likely to have something else in common too. This theory has been widely used in refining the searches of large IT engines such as Last.fm and Amazon.com. Every time you listen to a piece of music on Last.fm the system records your listening as your preference. It thereafter puts together all individuals that have expressed a preference for that particular song and tries to see whether they share more preferences for songs. In the meantime, experts teach the IT system to categorize songs and sounds according to music genders, themes, etc. Finally, once you search for a specific piece of music the IT system will filter the available information based on your search indicators and will recommend others that have been chosen by people with whom you share most similarities (Recommender system, n.d.).

33.5 APPLICATION OF THE THEORY TO THE AML/CTF SYSTEM

In the AML framework the end-user is the prosecution service. The information source it possesses is the financial sector, the criminal investigations, the administrative records – and these are VAST sources of information. So, how does the AML system make sure it discards redundant information as this flows towards the PPO and how does it add new relevant information – that, is, how does the successful AML system gather intelligence?

I apply a collaborative filtering approach to this information gathering process. Considering the dual nature of the information needed to combat ML – financial and criminal – the optimal filter system needs to be able to filter both financial and criminal information, preferably for the end-user. The recommender system must be able to relate the criminal offence to the financial information, thereby offering a link to the investigator between the financial scheme used to conceal the illicit money, and the predicate offence which yielded the illegitimate proceeds. I therefore propose a system where the FIU does both – filter and recommend with the help of an expert panel.

In the AML it has already been argued that both financial and criminal information is needed to build intelligence for the LEAs. The FIU should therefore collect information (both financial and criminal) and thereafter match a predicate crime related to a certain pattern of transactions. The basic assumption here is that criminals use similar patterns to commit crimes and similar patterns to conceal the proceeds from financially profitable violent or non-violent crimes. This means that once the FIU can recognize a pattern of concealing funds it can screen the transactions pertaining to such a pattern and offer them for further investigation to the LEAs. The role of the expert panel is to create and

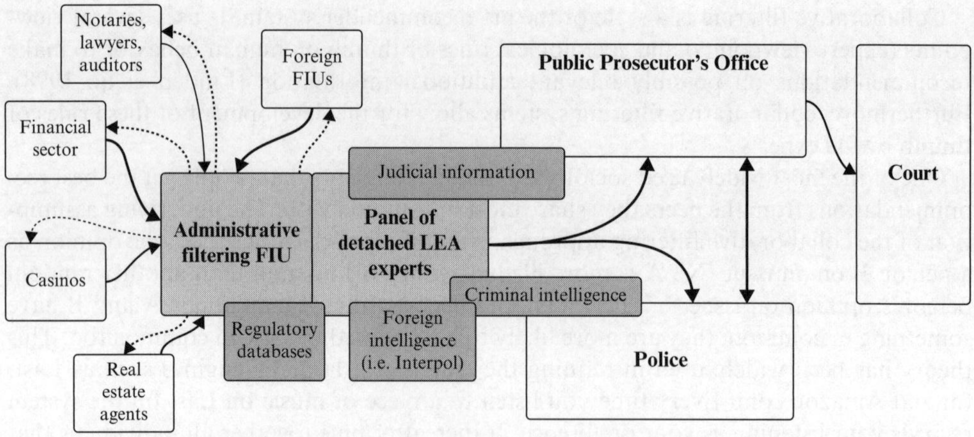

Note: In the figure above the continuous arrows show the ML/TF flows of information; dotted arrows represent the feedback given and received by the FIU; the thickness of the arrows reflects the intensity of the information flows – both in terms of quantity and quality; the dark grey boxes designate the databases relevant to the discovery, investigation and prosecution of ML.

Figure 33.4 An optimal AML information flow model – based on the filter/recommender system analysis

adapt the screens for these predicate crimes in terms of transaction patterns (i.e. make recommendations on which transaction patterns can be considered suspicious, in what circumstances). At the beginning, filters are harder to create but they can expand as long as the FIU uses expert information from the later investigative agents. Finally, the FIU will learn from the expert panel and the end-user will learn to use the output of the FIU in its investigations.

FIU – the optimal filter: If we look at the previous information flows, a first improvement would be to allow the FIU access to all databases: to be supplied with information from the reporting entities, and to be able to access national and international criminal databases. In its filtering capacity, the FIU would then have to cross-check information scattered across all of these different databases, and would therefore be the unique filter for doing so. Avoiding the differentiated filtering, as Figure 33.4 shows, allows the current AML system not to miss relevant data by impartially filtering. Cross-checking can and should be done by a capable IT filter system, so as to reduce the level of human error and at the same time to maintain a veil of confidentiality on the data that are more sensitive. Such a 'double blind' system has already been implemented in data sharing by the FIU.net and users were reporting themselves to be happy with this informational non-transparency to third parties (FIU.net n.d.).

Ensuring that the FIU correctly filters the information has another added value. It ensures that there will be no informational overload on the subsequent users. Just as in the case of vast amounts of online information that would be unnecessary to a user who performs a simple search on Amazon.com, a multitude of financial data would cripple the LEAs who would therefore have no other solution but to discard it altogether or to try to filter it themselves.

The expert panel – the optimal recommender system: An expert panel in the sense of a recommender system is needed to complement the analysis of the FIU with the expertise of latter stage users. Depending on what the end stage users are in each country, the expert panel should consist of a police representative, a representative of the regulatory bodies that have a role in the repression of ML and a representative for each prosecution service. An optimal expert panel has to serve three fundamental functions: it should analyze the intelligence provided by the FIU filter, thereafter direct it to the most appropriate end-user and, finally, it should, given the results of the LEA investigation, fine tune the filters of the FIU.

In an optimal system, the expert panel would therefore immediately adjust the information filters on the basis of the LEA analysis. In other words, the end-user would be able to immediately point out to the filter the relevance of certain transaction patterns and this feedback would allow the filter to better select information. The PPO would therefore be supplied with intelligence it can immediately use in its investigations and the FIU would be able to better reduce any information gap with respect to the transacting parties.

Improving current AML information flow systems: In terms of what FIUs can change in order to improve efficiency, the administrative types of FIUs need to know what is expected from them and what the end-users can do with the intelligence provided. The administrative FIUs therefore need to exhibit proactive behavior and involve LEA experts in their analysis. Conversely, the law enforcement and the judicial FIUs should have a backward looking attitude – in the sense of providing detailed feedback to the reporting entities and teaching the latter what patterns need to be picked up in financial transactions. These FIUs need to focus on efficiently filtering the information that reaches them and on connecting better to the financial sector and to the regulatory authorities.

These improvements have already taken place in the AML system of Belgium, the Netherlands and Portugal, among others. In Belgium, the FIU uses liaison officers from the LEAs and a detached prosecutor to fine tune their analysis and to target the cases at the most appropriate end-users. In the Netherlands, the FIU information is discussed by a Council formed of representatives of the end-users. This Council is also used as the main source of feedback for the FIU. Furthermore, in Portugal, the law enforcement FIU uses liaison officers from the other regulatory authorities in order to expand the databases available to the FIU but also to share knowledge with the latter concerning transaction patterns involving proceeds of crime.

33.6 CONCLUSION AND DISCUSSION

The war against money laundering is a relatively new war but one that has unfolded on an unprecedented global scale. The need for cooperation and coordination in this global fight was identified early on by the world's largest industrial powers, who created standard frameworks for combating ML. By means of peer pressure the international community has had to eventually implement these standards at a national level.

In this fight, intelligence gathering has been considered crucial in shifting the balance of power away from the money launderers. The current AML framework empowers the FIUs to collect and analyze this intelligence, and creates conditions for other auxiliary institutions to feed the FIU with information. Mutual evaluations and peer pressures seem to have induced (although not fully) convergence among the FIU's capacities to gather information. Furthermore, the relatively new focus on procedural convergence (both on the side of the FIUs as well as on the side of the prosecuting authorities handling white collar crimes) will have created a somewhat similar AML informational framework.

At the core of the success of any AML framework, therefore, lies the FIU's capacity to transform information in intelligence. The FIU does this in its filter capacity. With the help of economic and sociological theories we expose a possible efficiency boost – that is achieved once the current filter is standardized and matched with an appropriate recommendation system. Such an optimal system can be envisaged already in some EU Member States and would be focused on very large database compilation with large-scale IT filtering systems for the FIU and would shift the focus of the ML analysis towards a panel of experts from the LEAs.

The optimal FIU would thus have access to criminal records, international and national police and judicial intelligence, administrative records, and financial information. The FIU would consist of an administrative side that would be dominated by an IT filtering system with unlimited access to all of the above-mentioned databases, and an expert panel made up of financial, police and judicial entities with a double specialization in ML and in violent and non-violent financially profitable crimes. The expert panel would play the role of a recommender system attached to the FIU. In this capacity it would construct and adapt the filters of the administrative FIU, as well as analyze the intelligence created by the filters and distribute it to the (specialized) LEAs most capable to manage it. These experts must cover all the possible end-users and therefore be able to teach the administrative FIU system how criminals work and how to start from financial information and arrive at a predicate offence.

Despite this somewhat advanced solution to reducing the problem of asymmetric information, one needs to at least mention some of the limitations and cautions. For this solution to work, one needs to develop proper informational infrastructures – online databases that cover the knowledge accumulated by the public sector and by the regulatory agencies (divergences in their concerns and roles are further reported in the ECOLEF project).

Finally, we draw attention to the fact that the expansion of information processing tools allows the shifting of the balance of powers at an unprecedented scale in favor of the law enforcement agencies and of national governments. Because information is power, allowing the FIU access to administrative and law enforcement databases would give such a structure an unprecedented boost in power. We therefore recommend a careful consideration of the boundaries such an information system should have, as well as the enforcement of checks and balances systems to ensure that this power is not abused for private or political gains. For this reason, a double-blind IT solution to the cross-checking of databases seems to be a good solution for eliminating the possible temptation for the employees of the FIU.

NOTES

1. International Monetary Fund, World Economic Outlook Database.
2. See EU founded ECOLEF report, chapter 9 for a complete overview of the EU27.

REFERENCES

The 2005/60/EC Directive on the prevention of the use of the financial system for the purpose of money laundering and terrorist financing, downloadable at http://eur-lex.europa.eu/LexUriServ/site/en/oj/2005/l_309/l_30920051125en00150036.pdf

Akerlof, G.A, (1970), 'The market for "lemons": quality uncertainty and the market mechanism', *Quarterly Journal of Economics*, **84**(3), 488–500.

The Economic and Legal Effectiveness of Anti Money Laundering and Combating Terrorist Financing Policy (ECOLEF) (forthcoming).

European Public Prosecutor's Office (n.d.), In *European Commission*. Retrieved August 27, 2012 from http://ec.europa.eu/justice/criminal/judicial-cooperation/public-prosecutor/index_en.htm

FIU.net (n.d.), *FIU.net*. Retrieved September 12, 2012 from http://www.fiu.net/fiunet-unlimited/match/match3

Hanani, U., B. Shapira and P. Shoval (2001), 'information filtering: overview of issues, research and systems', *User Modeling and User Adapted Interaction*, **11**, 203–59.

International Monetary Fund, World Economic Outlook Database, downloadable at http://www.imf.org/external/pubs/ft/weo/2011/01/weodata/index.aspx

International Monetary Fund and the World Bank (2004), *Financial Intelligence Units: An Overview*, downloadable at http://www.imf.org/external/pubs/ft/fiu/fiu.pdf

Linden, G.D., J.A. Jacobi and E.A. Benson (1998), 'Collaborative recommendations using item-to-item similarity mappings', United States Patent, downloadable at http://patft.uspto.gov/netacgi/nph-Parser?Sect1=PTO2&Sect2=HITOFF&p=1&u=/netahtml/PTO/search-bool.html&r=1&f=G&l=50&co1=AND&d=PTXT&s1=6,266,649.PN.&OS=PN/6,266,649&RS=PN/6,266,649

Money laundering: an overview (n.d.), In *Cornell University Law School, Legal Information Institute*. Retrieved August 23, 2012 from http://www.law.cornell.edu/wex/money_laundering

Recommender system (n.d.), In *Wikipedia*. Retrieved September 12, 2012, from http://en.wikipedia.org/wiki/Recommender_system#Collaborative_Filtering

Ricci, F., L. Rokach and B. Shapira (2011), 'Introduction to Recommender Systems Handbook', *Recommender Systems Handbook*, New York: Springer, 1–35.

Simmons, B.A. (2000), 'International Efforts Against Money Laundering', in D. Shetton (ed.), *Commitment and Compliance: The Role of Non-binding Norms in the International Legal System*, Oxford: Oxford University Press, pp 244–63, downloadable at http://scholar.harvard.edu/bsimmons/files/MoneyLaundering.pdf

Thony, J.F. (1996), 'Processing Financial Information in money laundering matters, the Financial Intelligence Units, *European Journal of Crime, Criminal Law and Criminal Justice*, **4**(3) 257–82.

Verhelst, B. (2002), *The Financial Intelligence Units in the International Context*, the Egmont Group.

Wilson, C. (2008), 'Adverse selection', *The New Palgrave Dictionary of Economics*, 2nd edition, Basingstoke: Palgrave, Macmillan.

34. Evaluating anti-money laundering policies: where are we?

Barbara Vettori

34.1 INTRODUCTION

Although the international community began to focus its attention on money laundering a rather long time ago, there is still very little scientific knowledge about the effectiveness and efficiency of the countermeasures adopted to combat the phenomenon. The aim of this article is to contribute to the debate on the topic by discussing the reasons for this lack of knowledge and critically reviewing traditional (section 34.2) and new approaches (sections 34.3 and 34.4) to assess anti-money laundering (AML) efforts. Amongst the latter, a recent and promising strand of economic literature is discussed.

34.2 TRADITIONAL ASSESSMENT METHODOLOGIES BASED ON OUTPUT INDICATORS

The first international document to explicitly mention money laundering was the United Nations Convention Against Illicit Traffic in Narcotic Drugs and Psychotropic Substances, signed in Vienna on December 20, 1988. Although more than two decades have now passed since its adoption, there is still a lack of convincing empirical evidence on the extent of the phenomenon,[1] as well as the effectiveness of the measures adopted to combat it. It has also been observed that there is a close connection between these two knowledge gaps: since the effectiveness of counterpolicies should be assessed in terms of reduction of laundering activities, the inability to quantify the volume of the latter has hampered and still hampers understanding of the impact that policies have had on the phenomenon (Harvey 2005, p. 339).

Owing to these problems, existing attempts have mainly made use of output indicators related to the obligations and controls introduced by AML regulations. These provide a measure of the volume of activities undertaken by competent authorities to prevent and combat the cleaning of dirty money, but cannot say a great deal about the real impact of such actions on the criminal problem itself. This approach has been adopted, for example, by the Financial Action Task Force (FATF), an inter-governmental body set up in 1989 for the development and promotion of national and international policies against money laundering and terrorist financing. In 1990, the FATF drafted 40 recommendations, later amended with nine more on terrorist financing. Recommendation no. 32 states that:

> countries should ensure that their competent authorities can review the effectiveness of their systems to combat money laundering and terrorist financing systems by maintaining comprehensive statistics on matters relevant to the effectiveness and efficiency of such systems. This

> should include statistics on the STRs received and disseminated; on money laundering and terrorist financing investigations, prosecutions and convictions; on property frozen, seized and confiscated; and on mutual legal assistance or other international requests for co-operation. (FATF 2003)

Based on this recommendation, the FATF periodically gathers annual statistics from the various jurisdictions on the functioning of AML (and terrorist financing) systems, and more in detail on:

- suspicious transaction reports (STRs) (and other reports where appropriate under domestic law), received and disseminated: STRs received by the Financial Intelligence Unit (FIU), including a breakdown of the type of financial institution/ designated non-financial businesses and professions/other business or person making the STR; breakdown of STRs analysed and disseminated; reports filed on: (i) domestic or foreign currency transactions above a certain threshold, (ii) cross border transportation of currency and bearer negotiable instruments, or (iii) international wire transfers;
- money laundering (and terrorist financing) investigations, prosecutions and convictions, and on property frozen, seized and confiscated, that is: number of investigations, prosecutions and convictions; number of cases and the amounts of property frozen, seized and confiscated relating to (i) money laundering, (ii) financing terrorism and (iii) criminal proceeds; number of persons or entities and the amounts of property frozen pursuant to or under UN Resolutions relating to terrorist financing;
- mutual legal assistance or other international requests for cooperation: all mutual legal assistance and extradition requests (including requests relating to freezing, seizing and confiscation) that are made or received, relating to money laundering, the predicate offences and terrorist financing, including the nature of the request, whether it was granted or refused, and the time required to respond; other formal requests for assistance made or received by the FIU, including whether the request was granted or refused; spontaneous referrals made by the FIU to foreign authorities;
- other: on-site examinations conducted by supervisors relating to or including anti-money laundering (AML)/combating terrorist financing (CFT) and any sanctions applied; formal requests for assistance made or received by supervisors relating to or including AML/CFT, including whether the request was granted or refused. (FATF 2009a, pp. 38–39)

As noted by the FATF itself, these statistics are essential 'to assess the effectiveness of the implementation of the FATF 40+9 Recommendations and to deliver fair and accurate ratings' on each country (FATF 2009b, p. 9).

A similar methodology is used by other bodies involved in the fight against money laundering, including, for example, the Council of Europe, whose Committee of Experts on the Evaluation of Anti-Money Laundering Measures and the Financing of Terrorism (MONEYVAL), established in 1997, assesses non-FATF members based on the same kind of data (European Committee on Crime Problems 2010, p. 16).

More recently, the same approach has been adopted at the EU level, based on article 33 of the Directive on the prevention of the use of the financial system for the purpose of money laundering and terrorist financing by the European Parliament and by the Council of 26 October 2005 (Third Money Laundering Directive), which invites Member States, at paragraph 1, to ensure 'that they are able to review the effectiveness of their systems to combat money laundering or terrorist financing by maintaining comprehensive statistics on matters relevant to the effectiveness of such systems'. Paragraph 2 specifies that these statistics 'shall as a minimum cover the number of suspicious transaction reports made to the FIU, the follow-up given to these reports and indicate on an annual basis the number of cases investigated, the number of persons prosecuted, the number of persons convicted for money laundering or terrorist financing offences and how much property has been frozen, seized or confiscated'. Based on this provision, Eurostat, in cooperation with Directorate-General for Home Affairs of the European Commission, and with the advice of representatives from law enforcement entities, international organisations and academia,[2] has compiled a list of 23 indicators, grouped into the four key phases of money laundering proceedings. These are as follows:

- *for the reporting/intelligence phase*: 1. number of STRs filed by each category of obligated entities; 2. number of Cash Transaction Reports (CTRs) filed by each category of obligated entities; 3. number of postponement orders adopted on reported transactions; 4. number of money laundering investigations carried out independently by law enforcement agencies (without a prior STR); 5. number of declarations made in application to the EU Cash Control Regulation; 6. number of incorrect cash declarations or findings as a result of customs controls in the EU at external borders; 7. number of suspicious cash activities at the EU borders reported to the FIU (including those based on declarations and smuggling); 8. number of STRs sent to law enforcement and on which further analysis was made; 9. number of staff dedicated full time (or full time equivalent) to money laundering in the FIU;
- *for the investigation phase*: 10. number of cases initiated by law enforcement agencies on the basis of STRs sent by the FIU; 11. number of staff dedicated full time (or full time equivalent) to money laundering in law enforcement agencies; 12. number of cases brought to prosecution: originating from STRs, CTRs and independent law enforcement investigation;
- *for the judicial phase*: 13. number of staff dedicated full time (or full time equivalent) to money laundering in the judiciary; 14. number of persons/legal entities convicted for money laundering offences; 15. number of convictions for laundering proceeds of crimes committed abroad; 16. number of convictions for crimes other than money laundering originating from STRs; 17. number of sentences by type for money laundering offences; 18. number of unsuspended custodial sentences by length (as principle offence, as predicate offence); 19. number of freezing procedures (based on a court order); 20. number of confiscation procedures; 21. number of requests received for freezing orders from another EU Member State and the value of frozen assets; 22. number of requests received for confiscation orders from another EU Member State and

the value of confiscated assets; 23. amounts recovered from assets. (Tavares et al. 2010, pp. 11–12)

This approach is still based on output indicators, considering that, as stressed by the European Commission itself, it 'is limited to the linear monitoring of the anti-money laundering chain, from the filing of the suspicious transaction report through to criminal conviction' (Tavares et al. 2010, p. 5). However, it should be recognized that this attempt is more refined than the ones previously described, as shown by its higher level of detail. Moreover, it is regarded by the EU institutions themselves as a necessary first step in encouraging Member States, in the long run, 'to develop a cost/benefit analysis of their anti-money laundering scheme' (Tavares et al. 2010, p. 8). It therefore moves in the direction indicated by the new assessment methodologies described in the next two sections.

34.3 NEW ASSESSMENT METHODOLOGIES (1): COST/BENEFIT STUDIES

The academic community has recently sought to develop more sophisticated analyses which include economic studies. These studies, whose development has been prompted by the increasing complaints voiced by entities subject to AML legislation (primarily the banking system) about the burden of activities that it imposes on them, compare the costs and benefits of different legislative options for different social actors.

At present, however, few such studies have been carried out.

34.3.1 National Studies

A 2002 British study (HM Treasury and the Department of Trade and Industry 2002) performed a Regulatory Impact Analysis aimed at understanding the costs/benefits ratio resulting from the introduction of five requirements enhancing the transparency of the beneficial ownership of public and private unlisted companies. Thereafter, in 2005, a first Regulatory Impact Assessment estimating the costs and benefits of the various provisions set out in the Third Money Laundering Directive, including those regarding the disclosure of beneficial ownership, was performed in the UK to inform the British negotiating position on the Directive (Her Majesty's Treasury 2005).

In 2006, research was conducted to determine, in economic, competitive and ethical terms, the impact of AML regulation on financial operators in Luxembourg (Krieger-Faust 2006). With particular reference to evaluation of the economic impact of the regulation, the study discussed a variety of types of costs (i.e. transposition costs, recurrent costs, opportunity costs and externalities) and benefits (i.e. benefits for the community and benefits for banks). It concluded that the costs incurred by the Luxembourg banking system under anti-money laundering regulations were not negligible, although it was difficult to understand whether these costs were justified by overall benefits, because the latter are difficult to assess (Krieger-Faust 2006, p. 165).

More recently, in 2008, the case study method has been used to estimate the costs to Australian financial institutions of complying with the anti-money laundering

By requiring intermediaries to identify and verify the identity of the beneficial owner, the Directive has therefore opted, to express it in terms of the three OECD mechanisms, for the Intermediary Route.

This said, the aim of the study *Cost Benefit Analysis of Transparency Requirements in the Company/Corporate Field and Banking Sector Relevant to the Fight against Money Laundering and Other Financial Crime* was the comparison of two beneficial ownership disclosure systems in terms of the costs and benefits that may arise from their implementation in the 27 EU countries. The two systems – defined as model 0 and model 1 – were defined as follows:

- model 0 is the intermediary-based disclosure system embodied in the Third Money Laundering Directive. As seen, it relies primarily on financial and business intermediaries to obtain information about the beneficial ownership and control of companies. Intermediaries are required to identify, before establishing a business relationship or conducting a transaction, the natural person(s) who ultimately own(s) or control(s) their customer and/or the natural person on whose behalf a transaction or activity is being conducted. Whenever intermediaries suspect that money laundering is being or has been committed/attempted they have the duty to transmit a STR to the FIU, with details on the beneficial ownership of the client as well;
- model 1 is a new, hypothetical, up-front disclosure system where the duty to disclose beneficial ownership of public and private unlisted companies is placed on the same beneficial owner, who should notify details of his/her ownership to the company itself. In this system the ownership of 10 per cent of the shares of a public or private unlisted company is regarded as a sufficient threshold to be considered the beneficial owner. Should the real beneficial owner not be registered as a shareholder of the company, the duty is on any registered shareholder of 10 per cent or more of the issued capital to confirm the beneficial ownership of such shares. Information on beneficial ownership is gathered by the company, which is requested to enter it within a short period of time into a national Companies Registry, available online to Law Enforcement Agencies (LEAs) and to anyone interested.

The methodology used to compare costs and benefits arising from the two above described models was the following:

1. *Defining the two models in a way that allowed comparison.* This was done by expressing both systems in the form of five duties: (1) the duty to disclose the beneficial ownership of private and public unlisted companies; (2) the duty of monitoring and updating of information on beneficial ownership; (3) the duty of keeping records on beneficial ownership; (4) the duty to make this information available to FIUs/LEAs; (5) the duty to make such information available to the public.
2. *Identification of areas of incidence.* Eight categories/subjects/institutions on which the introduction of the two models was presumed to impact in terms of costs and benefits were identified: Government, LEAs, Intermediaries, Individuals,

Businesses, Wider Costs and Benefits, European Union and Member States, Human Rights and Data Protection.

3. *For each area of incidence, identification of cost and benefit items, both direct and indirect.*[4] As regards model 0, 39 cost items and 16 benefit items were identified; as regards model 1, 20 cost items and 12 benefit items were selected.[5]
4. *Defining how to measure (quantitatively or qualitatively) each cost and benefit item.* For quantifiable items (typically, direct costs/benefits), variables relevant to their expression in monetary terms were identified. For example, the following formula was used to calculate the beneficial ownership identification costs placed on intermediaries under model 0: average time devoted by banks to disclosing beneficial ownership (used as a proxy for average intermediary time) × banking sector hourly labour gross cost × number of total private and public unlisted companies registered in the national companies registry × estimated number of beneficial owners. In the remaining cases (typically, in relation to indirect cost/benefit items) researchers opted for a qualitative assessment.
5. *Data gathering to measure (quantitatively or qualitatively) the cost and benefit items*, by means of primary sources (i.e. questionnaires administered to six entities/professional bodies in each Member State) and secondary sources (such as official databases, documents and reports).
6. *Based on the collated data, calculation of the costs and benefits associated with each of the two models.*

The findings of the study are very detailed and include an estimation, for each area of incidence, of the costs and benefits of each of the two models within each Member State. A summary of these findings at the EU level is provided here.

At aggregate EU level, model 0 net direct cost[6] is estimated on a yearly basis at approximately 6,774 million euros, while net indirect cost is assessed at 10,143 million euros. As regards model 1, net direct cost is estimated at 125 million euros, while model 1 net indirect cost is assessed at 11,171 million euros. Net direct costs for model 0 are therefore greater than those for model 1 (the difference is approximately 6,648 million euros), while net indirect costs for model 0 are lower than those for model 1 (approximate difference 1,028 million euros).

Some more specific findings by some areas of incidence now follow. As regards the *Government area of incidence*, direct costs from model 1 are estimated at approximately 30 million euros per year, twice those arising from model 0. This difference is mainly due to public spending on the Company Registry improvements necessary to implement the integrated information sharing system foreseen by model 1. As regards the *LEA area of incidence*, direct costs related to model 0 are estimated at 9.2 million euros, three times higher than under model 1 (3 million). This difference is mainly due to additional STR analysis cost (6.7 million euros at EU level), given a 12 per cent increase in the annual number of STRs as the EU average due to the Third Money Laundering Directive. With reference to the *Intermediaries area of incidence*, net costs from model 0 are higher than those from model 1; this was to be expected, considering that most of the costs from model 0 are borne by intermediaries. For example, the beneficial owner disclosure process uses both ICT and employees' labour: for credit institutions, the former are assessed at 3.5 billion euros per year (1.12% of EU credit institutions 2005 total expenses), and for the latter at 260 million euros. As regards the *Individual area of incidence*, net costs from model 1 are higher than those from model 0 and amount to around 7 million euros due to filing (5 million euros) and updating beneficial ownership information (2 million euros). Regarding the *Businesses area of incidence*, net costs from model 1 are higher than those from model 0. Direct costs under model 1 are estimated at 104 million euros and are mainly due to keeping records of beneficial ownership information and filing it at the Central Registry (95 million euros) along with updating (9 million euros).

Along these lines, a 2009 study by Europe Economics has assessed the costs of compliance with a set of EU Directives, including the Third Money Laundering Directive. Compared with the study previously described, this one went beyond the beneficial ownership requirements; however, it paid attention to costs alone (benefits were not addressed). The methodology involved structured interviews with market participants in 19 Member States, namely 78 firms operating in four sectors: banks and financial conglomerates, asset managers, investment banks and financial markets. The focus was on two main categories of costs: 'one-off' costs (i.e. those incurred in transition to the new system) and 'ongoing' costs (i.e. those incurred after its implementation). Of all the Directives covered by the study, the Third Money Laundering Directive ranks third in terms of costs for banks and financial conglomerates. Mean one-off costs (mostly, IT and training costs) are estimated at 0.29 per cent of their 2007 operating expenses (Europe Economics 2009, p. vi);[7] while mean on-going costs are smaller (0.08%) (2009, p. viii).[8]

An on-going study is now conducting a cost/benefit analysis of anti-money laundering regulations within the EU on an even larger scale. This is the EU-funded project ECOLEF (*The Economic and Legal Effectiveness of Anti Money Laundering Policy and Terrorism Financing*), awarded by the European Commission, Directorate-General Home Affairs to Utrecht University (the Netherlands) in the context of the Prevention of and Fight against Crime Programme. It is a multidisciplinary research project studying the issue from a legal (constitutional law) and economic perspective. Amongst other things, it performs an economic analysis to determine whether anti-money laundering regulations across the EU are efficient, that is, whether they achieve their goal with minimum costs. To this end, it is about to carry out a cost/benefit analysis for each of the anti-money laundering policy instruments.

34.4 NEW ASSESSMENT METHODOLOGIES (2): THE ECONOMICS OF CRIME AND MONEY LAUNDERING

Another recent approach to the evaluation of money laundering policies has been launched in the Netherlands, with a study by Joras Ferwerda (Ferwerda 2009) following the law and economics strand of the literature referred to as 'the economics of crime', which explains criminal behaviour under the assumption of rational choice (Becker 1968). Ferwerda advocates the expansion of this concept to encompass more recent forms of criminality such as money laundering, therefore sponsoring the rising of what he labels the 'economics of crime and money laundering' (Ferwerda 2009, p. 906).

The hypothesis empirically tested by Ferwerda, using data from 17 countries,[9] was that '. . . anti-money laundering policy deters potential criminals from illegal behavior and therefore lowers the crime rate' (2009, p. 923). To test the hypothesis, the dependent variable, that is, crime rate, was measured using police-recorded crime statistics taken from the European Sourcebook of Crime and Criminal Justice Statistics.

The independent variable was anti-money laundering policy, or, to be more precise, four anti-money laundering policies. The starting points for the identification and measurement of these policies were the FATF's forty recommendations. In order separately to test the impact of different types of anti-money laundering policies on crime, the FATF recommendations were grouped into the following four policy areas:

- 'legal': this area includes certain key legal requirements (e.g. criminalization of money laundering, introduction of a criminal liability of legal entities);
- 'private sector': this encompasses the reporting duties placed on the private sector to prevent money laundering;
- 'public sector', that is, the required institutional building (e.g. setting up a FIU);
- 'international cooperation' includes recommendations related to international cooperation matters.

To measure the extent to which each country complies with the FATF recommendations, Ferwerda developed a new unique indicator based on the information included in the mutual evaluation reports on money laundering produced by FATF, IMF and the World Bank. These are the reports where FATF and FATF-style regional bodies assess the degree of compliance of a given country with the forty recommendations by assigning scores to each of them. Because the assessment reports vary in quality, shape and size, these scores are not of immediate use for comparative purposes. For this reason, Ferwerda created a database where scores were reassigned as follows: based on information taken from the mutual assessment reports, each country was given one of the following scores on each recommendation: 0 = no policy or action performed; 1 = only some policy or action performed/an attempt has been made; 2 = still a lot to be done; 3 = some problems or some sectors uncovered; 4 = minor shortcomings/considerations for improvement; 5 = comprehensive implementation. The database also specifies why a given score was assigned, that is, based on which comments of the assessment report.

Finally, four control variables were included in the analysis, since these may also affect crime rates: development (measured by income, more specifically: GDP per capita), corruption (using the average corruption score developed in a World Bank project), common law (as a dummy variable for common law countries), enforcement (i.e. law in action, measured using an index of public enforcement).

Using multivariate analysis techniques, Ferwerda concluded that the 'international cooperation' policy area is the one with the greatest impact on the crime rate. The higher the level of a country's compliance with FATF recommendations related to this area, the lower its crime rate.

Although this study has some limitations, mainly due to the data used to measure crime (as the author recognizes, police-recorded crimes are far from being a perfect crime measure), it is remarkable because it makes innovative use of output indicators in the money laundering field, using them in the context of explanatory studies.

34.5 CONCLUSIONS

This article has shown the gradual, still on-going, shift from traditional to modern approaches to the assessment of the effectiveness and efficiency of money laundering efforts.

With regard to the former, a methodology widely used by the international organizations leading the fight against these criminal phenomena relies on output indicators. These, as discussed, provide a measure of the volume of activities undertaken by the competent authorities to prevent and combat the cleaning of dirty money, but they cannot say a great deal about the real impact of such actions on the criminal problem itself.

With regard to the latter, two approaches have been discussed. First, studies comparing the costs and benefits of different legislative options for different social actors have been examined. These studies are not without shortcomings related to the impossibility of economically quantifying some crucial, yet intangible cost and benefit items, as well as to the necessary use of a great deal of imagination and of a set of assumptions to predict the future impact of legislative options which are either purely theoretical and/or not yet fully entered into force. Nevertheless, they are important for promoting the development of policies based (*inter alia*) on scientific knowledge about the impact of different regulatory options on different social actors.

The second, modern, approach to the assessment of AML policies, which is still in its infancy, has been developed within the law and economics strand of the literature. It opens the way to new developments in the law and economics realm and makes innovative use of output indicators in the money laundering area, using them to understand which types of anti-money laundering policies are more likely to reduce money laundering. Future studies in this promising area will hopefully further demonstrate the potential of this approach in the evaluation of anti-money laundering policies.

NOTES

1. For a review of the two main indirect methods used to estimate the extent of the phenomenon – i.e. the macroeconomic method and the microeconomic one – and on their respective shortcomings see Harvey (2004, 333–335).
2. The author of this article was among the academic experts consulted.
3. The description of the study and of its findings is taken from the final report of the research (Savona et al. 2007).
4. Direct costs have a direct, negative impact on 'balance sheets' through an increase in operating costs. These include the costs of establishing and running the two models in terms of human, financial and material resources. Indirect costs are costs which could potentially and indirectly have a negative impact on the subjects represented in the areas of incidence, for example by an increase in prices. They also include negative effects on competition. Direct benefits impact directly and positively on the 'balance sheet' by increasing revenues or reducing operating costs; indirect benefits are benefits which could potentially and indirectly have a positive impact on the 'balance sheet', but only if certain conditions occur.
5. By way of example, there follow some of the cost and benefit items identified for model 0: *Government area of incidence*: the (direct) cost of prosecuting and sentencing suspected money launderers; the (direct) benefit due to criminal asset recovery; *Law Enforcement Agencies area of incidence*: (direct) investigations costs; the (indirect) benefit of deterring intermediary connivance with criminals; *Intermediaries area of incidence*: (direct) costs for beneficial ownership identification; the (indirect) cost for clientele loss; (indirect) reputational benefits; *Individuals area of incidence*: the (direct) cost related to the reduced opportunities to hide

beneficial owner identity; *Businesses area of incidence*: (indirect) benefits from improved market efficiency. Some of the cost and benefit items identified for model 1 are the following: *Government area of incidence*: Central Registry (direct) costs; the direct benefit from the recovery of criminal assets; *Law Enforcement Agencies area of incidence*: (direct) investigation costs; *Intermediaries area of incidence*: clientele loss (indirect) costs; reputational (indirect) benefits; *Individuals area of incidence*: data filing (direct) costs; *Businesses area of incidence*: data updating (direct) costs.

6. This refers to the difference between total benefits and total costs.
7. The percentage turned out to be lower for investment banks (0.23% of their 2007 operating costs), asset managers (0.21%) and financial markets (0.16%).
8. On-going costs from the Third Money Laundering Directive were assessed to be 0.07%, 0.05% and 0.13% of the 2007 operating costs of asset managers, investment banks and financial markets respectively.
9. These are as follows: Australia, Austria, Belgium, Denmark, France, Germany, Greece, Ireland, Italy, Luxembourg, Netherlands, Norway, Portugal, Spain, Sweden, United Kingdom and the United States of America. As explained by the author, these countries were selected for the availability of FATF mutual evaluation reports and of comparable crime statistics and also because of the concentration of money laundering activities in European and North American countries.

REFERENCES

Becker, G.S. (1968), 'Crime and punishment: an economic approach', *Journal of Political Economy*, **76**, 169–217.

Europe Economics (2009), *Study on the Cost of Compliance with Selected FSAP Measures*, London, available at http://ec.europa.eu/internal_market/finances/docs/actionplan/index/090707_cost_of_compliance_en.pdf

European Committee on Crime Problems, Committee of Experts on the Evaluation of Anti-Money Laundering Measures and Financing of Terrorism (2010), *Revised Rules of Procedure*, Strasbourg, available at http://www.coe.int/t/dghl/monitoring/moneyval/About/Rules_en.pdf

FATF (2003), *FATF 40 Recommendations*, Paris: FATF.

FATF (2009a), *Methodology for Assessing Compliance with the FATF 40 Recommendations and the FATF 9 Special Recommendations*, Paris: FATF, available at http://www.fatf-gafi.org/media/fatf/documents/reports/methodology.pdf

FATF (2009b), *AML/CFT Evaluations and Assessments: Handbook for Countries and Assessors*, Paris: FATF, available at http://www.fatf-gafi.org/media/fatf/documents/reports/Handbook%20for%20assessors.pdf

Ferwerda, J. (2009), 'The economics of crime and money laundering: does anti-money laundering policy reduce crime?', *Review of Law & Economics*, **5** (2), 903–29.

Harvey, J. (2004), 'Compliance and reporting issues arising for financial institutions from money laundering regulations: a preliminary cost benefit study', *Journal of Money Laundering Control*, **7** (4), 333–46.

Harvey, J. (2005), 'An evaluation of money laundering policies', *Journal of Money Laundering Control*, **8** (4), 339–45.

Her Majesty's Treasury (2005), *The Third Money Laundering Directive: Regulatory Impact Assessment*, London: HM Treasury.

HM Treasury and the Department of Trade and Industry (2002), *Regulatory Impact Analysis: Disclosure of Beneficial Ownership of Unlisted Companies*, London: HM Treasury.

Howell, J. and P. van Reenen (2005), *Scoping Study: Cost Benefit Analysis of Transparency Requirements in the Company/Corporate Field*, Brussels: European Commission.

Krieger-Faust, S. (2006), *Impact de la lutte anti-blanchiment sur la place financière*, Luxembourg: Portails.

OECD (2001), *Behind the Corporate Veil – Using Corporate Vehicles for Illicit Purposes*, Paris: OECD.

Sathye M. (2008), 'Estimating the cost of compliance of AMLCTF for financial institutions in Australia', *Journal of Financial Crime*, **15** (4), 347–63.

Savona, E.U., M.A. Maggioni and B. Vettori (eds) (2007), *Cost Benefit Analysis of Transparency Requirements in the Company/Corporate Field and Banking Sector Relevant for the Fight against Money Laundering and Other Financial Crime*, Brussels: European Commission.

Tavares, C., G. Thomas and M. Roudat (2010), *Money Laundering in Europe: Report of Work Carried out by Eurostat and DG Home Affairs*, Eurostat Methodologies and Working Papers, Luxembourg: European Union, available at http://epp.eurostat.ec.europa.eu/cache/ITY_OFFPUB/KS-RA-10-003/EN/KS-RA-10-003-EN.PDF

Transcrime (2001), *Transparency and Money Laundering*, Trento: Transcrime.

Index

Index prepared by the publisher